FAMILY IN THE

5-31-12

1BP 8/05 22.95

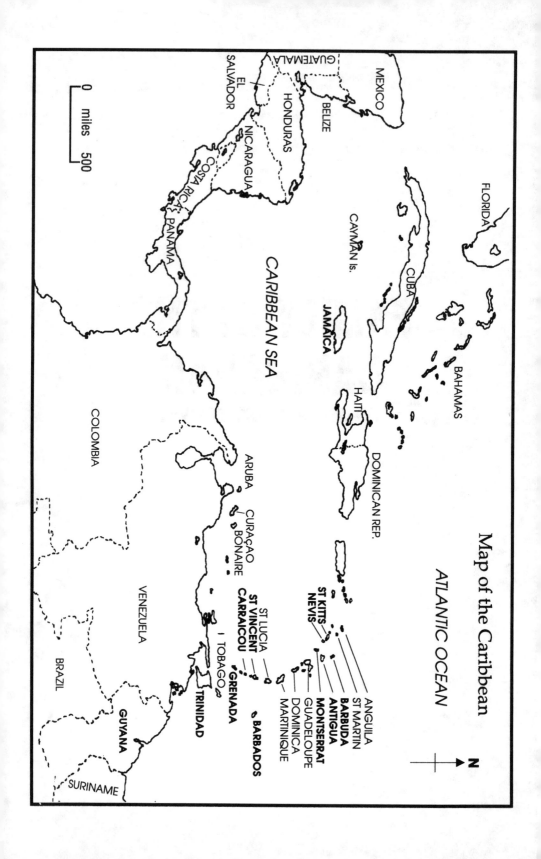

Map of the Caribbean

FAMILY IN THE CARIBBEAN

CARIBBEAN

THEMES AND PERSPECTIVES

Christine Barrow

Ian Randle Publishers
Kingston

James Currey Publishers
Oxford

Marcus Wiener Publishers
Princeton

First published in Jamaica 1996 by

Ian Randle Publishers
206 Old Hope Road
Kingston 6

ISBN 976-8100-75-3 paper

A catalogue record for this book is available from the National Library of Jamaica.

First published in the United Kingdom 1996 by
James Currey Limited
73 Botley Road
Oxford OX2 0B5

ISBN 0-85255-243-2 paper
A catalogue record for this book is available from the British Library

First published in the United States of America 1999 by
Markus Wiener Publishers
231 Nassau Street
Princeton, NJ 08540

Library of Congress Cataloging-in-Publication data
Barrow, Christine
    Family in the Caribbean : themes and perspectives / Christine Barrow.
    p.   cm.
    Previously published: Kingston , Jamaica : I. Randle, 1996
    Includes bibliographical references
    ISBN 1-55876-207-8 (hc : alk. paper), – ISBN 1-55876-208-6 (pb : alk. paper)
    1. Family – Caribbean Area. 2. Caribbean Area – Social conditions.
    3. Marriage – Caribbean Area. 4. Slavery – Caribbean Area.
    I   Title
    HQ576.8375   1998   98-43653
    S06.85'09729–dc21   CIP

Cover photos by Ronnie Carrington, Carrington Photo creations Ltd., Barbados.
Book and cover design by Michael Gordon
Printed by Data Reproductions Corporation

Contents

Author's Acknowledgements

My greatest debt of gratitude goes to Jack Alexander who, as is clear in the following pages, is himself a pioneer in the study of Caribbean family ideology and practice. His meticulous reading of the first draft provided invaluable detailed comment and insightful suggestions. I should also like to express great appreciation for Rhoda Reddock's useful comments on the first draft, particularly as she shared her intellectual expertise and experience on gender/women and family and on East Indian family patterns. I am indebted to them both, though I alone am responsible for the interpretations expressed here.

The library staff at the Cave Hill (Barbados) Campus of the University of the West Indies were most diligent and efficient in tracking down copies of articles not available locally. I am most grateful to Nel Bretney, Jeniphier Carnegie and Alan Moss. Appreciation also goes to Ronnie Carrington for the photographs on the front cover.

To my children, Jennifer and Geoffrey, many thanks are due for hours of proof reading and for their understanding and encouragement throughout.

Christine Barrow
March 1996

Dedicated to the memory of my parents
George Murray (1914-1989)and May
Murray (1916-1990)

Acknowledgements

The author and the publishers are grateful for permission to reproduce the articles presented in this volume and list below the original publication details.

Origins and functions

M. and F. Herskovits (1947) 'Retentions and Reinterpretations', *Trinidad Village*, New York, Alfred A. Knopf.

M.G. Smith (1957) 'The African Heritage in the Caribbean'. In V. Rubin (ed) *Caribbean Studies: A Symposium*. Jamaica, Instutute of Social and economic Studies, University College of the West Indies, pp. 34-46.

Extracts from T.S. Simey (1946) *Welfare and Planning*. London Oxford University Press.

R.T. Smith (1957) 'The Family in the Caribbean'. In V. Rubin (ed) *Caribbean Studies: A Symposium*. Jamaica, Institute of Social and Economic Research, University College of the West Indies, pp. 67-75.

Personal choice and adaptive response

H. Rubenstein (1980) 'Conjugal Behaviour and Parental Role Flexibility in an Afro-Caribbean Village', *Canadian Review of Sociology and Anthropology*, 17, 4, 330-337.

R. Dirks and V. Kerns (1976) 'Mating Patterns and Adaptive Change in Rum Bay, 1923-1970' *Social and Economic Studies*, 25,34-35.

S. Gordon (1987) 'I go to 'Tanties': The Economic Significance of Child-shifting in Antigua, West Indies', *Journal of Comparative Family Studies*, 18,3,427-443.

J. Gussler (1980) 'Adaptive Strategies and Social Networks of Women in St. Kitts'. In E. Bourguignon (ed) *A World of Women: Anthropological studies of Women in Societies of the World*, New York, Praeger.

K.F. Olwig (1993) 'The Migration experience: Nevisian Women at Home and Abroad'. In J. Momsen (ed) *Women and Change in the Caribbean*, Kingston, Ian Randle; Bloomington and Indianapolis, Indiana University Press; London, James Currey, pp. 150-166.

N.L. Gonzalez (1984) 'Rethinking the Consanguineal household and Matrifocality', *Ethnology*, 23, 1-12.

Ideology and Culture

Alexander, J. (1984) 'Love, Race, Slavery and Sexuality in Jamaican images of the Family'. In R.T. Smith (ed) *Kinship Ideology and Practice in Latin America*, Chapel Hill, University of North Carolina, pp.147-180.

Chapter 7 - 'Sex Role Differentiation', pp. 134-148. In R.T. Smith (1988) *Kinship and Class in the West Indies*, Cambridge University Press.

Extract 'Institutional and other Elements Influencing Mating Patterns', pp. 63-67. In G. Roberts and S. Sinclair (1978) *Women in Jamaica: Patterns of Reproduction and Family*, Millwood, New York, KYO Press.

J. Manyoni (1977) 'Legitimacy and Illegitimacy: Misplaced *Polarities in Caribbean Family Studies*', *The Canadian Review of* Sociology and Anthropology, 14, 4, 417-427.

M. Lazarus-Black (1991) 'Why Women take Men to Magistrate's court: Caribbean Kinship Ideology', *Ethnology*, 30, 2, 119-133.

Slave Families

Extract 'Mating Patterns, Parent-Child Relations, Kinship, and the white out-group' pp. 159-170 from O. Patterson *The Sociology of Slavery*, London, MacGibbon and Kee.

'Kinship and Sex Roles' pp. 32-42 from S. Mintz and R. Price (1976) *An Anthropological Approach to the Afro-American Past: A Caribbean Perspective*, Philadelphia, Institute for the Study of Human Issues.

M. Craton (1979) 'Changing Patterns of Slave Families in the British West Indies', *Journal of Interdisciplinary History*, X, 1, 1-35. (Reprinted in Beckles and Shepherd (ed) *Caribbean Slave Society and Economy*).

B. Higman (1973) 'Household Structure and Fertility on Jamaican Slave Plantations: a Nineteenth Century Example', *Population Studies*, 27, 3, 527-550. (Reprinted in Beckles and Shepherd (ed) *Caribbean Slave Society and Economy*).

Extract from 'Wives, Mothers and Family Structure', *Natural Rebels*, London, Zed Books Ltd.

East Indian Families

R. Bell (1970) 'Marriage and Family differences among lower Class Negro and East Indian women in Trinidad', *Race*, XII, 1, 59-73.

A. Niehoff (1959) 'The Survival of Hindu Institutions in an Alien Environment', *The Eastern Anthropologist*, 12, 3, 171-187

J. Nevadomsky (1980) 'Changes in Hindu Institutions in an Alien Environment', *The Eastern Anthropologist*, 3, 1, 39-53.

M. Agrosino (1976) 'Sexual Politics in the East Indian Family in Trinidad', *Caribbean Studies*, 16, 1, 44-46.

Child Socialisation, Relocation and Abandonment

Extract from 'The Development of kinship roles' pp.156-170 from E. Clarke *My Mother who fathered Me*, London, George Allen and Unwin Ltd.

H. Evans (1989) 'Perspectives on the Socialisation of the working-class Jamaican Child', *Social and Economic Studies*, 38, 3, 177-203.

Social Policy: State, Law and Church

R.T. Smith (1982) 'Family, Social Change and Social Policy in the West Indies *Niewe West-Indische Gids*, 56, 111-142.

Introduction:
Definitions and Themes

The conviction that the family, that is the co-resident nuclear family, is natural, universal and essential has faced its greatest test in the Caribbean. Family patterns in the region have been characterised as 'matrifocal', households as 'female-headed', men as 'marginal', conjugal unions as 'non-legal' and temporary, conjugal relationships as 'segregated' and children as 'outside' and illegitimate. This has been a source of bewilderment for researchers, as is evident in their obsession with studies of the family in the region and in the fundamental intellectual assumptions that have guided their research. How, they have asked, could the family, that most natural and immutable of all social institutions, have existed in Caribbean slave plantation societies, which were artificially engineered by grafting together racially and culturally varied migratory streams for economic production and profit? How could family life survive the subsequent mass migration of fathers and husbands? How could a moral social order be built on a deformed family cornerstone? Or, put conversely, how could seemingly normal adults be the product of these problem families? And why have Caribbean peoples apparently remained ignorant of the virtues of properly structured family life, refused to take advantage of social policies to reconstruct their own families and therefore; for generations, remained locked out of the Church and beyond the protection of the law?

The dilemma has its source in the definition of the family. Caribbean scholarship has had to make the choice either to accept the conventional ideological construction of the family as a co-resident, stable unit of husband and wife with their immature children or to redefine the family according to Caribbean meanings and realities. Both alternatives have characterised investigations of family patterns in the region.

Approximately half of the nearly fifty years of family studies has been dominated by the former perspective, as researchers concluded that conjugal relationships were 'promiscuous' and 'brittle' and family structures 'deformed' and 'disfunctional'. Since then, a number of developments have encouraged a change in interpretation, two of which we mention here. Firstly, Caribbean scholars have refuted the prevailing stereotypes of family life, replacing them with positive evaluations of resilience and adaptability; secondly, the recognition that similar family structures are common in Britain and the United States (extended female-centred kinship networks, for example, and matrifocal and single–parent families, the result of escalating divorce rates and other social phenomena) challenged the interpretation of Caribbean family relationships as 'unstable' and matrifocal structures as failed attempts to imitate the western ideal. However, it is only in the last 15 years or so that scholars have laid aside borrowed theoretical assumptions and related methodologies to ask: What is family in the Caribbean? and to answer the question in the light of ideology and experience historically and culturally patterned within the region.

The objective of this book is to review the development of family studies in the Caribbean. The intention is to show how we have arrived at present theoretical interpretations and methodological approaches and to point the way for future inquiry.

The Caribbean

The Caribbean, an arc of island states stretching from Belize in Central America southward through the Caribbean Sea to Guyana on the South American coast (see Figure I), is home to approximately 50 million people. Geographically separated, these countries nevertheless share the common history and contemporary imprint of discovery, plantation slavery and colonialism. Economic restructuring from monocrop (sugar and banana) production to the modernised mix of diversified agriculture with tourism, manufacturing and public sector expansion, created the boom years of the 1960s and early 1970s. Since then, Caribbean countries have confronted the paradox of formal political independence, gained since the early 1960s by all but a few smaller territories, with economic dependency. The crisis is most recently manifested in stabilisation and structural adjustment.

Caribbean social institutions like the family are not immune to these grand political and economic events. Modern Caribbean history began with the annexation of African slaves, European colonisers, Indian and white indentured servants and other minority groups. Racial hierarchies became less rigid with the evolutionary processes of cultural integration and social mobility, but the process has not been all one way. Race, class and culture continue to generate conflict and pull in opposite directions. Caribbean families have also dealt with a history of large scale demographic, economic, political and social change. Some of the more significant include reductions in infant mortality and fertility, aging grandparents and mass migration; state policies and programmes of birth control and social welfare; family images projected by tourist boards and foreign dominated mass media; educational and occupational mobility along with rising unemployment rates; prosperity with poverty. Within this Caribbean complex, family systems have consistently defied scholarly analysis, though it is quite clear that they are well-understood by those who live in them.

Themes

The book is constructed around six themes, each of which has been prominent in Caribbean family studies at one time or another. The first concerns *definitions of the family*. All writers on Caribbean family and kinship have acknowledged and emphasised the importance of the family as a fundamental institution of society. Not all have agreed, however, on what family is and what it ought to be, the differences being due mainly to the varying weight of ethnocentric bias. At one extreme are the early writers for whom families were universal and defined as nuclear, the married conjugal pair with their children living together under the same roof. Families so constructed performed certain functions such as reproduction and child–rearing that were essential to the survival of society. Arriving from Europe and North America armed with their theories and models, they looked aghast at Caribbean family forms, condemned them as deformed, unstable and not yet recovered from the annihilation of plantation slavery, and instituted restructuring policies to correct the problem. These biases have dominated the ideological perspectives of the State and public policy, the law and the Church in Caribbean societies and, with less excuse, have persisted until very recently in scholarly writing.

The second theme concerns the Caribbean debate between *plural society* and *creole society* perspectives. This is not the place for a detailed review of these contrasting sociological interpretations of Caribbean societies, the many critical points which they have generated (see Craig 1982) or the subsequent refinement of the models (see, for example, Smith 1991). Both models have, nonetheless, informed analyses of family in the Caribbean and we therefore proceed to examine them briefly from this perspective.

The plural society model, developed for the Caribbean mainly by Michael G. Smith (1960, 1965) postulates that Caribbean societies are characterised by an arrangement, not necessarily hierarchical, of discrete 'socio-cultural segments'. In these plural societies, there is 'a formal diversity in the basic system of compulsory institutions', which institutions comprise 'kinship, education, religion, property and economy, recreation and certain sodalities' (Smith 1960: 769). Plural societies are distinguished from culturally and socially 'homogeneous societies' and from 'heterogeneous societies' which share a common system of basic institutions, but practice different 'alternative' and 'exclusive' institutions (Smith 1960: 767). Class and occupational differences, for example, are characteristics of heterogeneous, not plural societies. Pluralism cannot therefore be equated with class stratification, for 'cultural difference and social stratification vary independently' (Smith 1960: 770).

In addition, plural societies are inherently unstable and the monopolisation of power by one socio-cultutal segment is therefore necessary to maintain the status quo. 'Given the fundamental differences of belief, values, and organisation that connote pluralism, the monopoly of power by one cultural section is the essential precondition for the maintenance of the total society in its current form' (Smith 1960: 772).

The plural society thesis has been criticised on many fronts, not least for its assertion that each social segment, reinterpreted by Smith to mean racial group (black, brown or white) or ethnic group (East Indian, Chinese and so forth), has its own unique culture of kinship, conjugality, descent, child socialisation and the like. The colonial mindset reinforced this interpretation by viewing indigenous Third World cultures as inferior and apart and black peoples as uncivilised and incapable of assimilation. If we add the anthropological predilection for in-depth study of small–scale communities or villages, with no written history and closed off from the rest of society, then the stage is set for the many false assumptions that have characterised Caribbean family studies.

The creole society model, on the other hand, draws heavily on structural functionalist theory. According to Lloyd Braithwaite (1960: 882), 'there must be a certian minimum of common, shared values if the unity of the society is to be maintained'. He, along with Raymond T. Smith (1967) and Edward Brathwaite (1971) emphasised synthesis and wholeness, as Susan Craig (1982: 155) put it, 'the consensus created by the integrative mechanisms of the creolization process'. Creolisation is interpreted as a process whereby Europeans, Africans and others interact, exchange and adjust culturally. But these writers differed on the direction that the process takes. Raymond Smith (1967: 234) referred to 'integrating around the conception of the moral and cultural superiority of things English' and Lloyd

Braithwaite (1960: 882) stated that the 'main common value element has been the sharing of the value of ethnic superiority and inferiority'. Edward Brathwaite (1974: 6), however, identified a dual process which includes 'acculturation, which is the yoking (by force and example, deriving from power/prestige) of one culture to another' and also 'inter/culturation', the unplanned and unstructured process by which African traditions are asserted.

The creole perspective allows researchers to escape the myopic focus on one socio-cultural segment. It took some time, however, before scholars shifted their attention from interpreting 'lower class Negro' family patterns as influenced by the 'white bias' of colonial society and therefore as second-rate imitations of the dominant European forms of the wider society, to an understanding of family principles and practices common throughout the social hierarchy. The assumptions built into these models have led researchers to ask whether family patterns in the Caribbean are peculiar to autonomous social and racial groups. Alternatively, are they in certain ways, characteristic of the wider social system as the conditions and evolutionary processes of social integration, cultural exchange cultural heterogeneity, and 'negative, regressive creolization' (Brathwaite 1977: 54) pull against each other.

The third theoretical theme, one which has also divided scholars of family in the Caribbean, is, whether to focus on *social structure* or *human action*. In the former approach individuals are seen to be constrained to behave in socially approved ways by social forces such as customs and laws passed down virtually unchanged from one generation to the next. Earlier investigators of Caribbean family were structural functionalists who adopted this theoretical perspective, though by the 1970s they were trying hard to soften the rigidity of their model by introducing notions of 'personal choice' and 'adaptive flexibility'. The resulting utilitarian analysis, apparent in some of these studies, is theoretically unsatisfactory and unsound as rational individual motivation replaces social and cultural dimensions. The influence of symbolic interactionism is evident in the latest studies of Caribbean family, which perceive individuals as actors who actively and creatively control the conditions of their lives. However, the recognition that they do so within a cultural system of symbols and meanings that makes sense of and guides actions is an important theoretical advance over the previous crude images of unrestrained, individual pursuit of self-interest.

Fourthly, we devote particular attention to the analysis of *gender roles* and *relationships* in Caribbean family studies, in particular the images of 'marginal men', 'respectable' women and 'matrifocal' or woman-centered families. These ethnocentric assumptions have also dominated, this time to misinterpret women and men. The image of male and female adults with distinct roles, separate but complementary, within a patriarchal nuclear family structure constitutes the functional ideal. Caribbean women were seen to conform and were portrayed in the literature as submissive, faithful wives and devoted mothers, fulfilling their child–care and housework responsibilities in the domestic domain. When demographic evidence was introduced, showing high levels of female-headed households and women's participation in the labour force, these images of female 'respectability' had to be redrawn. 'Wives' disappeared from the literature, as women were portrayed combining the roles of 'mother' and 'worker' — strong, dominant and in control of the distribution of resources from the centre of extensive female social networks. Images of men in the family have not undergone such a transformation in the literature. They have been continuously portrayed as 'marginal' to the family. For reasons of unemployment and poverty, the argument goes, they have been unable to function as husbands and fathers, these roles being defined essentially to mean economic maintenance and the exercise of familial authority which accompanies a successful breadwinner performance. It follows that if men are marginal, families will be matrifocal, maybe even matriarchal.

In terms of gender roles, recent approaches have also acknowledged the importance of understanding through the eyes of informants themselves as they explain the cultural principles which define 'motherhood', 'fatherhood' and other familial roles within Caribbean culture. Men and women may or may not express dissatisfaction with the non–performance or 'irresponsibility' of husbands, fathers and other kin, but it is important that they be allowed to do so themselves, rather than have researchers arrive at conclusions about male marginality by imposing culturally inappropriate models.

Fifthly, there is the question of *methodology*. Caribbean family studies have run the gamut in methodological variety. The interdependence of the results obtained from social inquiry and the methods used is well-known. Initial preconceptions of what constituted the family have shaped methodological approaches. For example, when family units were defined as co-resident groups so that family and household were assumed to be one and the same, the dominant methods of investigation were household surveys combined with the anthropological techniques of in-depth participant observation and unstructured interviewing of household members. Misconceived definitions along with inappropriate methodologies resulted in misunderstanding. Visiting unions were often ignored and researchers were never quite sure what to do with single-person households. Recent techniques adopted in Caribbean family research stress that informants must be allowed to talk during detailed unstructured interviews. The researcher listens rather than asks questions. Participatory methods that return research results to the community and archival research are also making an appearance. These techniques have gone a long way towards reducing the biases which previously resulted from imposed theoretical models and accompanying standardised field methods.

The sixth and final theme concerns the theoretical importance attached to *history* and *social change*. Investigations in the Caribbean began on a promising note in this respect, as the founding fathers of family studies sought the 'origins' of contemporary family patterns in the past. Their approach to the study of social change either identified similarities to African polygamous forms in contemporary family patterns and assumed that these had survived through slavery to the present, or concluded that families were deformed because of the destruction of plantation slavery. Both were subsequently dismissed as speculation and irrelevance. We do not, argued the structural functionalists who succeeded them, have the historical evidence to come to these conclusions and anyway, the important question is not: How did families in the Caribbean come to be as they are?, but, How do they function in contemporary society? Not only was history dismissed, but also social change, except in so far as short-term life-cycle changes were concerned. Deliberate attempts to reunite culture and history with family studies were reintroduced only recently as scholars investigated the ideology of family life by examining structural principles which were established generations ago. The Caribbean family culture, for example, of conjugal segregation together with mother-child unity and the association of marriage and legitimate children with status equals in contrast to non-marital unions and illegitimacy with women of lower status, has its roots in the past.

The image of the family as surviving unchanged over the years, or as undergoing significant transformation, continues to divide researchers. Early portrayals of Caribbean family life as virtually destroyed by the slave regime, but as potentially responsive to policies for reconstruction have been replaced by images of continuity in basic family structures and values, despite social policy, religious persuasion and legal discrimination and despite demographic improvements and marked socio- economic advances in standards of living. But while it may be true that marriage rates have remained just as low and illegitimacy rates just as high as ever, there is some suggestion, unfortunately not as yet systematically researched, that the younger generation is renegotiating gender roles and relationships, a process which has potential for significant change in Caribbean family patterns. Divorce rates, for example, are escalating across the region and there is evidence of significant creolisation and change in East Indian family patterns in Trinidad and Guyana.

Organisation

This volume is divided into two main parts. A critical examination of major theoretical trends is the subject of PART I. It contains four chapters that trace conceptual and theoretical developments in chronological order. PART II also contains four chapters, each of which examines a selected substantive perspective of Caribbean family studies. These chapters in PART II cater to more specialised interests, but are, nonetheless, informed by mainstream theory and therefore closely linked to PART I. PART II covers conjugal and family patterns among the slaves and among East Indians in the Caribbean, child socialisation and social policy. In both parts we have tried to strike a balance between theory, methodology and ethnographic narrative. At the end of each of the chapters in PARTS I and II, articles and selected extracts from books have been reproduced. These have been chosen for additional reading as core literature, illustrating major points and developments mentioned in the relevant chapter. The CONCLUSION summarises these theories and perspectives in order to point the way forward.

The potential scope of this book is vast, but there is only so much that a work of this kind can cover. Scholars from many disciplines — anthropology, sociology, demography, history, social work and social psychology — have focussed their research on family in the Caribbean resulting in a voluminous literature with a wide variety of theoretical approaches, research methodologies and conclusions. Researchers from the Anglophone Caribbean have joined with colleagues from the French, Dutch and Spanish-speaking countries. The resulting literature is plentiful and growing, but scattered. For this book we have tried to combine representative coverage with necessary selectivity, a most difficult balance to achieve. We have chosen research to represent a variety of disciplinary perspectives, but have, with regret, confined selection to the English-speaking Caribbean. Language barriers and the unavailability of resources for a thorough search of the literature in other languages have imposed this restriction. We have, however, sought to avoid the common tendency of confining coverage to the more developed and more researched Anglophone Caribbean countries and have deliberately included material on, for example, Nevis, Barbuda, Tortola and other less well-known Caribbean countries. Even then, we have had no choice but to leave out many exciting and worthwhile books and articles. Additionally, some important topics such as domestic violence have been omitted and others such as family law, and migration and family life mentioned only briefly. It is hoped that the bibliography at the end of this volume will help to make up for some of these gaps.

The original intention was to produce an introductory text for Caribbean undergraduate students in anthropology, sociology and related disciplines. The language is therefore simple and direct. But although this remains the primary purpose, we hope that this work will attract a wider audience, intellectually and geographically, with the result that international scholarship will give long overdue recognition and understanding to family in the Caribbean in its own right.

PART ONE

1
Origins and Functions

Virtually all of the founding fathers of Caribbean family studies were visiting anthropologists, sociologists and social welfare workers from Britain and the United States. They came from backgrounds in which the co-residential nuclear family structure headed by a man and based on stable marriage, with a clear division of labour between husband and wife, was the norm. They were firm in their belief that the family constituted the basic building block on which the whole moral and social fabric of society was constructed. All of them were concerned with 'lower-class Negro mating and family patterns' and one can imagine their confusion and dismay when, on arrival in the Caribbean, they were faced with what must have appeared to be an unending variety of odd and ever-changing family forms. What they found could hardly have been more different from what they knew at home. As Michael G. Smith (1970(1957): i), himself a Jamaican, explained their problem:

> The family life of West Indian 'lower class' Negroes or folk presents a number of equally important academic and practical problems. In this region family life is highly unstable, marriage rates are low, especially during the earlier phases of adult life, and illegitimacy rates have always been high. Many households contain single individuals, while others with female heads consist of women, their children, and/or their grandchildren. The picture is further complicated by variations in the type and local distribution of alternative conjugal forms; and, characteristically, differing communities, social classes and ethnic groups institutionalize differing combinations of them. Excluding legal marriage, mating is brittle, diverse in form and consensual in base among these Creole or Negroid populations.

Gender role definition and performance was also very different in the Caribbean. Husbands and fathers were seen as not fulfilling their function of providing economic maintenance and were described as 'marginal'. Conjugal relations were considered to be 'loose' and families 'matrifocal'. It is hardly surprising that most of these early investigators found great difficulty in interpreting the diversity and fluidity of Caribbean family patterns. In some cases this was clearly beyond them. They were also shocked that the family, that foundational social institution, was not up to standard; that is, of course, not up to their own standards at home. Guided by the theories and assumptions developed for the study of their own societies, they not only sought to make sense of what appeared to them as chaotic family structure in the Caribbean, but also in some cases to devise prescriptions for its reconstruction and moral upliftment. Their attempts to make sense of family forms in the Caribbean were later described as exploratory and impressionistic and the policies based on their conclusions as ethnocentric and misconceived. They nevertheless generated a profusion of studies that laid the groundwork for contemporary research.

For these early researchers, understanding Caribbean family patterns involved two major processes. Their first task, that of constructing concepts and typologies, we will explore in Chapter III. Their second task entailed providing an explanation for the existence in the Caribbean of family structures other than that of the nuclear family based on marriage and co-residence. In other words, the early investigators were searching for an understanding of family forms other than the norm in their own societies, an explanation for families which existed among those they referred to as 'lower-class Negroes' in the Caribbean. Their interpretations revolved around two major perspectives, the first was concerned with *origins* as they sought to find out how Caribbean family forms had come to be as they were; the second focussed on *functions* as they asked: How does the family work in contemporary society? This chapter explores and comments on these two approaches in early investigations of family in the Caribbean and, in the process, introduces representative case-studies.

Origins

The study of the family in the Caribbean began as an offshoot of the heated debate over how the New World Negro family in the United States had come to assume its contemporary form. The two protagonists were Melville Herskovits and E. Franklin Frazier. Both noted that Negro families were 'maternal' and extended, that common-law unions ('keeper' unions according to Herskovits and 'irregular' unions according to Frazier) occurred frequently and that rates of illegitimacy ('outlawed motherhood' according to Frazier) were high. Both were concerned that family form among the Negroes of the New World differed from the co-residential nuclear units of the mainstream culture of the United States. Both sought to provide an explanation for these unfamiliar family forms and both rooted their analyses in the past. But there the resemblance ended. For Herskovits, the origins of the Negro family were to be found in the African cultural heritage which had survived, albeit not completely intact, while Frazier dismissed this argument by claiming that the disruptive effects of slavery and the plantation system were responsible. Mintz and Price (1976: 33) contrasted their views:

> In one view, Afro-Americans were essentially Africans, whose commitments to their ancestral past made them culturally different from other Americans; in the other view, they were merely Americans, who had not been able to acculturate fully because of their oppression. Clearly, this controversy is far from dead, and a great deal of argument continues as to whether Afro-Americans have a different culture or different cultures, or are simply the victims of deprivation.

From the perspective of American cultural anthropology, Herskovits (see Article/Extract 1 at end of chapter) identified a 'scale of intensity of Africanisms' which persisted among Afro-American peoples of the New World. What he referred to as 'survivals' resemble as closely as possible the original African forms, for example, the practice of burying the umbilical cord of a newly-born child and planting a fruit tree over it or the ritual appearance of a mother and her young baby from their home nine days after the birth. 'Syncretisms' result from a process of identifying elements in the new culture with parallel components of the old, for example, Catholic saints with African deities. 'Reinterpretations' also compare the old and the new, but in circumstances where the parallel is less obvious, occurring 'in substance rather than form, psychological value rather than in name' (Herskovits 1973 (1945): 265-266). An example is the reinterpretation within the Caribbean of African polygamy as 'progressive monogamy', as successive rather than simultaneous plural matings, which occur when married couples separate and, without bothering to go through divorce procedures, form new conjugal relationships Herskovits (1958(1941): 168). The purity of African retentions is therefore reduced as we move from survivals to syncretisms to reinterpretations.

Herskovits proposed a 'scale of intensity of Africanisms' in the New World which, he claimed, varied according to the 'aspect of culture' in question and according to geographical location. With reference to the former, it is important and interesting to note that, in arguing the point, Herskovits (1973(1945): 261-262)did not totally deny the influence of slavery:

> Music, folklore, magic and religion, on the whole, have retained more of their African character than economic life, or technology, or art, while language and social structures based on kinship or free association, tend to vary through degrees of intensity that are noted.

> These differences are probably due to the circumstances of slave life, and confirm common sense observations made during the period of slavery. Slave owners were primarily concerned with the technological and economic aspects of the lives of their slaves, while the conditions of life as a slave also of necessity warped whatever patterns of African social structures the Negroes felt impelled to preserve. On the other hand, what tales were told or the songs that were sung made little difference to the masters, and few external blocks were placed in the way of their retention. In the case of religion, outer controls were of varying kinds and were responded to in varying degree, as is reflected in the intermediate position of this cultural element. Magic, which tends to go underground under pressure and can most easily be practised without direction — the force of the specific psychological compulsions here being of special importance — persisted in recognizable form everywhere, particularly since the similarity between African and European magic is so great that the one cultural stream must have operated to reinforce the other. The failure of African art to survive except in Guiana and to a lesser degree in Brazil is understandable when the life of the slave which permitted little leisure and offered slight stimulus for the production of art in the aboriginal African style or, indeed, in any other style is recalled.

Along with economic life, technology and art, African political and legal institutions stood little chance of surviving through slavery. Midway between the two extremes were social institutions such as the family. Herskovits also presented a tabulation showing that the scale of Africanisms varied according to geographical location within the New World. The 'Bush Negroes' of the Guianas were defined as the most African and the urban north of the United States was placed at the least African end of the continuum. The English-speaking territories of Trinidad and Jamaica fell between the two extremes (Herskovits 1973(1945): 260-261).

In terms of the family therefore, he concluded:

It goes without saying that the plantation system rendered the survival of African family types impossible, as it did their underlying moral and supernatural sanctions, except in dilute form. Only where Negroes escaped soon enough after the beginning of their enslavement, and retained their freedom for sufficiently long periods, could institutions of larger scope such as the extended family or the clan persist at all; and even in these situations the mere breakup in personnel made it unlikely that some manifestation of European influence should not be felt. In Dutch Guiana alone has the clan persisted; what forms the social structures of present-day Negro communities of Brazil take is unknown, but in Haiti and Jamaica larger groupings go no further than a kind of loosely knit extended family. Yet, on the other hand, slavery by no means completely suppressed rough approximations of certain forms of African family life. Even in the United States, where Africanisms persisted with the greatest difficulty, such family organization as existed during slave times in terms of the relationship between parents and children, and between parents themselves, did not lack African sanctions (Herskovits 1958(1941): 139).

In the study that Herskovits undertook along with his wife, Frances Herskovits, in a rural Trinidadian village called Toco, little in the way of family culture representing pure African forms was to be found. Though a few survivals persisted, the heritage was found to be 'functioning beneath the surface' (Herskovits and Herskovits 1947: 287), expressed in the form of reinterpretations, more in substance than in actual form. Several family characteristics, including the looseness of the conjugal bond, the close nucleus of mother and child, the importance of family support to the individual, the peripheral status of the father and the rituals of courting, birth and child socialisation, are not, they contended, pathological manifestations of the European family, but constitute retentions and subsequent reinterpretations of African custom (Herskovits and Herskovits 1947: 296).

Frazier's counter-argument was based on his observations of the Negro family in the United States. He claimed that 'the manner of the Negro's enslavement tended to destroy so completely his African culture' that only insignificant, soon to be forgotten memories remained.

These scraps of memories, which form only an insignificant part of the growing body of traditions in Negro families, are what remains of the African heritage. Probably never before in history has a people been so nearly completely stripped of its social heritage as the Negroes who were brought to America. Other conquered races have continued to worship their household gods within the intimate circle of their kinsmen. But American slavery destroyed household gods and dissolved the bonds of sympathy and affection between men of the same blood and household. Old men and women might have brooded over memories of their African homeland, but they could not change the world about them. Through force of circumstances, they had to acquire a new language, adopt new habits of labour, and take over, however imperfectly, the folkways of the American environment. Their children, who knew only the American environment, soon forgot the few memories that had been passed on to them and developed motivations and modes of behaviour in harmony with the New World. Their children's children have often recalled with skepticism the fragments of stories concerning Africa which have been preserved in their families. But, of the habits and customs as well as the hopes and fears that characterized the life of their forbearers in Africa, nothing remains (Frazier 1966(1939): 15).

At every stage in the process of forced migration, slaves were systematically stripped of their culture.

Even before reaching the United States, slaves had often been subjected to influences that tended to destroy the significance and meaning of their African heritage. Once in the New World, they were separated from friends and acquaintances and 'broken in' to the regimen of the plantation. Finally, they had to face the disdain, if not the hostility, of the slaves who had become accommodated and accustomed to the new environment (Frazier 1966(1939): 7).

The cultural vacuum left by the destruction of African family customs and beliefs was filled by attempts to adopt white planter ideologies as 'the slave tended to take over the attitudes and sentiments of his master toward religion, sex and marriage, and the other relations of life' (Frazier 1966(1939): 27). Frazier did, however, admit that the Caribbean circumstances in which there were larger concentrations of slaves on the plantations, might have facilitated African cultural survival. He noted, for example, evidence for the retention of polygamy in Jamaica, 'even today' (Frazier 1966(1939): 5-6, see also Frazier 1957: vii).

Frazier proceeded to trace the changes in Negro family patterns in the United States from the days of slavery. According to his interpretation, in the early days where male slaves were by far the numerical majority, family relations were reduced to animal lust.

When the sexual impulses of the males were no longer controlled by African customs and mores, they became subject only to the periodic urge of sexual hunger. Under such circumstances the males, as is generally true, seized upon the woman who happened to be at hand and with whom they had been thrown into closest contact (Frazier 1966(1939): 19).

As social and moral codes were developed, families became progressively stable and more permanent. Favoured slaves managed more successfully to assimilate 'western mores' and 'white civilization' and to establish nuclear families.

Subsequent events, such as Emancipation, the Civil War and mass migration to the North, disrupted family organisation. On the plantations and among the impoverished slum dwellers in American cities sexual relationships were characterised by promiscuity, family structures were 'maternal', relationships loose and children often abandoned. In contrast, stable nuclear family life, based on marriage, patriarchal authority and the 'subordination' of women, was to be found among those who managed to acquire land or gain some social mobility into the skilled artisan class and to adopt the culture and religion of American whites, albeit with limited success.

Frazier's main point then, is that family patterns are to be explained not by the loss or retention of the African heritage, but with reference to the changing social and economic conditions of life within America, specifically the exigencies of life on the plantations, slave and free, and in the cities and the impact of the white cultural patterns which the slaves and ex-slaves sought to imitate. The slave system totally destroyed African culture and there is no evidence to support the transfer, survival and retention of African family patterns. Therefore, to base an explanation on this is speculative and unscientific. Not only this, but for Frazier (1957: vii-viii) there seems to be little point in the exercise, since the 'real problem is not ... the discovery of African survivals, but rather the study of the organisation and role of the Negro family in a changing society or in a new society which is coming into existence'.

Echoing Frazier's views from the Caribbean were sociologists Fernando Henriques, Michael G. Smith and Dom Basil Matthews. Henriques (1973(1949): 321) made his position clear by contrast with that of Herskovits.

Professor Herskovits' view is that the original West African forms of the family survived in the Caribbean and in the New World generally. My own contention is that the forms of the family in the West Indies are *sui generis*. They are in fact a product of the peculiar conditions of slavery. To some extent these forms may have been influenced by the fact that slaves were largely drawn from polygamous groups, but the dominant influence has undoubtedly been that of slavery.

While certain components of slave culture such as 'verbal' religious traditions may have persisted, this was not the case with family forms which were controlled by the masters and forced into new shapes.

Patterns of family life could not survive as a verbal tradition. Whereas the slave could, and did, practise his magic and divination in secret, he could not perpetuate his ancestral family forms in secret. The pattern of his family life was governed by the will of his master. With the exception of the 'bush Negro' of Dutch Guiana who has, through isolation, evolved a matrilineal family pattern which owes little to slavery, the contemporary family structure among the New World Negroes can be distinguished as a phenomenon due mainly to the influence of slavery (Henriques 1973(1949): 322).

Smith (1957: 34-46, see Article/Extract 2 at end of chapter) provided a more detailed critique of the 'Afro-American research' of Herskovits and proceeded to conclude that the system of plantation slavery accounts for family form among the lower class in the Caribbean.

The persistence of high illegitimacy rates, unstable unions, and anomalous forms of domestic groups in the West Indies are all due to the same conditions. These conditions had their historical origin in slavery, especially in the mating organisation of slaves. West Indian slaves were not allowed to marry but they were free to cohabit consensually or to mate extraresidentially, as they pleased, except that slaves having different owners could scarcely establish a common home. Many old accounts of West Indian slavery describe these conditions. Slave children were the property of their mother's owner. Slaves could contract or dissolve unions informally, at will. Occasional references indicate that slave headmen often had two or more mates, living with one and visiting the others (Smith 1962: 260).

Under the system, the authority of males as husbands and fathers was eroded and family composition continually disrupted by the sale and removal of members. The result was the reduction of the family unit to mother and dependent children.

From the moral perspective of a Catholic sociologist, Matthews adopted a similar position by claiming that the plantation institution and not the African past is responsible for family form in the Caribbean. Attitudes and practices, with their foundation in the 'evils' of the plantation system, were established during slavery, producing a 'low grade mentality' which was carried forward, reinforced by the poor economic conditions and moral and social ills of the free plantation era and demonstrated most significantly in the persistence of 'random' and 'irresponsible' concubinage.

The plantation in freedom is the heir and repository of a vast New World tradition, a living tradition of customs and attitudes, adopted or adapted, established and developed within the institution of slavery and as a part of the institution (Matthews 1953: 30).

Thus the free plantation became, in its own right, the matrix of a complex of ideas and practices concerning marriage the roots of which went back into the system of slavery. The free plantation is indeed the inaugurator of the non-legal union as a social institution (Matthews 1953: 31-32).

Besides being of its very nature a favourable breeding ground for the non-legal union, the free plantation carried over from slavery a tradition of indifference to marriage in so far as the servile class was concerned. And so, the plantation — symbol of the social order of its day — can be seen quite clearly to preside at the formation of public opinion in the matter of non-legal unions for the populace (Matthews 1953: 32).

The debate between Herskovits and Frazier and those who followed their leads was not confined to the relatively straightforward task of identifying the origins of Negro family patterns, but was conducted also at the level of ideology, producing heated arguments concerning the identity and personality of New World Negroes. The Frazier following claimed that slave animal instincts replaced African culture and that the patterns of life which developed subsequently among Negroes in the New World were artificial and second-rate, no more than unsuccessful attempts to copy the standards of white super-culture. Herskovits and those supporting his position expressed the view that, although the African beliefs and practices had taken a battering during slavery and the hard years that followed, sufficient had been retained to make a valuable contribution to contemporary New World Negro culture. Herskovits explicitly stated that contemporary family patterns are 'not pathological at all', but reflect 'custom resilience and malleability' in the context of Caribbean circumstances (Herskovits 1947: 296). He concluded by warning of the dangerous implications of Frazier's views for Afro-American identity and racial tension in the United States.

To accept as 'moral' only those values held moral by the whites, to regard as 'culture' only those practices that have the sanctions of a European past is a contributory factor in the process of devaluation, if only because to draw continually such conclusions has so cumulative an effect. A people without a past are a people who lack an anchor in the present. And recognition of this is essential if the psychological foundations of the interracial situation in this country are to be probed for their fullest significance, and proper and effective correctives for its stresses are to be achieved (Herskovits 1958(1941): 185-186).

It is unfortunate, therefore, that the generation of anthropologists and sociologists who carried forward the study of family and kinship in the Caribbean were influenced more by Frazier's perspectives. During the 1950s and 1960s, the views of Herskovits were discredited and it is only recently that there has been a revival of interest in and an appreciation for his position. For example, the work of Sidney Mintz and Richard Price, which we examine in more detail in Chapter VI, also adopted an anthropological culture-history approach, which they claimed 'refines — rather than discards or disproves — earlier approaches' (Mintz and Price 1976: 43). They acknowledged their debt to Herskovits although, instead of defining their task as the identification and classification of overt socio-cultural forms and explicit beliefs, they were more concerned with culture at the level of 'cognitive orientations', that is cultural principles, assumptions and understandings, and sought to interpret the social process whereby enslaved peoples kept alive African ideas as they created and remodelled culture and established social institutions and communities in the Caribbean.

Functions

The period of family studies starting from the end of the Second World War was dominated first by social welfare workers and then by social anthropologists. They shifted the focus of attention from origins to functions, to a concern with the functioning family or, from their perspectives, with the malfunctioning family. Within this general approach, two major trends can be identified; the first has become generally known as social pathology, the second, as structural functionalism. We examine them in turn.

Social pathology

The objective of the investigators who viewed family in the Caribbean from the perspective of social pathology was not to provide a theoretical explanation, but to investigate Caribbean family structure as a social problem. In this, they were prompted by the conclusions of the West India Royal Commission (Moyne Commission) of 1938-1939, which travelled through the British Caribbean colonies collecting evidence on social and economic conditions. As M. G. Smith (1970(1957): iv) explained:

> The numerous practical or social problems presented by the characteristic patterns of West Indian (Creole) mating and lower class family life have attracted continuous attention ever since 1938 when a Royal Commission appointed by the British Parliament to survey the social and economic conditions of this region and to recommend appropriate programmes for action, dwelt on the evident 'disorganisation' of family life and on the apparent increase of 'promiscuity' as against faithful concubinage, the 'common law' or consensual cohabitation which has hitherto been accepted as the Negro peasant's equivalent of marriage and the basis of his family life.

The language of the commissioners is significant. Concerning the family, for example, their report stated,

> the argument that the man is the head of the household and is responsible for the financial upkeep of the family has less force in the West Indies, where promiscuity and illegitimacy are so prevalent and the woman so often is the supporter of the home (Great Britain, West India Royal Commission 1945: 217-220).

To remedy the situation, a band of social welfare workers was sent from London by the Colonial Development and Welfare Office, perhaps the most well-known of whom is Thomas Simey.

From the perspective of social welfare and administration, Simey's main task was to devise a programme to deal with the social problems of Caribbean society. For him, these problems had their roots in contemporary family life which, in turn, was profoundly affected by the prevailing economic situation, specifically by the poverty he described as the 'most striking fact about West Indian peoples' and the 'first factor which moulds the West Indian personality' (Simey 1946: 91). From this perspective, Simey (1946: 47-48,53) criticised the work of Herskovits as an impossible foundation for social policy, while identifying with that of Frazier. He described Frazier's book, *The Negro Family in the United States*, as a 'work so penetrating that it is not only an indispensable guide to the social problems of the West Indies, but also ranks as a major contribution to the general science of sociology' (Simey 1946: 49).

Simey (see Article/Extract 3 at end of chapter) found kinship patterns in the Caribbean to be severely lacking in many respects. He described family life as 'loose' and unstable and relationships as 'casual'. Conjugal ties were occasionally faithful and enduring, but more often 'promiscuous' and 'transitory'. Fathers may have done their best, but their contacts with their children were irregular and, as a result of poverty, they were unable to provide economic support. Children, though loved, were illegitimate, effectively fatherless, unschooled and subject to 'severe', erratic parental discipline. His inquiries in Jamaica found that many boys of between 12 and 16 years of age had left home to join street gangs (Simey 1946: 15-16, 84, 88, 89-90).

Simey pursued the argument from the family to the wider society. For him and for others who followed his lead, the family is the 'outstandingly important social institution of the West Indies', so that if the family failed to live up to certain standards, that is western, Christian standards, then the whole fabric of society would suffer the consequences (Simey 1946: 79). The crisis in Caribbean family life, therefore, brought with it a range of social problems, juvenile delinquency in particular. In other words, the problems of society are ultimately attributable to the inadequacies and weaknesses of the family. It is poverty, in turn, which has created these families. Resorting to a level of crude economic determinism in an effort to prove his point, Simey (1946: 91-92) linked the lack of food, the absence of a shared family meal and the lack of dining tables and chairs with family looseness. (For further discussion of Simey's approach from the perspectives of social policy, see R. T. Smith 1982)

The mandate of these colonial officials, as social welfare workers, was not merely to identify the problems of family life among the poor in the Caribbean, but also to do something about the situation. Their central concern was how to persuade people to adopt the superior co-residential, nuclear family sanctioned by marriage and producing legitimate children. Several social policies were set in train in an effort to alter the structure of lower-class Negro families and, in the process, to uplift the moral and social well-being of that sector of Caribbean societies. Perhaps the most notorious of these efforts was the Mass Marriage Movement of Jamaica.

To halt this presumed spread of 'promiscuity', in 1944-5 Lady Huggins, wife of the then Governor of Jamaica, launched an island-wide campaign to marry off consensually cohabiting couples and any others whose mating status and relations seemed to warrant this. This Mass Marriage Movement was initiated in response to the Royal Commission's demand for 'an organized campaign against the social, moral and economic evils of promiscuity'. However, being based on ignorance of Jamaican folk society and family life, the movement was equally misconceived in its methods and goals, and proved unsuccessful. At its greatest impact the movement lifted the Jamaican marriage rate from 4.44 per thousand in 1943 to 5.82 in 1946. By 1951 the marriage rate and the correlated illegitimacy ratio among annual births had reverted to their earlier level. By 1955 the Mass Marriage Movement had petered out.

Several conditions ensured the failure of this Mass Marriage Movement, despite the energy and skill with which its director, Lady Huggins, marshalled the churches, schools, press, radio, welfare agencies and 'national' associations behind it. Above all, the campaign was based on the erroneous notion that because the elite and lower classes employed a single word, marriage, to denote a particular conjugal institution, this had identical or very similar meanings, value and significance among these social strata. We now know that this view is only superficially correct .... Being thus conceived in error, the Mass Marriage Movement could hardly succeed; and its early signs of failure indicated the need for systematic sociological studies of those unfamiliar familial institutions with which the problems of 'promiscuity', marital instability, defective paternity and child socialization, high illegitimacy were all evidently linked, though in obscure and problematic ways (M. G. Smith 1970(1957): iv-v).

M. G. Smith (1970(1957): vii) concluded his discussion of the campaign on a note of caution concerning the lessons to be learnt from the fiasco.

If the Mass Marriage Movement did little else, it should surely have served to demonstrate this vital need for adequate knowledge of West Indian social conditions in advance of the 'organized campaigns' mounted to remedy or reduce them. Intensive sociological research designed to elucidate the forms, 'causes' and implications of West Indian family organization should thus rank very high on the list of essential steps towards the reconstruction and development of local society; and the very limited and costly advances achieved by various schemes of social development launched during the past twenty years merely demonstrate the fundamental character of this need for scientific knowledge of these social conditions before proceeding with further schemes of this sort.

As we shall see in the next section, the challenge was taken up by a number of researchers, as they embarked on intensive studies of Caribbean lower-class family life.

Structural functionalism

The structural functional perspective was introduced into the Caribbean in the early 1950s and marks the next stage in the development of family studies in the region. With this new phase, the concentration on 'lower-class, Negro family and mating patterns' continued, but the approach was different. It was dominated by anthropologists trained in the British structural functional tradition. For example, Edith Clarke, Fernando Henriques and Judith Blake conducted research in Jamaica, Raymond T. Smith in British Guiana (now Guyana), Sidney Greenfield in Barbados and Michael G. Smith in Grenada, Carriacou and Jamaica. The two classic ethnographies of this period, *My Mother Who Fathered Me* by Edith Clarke and *The Negro Family in British Guiana* by Raymond Smith, provide the basis for detailed discussion in this chapter. This is preceded by some general points concerning the methodology and theoretical assumptions of structural functionalism that influenced the work of these researchers.

True to their anthropological training, the structural functionalists investigating family in the Caribbean conducted detailed, rigorous fieldwork. Their meticulous approach to data collection constituted an important advance over the previous superficial social pathology investigations, which, as we have seen, were loaded with undisguised ethnocentrism and which provided the basis not only for an assumed understanding of family form, but for some very misguided attempts to remedy what were seen as its serious shortcomings. As Sir Hugh Foot (1970(1957): 9), Governor of Jamaica, wrote in the preface to Clarke's book,

we are constantly reminded of how little we know of the attitudes and suspicions and weaknesses and aspirations and all the fine qualities of the country people. In housing when we came to carry out the big programme of reconstruction following the 1951 hurricane, again we discovered how little we knew about the way the ordinary Jamaican families live. It has been the same in carrying out all branches of Government policy —

in our health services, in our education and in industry. We build the super-structure without a real knowledge of the foundations.

In every aspect of national life, and specially in the fields of labour and land tenure, Edith Clarke has shown us how important and urgent it is to base policy on knowledge acquired and recorded without bias and without sentimentality.

Indeed, for M. G. Smith (1962: 12) revised methodologies were essential if researchers were to avoid the premature, derogatory labelling of Caribbean family structure.

Various authorities have simply written off the West Indian family as chaotic and disorganized. Others have accepted this disorganization as a fact and sought to account for it by slavery or by the persistence of Africanisms in a modified form. I would suggest that the characterization of West Indian family relations as 'chaotic' or 'systematic' should await analyses based on sufficiently comprehensive materials to provide an accurate model.

Both Clarke and R. T. Smith immersed themselves in village communities in their respective territories for an extended period of time. For Clarke, fieldwork extended over two years, while for Smith, the period was 19 months. They combined their in-depth techniques of participant observation and unstructured or 'free' interviews with the collection of statistical data on household composition and conjugal union status. While R. T. Smith stuck closely to the role of the academic, Clarke combined hers with that of social administrator and 'Jamaican patriot' with a family heritage of commitment to improving the lot of the poor in Jamaica (Foot 1970(1957): 7-10). R. T. Smith (1971(1956): 228) trod more carefully, claiming, for instance, that it was 'not within our competence to discuss the psychological implications' of the presence or absence of a father-figure for the socialisation of children, though he did link companionate unions with inadequate child care and delinquency (R. T. Smith 1957: 69). Clarke, on the other hand, was more inclined to pass judgement, arguing that the family was not as it ought to be in this regard. We examine her position on childhood socialisation in more detail in Chapter VIII.

The theoretical assumptions of structural functionalism reoriented these researchers away from the investigation of origins to the study of functions, that is, to how things worked in contemporary perspective. To answer this question they redirected attention from history and culture to social structure. R. T. Smith (1971(1956): 231-232) illustrated this shift in focus in a critique of the Herskovitses study in Trinidad, highlighting from the perspective of structural functionalism, what he saw as their shortcomings and omissions.

Our contention is that the Herskovitses fail to analyse the contemporary social system fully; treat structure and culture as being of the same order of generality; and fail to recognize that these two orders of social facts need to be treated within different frames of reference. Cultural symbols which are clearly derived from Africa may serve as vehicles for the expression of new values in Toco, or in the West Indies generally, and the tracing of their origins and their new integration into a coherent system is an important task for anthropology, admirably tackled by the Herskovitses .... However, the study of social structure does not respond to the methods used by Prof. and Mrs. Herskovits, and the prior task of sociology in this field is the elucidation of the social structure of a functioning system within a general theoretical framework which permits of comparative study at a higher level of abstraction than the purely descriptive.

Essentially, the structural functionalists were asking how the interrelated parts of a system functioned to meet the needs or 'functional prerequisites' of the total structure. The necessary integration between the parts of the system to maintain the order and stability of the whole is provided by value consensus and patterned relationships. The emphasis of the model is on consensus and solidarity, not strain and conflict. Seen in this light, the family is still an indispensable institution, the importance of which lies in its contribution to the integration and smooth working of the society. Towards this end, the family performs several important functions. R. T. Smith (1957: 67-68)(see article 4 at end of chapter) identified six such functions to include child care, sexual services, domestic services, economic support, managerial functions and status-defining functions. As regards child care, for example, a major function of the family is the socialisation of the young, to instil social norms and values so that they will become integrated adult members of society. In order to properly and efficiently fulfill these functions, male and female roles and relationships ought to be separate, complementary and asymmetrical. Women's roles as wife and mother involve household chores and child care in the domestic domain, as an extension of biological reproduction, while men, in their roles as husbands and fathers, earn economic support for the family. Women should submit to the authority of their husbands. Additionally, from the perspective of structural functionalism, the society comes before the individual and social institutions, especially the family, are there to create, mould and control their members.

The structural functional model stresses stability, and the researchers went to considerable lengths to point out the distinction between their approach and that of the earlier investigators. Clarke, for instance, condemned the search for the historical roots of the Caribbean family either in slavery or in European and African culture as 'dangerous' and 'sterile'. She stated her position as follows:

> So far as the family is concerned there are still profound class differences in form, in household structure, in the basis of the union in marriage or concubinage and in the parental roles. And it is our thesis that these differences are not explicable either by reference to the different inherited cultural patterns or solely by the historical facts of slavery.

> The important point for an understanding of the contemporary situation is that conditions which make it impossible for men to perform the roles of father and husband as these roles are defined in the society to which they belong, **persist in present-day Jamaica** and it is in conditions as we find them today that we shall most profitably look for the explanation of the 'unstable' features of family life to which such prominence is being given (Clarke 1970 (1957): 21) (Emphasis in original).

In like manner, R. T. Smith (1971(1956): 228) made the following claim:

> Writings on New World Negro family organization have tended to concentrate to some extent on the controversy as to whether the form of the New World Negro family is the result of the peculiar conditions obtaining on the plantations during the period of slavery or whether it can be seen as a modified survival of an 'African' family pattern. Equally plausible theories supported by historical evidence have been advanced on either side, and the polemical discussions have brought to light a considerable body of information and have been productive of many profound insights. It would seem, though, that there is a need for synchronic analysis, which attempts to understand the working of the system without any pre-conceptions as to its previous states. There is

always a danger that the prior task of sociological analysis may be side-stepped when historical factors are prematurely introduced as 'explanatory' devices.

R. T. Smith was of the view that investigations over a limited time span were sufficient to achieve the main task, that is, to identify regularities in family patterns. He did, therefore, introduce a short-term time dimension by identifying changes which occur during the life cycle of the family, an exercise which we shall examine more closely in Chapter III. But he claimed to have deliberately avoided a more long-term dimension because of the faulty memories of his informants. Most importantly, however, he considered this unnecessary for he concluded that there had been little real change in family patterns over the years in the communities he was studying.

He provided the following justification for his approach:

> We are perfectly aware of the fact that we are in some senses transforming a pattern of synchronic distribution of types of household groups into a pattern of distribution along a time axis, but there is some justification for this in that the age of the household head is in fact a point on a time scale, and our observations are backed up by individual life histories. Under actual field conditions it proved extremely difficult to get detailed histories of particular households as opposed to individuals, and it has been felt to be more satisfactory to deal with distributions which could be actually observed and did not depend on the memories of informants, particularly relating to their childhood. In a system such as this, where there is a fair amount of movement from household to household, and accretion and shedding of members of the household group, there tends to be selective remembering concerning the exact constellation of kinsfolk who were members of the household group when the informant was a child. On the other hand, the case histories of individuals and the general comments of informants do not suggest that there was any great difference in the general pattern of domestic life say fifty years ago. It therefore seems justifiable to regard existing households as representing different stages of development though it is less accurate than actually observing a developmental sequence over a period of years. We have tried to present as clear a picture as possible by combining observed distributions with a case-history approach (Smith 1971 (1956): 112).

But how exactly did the structural functionalists interpret Caribbean family structure? We proceed with a more detailed analysis of the work of Clarke and R. T. Smith as represented in the two pathbreaking studies written at the time. We then highlight the notion of 'matrifocality' which dominated their work and which, even after much attention and criticism, has survived to the present as an important analytic concept in the understanding of Caribbean family patterns.

Edith Clarke: *My Mother Who Fathered Me*

For Clarke, the explanation of family patterns was to be found in community organisation. A comparison of the three Jamaican communities or 'Centres' in which she studied and which she fictitiously named Sugartown, Mocca and Orange Grove, showed community life to differ significantly and it is to these differences that she attributed variations in family life.

Life in Sugartown was dominated by the sugar industry which formed the economic base of the community. Population size, geographical mobility and economic well-being all fluctuated with the seasonality of sugar. Residents lived in overcrowded shacks, making 'any sort of decent home life within them impossible for the majority of the population' (Clarke 1970(1957): 23). Mocca was a small, mixed farming community in which members survived in extreme poverty year round. Most of the villagers could, however, trace ancestral roots back for many generations and kinship solidarity was strong as 'family and kindred cling together, united in the struggle to find a means of livelihood' (Clarke 1970(1957): 23). Orange Grove was a more prosperous village of citrus farmers in which income was relatively high and steady. Economic activity in Mocca and Orange Grove, in contrast to Sugartown, was based on the household group and entailed 'constant, intimate cooperation' (Clarke 1970(1957): 183). Only in Orange Grove, however, was there cooperation at village level as meetings and activities were organised and local committees established to provide community services. In Mocca, on the other hand, 'neighbourliness is not as operative' (Clarke 1970 (1957): 183), and in Sugartown 'any comprehensive forms of cooperation embracing the community as a whole — men, women and children — had no part' (Clarke 1970(1957): 186). The population of Sugartown was diverse and highly mobile with patterns of behaviour and values contrasting between the permanent residents and the immigrants.

> Where Mocca and Orange Grove were integrated by kinship bonds and a common pattern of life, and organized to permit of constant intercommunication, exchange of ideas and the transmission of approved modes of conduct, Sugartown presented itself as a collection of disparate un-assimilated and opposing aggregates (Clarke 1970(1957): 188).

Clarke's interpretation of family structure in these three communities was comprehensive. Here we summarise her conclusions in relation to conjugal unions, attitudes and practices in terms of sex and procreation, extended family households, illegitimacy and the residential separation of parents and children.

In Orange Grove marriage was clearly the preferred form of conjugal union with the proportion of married couples amounting to 75 per cent. Corresponding figures for Mocca and Sugartown were 35 and 26 per cent respectively (Clarke 1970(1957): 90). Clarke attributed these differences in rates to economic conditions, social status and the stability of the relationship between the couple, each of which was perceived as a function of community organisation. As she explained,

> marriage cannot be considered at all unless the conditions proper to it are fulfilled or appear capable of fulfillment. And some of these conditions place marriage beyond the reach of large numbers of the population, while others make it necessary to postpone marriage until after a preliminary period of cohabitation (Clarke 1970(1957): 78).

Economic preconditions were considered to be all-important.

> It is not considered correct for a man to propose marriage unless he owns a house and, preferably a bit of land. 'A man should not marry and live in a rented house.' The cost of the wedding itself with the extravagant expenditure on clothes, finery and food for the wedding feast often exhausts all the man's savings. But what is more significant is that he is expected to support his wife in a higher status than that which is accepted for a concubine. Concubinage is recognized as a partnership in which there is equal responsibility between both partners in practical affairs. It is considered right and proper for the woman to do any form of work to assist in the maintenance of the home. Marriage, however, is expected to bring about 'a change of life', to release the woman from the anxiety and drudgery of earning her living, to transform her 'from a common

woman to a lady'.... It is derogatory for a wife to 'go out to work' (Clarke 1970(1957). 78).

Orange Grove was the only one of the three communities with the wealth and economic stability required to fulfil these expectations. But economic factors were not the only important ones, for marriage was also associated with social status and social mobility and with community pressure to reinforce the ideals of respectability. Again, Orange Grove was the exception.

Only in Orange Grove among our Centres is society so organized that pressure can be deliberately exercised on the behaviour of individuals. Here marriage has the sanction of respectability and is also the hall mark of status. A small farmer who acknowledged having been promiscuous in his youth when he travelled about the Island said he would never have thought of marriage in those days, but when he returned to Orange Grove and began to farm he married 'to satisfy the public — if he had not, discrimination would have come right in their midst'. In Sugartown individual behaviour and personal relations were not subject to the vigilant criticism of kin or neighbours to anything like the same degree. Apart from the religious incentive, there was no social disapproval of concubinage nor bias towards marriage among the workers or the old families. In Mocca, where family and kin are stressed, public opinion was exerted towards the maintenance of unions and the recognition of parental, conjugal and kinship responsibility, without any particular stress on marriage (Clarke 1970(1957): 82).

Conjugal stability was also a prerequisite to marriage.

Marriage occurs, therefore, as a latter stage in an association begun in concubinage and is an indication that the economic conditions regarded as obligatory have been fulfilled and that the contracting parties have approved one another sufficiently to risk the change in status and responsibilities which marriage implies. It marks the end of a free association which can be dissolved at any time at the will of either party .... Marriage, occurring after a period of cohabitation is, in other words, the affirmation of stability; the seal on a proven conjugal union (Clarke 1970 (1957): 84).

Clarke also identified gender distinctions in conjugal roles and relationships. Women gain respectability through marriage and certain qualities make a good wife.

Fidelity or the intention of being faithful is the first. A woman should show that she can be discreet and that she can justify the higher degree of confidence and trust which a wife has a right to expect. She should bear with poverty, if it comes their way, without discussing it with neighbours. She should not be familiar with any one not her own equal .... She must be able to cook, too, and wash and do housework (Clarke 1970 (1957): 83).

By contrast, maleness is enhanced by sexual prowess and experience (Clarke 1970(1957): 91, 105). Though it is not always possible, for example in the circumstances of Sugartown, the couple ideally maintains a clear division of labour.

Another farmer also in the upper class bracket in Orange Grove told us that his wife did not milk the cow or help with the farm work, not even the light work. It was not the custom if they were delicate, only if they were of a rough disposition. She used to have a kitchen garden. He made it but she called it hers, but she did not do the work herself. He really did not like the idea of seeing his wife working in the fields. She did all the housework and looked after their six children. She cleaned the floor and scoured the pots and pans (Clarke 1970(1957): 144).

Another farmer's wife told us that she and her husband each have their own work to do; his in the field and hers in the home with the children. She does not like field work and she does not interfere with it (Clarke 1970(1957): 145).

Parenting is a woman's responsibility.

The man is satisfied by the proof of his virility and does not necessarily accept any of the obligations and duties of parenthood. These are generally accepted as the woman's responsibility and there is no public censure if he does not acknowledge or fulfil them (Clarke 1970(1957): 96).

Clarke also examined variations between the three villages in terms of attitudes to sexual activity and procreation. In Orange Grove extramarital affairs were a 'serious breach of the social code' and sex was not a topic for discussion.

Among the upper class farmers and their wives it was difficult, if not impossible to discuss the subject of sex. Whenever it was introduced it was shied away from, either with shocked surprise or a refusal to admit that irregular sex relations ever took place. The comment made on our inquiry by one Orange Grove citizen was that 'when he heard the rumour that we were asking sex questions he did not credit it for he thought that we could not be so out of order' (Clarke 1970 (1957): 90).

In Sugartown where 'casual concubinage and promiscuity' were common, attitudes could hardly be more different.

In Sugartown, by contrast, sex was a favourite subject of conversation with both men and women. Men enjoyed talking about their sexual prowess, the number of children they had fathered and the number of their conquests, referring with especial pride to any relationship with a virgin. Both men and women regarded sexual activity as a normal part of adult and adolescent life, and there was never any attempt to temper the discussion if children were present. Childish and adolescent precocity was on the contrary, regarded with tolerant amusement and, in the case of boys, with admiration (Clarke 1970(1957): 91).

By contrast, in Mocca stable family life and kinship solidarity were most valued. Little emphasis was placed on respectability.

In Mocca, where the conjugal pattern is concubinage for life, the family is all important and there was not the least hesitancy in discussing the outside children in the household nor any difficulty in getting particulars in regard to their different fathers. Here illegitimacy has no social significance. At the same time there is little open discussion of sex, and none before their womenfolk. The stress here is on kinship and any extra-conjugal relationships which threatened to disrupt an existing union would be regarded as a serious matter by the family of the injured party. Here, as in Orange Grove, promiscuous or casual affairs were surreptitious and furtive compared with Sugartown where they were carried on openly and where they had greater social importance because of the number of children born to couples who only came together for the period during which work was to be had on the sugar estate (Clarke 1970(1957): 92-93).

Another aspect that we examine here is the extended family household. Clarke's three communities also exhibited differences in the proportions of households consisting of kin in addition to a man, his conjugal partner and their biological or adopted children. She related the prevalence of these households to conjugal union type, kinship solidarity and economic security.

> We are dealing with family groups with children or other kin present. Among such family households in Sugartown, two-thirds are of the simple family type containing children and about two-thirds are based on concubinage; among those based on marriage 43 per cent are of the extended type and there is a much smaller proportion (27 per cent) of those based on concubinage that are extended by the inclusion of other kin. In Mocca, the emphasis on concubinage rather than marriage among these family groups is again clear, but there is a greater tendency for them to be of the extended type than is the case in Sugartown, and this is true for those based on concubinage as well as for those based on marriage. This ties in with the greater solidarity of the kin in Orange Grove and Mocca as compared with Sugartown. In both Centres, the extended family households are approximately equally divided between marriage and concubinage. In Orange Grove, almost as many households are of the extended family type as are of the simple family type with children (Clarke 1970(1957): 122-123).

The final dimension to which we turn our attention is childhood. For Clarke and other structural functionalists, the most important task of the family is that of rearing and training children to become properly socialised adults. Successful performance of this function depends on family structure, that is, on how closely the family conforms to the nuclear ideal. Clarke therefore expressed concern at illegitimacy and the residential separation of parents and their children.

Rates of illegitimacy were relatively high in Sugartown (37 per cent) when compared with Mocca (9 per cent) and Orange Grove (7 per cent) (Clarke 1970(1957): 120). Parallel distinctions were apparent in the proportions of children who were of married parents and living with both father and mother. In Orange Grove 69 per cent of children had what Clarke described as the 'advantage' of living with both parents and, of these, 85 per cent lived with their married parents. Figures for Mocca were 56 per cent and 42 per cent respectively and for Sugartown 50 per cent and 44 per cent (Clarke 1970(1957): 128-129). Conversely, while 23 per cent of the children in Sugartown lived with their mothers only, that is in households from which fathers were absent, the comparative figures for Mocca and Orange Grove were 17 per cent and 15 per cent respectively. These distinctions correlated with the following variations in the performance of fatherhood responsibilities:

> There was no adult pattern of male conjugal or parental responsibility in the Sugartown community as a whole for the young boy to imitate or be influenced by. On the contrary, his early sex-play was regarded with amused indifference, if not admiration, by the older men and he early learned the general attitudes of his seniors that children are primarily if not solely 'woman's business'. It was not part of the social ethic that he should provide for his girl and their children. In fact, his own personal home life as well as that of the majority of his playmates and companions, might demonstrate the exact opposite. There were, of course exceptions, and important exceptions, among the old families and permanent residents of Sugartown. But on the whole it is to Orange Grove and Mocca that we have to turn to find examples of fathers lavishing care

and affection on their children and carrying out their conjugal and paternal duties'
(Clarke 1970(1957): 98).

As we examine the question of child socialisation in Chapter VIII, we will revisit
Clarke's community studies and note her expressions of grave concern about what
she sees as the inadequate patterns of child rearing and training, particularly in
terms of father absenteeism; hence the title of her book, *My Mother Who Fathered Me.*

Raymond T. Smith: The Negro family in British Guiana

Smith, conducting fieldwork in a coastal region of Guyana, also studied in three village settings. These he named August Town, Perseverance and Better Hope. August
Town was established soon after emancipation as ex-slaves bought land which was
previously incorporated into cotton estates. Perseverance, a semi-aquatic village, was
founded somewhat later as settlers first established themselves on abandoned estate
land as squatters and subsequently, in the latter 1800s, legalised their occupation of
the land. The origin of Better Hope as a post-emancipation village is similar to that
of August Town, but the two villages differ today in that Better Hope is more closely
located to the capital city, Georgetown, and therefore more subject to urban and
governmental influences.

From the time of establishment, the villages were characterised by community cohesion, social homogeneity and egalitarianism, based on ethnic identity as 'black
people', common culture, particular place in the total social system and performance of 'tasks in the occupational system, being all-replaceable one by another (allowing for sex and age differentiation of course)' (Smith 1971(1956): 219). As
Smith further explains:

> The main village group forms a localized sub-system of the total social system, but it is
> itself differentiated internally, without however producing any significant social stratifi-
> cation within itself. The 'band' of status differentiations within this group is narrow
> and non-institutionalized, and in fact the main pressures are operating to prevent its
> becoming wider, or in other words to prevent significant status differences from devel-
> oping beyond a point which would destroy the solidarity of the group, and conflict
> with the major values of the total system (Smith 1971(1956): 211-212).

Village solidarity was reinforced by family activities and by the need to cooperate to
construct and maintain dams, sluice gates and trenches to deal with the ever present threat of flooding by sea water, an ecological problem which had the 'effect of
imposing a pattern of corporate life almost as a condition of existence' (Smith
1971(1956): 23). However, community spirit was weakened by two conditions of life
in the villages, namely the high levels of male migration in search of employment
and cash wages, which made it difficult for men to participate in communal activity,
and the increased dependence on the local government system for administrative
control of drainage and irrigation, with the corollary that voluntary co-operation
was replaced by cash payment. Nevertheless, village unity continued to be expressed
in kinship ties, village endogamy and informal ceremonies, such as the wake, rather
than through the institutions of village council, church or school (Smith
1971(1956): 204-205).

Following structural functional assumptions that all social systems have certain
functional requirements and that families fulfil some of these, the central task

which R. T. Smith set for himself was to provide an understanding of how family was structured in the three villages in order to cater to these needs. As he put it,

> we are interested in knowing, firstly, the kind of form taken by these family units in terms of their internal relationships, and secondly, their relationship to other structures in the society. The latter is, in this case, really another way of asking why the family system takes that particular form. We need not concern ourselves unduly with the fact that the domestic unit meets certain 'needs' such as the need for shelter, for sexual satisfaction or for nourishment, for these are 'givens' as far as we are concerned. It is the way in which these needs are satisfied that interests us as sociologists (Smith 1971(1956): 146).

For Smith to provide such an interpretation, it was essential to view the family and community within the context of the total society. Indeed, he was critical of those structural functional perspectives which isolated village communities and investigated them as autonomous social units with well-defined boundaries.

> This book deals primarily with certain aspects of the social structure of three village communities in the coastal area of British Guiana, but in attempting to arrive at an adequate understanding of these relatively small sections of the population we are obliged to consider features of the total society of British Guiana, so interdependent and functionally related are the local communities and the total society of which they are a part (Smith 1971(1956): 4).

The comparative dimension drawn for his study was therefore between community and total society, not between the three communities as was the case with Clarke's study. Although Smith recognised distinctions between the three villages in terms of economic prosperity and urban influences, they were not treated as theoretically significant. Conclusions drawn from one village were generalised to the others and extended to other coastal Negro villages, though not without some reservation.

A number of characteristics of family form in the three villages were identified. In order to summarise them here, we group them around two distinct though overlapping complexes which were identified in the book. The first refers to the incidence of common-law relationships and village endogamy; the second combines weak conjugal ties, male marginality and strong mother-child bonds.

Common-law unions were seen as a 'symbol of class differentiation' (Smith 1971(1956): 181) and an appropriate form of conjugal union in the villages, carrying no social stigma or negative sanction. The transition from common law to marriage was described as 'somewhat meaningless' from the perspective of village family relationships. It made no difference to the status of the male, nor to the rights and responsibilities between the couple. Indeed, in some cases the relationship deteriorated, prompting villagers to conclude that marriage was 'wrong' for themselves (Smith 1971(1956): 181). At the same time, marriage was the most common form of conjugal union in the three villages, for men and for women (Smith 1971(1956): 116-119) and had to be understood, according to Smith, by recognising that the village was not isolated from the values of mainstream Guyanese society which legally acknowledged and religiously sanctioned marriage as the only acceptable form of conjugal union.

Similarly village endogamy, which represented the choice of a partner who was well-known and of similar background, made logical sense when viewed from this perspective.

The emphasis which is placed upon the desirability of marrying within the village is explicable if it is seen in relation to the total social structure of the colony and the place of the lower-class Negro group within it. For a person born in one of our villages, the village represents one of his main points of social reference; it is the place to which he 'belongs', and in which he feels secure. Since the majority of villagers are not concerned with improving their social status through marriage they do not seek a partner who could help them improve that status. If they enter a union with someone from another part of the colony they will perforce have to form new and difficult relationships with strange persons, an experience which can be avoided by marrying someone whose family and background they know already. If one marries a fellow villager then one can also be in close contact with one's own family of orientation and especially one's mother (Smith 1971(1956): 187).

From the perspective of functionalism:

Village endogamy results in a proliferation of intra-village kinship ties which actually militate against internal status differentiation between families, and it thus contributes to the solidarity of the group and its unitary character in the total social system (Smith 1971(1956): 187).

As part of the second familial complex, Smith saw conjugal relationships as weak and gender roles as distinct. The family is essentially woman's business in her roles as mother, wife and grandmother. 'The kitchen is the province of the woman' (Smith 1971(1956): 57) and her daily routine is occupied with cooking, cleaning, ironing, mending and collecting firewood (Smith 1971(1956): 75-77). For Smith, women are also carriers of respectability which is evidenced in marriage and church attendance (Smith 1971(1956): 179,180). Men, on the other hand, are 'marginal' to the family. However, although women own property, including houses and land, (Smith 1971(1956): 59) and there are income-generating opportunities for them, very few have jobs, for this reflects adversely on their spouses' ability to provide economic support (Smith 1971(1956): 75). Women 'cannot be economically self-sufficient' (Smith 1971(1956): 226) and they are for the most part dependent on their male partners and subject to their authority and control. Male household headship is socially prescribed:

The role of husband-father as head of the household, responsible for the group and being the chief provider of cash and economic resources is well established in the system and those households which are headed by females are almost by definition without a male head. Thus women will often say that they are poor and have to work hard because they have no husband to take care of them. The absence of a male is thought of as a deficiency in this sense (Smith 1971(1956): 79).

Smith assumed that the family is structured around the roles and relationships of mother, father and child and that the central problem for investigation is the way in which they fit together.

There is a sense in which we can take for granted the fact that the mother-child relationship will be a close one in any society, and the real problem then begins to centre on the way in which masculine roles are integrated into the family system, and the way in which the mother-child relationship is structured to fit in with the general structure including the masculine role pattern (Smith 1971(1956): 224-225).

The 'marginal' male and the corresponding enhancement of the role of the mother were understood with reference to the minimal functions that the father or husband performed within the Negro family situated on the lowest rung of the ladder of Guyanese society. The father did not have exclusive control over land or any other means of family livelihood. Neither did he function as the head and leader of a unit of production typically the case in peasant society. He played no part in social placement by defining the social status of members of his family or in the socialisation of his children, often doing 'no more than just existing as a father-figure' (Smith 1971(1956): 258). The corollary of male marginality is matrifocality.

Matrifocality

The existence and persistence of matrifocality in the lower-class, black household and family structure is a question that has preoccupied virtually every investigation in the Caribbean. The first scholars of family structure, while they may not all have used the term matrifocality, were essentially concerned to understand and explain the same phenomenon. They identified what they described as truncated and inadequate family structures in which males avoided their responsibilities as fathers and conjugal partners and in which women, as a result, were overburdened and could not single-handedly manage adequately to socialise children and ensure economic support for household and family members. We also saw that they put forward several different and conflicting explanations. Matrifocality was variously attributed to the African heritage, the slave system, poverty, community organisation and contemporary socio-economic circumstances, specifically the inability of males to acquire the occupational status and the income necessary to fulfil the role of husband and father. All of these perceptions, to a greater or lesser extent, reflected the ethnocentrism of the scholars writing at the time by identifying matrifocality as a pathological or deviant variant of the ideal nuclear household and family. In a later work, R.T. Smith (1973: 31) recognised the problem.

> The logical implication of the argument is that the emphasis on 'matrifocality' and the efforts to account for, or to explain it - rather than to show it as one of the several ways of organising the domestic arrangements represents the ethnocentric projections of scholars who appear to be unable to break away from the restrictions imposed upon them by their own cultural tradition.

Accordingly, matrifocality was interpreted as a characteristic form of lower-class Negro family and household structure which deviated from the nuclear norm. It was found alongside male marginality.

> The household group tends to be matri-focal in the sense that a woman in the status of 'mother' is usually the **de facto** leader of the group, and conversely the husband-father, although **de jure** head of the household group (if present), is usually marginal to the complex of internal relationships of the group. By 'marginal' we mean that he associates relatively infrequently with the other members of the group, and is on the fringe of the effective ties which bind the group together (Smith 1971(1956): 223).

The key to the explanation of matrifocality, therefore, lay in the peripheral role of the male in family and domestic activity which, in turn, was explained by the low level and character of his participation in the wider socio-economic system.

In the lowest status group the only basis for male authority in the household unit is the husband-father's contribution to the economic foundation of the group, and where there is both insecurity in jobs where males are concerned, and opportunities for women to engage in money-making activities, including farming, then there is likely to develop a situation where men's roles are structurally marginal in the complex of domestic relations. Concomitantly, the status of women as mothers is enhanced and the natural importance of the mother role is left unimpeded (Smith 1971(1956): 227-228).

In a review of the concept of matrifocality as he expressed it in *The Negro Family in British Guiana*, Smith (1973: 142) stated that he 'tried to set out the major dimensions of the problem ... rather than attempting a "definition" of matrifocality'. In this article, he was anxious to distinguish himself from those who saw matrifocality as female dominance and as a distinct type of household structure. He interpreted it as the focus of domestic relationships centred on the mother figure, rather than her headship, and as a final phase in the life cycle of the domestic group.

Smith (1973: 125) identified matrifocality as a 'property of the internal relations' in accordance with which '**it is women in their role as mothers** who come to be the **focus** of relationships, rather than head of the household as such' (emphasis in original). He elaborated by describing how the matrifocality of the domestic group increases over time.

> During the period of early co-habitation (which may or may not be based on legal marriage), the woman is fully occupied with child-rearing and maximally dependent upon her spouse, but while men contribute to the support of the household they do not participate very much in child-care or spend much time at home. As the children grow older, they gradually begin to drop out of school to help with household tasks or with jobs on the farm and running errands. The woman is gradually freed from the constant work of child-care and when the children begin to earn, they contribute to the daily expenses of the household. It is at this stage that one begins to see more clearly the underlying pattern of relationships within the domestic group; whereas the woman had previously been the focus of affective ties she now becomes the centre of an economic and decision-making coalition with her children (Smith 1973: 124-125).

For Smith, therefore, the matrifocal quality of domestic relationships occurs independently of a male presence and is clearly distinguishable from female household headship. In other words, matrifocality is present and increases whether or not the husband-father is resident and whether or not he is the head of the household. What this developmental pattern also indicates is that, although the essence of matrifocality is the 'focus of affective ties', this shifts with time towards an 'economic and decision-making' basis, implying a change in favour of the woman in the balance of gender-based household authority.

Summary: Structure and values

The social welfare workers and anthropologists who set the stage for family studies in the Caribbean came from abroad, mainly from Britain, the colonial mother country. They developed a fixation with lower-class Negro 'mating' and family structures. Middle and upper-class families appeared to be 'normal', but those of the lower class were different from anything they had ever known. These 'irregular' patterns, therefore, required scholarly explanation and, for some, social policies to rectify the deficiencies.

For Herskovits and Frazier the explanation was to be found in the past. Lower-class Negro family forms had their origins respectively, in Africa or in the slave plantation regime. But in neither case did these scholars limit themselves to a study of the family. Herskovits examined all aspects of culture from economics and technology to religion and magic and, although Frazier devoted one book to the study of the Negro family in the United States, his other works covered other areas of concern.

When the social anthropologists took over, however, the obsession with lower-class Negro family forms took root. The structural functionalism that dominated their studies contained definite ideas about family life. Accordingly, the family was defined as universal, nuclear in structure and performing several vital tasks for the social system. It followed, therefore, that if there was something wrong with this family structure, then a number of serious social problems would inevitably occur. The family, for example, was seen to play a crucial role in the socialisation process, moulding and training young children to take over the society as responsible adults. Badly-raised children who grew into juvenile delinquents and a number of other family-based problems threatened the whole social and moral fabric of society. These assumptions dominated the Caribbean family studies of social anthropologists during the late 1950s and early 1960s, defining what they saw and how they interpreted it.

The structural functionalist interpretations constituted an important advance over the crass ethnocentrism of the social pathologists, who had come to conclusions about chaotic and disorganised Caribbean family structures on the basis of virtually no data and who were more interested in doing something about 'the problems' than in conducting methodologically sound investigations. The systematic and meticulous fieldwork conducted by the anthropologists as they observed and participated in the lives of their informants for extended periods of time, provided a detailed body of information on family patterns from several different Caribbean territories. But their interpretation of this ethnographic data was controlled by the ideological and theoretical assumptions of their model. As we shall see in the following chapter, the model defined the family for them as a co-residential nuclear unit, ideally and in practice. Gender roles and relationships were also prescribed. Men were breadwinners and authority figures so that where they did not live up to expectations, they were described as 'marginal' and families as 'matrifocal'. Despite the fact that men did not perform these familial duties, they were still assumed to be household heads, and yet their familial authority was said to depend on the economic support they provided. Women were assumed to conform to the values of respectability (for more detail see Wilson 1969, 1973). They were confined to the domestic domain, spending 'a greater part of their time within their own house and yard' (Greenfield 1966: 106) immersed in motherly and wifely duties under the authority of their male partners. They were modest and obedient and exhibited proper standards of fidelity and morality. We reiterate an earlier statement concerning the resulting discrepancies between the image and the reality of Caribbean women's lives.

> These stereotypes and standardized portrayals of women are distorted and misconceived. They present a pattern of submissiveness, a preoccupation with home, motherhood and domesticity and an economic security derived from dependence on a man which is highly unlikely in the circumstances of poverty, unemployment and economic uncertainty in which many Caribbean women live (Barrow 1988: 162).

Structural functionalism also steered these researchers towards an image of pluralist Caribbean societies with self-contained villages and Negro cultural segments with distinct family norms and by extension, for some (Henriques 1953), to conclude that Negro families were the same throughout the Caribbean. There were occasions, however, when evidence of cultural integration appeared in their work. For example, the seeds of what was later to become the Creole model of Caribbean society were evident in R. T. Smith's claim that the matrifocal family was not a distinct sub-cultural type, 'a matter of degree rather than some absolute quality of the system' (R. T. Smith 1957: 70), and his recognition of the influence of mainstream Guyanese marital values in village life. Structural functionalism gave priority to the study of social structure so that family structures and the way in which they functioned to fulfil certain needs constituted the main focus of Caribbean family studies. Furthermore, R. T. Smith noted similarities of family structure in culturally and ethnically different social groups, East Londoners and Scottish miners and so on, and proposed an extension of the approach to include comparative studies of families in contemporary social systems with similar structural features. Thus the comparative study of social structures was in, culture was no longer important and history was dismissed as speculation. Finally, structural functionalism, by emphasising the needs of the system, presented a picture of individuals constrained by society, by the family in particular. The family functioned to model individuals into socially acceptable adults who assimilate social values and conform to social norms and who must accept this as inevitable. As we shall see in Chapter IV, the next stage in the theoretical development of Caribbean family studies involved attempts to introduce the individual into structural functionalism through the concepts of 'personal choice' and 'adaptive flexibility'.

READINGS

M. and F. Herskovits

TRINIDAD VILLAGE

In analyzing the culture of the Toco Negroes, we are confronted with an intricate and subtle example of cultural integration. The processes of human civilization in change under contact, operating in terms of the specific historic sequences that stripped the Africans of certain of their ab-original institutions and made for the kind of adaptation their descendants achieved, have produced the psychological complexities that have been seen to exist behind a façade of cultural simplicity.

Historically considered, the roots of Toco culture lie in Europe and Africa. Yet neither the institutions under which its people live, nor their attitudes toward their ways of life are at any single level in full consonance with either European or African tradition. For where, as in Toco, the power and prestige of the European stock have effectively set the tone of convention in European terms , retentions of African custom in immediately recognizable form are relatively few. The structure of society, its economic base, its political controls, its religious practices have been seen to be in large measure European. The validation of these forms of behaviour is at the same time seen to lie in traditions that give to them meanings not shared by Europeans. What has happened is that the African contribution to this culture, functioning beneath the surface, and giving its own significance to European institutions and beliefs has more often been made in terms of reinterpretations of African custom than as full-blown retentions of African ways of life.

We may now look back at this culture in the light of the hypotheses advanced in our opening pages, indicating what of African custom has been retained, how this was integrated with the European conventions that were accepted, and how both these were re-interpreted in terms of one another. In doing this, we shall refer not only to relevant aspects of the cultures of West Africa and the Congo, but also to similar adjustments achieved by Negroes in other New World areas. For only in such terms of reference is it possible to assess the underlying significance of this body of custom in New World Negro culture and, more importantly, in the wider sphere of the processes of change in human civilization as a whole.

It has been shown that both legal marriage and the informal union termed 'keepers' share in the formation of the Toco family; that both these enjoy social sanction, though they are endowed with differing degrees of prestige; and that in terms of the patterns of Toco conventions there thus is in this dual system nothing reprehensible. We are, indeed, here faced with one of the most interesting series of reinterpretations to be found in the entire range of Toco or, for that matter, of New World Negro custom. For here is a translation, in terms of the monogamic pattern of European mating, of basic West African forms that operate within a polygynous frame.

In West Africa and the Congo, where the children born of a mating belong to the man's family, and are under his control, certain ritually decreed fees must be paid to a prospective bride's family, and certain tasks must be performed for her father and mother. Should the girl merely join the man and form a union, living together without his paying these fees and discharging these obligations, children born to the couple remain under the control of the woman, or her family, no matter how enduring the match.

In Trinidad, practices governing the payment of fees, or the control of children have disappeared. What is left is the classification of unions into marriage and keeper types, the looseness of the bonds that bind a man and woman in a union — here applying to both classes of matings — and the attitudes derived from the existence, in Africa and later under slavery, of the nucleus of mother and children as the basis of the family structure.

The substance, if not the form of the obligations of a suitor toward the parents of the girl he wishes to marry are to be discerned in legal marriage. The formal letter, which under the law carries contractual force, is the reinterpretation of what, in Africa, are addresses to the parents of the girl made through an elder member of the family acting as an intermediary, and the contractual nature of betrothal; in Haiti, it is known as the *lettre de demande*. The investigation of the family of the young man by that of the girl, and of her family background by his, is similarly fundamental in African practice. The informal convention that a young man work for a few days during the planting season in the garden of his girl's father is a truncated expression of the African requirement that he prepares a field for his prospective father-in-law; though there, unlike Toco, he continues to do this or a comparable task periodically after his marriage. The contributions of food given if a close relative of a fiancé or spouse dies, not mandatory in Toco, is one of the most rigorously observed requirements of a man or woman in West Africa. The need to obtain the consent of the ancestors to the match, by holding a reel dance and giving the *sakara* sacrifice, is entirely African, deriving from the sanctions of the ancestral cult which, in uninstitutionalized form, are represented in Toco by the beliefs in the power of the dead members of the family that, as has been seen, function widely there.

It would be expected that with the disappearance of the sib, and the tradition of counting descent on only one side of the family, African patterns of exogamy would also disappear. In Toco, all that remains of this is a feeling on the part of the old people that one should not marry a second cousin, though even this rule is being dismissed with the dictum, 'Second cousin no family'. Only fragmentary, also, are the retention of West African traditions of the sororate and levirate. There, when a man dies, his brothers and sons customarily marry his wives, and among some West African peoples, when a wife dies, the widower takes one of her sisters. In Toco, however, such marriages are sanctioned only if the original mating produced no offspring.

In all matings, the importance of 'having the family behind you' is to be looked on as the retention of a complex of attitudes and relationships so deeply rooted in African culture that not even the experience of slavery could change it. Europeans also have family ties that strike deep, yet the quality of this feeling is one which, in kind and degree, is quite different from that of Europe. One recalls the shocked reactions in the courtroom when a mother and son bitterly contested the ownership of a plot of ground. A woman does everything she can to obtain the consent of her parents before entering into a marriage or a 'keepers' relationship of which they are inclined to disapprove; a wayward daughter is brought under control by a rite denouncing her conduct to the ancestors. All this is a part of the pattern which, with the sanctions imposed and guardianship granted by the spirits of the family dead, gives stability to family life in full African fashion, even where unions often do not endure.

This also explains the importance of the household in the rearing and training of children. In essence, this is based on the retention in Toco of the nucleus of African kinship structures which, as explained, consists of a mother and her children living in a hut within her husband's compound, also inhabited by her co-wives and their children. That this nuclear unit has evolved into such a household as the one headed by the elderly woman, previously described in detail, where her grown daughters are still more or less under her direction and some of their children entirely given over to her care, merely represents in one respect the logical development of this African institution under the influence of slavery and of the particular socio-economic position of the Negroes after slavery was abolished.

Further examination of this household reveals attitudes that are to be ascribed to other reinterpretations of African custom. We have seen that in this grouping, since the father assumed financial responsibility for a daughter and subsequently for her first child, these two members remained under his guardianship. Unlike the case in West Africa, in Toco the concept of the children 'belonging' to a man has neither ritual nor economic import. Nevertheless, whenever the man provides the support of children born to him, his authority over them is recognized. Of equal significance is the attitude of the woman who heads this household toward the grandchild she has supported from infancy. She had been given no contributions towards the child's rearing, and therefore the child's mother could make no claim on it.

Thus in considering the forms taken by the family and the behaviour associated with it, we are faced with a retention of African custom that has been reinterpreted so drastically as to make the resulting institutions not only susceptible of description as pathological manifestations of the European family but ones which, in fact, have been frequently so described. Nevertheless, as we have seen, these forms of the family are not pathological at all, but rather demonstrate how tenaciously a tradition can be held to, and how the process of reinterpretation can give to custom resilience and malleability in the face of new circumstances.

In examining the customs surrounding birth and training of children during the first years of their lives we shall find it useful again to recall our hypothesis that in the New World the process of stripping from the Africans the larger institutions in their culture left them only the more intimate aspects of earlier ways of life, for here retentions of this order abound. That abortion is held socially repugnant and must be practised, if at all, in secrecy, is not particularly restricted to Africa; but that the enforcing sanction is in the fear that the ancestors, in their resentment, will cause barrenness is African. Another Africanism is found in the fact that a diviner is consulted when a woman has a first pregnancy, or has experienced miscarriages, or her previous children have died.

Notifying the family dead that a first child has been conceived, and asking their aid and that of the saints — transmuted from the African deities, although here European belief enters as well — for a good parturition or, should there have been a series of stillbirths, for the survival of the infant, is similarly in accordance with African custom. The measures taken by the lookman to counteract the evil magic that, in Toco, is believed to have 'tied the baby' in the womb of the mother, or where a woman is held to have a 'jumby belly', represent retentions of African belief and behaviour in forms but little changed.

Toco has carried over from Africa many of the practices surrounding childbirth, and many of the beliefs concerning the significance of various characteristics of the newly born child. Depositing the umbilical cord in a hole over which a fruit-bearing tree is planted is found in many parts of Africa, though there the tree usually becomes the property of the child. In Africa, as in Toco, it is held that a baby with extra fingers or toes will be lucky, and that an infant born feet foremost is a dangerous being. The custom of giving a child born after a series of miscarriages a 'funny' name, acting toward it as though it were disliked, dressing it poorly, taking precautions to nullify the magic that had caused the previous still-births, and vowing the child to a saint — reinterpreted from African deities — all constitute a complex, widely spread among those who live in the areas from which the African ancestors of the Toco Negroes were obtained.

The African derivation of the cult of twins can be localized, for its form indicates the influence of the 'Yarriba' component in the Trinidad Negro population. The fact that twins are held to bring good luck, the elaborateness of the rite of emergence from the house held for them, as compared to that for ordinary infants, their being taken to nearby houses to receive gifts that must be given in two equal parts, and the customs that follow the death of one of the pair are all variants of the Yoruban-Dahomean tradition, even to some of their details. These customs are also found in Brazil, Guiana, Haiti, Cuba, and elsewhere in the New World in similar specific form, where twins are given either their Yoruban or Dahomean designations *ibeji* or *hohovi*. In the Gold Coast, the Ashanti regarded twins as so important that, if they were girls, they became wives of the king, if boys, his servitors; and they were brought to him in a golden bowl. But eastward of the Yoruba, twins are destroyed at birth, for the respect in which the more westerly peoples hold them, because of the supernatural power they are believed to wield, turns to fear.

Other Africanisms found in the care of infants and rearing of children, in addition to the rite of emergence of mother and child from the house nine days after birth, as already mentioned in the case of twins, can be reviewed briefly. Baptism is a Christian rite, but the interpretation of its need to keep the child from joining the spirits of the forest is African; while the one baptismal name that in Toco is held secret is the counterpart of the 'real' name given an infant in Africa, a name whose use exposes him to the force of any magic set against him. That an infant must never be left alone or, if this is unavoidable, must have magical or supernatural protection is a tenet of belief found everywhere in West Africa, its reinterpretation in Toco being manifested in placing an open Bible or prayer book at the side of the child whose mother is urgently called away from it, and has no one with whom to leave it.

The convention of giving an infant a gift when the first tooth appears, and the little ceremony performed when the first deciduous tooth falls out, come directly from Africa. In Dahomey as in Toco, this first tooth is thrown on the roof of the house — though by the child rather than the mother — and a little dance is held by its playmates, who sing,

"I don't want the teeth of a pig,
They're big!
I want the teeth of a goat,
They're small!"

The experiences — almost inevitably, it would seem, traumatic in effect — of those who soil the sleeping-mat are paralleled in West Africa, even to attaching a live frog to the offender, and sending the child out in the street to be shamed by the taunting songs of its playmates.

Other aspects of growing up which are African either in form or sanction include the manner in which a child is trained in household duties or in working the field, the importance for black magic of a girl's first menstrual cloth, the punishment of wayward children by the ancestors. But most important, to return to the household as a unit, are the attitudes toward father or mother. Here we must once again refer to the hypothesis advanced in the first chapter of this work, since the instances of the relationships within the household that were given show how, in the lower socio-economic strata of Toco society at least, the father, as in Africa, remains on the periphery of the nucleus constituting the household, whose center is the mother, a grandmother, an aunt.

M. G. Smith

THE AFRICAN HERITAGE IN THE CARIBBEAN

The concept of an African heritage in the Caribbean and the New World is not exactly a new one, and its discussion or application cannot help being influenced by previous thinking and research. It is thus both necessary and valuable, before attempting to assess it, to glance backward for a moment at the state of anthropology in which this interest developed.

I think the contrast between anthropology before and since the first World War offers the most direct route to an assessment of present Afro-American studies, in so far as these are conceived in terms of acculturation. Until the time of Malinowski's death, there were three major competing notions about anthropology as a discipline and about the nature of its data. In Malinowski's view, culture was an empirical functional system which included social relations and which lent itself to synchronic studies rather than historical research. In the view of Boas and his students, culture was a historical continuity, the systemic aspects of which could not be predicated in advance of detailed study. In the theory of Radcliffe-Brown, culture was the process of social life, and society as a natural system was the focus of interest in synchronic research.

The ways in which these differing approaches handled historical studies of society or culture varied a good deal. Kroeber's paper on culture as a super-organic, self-determining system, timeless and spaceless,(12) represents an extreme of idealism and reification, while his careful mapping of cultural areas in California(11) represents an equally impressive contribution to ethnology by the study of trait-distribution. Malinowski's search for a zero point at which to begin the study of cultural change(14) was partly an attempt to apply the postulate of the functional equilibrium of culture to diachronic systems without indulging in historical reconstruction or speculation. Radcliffe-Brown ignored this problem, but Robert Redfield, whom he influenced, attempted to combine cultural and sociological data and to develop a typology of change in which spatial position might substitute for time(15). Ultimately, the central conflict between these approaches revolved about conceptions of the nature and relations of culture and society on the one hand, and of diachronic and synchronic anthropological studies on the other.

These differences are still important today; but, as I understand the literature, their former exclusiveness seems to be dissolving. Since the war, it seems that the duality of anthropological data has been recognized increasingly, and the area of agreements about the interdependence of culture and society, and of diachronic and synchronic research, has widened correspondingly. I think few anthropologists today would deny that social structure is embodied in cultural process, or vice versa; and few would hold that, where materials are available, historical research is either outside or exhaustive of the anthropologist's legitimate interests. As I see it, there is now emerging a debate about the nature of anthropology as a natural science, a branch of history, or an aspect of moral science. Fortunately, our subject is broad enough to include all these and other approaches. But the important point to note is that this present debate progresses on the basis of common understanding about the basic materials of interest to anthropologists, culture and society. As Firth has put it clearly: 'Society' emphasizes the human component, the people and the relations between them; 'culture' emphasizes the component of accumulated resources, non-material, and material, which the people through social learning have acquired and use, modify and transmit. But the study of either must involve the study of social relations and values, through examination of human behaviour(7).' Bidney, whose recent book discusses the most prominent theories of culture and society, shares a similar view(2).

I think this recognition of the mutuality, difference, and interdependence of culture and society has important implications for the study of social and cultural change in general, and for the problem of the African heritage in the Caribbean in particular. If we reject the views of Durkheim and Kroeber, that society on the one hand, or culture on the other, is primary and self-constitutive, then we must admit their equal significance in the study of any process of change. This means in fact that the study of acculturation or cultural change cannot be complete without parallel study of social change; that acculturation studies include studies of assimilation; that enculturation is an aspect of socialization, or vice versa. If this is so, it follows that the study of African heritage in purely cultural terms is not adequately conceived and cannot by itself reveal the processes and conditions of acculturation. Thus, if acculturation, rather than the simple identification of elements as African or other, is the aim of such study, we must study the relevant social and cultural conditions equally and simultaneously. In this respect, it is specially of interest to determine the structural correlates of persistence with or without change on the one hand, and the conditions of disappearance, loss, or new developments on the other. Discrimination of persistence through the functional consistency or appropriateness of traits to particular structural contexts permits some grasp of the structural conditions typical of varying degrees or processes of acculturation; and the comparative scope of inquiry allows further precision in their formulation. But to achieve these results and to follow this method, certain initial ambiguities must be ruled out.

The ambiguous relation of cultural process and social organization is especially significant. In one definition, culture includes or presupposes the inclusion of social organization; in another, it is characteristically the activity and content of the social organization. Now if the African cultural heritage is taken to include African patterns of social organization, these specifically social elements of the potential heritage must not be confused with the social contexts in which their persistence or disappearance took place. We must, in other words, keep the New World social context which is the matrix of the acculturation process clearly distinct from those Old World social forms which are included in the possible heritage whose form and function is under study. I think this distinction necessary even where simple identification of African elements is the purpose of study.

But the ambiguities against which we must guard our enquiry are many and serious. There is ambiguity in the concept of an African inheritance itself. Such a concept presupposes a uniformity and uniqueness of African cultures which ethnography does not support. For example, spirit-possession is commonly taken to be an element of African culture persisting among the New World Negroes who practise it. But there are numerous tribes of West Africa among whom spirit-possession is not to be found. Moreover there are many other peoples, including whites, among whom this practice has been reported(4). Similarly, ancestor worship is neither universal among nor peculiar to African societies. Nor is polygyny, and so on. Where tribal attribution can be directly established for elements of the African heritage, these difficulties of formal correspondence tend to disappear, although functional problems remain. But where this tribal ascription is not clearly evident, the types of ambiguity which lurk within the unitary concept of an African inheritance are great indeed. And in my view fairly precise and extensive qualification of this indefinite concept of an African heritage is necessary if it is to prove serviceable for scientific purposes, and to exclude spurious or dubious attributions.

Another serious source of ambiguity derives from the inverted order of this study of African heritage. Instead of starting at the beginning of the process of culture contact and change and then tracing its development up to the present, we start at one end of such a process and try to reconstruct hypothetical courses of development for attributions of varying status and value. This procedure is of course unavoidable if the enquiry is to be pursued at all. It is unavoidable for historical reasons; but precisely because the history of acculturation processes is not sufficiently open to us, it is essential that the greatest care be taken to distinguish between attributions according to their specificity, character, and evidential basis. Failure to make these distinctions clearly and consistently confuses valid and invalid attributions from the start, and thereby confuses thoroughly the hypotheses developed to account for persistence of these attributions. Hypotheses developed to 'explain' the acculturation history of accurate ascriptions may be sound or unsound. Those developed about invalid ascriptions, can only be unsound. Confusion of valid and invalid ascriptions or of specific and indeterminate cultural predicates, therefore conduces to the confusion of hypothetical acculturation histories for ascriptions of all types in a manner which begets controversy rather than cumulative understanding of these acculturative processes. To protect the enquiry against this unnecessary admixture of the sound and the unsound, something like a rigorously critical methodology is requisite.

Ambiguities also develop through the uneven historical materials which bear on African cultural persistence. In some cases, these materials might be sufficient to indicate factors in the processes of acculturation, and their relative weights. In other cases, they may serve as guides to the relative probabilities of competing hypotheses. In yet other cases, they may offer little or no information at all. In all cases, however, supplementary analyses of the institutions or customs under study are necessary to provide hypotheses about their distribution in the area of interest; and these analyses must focus on the functional relations of the forms under study with other social practice, and with varying social conditions and contexts. Checks provided by comparative studies of the distribution of these traits will then serve to refine the hypotheses developed through functional analyses, and may perhaps increase our understanding of the acculturation process at work. But if the study of African cultural persistence is conceived in terms of acculturation rather than the simple identification or attribution of elements, it is necessary to include both lost and persistent culture-traits of African origin as far as these can be established by distributional studies based on African ethnography, and as far as they are known to be present in or absent from the New World areas of interest. In the study of lost forms also, historical and functional approaches must be combined to develop specific hypotheses relating to the conditions of disappearance or change. The same point holds true for new developments among the New World Negroes such as the Calypso or steel-bands.

Yet other ambiguities in this enquiry develop with reference to the distribution of elements of African heritage among New World populations, Negro or other. For instance, if jazz, which is regarded as a part of the African heritage, is found among the whites also, then we must examine its distribution among whites in the same way that we examine the distribution of African-type folk tales or head-ties among the Negro population. But in these studies of distribution, it is not sufficient merely to report the place-names where items of imputed African provenience are to be found. This tells us nothing at all about their distribution within such areas, their centrality or marginality. It is surely far more informative and important to know the conditions within which such items are to be found characteristically and marginally, the socio-economic levels and organizations of which they are typical and not typical, and their functional values in either context.

Granted these ambiguities, it is especially important in discussing or investigating the African heritage in the Caribbean to define what we mean by each of these terms. Without such definition, discussion and enquiry alike dissolve into amorphous and chaotic forms. Definitions will of course vary with purpose; but I suggest that the enquiry and discussion can gain a great deal in precision and development from the initial adoption of definitions which rule out, or at any rate, distinguish sharply, ambiguous or uncertain attributions. Some of the ambiguities facing study of this general problem have already been mentioned. In directing attention towards these ambiguities, I am simply presenting evidence which indicates the need for a more refined methodology than at present characterizes this area of research, and also for a more precise and less hypothetical system of categories.

The Caribbean as a geographical region appears to present few problems of definition. Socially, however, the area is not a unit. It is differentiated internally by different metropolitan associations, by various religious, linguistic, and cultural affiliations, by different racial-population ratios, and by historical differences, particularly with regard to African slavery and its abolition. Clearly differentiae of this order rule out the possibility of a uniform pattern of African heritage in this area, at the same time that it raises problems and possibilities of comparison with it.

This brings us face to face with the problem of defining the African heritage itself. A heritage is something inherited, handed down; loosely speaking, heritage and tradition can be equated. But in areas where change is proceeding, that which is handed down may not be traditional in the usual sense, or not equally so in its parts. Presumably the idea of an African heritage refers to that which is handed down and is African in origin. Such a heritage has three major aspects: the biological, the social, and the cultural. For the study of an African heritage, it is necessary to examine all three in their relations one with the other and with relevant conditions in the wider society.

Biological or racial heritage normally provides a common basis of group identification and differentiation in multi-racial societies such as the Caribbean contains. In such contexts, groups develop stereotypes about one another and about themselves also. George Simpson's work on the Ras Tafarites of West Kingston, Jamaica(17), provides a neat illustration of this, a case in which the African heritage functions as an ideological postulate, as a myth which permits withdrawal into defensive escapist cult-groups; and clearly a case in which the postulate of African heritage does not correspond with cultural reality. This instance is of course far from peculiar in the ideological racism it represents. As far back in Jamaican history as we care to go we can find equally clear examples of this ideological racism(13). In multi-racial societies, especially with relation to their internal differentiation and classification, we are not merely confronted by differences of a biological character, but are faced with conflicting interpretations based on other non-genetic dimensions, predominantly, of course, on social and cultural practice.

In the British West Indies particularly, this social aspect of African inheritance is obvious, historically unambiguous, and important. The African *qua* African was imported as a slave. He was not so much a person as property until emancipation was enacted in 1838. His relations with his European masters during this time are thus not fully analyzable in terms of race relations. The statuses of slave and slaveowner and their interpretations are at least as important. Moreover, we must recognize that ever since emancipation, Negroes have occupied the lowest position of any biological group in the societies of the British Caribbean; and although there is no clearly drawn race or caste line in these areas, prominence and prestige, wealth and power, have historically been distributed in terms of light pigmentation. At the same time, both during and since slavery, Negroes have been subordinated, exploited, excluded from certain institutional systems characteristic of the dominant groups, and subjected to special acculturative pressures in particular fields. For example, Christianity, membership in the formal political system, education and formal occupational association were not always open to Negro participation. On the other hand, pressure has been directed at Negroes to alter their marital habits, as for instance in the mass-marriage movement of Jamaica. Thus a peculiar distribution of acculturative pressures and processes is intimately bound up with the historical status and role of the Caribbean Negro. And this social background to acculturation compels us to devote equal attention to the processes of assimilation, social differentiation, and acculturation in any scientific study of the African heritage. Moreover, the principal historical changes in the social status of Negroes in this area entail, within these frameworks of social transition, diachronic analysis of their socio-cultural organization and its characteristics. The recent rise of trade unionism, of political-party movements based on universal suffrage, and of ministerial systems of government are themselves decisive conditions promoting further changes in cultural process and social structure alike, both within the Negro stratum and in the total society.

With biological and social inheritance we are dealing with accessible and clearly determinate conditions. Biological characters tend to be highly constant and history provides a fair record of the continuity or change of social position and conditions. But cultural inheritance is not so easily definable. The type and degree of persistence or continuity to which it refers is definable variously, according to the precision or type of interest.

In the study of African cultural persistence in the Americas, we are handicapped by lack of ethnographies of the area from which migration occurred, which describe these areas at the time of migration. It has therefore been necessary to extrapolate backward, using contemporary ethnographies of these regions as evidence of the cultural conditions from which the migrants were drawn. But such a postulate rests on assumptions of cultural stability and immobility which are dubious in the extreme, particularly with regard to the West African area; and these assumptions in any case are unverifiable.

Moreover, we are faced with the problems of marked cultural dissimilarities within the West African regions from which the bulk of Caribbean Negroes trace descent. Even when the influence of Islam in this area is excluded, there remain sufficiently important differences of culture for reference to or definition of a cultural pattern as characteristic of this area to remain highly suspect(8). If this is true of Africa, it can hardly be untrue or unimportant in relation to African cultural continuities among New World Negroes. Where traits or complexes can be ascribed to particular tribal traditions, such as Ibo, Dahomey, Kongo, Mandinka, Yoruba, or Akan, this type of problem disappears. But without such tribal attribution, the simple description of a trait or complex as African must often consist in question-begging, and may often be quite spurious.

Faced with the relative instability of cultural traits, the diversity of African cultures, and the relative lack of historical records detailing the processes of transmission of African culture in the New World, we are unavoidably committed in the study of this heritage to put the cart before the horse and to start with end-effects, real or assumed, and then try to work back through their hypothetical processes of persistence, development, or change to some particular tribal culture or to some undifferentiated 'African' culture. In an enquiry of this type, it is therefore especially urgent that we should distinguish as sharply as possible between precise and indefinite forms and between specific and indeterminate attributions. The alternative is simply to perpetuate a wayward enquiry based on poor methodology and to invite the substitution of speculative derivation by the multiplication of indeterminate concepts and hypotheses in place of the search for demonstrable relations.

I suggest that the distinction between specific and general attributions is basic to the fruitful pursuit of our enquiry. By a specific attribution, I mean the ascription of cultural traits to particular cultures in Africa, as Bascom has done with Afro-Cuban divination practices(1) or Herskovits(9) and Deren(5) have done with certain spirits and rituals of Haitian *vodun*. All ascriptions which lack this tribal reference must be classified as general or indeterminate simply because their conceptual assumptions of a general African culture are of this character. I would give as examples of this indeterminate attributions, Herskovits' concept of serial polygyny or of spirit-possession(10).

Both specific and general ascriptions presuppose correspondences of form. Both may be accurate and useful. But since the particular forms to which attribution is made are more easily demonstrable in specific ascriptions, these enjoy a greater certainty and precision than do general attributions, and they offer more rewarding leads for initial study.

Both specific and general ascriptions may be formally identical with African originals, or they may be somewhat changed. Thus the serial polygyny or spirit-possession mentioned above are not identical with the African institutions to which ascriptions of either are made. I therefore suggest a secondary classification, cutting across the distinction in terms of specific and generalized ascriptions, to differentiate those forms which persist without change, those which have persisted but show change, and those which have not persisted at all.

Our categories of cultural persistence therefore have six divisions:

Degrees of Change:	ASCRIPTIONS	
	Tribal	General to Africa
Unchanged forms:		
Changed forms:		
Lost forms:		

I suggest that these six different classes of suspected persistence are not evidentially equal and will vary correspondingly in their utility for research. Briefly, it seems that formally unchanged patterns of specific tribal derivation offer a firmer basis for acculturation research than do changed forms of indeterminate or specific tribal provenience. And although it is of course impossible to establish fully that any particular pattern is completely lost, the hypothesis may be admitted for working purposes in relation to particular patterns in defined areas, such as, for example, the withdrawal of women from farm labour, which I will discuss later.

So far we have been talking purely of forms. To grade and classify ascriptions in terms of probable scientific utility we have constructed a simple grid which focuses on specificity in ascription and identity of form, without any implication about the process of persistence. In my view it has been a great source of confusion in the study of our African heritage to classify forms in terms of hypothetical acculturative processes. If our enquiry in this field is to advance, we must distinguish carefully between three aspects, attending to each separately and in turn. Form is one thing, function is another; process, the third, is the ultimate goal of our analysis.

To make ascriptions simultaneously in terms of process and form is to forestall the study of either separately and of acculturation altogether. Yet this is the method of Herskovits and his associates, whose classifications of traits simply consist in distinctions between retentions, or survivals, reinterpretations, syncretisms, and reintegrations. These are of course processual categories, which may be useful or otherwise in analysis of the processes of acculturation. But they can only beget obscurity when applied to the classification of forms. The type of obscurity thus begotten is mainly obvious in the ambiguity of attributions which this method permits. For example, family organization among Caribbean Negroes is classifiable along these lines as a reinterpretation of West African patterns, when they may be nothing of the sort. And patently spurious ascriptions are possible by this method of classification. Thus Herskovits(10, p. 234) and Simpson(18) both regard baptism and the use of water in the religious practice of New World Negroes as evidence of African cultural persistence through reinterpretation. This is hardly fair. Such uses of water have figured prominently in European Christianity for nearly two thousand years(6). Ascriptions made on the basis of form and process simultaneously are inevitably hypothetical and of ambiguous status. I suggest that form alone provides a sufficiently unambiguous referent for ascriptions, and that we can only proceed to search for process by enquiry into the history and functional relations of ascribed forms.

The functional aspects or values of competing forms have hitherto attracted insufficient interest among Afro-Americanists involved in the study of cultural persistences. Yet its implications for their enquiries are important and various. I shall try to illustrate some of these by certain data drawn from my own experience. Land tenure among the Caribbean peasants, most of whom are of African descent, provides a neat instance. By and large, in most of the British Caribbean islands, the rural population practises a type of family tenure of land which differs markedly from that of the common law and has certain superficial parallels with some Africans systems of tenure. These resemblances led Edith Clarke, who first described this institution systematically, to speak of 'the peasant theory of land tenure, reflecting West African principles'(3). This system of tenure is not peculiar to Jamaica. It is also found among the peasants of Carriacou, a small island off Grenada. There also it bears some superficial resemblances to certain West African systems of tenure. I made a detailed study of the development of this system of folk tenure on a Government Land Settlement established with all regard to the forms and procedure of law. I then found that this customary tenure had developed as a functional adjustment of the population of the Settlement to their social and individual circumstance under the pressure of certain measurable conditions such as migration, population increase, death-order of spouses, and the like(21). In this case African cultural persistence cannot be admitted, partly because the legal establishment of the Settlement broke with this tradition, and more importantly because the development of customary tenure which followed after was governed by demographic conditions.

Other instances of formal parallelism developing on purely functional grounds and in historical conditions which rule out African persistence can be taken from the field of labour organization. In many rural areas, production for subsistence and exchange is commonly found together with *ad hoc* wage labour. When slavery obtained, this balance was paralleled by the distribution of slave labour-time on their subsistence holdings or their masters' cultivation. These distributions were characteristic of slavery in West Africa and the Caribbean(20). Now, as West Indian slaveowners controlled the time allocations of their slaves, and as the owners were Europeans, this formal parallel cannot be interpreted as an instance of African heritage or cultural persistence.

Since the abolition of slavery among the Hausa of West Africa, and in the British Caribbean, there has been a progressive withdrawal of women from manual farm labour. Women are still important helpers in light farm tasks such as harvesting, but in areas of mixed production for subsistence and exchange by small-scale farming, they are otherwise marginal to the field labour force. In both Hausaland and Jamaica, women were actively engaged in manual field work under slavery. The parallelism in development is thus quite real and could conceivably be mistaken for persistence of African cultural traditions. This would of course be inappropriate.

The basis of this withdrawal of women from farm labour consists in the status transition from slave to free. Under slavery, women as well as men were subject to compulsory farm labour. While the abolition of slavery in both areas provided the opportunity to assert the status of freedom, it did not of itself indicate how to do so. In Jamaica, where British land law prevailed and the masters controlled the sugar-producing plains, there was a prompt and substantial exodus to the unoccupied hill country. Among the

Hausa, where title to land is based on use and occupancy, this problem did not arise, and the ex-slaves remained where they were. But in both areas women withdrew from manual field labour. In this way they were able to assert their new status as free persons, not merely for themselves, but for their husbands and families also. The contrast in Jamaica today between the hill-folk, descended from those who left the estate areas, and the population of the plains, descended from those who remained in the sugar belts, is especially clear in this particular. In the plains, women continue to carry out cane-weeding and other manual field tasks on and off estates. In the hills, their participation is highly marginal. Thus, in the Top Hill District, St Elizabeth parish, Jamaica, last year I found that only one woman, an aged destitute, still worked in the fields for cash. The point here is that in Jamaica the same stimulus, abolition of slavery, has developed different reactions, withdrawal or continued participation of women in farm labour, according to different conditions. And that one of these reactions, the withdrawal typical of the women in Jamaican hill country, is identical in form with that observed among the Hausa.

Here we have a formal parallel of negative character, that is, one which could presumably be interpreted as the loss of an original pattern. But this trait is characteristic of neither area entirely. In Africa, for example, among the Ibo, Yoruba, and Nsaw, women engage actively in farm work. In Jamaica, in the sugar belt, although not in the hills, they still practise field labour. The instance we are discussing therefore illustrates how complex problems may arise even where formal identities obtain. This complexity develops due to the diversity of African cultures, the diversity of Caribbean practise and its distribution, the impact of common or different historical conditions and their influence on the pattern in question, and the variable functional conditions of its development in the Old or the New World.

Wage-labour forms for farm-work among Hausa and Jamaicans in rural areas are strikingly similar. Hausa *kodago* patterns are either job or day work. In Jamaica also, day work and job, piece or task work, are the two major modes of arranging wage labour on farms. This type of resemblance suggests community of origin. In my view the suggestion is both erroneous and unnecessary. It is erroneous since such patterns have developed in either area after the African migration to the Caribbean had ceased; in fact, after slavery had been abolished. It is unnecessary since there is a simpler more general explanation of both developments. This explanation also is functional in character. It consists in the fact that cultivators engaged in subsistence production and dependent also on exchange activity for the cash income necessary for certain unavoidable outlays will have to sell their labour to the extent that their demands for cash cannot be met in any other way, as, for example, by trade or craft production. But since these wage-workers are primarily committed to subsistence cultivation, they will not normally be able to engage in long-term labour contracts during the farming season, when their labour will be most in demand locally, nor will they normally be free to migrate at that period in search of continuous work. The appropriate labour contract for such people is therefore one which allows them to attend to their farms as the cultivation schedule requires. This can be provided either by short-term day engagements, or by the type of job, piece, or task-work pattern which allows the labourer to dispose of his labour time as he sees fit.

I have devoted some time to these instances taken from the field of labour organization because the functional values of different types of work organization in different conditions are easily appreciated, and because it is in this respect that the historical record of West Indian slavery is probably most helpful to us. I have been concerned with showing that despite formal parallelism between specific or general African arrangements and certain West Indian practices, African cultural persistence cannot be predicated for these forms simply because of the massive historical discontinuities which slavery produced. Yet these discontinuities do not prevent Herskovits from treating all forms of co-operative farm work among males, such as *gayap* in Trinidad, *combite* in Haiti, *troca dia* in Brazil, or 'lend-day' in Jamaica, equally as instances of African persistence(10, pp. 62, 290-91), despite their highly dissimilar constitution(22). While *gayap* and *combite* are *ad hoc* groups of several individuals, sometimes a score or more, *troca dia* and 'lend-day' are reciprocal and recurrent arrangements between two individuals. These categories of co-operation thus exhaust the probable forms of farm-labour co-operation. In other words, in terms of this approach any case of co-operation in farm work, whether between two or more persons and whether recurrent or merely occasional, is ascribable to African tradition. Now it seems to me that even if we ignored the historical data on this matter, such attributions weaken the study of African cultural persistence by swelling the claims for such persistence through the inclusion of dubious items. It is my contention that functional imperatives may produce parallel forms in similar conditions without the persistence of African traditions being necessary. I think that if the classification of all free co-work in farming as African persistence is admitted, there should be no objection to regarding all forms of mating practice as equally African.

A sufficient number of examples have now been given to illustrate the principal methodology prerequisites for fruitful study of African cultural persistence in the Caribbean and other areas of the New World. I shall attempt to state these conditions simply.

(1) Where specific tribal prototypes cannot be established, the items of African attribution must be demonstrable features of all the principal African cultures contributing to the area in which they are reported.

(2) They must also be features of a type, the persistence of which in Africa as well as the New World would appear to be more probable than their change or disappearance during the period since migration has ceased.

(3) The distribution of these features among the American Negro population must be general, measurable, and linked to known conditions.

(4) There must not be any historical evidence suggesting discontinuous transmission of these attributed traits among the New World Negroes or their recent introduction from Africa.

(5) Traits regarded as evidence of the persistence of African cultural forms must be formally peculiar and distinct from the customs or institutions characteristic of all other cultural groups within the society of their location.

(6) Identities or similarities of form must be shown between the traits of imputed African provenience and the African models from which derivation is traced.

(7) Even where formal identities and historical continuities can be demonstrated, traits which reflect necessary functional adjustments to New World conditions must be distinguished as a group from others for which functional values have not been established. This distinction is of course essential where historical discontinuities in the transmission of African patterns are known or suspected.

This battery of conditions, which should be satisfied before indeterminate attribution is admissible, is simply designed to preserve the specificity of our subject matter, to allow easy verification, and to permit the progressively precise understanding of the processes of acculturation and assimilation at work. Where specific tribal derivation is evident, the enquiry shifts promptly to structural-functional analysis of the traits and contexts concerned; and, on the basis of hypotheses developed therein, attempts to assess the weight of all factors at work in the acculturative process by historical and comparative studies of the custom in question in the various New World *milieux*. It seems quite probable that detailed attention to specific and obvious African traits along these lines will lead gradually to the development of sufficient knowledge about the acculturative processes involved in their persistence, change, or loss, and will reduce the difficulties which at present face enquiries about traits of indeterminate form and origin. We must, in other words, build from the clearly known to the less clearly known, from the concrete and particular to the general.

REFERENCES

1. BASCOM, William R. (1952) 'Two Forms of Afro-Cuban Divination", in *Acculturation in the Americas*, ed. by Sol Tax, Chicago, University of Chicago Press, pp. 169-79.

2. BIDNEY, David (1953) *Theoretical Anthropology*, New York, Columbia University Press.

3. CLARKE, Edith (1953) "Land Tenure and the Family in Four Communities in Jamaica", *Social and Economic Studies*, Vol. I, No. 4, pp. 81-118. Jamaica, University College in the West Indies.

4. DAVENPORT, F. M. (1905) *Primitive Traits in Religious Revivals*, New York, Macmillan Co.

5. DEREN, Maya (1953) *Divine Horsemen: The Living Gods of Haiti,* New York, The Vanguard Press.

6. DILLISTONE, F. W. (1955) *Christianity and Symbolism*, London, Westminster Press, Chap. VII.

7. FIRTH, Raymond (1951) "Contemporary British Social Anthropology", *American Anthropologist,* Vol. 53, No. 4, pp. 474-89, p. 483.

8. FORDE, Daryll (1953) "The Cultural Map of West Africa: Successive Adaptations to Tropical Forests and Grasslands", *Transactions of the New York Academy of Sciences*, Series II, Vol. 15, pp. 206-19.

9. HERSKOVITS, M. J. (1937) *Life in a Haitian Valley,* New York, Alfred Knopf.

10. HERSKOVITS, M. J. (1941) *The Myth of the Negro Past*, New York, Harper Bros.

11. KROEBER, A. L. (1920) "California Culture Provinces", *University of California Publications in American Aroheology and Ethnolgy*, No 17, pp. 151-69.

T. S. Simey

WELFARE AND PLANNING IN THE WEST INDIES

1. Professor Herskovits concludes that the status of the Negro family, and most of the other forms of Negro life, was determined by the play of various forces brought to bear on the Negro in the New World, 'projected against a background of aboriginal tradition'. Slavery, he argues, did not 'cause' the maternal family; it tended rather 'to continue certain elements in the cultural endowment brought to the New World by the Negroes'.[1] But many of the characteristics of the Negro in the New World were not transplanted from Africa at all. It has, for instance, been pointed out that the Negro slave saved himself from the deterioration experienced by the American Indian and the Carib by the development of the qualities of gentleness, religious escapism, and personal loyalty to his master, which he can hardly have shown in his native Africa.[2] What is most interesting and significant about the formative influences of the Emancipation period is not so much the material which lay ready to hand when the new societies were being shaped as the needs which influenced the West Indian peoples in making use of one piece of material and in rejecting another, and in creating entirely new structures at times to meet them. African origins and the institution of slavery in itself are of little importance today compared with the processes of selection, rejection, and invention, which *still* operate.[3] The final judgement in evaluating the approach to West Indian social structure through Africa must therefore be that such an approach is of importance in so far as it 'loosens our thinking', particularly amongst those who have received no training in the comparative study of social institutions, and tend to think of family organization entirely in terms of Europe and North America. It would be quite impossible to construct a social policy on the assumption that African origins bulk sufficiently largely in the West Indian scene to make it feasible to establish a matriarchy on a stable basis as a halfway house between the Western and the African families. Social development has gone much too far to make this possible even in the remotest sense in the West Indies. It is thus much more important to study the forces that have made the West Indian family different from the African family than to endeavor to discover the respects in which identities may be said to exist.

It may be assumed that the most potent of these forces was slavery, and there is no need to go farther back than the plantation, with its labour force of slaves, to find a plausible and even compelling explanation of many of the features of the West Indian society of today.[4] (Simey 1946: 47-48)

2. The theory that the social institutions of the Negro peoples of the New World have been mainly shaped by the economic forces brought to bear on them during the period of slavery and later (but especially during the period of slavery) has, unlike the rival theory that the more important factor is the inheritance of culture patterns from Africa, a vital bearing on administrative issues today. More has been done towards clearing the ground for the work of social reconstruction in the West Indies by the placing of the institution of slavery in its historical and economic context than perhaps in any other way. (Simey 1946: 53)

3. The prevailing type of West Indian family which is encountered over and over again in all the colonies is very loose in organization. It is rarely founded on the ceremony of marriage, and the relationships between its members are very casual indeed. There is little control over the children, who may receive plenty of maternal affection (tempered by explosions of emotion), but little in the way of careful general upbringing. Children are highly prized and warmly loved. They are desired for their own sakes, and a child whose mother is too poor to look after it will be readily 'taken in' by another family group. Informal fostering of children in this way is one of the outstanding features of West Indian social life.

The relationship between a man and his children under this form of family organization is by no means regular or close. A man will do his best to care for his children,[5] as a rule, but the insecurity of his position in the family and his poverty make it very difficult for him to discharge obligations of parenthood which are accepted without question in Great Britain and North America. The illegitimacy rates common throughout the West Indies vary from 60 to 75 per cent of the total number of births. On the other hand, this figure is not to be taken at its face value, for the institution known as 'faithful concubinage' may unite parents in an association which endures for a lifetime; where these relationships obtain the family may be said to exist in much the same way as it does in peasant communities throughout the world. Nevertheless, the relationship between the parents is generally a transitory one, and even though the man is more often the wanderer, mothers frequently move from one household to another, taking their children with them. A man will accept the children of the woman with whom he is living into his household without question, and will bestow on them a degree of care and attention certainly not inferior to that which he bestows on his own children. Even though both fathers and mothers exhibit so many good intentions in regard to their offspring, however, the environment in which children are brought up is very far from satisfactory. Only about half the children between 6 and 15 years of age attend school at all regularly, a state of affairs which is common to all West Indian Colonies.[6] (Simey 1946: 15-16)

4. Such evidence as there is, therefore, goes to show that in the majority of cases the relationships between the sexes which lead to the procreation of children are temporary, and the institution of marriage is unstable.

The family group is, indeed, one which is brought together in a very casual way
....

More or less promiscuous sex relations are regarded in the West Indies as normal behavior .... (Simey 1946: 84)

5. The individual in the West Indies grows up in an environment which is fundamentally different from that of Great Britain or North America in that close association between father and child may be regarded as an exception rather than a general rule. The fact of illegitimate birth is one completely taken for granted. An illegitimate child does not consider himself disadvantaged thereby, since legitimacy is an exceptional status rather than illegitimacy.[7] This cannot but have a most important bearing on the development of personality. Although another male adult, or a number of male adults, can probably act as satisfactory substitutes for the father in guiding the development of the child, it is doubtful whether there can be said to be *any*

effective father-substitutes at all for large numbers of West Indian children. (Simey 1946: 88)

6. The everyday relationships between parents and children are explicable as a cul-
ture-trait inherited from the European dominant caste in the early nineteenth century. Children may run wild outside the home, but inside it the authority of the
mother (and, where present, the father) is absolute. The child is severely disciplined, and vigorously whipped for misdemeanours at home and in school. He is
expected to be strictly obedient, to be 'seen and not heard', and generally to behave as a good Victorian child should. In consequence, West Indian people are
thought of as very old-fashioned in Harlem, whilst they in turn are apt to regard the
educational methods prevalent in the United States unfavourably, as it is thought
that far too much liberty is allowed children in the New York schools. The tensions
of adolescence are acute because many young people are aware that the West Indies are behind the times in this regard, and resist a form of discipline abandoned
by parents in western countries many years ago. A child will often leave home to
go to live somewhere else after a pitched battle with his parent or parents at this
stage of his development.[8] An added element of instability is, moreover, introduced
into the patriarchal family by reason of the fact that parental authority is difficult to
maintain in a society in which a son, resentful of his father's attitude and discipline,
finds it relatively easy to take himself off to another household. Boys accordingly
tend to break loose from family ties as soon as they are able to look after themselves. The striking fact was revealed during inquiries conducted in one area in Jamaica that, out of twenty-one households studied, only five had males in them
other than husband or father, and boys of under 14 years of age. In a surprisingly
large number of cases the boys had simply run away, and a large gang of boys of
between 12 and 16 years of age wandered about, sleeping in empty premises and
begging or stealing their food.[9] This should not be taken to imply that Jamaican or
West Indian children are cruelly or even unkindly treated; on the contrary, the common people are naturally kind and generous to children. Nevertheless, the lack of
organization in family life, and of standards of behaviour generally, subject the child
to gusts of emotion. The adult is not schooled in self-control, and outbursts of temper are frequent when children are rather more than usually irritating. The child is
indulged and petted when the mother is in the mood, and scolded and beaten un-
mercifully when another mood has taken possession. Children thus suffer from excessive anxiety and feelings of insecurity. (Simey 1946:89-90)

7. In discussing the social structure of the West Indies the obvious starting-place is the
family,[10] for it is, even when quite ephemeral, the outstandingly important social institution of the West Indies. Slavery left its mark deeply imprinted on the family,
and it is thus in the strengths and weaknesses of family life that the characteristic
features of West Indian social organization are most clearly displayed.[11] (Simey
1946:79)

8. It is probably shortage of food as much as anything else which is responsible for
the common West Indian practice of scraping meals together anyhow, and eating
food whenever it is available. The common family meal is one of the strongest ties
of family life, since the sitting together at a common table involves the sharing of
many more things than food, but this is rarely made a practice by the masses in the
West Indies. Adults and children alike gather their food together in a tin dish or
plate, and eat it at any time and in any place round about the home which may be
convenient.[12] (Simey 1946:91-92)

NOTES

1. Op. cit., p. 181.

2. James Parkes, *An Enemy of the People, Antisemitism*, Penguin Books, 1945, p. 91.

3. Dr. M. Fortes recognizes the continued existence of West African culture traits in the West Indies, as demonstrated by Professor Herskovits, but concludes that the scanty research which has been accomplished prevents the assessment of the relevance of this fact to modern social problems. 'An Anthropologist's Point of View' in *Fabian Colonial Essays*, Allen & Unwin, 1945, pp. 228-9.

4. The inheritance of the plantation tradition and its consequences on contemporary social life in the Southern States of North America have been analysed by Charles S. Johnson, in *Shadow of the Plantation*, The University of Chicago Press, 1934. Much of the argument in this book illuminates the social structure of the British West Indies.

5. This view by no means commonly accepted amongst the upper and middle classes in the West Indies. The Jamaica Nutrition Committee reported in 1937, for instance, that whilst the bulk of male workers earned an average of 14s. a week, women earned much less. 'The situation is even worse than it appears when it is realized that 71 per cent of all births are illegitimate and that a large proportion of men in this group fail to undertake their paternal and family responsibilities wholly or partly. It is common for the woman of the labouring class to bear all or most of the family burden, and she must do this on her wages of usually about 5s. per week, intermittently earned in a good many cases. One of the chief reasons for destitution and the need for parochial aid arises from this irresponsibility of the male parent.' *Report*, para. 4.

6. Statistics of school attendance are given in the *Report of the West Indies Committee of the Commission on Higher Education in the Colonies*, 1945, Cmd. 6651, Appendix 2. The illiteracy rate for Trinidad as given by the Census of 1931 was 28.5 per cent.; that given by the Jamaican Census of 1943 was 23.5 per cent. See Appendix II.

7. A common practice during the war years was for Jamaicans joining the H. M. Forces to have their photographs printed in one of the local newspapers. 'Private A, son of Miss B' was a common caption appearing under them, which occasioned no local comment.

8. Here again the experiences of the British West Indies is borne out in St Thomas, where 'the childhood environment is characterized by three general features: the relative leniency of disciplines controlling the satisfaction of the biological needs including sex, the relatively rigid domination by adults and the severity of methods by which adult domination is imposed, and the relative insecurity resulting from the lack of stable family organisation, the division and invidious inequalities within the society at large, the importance of supernatural forces, and, in the lower class, the uncertainty of the satisfaction of subsistence needs'. Campbell, op. cit., pp. 44-5, 49-50.

9. Information supplied by Mr Lewis Davidson.

10. The family discussed in this chapter is the Negro family. No reliable information is available concerning the East Indian family in the West Indies.

11. The typical features of West Indian family life obtain throughout the Caribbean. See, for instance, A. Campbell, *St. Thomas Negroes – A Study of Personality and Culture*, Psychological Monographs, The American Psychological Association, Inc. vol. iv, no. 5, 1943, p. 40.

12. For example, in St Thomas, Campbell, op. cit., p. 40.

R. T. Smith

THE FAMILY IN THE CARIBBEAN

This paper does not attempt to cover every aspect of family organization nor to review the literature on the family in the Caribbean. Instead it will discuss the problem of relating variations in the form of family structure to other factors in the social system, using the author's own field material for purposes of illustration.

It is convenient to begin by examining the structure and activities of household groups. These are easily isolated for study and most writers are agreed that the main functioning family unit in the Caribbean is a household group. It will be defined as a group of people occupying a single dwelling and sharing a common food supply. The term 'family' can be used to denote many different types of group, depending upon its definition and qualifications, and it is also used to refer to an institution, i.e., a stand-ardized mode of co-activity (6, p. 108). In discussing the household group as a family unit, this distinction between the mode of co-activity and the group which activates it will be made. Although kinship ties extend beyond the household group, no organized enduring group structures based upon kinship and comparable to a corporate lineage are reported for the larger territories, though M. G. Smith speaks of patri-lineages in Car-riacou(9), and of course the Bush Negroes of Surinam are another special case(4).

As a preliminary step in analysis it is useful to distinguish the following elements of household group activity. The comments refer to the situation in Negro villages in British Guiana but the elements themselves can be generally applied.

1 *Child Care:* This is an almost universal activity of household groups and is normally under the control of a woman in the status of 'mother', who is not necessarily the bio-logical mother of all the children in the group. Males do not participate directly in this activity, but the existence of the role of 'father' is important to the socialization process and male contributions to the household economy are essential in the majority of cases.

2 *Sexual services:* Within the household these are provided only between spouses in non-incestuous unions[1], but they may be provided across the boundaries of household groups between persons who will be referred to as 'lovers'.

3 *Domestic services:* These are provided by adult females for all members of the house-hold group, and consist mainly of cooking and washing clothes. They are rarely pro-vided across the boundaries of household groups.

4 *Economic support:* Economic support is provided by adult males and channelled to the woman in the status of wife-mother or mother. It consists mainly of cash with which to buy essentials such as certain kinds of food, clothing, and other consumer goods but it also includes farm produce. It may also be provided by males outside the household group in return for sexual services or as a paternity obligation. In a few cases economic support may be wholly provided by female members of the household through their trading, farming, or wage-earning activities. But this is rare.

These are the four main elements relevant to a discussion of the village data but two more may be added since we shall need them later on for comparative purposes.

5 *Managerial functions:* This only applies in cases where a farm or business provides the basis of the household economy and where co-ordination of activities in the owner-ship and operation of the enterprise invests one person with some measure of control over the other members of the group.

6 *Status-defining functions:* This occurs where the definition of the status of the house-hold group in the society at large depends upon the activities of one or more of its members and not primarily upon the ascribed characteristics of the whole group. Status-defining functions will normally refer to the activities of males in the external occupa-tional system, but this element will not be considered present if that activity does not confer a higher or lower status than if it were absent.

In these Guianese Negro villages, household groups, with few exceptions, come into being when a man and a woman enter a conjugal union and set up house together. The relationships between the members of a newly constituted household group may have been in existence for some time and the couple may have several children as a result of their previous ties as lovers. The woman may have been providing the man with sexual services in return for a measure of economic support, but until they live together there is no explicit recognition of the man's exclusive rights to her sexual services. Also she is unlikely to have provided him with domestic services while they were living in separate households.

Young women tend to remain in their parents' households during the period of maximum instability in their sexual relationships, and they may have several children by different men before they acquire a more permanent lover. Once they go off to live with a man in a separate house, the relationship is usually much more stable regardless of whether they are legally married or not. The majority of unions endure at least until the woman finishes her period of child-bearing.

The position may be rather different in an urban or semi-urban area where women live with a series of common-law husbands, perhaps sending any offspring to be cared for by their mothers. In such areas there are usually more employment opportunities for women, particularly as domestic servants. A companionate type of union may develop with an absence of child-rearing functions or a very inadequate type of child care leading to delinquency and so on. But even in urban areas this is not likely to be the predominant type of household(1).

Once the household group is established, its size gradually increases by the birth of children, and their care takes up a good deal of the time and energy of the mother.

All household groups in these Guianese communities are kinship groups, and a detailed examination of the categories of kin which are included shows that there are definite regularities in their composition. In households with male heads, the largest single category of kin is children of the head and his spouse, followed by daughter's children. A small proportion of other kin is found, but these are mainly children of a deceased sister of the head or his spouse. Households with female heads contain a large proportion of the head's daughter's children and a larger proportion of her siblings' children than is found in households with male heads. These differences in the composition of household groups are related to the fact that households with female heads grow out of the male-head type, and the increase in the number of persons related to the 'mother' (whether she is in the status of spouse or of head) reflects her increasing authority within the group as she grows older. The proportion of kin more distantly related to the head than sibling's grandchild never exceeded 1.5 per cent in any of the communities studied(10, Ch. IV).

During this early stage in the life of the household group the woman is quite dependent upon her spouse for economic support, for he is the sole provider for herself and her small children. She becomes less completely dependent upon him as her eldest children begin to leave school and to enter the labour market, thereby acquiring the means to make some contribution to the economic support of the group. Sons rarely work with or for their fathers, but they always give support to their mothers, who perform domestic services for them. Although young men rarely set up a household of their own before they reach the age of twenty-five, they do begin to have affairs with young women and to divert part of their earnings to the support of children they may have fathered. They do not normally bring a spouse to live in their parents' household, nor can they expect at an early age much assistance in setting up a household of their own. Gradually they accumulate enough capital to provide for a house of their own and they may then enter into a conjugal union.

Girls of the household group help their mother with domestic tasks and child-rearing. They too may go out to work if there are employment opportunities locally. Almost certainly they will begin to have affairs with young men, and it is likely that they will have their first child while living with their parents. The girl who has children while living in her mother's home will relinquish many of the functions of child care to her. However, some girls contract a legal marriage before having a child and others marry when they are pregnant.

From now on men in the status of husband-father begin to drop out of the group, usually because they die, but also because they may just leave the group to go and live alone, or to enter another union. Whether they leave or not, the focus of authority and control gradually shifts to the wife-mother, so that, irrespective of whether there is a husband-father present, the household group at this stage can be referred to as 'matrifocal'. The fact that women generally live longer than men means that there is a large number of widows, and these women just automatically become household heads. Sons and daughters begin to leave as they develop sufficiently stable relationships with a lover to set up a household of their own, but daughters will usually leave some of their children to be cared for by their mother. Some women spend the whole of their child-bearing period in their mother's home, having no more than casual affairs with a series of men from whom they receive some economic support.

There are really three phases in the development cycle of the household. In the first phase, young men and women are forming relationships with a series of lovers and becoming parents without living with a spouse. This is really a latent phase for it is only when they enter phase two and begin to live together that the life of a new household group can be seen to begin. The second phase involves the isolation of nuclear family unit in its own house. In the third phase the household has become matrifocal, and it usually includes the members of a three generation matri-line: mother, daughters and maybe sons, and daughters' children. At this stage it may also incorporate other categories of kin, more particularly the mother's sisters or sisters' children. Clearly, phase one and phase three of this cycle overlap in time. In some cases the second phase may be by-passed completely, and in others it may be extended either way so that phases one and three disappear completely. In the villages under discussion all three phases normally exist as a part of the system.

A striking characteristic of the system is the close relationships between mother, daughters and daughters' children, relationships which are rooted in the activity of child care. However, there is no discrete type of household group which contains only the members of this primary coalition. If families are viewed as units with a time dimension, then it can be seen that the vast majority of women spend at least a period of their lives in some sort of conjugal union. Matrifocality, a feature remarked upon by every writer on the New World Negro family and by many writers on Latin American societies, is a matter of degree rather than some absolute quality of the system. So far as this writer is aware, one never finds a whole community made up of households in which there is no husband-father.

In the absence of any enduring group structure to organize the economic support of women and children, males provide this support in their roles as husbands, sons, and lovers. There is a limit to the extent to which men, in their role as sons, can provide support for the household. Once the mother dies, the system breaks down and men do not give economic support directly to their sisters. Outside the mother-son relationship economic support is closely bound up with the provision of sexual services, and the brother-sister relationship is subject to a strict incest taboo. The system permits a woman with children to select a male in the status of husband, common-law husband, or lover from a wide range of possible individuals. The strength of the ties between mothers and child-bearing daughters is directly related to the way in which men perform their roles in the family system. An analysis of the time sequence of household group development shows up the changing position of mothers and children in relation to the sources of economic support and the varying structural arrangements which go with it.

Professor and Mrs Herskovits have pointed out that on the New World slave plantations it was impossible to maintain those fields of male activity, such as the clan and the extended family, which had been important in Africa. While the mother-child cell remained relatively intact, the male's functions as production manger, ritual leader, and jural head of the lineage disappeared(5). There is much more in this than a statement of historical fact, and it is profitable to follow up this lead and to examine the contemporary social system in order to see how the functions of males in the society at large react back upon their status in the family structure.

It was mentioned earlier that managerial functions and status-defining activities are absent from the type case we have been examining. Farming is certainly a part of the economic life of the village, but it does not mobilize household or kinship groups for work under the direction of one person. A minimum of labour and enterprise is expended on the small scattered holdings which comprise these farms, and the focus of attention is wage labour in large-scale organizations such as plantations, government works, bauxite mines, etc. In other parts of the Caribbean an entirely different situation exists. In Jamaica, for example, there are areas such as Miss Edith Clarke's Orange Grove(2) where the management and operation of medium-sized farms introduces a new element of co-activity into the household group and results in a greater emphasis upon the position of husband-father. Jamaica is typical of situations where complexities arise from the range of variations according to ecological area, and these variations provide one useful basis for comparison.

In spite of variations, the general type of family structure I have outlined for the Guianese village seems to be fairly widespread in the Caribbean, and something very like it is found in other parts of the world. It is never the norm for a total society and one may venture the suggestion that it is always found under certain conditions. It is characteristically confined to low-status sections of a more inclusive society, such sections being differentiated primarily on the basis of ascriptive criteria[2]. They may be differentiated on the basis of ethnic, occupational, or cultural factors. Membership in such sections is almost invariably defined by birth, though it is not patrifiliation which in itself determines membership in the group. Apart from the broad differentiation between children and adults and the hierarchical differentiations within household groups, there is no significant degree of hierarchical differentiation within such sections. But they are integrated into the larger society of which they are a part in such a way that their members all fill subordinate roles in wider systems of organization. There is, at best, very limited possibility of upward social mobility. The importance of cash income from wage labour in the Guianese case has already been stressed, and this, or the corollary that ownership of income-producing property is a marginal consideration, seems to be another associated feature. It is unlikely that this system will develop in a situation where the ownership, control, and use of real property is the sole basis of family economy, as it is in a true peasant society.

However, it is never the absence of productive property which alone determines the form of family structure. This is easily borne out by an examination of the West Indian middle class. (This term is used loosely because we are not concerned with an exact description of the status system here). Within such middle-class sections there is a fairly wide range of internal status differentiation and the definition of status is a task of the household group. There are several factors which militate against the development of an isolated nuclear family whose status is defined by the occupation of the husband-father, as in the urban middle class in the United States(7). There is generally less mobility, both spatial and hierarchical, and ethnic factors, which are the basis of ascribed status, are constantly reasserting themselves. Braithwaite comments upon the lack of authority of the Trinidadian middle-class husband-father, but he gives little indication of the variations in this condition either over time or within the middle class as a whole. He does state unequivocally that '...the status of the kinship group derives from the occupational and social status of the father'(1, p. 103). Marriage and co-residence are necessary preliminaries to child bearing and one does not find unmarried daughters with their children living in the parental home. The lack of authority of the husband-father may be marked, particularly in a situation where it is common for men to validate their occupational status by marrying lighter coloured women, and where they may have to keep incrementing their occupational status in order to prevent the centre of status interest from swinging back onto the wife-mother. So long as the man's income provides the basis for the style of life that is important in maintaining the status of the whole group, then there is a point beyond which his position in the family is unlikely to deteriorate.

In the lower class where neither status definition nor managerial functions are important male activities, the husband-father role is extremely circumscribed. It does not disappear; there is never complete promiscuity; and the incest taboo operates with full force. In rigidly stratified societies such as that of British Guiana, where social roles are largely allocated according to the ascriptive criteria of ethnic characteristics, the lower-class male has nothing to buttress his authority as husband-father except the dependence upon his economic support. The uncertainty of his being able to carry out even this function adequately because of general economic insecurity undermines his position even further.

One of the problems in discussing family structure is to pin down the large number of factors influencing it and to separate out those which appear to vary significantly from one society to another or from one group to another. In the first half of this paper an attempt was made to show that one set of apparent variations can be reduced to greater order by taking into account the changes which occur over time and by discussing family structure as a cyclical process. Variations over time are thus a part of the system, and what appear top be different types of family viewed simultaneously are perhaps different growth stages of the same system.

Another point made was that there is a significant relationship between the form of family structure and economic and status factors. Variations within and between status sections and between different ecological areas are best seen against the background of the structural differentiation of the total society. At its simplest such a view can concentrate attention upon the role of husband-father or upon the dual role of males in the family and in the total social system.

Although this paper has dealt with Negro groups, there is no reason why the method of analysis cannot be applied generally, regardless of ethnic factors. Cross-cultural typologies may be constructed when it is decided what the theoretical basis of their establishment shall be. It is suggested that in the case of the family the typology must rest upon some prior consideration of structure and function rather than upon a simple list of elements which may or may not be present (e.g., presence or absence of legal marriage, particular forms of child-training techniques, or specific bases of family economy).

The type of family system with which this paper has been primarily concerned bears some resemblance to those reported from other societies culturally and ethnically dissimilar. A short report on certain aspects of the family in a section of East London deals with the existence of what Young refers to as the 'matrilateral' family(12). Dealing with a random sample of ninety-six working-class families, he concludes that the close relationships between 'Mum' and her daughters and daughters' children is related to the insecurity which working-class women have to face in a situation in which males may easily become unemployed, die, or just desert their wives. Superficially at least, there are marked resemblances between these families in London's East End and those in a Scottish mining community reported on by Miss Wilson(11)[3]. In the latter community there appears to be a basic correlation between the nature of lower-status family relations and the relative absence of vertical social mobility. In both the East London and Scottish studies, the evidence suggests that the existence of a three generation matriline with an emphasis upon the matrifocal household group is associated with a social structure in which males neither control income-producing property nor wholly determine, by virtue of their occupational or political role, the status position of their families of procreation.

Similar types of family structure are also found in some Latin American countries where the culture is predominantly Iberian, often mixed with aboriginal Indian elements. The Peruvian village of Moche is an outstanding case which has been discussed elsewhere(3)[4]. The Paraguayan town of Tobati described by E. R. and H. S. Service provides an interesting comparative case, especially as the authors submit some quantitative data on household composition which show quite clearly the tendency toward matrifocal families in the lowest status group of the gente(8).

In all these cases there is a definite similarity to the Caribbean lower-class matrifocal family pattern, and although much research needs to be done to determine the degree of structural similarity, at least they shift our attention from a purely historical treatment of Caribbean Negro family patterns. There is no doubt that the present position of the Negro group and the Negro family system had their origin in the extreme type of society created by plantation slavery. Even so, it may be less profitable to regard slavery as the cause of present-day family structure than to examine the correspondence between the various parts of the contemporary system. In this way it is possible to widen the comparative framework to include societies with a different historical background but similar structural features, as well as to recognize the fact that Negroes participate at higher status levels in the present society and live in varying types of family system.

A correct use of the comparative method requires more than a search for identity between particular structural features in widely differing societies. We must also explain such negative cases as there may be, or comparison leads nowhere. In this respect the East Indian community in the Caribbean forms an extremely valuable test case. In British Guiana the economic position of Indians is in many ways similar to that of Negroes, but their family system is quite different. This is not merely a matter of cultural persistence. A number of group structures have been developed in which males play important roles, and there is an Indian status system which is distinct from that of the total society. This is not to say that Indians do not participate in the ranking system of the total society, for they certainly do, but they have not been ranked at the bottom of a scale of colour values as Negroes have, with all that that implies so far as social mobility is concerned.

It is apparent therefore that in speaking of the family in the Caribbean we are dealing with a number of varying types, which we may either distinguish and classify in terms of a series of specific characteristics, or which we may attempt to distinguish in terms of their structural characteristics and functional relation to other elements of the social structure.

NOTES

1. Because of the existence of different kinds of marital status, the terms 'spouse' and 'conjugal union' are used without differentiation between legal and non-legal unions. The terms do imply co-residence.

2. It may be that in some cases the status sections so differentiated are very small and marginal to systems of differentiation according to achievement criteria. An example would be small pockets of slum dwellers in an otherwise open-class type of society.

3. See (10, pp. 247-51) for a fuller discussion of this work.

4. Discussed in (10, pp. 2401-15)

REFERENCES

1. BRAITHWAITE, L. (1953) 'Social Stratification in Trinidad', *Social and Economic Studies*, Vol. 2, Nos. 2 and 3, Jamaica, University College of the West Indies.

2. CLARKE, E. (1953) 'Land Tenure and the Family in Four Jamaican Communities', *Social and Economic Studies*, Vol. 1, No. 4, pp. 81-118. Jamaica, University College of the West Indies.

3. GILLIN, J. (1945) *Moche: A Peruvian Coastal Community*. Institute of Social Anthropology Publication 6. Washington, D.C., Smithsonian Institution.

4. HERSKOVITS, M. J. and F. S. (1934) *Trinidad Village*. New York, McGraw Hill Book Co., Inc.

5. HERSKOVITS, M. J. and F. S. (1947) *Trinidad Village*, New York, Alfred A. Knopf.

6. NADEL, S. F. (1951) *The Foundations of Social Anthropology*. London, Cohen and West, p. 108.

7. PARSONS, Talcott (1954) *Essays in Sociological Theory*. Glencoe, Illinois, The Free Press.

8. SERVICE, E. R. and H. S. (1954) *Tobatí: Paraguayan Town*. Chicago, University of Chicago Press.

9. SMITH, M. G. (1956) 'The Transformation of Land Rights by Transmission in Carriacou', *Social and Economic Studies*, Vol. 5, No. 2, pp. 103-38. Jamaica, University College of the West Indies.

10. SMITH, Raymond T. (1956) *The Negro Family in British Guiana*. London, Routledge and Kegan Paul Ltd.

11. WILSON, C. S. (1953) *The Family and Neighbourhood in a British Community*. Unpublished M.Sc. Dissertation, Cambridge University Library.

12. YOUNG, M. (1954) 'Kinship and Family in East London', Man, Vol. LIV, Article 210.

2
Labels and Typologies

As a preparatory step in their efforts to understand and explain family structure in the Caribbean, researchers, especially those to whom we referred in the previous chapter, undertook the task of classifying the diverse family forms they found in their field sites. In this exercise, they linked their classifications with those adopted by Caribbean demography, in particular by the census conducted at regular, usually ten-year intervals. With this as a base, they devised typologies in order to make sense of the wide variety of families by classifying them on the basis firstly, of conjugal union type and secondly, of household composition. We deal with these in turn, taking time also to examine demographic studies on the correlation between conjugal union type and fertility.

Conjugal unions

The classification of conjugal unions constituted a preliminary exercise integral to the formulation of family typologies. Marriage was considered to be the most important union and other types were identified as less satisfactory alternatives or breakaway forms. Thomas Simey, for example, identified what he called the 'Christian family' based on marriage, in comparison with which 'concubinage' and 'companionate unions' were described in negative terms, as being unstable and not sanctioned by law and the Church. Edith Clarke also contrasted marriage and concubinage. She did so on the basis of distinctions made by her informants.

> In our search for our informants' own distinctions between marriage and concubinage it became clear that these institutions were not regarded as alternative forms of conjugal association between which any individual was free to choose. In contrast to concubinage which begins as an informal arrangement and involves no conjugal or parental ties that cannot be easily broken, marriage is regarded as a serious and responsible step (Clarke 1970(1957): 77-79).

Marriage is 'the respectable form of union', 'approved', 'formally entered into' and involving prescribed spousal rights and responsibilities. The classification of conjugal union status adopted by Raymond Smith utilised census data modified by the addition of several more categories appropriate to the situation which he found in his Guyanese field sites. The result was a proliferation to the following eleven categories which he describes as a 'convenient set of working definitions':

1. Married — Legally married.

2. Common-law married — Where a person is living in the same house as their partner without being legally married. This category definitely implies cohabitation.

3. Single mother or single father — Where a person is the biological mother or father of a child or children which he or she recognizes, but has never lived with a member of the opposite sex in a marital or common-law union.

4. Single — Where a person has never had any children and never lived with a member of the opposite sex in a marital or common-law union.

5. Widower.

6. Widow.

7. Common-law widower.

8. Common-law widow.

9. Separated.

10. Common-law separated.

11. Divorced — Only refers to those cases where a divorce has been granted by the courts (Smith 1971(1956): 96-97).

Two major criticisms have been directed towards this typology, both originally expressed by Michael Smith. The first is what he referred to as the 'arbitrary exclusion' of extra-residential or visiting unions (Smith 1970(1957): xiv, 1962: 222-223). Indeed, in arriving at this typology, R.T. Smith appeared to be at odds with his own fieldwork evidence. He reported, for example, that sexual linkages occur between young men and women while both are still living in their parental households, but concluded that these are not 'real conjugal relationships' (Smith 1971(1956): 184-185). Although these relationships are variously described as 'well-established', 'enduring' and 'semi-permanent', since co-residence may be 'considerably delayed' and children born within them (Smith 1971(1956): 109, 110, 135, 121), they are interpreted as lacking in authenticity, as merely a preliminary stage to the real thing.

This period when 'young men and women are forming relationships with a series of lovers and becoming parents without living with a spouse' is described as a 'latent phase', existing in anticipation of a co-residential union (R. T. Smith 1957: 70). The first case-study which was presented (Smith 1971(1956): 122) was that of John and Emily Richmond who were in an extra-residential relationship which lasted for five years and saw the birth of two children, before they moved in together. Presumably that period of their lives would have been ignored altogether if they had not subsequently established co-residence. With this overemphasis on the importance of co-residence to definitions of conjugality, it is hardly surprising that Smith finds it 'quite remarkable' that there is no ritual or ceremony to give social recognition to the start of a co-residential union. That relationship might indeed have started several years before.

> We have taken common residence as our criterion of marriage and common-law marriage, because it almost invariably coincides with marriage anyway, unless the couple are separated or one of them is temporarily away, and because it is only in the context of common residence of some sort that the mutual rights and obligations of a common-law couple become explicit. A man and woman who do not live together and yet have established an enduring relationship involving the birth of several children will have very close ties and mutual expectations, but until they begin to live together these ties will not have the stamp of authenticity, and it is doubtful if much is to be gained by coining a new word for such a relationship. In Perseverance one hears the term 'frenning' which is common in Trinidad also, but in August Town it is customary to use the term 'keeper' to indicate both common-law unions involving common residence and those few cases where a man and woman have a well established relationship without living together. The dividing line is difficult to draw precisely, because the building up of such relationships is a gradual process, and moving into a house together is just one point on the line of development. Here we are not dealing specifically with marriage and mating and so we can ignore these considerations for the time being and work on our original assumption that common residence is a basic criterion of an effective conjugal tie (Smith 1971(1956): 109-110).

The second point of criticism of R.T. Smith's classification of conjugal union types was levelled at his claim concerning the similarity between common-law and marital relationships, that 'there is no difference in the customary rights and duties of the couple towards each other whether they are married or not', and the corollary of the 'almost complete absence of any social disabilities incurred by the illegitimate child'. Any identifiable distinctions between the unions in terms of authority and economic security are minor and more a function of household ownership and legal prescription than conjugal union type (Smith 1971(1956): 178). But William Davenport (1963: 425-235) and, as we noted in the last chapter, Edith Clarke pointed to changes in a woman's lifestyle, social status and economic security after marriage. And M.G. Smith's critique was based on his own fieldwork findings in Carriacou, Jamaica and Grenada. In Carriacou marriage is obligatory for all men and consensual cohabitation is forbidden and in rural Jamaica and Latante in Grenada marriage 'marks the maturity of couples' and common-law relationships are a distinct stage between visiting and marital relationships (Smith 1962: 245-252).

The contemporary classification of conjugal unions used for Caribbean census tabulations and adopted by demographers and more recently by anthropologists and sociologists, has corrected these earlier misconceptions by recognising visiting unions and by identifying common-law and marital unions as two distinct types.

However, the continuing limitations of census classifications are recognised, for example, in terms of dealing with broken visiting unions.

> Two features form the basis of this classification. The first is the presence or absence of legal sanction attaching to the union; the second is whether or not the couples share a common household. Thus a union which is legally sanctioned, that is established before an accredited marriage officer, and in which the partners share a common household constitutes a formal marriage. Where the partners live together in the same household but the union does not have any legal sanction, then the union is designated common-law. A union between a couple in which there is no legal sanction and in which the partners do not share a common household is termed visiting. It is relatively simple, in terms of this typology, to identify all females of married or common-law unions which have been broken by the death of the male partner or by some form of separation. Women of such broken unions are, in censuses, classified as previously living with husband or common-law partner. In the context of a census, however, it is not easy to extend this classification of broken unions to visiting types. No such problems, however, should be encountered in the case of a properly ordered survey, which could easily accommodate all types of unions and all forms of broken unions (Roberts and Sinclair 1978: 2-3).

In their in-depth study conducted in Jamaica, Roberts and Sinclair (1978) provided more detail on the distinction between the three types of union and found it necessary to add a fourth, namely the 'casual relationship'. We proceed by summarising their conclusions.

Visiting unions predominate at the early stage of union formation, the average of entry at 20.6 years of age being lower than that for entry into common-law or marital unions. The majority of women move to another union type at 20 to 25 years of age, mostly into marriage, less frequently into common-law unions. Detailed information on the nature of the relationships reported in this study challenged the stereotyped picture of visiting unions as short-lived, loose and concerned mainly with sexual gratification. The partners in the study met on average over three times weekly, generally at the home of the woman. Contacts between the fathers and their children were regular as were family outings for entertainment. Discussions and future planning for family well-being occurred, conjugal faithfulness was expected and in many cases the relationship strengthened over time.

The union between common-law partners has not been legally or religiously sanctioned, although the couple share a common household. Age at entry varies considerably, with the average for the women in the sample at 21 years. There is also a strong possibility that these unions will be converted to marriage, though not to the same extent as the visiting unions. The age at entry into marriage is highest of the three union types, averaging nearly 24 years. However, many of the women who marry have, as suggested, been previously involved in visiting or common-law unions.

It is interesting to note that Roberts and Sinclair introduced a fourth type of conjugal relationship which they refer to as the casual relationship. They identified this as a 'subset' of the visiting union type and claimed that evidence from their informants necessitated its inclusion. Although, as indicated above, there were many visiting unions reported in the study which endured and strengthened over several years and in which cohesion and commitment developed between the partners and their children, there were others which never reached this stage, but ended after the first pregnancy. These casual relationships generally happened between sexually experimenting teenagers, aged 16 to 19 years, often while still at school, with the pregnancy in many cases an accident, the shock result of a single sexual contact.

Labels and definitions of conjugal union types in the Caribbean have become increasingly indigenous. As Berleant-Schiller (1972: 79) put it,

> we have come to let the Caribbean materials teach us. We have come less and less to impose parochial presuppositions.

She suggested, however, that we take the process further, for example, by removing the 'artificial variable' of legality from our notions of marriage. Adopting an ideal, jural view limits our understanding of Caribbean conjugality, especially the alternative unions which are also functionally and socially accepted. There may be no common essential element to marriage. We should therefore, she proposed, recognise as marriages the wide variety of relationships which entail different rights and duties between conjugal partners and examine these within the ecological, economic and demographic context of the Caribbean, rather than assume and search for universal criteria and essential characteristics.

Conjugal union and fertility

Demographers exploring conjugal union types and distinctions have devoted much attention to the correlation between each of them and fertility levels. Census categories based on British classifications originally simplified the Caribbean situation by dividing women into those who were married and those who were not, with the assumption that only the former were exposed to the risk of childbearing. By the 1946 census the common-law category had been introduced, though women in visiting unions were still classified as single and therefore not at risk. Writing as a demographer, Roberts emphasised the need for classifications of the family which shed light on fertility differentials. From this perspective, conjugal co-residence or extra-residence becomes the most crucial variable.

> Classifying family unions in these populations, and delineating major features of the types identified, pose weighty problems, many of which are more relevant to the anthropologist than to the demographer. A fairly extensive literature outlining results of field enquiries as well as proposing theoretical frameworks of study and hypotheses on structure and function is developing. The writings of M. G. Smith, R. T. Smith, E. Clarke and W. Davenport are of special significance both in terms of field work and theoretical treatment of the subject. Our concern in the demographic context is not so much with structure and function of the family as with certain social variables which permit the division of families into useful categories, and which may also help to throw light on levels and differentials of fertility. Many of the variables treated by writers on the West Indian family - such as prevailing sex ratios, family and household composition (especially in terms of the absence or presence of the male) - are of relevance in the demographic approach. One which probably receives less notice in works on the West Indian family, is intensity of exposure to the risk of childbearing, which may depend largely on two basic factors, cohabitation of spouses and, to a smaller degree, legal sanction of these unions. In practical terms this may be measured by the frequency of sexual intercourse between the woman and her partner (Roberts 1975: 105).

By 1960 Caribbean census categories were recognising non-residential conjugal unions and correlations between fertility levels and conjugal union types were well-established. Since then, different indices have been used for the measurement of fertility in relation to conjugal types. The analysis is statistically complex and we simplify here by identifying three studies which use three different indices of conjugal unions, namely union type, already mentioned, as well as number of partnerships and number of partnership dissolutions.

The general conclusion presented by Roberts and Sinclair (1978: 51-53) indicated that childbearing was found to begin earlier in visiting unions when compared with common-law unions and marriage. However, the spacing between births is more lengthy, indeed many unions are dissolved after the first birth and there is some time lapse before another union is formed. Additionally, women in these unions end their childbearing at a relatively low age. These points explain the lower fertility level associated with visiting unions. Fertility levels for women in common-law unions are relatively high for, although they enter them later than women in visiting unions, birth spacing is considerably shorter and they continue childbearing for a longer period of time. Within marriage, the average age at the birth of the first child is relatively high. However, marriage fertility rates are the highest of the three union types, a phenomenon explained by the short period between births and the higher age at birth of the last child.

Fertility levels were found to be significantly lower among women in visiting unions when compared with those in common-law relationships or marriage. Comparing the latter two, fertility levels in marriage have been found to be higher, a conclusion to be expected since these unions in general last longer than common-law unions. This explanation is assumed to be based primarily on the spacing of births which, in turn, is viewed as a function of the amount of time women spend in or out of partnerships and therefore their differential exposure to the risk of pregnancy. Thus women in visiting unions live apart from their partners and spend more time out of conjugal relationships during which periods they are not exposed. The paradox was that these prevailing mating patterns, though viewed as socially unacceptable, did constitute a fertility depressant so that any attempt to change them by involving women in more stable unions, particularly by encouraging marriage, would automatically increase a fertility rate already considered to be too high. This prediction constituted a source of concern for sociologists many of whom, as we noted earlier, also had an interest in social policy. Judith Blake (1961: 248-250), for example, claimed that a shift to stable marital unions in Jamaica would increase fertility rates by an estimated 30 per cent.

Ebanks, George and Nobbe approached the question from another perspective and came to an entirely different conclusion concerning the correlation between union stability and fertility levels. Instead of viewing union stability as a function of union type, they defined it with reference to the number of partnerships in which a woman has been involved. Working in Barbados, they conducted a survey of 4199 women of lower and lower-middle socio-economic status, aged between 15 and 50. Short-term, casual relationships were excluded by focussing on unions of three or more months duration which involved 'intimate relations with a partner' (Ebanks, George and Nobbe 1974: 451). The general conclusion which they reached from this investigation was that there was a positive correlation between fertility levels and number of partnerships. In other words, the general pattern is that a woman's fertility increases with an increase in the number of partnerships in which she engages. The conclusion that union stability lowers fertility was much more comfortable for those whose mission it was to encourage union stability through marriage.

By way of providing an explanation, albeit tentative and incomplete, for this alternative evidence, the researchers made a number of points. They claimed that differential contraceptive use did not affect the overall result, since women who change partners relatively frequently are just as likely to use contraceptives as those who do not and women with the fewest partnerships are the lowest users. Additionally, there is often little time or indeed, some overlap between partners in visiting unions in particular, and these unions often terminate when the woman becomes pregnant, so that it is possible that much of the time spent between unions occurs when women are in fact pregnant. If the next union commences soon after childbirth, then overall fertility will not necessarily be affected. They also argued that women try to stabilise unions by having a child or children from each partner, a factor which would also increase fertility levels in the more unstable unions (Ebanks, George and Nobbe 1974: 459-460).

In a more recent article, Lightbourne and Singh (1982) also explored the relationship between mating patterns and fertility and made an important contribution to this debate. Their report was based on the results of the World Fertility Survey conducted in Jamaica and Guyana between 1975 and 1976. Without going into detailed statistical analysis, we summarise three important points from their work.

Firstly, in response to the earlier correlations identified between fertility levels and union type, they noted that there are in fact a number of births which occurred outside of any of the three union types commonly identified. The proportion of these births, they claimed, has remained fairly constant, constituting 14 per cent of all Jamaican births and 6 per cent of births within the non-Indian Guyanese population. These births probably occurred within what Roberts and Sinclair would call casual relationships and, although presenting a problem for conventional demographic measurement, are obviously significant enough for inclusion in any analysis of fertility levels.

Secondly, the researchers proposed that partnership dissolution is a more significant variable for testing the correlation between mating patterns and fertility levels than are either union type or the number of partnerships. By emphasising the number of partnership dissolutions, 'separated women' were included as a distinct category and measurement became more accurate. They explained as follows:

> As an example which illustrates why number of partnerships is not the ideal variable for testing the effects of partnership instability on fertility, suppose that 100 women enter partnership at age 20, that 50 of these partnerships persist to age 50, but that 50 terminate at age 30. In addition, suppose that among the 50 women who terminate a first partnership at age 30, 25 remain permanently partnerless until age 50, while the other 25 enter new partnerships at age 31. Finally for the sake of simplicity assume that women bear 0.2 children per year until age 50.

> The naive analyst would observe that in a group of women age 50, those with one partner would average 4.67 births while those with two partners would average 5.8 children per head. While he would be perfectly correct in concluding that an increasing number of partnerships was associated with increasing fertility, our example makes it clear that we would be wrong to assert that instability of partnerships was positively associated with increasing fertility. Our example tells us that if all 100 women had remained in partnership from age 20 to 50, they would have had on average 6.0 births each, and that instability of partnerships was responsible for reducing fertility to a mean of 4.95 children per woman.

> From this example it is clear that to measure instability of partnerships by the number of partners is not the best procedure. It is also clear that the right conclusions about the effects of instability on fertility would be drawn if the measure used were the number of partnership dissolutions. Then the 50 women with no dissolutions have on

average 6.0 children per head, while for the 50 with one dissolution the average is 3.9 correctly reflecting the true effects of dissolution on fertility in our simulated population.

For these reasons we use number of partnership dissolutions to test whether instability of partnerships acts as a fertility depressant. Women with no dissolutions and one partner form the most stable group, those with one dissolution and one or two partners follow and so on (Lightbourne and Singh 1982: 224).

The broad and general findings of their study showed that women with more partnership dissolutions achieve higher fertility rates for the same amount of exposure to the risk of pregnancy. Thus they concluded that women with fewer partnership dissolutions are practising fertility control to a greater extent, this point being linked to the previously noted tendency to desire children within each new partnership.

Thirdly and importantly, Lightbourne and Singh concluded that marked changes have occurred over time in the Caribbean in terms of the correlation between union status and fertility, a major contributing factor being the increased availability and use of modern techniques of contraception. Statistical information collected in the 1940s and 1950s indicated a close correlation between union type and fertility. As the study by Roberts and Sinclair pointed out, married women showed higher fertility rates than those in common-law unions and women in visiting unions have the lowest rates, these variations being attributed to differential levels of exposure to the risk of pregnancy. Statistical evidence from the 1970s, however, showed that women in common-law unions have outpaced married women to become the most fertile and that the gap between those in marital and visiting unions has been significantly reduced. The conclusion drawn is that fertility levels have increasingly become a matter of personal choice, related to the voluntary use or non-use of effective contraceptive techniques, and are no longer a function of exposure to the risk of pregnancy defined as being in or out of a partnership or a particular type of union. Women in stable marital unions with one partner thus cease childbearing once desired family size is reached, whereas those who enter several partnerships are motivated to have children within each new relationship.

Household composition

The typologies constructed for household composition incorporate conjugal union distinctions and also follow closely those categories used for the population census. There were in fact some researchers who, in their investigations into family patterns in the Caribbean, relied totally on the census for classification and statistical data on which to base their interpretations of household and family in the Caribbean. This, of course, reinforced the assumption that the household contained the family, a conclusion that has come under much censure.

The first typology of interest here was formulated by Simey from data on 270 rural Jamaican families collected by Lewis Davidson in the preparation of a report for the Presbyterian Church of Jamaica (Simey 1946: 82). Although he recognised the limitations of his data base as 'small in size' and not 'truly "random" from the statistical point of view' (Simey 1946: 83), he nevertheless proceeded to use it as the basis on which to design a classificatory system and to identify the relative frequency of each type. The typology also reflects Simey's assumptions that what constituted the family was, or at least ought to be, nuclear in composition with members residing in one household and his major concern with 'weak' family structure, low marriage rates and high levels of illegitimacy. He identified four family types as follows:

Christian families: patriarchal domestic units based on legal, Christian marriage;

Faithful concubinage: patriarchal domestic units based upon a union which is neither legally nor religiously sanctioned;

Companionate unions: cohabiting unions of less that three years duration;

Disintegrate families: households containing women, children and grandchildren (Simey 1946: 82-83).

Christian families constituted 20 per cent of the total, those based on faithful concubinage, 29 per cent, and the combined total of companionate families and disintegrate families, 51 per cent.

This four-fold typology gained widespread acceptance. It was, for example, adopted by Fernando Henriques with only slight modification in terminology for his classification of domestic groups in Jamaica. Thus Henriques acknowledged his debt to Simey for the nomenclature of types A and B, but reduced the negative bias by replacing the label 'disintegrate family' with 'maternal or grandmother family' and 'companionate family' with 'keeper family' to arrive at the following classification:

A: Christian family;

B: Faithful concubinage;

C: Maternal or grandmother family;

D: Keeper family (Henriques 1953: 109).

The problem arose as Henriques attempted to identify the proportions of each family type. Relying on census data for Jamaica which classified households by a different set of criteria, namely sex and marital status of the household head, he produced an unsatisfactory correlation between the two classificatory systems which provided only rough estimates of the proportional distribution of each of his household types (Henriques 1953: 115-117).

The classificatory system used by Edith Clarke and adopted by Sidney Greenfield (1966: 137-139) showed similarities, though it was more detailed and complex, reflecting the process by which she constructed it. Instead of bending and stretching census categories, she attempted to create a typology to fit the range of household types which she identified during her fieldwork in Jamaica and also, importantly, to suit the culturally specific questions which she intended to pursue in relation to this ethnographic evidence. Also emphasising the household, which she referred to as the 'residential grouping', her typology contained six basic types which were then further subdivided.

(A) simple family type households consisting of a man and woman with or without their children and possibly adopted children and non-kin persons; (B) extended family households, being an extension of simple family by the addition of other kin; (C) and (D) denuded family households, containing either a mother, or a father, living alone with his or her children. These might be either of the simple or the extended type; (E) single person households and (F) sibling households. These were the main types. They were found, however, to be insufficient for the sort of analysis we required. For example, in a Type A simple family, defined as a man and woman living together with or without their children, it could not be assumed that all the children were children of **both** the man and the woman. Two aspects of the parental relationship with which we are concerned are, firstly, the extent to which this separation occurs and the circumstances in which it most commonly occurs, and secondly, what happens to the children of previous unions when a new union is contracted. It was, therefore, necessary to subdivide this Type into two main groups, (I) a **primary** type containing the children of the couple only and (II) a **secondary** type showing the presence of outside children. Thus II(a) showed households containing outside children of both the man and woman, II(b) those with outside children of the man and II(c) with outside children of the woman. Since adoption, in all its meanings in this culture, is the subject of special discussion, it was also desirable to isolate households in which there were adopted children. This was done in II(d). In all these sub-types the figures were shown in relation to the presence or absence of own children or outside children. A final subtype (III) distinguished childless households (Clarke 1970(1957): 117) (Emphasis in original).

For 'simple family' (Type A) and 'extended family' (Type B) households, a distinction was made between those based on marriage and those on common law unions. 'Extended family' households were further divided into sub-types as follows:

> Firstly, a kinship discrimination between households consisting of direct descendants of the couple and those including siblings and descendants of siblings; and secondly, within these sub-types, a distinction between households containing two, three or four generations (Clarke 1970(1957): 118).

Additionally, the 'denuded simple' and 'denuded extended' households (Types C and D) and the 'single person' households were further differentiated according to whether they were based on a male or female adult. And again, the presence or absence of children (own, outside or adopted), other kin and non-kin was also an important criterion (Clarke 1970(1957): 127). Ultimately, the refinement of the typology by the seemingly endless proliferation of types in order to provide a category for each and every one of the households in her sample from the three Jamaican villages, becomes unmanageable and the statistical distribution of each increasingly meaningless.

R. T. Smith noted the great variety of household types which he identified during his fieldwork and the difficulty of identifying anything which could be considered the norm.

> In British Guiana Negro communities, individual households do appear to exhibit a wide variation in the categories of persons who make up their membership, and a cursory examination of August Town was sufficient to make it quite clear that there was no superficially apparent norm of domestic grouping. Over 300 houses in the village seemed to contain a somewhat bewildering array of occupants, and although one could draw up a list of various 'types' of grouping it seemed necessary to make a

comprehensive survey of all households in order to introduce an element of certainty into any discussion of what is 'normal' for this community (Smith 1971(1956): 96).

Smith was critical of attempts to produce household typologies by imposing a few rigid categories on this wide variation. His solution to the problem was to provide an overall statistical picture of the 449 households in his sample as they existed at the time of his investigation. He did this by identifying one member of each household, male or female, as the 'household head' and then enumerating each of the other residents in terms of relationship to this head. An extensive range of kin was thereby classified and included a total of 44 categories of kin and non-kin in male headed households, and 29 for those headed by a woman (Smith 1971(1956): 99-101).

Smith (1971(1956): 102-103) claimed that this statistical enumeration enabled him to arrive at a number of conclusions. Households, he argued, whether headed by males or females, are kin groups. Very few non-kin members were resident in his sample of households. They are predominantly male headed with the rights and responsibilities of the conjugal partners clearly defined. More often than not, they are 'two generational groupings, devoted to the rearing of children'. They are based on a co-residential union and the majority of the children of the household are the off-spring of both the male head and his spouse. Female-headed households are not as common and generally comprise three generational groupings of a grandmother, her adult daughter and her grandchildren, in the absence of a male conjugal partner.

Having produced this statistical overview, Smith did not then proceed to create a typology by reorganising all of these households into categories. He deliberately avoided such an exercise, claiming that it would not only distort by forcing households into categories to which they do not belong, but would also perpetuate a static approach. Referring to his statistical overview of household composition, he argued as follows:

> These tables present us with an over-all picture of the situation as it existed in the three villages at the time of the study, and if we so desire we could go on to develop a synchronic classificatory scheme in much more detail. Synchronic in this sense would mean at that point in time at which the field-study was carried out, or the phenomena observed. This is essentially the process followed by the writers who have drawn up lists of family types. The limit to the number of such types would be determined only by the range of variability of our data, and the range of variability is fairly extensive. Thus we could have elementary or nuclear families based on marriage and on common-law marriage; three generation families with a female head; two generation families with a female head; families including collateral kin of either the male head or his spouse; and so on until we had exhausted our range of variations. This procedure would be no more valueless than squeezing all our 'types' into three or four procrustean categories and leaving it at that (Smith 1971(1956): 106).

Up to this point Smith made a number of valid criticisms concerning the construction of typologies to deal with Caribbean family types. It was when he proceeded in his attempt to introduce the dimension of time that his analysis moved to shaky ground. He formulated a model to trace life-cycle changes in household structure by rearranging his synchronic ethnographic data into a presumed chronological order. While he recognises the limitations of this reinterpretation, he nevertheless goes ahead, adding a few case-studies which, one can only assume, are intended to carry the weight of his conclusions concerning the life cycle of the domestic group.

Two important additional criticisms, the first from Nancie Solein (1960) and the second from M. G. Smith (1962), were directed at R. T. Smith's earlier work and, by extension, at other attempts to classify family life in the Caribbean. R. T. Smith, who as we shall see later has conducted a thorough rethink of his approach and who now leads the field in recent interpretations of Caribbean family life, acknowledged their validity.

> Two major criticisms were levelled at my early work; neither of them goes far enough. The first was to equate household composition with family relations, since it leads to a neglect of inter-household ties .... The second was that I had ignored, or minimised, the importance of the mating system in giving rise to a variety of household types (Smith 1978: 341).

The first point, that of assuming that the household and family are coterminous, that the 'main functioning family unit in the Caribbean is a household group' (R. T. Smith 1957: 67), clearly followed from the ethnocentric assumptions of the early functionalist writers for whom the most important task was to identify a social unit that undertook domestic functions such as child socialisation and economic maintenance. According to their interpretation, the family group had to be co-residential in order to perform these tasks effectively. The household thus became the most important domestic unit and the assumption was that it contained the family as was the case in their own societies.

Clarke suggests that ethnographic convenience predisposes the researcher to select the household as a unit of analysis and identifies the consequent dilemma of starting fieldwork in the Caribbean.

> The anthropologist in search of the family **sees** first the house, surrounded by other houses in yards on family land: separated by barbed wire fences, along village streets or country roads; appearing as a thatched roof in the distance, emerging between trees of breadfruit, ackee, or mango on the edge of a yam field; or as a white painted wooden cottage behind regular lines of orange trees with their green and yellow fruit. Within that house, be it hut or cottage, is contained, for some time of the day or night, part of the group which he is about to study.

> But what part of it? Will he find the majority of these households to contain parents and their children; or mothers only with their daughters and their daughters' children; or a man and a woman with some only of their offspring? Or, instead, will he find a heterogeneous collection of kin, brought together by some new pattern of association, based on a system of relationships fundamentally different from that found in other societies elsewhere? (Clarke 1970(1957): 28-29).

Rather than look for answers to these questions from within the Caribbean, many researchers have just assumed that within the household lives the family. As Solien (1960: 101) stated:

> There has been a tendency to identify the family with the household, a procedure which ... has some precedent in anthropological usage. However, the situation in these societies differs so much from those described in other parts of the world, that great difficulty often arises when one tries to apply the classical concepts of 'family' and 'household' in Afro-America. Unfortunately, too often the writer merely glosses over the conceptual difficulty, using the terms interchangeably without defining them, and as a result there is much confusion in the literature.

It is apparent that most anthropologists think of a family as a co-residential group within which there is at least one conjugal pair plus at least some of the offspring of this pair. Various extensions of this unit may occur typically in different societies, such extensions being based upon kinship ties (consanguineal and/or affinal) between other persons and one member of the original conjugal pair. Conversely, the household generally refers to a group of persons who live together and co-operate in at least some if not all domestic affairs. A family unit of some type is generally assumed to be the nucleus of the household, though there may also be present some unrelated persons (Solien 1960: 102).

The references which some researchers made to census data on household composition reinforced this perception. There were indeed those who relied totally on the census for quantitative information on what they claimed were family structures, but were really household types. The 1960 Caribbean census, for example, defined the family as,

> two or more persons living together in the same household and bound together by ties of marriage or kinship (Quoted in Roberts 1975: 104).

Several writers appeared to recognise the importance of extra-residential kinship ties especially those linking to fathers and conjugal partners, but seemed unable to incorporate these into their typologies and theoretical paradigms. Henriques, for example, recognised that not all of the functions assumed to be the responsibility of the family are necessarily performed within the household.

> A domestic group does not depend on the presence of cohabitation. Its presence helps to determine the type of family, but not the existence of family (Henriques 1953: 110).

But the implications of the point for trans-household functional linkages were left unexplored.

Similarly, Greenfield emphasised the point with reference to the role of the father. Extra-residential males, he claimed, can and do perform their roles as fathers adequately, if not on occasion better than those who live with their children, a fact that would be ignored if investigation and analysis were confined to the household.

> The role of father does not necessarily require co-residence with either the children or their mother .... A man can be an 'excellent' father even though he does not live in the family dwelling. Evidence of this can be seen in the cases examined where the father works out of the island, returning only irregularly for visits. Though the young children know very little of him as a person, they learn that he is a good father because he provides money for all that they require. A number of informants spoke very highly of fathers who went to Panama and the United States and sent support back home. Though not actually knowing him, the fact that 'my father gave me everything' was enough to bring warmth and approval to their faces. An opposite reaction was sometimes given by persons who spent all of their lives in the same home as their father. 'He ain't done nothin' for me, he ain't no use, father wha!' would be the normal reaction to a man who never provided money for material goods ....

> Since fatherhood does not necessitate co-residence, a family can exist and function in the normal way even in cases where the father does not inhabit the same dwelling as the other members of the group. By limiting ourselves to interaction within a given household we would miss this behaviour (Greenfield 1966: 140-141).

Unfortunately however, having made this important point, Greenfield then slipped back into misconception by providing a classificatory system which combines household and family and which cannot therefore be satisfactorily used to understand the role of the extra-residential father. He identified two types of family, namely the 'complete' and the 'incomplete' family. The former is one in which 'the husband-father, wife-mother and child-sibling roles are played by distinct individuals and the normal sexual divisions of labour are maintained', while the latter is either without an adult male functioning as husband-father or, less frequently, without an adult female performing the role of wife-mother (Greenfield 1966: 142). The 'complete' family lives together in a 'nuclear' household. The 'incomplete' family, described as 'the mother-centred or matrifocal family' in which 'the mother-child relationship is the basis of organisation', is identified with the 'subnuclear' household. Neither of the two alternatives leaves room for the recognition and analysis of the nuclear family which is not co-resident or of the matrifocal family in which a kinship role is performed by a non-resident member. Paradoxically, the role of the extra-residential father, which Greenfield already noted as important, is likely to be underestimated or even omitted entirely from an analysis based on his own classification. In the final analysis, Greenfield (1966: 139) concluded:

> Understanding the family necessitates moving into the household and examining the interaction of the persons who reside within the physical structure.

Solien, although also theoretically rooted in the structural functional tradition, was the first to devote systematic attention to the distinction between family and household.

> I suggest that in order fully to understand Afro-American society it is necessary to view it in terms of household units on the one hand, and family units on the other. I would maintain that many, if not most, individuals belong to both a family and to a household. At times the two units coincide, but quite often they do not (Solien 1960: 104).

To support the importance of this distinction, she drew on her own field work among the Garifuna (Black Caribs) of Guatemala.

> The nuclear family unit among the Carib may be scattered in several different households. For example, the husband-father may be living with his own mother, one or more children may be with their maternal relatives or with non-Caribs, while the mother may be working and 'living in' as a maid in one of the port towns. Some may then assert that under such circumstances this no longer constitutes a family unit. However, if the nature of the personal interrelationships among the group members is considered, it may be seen that there exists a pattern of affective and economic solidarity among them. It is true that many such groups are extremely brittle and unstable, but they do exist for varying lengths of time. And for their duration the members think of themselves as a unit; when questioned as to their family connections they will immediately name and locate their primary relatives. Furthermore, there is some economic co-operation among them, the man generally contributing a part of his wages (or money from the sale of cash crops) to the woman and the children. The woman too, if working, may give money to the man, and certainly sends clothing and money to the household(s) in which her children are living (Solien 1960: 104).

The resulting conceptualisation of the family was based on relationships of kinship and affinity, while households are defined according to co-residence and domestic functions.

> I propose that the family be defined as a group of people bound together by that complex set of relationships known as kinship ties, between at least two of whom there exists a conjugal relationship. The conjugal pair, plus their offspring, forms the nuclear family. Other types of family may be defined as extensions of the nuclear type, each being identified by the nature of the relationship between the conjugal pair (or one member of that pair) and other members.

> The household, on the other hand, implies common residence, economic co-operation, and socialization of children. Although the members of the household may be bound by kinship relationships, no particular type of tie is necessarily characteristic. In any given society a particular family may or may not form a household. Conversely, a household may or may not contain a family. Although it is probably useful to make an analytical distinction between the two concepts in all cases, the investigator must be particularly careful to examine the structure and functioning of both types of units in those societies in which their membership does not coincide (Solien 1960: 106).

It is possible, therefore, to recognise what she called a 'non-localised family', that is a situation in which family ties continue to function although the family members do not live together under one roof.

However, as the above quotation also indicates, Solien continued to view the conjugal union as an essential component of a family. In this she remained true to functionalism which perceives the co-residential family as 'normal' and claims that the grandmother-mother-children unit 'rarely becomes differentiated as a functional whole' (R. T. Smith 1971(1956): 160). Thus with reference to a social unit consisting of a mother and her children only, she stated: 'I would not call this unit a family at all ... it is on a lower level of organization than a family' (Solein 1960: 105). Female-headed households therefore, if they are recognised at all, are assumed to occur at the end of the domestic cycle.

> Female heads of households are nearly all women who have passed the menopause, and consequently finished their period of child-bearing .... Whilst most of them are widows, common-law widows, or separated, a few have passed straight from being daughters to being mothers and household heads without even having lived in any kind of marital or quasi-marital union with a man. The position of female heads is largely defined by the fact that they are mothers and grandmothers, and the household with a female head grows naturally out of the other type of household group (R. T. Smith 1971(1956): 65).

> A woman's elevation in status to titular headship of a household usually comes about through the death of her husband or common-law husband, and from the age of 60 years onward there are forty-nine female heads of households in August Town as compared with forty-eight male heads (R. T. Smith 1971(1956): 119).

And yet only half of the female household heads in Smith's three Guyanese villages were over sixty years of age. Since these matrifocal units are definitely based on kinship relationships and are common in the Caribbean, it seems odd to stipulate that a conjugal union must also exist before we can consider them to be families. It might be more appropriate to continue to recognise them as 'maternal' or 'grandmother' or 'keeper' families. The recognition of extra-residential conjugal relationships does not mean that they exist for all families.

Rubenstein (1983) picked up the point from Solien. He noted that, once the distinction between family and household had been clarified by her and generally accepted, attention shifted from the household as the unit of analysis to the family, as well as to other areas of interest. Concomitantly, it was thought that whereas the household could be studied as a bounded, corporate group, the family could not.

He proposed a return to unfinished business by revisiting the domestic group, by conducting a comprehensive examination of structures and functions, treating the domestic group and the family on the same level of analysis and, in doing so, distinguishing between co-residence and domestic functions and between domestic group and household. He also stressed that the fluidity of both the household and the domestic group would be better captured by an approach based on the concept of 'network' rather than 'group'.

This brings us to the second point of criticism of R. T. Smith's earlier work, that is the underestimation of the influence of conjugal union type in the process of domestic group formation. Indeed, this seems to have been a deliberate intention on his part. He contrasted his approach with those of Henriques and Simey:

> Some writers on the West Indies have tended to place the primary emphasis upon the marital relationship, and to classify households according to the type of conjugal union (or absence of it), on which they are 'based'. We are approaching the problem from a somewhat different point of view in that we are stressing the various constellations of relationships which exist within these groups at different stages of their development (Smith 1971(1956): 108).

For M. G. Smith (1962: 245) on the other hand, conjugal unions are important regulators, or in his words 'structural determinants', of parental roles and household composition. As he put it,

> the alternative mating forms which regulate the allocation of parental roles also regulate the constitution and growth of domestic units. They do so in various ways; by permitting mates to live together or to live apart with their own kin; by bringing into being new households based on cohabitation, whether childless or not; and by bringing into households new members whose parents do not live together. In this system, the extra-residential mating form permits persons to live alone or with their siblings, their children or their grandchildren, while maintaining conjugal relations. The same mating form also entails the domestic isolation of some mothers and their children, as well as the domestic association of single mothers and their own mothers, or single mothers and their collateral kin. These latter associations may occur in homes with male heads, as well as in those without. They may be interrupted when the woman resumes consensual cohabitation or marries, as well as by the widowhood or death of the household principal with whom she lives. The entire complex of domestic relations, the range and variety of domestic forms, the patterns of isolation and association, all are regulated by the system of mating alternatives and its associated parental roles (Smith 1962: 224-225).

This new focus enables us to include extra-marital conjugal unions as an important and distinct type, co-existing as an alternative to marriage and common-law unions, not as a different stage in a developmental cycle. According to M. G. Smith (1962: 265), the West Indians who mate extra-residentially have conjugal unions which are just as real as their domestic ones. The important distinction between conjugal and casual relations is their public recognition, and the regulation of mating and parenthood within them.

Women who head households and are engaged in visiting unions form part of the system of mating and parenthood publicly recognised in the Caribbean and must also be theoretically acknowledged and analysed. With this perspective also the mistake of identifying family with household group and the dismissal of childless couples and households of adult 'single' siblings become inconceivable.

Conclusion

Situated between data collection in the field and theoretical interpretation, the tasks of classifying and building typologies of conjugal unions and family forms were important ones for these investigators of Caribbean kinship. At every stage, however, their ethnocentric ideas of how families should be structured and how they should function dominated the process. The typologies adopted by anthropologists and sociologists were often linked with census categories, which also had their origins in Britain and incorporated the same biases. These ideas influenced what they saw and how they labelled, classified and interpreted it.

Labels and typologies reflected their assumption that families were nuclear, based on a co-residential conjugal union with all members living in the same household. Family life structured as 'faithful', 'Christian' and 'stable' was contrasted with matrifocality which was 'disintegrate', 'denuded' and confined to the end of the life cycle when the important function of child socialisation had been completed. Functioning male partners and fathers who lived elsewhere often remained invisible and, even when the investigators corrected themselves in this regard, real families were still defined to include a conjugal union.

For the researchers of family life mentioned in this and in the previous chapter, it was important to quantify conjugal unions and family/households to give a precise indication of the prevalence of each type. Some attempted to generalise statistically to the wider society and in doing so distorted data by forcing correlations with national census data. Others were content to deal with conjugal and family structures within the communities they studied, but in their attempts to deal with what must have seemed an infinite variety of types, they produced more and more extensive and sophisticated typologies, a process which Smith (1988: 10) has recently described as 'the refinement of error'. On occasions, it seemed that the creation of synchronic typologies became an end in itself rather than a step towards the interpretation and understanding of family dynamics. The process also reinforced notions of a plurality of family forms. Specifically, a dual system was perceived in which abnormal forms were measured against properly constructed marriages and co-resident nuclear families and found wanting.

3
Personal Choice and Adaptive Response

This phase of Caribbean family investigations, conducted during the 1970s and beyond, remained firmly grounded in structural functional theory, but bent the framework of that model to allow for personal choice and to admit the concept of 'adaptation'. This departure constituted a conscious attempt to soften the rigidity of structural functionalism, the overly deterministic view of human action and the focus on social structure and stability, and to respond to charges of persistent ethnocentrism. Accordingly, behaviour and relationships within black, lower-class families were perceived not as social problems, but as culturally appropriate solutions to the problems of living in socio-economic circumstances of deprivation and uncertainty. Correspondingly, a host of new adjectives and labels were adopted. Family patterns were described as 'adaptable', 'flexible', 'elastic', 'fluid', 'malleable', 'adjustable', 'labile' and so forth. Hyman Rodman (1971: 197) explained the approach:

> As the middle class critic sees lower-class life it is characterized by 'promiscuous' sexual relationships, 'illegal' marital unions, 'illegitimate' children, 'unmarried' mothers, 'deserting' husbands and fathers, and 'abandoned' children. These are typically viewed in a gross manner as, simply, **problems** of the lower class. According to our perspective it makes better sense to see them as **solutions** of the lower class to problems that they face in the social, economic, and perhaps legal and political spheres of life (Emphasis in original).

Family patterns were perceived as informal and flexible, thereby enabling individuals to make personal choices from a number of alternative patterns and families to develop 'adaptive mechanisms' to ensure survival and to take advantage of what economic opportunities exist. These were no longer seen as a deviant form of society's ideal. On the contrary, the fluid, adaptive quality of the family was viewed as a *positive* response to adverse circumstances of poverty and of unemployment, especially among males.

The choice of field sites and informants, however, remained virtually unchanged. Indeed, it appeared that these continued to be determined by the theoretical assumptions adopted. In order to show that conjugal unions, families and households were structured as adaptive responses to deprived economic conditions, village settings chosen for research had to be poor and marginalised with little opportunity for improvement and social mobility. It also happened that the structural functional anthropologists' preference for small, mainly rural, black or Afro-Caribbean communities was perpetuated.

In this chapter, we make use of several examples of ethnographic studies in a variety of Caribbean islands to critique, in turn, the concepts of personal choice and adaptive response.

Personal choice

The notion of personal choice in family relationships has been explored furthest in the work of Rodman within the black, lower-class community of Coconut Village in Trinidad. Villagers live in poor quality, closely-packed, small (two-room) mud houses on land insufficient to provide a livelihood. Farming is therefore supplemented by casual employment and economic activity as opportunities arise. Socio-economic equality and community cohesion characterise the village. According to Rodman (1971: 38) 'occupational differences do not serve to mark off one worker from another' and 'there is no group of villagers that keeps itself apart from the others: even the shopkeeper's children mingle freely with all of the villagers'.

Rodman (1971: 176) intended his study to be 'a step toward a general theory of lower-class family organisation' and, to this end, he adopted a functionalist perspective. 'It should again be emphasised that the theory is functional rather than historical — it is an attempt to explain the contemporary relationships of lower-class life rather than its historical development' (Rodman 1971: 186). His allegiance became clear in his work as he followed the logic of the earlier structural functionalists in explaining family structure and relationships as a result of the inability of men to fulfill their economic roles.

> The man's role as worker-earner lies at the centre of an explanation of lower-class family relationships in Trinidad. The man is expected to work and to earn for his family; his status within the family hinges upon how adequately he provides. Unfortunately, the lower-class man is involved in much unemployment, under employment, poorly paid employment, and unskilled employment. Because of these handicaps in his occupational role he is frequently unable to fulfill his provider role. This situation is so all-pervasive that it has ramifications for the entire system of family and kinship organization (Rodman 1971: 177-178).

According to Rodman, male economic inadequacy is the pivotal structural factor which explains a sequence of family characteristics including male marginality, loose conjugal relationships and 'marital shifting', the importance of the maternal role and patterns of 'child-shifting'. Because males are unable to fulfil the economic provider responsibilities of their roles as husbands and fathers they lose authority and esteem in the family and seek gratification elsewhere, mainly in relationships with male peers or with other women. Economic uncertainty and suspicions of infidelity strain the marital relationship with the result that alternative and, for the male, less-demanding unions such as 'friending' (more commonly known in the literature as visiting) or 'living' (common law) develop and the incidence of conjugal partner change or 'marital-shifting' is frequent. The attitude between spouses is casual and 'separations are taken in stride as part of the normal course of events' (Rodman 1971: 181). Additionally, it follows from the frequency of non-legal unions that the birth rate for 'outside' children is high, that is children conceived with someone other than the person to whom one is married or with whom one is living. In this context of frequent conjugal union dissolution, the woman is often left with full responsibility for her children, legitimate and illegitimate. The pattern of 'child-shifting' provides her with a solution to the problem.

> She cannot both **care** and **mind** her children, and so she turns their care over to a female relative while she takes on the job of **minding** them financially .... In present-day Trinidad the child-shifting pattern ... permits the redistribution of children into households where they can be taken care of, and it makes it possible for the mother of the child to work and to contribute financially to her child's support. In such a case the child may be 'mothered' by a female relative of his mother and 'fathered' by his mother (Rodman 1971: 183) (Emphasis in original).

What is evident in this analysis is the high degree of flexibility and the range of choices and alternative patterns of family role definition and conjugal and kin relationships. According to Rodman, this occurs as a result of a lower-class response to the society's dominant value system which involves either 'stretching' or ignoring these values.

> By the value stretch I mean that the lower-class person, without abandoning the general values of the society, develops an alternative set of values. Without abandoning the values of marriage and legitimate childbirth he stretches these values so that a non-legal union and illegitimate children within that union are also desirable .... The result is that the members of the lower class, in many areas, have a wider range of values that others within the society. They share the general values of the society with members of other classes, but in addition they have stretched these values, or developed alternative values, which help them to adjust to their deprived circumstances (Rodman 1971: 195).

Alternatively, the individual may pragmatically ignore the values of society altogether and fully open the range of alternative behavioural codes and personal choices. At this point, individuals move beyond 'stretching' social values. They no longer concern themselves with developing alternative values, but 'react to circumstances pragmatically rather than normatively: they are neither guided nor hampered by allegiance to any set of values' (Rodman 1971: 195).

Pragmatism, according to Rodman, is evident in lower-class kinship relationships which exhibit high levels of the following four 'general structural characteristics':

> (1) individualism — narrowly defined as the extent to which the individual remains unbound by strong ties of kinship; (2) personalism — the extent to which the content of a kinship relationship grows out of interaction (instead of being prescribed by the formal tie); (3) replaceability —the extent to which it is possible to replace one person by another in a given kinship role; and (4) permissiveness — the extent to which there exists a variety of permitted patterns of behaviour in a given situation. All four of these characteristics are closely related and each represents a continuum along which any group can be ordered. Lower-class Trinidad would be at the high end of the continuum for each characteristic (Rodman 1971: 159).

These characteristics maximise personal choice. The individual is not constrained by conjugal or kinship ties shaped by culturally prescribed responsibilities and expectations, but is able to choose which ties to pursue and which to de-emphasise or drop altogether and, in response to the pressure of circumstances, to select from a wide range of alternative behavioural patterns. These are the characteristics of the lower-class individual, referred to by Rodman (1971: 196) as the 'circumstance-oriented man'.

> He cannot be too much bound by inner standards or others' standards because this would divert him from his major task. He must steer a course according to the circumstances about him. Not being bound by formal kinship ties, and with freedom to emphasise the personal element in kinship relations, the lower-class person is better able to meet life's exigencies.

The adoption of a perspective which highlights human action by emphasising the individual and personal choice introduces a welcome ease to the rigidity of previous structural functional interpretations of family patterns in the Caribbean, which denied the individual a place in the analysis by emphasising the enormous weight of social structure. But it is with Rodman's notion of pragmatic, personal choice that a difficulty arises, for in reinstating the individual he eliminates the social and cultural. Personal choice appears to take place within a context virtually devoid of values and norms. When taken to extremes in this way, a picture is presented of unrestricted options, of situations in which individuals freely go about satisfying their own immediate self-interest with little regard for anything or anyone else. It is difficult to reconcile Rodman's insistence in a footnote that he is not describing situations of 'chaos, anarchy or amorality' (Rodman 1971: 200) with his description of valueless, normless, circumstance-oriented behaviour within family relationships.

Adaptive response

The concept of 'adaptive response' perceives the family as structured and as functioning in response to conditions of economic marginality and poverty. It is closely linked to the notion of personal choice and is also introduced in Rodman's work. But whereas Rodman focussed more on the individual and personal choice, those writers who emphasise adaptation have tended to take a wider social unit of analysis and to emphasise the way in which conjugal, kinship and household patterns constitute culturally appropriate adaptive responses and strategies for survival within these circumstances. We proceed by highlighting and summarising the adaptive response perspectives adopted by a selection of studies as they have dealt with conjugal unions and parenting roles, with marriage and extra-legal unions, with child-shifting and with kinship networks. Finally, we revisit matrifocality from this perspective and compare the resulting images of women with those from the literature on female-headed households.

Conjugal unions and parental roles

Hymie Rubenstein (1980, see Article 1 at end of chapter) examined family patterns in a Vincentian rural, peasant community of 2,245 inhabitants which he fictitiously named Leeward Village. Unemployment and underemployment characterise the village economy and those that are employed are engaged in unremunerative, low-income occupations. Rubenstein specifically highlighted conjugal relations and parental roles and concluded that these are 'appropriate adaptive mechanisms' within the context of economic poverty and stagnation and a stratification system characterised by upper and middle-class monopolisation of resources. Making a strong plea for an analytical approach which replaces the structural functional concentration on statistical analyses of mating patterns and household composition with a detailed understanding of 'folk' concepts and systems, he specifically examined extra-residential unions, clandestine as well as publicly recognised, and alternative patterns of parenting.

Rubenstein (1980: 332) acknowledged the acceptance of the nuclear family household based on an enduring marital bond as the ideal among villagers. But in Leeward Village, the adoption of clearly defined conjugal and parental prescriptions and obligations that go with this pattern are both inappropriate and impossible. Less than one-third of the households are so constituted, extra-residential unions are the most common form and parental responsibilities are not allocated to the mother-wife and father-husband in accordance with this ideal. Borrowing from Rodman (1971), Rubenstein claimed that the villagers have 'stretched' the values of the dominant social system to develop flexible alternatives which are socially and economically viable for them. Accordingly, extra-residential unions are usually short-lived. Lacking well-defined social obligations, they can be terminated at will and with little difficulty. Associated with these unions is a variety of parenting patterns. Parental responsibilities for children, including 'owning' (accepting paternity of), 'minding' (financially supporting) and 'caring' (rearing), are distributed and allocated not only to those identified as biological and social parents, but also to extended family and community members in order to ensure as adequate a performance as possible in the circumstances in which villagers live. The flexibility of conjugal unions, especially extra-residential unions, and of parental role behaviour allows villagers to respond quickly to socio-economic constraints and also to incentives, for example, to labour and migratory opportunities (Rubenstein 1980: 336).

Marriage and extra-legal unions

Robert Dirks and Virginia Kerns (1976, see Article 2 at end of chapter) investigated conjugal union patterns in Rum Bay, a small, rural village inhabited by approximately 400 people, situated in Tortola in the British Virgin Islands. Villagers are culturally homogeneous for, although property ownership differs, this has a negligible effect on lifestyle. Agricultural activity occurs, but is not prominent and villagers turn their energies to whatever economic opportunities arise. The village is poor and, along with other Virgin Island communities, it is also dominated and marginalised within the international economic system of resource monopolisation (Dirks and Kerns 1976: 36).

> Excluded by metropolitan corporate interests from direct access to and control over the most rewarding resources in their environment, the people of the Virgin Islands have been caught up in a constant struggle to adapt to a changing assortment of available exploitive opportunities. In accordance with decisions made in foreign boardrooms, capital has been invested and withdrawn from a succession of resource domains. These decisions have contributed to a history of major ecological changes for the inhabitants of the island (Dirks and Kerns 1976: 36).

The main purpose of these two scholars is to test 'the general hypothesis that the level of marriage and extra-legal alliances expressed in Afro-Caribbean communities is a dynamic adjustment to economic environment' (Dirks and Kerns 1976: 35). In doing so, they added the perspective of ethno-history to that of synchronic adaptation. In other words, community conjugal union patterns are perceived as the result of accumulative cultural continuities combining patterns from recent historical periods, from Africa and from the slave era as well as flexible responses to economic conditions of insecurity and a lack of employment opportunities. Conjugality is a product of both cultural tradition and economic environment and methodologies must allow for this by combining both perspectives (Dirks and Kerns 1976: 35).

The inhabitants of Rum Bay have experienced a history of significant economic change and instability as resource domains and accompanying employment opportunities have opened and closed. By viewing mating patterns as an 'adaptive strategy', it is possible, according to Dirks and Kerns (1976: 36), to investigate them as a response to the changing economic opportunities over the years. Seven distinct historical periods are identified. During the periods when migratory wage work was widely available to community members, marriage rates were significantly higher than for those periods when such employment was scarce and people survived on inadequate and insecure local subsistence production. Dirks and Kerns (1976: 45) therefore concluded that a historical correlation exists between an insecure resource base, few income-generating opportunities and non-legal unions on the one hand, and employment opportunities and marriage on the other.

Additionally, contemporary ethnographic observations in Rum Bay indicate that 'mating alliances can be viewed as organization strategies which involve different sorts of reciprocity, which offer different kinds of pay-offs, and which are advantageous under different circumstances' (Dirks and Kerns 1976: 46). From this perspective, the researchers provided a rationale for the change of union patterns at different stages of the life cycle among the men of Rum Bay. Young men are subject to many demands on their earnings, including remittances to their families of origin and peer group expenses, leaving little to invest in the development of stable conjugal relationships. Extra-legal unions, with minimal, short-term obligations and characterised by balanced reciprocity or, on occasions, advantage to the young men, are therefore appropriate and prevalent at this stage in their lives. By the time they reach their mid-twenties, when obligations to their families of origin are often reduced and more stable employment secured, marriage becomes a more attractive long-term investment, providing a wife to protect property during periods of migration, to bear legitimate children who later in life tend to be more supportive and to secure representation in religious and political domains. Marriage also brings with it respectability within the community and general security for the future. Different conjugal unions therefore, require different reciprocal economic expectations and are appropriate strategic adaptations to the circumstances in which village men find themselves at different life cycle stages (Dirks and Kerns 1976: 49).

Child-shifting

Sally Gordon (1987, see Article 3 at end of chapter) examines 'child-shifting' in two Antiguan villages, one peri-urban, the other rural. Villagers in both locations are poor, indeed the more urbanised is described as approximating an 'urban slum' (Gordon 1987: 428). Although diverse economic opportunities are open to them, they have no control over these. As is the case in other marginalised Caribbean communities, economic options are very limited, externally controlled and highly variable.

'Child-shifting' is defined as fosterage involving the 'reallocation of dependent or minor children to a household *not* including a natural parent' (Gordon 1987: 427). In her sample of 49 households, she finds 41 cases of child-shifting spread over 21 households (42.9 per cent). The reasons that children are moved from one household to another are varied and include 'abiding conditions' which prompt child-shifting because 'the child wanted to live with X, or X "asked for" the child' (Gordon 1987: 437) as well as 'singular events', in particular the migration of a natural parent or caretaker. Gordon adds to this a structural rationale. Child-shifting is perceived as a domestic 'responsive strategy' (Gordon 1987: 442) to economic circumstances whereby the costs and benefits of child rearing are relocated among households by shifting children from those less economically secure and less able to support them to those which are better off. Household size and composition is thereby controlled by balancing and managing dependency in relation to resources (Gordon 1987: 438). The relationship between flexible household composition and economic survival, especially through migration, is therefore perceived not only as complementary but also as necessary (Gordon 1987: 422-423).

Kinship networks

Several recent investigations of family in the Caribbean have identified female-dominated kinship networks, often extending abroad to incorporate migrant ties. They are seen to be created and cultivated by women as adaptive strategies for survival in circumstances of poverty and deprivation. Judith Gussler (1980, see Article 4 at end of chapter) conducted her investigation in a village setting in St Kitts (St Christopher) in which economic and employment opportunities are severely limited and people attempt to secure a livelihood by engaging in multiple income-generating activities. Villagers are also highly mobile and migration to escape St Kitts, perceived by villagers as an island of 'limited good', to the 'economic abundance and opportunity' of the world outside is an important economic strategy. Within this context of virtually non-existent economic resources, it is human relationships that constitute the most important resource in which to invest and which to tap now and in the future. Gussler referred to the 'adaptive opportunism' of the women of St Kitts as they seek out economic support, in particular by building networks over the years incorporating men (children's fathers), their own children, friends, employers and others, at home and abroad. It is usually not until the later stages of their life cycles that women have developed significant kinship networks. Gussler (1980: 202) described the lifestyle of one of her informants, a great grandmother, economically successful and supported by an extensive network of 'children, grandchildren, nieces, nephews, and their kin — who provide her with all kinds of goods and services, and she speaks of her success in terms of these social resources'. Having children is especially important to ensure a comfortable old age. But as we shall see in Chapter VIII, not all women have children and not all of them are successful in their efforts to develop supportive kinship networks.

This study added the important dimension of cross-class comparison, which is generally omitted in investigations of Caribbean families. Gussler reported that women of higher socio-economic levels are, to a greater extent, tied to home, to the private domain. Their lives are more constrained and restricted than those of their lower-status counterparts. In contrast to the large and widespread networks developed by the poorer village women, theirs are narrower and more secure, with ties which are significantly fewer, but which are more stable and which link them with persons whose support is more reliable (Gussler 1980: 208).

The investigation by Karen Fog Olwig (1993, see Article 5 at end of chapter) of women and kinship networks was conducted in Nevis where family life is influenced by migration even more than in the sister island of St Kitts. Once a male-dominated phenomenon, women have now taken over, constituting 55 per cent of the migrants from Nevis between 1970 and 1980 (Olwig 1993: 162). The economic circumstances in Nevis are such that farming generates limited income and wage employment for women in tourism or light industry is irregular, poorly paid and inadequate as a source of livelihood. For the majority of women, therefore, economic security and respectability depend on building a supportive network at home and especially abroad (Olwig 1993: 154).

Kinship networks are concentrated on the relationship between mother and child, especially mother and daughter. Indeed, men (children's fathers) are often absent, contact having been broken when they migrated. Permanent obligations to help support one's mother, preferably by achieving success abroad, are instilled into children from an early age. The situation of a mother with adult migrant children contrasts markedly with that of a childless woman, supporting the conclusions reached by Gussler for St Kitts. Mrs L, for example, had seven migrant children, all of whom, especially the daughters, had honoured their obligations by sending remittances. The money they sent paid for an extension to her home and the installation of electricity and water. They also sent food and clothing and ensured economic security in her old age (Olwig 1993: 156).

Olwig also traced the changing structure of networks developed by women who migrate both to St Johns in the US Virgin Islands and to Leeds in England. Leaving the protective family network at home, their situation is more complex and more demanding when compared with the women left in Nevis and also with migrant males. As important members of their households in Nevis, they feel a strong obligation to remit to their mothers, especially if they received money from a mother to pay the fare for their passages abroad, if they have left their own children at home to be cared for by her and if she has used her extensive network abroad to make arrangements for her migrant daughter to settle in and find work. Male migrants, on the other hand, generally pay for their own passages and are assisted by their friends in their new location (Olwig 1993: 157).

Obligations to Nevis are, however, reduced over the years, especially for those women who have migrated as far away as Leeds. They no longer feel any close attachment to the island and express little interest in returning. Correspondingly, their networks are relocated to England as Nevisian family members are replaced by those within the migrant community. The successful woman migrant restructures her network, balancing her obligations to the Nevisian component with the resource input required to develop a supportive network in her migration destination and, in the process, gradually reducing the former while building up the latter.

Matrifocality

As we noted at the end of Chapter II, the concept of matrifocality as a distinguishing feature of lower-class, black Caribbean family and household structure was first put forward by the structural functional writers of the 1950s and 1960s to explain what for them was the atypical characteristic of female-centred or female-dominated household groups and kinship networks. Recent explanations have attempted to remove these biases by reinterpreting matrifocality as an 'adaptive mechanism' occurring as women, in particular, deliberately choose certain survival strategies in order to cope with inadequate and uncertain male support in circumstances of poverty, unemployment and male migration.

The term matrifocality has been used interchangeably with several other concepts including, 'mother-centred', 'female-centred' or 'woman-centred', 'matriarchal', 'female-headed' and 'grandmother family'. The result is considerable confusion and discrepancy. As Gonzalez (1970: 231-232) pointed out,

> not only is it extremely difficult to find explicitly stated definitions of matrifocality, but there is much variance in its meaning as implied by the diverse usage of the term. In some cases matrifocality seems to imply that women are somehow more important than the observer had expected to find; in other words, that the general status of women in the society is 'rather good'. This, of course, implies that the observer had certain ideas concerning the usual or proper balance of status between the sexes before he made the study. Without knowing the individual scientist's value position, then, it becomes difficult to evaluate qualitative statements concerning the 'importance of women'.

> In other cases the anthropologist has seemed to mean that women have a great deal to say about how the money or income is spent, which in fact says quite a lot about the culture in general. But for still others the term is taken to mean those households in which the woman is the primary **source** of income. At times, as in US census materials, for example, the term 'woman-headed' means that there is no resident male in the household. Yet there are many societies which have been characterized as matrifocal in which men were indeed members of the households.

Having said this, however, two main criteria defining matrifocality emerge from the literature, firstly, the mother/woman as the central focus of relationships and secondly, her authority and dominance within the family. Gonzalez combines both criteria in her conceptualisation of matrifocality as she highlights the presence of the stable mother-female figure and her extended kin and also identifies maternal disciplinarians.

> Within the domestic context, the mother-figure would be least likely to have multiple or shifting allegiances to different households and or families. Rather the female (or females) who fills the role of mother would tend to be the stable figure around whom other members cluster, whether or not they are physically present ... one would normally expect to find that when members of the extended family are included in the household, these are more likely to be relatives of the mother than of the father. Similarly, one would expect to find that personal contacts occurred more frequently with mother's kin than with father's kin (Gonzalez 1970: 233-234).

The extent to which women's decision-making is free from male authority is also a critical factor in this analysis.

> In terms of decision-making or patterns of authority, here again one would expect that in societies labelled 'matrifocal' women would be free to make decisions concerning the household and to discipline children, although this is not to suggest that they never call upon males for assistance or guidance in these matters. The crucial issue would be the possibility, given the value system of the society, for women to even consider making decisions without calling in a male authority figure (Gonzalez 1970: 234).

From the perspective of the children living within a matrifocal household and family system, one would expect that, 'the maternal figures would be strongest, most stable and most dominant; they would see their mothers as being not only nurturing, but disciplinary figures' (Gonzalez 1970: 234).

The rationale for the existence of matrifocality presented by Sidney Greenfield in an article published in 1973, reduced somewhat the bias of earlier structural functionalism, including that of his own work, by claiming to deal with matrifocality not as unique and odd, but as one of a variety of domestic arrangements that constitute 'an adequate adaptive response to a particular set of circumstances' and which therefore 'should be expected' (Greenfield 1973: 31, 32). He related the development of matrifocality to the domestic division of labour between men and women. In typical peasant households, for example, matrifocality is limited because 'males generally perform (or are assigned to perform) the most highly-valued tasks and hence tend to be dominant and focal in their domestic groups' (Greenfield 1973: 42). Matrifocal elements, however, may creep into this system as women's economic activity, for example in marketing agricultural produce, increases and this tends to occur during the earlier and later phases of their adult life cycle when they are not preoccupied with the care of young children (Greenfield 1973: 39-40). As plantation labourers, men are 'unable to earn sufficient income to support a mate and children', while the women manage, 'often with greater regularity than the men, to obtain jobs that paid almost as much as men could earn' (Greenfield 1973: 43). The woman, therefore, becomes the family breadwinner and may join forces with female kin, especially her mother or sisters, who will assist her as she shoulders the task of income generation in addition to child care and domestic duties. These women 'work together to provide for themselves and their children in a household in which the only adults, until their sons grow up, are females' (Greenfield 1973: 43). Full matrifocality, as it were, results as women take total responsibility for providing economic support, assume dominance and head the household in the absence of adult males as fathers and conjugal partners. The explanation for matrifocality, therefore, is to be found in external economic circumstances, specifically employment opportunities which require domestic groups to adapt, restructure and reallocate economic roles thereby modifying nuclear family form and organisation.

> The key factor with respect to focality and dominance is not the traditional division of labour and the tasks performed by the sexes. Instead, it is a question of employment possibilities and wage levels — factors external to the domestic group. Where males obtain jobs at more than minimum salary levels, the nuclear family household with a male head is the rule. Where men cannot find employment and women get jobs at the lowest wage levels as an alternative to starvation, they automatically become the household's breadwinner, thereby gaining the authority and relative importance that goes with the task. Should the unemployed male leave home, his mate — along with the kinswomen she brings to help — becomes the hub of a matrifocal household. To say that women are dominant and focal in such households is true, not as the result of traditional arrangements and the allocation of activities, but rather as a matter of default in which women, in desperation, somehow do what their men are unable to do (Greenfield 1973: 44).

In the final analysis therefore, Greenfield reinforces many of the assumptions of structural functionalism. These include the focus on the household as the unit for analysis, the notion that domestic structures and relationships are moulded and controlled by external economic forces and that matrifocality constitutes a modification of traditional nuclear family households in circumstances where members, women and men, can do no better.

Gonzalez (1970: 232) also made a plea for a favourable re-evaluation of matrifocality 'with a view toward explaining the distribution of the form in adaptive, evolutionary terms'. From this perspective and with reference to her own fieldwork among the Garifuna (Black Caribs) as well as information from other studies, she searched for 'structures, institutions, or circumstances which have been thought to coincide with or induce matrifocality cross-culturally' (Gonzalez 1973: 234). She found no necessary correlation with African origin or slavery, or with stable or unstable marriages and the strength or weakness of conjugal relationships, or with consanguineal households, or with the presence or absence of residential men. Matrifocality is, however, associated with the development of modern society and with bilateral kinship. As she explained, modernisation entails both the separation of domestic and jural domains and the enlargement of the sphere of domestic responsibility to include a range of intermediate or 'supra-domestic' functions which occur outside the household and include schooling, public health and consumer purchasing. With the relocation of male activities to the jural domain and their absence from the domestic and supra-domestic scene, women's roles in that sphere expand in content and importance. Bilateral kinship provides the necessary flexibility to allow this gender role restructuring to occur and thereby to ensure that 'the vital functions continue even in the absence of the husband-father figure' (Gonzalez 1973: 243) and that the family survives to provide security and stability for its members despite the circumstances of high levels of male migration, unemployment and poverty. According to Gonzalez, this perspective allows the researcher to take a new look at matrifocality.

> Instead of concentrating upon the negative aspects of matrifocality I suggest that we look to the possibility of its offering a selective advantage for the sub-society under certain conditions of strain in the adaptation of the latter to the industrial system (Gonzalez 1973: 242).

In her earlier analysis, Gonzalez linked matrifocality with domestic groups which were 'consanguineal' as distinct from those which were 'affinal' (conjugal). The former are composed of members related by consanguineal (blood) ties with no members linked in a conjugal union, the latter are based on a conjugal relationship. The consanguineal household was thus perceived as an adaptive response to poverty and male migration. In a later article, Gonzalez (1984, see Article 6 at end of chapter) recognised that this interpretation did not fully fit the facts; it did not explain the existence of approximately equal numbers of consanguineal and conjugal households or the persistence of this ratio as the incidence of female migration increased relative to male. Her reassessment questioned the validity of the whole exercise of identifying distinct household types given the fluidity of household composition among the Garifuna. Individuals resided in a variety of domestic situations during their life-times and households are described as 'ephemeral, transitory agglomerations of kin' (Gonzalez 1984: 7).

This reinterpretation blurred the distinction between the conjugal and consanguineal households and Gonzalez found it more useful to view all kin groups as variations on a set of 'common ideational themes' (Gonzalez 1984: 8). She identified three such themes, namely matrifocality, individualism and migration. Of primary interest to us here is matrifocality, which was explained by the historical process according to which women have become central in Garifuna society. The former roles of men have either disappeared, as with hunting and fishing, or have opened up to female participation, as in the case of migration and religious leadership. The Garifuna matrifocal social order parallels that in other parts of the world where the balance in the importance of gender roles has been tipped in favour of women (Gonzalez 1984: 8-9).

Within the household, mature women are the decision-makers. They control the pool of available labour, maximising membership and income by drawing contributions from adult sons and daughters, and manage ceremonial functions, in particular honouring the dead ancestors (Gonzalez 1984: 6-7). The important point is that matrifocality with loose marital relationships and residential flexibility are characteristics of *all* households, an 'adaptive strategy which has enabled the Garifuna to survive and flourish' (Gonzalez 1984: 10).

Female — headed households

Many scholars who have studied the family in the Caribbean have adopted the perspectives discussed so far in this chapter and identified adaptive strategies to ensure survival and, on occasions, even success. However, the Women and Development literature has concentrated the analysis on 'female-headed households', usually portraying a very different picture of Caribbean women and coming to very different conclusions concerning their economic welfare and survival. Accordingly, women who head households survive in poverty, in circumstances in which there is often no choice of economic strategy and little success in ensuring sources of support. Before examining these images of women, however, we take a brief look at the definition and prevalence of female-headed households in the Caribbean.

The conceptualisation of 'female-headed' is problematic. Sometimes it is defined as 'female-centered', as one and the same as Raymand Smith's original concept of matrifocality. More recent definitions, however, incorporate notions of female authority. And yet, a woman's dominance in the household does not necessarily coincide with female-headship. There also remains the question of whether or not a household can be defined as female headed if a resident adult male is present as conjugal partner, father or brother. Investigations of female-headed households in the Caribbean have generally been conducted by demographers and have relied heavily on census data. While, as we have noted, census categorisation has become more sophisticated and more relevant to Caribbean realities, problems remain. The identification of who heads the household continues to be ambiguous and subjective. Often the person who is defined as household head by the interviewee is so recorded. A number of criteria may be called on to justify the response, such as economic support, decision-making, ownership of the house and land, just being 'the man of the house' or, alternatively, being the woman at home regularly, not all of which correlate to produce an agreed, sociologically valid definition.

Bearing these points in mind and also that there is a limit to what census data collection methods can do to reflect the complexities and variations in the relationships and respective duties and responsibilities of adult males and females, investigations of female-headed households are, nevertheless, informative. Indeed, judged against the comparable database provided for other Third World countries, the Caribbean census has received high praise for 'providing a wealth of information on female heads of household' (Buvenic and Youssef 1978: 55). According to census figures, the proportions of female-headed households in the Caribbean in 1980 averaged 36.7 per cent of all households with a high of 45.6 per cent in St Kitts and a low of 24.4 per cent in Guyana, the latter being due to a predominance of East

Indian households which, as we shall see in Chapter VII, are culturally and historically constructed with male authority and headship.

A number of reasons have been put forward to explain the prevalence of female-
headed households. Important is the distinction made between the Caribbean
situation and those elsewhere in the Third World where the phenomenon is considered to be relatively recent.

> International data reviewed on the socioeconomics of women heads of household sug-
> gest a direct linkage between processes of modernization — particularly those stem-
> ming from economic development and its policies — and the rise of households
> headed by women. What is occurring in developing societies today with respect to this
> phenomenon are neither isolated instances nor traceable to specific ethnic/cultural
> heritages. Rather, most studies suggest that explanatory factors for female family head-
> ship should be sought in both internal and international migration; mechanization of
> agriculture; the development of agribusiness; urbanization; overpopulation; lower class
> marginality and the emergence of a class system of wage labour — all of which are inte-
> gral parts/ consequences of rapid economic transformation ....

> It is women among the poor, be it in Central and South America, in sub Saharan and
> North Africa, in Asia, who are increasingly becoming the sole or main economic
> provider of their families. In almost all these societies, this group of women are ill pre-
> pared to assume such responsibility. The suddenness of this new role that women are
> called upon to fulfill is, in many instances, traumatic. This is particularly true in social
> settings which, up until recently, have staunchly upheld the tradition of stable family
> systems and male headed households (Buvenic and Youssef 1978: ii-iii).

The Caribbean, on the other hand, has a tradition of female-headed households
and women's involvement in economic activities to support their families and
households which pre-dates modernisation by more than a century, stretching back
to the days of slavery. Female-headed households in the Caribbean also predominated during those periods when male migration had a dramatic effect on sex ratios
in the population. For example, by 1921 the exodus of men from Barbados, mainly
to Panama to assist in the building of the canal, left a sex imbalance of 679 males to
every 1000 females. Within the productive and reproductive age groups the proportion of males was only 526. The female numerical surplus resulted in a high proportion of female-headed households. As Joycelin Massiah (1983: 11) has claimed:

> The continued deficit of males in this crucial age-range meant that significant numbers
> of females were required to manage their households single-handedly. It may be ar-
> gued that it was during this period that the phenomenon of female household heads
> took firm root in the region.

But the prevalence of female-headed households cannot be explained solely with
reference to unbalanced sex ratios. To continue with the case of Barbados, the ratio
of males to every 1000 females evened out to 911 by 1990, but the percentage of
households headed by females has remained high, at 43.5 per cent.

An additional demographic reason advanced for female-headed households
concerns female longevity combined with age at marriage and the low remarriage
rates among widowed women. Though the gap has recently narrowed, Caribbean
women's life expectancy has consistently outpaced that of men by approximately
5 years. Women also tend to marry men older than themselves by approximately
5 years. This means that they usually outlive their spouses. It is also unusual for

widows to remarry and form households headed by their new husbands. This combination of factors explains the high level of female-headed households towards the end of the life cycle.

The question of personal choice of conjugal union status and residential patterns is also relevant to this rationale for the existence of female-headed households in the Caribbean. Much of the recent literature including the articles reviewed earlier in this chapter suggests that women in particular are deliberately choosing independence and freedom from male dominance. For Massiah's informants,

> the theme of independence loomed large. One of them commented: "Being single fits in with my independent thinking." Another said of her visiting union: "I like freedom, so I'm keeping it like it is" (Massiah 1983: 41).

Increasing levels of union dissolution and divorce, with petitions brought before the courts more by women than by men, are also cited to support the argument. Additionally, as we shall see in more detail in the next chapter, Jamaican women are reported not only to be able to survive with minimal male support, but also avoid co-residence and favour visiting unions since they thus maximise freedom from domestic responsibility for a male partner and from conjugal violence (Roberts and Sinclair 1978: 65-66, 249). These arguments suggest the need for a Caribbean reinterpretation of the conclusions reached by Buvenic and Youssef that modernisation has negatively affected the status of women, creating female heads of households in the midst of poverty. If Caribbean women chose to head households and enter extra-residential visiting unions, this suggests a level of female economic autonomy and well-being.

However, the link between female-headed households and economic welfare as explored for the Caribbean by Massiah (1983) indicates that women who head households are less well-educated than their male counterparts or the adult female population in general. Although they are more likely to be employed, as one would expect, their occupations are comparatively menial, badly paid and insecure, concentrated in the informal and marginal sectors of Caribbean economies and unprotected by state benefits and insurance. This study also challenges the portrayal of female heads as embedded and supported within extensive kinship networks. Massiah claims that family support is not always available or adequate and reports that many female heads of household have no choice but to face the shame of dependence on welfare assistance provided by the state. An examination of 38 female welfare recipients in Barbados showed that a clear majority (30) were heads of households with no partner resident. Their average age at the time of their first visit to the Welfare Department was 33 to 34 years, that is in the middle of the working and child-bearing phases of their lives. All of these women had young, dependent children, the average number being four per woman, and all but three of them were unemployed. In terms of family network support, this was not forthcoming. Extended family members living in the same households were generally older and/or incapacitated dependents and child support from non-resident fathers was virtually non-existent.

> It has been argued that ... many women deliberately cultivate a series of partners with the specific intention of collecting several support payments. In this way, they can be assured of a steady income without themselves having to be engaged in economic activity. Fathers, however, do not appear to contribute with any degree of regularity, if they contribute at all. Of the seventy-six men involved, twenty-one provided support of some kind as they were able. Another twenty-six provided no support, either because they refused to do so, their whereabouts were unknown or they preferred to go to gaol rather

than honour a court order. Another fourteen had migrated, nine were deceased and six were ill, five of them mentally. Once again, another possible source of income proves chimerical (Massiah 1983: 52).

Massiah (1983: 58) also included the following important quote from one of her informants which introduced values into the argument to show that multiple unions for women are disapproved of culturally. 'I don't like the idea of moving in with a man and having to move out, then moving in with another ... I don't believe in having children from different men.' What all this meant for these women was that they had no alternative but to rely on welfare benefits which constituted their principal and, in several cases, sole source of support.

There may well be women in the Caribbean who choose to head households and to cope without a man and who manage reasonably well economically, even improving their standards of living. Indeed, the literature implies that this may be true of women who, at the later stages of their life cycles, are supported by adult-working offspring. Census data for 1980 for the Caribbean, however, show that nearly half of the women who head households are under 50 years of age and therefore may not have reached this stage. Low education, menial employment if any, minimal family support and persistent poverty are the norm for them and many have no option but to turn to welfare benefits in order to survive. It is this evidence which has led researchers to conclude that,

> women heads of households might be a very special group among the poor worthy of the full attention of policy-makers concerned with improving the quality of life of the poorest of the poor (Buvenic and Youssef 1978: 1).

Massiah (1983: 34) repeated this conclusion for the Caribbean, also describing women who head households in the region as the 'poorest of the poor', the most vulnerable and as 'firmly placed among the disadvantaged sections of Caribbean populations'.

Conclusion

By incorporating the notions of personal choice and adaptive response, scholars introduced several positive developments into studies of family in the Caribbean. For one thing, they were no longer as preoccupied with the statistical identification of regularities in mating patterns and household composition. While some of the writers examined in this chapter retained quantitative methodologies, household structure was no longer the major focus. They reintroduced the perspectives of human action, of individuals making conscious choices and creatively constructing their own lives, though on occasions we were presented with pictures of rampant utilitarianism. The writers whose articles we have reviewed in this chapter concerned themselves with relationships between spouses and between parents and children and with questions about what options were available to people and why they chose to behave as they did.

With these developments also, scholars modified their ethnocentric definitions of what constitutes a family to include Caribbean patterns, not as disorganised or 'denuded' versions of nuclear family ideals, but as legitimate family types. The earlier negative evaluations were replaced by positive ones. Matrifocality, extra-residential unions and alternative patterns of parental responsibility were studied in their own right and were perceived as flexible family forms, appropriate and viable in the socio-economic conditions in which people lived. Nuclear families, each residing within and confining familial functions such as child-rearing within household boundaries, were still seen as part of the village value system. But the nuclear family was no longer an unqualified ideal to which villagers made all efforts to aspire, rather it was generally perceived as unattainable and inappropriate, so that villagers either 'stretched' these values or developed alternative patterns which were suited to their economic circumstances and were also positively sanctioned within the village communities. Marriage, for example, carries with it expectations of permanence, co-residence and the fulfillment of obligations, especially on the part of husbands as sole economic providers for wives and children. Within village conditions of scarce and uncertain economic resources, this may never be possible or at least not until the later stages of the life cycle. For much and sometimes all of their lives, men can neither afford to establish a marriage (involving as this does an expensive ceremony and the provision of a home) nor to maintain it subsequently by supporting a dependent (non-working) wife and several children. The rigidity of nuclear family structures and conjugal and parental role prescriptions were seen as unrealistic, unworkable and a disadvantage in these circumstances, except perhaps towards the end of the life cycle. On the other hand, the flexible, extra-residential patterns of non-legal unions and child-shifting constitute appropriate adaptive mechanisms in response to economic conditions. They were no longer seen as a problem, but as a cultural solution to a problem, the problem being the adverse and unstable conditions of poverty and marginalisation within which people live.

The assumption of village autonomy and self-sufficiency which underpinned previous structural functional community studies was retained to some extent. However, several authors sought to change this by incorporating themes from development theory and locating their villages of investigation as marginalised and dependent at the periphery of an exploitative global economic order. Their perspectives were therefore more complete than some of the earlier notions of village-based male marginality. Having said this, however, the concentration on lower-class, black family forms persisted. Though some comparisons were made between the better off and the less well-off villagers, these tended to reinforce pluralistic notions by stressing class distinctions in family patterns.

Apart from identifying changes in family patterns during the life cycle of individual men and women, most of these studies were essentially synchronic, perhaps not surprisingly since this was the case with their parent model. Dirks and Kerns, however, attempted to combine ethno-history with functional analysis in order to test the correlation between marriage, on the one hand, and migration, employment opportunities and economic prosperity, on the other, during specified historical periods. In the process they confirmed their hypothesis. But for Gonzalez, the result of a similar exercise raises important methodological questions as she finds that the ratio of household types remained unexpectedly constant as migratory patterns experienced marked changes over time. Her recognition that fluidity and flexibility of household composition were characteristic of all households blurred the class distinction previously assumed to exist between Caribbean household types. This, along with her idea that all kin groups are variations on a common set of 'ideational themes', helped to pave the way for the next theoretical phase in the study of family in the Caribbean, which we explore in the following chapter.

Perhaps the most significant criticism of these writers concerns their underlying assumption that family structure and relationships are economically or environmentally determined and that cultural principles and values have no real part in the analysis of family patterns. Their argument seems to be that since communities are culturally homogeneous, differences in local tradition are minor and have little to do with prevailing conjugal and family patterns. These must therefore be a result of varying and fluctuating circumstances, especially economic conditions. This argument has been put to the test in several ways, two of which we mention here and follow through in later chapters. If conjugal and family patterns vary with prevailing socio-economic conditions then, firstly, why have they not changed significantly with the developmental progress and improvements in standards of living that have occurred in Caribbean countries? And secondly, why do East Indians, who live in the same conditions of poverty and marginality, have very different family patterns?

The final point that we make here concerns the changing images of women within the family. It is possible that in their efforts to remove completely the heavy-handed ethnocentrism of the past, scholars ended up with overly positive images by portraying the family as resilient, flexible and adaptable and women, in particular, as matriarchs adopting the strategies that accompany such family forms to control the distribution of resources through kinship networks, thereby ensuring survival and even success. Lower-class, Afro-Caribbean women do indeed inhabit a cultural context in which visiting and common-law unions, matrifocality and female economic autonomy are traditionally accepted and immune from community condemnation and they do also devote considerable time, energy and ingenuity to the search for economic support for themselves and their dependents, especially children. However, to conclude that they succeed in their efforts may well be misconceived for the majority. As in-depth study on strategies for survival used by Barbadian women concludes:

> The existence of these alternative, culturally acceptable codes of conduct implies flexible behavioural patterns and a choice among several potential sources of support. Indeed, our informants recognise the need to keep all options open by changing strategies in their efforts to seek and cultivate new support sources. However, in reviewing their lives, it is clear that on many occasions changes in strategies and sources of support have occurred not as a result of a free choice among several options, but because there was no alternative ....

> In this context of poverty and uncertainty, limited options and little control, women remain economically vulnerable and economic security is elusive (Barrow 1986: 168-169).

Not all Caribbean women who head households find themselves at the end of their life cycles surrounded by supportive adult sons and daughters and extensive kinship networks that cross national boundaries to include better off migrants.

Many are childless and destitute and others are still in their reproductive years with dependent children to support and no alternative but to depend on welfare. Neither marital shifting nor child-shifting are necessarily the painless operations that we are sometimes led to believe. Most women disapprove of the practice of multiple partnering and would avoid it if they could. In other words, for these women so-called 'adaptive mechanisms' are not always freely and easily chosen and do not always work.

The critical response from a theoretical perspective to those who adopt the adaptive response perspective has been in the form of a plea to redirect attention to kinship ideologies and cultural ideas and values and to investigate family patterns from within, rather than as a result of external factors, economic or otherwise. There is a need to understand the conceptual structures and subjective interpretations of informants themselves, but, in doing so, investigators should do much more than just record informants' rationalisations of familial behaviour whether through personal choice, because they like or dislike a relative, or economic necessity, because they can or cannot afford whatever the practice. The proposal is to wipe the slate completely clean of persistent ethnocentrism and return to the fundamental question of defining kinship within the Caribbean cultural context. Such an approach is intended to avoid the trap of synchronic economic reductionism and should therefore respond to the above criticisms by introducing cultural comparisons across race and class and by reinstating kinship ideology and history. In the following chapter we proceed with these new theoretical developments.

READINGS

H. Rubenstein

CONJUGAL BEHAVIOUR AND PARENTAL ROLE FLEXIBILITY IN AN AFRO-CARIBBEAN VILLAGE

Theoretical speculation has sometimes run ahead of the collection of detailed ethnographic data in Afro-Caribbean family research. An investigation of extra-residential mating and the parental roles it creates in Leeward Village, a peasant community in St Vincent, reveals a folk system in which a variety of behaviours are permitted and in which actors are constantly being replaced. The variability and flexibility of this system are the expression of distinctive lower-class mating and parenting values which help villagers cope with Vincentian economic stagnation and class stratification.

Dans la recherche sur la famille Afro-Caraibe, la speculation purement théorique a partois largement devancé la collecte de matériaux ethnographiques précis. Une enquéte sur l'accouplement extra-résidentiel et les roles parentaux ainsi créés à Leeward Village, une communauté paysanne de St. Vincent, a révélé un systeme de caractère populaire (folk) qui permet une diversité de comportements où les acteurs sont en situation de constant remplacement. La variabilite et la flexibilité de ce système sont l'expression distincte des valeurs particulières liées à l'accouplement et au parentage de la classe moyenne. Cette situation semble faciliter chez ces villageois l'adjustement à la stagnation économique et à la stratification sociale de St. Vincent.

INTRODUCTION

For many years researchers have been intrigued by the complexity and variability characteristic of most aspects of family organization within the lower class of black West Indians. A host of theoretical frameworks have been employed to explain the high incidence of such phenomena as extra-residential unions, illegitimate births, late entry into marriage, and households headed by females. These and related features of family organization have been explained by the following: the influence of the African heritage (Herskovits and Herskovits, 1947); the operation of slave society (Cohen, 1956; Freilich,

1961); family organization in England (Greenfield, 1966); cultural pluralism (M. G. Smith, 1965); the culture of poverty (Rodman, 1971); class and racial differentiation (Henriques, 1953; R. T. Smith, 1956), male wage-labour migration (Gonzalez, 1969; Otterbein, 1965); and community organization (Clarke, 1966).

This emphasis on explanation is so well established that rarely is it given any justification. Thus Otterbein (1965: 66) seems to be belabouring the obvious when he gives the following rationale for an analysis of Caribbean family organization.

The problem of this paper is to explain the variability which occurs among Caribbean family systems. If this is to be accomplished, it is not sufficient merely to describe the attributes and dimensions of such systems; rather, it is also necessary to locate and identify the conditions and factors within the socio-cultural system which accounts for the variability. In other words, I will not only analyze family systems in terms of the most significant dependent variables but will also seek to discover the independent variables to which thee variables are functionally related.

It is my contention that explanation on the basis of independent variables, be they diachronically or synchronically rooted, has sometimes prematurely preceded detailed ethnographic investigation in Caribbean family studies. This assertion may seem rather curious in view of the apparent vastness of the literature in this area of Caribbean social organization. Yet the plethora of models and explanations alone suggests that not enough attention has been paid to the details of the systems in question. Folk systems have occasionally been by-passed, as is strikingly revealed by the preoccupation, beginning with the studies of R. T. Smith (1956) and Edith Clarke (1966), with statistical analyses of mating arrangements and household composition. One of the strongest proponents of the quantitative approach, M. G. Smith (1962a:7, 12-13), justifies it as follows:

> Field studies of the West Indian family organization are forced to rely heavily on household composition data in view of the *lack of reliable explicit rules* about family relations .... In such culturally heterogeneous societies as the West Indies, *we cannot expect informants to provide reliable generalizations* about family forms and relations .... *Analytic complexity enjoins a quantitative treatment*, since it is only by trying to relate frequency distributions of various kinds that we can determine the structural principles at work and assess their relative significance for the system as a whole. Moreover, *only this type of treatment enables us to see whether the raw materials do or do not reveal a systematic order* (my emphasis).

Smith neither defines what he means by 'reliable explicit rules' and 'generalizations' about family organization nor does he prove that such rules or generalizations can only be elicited through 'quantitative treatment'. Though clearly defined jural or moral rules may be absent, however, this does not mean that 'the structural principles at work' cannot be derived through analysis of material gathered from cognitive orientations of selected informants. Similarly, the absence of folk rules does not mean that structural principles of family organization are best derived by 'relating frequency distributions of various kinds'.

I wish to illustrate my contention that folk systems have not been given as much attention as they deserve in Caribbean family studies by analyzing the kinds of parental roles which result from extra-residential mating unions. Conjugal unions in which the partners live apart from each other have not received a great deal of attention. R. T. Smith (1956: 109), for example, treats extra-residential mating as a rather inconsequential conjugal form, while M. G. Smith (1962a: 32; 1962b: 168) and Philpott (1973: 118) insist that sexual unions are worthy of study only if they can be shown to be publicly recognized. I suggest that extra-residential unions, whether publicly recognized or surreptitiously carried out, deserve special care in their treatment. This is because they dramatically reveal the elements and principles informing the organization of all forms of parental behaviour. Rights and duties which intermesh within unions based on consensual or legal cohabitation, and are difficult to factor out, appear as separate or semi-independent parental roles within the extra-residential union. An analysis of the extra-residential union provides insight into the form and content of elements composing parental role behaviour and into the conditions and situations wherein some or most of these ingredients coalesce. To illustrate this need for more careful studies of folk concepts and taxonomies in Caribbean family research, I will describe the elements associated with parental role behaviour in Leeward Village, a peasant community in the Eastern Caribbean island of St Vincent. The complexity of parental roles in Leeward Village is due, in part, to the fact that the parent-child relationship is multi-stranded in most societies, simultaneously incorporating several different functions and patterns of behaviour (Goody, 1971: 332).

ISLAND AND VILLAGE BACKGROUND

St Vincent is a hilly, volcanic island covering an area of 133 square miles and containing over 90,000 people, most of whom are descendants of black slaves who were transported to the island during the eighteenth and early nineteenth centuries to work as labourers on the large sugar plantations that then dominated the local economy. Since Emancipation in 1838, island economic life has featured a decrease in the number of large estates, an increase in the importance of small-scale peasant cultivation, and short periods of economic stability based on the overseas sale of such crops as arrowroot, bananas, cotton, various starchy tubers, and, most recently, tobacco.

St Vincent is one of the poorest countries in the entire region. A report published some ten years ago argued that the per capita income of islanders 'is probably the lowest in the Western Hemisphere with the possible exception of Haiti' and that,

> ... most of the people on the island are living in a way which, in terms of material and environmental conditions, could scarcely be far removed from the situation as it was under slavery (University of the West Indies Development Mission, 1969: 4, 9).

Most islanders are black, rural dwellers, barely subsisting by means of peasant cultivation, agricultural wage labour, small-scale retailing, fishing, unskilled manual labour, domestic service, and semi-skilled independent trades. A large portion of the teenage and young adult population and much of the adult female population are unemployed. Underemployment is an even more serious problem affecting large sectors of the lower class work force.

Leeward Village is the fictitious name of a large rural community on the Caribbean coast of St Vincent. Nearly all of its 2,245 inhabitants are members of the island lower class. They dominate such unremunerative and low-status occupations as peasant and wage-labour agriculture, small-scale commercial fishing, petty-commodity retailing, semi-skilled and unskilled trades, and government manual wage-labour. Paralleling the national situation, many potentially productive persons are regularly unemployed and almost always underemployed.

EXTRA-RESIDENTIAL MATING

The inhabitants of Leeward Village are well aware that parenthood is a complex institution often composed of several discrete patterns of behaviour, with functions divided among various actors. But like their counterparts elsewhere in the region they view the nuclear family household, founded on the life-long marriage of husband and wife, as the ideal arena for sexual congress, reproduction, child care, and economic co-operation. Yet with less than one-third of village households composed in this way, deviations from the ideal are the rule rather than the exception, The presence of extra-residential mating as a socially acceptable mating form accounts for much of this deviation.

Males, whether married or not, are given complete sexual freedom and while sexual activity for young teenage girls is felt to be inappropriate, those who are more mature are permitted to engage in premarital mating unions without community censure. Depending on the dominant characteristic of the union, extra-residential mating is variously termed *liming, talking, pass-by, friending,* and *keeping,* and extra-residential mates are referred to and refer to each other as friend, *girl friend/boy friend,* and *keeper.* Extra-residential mating is the most common village mating form. For nearly all villagers, it is the first union into which they enter, and a great many elderly women have never participated in any other type of union. *Friending* is popular with nearly all males including those who are currently married. Many women who have never participated in a co-residential mating union have produced all of their children in one or more extra-residential unions with married men.

M. G. Smith (1962b: 168) restricts the term 'mating'

> ... to those unions which involve conception, co-habitation, or community consensus and familial action. Where paternity is disputed, I cannot speak of mating. Where the community and kin of a couple who live apart regard them as mates, the relation possesses duration and the tolerance, if not approval, of the partners' families, as well as public recognition. We cannot speak of clandestine or casual relations as mating, since such relations lack public recognition or family sanction.

I disagree with Smith. Clandestine unions are such an integral part of the entire Leeward Village mating system — and I suggest that the same holds elsewhere in the Caribbean (cf. Freilich, 1961, 1968) — that their denial would obscure many of the system's basic components. Some of the village terms to describe extra-residential unions are usually reserved for these unrecognized relationships. The term *liming*, when used to refer to an ongoing extra-residential affair, implies that the union has not yet become well established, that it may never become regularized, and that its existence is not widely known or acknowledged. Similarly, the terms *talking* ('He an she are *talking good*') and pass-by ('He just *pass-by* and they make a child') also refer to short-term irregular unions. Among young teenage girls the fear of parental punishment constrains them to keep their mating secret. There is also an effort to keep unions which are based on a direct exchange of sex for money from becoming public. A man gains little prestige from such 'unions' and may even lose the esteem of his peers for *running whores*. In addition, since it is likely that he is also in a more stable union, his regular partner may make a fuss about his philandering, particularly if she believes that he is expending resources that should go to her instead. Similarly, the female partner in the irregular union may also be part of a more stable union and only *makes fares* to supplement her income. Finally, a few married women whose husbands have migrated overseas engage in carefully concealed unions so as not to place their marriages in jeopardy.

Some extra-residential unions last for several years and there are a few which have been extant for over twenty years. The majority, however, are short-lived affairs lasting no more than a year or two. Extra-residential mating unions may be terminated when either partner wishes to do so. Since they are non-legal and do not involve the kinds of material obligations associated with co-residence, they appeal particularly to lower-class males; they permit sexual gratification and the gaining of prestige (if a number of partners are involved simultaneously or consecutively) without the need to enter a legal or consensual union in which the economic expectations may be difficult or impossible to meet.

The absence of well defined rights and responsibilities linking extra-residential partners is one of the primary reasons many unions of this kind are terminated after a short period of time. The female partner is expected to be sexually faithful to her partner, who, in turn, is obliged to reciprocate with regular or periodic gifts. Beyond this, little is specified about the way the union should be acted out or what obligations the partners owe to each other. Various types of behaviour therefore are permitted. Some women regularly wash and cook for their non-resident boyfriends, while others never do so. Some unions are very intimate, while others are rather formal and confined to sexual release. Some unions involve constant visits between households, while others are based on brief encounters in deserted spots or in the home of a third party. Some unions require considerable economic assistance from the male, while others are characterized by small or infrequent gifts. There is a measure of male sexual exclusiveness in certain unions; others represent an expression of the male desire to have concurrent affairs with several women. Some show promise of being a prelude to marriage; others are simply fleeting affairs soon to be terminated.

PARENTAL ROLE BEHAVIOUR

When a child results from an extra-residential union, the genitor normally is expected to *mind* [financially support] the offspring, thereby acquiring the rights and responsibilities associated with the role of pater. These include the obligation to provide the child with a surname and a class of socially recognized kin, the right to expect obedience and respect from the child and to punish the child for wrongdoing, responsibility for some of the child's actions, and the right (but not obligation) to make the child an heir. *Minding* a child, in turn, presupposes *owning* [accepting paternity of] the child. Whether a child is *owned* by the genitor is often a complicated issue. Some children are not owned at all; others are *minded* by men who do not own them. Occasionally a child is *owned* by two men, and in a few cases paternity changes over time. Privately some men admit that they have sired children who are owned by other men. There is reason then to distinguish between the pater (the social father), the genitor (the person socially acknowledged to be the biological father), and the genetic father (the actual biological father) (Barnes, 1961).

Although some women succeed in forcing reluctant genitors to accept the ownership of their child through a maintenance suit, admission of paternity normally rests with the man. If he has no cause to doubt her fidelity or his siring of their other children, a man will not question his girl friend's pregnancy. On the other hand, a man may deny that a child is his, sometimes claiming that he never engaged in sexual relations with her or that he paid for her services. He may attempt a denial if the woman who tries to give [assign paternity of] the child to him is known to be rather promiscuous, if the child bears no physical resemblance to him, if their relationship was very brief or furtive, or if he is unable or unwilling to support the child. If a man does decide to own the child this normally indicates that he is willing to mind it as well. But not all men who own their children subsequently mind them, and a child may be minded by someone who does not own it. In cases where the father does not own his child, or owns it but does not mind it, the burden falls on either the mother who is then said to mind her own child or on the mother's mother or some other relative who minds it for her. A further complication may arise when a father does not own his child but his own mother acknowledges that the child is her son's based on a physical resemblance between child and father and/or other close kin. In such event the son's mother is said to own the child although this implies no obligation that she support it.

A child also may be disowned by a genitor who claims that he made an error in accepting paternity. Such a disclaimer may occur if the growing child begins to resemble the father less and less, if it is discovered that the woman was also mating with another man at the time of conception, or if it is found that she has also *given* the child to someone else. In all of these cases the discovery is usually based on gossip conveyed to the man by kin or friends. For example, when Kevin Charles (a pseudonym) heard that his daughter from an extra-domestic union was not his, he changed his mind about arranging for mother and daughter to join him in England, where he had migrated during the woman's pregnancy. He wrote a letter, an excerpt from which follows, to a close family member explaining his decision:

> Well Noreen I saying this but I know you would all not like to hear such but I am sorry about this child affairs. Well I have heard that the child is not mine and how its black and I don't decide to mind no other man's child. What so ever they get when I was at home let them make that do. I am entirely finish. I even had the birth paper but I am going to send it back to them without a line. My child is not suppose to be so black as I heard from those fellows that came up late. Its up here I hear everything.

Children who are both *owned* and *minded* by their non-resident fathers usually take their surnames, although this does not necessarily imply that they will be incorporated into their circle of kin. As illegitimate issue they have no legal claim to their father's property or to the property in which the fathers have shares. In addition, the continuing viability of a mating union directly affects the support that such children receive, suggesting that *minding* in the extra-residential union is contingent on continuing sexual access to the mother (Sanford, 1975: 170). More than half of the village children under the age of fifteen who were produced in now defunct extra-residential unions receive no support from their fathers. Only a few illegitimate children over this age receive support if they are the product of defunct unions. On the other hand, early cessation of support means that the father cannot expect to receive the affection, loyalty, respect, productive labour, or economic assistance of his children in old age.

A woman whose child no man will *own* or *mind* will state that she is both mother and father to the child. This implies that when a genetrix also assumes the role of pater all parental rights and duties belong to her; it confirms the view that the mother-child relationship is the most important of all consanguineous ties among lower-class black West Indians (Clarke, 1966: 142; Rodman, 1971: 80-9; R. T. Smith, 1956; Wilson 1973: 135). Villagers will state that it is the duty of a mother to *care* [rear] her child and, if the father is not supporting it, to mind it as well. However, as elsewhere in the Caribbean (Clarke, 1966: 99, 177-81; Gonzalez, 1969: 52-3; Sanford, 1974, 1975), maternal rights and duties in Leeward Village may be temporarily or permanently transferred to or shared with others. Some mothers neither *care* nor *mind* their children; some *care* them without *minding* them; others *mind* them but do not *care* them.

Nearly one-quarter of the village children under the age of fifteen are living in homes which do not contain their biological mothers. Some seventy per cent of these children are at least partially supported by their non-resident mothers, who thereby affirm the right to physical custody over them. Most of these are temporary arrangements in which the genetrix asks the fosterer to *keep* the child for her. If the arrangement continues for a long period of time — several years or more — and support from the genetrix is low or irregular, the fosterer assumes greater rights over the child and may even become the child's social mother or mater. Even in temporary arrangements, day-to-day nurture and training rests with the fosterer, often the child's maternal grandmother, who also acquires the right to discipline the child and to expect help with household chores.

A genetrix *cares* but does not *mind* her children if *minding* is being carried out by the children's father(s) or has been delegated to some other household member. If a child is not being *minded* by its father and if the mother has no means to support it herself, the rights and duties associated with *minding* again tend to fall on the mother's mother. If the genetrix remains a household member, various parental rights and duties associated with nurture, grooming, nursing, discipline, and training are shared among the genetrix, grandmother, and other capable household members. The right to assign temporary or permanent custody of the child to some other party is retained by the genetrix even if she does not *mind* the child and only plays a small part in the rearing process.

Where *caring* is either fully delegated by a genetrix or shared with other household members, the growing child often tends to 'adjust' the normal system of kinship terminology to fit the actual content of the roles being performed on its behalf. A mother may be addressed by her first name, by a nickname, by the term *tantie*, which is usually reserved for a parent's sister, and by the ideal terms associated with the role of genetrix. A mother's mother may be addressed by a nickname and by the ideal terms associated with motherhood. A biological mother may be addressed by the term *tantie* or called by her first name even if she is a resident household member when her own mother or older sister is either the most dominant household member or the person most responsible for the child's day-to-day care (cf. Rodman, 1971: 145-55; R. T. Smith, 1956: 143-6, 162). It would be both confusing and inaccurate for a child growing up in this situation to address both women by the same term, and the child is permitted to select the term which most closely corresponds to actual behaviour. In some cases a kind of compromise is reached with the child calling the genetrix, *mommie*, and the mater, *momma*.

Minding and *caring* result in the permanent transfer of rights over the child from the biological mother to the mother-substitute if the child has been transferred at an early age and the mother does not *mind* it. This often happens when destitute mothers give their children to distant kin or even non-kin for *minding* and *caring* in the hope that the children will be adequately looked after. In many of these cases the transfer is initiated by childless couples or elderly women with no resident children or grandchildren to assist with domestic duties and the running of errands.

ANALYSIS

I have now described some of the elements constituting one type of conjugal behaviour — extra-residential mating — in Leeward Village, and the variability in the content of the parental roles that result from it. While I have employed the distinctive folk perspective and nomenclature of lower-class villagers themselves, many of the features dealt with should be familiar to Afro-Americanists even if their ethnographic treatment so far has been less than satisfactory. Thus, in the Caribbean literature there is the occasional brief discussion of, or passing reference to, such topics as eligibility for parenthood, the establishment of paternity, the assignment of kinship terms and surnames, rights and duties concerning children, fosterage and adoption, the sharing and division of parental roles, and male domestic marginality (Clarke, 1966: 84, 95-6, 98, 100, 106, 108, 141-2, 176-80; Gonzalez, 1969: 52-4, 60; Greenfield, 1966: 104-6, 112-3, 120-3, 140-2; Horowitz, 1967: 55-6; Rodman, 1971: 75-82, 145-55; Sanford, 1974, 1975; M. G. Smith, 1962b: 194-8, 211-12, 226-35; R. T. Smith, 1956: 142-7, 158-9). What is clearly missing in the individual studies is the detailed, synthetic treatment of the multiple features of and linkages between conjugality and parental roles, which can only be obtained through systematic investigation within and among particular Caribbean societies. While such an undertaking was well beyond the scope of a short paper, I have attempted to show both the kind of issues that need to be reviewed and the direction further research ought to be taking. Although my purpose has been undeniably ethnographic, the presentation would remain incomplete without an attempt to explain the presence and significance of the features of conjugal and parental role behaviour that I have described. This task requires a different kind of analysis from the one presented up to this point, namely one which lies outside of the cognitive orientation and systems of explanations of the actors involved.

Although I have portrayed St. Vincent as a poor country, by no means all Vincentians are poor. From an etic perspective it is useful to divide the island population into three hierarchal social classes whose member share differential access to productive resources, wealth, and positions of power. Pheno-typical differences continue to parallel differences in privilege, prestige, and lifestyle with the upper and middle classes containing most of the island's white and racially mixed persons except for a category of poor whites (locally termed *Bajans* to distinguish them from 'real' whites) whose ancestors migrated from nearby Barbados at the end of the nineteenth century. While these two classes (which also include a growing black component) together form less than ten per cent of the island's population, their members monopolize the most important social, economic, and public-service facilities in the country, including the political and legal systems, the traditional Christian churches, the educational apparatus, the medical and health-care institutions, the plantation system, the import-export sector, the overseas commercial banks and insurance companies, all major retail outlets, and the fledgling tourist and manufacturing industries.

Although lifestyle and life-chance differences clearly demarcate the three classes, mainstream Vincentian culture which is the local manifestation of British-derived traditions influences the behaviour of all islanders. Lower class persons are required to recognize and manipulate many of the norms, values, symbols, and behavioural patterns typical of middle and upper class members of the society (Rubenstein, 1976). They are encouraged particularly to adopt mainstream patterns of respectable behaviour. For example, the clergy, secular members of the dominant categories, and peers who have chosen to accept the over-arching moral code, actively and deliberately urge those 'living in sin' to regularize their unions in accordance with the societal norm of legal, Christian marriage. In this way the nuclear family household founded on legal marriage has come to be acknowledged by Leeward villagers as the ideal arena for sexual activity, procreation, and the performance of such domestic activities as the common preparation and consumption of food. The result of adherence to mainstream norms of respectable mating which imply the economic viability and self-sufficiency of its head, the husband-father, this household arrangement carries higher prestige than any of the many competing village household configurations.

Where does all this leave the folk system of parental role behaviour that has already been described? In particular, how can we account for a system which clearly does *not* generate stable, Christian nuclear families when there exists an ideal system which most villagers view as the most appropriate one for acting out parental and family activities?

The answer lies in the utility of choice and flexibility in an otherwise extremely constraining social and economic environment. While the dominant notion of marriage as the only appropriate arena for mating and reproduction may be accepted as an ideal among most lower-class villagers, many are unable to realize their non-legal unions (common-law cohabitation and extra-residential mating) for the simple reason that they cannot fulfil the culturally defined expectations associated with marriage. Legal unions and stable, independent nuclear family households are unavailable to many because their material prerequisites — a reliable income source, a church wedding followed by an elaborate reception, a house and furnishings — cannot be met, given the monopolization of limited island economic opportunities by members of the middle and upper classes. Recognizing a similar situation among poor black peasants in Trinidad, Rodman (1971:195) argues that the effect of this blockage has been that

> ... the lower-class person, without abandoning the general value of the society, develops an alternative set of values. Without abandoning the values of marriage and legitimate childbirth he stretches these values so that a non-legal union and illegitimate children within that union are also desirable .... The result is that members of the lower class, in many areas, have a wider range of values than others within the society. They share the general values of the society with members of other classes, but in addition they have stretched these values, or have developed alternative values, which help them to adjust to their deprived circumstances.

The distinctive Leeward Village folk system of conjugal and parental role behaviour is a clear example of the development of a socially viable alternative or 'stretched' value system. The significance of such a system lies in the manner in which it serves to reflect general Vincentian economic stagnation and middle and upper class resource monopolization. Operating as they do within a socio-economic system characterized by restrictions on social mobility and economic well-being, the best interests of most villagers would not be served by a highly ascriptive set of reproductive and parental roles with clearly defined, obligatory rights and duties attached to persons linked in pre-determined ways. Rather, a variable and malleable pattern of mating and parenting which permits adjustment to changing circumstances would seem a most appropriate adaptive mechanism, given the marginal social and economic situation which defines the lives of most villagers. In short, the flexibility of conjugality, parental role behaviour, and associated elements of kinship and domestic organization (such as kinship terminology) permit villagers to respond quickly to changes in social and economic incentives and constraints. Inability to support a mate and offspring because of loss of employment, the need to transfer the responsibility for child rearing to a closely related female when wage labour opportunities arise unexpectedly, the addition of household members through closely spaced births, and the periodic though unpredictable availability of labour-migration opportunities all place a premium on flexibility and maneuverability in mating and parenting. The result has been the creation of a social system in which roles are achieved rather than prescribed, in which actual behaviour, rather than customary usage or social convention determines conjugal and parental positions and activities appropriate to those positions.

The complexity of parental role behaviour within the extra-residential union also suggests that such basic kinship categories as 'mother' and 'father' are composed of separate 'social identities (Goodenough 1965) whose elements co-occur only when legal marriage leads to the establishment of nuclear family households. The existence of these component identities is made obvious by the manner in which villagers themselves factor out parental roles, underscoring the need to pay closer attention to folk descriptions and classifications in analyses of Afro-Caribbean family life.'

NOTES

1. Only Freilich (1961, 1968) has dealt in any systematic way with secret mating in the Caribbean. Although he was concerned only incidentally with showing their relation to parental role behaviour, his analysis of clandestine unions in a Trinidad village clearly shows that they form an integral part of the entire family system.

2. Field work in St Vincent was carried out betwen September 1969 and Ocober 1971 and between April 1972 and August 1972. Research was made possible by a Canada Council Doctoral Fellowship, a Centre for International Studies (University of Toronto) Fellowship and Research Grant, and a Province of Ontario Graduate Fellowhsip.

3. The State of St Vincent also includes most of the Grenadines, a chain of small islands strung between the mainalnd and neighbouring Grenada to the south.

REFERENCES

Barnes, J. A. 1961. 'Physical and Social Kinship' *Philosophy of Science* 28:296-9.

Clarke, Edith 1966 *My Mother Who Fathered Me: A Study of the Family in Three Selected Communities in Jamaica*. London: Allen and Unwin.

Cohen, Yehudi A. 1956 'Structure and Function: Family Organization and Socialization in a Jamaican Community', *American Anthropologist* 58:644-86.

Freilich, Morris 1961. 'Serial Polygyny, Negro Peasants, and Model Analysis', *American Anthropologist* 63(5):955-75.

1968 'Sex, Secrets and Systems', pp. 47-62 in Stanford N. Gerber (ed.), *The Family in the Caribbean*. Proceedings of the First Conference on the Family in the Caribbean Rio Piedras, Puerto Rico: Institute of Caribbean Studies, University of Puerto Rico.

Gonzalez, Nancie L. Solien 1969 *Black Carib Household Structure: A Study of Migration and Modernization*. Seattle University of Washington Press.

Goodenough, Ward H. 1965. 'Rethinking "Status" and "Role": Toward a General Model of the Cultural Organization of Social Relationships'. pp. 1-24 in Michael Banton (ed.), *The Relevance of Models for Social Anthropology*. ASA Monographs I. London: Tavistock Publications.

Goody, E. N. 1971. 'Forms of Pro-Parenthood: The Sharing and Substitution of Parental Roles'. pp. 331-45 in Jack Goody (ed.), *Kinship: Selected Readings*. Baltimore: Penguin Books.

Greenfield, Sidney M. 1966 *English Rustics in Black Skin: A Study of Modern Family Forms in a Pre-Industrialized Society*. New Haven: College and University Press.

Henriques, Fernando 1953, *Family and Colour in Jamaica*. London: Eyre and Spottiswoode.

Herskovits, Melville J., and Frances S. Herskovits 1947, *Trinidad Village*. New York: Alfred A. Knopf.

Horowitz, Michael M. 1967, *Morne-Paysan: Peasant Village in Martinique*. New York: Holt, Rinehart and Winston.

Otterbein, Keith F. 1965, 'Caribbean Family Organization: A Comparative Analysis'., *American Anthropologist* 67:66-79.

Philpott, Stuart B. 1973, West Indian Migration: The Montserrat Case. London School of Economics *Monographs on Social Anthropology* No. 47. London: Athlone Press.

Rodman, Hyman 1971, *Lower-Class Families: The Culture of Poverty in Negro Trinidad*. London: Oxford University Press.

Rubenstein, Hymie 1976, 'Incest, Effigy Hanging, and Biculturation in a West Indian Village', *American Ethnologist* 3:765-81.

Sanford, Margaret 1974. 'A Socialization in Ambiguity: Child-Lending in a British West Indian Society', *Ethnology* 13: 393-400.

1975, 'To Be Treated Like a Child of the Home: Black Carib Child Lending in British West Indies Society'. pp. 159-81 in Thomas R. Williams (ed.), *Socialization and Communication in Primary*

Groups. The Hague: Mouton.

Smith, Michael G. 1962a. *West Indian Family Structure*. Seattle, University of Washington Press.

1962b. *Kinship and Community in Carriacou*. New Haven, Yale University Press.

1965. *The Plural Society in the British West Indies*. Berkeley, University of California Press.

Smith, Raymond T. 1956, *The Negro Family in British Guiana: Family Structure and Social Status in the Villages*. London, Routledge and Kegan Paul.

University of the West Indies Development Mission 1969, *The Development Problem in St Vincent*. Kingston, Jamaica: Institute of Social and Economic Research, University of the West Indies.

Wilson, Peter J. 1973, *Carib Antics: The Social Anthropology of English-speaking Negro Societies of the Caribbean*. New Haven: Yale University Press.

R. Dirks and V. Kerns

MATING PATTERNS AND ADAPTIVE CHANGE IN RUM BAY, 1823-1970

INTRODUCTION

Anthropologists and sociologists have been analyzing aspects of West Indian family and domestic life for many years now. Much of their work has concentrated on conjugal patterns, especially amongst various Afro-Caribbean populations where a high incidence of extra-legal unions exists. Ethnocentric concern arising from middle-class morality may have inspired some of the work in this area, but most seems founded on a genuine fascination with a clear and quantifiable manifestation of cultural pluralism. In the microcosmic realm of mating relationships, the issue of pluralism boils down to some specific, straightforward questions: What explains the simultaneous accommodation of disparate yet closely related conventions like formal marriage and its extra-legal counterpart? How can these plural forms co-exist, particularly in small and otherwise rather homogenous communities?

Answers to such questions frequently have assumed the form of ethnohistorical explanations. References have been made to the pluralizing influence of traditions from Africa [e.g., Herskovits and Herskovits 17], England [e.g., Greenfield 14], and plantation slavery [e.g., Freilich 12, Matthews 20, Smith 27]. Essentially, these studies identify probable sources of evolutionary input contributing to the *general* structure and organization of mating alliances. But ethnohistorical research on the origins of Afro-Caribbean conjugal patterns has its limitations. Since the replication of cultural patterns is never an exact process, we are left wondering by what means the present has remained faithful to the past. What are the immediate factors that have contributed to the maintenance of Old World and slave traditions from one generation to the next right down to the present day? Further limits appear to be defined by an inability to offer acceptable explanations for *particular* differences among contemporary communities. The relative proportion of legal and extra-legal unions varies widely from one place to another, even where cultural heritage seems fundamentally the same. Contemporary variation has not been explained convincingly by attempts to document substantially different acculturative histories. A third difficulty standing in the way of a purely ethnohistorical interpretation is the fact that a high frequency of extra-legal mating is also characteristic of many communities with very different cultural backgrounds. This suggests that factors other than the force of tradition must contribute toward a convergence of patterns.

When it comes to dealing with contemporary similarities and differences between groups, various economic and environmental explanations appear more successful.

These rest on the hypothesis that extra-cultural pressures are responsible in large measure for the relative incidence of legal and extra-legal unions. The overall organization of a community mating pattern is seen as a label rather than as a fixed cultural endowment. Research along these lines has shown that high frequencies of extra-legal relationships correlate with economic insecurity and a lack of employment opportunities [e.g., Clarke 3, Otterbein 21, Rodman 25]. At best, these correlations are founded on comparisons of distinct groups *assumed* to be culturally similar, though demonstrably subject to dissimilar economic conditions. Such studies are intuitively persuasive and add an extra dimension to our understanding by suggesting that the plural forms inserted into tradition during the course of culture history become manifest at various levels in accordance with environing circumstances. They further suggest that the economic resource base available to individuals is related causally to the immediate organization of their mating relationships.

It is important to bear in mind that, while Afro-Caribbean mating patterns may be environmentally sensitive, studies thus far actually have not verified this hypothesis. There are two reasons for this. To begin with, the alternative hypothesis has not been ruled out. By their very nature, synchronic comparisons cannot distinguish between the effect of environment and cultural tradition. It remains entirely possible, despite the lack of convincing demonstration to date, that minor differences in local acculturative experience actually do account for observed differences in the relative proportion of mating arrangements. A critical test bearing on the influence of economic environment should be able to control for variation in culture history more positively than by assumption. In the second place, and perhaps more basic, the verification of statements regarding causality depends in principle on the demonstration of a diachronic process. Studies without a temporal dimension cannot confirm causality. Hence, comparative correlational studies aimed at explaining the variable frequency of mating relationships also have inherent limits. To push beyond these limits, a synthetic approach is required, one that combines the strengths of ethnohistory with those of socio-economic environmental analysis.

This study attempts such a synthesis. It is a specific test of the general hypothesis that the level of marriage and extra-legal alliances expressed in Afro-Caribbean communities is a dynamic adjustment to economic environment. As a community-specific test, it is only a first step in the direction of more general conclusions. However, despite its specificity, the study we describe avoids some of the methodological shortcomings apparent in previous efforts. Because our data are drawn from a single, small, homogeneous community, its residents largely alike in terms of acculturative exposures, we can be quite certain that variations in local tradition have little to do with the establishment of one or the other type of conjugal bond. Furthermore, in contrast to the comparative method, we introduce data indicative of diachronic change by showing close parallels between environmental fluctuations and the relative frequency of mating forms. Our data show regular change in the proportional incidence of mating relationships over a span of nearly a century and a half (1823-1970).

THE COMMUNITY

Rum Bay is a rural community on the island of Tortola, British Virgin Islands (BVI). The main settlement and the surrounding hillsides are populated by some 400 black people. It is important to establish from the outset that virtually all of the inhabitants have some interest in local land. Nevertheless, agricultural activity is not prominent. Residents sometimes identify themselves in connection with an occupational specialty such as taxi driver, hotel worker, or carpenter, but in reality the people of Rum Bay direct their efforts wherever a relatively rewarding opportunity can be found. The ownership of shops, vehicles, and other capital introduces some socio-economic stratification into the community, though impact on life styles is negligible.

Like a great many other communities throughout the Afro-Caribbean, Rum Bay is a constituent unit within a neoteric society [cf. Gonzalez 13]. Excluded by metropolitan corporate interests from direct access to and control over the most rewarding resources in their environment, the people of the Virgin Islands have been caught up in a constant struggle to adapt to a changing assortment of available exploitive opportunities. In accordance with decisions made in foreign boardrooms, capital has been invested and withdrawn from a succession of resource domains. These decisions have contributed to a history of major ecological changes for the inhabitants of the islands.

Faced with unstable conditions, adaptation in Virgin Island communities, as elsewhere, demands a high degree of flexibility in terms of organizational strategies. Viewing mating alliances as a kind of adaptive strategy, our data allow us to examine the extent to which certain features of Rum Bay's mating pattern have been responsive to this history of changing economic opportunities. More specifically, the available data enable us to analyze three features of Rum Bay's mating organization across periods of socio-economic change: (1) the proportional frequencies of legal and extra-legal mating alliances, (2) the mean annual frequencies of marriages contracted in Rum Bay, and (3) the mean ages at which males and females first enter formal marriage.

In the following sections of this paper, we present a descriptive outline of the socio-economic changes encountered by the residents of Rum Bay. These changes are described in terms of opening and closing resource domains. Next, we discuss the historical data that are available on local mating patterns and present a comparative analysis of that data within and between periods of socio-economic change. Finally, we introduce some ethnographic data concerning contemporary mating patterns. These data are used to construct a model of the adjustment process influencing the selection of alternative types of unions and to delineate more clearly some of the theoretical implications of our historical findings.

SOCIO-ECONOMIC CHANGE IN THE BRITISH VIRGIN ISLANDS

Surveying the history of the BVI, it is possible to discern seven major socio-economic periods between the years 1823 and 1970. These periods are differentiated by marked changes in the resource domains open to the inhabitants of Rum Bay and their fellow islanders. Unfortunately, historical sources do not offer the sort of consistent data necessary to construct a quantifying index, having power to delineate one period from the next with truly unambiguous rigour. Despite this drawback, it is possible to characterize each period by the appearance and disappearance of certain economic opportunities due to technological, business, and political events emanating from the metropolitan centres of America and Europe. Some of these events are dramatic, others less so. In either case, the dates marking the onset of each period should be taken to represent a somewhat arbitrary starting point for a general trend in the direction of prosperity or decline.

Period I (1823-1833): The first years for which mating data for Rum Bay are available include the final full decade of slavery. This period has been described in detail by Dookhan [9, pp. 137-186]. Labouring on eight small plantations, Rum Bay's slaves depended on estate owners and overseers for their welfare. Mountainous topography and erratic rainfall militated against the development of Tortola as a prosperous sugar island and there is some indication that planters attempted to make up in labour intensity what they lacked in natural resources. For their efforts, slaves were 'compensated' with simple clothing, rights to provision grounds and pasture, plus small supplementary doles of imported foodstuffs. At best, this afforded a bare subsistence.

Period II (1834-1849): Emancipation in 1834 opened a brief period of expanded economic opportunity, allowing the people of Rum Bay somewhat more than a subsistence-level existence. For most of the Black population, the post-Emancipation era began with compulsory apprenticeship, a scheme that paid ex-slaves for any work in excess of a 45-hour weekly obligation. Apprenticeship lasted until 1838 and thereafter most women withdrew as full-time members of the labour force [Dookhan 9, p. 240]. Men who continued in plantation work earned about six pence per day as well as the use of a dwelling house, garden plot, pasture, and free medical attention. These extras were said to double income [Gurney 15, p. 27].

By the mid-1840s, BVI sugar interests were in serious financial trouble and began to convert to a metairie system [Dookhan 9, p. 248]. This shifted risk to agricultural labourers and probably reduced their cash income to some extent. Yet, despite difficulties, island-ers continued to enjoy relative prosperity by virtue of access to St Thomas's thriving markets less than ten miles to the west.

St Thomas's importance as a market centre for labour and produce during these years derived from a combination of political, geographical, and technological factors. Danish neutrality in international affairs was attractive to shippers [Knox 19]. In addition, for sail-ing vessels bound to and from Europe, St Thomas was perfectly situated astride the shipping lanes of the Eastern Caribbean. Transoceanic as well as inter-island vessels were loaded and unloaded at St. Thomas, creating a great demand for labour and pro-duce. British Virgin Islanders eagerly supplied both in the years following Emancipation [Dookhan 9, pp. 257-8]. A portion of the relatively high wages earned in St Thomas was returned to local communities such as Rum Bay, where it was used to establish inde-pendent households and eventually to purchase the land of defunct plantations [Dook-han 9, pp. 258-265].

Period III (1850-1879): While no single occurrence punctuates the start of this period, by 1850 events of the previous decade and some developing trends were beginning to have an impact. The effect was to constrict previously expanding horizons.

Although freedom had increased the fortunes of the rural folk, the BVI economy as a whole was far from healthy. The first unequivocal sign occurred in 1847, when a major sugar estate collapsed, throwing over 1,000 people out of work [Dookhan 9, p. 243]. The severity of this blow for a population of only 6,500 cannot be overemphasized. The abil-ity of St Thomas to absorb those looking for wage work was curtailed seriously in 1848 when the Danes released their own slaves. Four years later, Knox [19, pp. 122-131] de-scribed St Thomas as full of unemployed. The demand for dockhands declined through-out the 1850s and 1860s with the decreasing use of wind-driven vessels. Steamships were able to call directly at British and Spanish ports previously served by inter-island craft and the importance of St. Thomas as a trans-shipment point waned [Westergaard 29, p. 252]. The port continued as a coaling station, but it never regained the stature of former years.

In response to these turnabouts, British Virgin Islanders increasingly came to rely on home-based, cattle-raising, small-scale cultivation, and fishing. As peasant proprietors, they were frustrated by droughts, a major hurricane, heavy taxation, and a declining market for their produce [Dookhan 9, pp. 230-275]. However, by this time much of the land was their own and it provided a haven in the face of a depressed regional econ-omy.

Period IV (1880-1921): By 1880, a new economic opportunity presented itself to the people of the BVI. While the commercial decline of St Thomas continued, international events precipitated a demand for labour further afield. During the Cuban Ten Year's War (1868-1878), some sugar capital withdrew from Cuba in favour of Santo Domingo where the industry took root and grew steadily [Fagg 11, p. 150]. Beginning in 1880, island men responded in increasing numbers to the new demand for labour in Santo Domingo [Har-rigan 16, p. 96]. For 40 years, foreign canefields provided British Virgin Islanders with a major source of cash income. Many never returned from the work abroad. Between 1871 and 1881, the population of the BVI declined no less than 21 per cent [cf., Cumper 4, p. 9, Watkins 28, p. 139]. The savings of those who did return were used to maintain or acquire additional land, purchase livestock, and build dwellings.

Period V (1922-1931): In 1917, the United States purchased the former Danish Virgin Islands. At first the change in government in the neighbouring islands had no palpable effect on BVI society. In November 1921, that changed, as the Prohibition Amendment to the U.S. Constitution took effect in the American Virgin Islands. Overnight, canefields again sprang up on the slopes of Rum Bay as British Virgin Islanders responded to the demands of their thirsty American neighbours. Ancient distilleries worked to capacity. Captains of sailing vessels in the British islands, already adept at smuggling through eco-nomic necessity [Dookhan 9, pp. 278-9], transferred their skills to the illicit liquor trade. The attempts of the colonial government to suppress the trade were eventually success-ful [Harrigan 15, p. 183]. Still, while it lasted, the business of distilling and exporting rum created a busy cash-crop market in the BVI. Gradually, however, this Prohibition-in-duced prosperity was submerged beneath the oncoming wave of economic depression.

Period VI (1932-1941): With the advent of the Depression, there were few nearby opportunities for employment. Once again, British Virgin Islanders sought work overseas. However, with few jobs available, those who remained in the islands received little in cash remittances. Having few dependable local sources of cash, the land again served as a means for subsistence for large numbers of people.

Period VII (1942-1970): For the past three decades, the U.S. Virgin Islands have been the recipients of an unprecedented amount of metropolitan investment. During World War II, military construction and shipping provided cash income-earning opportunities for all able-bodied Virgin Islanders. After a brief recession of activity in the late 1940s, the expansion of tourism opened a new niche for islanders. At any given time during the 1950s and 1960s, more than ten per cent of the population of the BVI was employed in the American islands [Harrigan 6, p. 157], particularly in the construction of tourist facilities and the provision of tourist services. Agriculture and livestock production sank to new lows in many BVI communities, including Rum Bay, as islanders exploited attractive cash-earning opportunities off-island [Dirks 5, pp. 86-101].

It should be mentioned that in the mid-1960s a surge of investment, mostly in the tourist industry, stimulated growth in the economic activity of the British islands themselves. The job opportunities created by this growth attracted many migrants back home as well as a large number of labourers from outside the archipelago. These 'down-islanders' helped fill the vacuum left by native emigrants who continued to find higher wages in the American islands. The social impact of the down-island labour force on Road Town, where development works centred, proved considerable. However, the effect of this influx on the rural areas seemed minimal. In fact, the half dozen or so immigrants who found work in Rum Bay were excluded quite rigorously from most aspects of community life [Dirks 8, p. 106].

It is evident that since 1823, the people of BVI have been faced with a series of fundamental changes in the resource domains open to them. For the residents of communities such as Rum Bay, these changes have been neither predictable nor controllable. At times, large numbers of them have been attracted overseas by opportunities to earn cash incomes. At other times, they have concentrated on local domains. The availability of cash coupled with migratory and sedentary means for gaining a livelihood are important variables to which local populations have had to accommodate themselves in order to assure their continuity. A flexible mating pattern has been one means for adapting to these fluctuating conditions.

SOURCES AND ANALYSIS OF MATING DATA

Data on Rum Bay's mating pattern were obtained from two sources: the Methodist baptismal records (1823-1965) and the Methodist marriage registry (1880-1970) for the BVI.[2] The use of Methodist records is appropriate to the countryside of Western Tortola where church membership runs nearly 90 per cent. Rum Bay itself was completely Methodist until the late 1960s when a handful of residents started a small Baptist congregation. This very recent development aside, corporate life traditionally has centred around the church congregation and powerful sanctions have insured a Methodist baptism for all infants [Dirks 5, pp. 182-229; 6, p. 576]. Fortunately, over the years Methodist ministers have recorded the marital status of each baptized child's parents. Unions productive of baptized infants consequently provide a sample of the frequency of legal and extra-legal mating alliances. This sample incudes 402 cases spanning a 142-year period.

Our sample appears to be representative of mating alliances among the entire population of Rum Bay. However, certain assumptions are necessary. While the sample includes only those couples producing children who survive a matter of days or weeks until baptism, it is assumed not to be biased either in the direction of legal or extra-legal mating by this fact. Within the context of the Caribbean region, Roberts and Braithwaite [4] have shown that there is little, if any, difference in fertility between legally mating and extra-legally mating couples who are cohabitants.[3] On the other hand, extra-legally mating couples who do not cohabit do have lower fertility rates than the former. As the baptismal records do not indicate the residential status of extra-legally mating couples, there is no way to determine the number of co-residential and extra-residential couples included in the sample. However, since it is the *change* in the proportional frequency of mating types that is important here rather than the absolute frequencies, and since only a single baptized infant is required for inclusion in our sample, this fertility factor should not significantly affect our results.

The recent tendency for BVI women to bear their children in the American Virgin Islands should be mentioned as an additional factor bearing on the reliability of the sample. Children born on American soil are automatically granted the status of U.S. citizenship. This promises them a future competitive advantage over the children of other island women in securing employment in the U.S. islands and on the continent. According to Harrigan [6, p. 171], a sample of four years between 1956 and 1966 indicated that from 26 per cent to 46 per cent of the annual births to all BVI women took place in the U.S. Virgin Islands. Since the birthplaces of Rum Bay infants are not recorded, it is impossible to determine the precise degree to which Rum Bay conforms to this general pattern. What is certain is that this is a relatively recent phenomenon, especially characteristic of the post-World War II years. Because it is recent and because there is no indication that BVI women giving birth off-island typically engage in one type of mating union rather than the other, we have assumed that the sample is not biased by these events.

In preparing the baptismal record data for analysis, each mating couple was counted only once, regardless of the number of baptized infants produced. In cases where a couple had a succession of offspring and appeared repeatedly in the church records, a single record entry was randomly selected and used to assign the couple to a socio-economic period. For the purposes of the sample, this same entry was used to determine the marital status of the couple. In cases where a couple had only one child, this procedure of random selection was unnecessary. The effect of organizing the data in this manner was to render the statistics for each socio-economic period independent of each other and suitable for comparison both within and between sample periods. The frequency of legal and extra-legal mating was then tabulated for each socio-economic period and adjacent periods were compared. At the .05 level, chi-square tests on the frequencies were significant in all comparisons except in the case Period V (1922-31) versus Period VI (1932-41). The hypothesis of no difference was therefore rejected in five of the six comparisons. These comparisons are summarized in Table 1.

TABLE 1   *Frequency of legal and extra-legal mating in Rum Bay*

		Extra-Legal		Legal		
	Period	#	%	#	%	Chi Square
I	(1823-1833)	34	85.0	06	15.0	14.07*
II	(1834-1849)	25	47.2	28		
II	(1834-1849)	25	47.2	28	52.8	6.44*
III	(1850-1879)	30	73.2	11	26.8	
III	(1850-1879)	30	73.2	11	26.8	8.31*
IV	(1880-1921)	38	45.8	45	54.2	
IV	(1880-1921)	38	45.8	45	54.2	6.89*
V	(1922-1931)	24	72.7	09	27.3	
V	(1922-1931)	24	72.7	09	27.3	2.40
VI	(1932-1941)	29	87.9	04	12.1	
VI	(1932-1941)	29	87.9	04	12.1	6.57*
VII	(1942-1965)	77	64.7	42	35.3	
TOTAL: I-VII						
(1823-1965)		257	63.9	145	36.1	

*significant at .05 level

The second historical source, the Methodist marriage registry, yielded two sorts of information: the dates at which marriage ceremonies were performed and the age of the two partners to the union. Table 2 lists the total and the mean annual number of marriage ceremonies in Periods IV through VII, the only periods for which this type of datum still exists.

Using an analysis of variance, each hypothesis of no difference between the means of adjacent periods was retained (see Table 3). That is, the mean annual number of marriage ceremonies performed in Rum Bay shows a consistency across socio-economic periods.

TABLE 2   *Frequency of marriage ceremonies in Rum Bay*

	Period	Total Marriages Per Period	X per Year
IV	(1881-1921)	78	1.9
V	(1922-1931)	16	1.6
IV	(1932-1941)	21	2.1
VII	(1942-1970)	38	1.3

TABLE 3   *Analysis of variance summary for number of marriages per year*

Source	df	ms	F
Group	3	2.37	
Within	87	2.86	.83
Total	90		

The second type of data provided by the marriage registry is a sample of male and female ages at the time of marriage. A summary of mean ages at first marriage is presented in Table 4. Only first marriages were considered in order to rule out factors such as remarriage after the death of a spouse or divorce, which might obscure an otherwise meaningful pattern.

TABLE 4   *Mean age of males and females at first marriage*

	Period	Males	Females
IV	(1880-1921)	27.8	24.4
V	(1922-1931)	35.1	26.2
VI	(1932-1941)	31.3	26.1
VII	(1942-1970)	28.2	22.5
TOTAL: IV-VII			
(1880-1970)		29.2	24.3

Some significant variations in the mean age at first marriage were evident across socio-economic periods. As shown in Table 5, an analysis of variance of the mean age for males resulted in a significant F-ratio. Therefore, the hypothesis of no difference in age at first marriage for males was rejected. As a follow-up to this, the Sheffe test was used to test the difference between all period means, taken two at a time. On this basis, no significant contrasts were found.

TABLE 5   *Analysis of variance summary for male age at first marriage*

Source	df	ms	F
Group	3	197.33	5.83*
Within	107	33.85	
Total	110		

*significant at .05 level

As Table 6 illustrates, an analysis of variance of the mean age for females entering their first marriage also resulted in a significant F-ratio. However, once again the Sheffe test failed to show any significant contrast between the means when periods were compared two at a time.

TABLE 6 *Analysis of variance summary for female age at first marriage*

Source	df	ms	F
Group	3	69.63	2.56*
Within	107	27.17	
Total	110		

*significant at 0.5 level

DISCUSSION OF DIACHRONIC DATA

Analysis of the mating data available in Rum Bay's Methodist registries produces some varied outcomes. Using marriage registry data, we find no significant variation in the mean number of marriage ceremonies conducted in Rum Bay across the last four socio-economic periods. This could be the result of demographic changes in the community, a situation in which marriage frequencies remain constant while the percentage of the population contracting marriages fluctuates. Since no demographic data spanning these periods are available specifically for Rum Bay, we have no way to ascertain if this is the case.

The mean ages of both males and females at the time of their first marriage do show significant variation within the span of years represented by Periods IV through VII. Sample ages are generally higher in periods in which the labour force is largely sedentary than during periods marked by recurrent mass migration. However, when adjacent socio-economic periods are compared two at a time, significant contrast between the means are not found. Perhaps the lack of significance in connection with this follow-up can be attributed to the conservative nature of the test. In any case, it is in comparing the proportional frequency of legal to extra-legal mating between socio-economic periods that significant results regularly appear. These differences correspond to a changing pattern of cash availability and migration for the people of Rum Bay (see Figure 1).

FIGURE 1 *Changes in the percentage frequency of marriage across socio-economic periods*

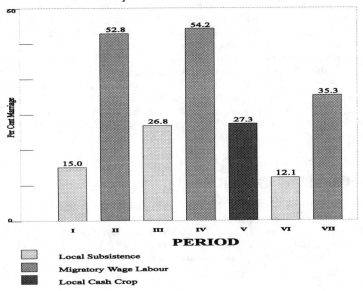

During Periods II (1834-49), IV (1880-1921), and VII (1942-70), periods during which wage work was widely available at off-island locations, the sample marriage rate for the community ranges from a high of 59 per cent to a low of 35 per cent of all unions productive of baptized infants. During Periods I (1823-33), III (1850-79), and VI (1932-41), periods during which cash employment opportunities were generally scarce and local subsistence production prevailed, the rate of legal marriage ranges from a high of 27 per cent to a low of 12 per cent. During Period V (1922-31), the single socio-economic period in which local crop production provided any notable source of cash income, the proportion of marriage to extra-legal unions again falls within the low range, the legally married comprising only 27 per cent of the couples listed. It is significant that during this period the opportunity to earn a good cash income was rather brief and tenuous, the rum market being exploited in the midst of official moves against it. This suggests that both an insecure resource base and a shortage of cash income-earning opportunities contribute to the relatively high proportion of extra-legal mating in Rum Bay. Furthermore, it is apparent that a relative plentitude of cash income-earning opportunities is related to a comparatively high proportion of marriages. It is noteworthy that these conclusions, drawn from a diachronic analysis of mating patterns in a single community, are in basic agreement with those presented by Otterbein [21] on the basis of comparative analysis of contemporary mating organization in 20 Caribbean communities.

Otterbein [21, p. 73] found a positive correlation between the opportunity for men to earn and save cash — a variable operationalized in terms of recurrent migratory wage labour — and a relatively high proportion of legal marriage in a community. In explaining this correlation, Otterbein reasoned that a prevalent pattern of migratory labour enables a large segment of the adult men in a community to finance a marriage and thereby meet the normative expectations of Afro-Caribbean culture. In other words, from Otterbein's perspective, a widely-held cultural value apparently motivates marriage while the lack of income-earning and saving opportunities constrains the fulfillment of this value norm.

The explanation offered by Otterbein has potential diachronic application. In Rum Bay, where marriage is the expected status among adults, individual life histories show a close temporal coincidence between the attainment of a relatively secure source of income and first marriage. Furthermore, on the community level, the historical covariance between opportunities to earn and save cash and comparatively high proportions of legal mating seems to indicate the long-standing existence of a value promoting legal marital alliances under favourable economic circumstances. Indeed, the stabilization of conjugal bonds and family life was one of the outstanding goals of the early missionaries to the slave communities [Dookhan 9, p. 70]. Certainly the uniform fluctuations of the mating pattern data suggest that no dramatic change in values or any other aspect of the mating system has disturbed its fundamental historic continuity. Several questions arise: How are we to explain the presumed persistence of the cultural value associated with marriage? What social and economic advantages accrue to those contracting marriages that are best realized under conditions of relative prosperity? Are there any advantages associated with extra-legal mating, especially when opportunities to earn a cash income are scarce? The historical record is silent on these points. However, by turning to contemporary ethnography, inferences can be made with regard to the dynamics of Rum Bay's mating system. On this basis, our position is that mating alliances can be viewed as organization strategies which involve different sorts of reciprocity, which offer different kinds of pay-offs, and which are advantageous under different economic circumstances [cf. Horowitz 8].

ETHNOGRAPHIC OBSERVATIONS

In Rum Bay, unmarried, extra-legally mating males fall into two general categories. One consists of young men ranging in age from mid-teens to late twenties. Although many young men migrate permanently from the community, those who maintain either a temporary or fixed presence reside in the households of their mothers or other close consanguines. The second category encompasses men of relatively advanced age. These men reside in all-male households. Only two unmarried men live with their extra-legal mates in Rum Bay.

The young men of Rum Bay are mostly unskilled labourers. They can expect to earn only a sporadic cash income during their early working years. Occasional employment can be found on Tortola but more rewarding work is located in St Thomas. For the most part, positions there are temporary, being linked to the tourist season or the duration of a construction project. As a consequence, the working year is likely to be interspersed with periods of unemployment that often last for several months. Many young men spend a part of this time residing in their natal households. A migrant's welcome home is insured by the regular remittance of a portion of his earnings [Dirks 7].

Migrants feel a powerful obligation to send a share of their earnings to their families [cf. Philpott 23]. Not uncommonly this sense of obligation is matched by sizeable remittances comprising as much as 25 per cent to 50 per cent of an unmarried worker's income. For many sedentary adults — women involved in child care, the elderly, and any others unable to earn a sufficient cash income — remittances are essential sources of support. For the migrant, they are important in protecting his rights among his kinsmen, including his interest in family lands, and in providing him with a measure of respectability in the community. Given these functions, remittance obligations cannot be avoided with impunity by those who plan to return to Rum Bay at a future date.

Another fundamental drain on the personal resources of a young worker is the necessity to build a wide network of friends in communities throughout the Virgin Islands. An extensive personal network is of the utmost importance as a source of intelligence and aid in locating and securing sources of cash income [Dirks 6, p. 573], particularly in the face of the difficulties that await the alien in the labour markets of the U.S.V.I. [Dirks 8]. The individual bonds that go into the creation of a network are expensive to maintain. Considerable outlays of cash are required to carry on the rounds of convival drinking and entertainment that symbolize active friendship between men. To be 'tight', to neglect the exchanges called for in the cultivation of open friendships, is to court isolation.

Given remittance obligations and other expenses, the personal resources of most young men are under a heavy strain and their capacity to invest in other social domains is limited. Marriage in the BVI apparently always has called for a rather substantial outlay of cash [cf., Eadie 10], one that few young men can afford easily. Thus, the conventional attitude adopted at this point in life is far removed from one that might be interpreted as domestic. Young men are quite forthright in asserting preference for sexually attractive girls who make minimal demands on them. This simply reflects the impinging constraint of limited means. The economics of extra-legal unions at this stage tend toward balanced or negative reciprocity.[4] In the latter mode, an alien woman standing outside the sphere of the community might offer the chance for a short-term relationship with mutually exploitative undertones. At the balanced end of the spectrum, less exploitation and greater altruism is evident. In the local idiom, a woman has a child 'for' a man. The implication is one of gift; the expectation is one of reciprocity. Giving birth is supposed to entitle a female to financial contributions from the father for the support of the child. The contribution received by the mother may be very small and irregular. Nevertheless, for many women, particularly those from less than well-to-do households, childbirth often presents their only claim to cash.

By their mid-twenties, most men in Rum Bay experience a shift in impinging social and economic pressures. They reach a point where cash savings are possible; they find a 'station job'; a position that seems to offer a fairly stable income for the foreseeable future. At the same time, remittance obligations are frequently reduced by the death of parents and/or the maturation of siblings and convival spending begins to slacken. The acquisition of relatively steady employment negates the value of many network bonds; these are deactivated through disuse. At this stage in a life cycle, those who continue to 'carouse' at the same level as their juniors are viewed by community members in a negative light. They are accused of wasting their lives. It is recognized at this juncture, during the prime working years of a man's life, that the establishment of a marriage is a prudent move. As a reaction to increased income, social realignments, and community pressure, men undertake a reallocation of their personal resources. An important step in this reallocation is the construction of a dwelling house using accumulated savings. In Rum Bay, as throughout most of the Afro-Caribbean, house-building is an important first step toward marriage [Otterbein 21, pp. 72-4].

Marriage is a future-oriented institution. It involves attention to the formation of a stable relationship that promises pay-offs quite unlike those associated with extra-legal unions. In Rum Bay, where a woman is often portrayed as a 'weak vessel', a man as in need of a 'safe harbour', marriage is seen as offering mutual protection against the inclemencies that are bound to beset life. For women, this assurance lies in an enforce-able legal claim to financial support and property as well as any tangibles that may derive from their respectable status in the community. For men, faced with potentially disastrous possibilities such as an injury, a sudden and sustained loss of employment, and the inevitable disability of old age, marriage assumes what might be described as an even more protective character. 'Lawful' children and a sedentary representative of his home interests are critical to a man's future security.[5]

In Rum Bay, marital alliances are founded on a couple's willingness to enter into a long-term economic commitment and the male's demonstration of his capacity to do so. Many extra-legal unions are eventually converted into legal ones. This is particularly true of those extra-legal relationships carried on during an engagement to marry. These unions may produce several offspring prior to their legalization, the marriage being delayed until the male accumulates sufficient cash to complete the construction of a dwelling house for his mate. In such cases, there may be every intention of implement-ing a long-term relationship but, without a material demonstration of a financial commit-ment and the ability to complete the task of house-building, the union continues to be organized along extra-legal lines. Fieldwork in Rum Bay uncovered only a single case of an individual who married prior to the construction of a dwelling house.[6] This couple took up residence with the wife's mother. Under pressure from kinsmen, the marriage proved unhappy and short-lived. We suspect that the reason behind this conservative economic attitude toward marriage is a history of a high rate of economic failure on the part of men.

Failures have been highly visible in community life. Twenty per cent of the men over 40 years of age who currently reside in Rum Bay have never legally married. Another six per cent are divorced or separated. All live in a state of relative poverty, without savings, without support from their offspring, their age or a physical disability keeping them from effective competition in the regional labour market. Such men merit little respect in the community. Their failures are attributed to previous imprudent and squanderous be-haviour and a subsequent inability to attract or hold a wife. Thus, disregard for financial responsibility can be seen to have unfortunate social results.

Of vital interest to all men in the community is land. As the only available resource over which individuals can exercise direct control and as an enduring element in the environment of notoriously unstable opportunities, land is synonymous with security in Rum Bay. In a very real sense, islanders bank on land, counting on it to feed a man and his family during hard times, to support the elderly, to provide the ever-ready potential for emergency income through rental or sale. During periods when income-earning op-portunities are relatively good, individuals seek to transform cash and other assets into solid personal resources within their home community. Since the local land base is finite, these simultaneous efforts to effect such a transformation inevitably result in com-petition. Given the pressure on land, a general lack of documented ownership, and a system in which physical occupation is the only secure tenure, there is no quicker way to lose one's land claim than to leave a holding unprotected. This creates a problem for a worker who must migrate off-island for extended periods. It is in this context that the sedentary component of the community, particularly women, is important.

While men are absent from the community, women remain behind to protect their property claims, land that might otherwise be seriously threatened by the predations of others. With relatively undivided loyalties, a wife vies with a mother as the most de-pendable representative for a temporary migrant. Because a mother ages, sisters marry, and ties with extra-legal mates often prove fragile, a legal wife can in many cases best see to the protection of a migrant's property. She does so by occupying it. Often she maintains a dwelling house on the land as well as a small garden and a herd of livestock. In effect, she may replace consanguineal females in protecting the birthright and the future of her spouse.

A wife's services extend beyond property maintenance. A spouse can be expected to bear lawful children and thereby provide a number of future contributors to the support of the household. The relationship between 'unlawful' children and their fathers is regarded as being of a more tenuous nature than that which pertains to lawful offspring. Wives also represent their husbands in church affairs. This is important in so far as the Methodist congregation in Rum Bay is the only corporate group in the community with direct access to government. This access is provided through a church hierarchy in which authorities either have considerable influence with civil government or directly occupy government posts themselves. Since migratory labour and various other behaviours bar most men from full church participation in their younger years, it is their wives who are in the best positions to secure political patronage for them [Dirks 6, pp. 576-7]. Thus, a woman can apply to one of the local preachers for assistance in finding work for her unemployed husband, perhaps on a public works project.

SUMMARY AND CONCLUSIONS

In Rum Bay, most extra-legal mating relationships are initiated under a mode of reciprocity that favours the maximization of short-term social and economic interests. As such, extra-legal unions are of specific value to those persons who find themselves in extremely marginal positions within the regional economy. For those who face the continuous problem of securing access to resources of great immediate utility, competing expenditures and the demands for personal flexibility effectively preclude much investment in stable, long-term social relations that promise minimal present benefit. Marriage, on the other hand, is generally contracted by the people of Rum Bay with the prospect of an enduring, generalized exchange relationship. These unions require investments that promise minimal immediate return. Instead, their value lies in the maximization of long-term objectives: e.g., respectability and power in the local community, supportive offspring, and old-age security. Marriage alliances are particularly attractive to individuals who are relatively secure in terms of immediate resource needs. Thus, marriage and extra-legal conjugal unions have complementary strategic values that arise from the nature of the reciprocity and the expected pay-offs involved. In relating these findings from contemporary ethnography to diachronic shifts in the percentage frequencies of legal and extra-legal mating, an appreciation of the role of house-building is essential.

The custom of house-building in connection with marriage seems to be a very old tradition among the black peoples of the Eastern Caribbean. It almost certainly extends back to the latter years of the slave era. While there is no direct evidence for this in the scanty literature on Tortolan slavery, the situation on Tortola was probably not unlike that of St Vincent, a cognate society with good documentation. With reference to St Vincent, Carmichael [2, I, p. 131] reported that male slaves 'get wives' at about 18 or 19 years of age "when ... they have houses of their own". A young man built his own dwelling with the help of friends and held a feast on the night he took possession of it. The size and style of the structure were indicative of the new householder's rank [Byam 1, p. 107; Carmichael 2, I, p. 128]. It appears, then, that house-building not only served to place a roof over one's head; it also served symbolic functions, making statements about status and worth. In contemporary Rum Bay, the act of house-building continues to do both.

Undertaking the construction of a house indicates a man's increasing financial ability and readiness to marry. In a very real sense, house-building is as much a part of the marital sequence as the ritual attending religio-legal matrimony itself. In fact, it has priority over marriage ritual, which ordinarily cannot proceed until house-building has been completed.

In this way, the cultural rule calling for the building of a house serves as an intermediate control over marriage in the community, requiring the availability and accumulation of a certain amount of cash before construction can be completed and a marriage can be contracted. Through the house-building rule, the state of the regional economy feeds back on the pattern of relations existing between couples in Rum Bay. During those periods when cash is readily available, the mean age of those contracting their first marriage is at its lowest point. At the same time, the percentage of productive legal unions is at a relatively high level. Conversely, during those periods when access to cash income is minimal and house-building funds are scarce, the community exhibits a relatively high percentage of extra-legal unions. Marriages are entered into at a relatively advanced age. Such changes apparently occur without any conscious or unconscious alteration of the positive value attending marriage. Both individual behaviour and the relative proportion of alternative mating forms in the community are adjusted and synchronized with prevailing economic conditions by means of the house-building rule. In this respect, the organization of mating alliances in Rum Bay appears as the cultural analog of the biologists' 'scaled trait': a behavioural adaptation fixed at some point in the evolutionary scale among a minority of communities subscribing to a two-choice mating pattern, in which extra-legal co-residential unions are quite rare [cf., Otterbein 22, p. 138]. In other communities like Rum Bay and in those with a wider range of choice, it remains to be seen to what extent socio-economic change influences the dynamics of connubium.

In calling for subsequent studies of the type described here, it is imperative to draw explicit attention to some obvious shortcomings in our work. We have already pointed out our inability to give sharp, quantitative definition to points of socio-economic change. Our statistical sample is small. Good census data and vital statistics spanning the study period in its entirety are wanting. At this point, we are in a position only to acknowledge the kinds of data we lack.[7] Hopefully, this does not detract from the accomplishment of our fundamental goal. What we have tried to show in this article is simply this: The plurality of conjugal forms in Rum Bay can be understood as a response to an environment in which fully adult and sexually active individuals cannot uniformly count on access to stable income-earning opportunities. The specific proportion of legal and extra-legal unions varies over time in a way that appears linked to cycles of increasing and decreasing access to such opportunities. Historical changes in technology, the directions of metropolitan investment, and the international political scene have had an important effect on the mating patterns of Rum Bay in so far as they have affected the economic security and cash income of community members. The histories of other island groups are likely to contain other incidents of particular importance in this regard.

This certainly does not mean that research must return to particularism. It does mean that a greater reliance on diachronic data is in order, especially for those of us who are interested in non-traditional societies on the margins of the industrial world where the repetitive economic ebbs and flows of the metropolis often have exaggerated effects. An accurate description of such a population, one which is confronted by a regularly fluctuating resource base, must provide an account of the entire ecological cycle confronting it. Anything less may result in a failure to identify the flexibility of a given institution. It may lead to the mistaken notion that an observed change is absolute when in fact it is reversible and simply one point in a long-standing and stable equilibrium.

NOTES

1 Rum Bay is a fictitious name, a pseudonym for a settlement where data on mating patterns were compiled by the senior author during the course of fieldwork on Tortola from September, 1969 through June, 1970. The research was supported by a Hokin Foundation fellowship administered under the auspices of the Caribbean Research Institute, College of the Virgin Islands. The Reverend Desmond Mason of the Leeward Islands Methodist Conference kindly made church records available. We wish to thank Drs Keith Otterbein and Kenneth Strand for their suggestions during the preparation of this paper.

2 Baptismal records for 1966-70 were unavailable for research. Period VII thus terminates in 1965 instead of 1970 where baptismal records are the source of data. Marriage registry books prior to 1880 could not be located and presumably were destroyed.

3 Roberts and Braithwaite [24] state that for Trinidad the method of classification of data determines whether legal or extra-legal mating has a higher fertility. We assumed this holds true elsewhere, including the BVI.

4 Marshall Sahlins [26], an anthropologist with a long-standing interest in domestic and familial economics, developed a formal typology of reciprocity based on the immediacy and equivalency of returns. According to his scheme, balanced reciprocity involves the exchange of roughly equivalent values with little delay. The maintenance of social ties tends to be as important or more important than the economic side of the relationship. Negative reciprocity, on the other hand, is characterized by transactions aimed at utilitarian advantage. Reciprocity of this type is more impersonal than balanced reciprocity.

5 Of course, extra-legal mating activity does not terminate altogether with marriage. Indeed, the continuation of such unions remains a viable feature in the lives of many married persons. This is especially true for men who continue to work in St Thomas while they maintain their wives and children in Rum Bay.

6 We have no directly comparable data on marriage prior to house-building for the BVI as a whole. Our impression based on informants' statements is that the pattern is customary and holds throughout. British Virgin Islanders exhibit a strong preference for neolocality. In 1960, for example, only 7 per cent of the islands' married women resided in extended households as junior members. Most of these probably represented temporary accommodation to the absence of a husband working off-island.

7 The data included in this paper were collected originally for a study of local-level politics, not for the purpose of the research described here.

REFERENCES

BYAM, Sir Ashton, "Testimony on the Slave Trade", *House of Commons Accounts and Papers*, Vol. 29, 1790.

CARMICHAEL, Mrs., *Domestic Manners and Social Conditions of the White, Coloured and Negro Populations of the West Indies*, 2 vols., New York: Negro Universities Press, 1969 (1883).

CLARK, Edith, *My Mother Who Fathered Me*, London: George Allen and Unwin, Ltd, 1957.

CUMPER, George, *The Social Structure of the British Caribbean (excluding Jamaica)*, Part II, Extra Mural Department, University College of the West Indies, n.d.

DIRKS, Robert, "Networks, Groups, and Local-Level Politics in an Afro-Caribbean Community", Ph.D. dissertation, Case Western Reserve University, Ann Arbor: University Microfilms, 1972.

—"Networks, Groups and Adaptation in an Afro-Caribbean Community", *Man* (N.S.) Vol. 7, No. 4, December 1972.

—"Remittances for Security: Pressuring the Tolian Migrant", paper presented at the annual meeting of the American Anthropological Association, Toronto, 1972.

—"Ethnicity and Ethnic Group Relations in the British Virgin Islands", in John Bennett (ed.) *The New Ethnicity*, St. Paul: West, 1975.

DOOKHAN, Isaac, "A History of the British Virgin Islands", unpublished Ph.D. dissertation, University of the West Indies, 1968.

EADIE, Hazel, *Lagooned in the Virgin Islands*, London: Newness, 1931.

FAGG, John Edwin, *Cuba, Haiti, and the Dominican Republic*, Englewood Cliffs, N. J.: Prentice-Hall, 1965.

FREILICH, Morris, "Serial Polygyny Negro Peasants, and Model Analysis", *American Anthropologist*, Vol. 63, No. 5, October 1961.

GONZALEZ, Nancie L., *Black Carib Household Structure*, Seattle: University of Washington Press, 1969.

GREENFIELD, Sidney M., *English Rustics in Black Skin*, New Haven: College and University Press, 1966.

GURNEY, John Joseph, *Familiar Letters to Henry Clay of Kentucky Describing a Winter in the West Indies*, New York: John Murray, 1840.

HARRIGAN, Norwell, "A Study of the Inter-Relationships between the British and United States Virgin Islands", St Thomas: Caribbean Research Institute, n.d.

HERSKOVITS, Melville and Frances HERSKOVITS, *Trinidad Village*, New York: Alfred A. Knopf, 1947.

HOROWITZ, Michael M., "A Decision Model of Conjugal Patterns in Martinique", *Man* (N.S.) Vol. 2, No. 3, September 1967.

KNOX, John P., *An Historical Account of St Thomas*, New York: Scribner, 1852.

MATTHEWS, Dom Basil, *Crisis of the West Indian Family*, Trinidad: Extra-Mural Department, University College of the West Indies, 1952.

OTTERBEIN, Keith, "Caribbean Family Organizations: A Comparative Analysis", *American Anthropologist*, Vol. 67, No. 1, February 1965.

—*The Andros Islanders*, Lawrence: University of Kansas Press, 1966.

PHILPOTT, Stuart, "Remittance Obligations, Social Networks and Choice among Montserratian Migrants in Britain", *Man* (N.S.), Vol. 3, No. 3, September 1968.

ROBERTS, George W. and Lloyd BRAITHWAITE, "Fertility Differentials by Family Type in Trinidad", *Annals of the New York Academy of Sciences*, Vol. 84, 1960.

RODMAN, Hyman, *Lower-Class Families: The Culture of Poverty in Negro Trinidad*, New York: Oxford University Press, 1971.

SAHLINS, Marshall, "On the Sociology of Primitive Exchange", *The Relevance of Models for Social Anthropology*, A. S. A. Monographs 1, London: Tavistock.

SMITH, M. G., *West Indian Family Structure*, Seattle: University of Washington Press, 1962.

WATKINS, Frederick Henry, *Handbook of the Leeward Islands*, London: West India Committee, 1924.

WESTERGAARD, Waldemar, *The Danish West Indies*, New York: Macmillan, 1917.

Sally W. Gordon

'I GO TO 'TANTIES': THE ECONOMIC SIGNIFICANCE OF CHILD-SHIFTING IN ANTIGUA, WEST INDIES

Child-shifting or fosterage has elsewhere been noted to occur in the West Indies (e.g. Clarke 1957; Olwig 1981; Powell 1982; Roberts and Sinclair 1978; Rodman 1971) and, in different forms, throughout the world (e.g., Carroll 1970). The reallocation of dependent or minor children to a household *not* including a natural parent often benefits two households, both the child-giver and the child-receiver, and does not occur from any lack of affection for the child (cf. Powell 1982: 144). As Smith (1978: 353) notes. 'Close and imperishable bonds are formed through the act of 'raising' children, irrespective of genetic ties, and informants will state quite clearly that these relationships are just as strong as 'real' kinship ties'. Consider, for example, the gentle affection embedded in the following scenario:

> Nellie is a 75-year-old widow living with her 28-year-old "adopted" son. Her first pregnancy did not occur until she was 42, at which time she married her boyfriend of many years. Unfortunately, that pregnancy ended in a still-born child. Several years later, when it was apparent that she would indeed have no children of her own, she took her sister's grandson (her

sister's daughter's son), then about 3 years old; she has long since forgotten the details of that child's situation at that time. Although she had previously planted cotton on an estate, the opportunity to raise a child which she couldn't have prompted her to stay home, sewing clothes for other people out of her home to supplement her husband's irregular income as a carpenter. Indeed she notes with pride that her husband built their house himself, a small house (about 400 square feet) but comfortable by West Indian standards and sturdily erected on a concrete foundation. She continued to sew until only four years ago when, at 71, her eyes began to fail. A year later her husband of 30 years died, but he had by then trained their "adopted son" as a carpenter. That son, now 28, still lives with and supports his "tantie". Nellie's sister's son, now 49, has been working in England for many years; he has also sent money and gifts to them over the years and continues to pay for the insurance on their house, thus having helped to support his sister's son and his mother's sister[1]

This discussion will examine some of the details of child-shifting in Antigua, West Indies and the significance of this pattern for household economic strategies. Although such arrangements might last for periods ranging from a few months to several years, indeed perhaps an entire childhood from birth to independence, here only those shifts lasting more than one year will be examined. Adequate data are more available for longer, seemingly more permanent shifts; conversely, shorter adjustments occur fairly often and with little drama, so the details of such were often forgotten or only vaguely recalled by informants.

The initial research on which this analysis is based was undertaken in two villages in Antigua, one peri-urban area near to the sea and the other a more 'rural' or agricultural inland village.[2] In both villages diverse economic options were available to residents, although the more urban settlement was generally 'poorer,' approximating what some might label an 'urban slum.' A sample of 50 households, 25 in each village, was selected randomly in each village. (In some measures only 49 households are used as a sample because of highly erratic data from 1 household in certain matters).

THE PATTERNS OF CHILD-SHIFTING

For the purposes of this discussion, three types of child-shifting will be distinguished as follows: (1) historical child-shifting, (2) current, incoming children, and (3) current, outgoing children.

1 Historical child-shifting: Evidence for child-shifting having occurred during the childhoods of adults who were interviewed was drawn largely from the residential histories elicited from a principal respondent (PR) in each household in the sample.

2 Current child-shifting: Evidence of currently fostered children was based largely on two kinds of data.

    (a) Current, incoming: Based on household membership inventories which included children who had lived with the PR for at least one year but neither of that child's parents as coresidents.

    (b) Current, outgoing: Based on kin inventories which included reference to minor children of the principal respondent who had not been coresident for one year or more.

This discussion of child-shifting, either historical or current, incoming or outgoing, does not address the possibility of a person potentially being perceived as a 'member' of two households simultaneously; subsequent data from Antigua suggest that such is a real possibility, as do other studies from the West Indies which make reference to 'absentee membership' (e.g., Moses 1977; Solien 1981; Walker 1968) as well as some studies from other parts of the world (e.g., Arnould 1984; Douglas 1984; Mueller 1977; Stack 1974). Furthermore, this does not deal with the thorny problem of defining a household in the West Indian context, a discussion of sufficient depth to require a separate treatment (see Goody 1972; Netting and Wilks 1984; Smith 1978). It is clear from this research that coresidential group is not a bounded, autonomous, economic or social unit. Philpott, among others, has noted that while the household is the basic unit of social life as conceived by Montserratians (the population of a nearby West Indian island), 'the study of familial ties which cross household boundaries has been neglected' (1973: 113). Nonetheless, for the purposes of this research, a dwelling was considered an operationally-definable unit of analysis, and coresidence was identified by those interviewed.

The frequency of child-shifting among the 49 sampled households clearly indicates that the phenomenon is of sufficient scale to merit attention. There were 41 clear episodes of child-shifting spread over 21 different households (42.9% of the sample). In some cased PR's had themselves lived a large part of their childhoods with a non-parental caretaker and were also currently involved in a reallocation of children, either as givers or receivers. Furthermore, there were three households which simultaneously had incoming and outgoing children.

Table 1

	Incoming	Outgoing	Historical (i.e., Child-shifting is a 'completed' event)
Number of households	12	7	11
Number of 'children' shifted	24	10	14
Male	12	4	3
Female	12	6	11
Number of episodes*	16	8	12
Number of relationships represented**	18	8	12
Average ages of children now	11.64 years old	12.7years old	not applicable
Average length of stay	6.8 years	8.53 years	8.86 years
Average age at which shifting occurred	4.83 years	4.1 years old	5.36 years old

*If more than one child in the same relationship to child-receiver, e.g., a woman taking a daughter's three daughters, move as a unit, that is counted here a one episode of child-shifting. Also, if all the offspring of a child-giver move in with the child-receiver sequentially as each is born, that here is considered to be one episode.

**If in an episode, the child-receiver cares for daughter's daughter and daughter's son, two relationships are represented in that episode.

Some households are thus represented more than once. This level of frequency is comparably scaled with other calculations. For example, Olwig (1981) reported that 29% of the children in a sample of 46 households in St Johns, Danish West Indies were living with neither parent. Similarly, Roberts and Sinclair (1978: 162) estimated that 30% of women of child-bearing age had shifted at least some of their children. Indeed one needs only to listen to obituaries on the local radio to ascertain the commonness of child-shifting. 'We regret to announce the death of Emma George, age 72. The following people "called her mother": .... Here follows a list of as many as 40 people who had at one time lived with the deceased woman, perhaps only about eight of them her 'natural' children.

Who Are the Children? The 'children' currently living with a non-parent for at least the previous year included a few young adults who lived with their current caretakers since dependent ages or childhood, i.e., they did not enter their current households as autonomous adults. The age and sex breakdown of those fostered is also indicated in Table 1.

Clearly boys and girls were fostered with equal frequency. (The cases of completed or historical child-shifting were drawn from the residential histories of adult PR's; since that sample was disproportionately female, there is no necessary implication that the sex ratio of shifted children was formerly less balanced than today). Although in this small sample the outgoing children are slightly older than incoming children, and accordingly have been in their current households for a longer time, there is no evidence to suggest two disparate phenomena, merely 'two sides of the same coin'. This is reinforced by noting that the average ages at which the shifting occurred are very similar for both in-coming and outgoing children.

It is also clear that a substantial majority of these events occurred during early child-hood: the distribution in the age of those given in fosterage is represented in Table II. Thus 66.7% of the cases of incoming children (16: 9 boys and 7 girls), 70% of those of outgoing children (7: 3 boys and 4 girls), and 50% of the historical episodes (7: 3 boys and 4 girls), illustrated shifting at age 5 or younger. More interestingly, those ages 12 and over, 4, incoming (2 boys, 2 girls) and 2 outgoing (1 boy and 1 girl), were evenly divided by sex. This suggests that older children were not lent or received for sex-spe-cific labor or tasks (see below, reasons for fosterage). In some agricultural settings when the desirable sex and birth order complement of children is not naturally occurring, fos-terage is a mechanism for manipulating household membership to accomplish tasks often performed by unpaid household labor (e.g., Carroll 1970: 135; Lieber 1970: 180; Mamdani 1972). Indeed large families can constitute essentially an economic resource in both agricultural (e.g., Mamdani 1972; Tilly 1978) and urban (e.g., Hackenberg et al. 1984) settings (see also Nag, White and Peet 1978). Although other studies document the labor contributions of children (e.g., Cain 1980; Hart 1980; Nag 1972; Nag et al. 1980), such would not appear to be a strong or primary motivation among West Indians.

Table 2 *Age of children at the time of their being given in fosterage: Disaggregated by sex*

	Incoming		Outgoing		Historical		
	Male	Female	Male	Female	Male	Female	Total
At birth	4	2	3	3	3	4	19
0-2 years of age	2	5	—	1	—	—	8
3-5*	3	—	—	—	—	—	3
6-8	1	2	—	—	—	2	5
9-11	—	1	—	1	—	2	4
12-14	—	1	—	1	—	2	4
15-17	2	—	1	—	—	1	4
18-20	—	1	—	—	—	—	1
	12	12	4	6	3	11	48

*One adult respondent was uncertain of the child's age when he came to her but did recall that the child was not yet in school: that child is here included in the 3-5 age range, and in numerical calculations he was estimated at 3 years of age.

Who Receives Children? The average ages of the principal adults when the shifting oc-curred and of all members of the households in which fostered children currently reside clearly indicates that children are going from younger to older households and caretak-ers. (The data on household membership among historical cases of child-shifting are not sufficiently complete among enough cases to allow for comparison).

	Incoming (i.e. receiving households)	Outgoing (i.e. sending households)
Average age of all members of households currently incorporating a shifted child	30.85	16.32
Average age of principal adult when shifting occurred	50.17	24.6
	(i.e., child-receiver)	(i.e., child-giver)

This is not particularly surprising since some increasing economic well-being with age (e.g., Comitas 1973: Hackenberg et al. 1984) implies more capacity to absorb dependent members. Conversely, younger adults and households are often more economically vulnerable or marginal, hence have less capacity to support the social or economic strain of additional dependents. Other reports of child shifting include economic stress as a triggering mechanism (e.g., Olwig 1981: 72; Rodman 1971: 183).

It is also not surprising that the vast majority of shifting occurs among close kin. (There were only two episodes of non-kin fosterage, one a mother's friend and the other a highly-respected local nurse). Although the children in question are nearly evenly divided between boys and girls (sons and daughters), the kin relationships with the child-receivers which can be clearly defined are disproportionately traced through female kin as follows:

	Number of episodes	Number of children
Sister's kin	8	10
Brother or brother's kin	4	4
Daughter's kin	8	13
Son's kin	3	3

It was interesting to note, however the prominence of sib relationships in child-shifting. Lateral (i.e, sibling) and lineal (i.e., parental) ties were equally common, contrary to the possible expectation that a maternal tie might be most common. Philpott (1973) has also noted that West Indian sibling ties tend to be tangible and enduring (p.115); indeed he found siblings to be most frequent source of support or mobilizing passage money for a migrant (134). Although Philpott acknowledges that the strength of sibling ties is more an artifact of coresidence than of the structure of the kinship system, and Rodman (1971: 98) describes the strength of sibling ties as situational (an observation with which I would agree), Rodman (1971: 93) has also observed very brittle sibling ties with many obstacles to their lasting relationships. This research, however, has indicated very frequent economic support with nearly equal frequency, women are far more often the recipients of such assistance. Perhaps the nature, utilization, and variability of sibling relationships is a fruitful area of future inquiry (also Rodman 1971: 98).

Table 3 *Kin relationship between child and child-receiver*

	Incoming		Outgoing**		Historical**		Total	
	Number of episodes	Number of children	Number of episodes	Number of children	Number of episodes	Number of children	Number of episodes	Number of children
Sister's daughter	3	3	—	—	—	—	3	3
Sister's son	3	5	—	—	—	—	3	5
Sister's daughter's son	1	1	—	—	—	—	1	1
Husband's sister's daughter	—	—	1	1	—	—	1	1
Brother	1	1	—	—	—	—	1	1
Brother's daughter	1	1	—	—	1	1	2	2
Husband's brother's daughter	1	1	—	—	—	—	1	1
Daughter's daughter	1	3	1	2	1	1	3	6
Daughter's son	2	4	—	—	1	1	3	5
Daughter's daughter's daughter	—	—	1	1	—	—	1	1
Daughter's daughter's son	—	—	1	1	—	—	1	1
Son's daughter	—	—	—	—	1	1	1	1
Son's son	1	1	1	1	—	—	2	2
Niece (unspecified)*	1	1	—	—	1	1	2	2

Great niece (unspecified)*	1	1	—	—	—	—	1	1
Cousin, female (unspecified)*	1	1	—	—	—	—	1	1
Mother's cousin female (unspecified)*	1	1	—	—	—	—	1	1
Non-kin	—	—	—	—	2	2	2	2
No data or unclear	—	—	2	3	5	7	7	10
Alone	—	—	1	1	—	—	1	1

*More specific kin relationship could not be identified by respondent.

**Kin relationship traced from point of view of receiver in the interests of parallelism

Furthermore, birth order was a more present factor than might have been expected among child-receivers. Of the 12 principal adults (PA's) receiving children, there were unambiguous data on their position in birth order for 8 of them. (There were no data on birth order for 4 of those PA's; 2 of them were elderly women whose siblings were deceased, and the other 2 reported being not close to their sibs, i.e., 'they don' study me and me no care,') Of the 8 for whom there were data, 6 were the eldest in their sibling sets, all but one of whom had assumed responsibility for younger siblings and/or sib's children. The other 2 receiving adults were also receiving sib's children and in fact were receiving partial support *from* all of their elder siblings. This suggests that elder sibs might feel a special responsibility to their sibling set, although siblings at all positions in birth order are often mutually supportive.

There are other indications that the eldest might have a distinctive role. For example, they assume greater responsibility for the supervision of family land and care of sibling's children, thereby foregoing the option of migrating (data from Anguilla, Walker 1968). (Philpott also refers to inheritance, often by a daughter, of 'family' housing as 'compensation' for 'giving up the opportunity to migrate' (1970): 16) in the Montserrat setting: it is not, however, an artifact of birth order in this case). The role of birth order in economic behavior, including child care which allows *sibs* to activate certain economic options, therefore might well be another important area of future research in the West Indies.

CHILD-SHIFTING RELATIVE TO UNION STATUS

The union status of current child-givers and child-receivers, despite the average age differential, did not vary in a conclusive manner. (There were not sufficiently clear data on enough of the historical child-shifting episodes to allow for comparison). Despite the small sample, there were some apparent patterns. For example, married women, whether or not the husband was resident, did not shift children out. As noted below, however, this could be an artifact of married women having more attenuated kin ties therefore fewer options for child-shifting arrangements. Also, outgoing children were more likely to come from visiting relationships than from any other kind of union (3), but there were also several women (4) who had received children despite being engaged in no union at the time. Given the frequency with which male partners do not wholly support their children, it would not be surprising if women decided to give or receive children relatively independent of their union status. Indeed, women often engage in and nurture social relationships, principally with other women, which become or also serve as an economic resource (cf. Justus 1981: 440-41, 445; Massiah 1982: 85; McKenzie 1982: x on female solidarity).[3]

From a woman's point of view, particularly if she has children, the issue of engaging in a union of any type seems in part an economic judgement. It is interesting to note two patterns in the frequency of unions as follows:

1 No woman in this sample over age 54 is engaged in a union , an the vast majority of the women currently engaged in a union are 19-39 (73%); indeed the average age of women involved in any type of union is 33.1. Similarly, a decreasing percentage of each age cohort of women participates in unions. Clearly unions correspond to the years of

maximum economic stress (cf. Smith 1978: 345). It is as though mates are more common when they are more 'valuable' economically.

Table 4   *Union Status of Child-Shifting Adults*

	Current union status		Union status at time of shift	
	Incoming	Outgoing	Incoming	Outgoing
No union	3	2	4	—
Visiting	3	2	1	3
Residential, not married	2	3	1	1
Married, not residential	2	—	1	—
Married, residential	—	—	2	—
Widowed	2	—	1	—
Union shift-concurrent with child-shift (non-marital, residential union dissolved)	—	—	2	2
Unclear/no data	—	—	—	1
	12	7	12	7

2   There is an *inverse* relationship between the availability of lineal and lateral kin and the frequency of unions. A disproportionate percentage of the women engaged in unions particularly *marriages*, either have no siblings or report being not very close to their sibs. Furthermore, the frequency of marriage *declines* exactly as a woman has more siblings, and women with more siblings are far less likely to marry if they engage in any union at all. Moreover, more unioned women have attenuated lineal kin ties, e.g., mother is deceased, more often than among similarly aged but non-unioned women.

This suggests that women are *more* likely to marry or engage in a union when lateral and lineal kin ties are *less* likely to be significant economic resources or at least constitute a diminished social network as a resource base. It appears that when women *do* have lateral and/or lineal kin networks on which they can rely for economic and social support, they are *less* likely to engage in unions and *far* less likely to marry. In other words, if the 'resource base' of their own kin is attenuated or is one to which they feel they have only limited access, they are more likely to nurture another relationship — a union — as an alternative strategy to help them meet the economic exigencies of child rearing. Although males provide some support to their children more frequently than is often suggested, it is rarely total support, and they are certainly not perceived as equally reliable as one's own kin and therefore constitute an alternative, even a 'second choice,' economic strategy.

This does not mean to imply, however, that union status does not influence allocation of responsibility for children. Consider, for example, the following scenario:

Erna Mae at 22 had 5-and 3-year–old daughters by two different fathers. One of the two fathers had always contributed money and vegetables grown on family land to his child's maintenance. About 1 1/2 years ago, Erna Mae's current boyfriend, not the father of the children, moved in with her. At that time the 3-year–old daughter moved to her father's kin in a different village, but the 5-year–old remained with her mother. Not only is the boyfriend employed, but also his aunt helped Erna Mae initiate a small business in her home selling clothing to other women in the village. With the coresidence of an adult, employed male and the added income from her small business activity, Erna Mae felt confident in assuming total responsibility for her 17-year-old brother; since their mother died about 10 years ago he had been living with his mother's sister. A few months later Erna Mae's 19-year-old sister also moved in with her 6-month-old child. This sister worked at a local factory, but the nature of Erna Mae's business allowed her to care for her own 5-year-old and her sister's 6-month-old son during the day. As the eldest of 10 children, Erna Mae felt some responsibility for her other siblings; accordingly she has been helping to pay the school expenses for 16 and 14-year-old sisters and a 12-year-old brother, each in a different village with different kin. The onset of Erna Mae's current union thus allowed her to assist her sibling set, although it also prompted the shifting of her youngest daughter to her former mate's family.

This scenario illustrates not only assumption of responsibility for siblings by both Erna Mae and her boyfriend, but also that a new union can trigger reallocation of responsibility for children, having created different social and economic options for a woman. Similarly, one household acquired an incoming child as a husband moved out, and in another, when a residential non-marital union dissolved, a child was shifted to other kin. The impact of unions on residential arrangements is further illustrated by the following:

> Enid is now 51. She and her husband have been married for 25 years, but he has not lived with her for several years. Although he is still living in another village in Antigua, he does not provide regular support to Enid and their only child, a 24-year-old daughter. About 10 years ago, Enid's elderly aunt, her mother's sister, moved in. At the same time Enid's husband's brother's daughter, then 8-years-old, joined the household. Enid works part-time cleaning in a store and also sells cold drinks from her house. When she is out of the household working, her aunt has been able to mind both the small business and the children over the years. Her daughter was able to find her first job in a small shop about a year ago, at which time Enid's 15-year-old sister's son moved in. Although that sister is unable to provide any assistance in supporting her child, their brother, a skilled professional working in Canada, sends money regularly to supplement their household income. Enid has thus raised her husband's brother's daughter for many years, her mother's sister, and, more recently, her sister's son as well as her only child.

THE REASONS FOR CHILD-SHIFTING

Who Gives Children? It has already been noted that child-givers tend to be younger than child-receivers, hence likely more economically vulnerable, perhaps having less of a 'security net' with which to absorb social, personal or economic stress. When PR's were asked why such a shift of a child occurred, they most often said that the child wanted to live with X, or X 'asked for' the child. Such a nondramatic response suggests an abiding condition as opposed to a singular event which precipitated the shifting of a child. The frequency of such a response might suggest, however, a convenient 'public' reason which disguises other reasons, e.g., other forms of stress. Beyond that, other reasons for child-shifting were offered as follows:

Table 5 *Other specific reasons provided for child shifting*

Reason	Number of episodes
Migration of natural parent	5
Death of natural parent or other caretaker	4
Birth of another child/another pregnancy	2
New union	2
Receiver had no children of own	2

It is also interesting to note that of the 11 historical episodes of child-shifting, i.e., 'completed events' as opposed to transactions in progress, in 6 of those cases the child at some time *returned* to the natural parent(s). This is no doubt related to the fact that child-shifting is an age-lined phenomenon, i.e., younger mothers have less ability to assume the social responsibility of parenthood or sustain the attendant economic responsibility (Jagdeo 1982, 1984; Rodman 1971). When the parent is better able to absorb dependents at a slightly later age, the child returns. This also reinforces the observation that children are not shifted out from any lack of affection for the child but rather from inability to maintain the child (cf. Philpott 1973: 140) and/or a *greater* need or supportive capacity on the part of the child-receiver. This system therefore reallocates the costs or responsibilities *and* the benefits of child-rearing.

The most commonly listed 'event-related' reason for shifting children was that of a parent's migration. At the very least migration is a mechanism for redistributing people, thereby adjusting the supply and demand equation within a household; emigrant kin not only reduce 'demand' on a household's resources but also often increase 'supply' in the form of remittances. Furthermore, in a setting with a limited economic base common to LDC's generally and small territories with a fragile ecological base in particular, migration constitutes 'economic niche expansion' (Richardson 1984: 180). In other world areas as well as the West Indies there is documentation of fosterage as a strategy to assure the welfare of children of migrating parents (e.g. Fischer 1970: 296; Hooper 1970: 65; Jagdeo 1982; Stack 1974). Although West Indian males engage in migration more frequently than do females, the autonomous migration of women from the West Indies is quite high by Third World standards (Youssef 1979). Since women typically bear the primary responsibility for children, mechanisms accommodating female migration thus would be expected.

Inasmuch as (a) migration is virtually institutionalized throughout the Caribbean (e.g., Patterson 1978; Richardson 1983), and (b) migration is typically an age-graded phenomenon with people of peak reproductive years comprising the largest percentage of migrants (e.g., Philpott 1973; Walker 1968; Wood 1980; Youssef 1979), it is not surprising that strategies accommodating migration by rearranging household composition would be traditional. Migration as an age-graded strategy or option affects younger adults not only because of any greater 'employability' they might have but also because they face the greatest economic stress from supplementing the support of both a descending generation (e.g., children) and an ascending generation (e.g., parents, parents' siblings) at approximately the same time. Furthermore, migration is often deemed to be a highly elastic economic strategy (e.g., Philpott 1973; Richardson 1983), and household composition in parallel fashion is non-prescriptive and elastic (e.g., Douglas 1984). Others have given attention to the impact of migration on domestic group organization (e.g., Arnould 1984; Boserup 1970; Kunstadter 1984; Richardson 1983; Smith 1978; Sudarkasa 1977), but there is relatively less examination of the complementarity between flexible household composition and migration as a prevailing economic option (an exception is Philpott 1973). Indeed studies which bemoan the 'disorganization' of Afro-Caribbean family structure essentially ignore the reciprocal or circular character of domestic structures and the economic context, in the West Indian case a context which includes migration as a traditional economic option with a long history (cf. Patterson 1978).

Reasons for child-shifting such as those listed above are not necessarily unique to the West Indian context. Clearly child-shifting relieves parents who cannot themselves provide for the child's welfare, in some cases because they simply do not have access to sufficient resources to adequately care for the number of children they have (e.g., Fischer 1970: 308; Lieber 1970: 179). Conversely, there is documentation elsewhere of the value of fosterage as a mechanism for providing children to those who have none (e.g., Goodenough 1970: 316; Howard *et al.* 1970: 45; Lieber 1970: 175; Ottino 1970: 101). In such cases there is a clear expectation that the shifted child is an adult, would contribute to the caretaker's support in her old age part of the normative child/caretaker relationship. As such, children are perceived as a 'resource' to be 'shared' (Carroll 1970: 125; Howard et al. 1970: 45), and fosterage a means of 'evening out access to children' (Wilks & Netting 1984: 15). Thus both the economic costs and benefits are being redistributed throughout the community, despite the fact that those 'benefits' in terms of support from future income might be years in coming (cf. Cain 1980; Fischer 1970: 296; Gonzalez 1969; Hackenberg *et al.* 1984; 1980; Hooper 1970: 66; Mamdani 1972; Nag *et al.* 1980; Ottino 1970: 101; Tilly 1978).

Indeed it is clear that fosterage generally serves to 'distribute the responsibilities and rewards of parenthood more evenly throughout the population' (Goodenough 1970: 337). More specifically, fosterage provides a means of levelling household size or achieving a culturally or economically desirable household composition, hence constitutes a mechanism to maintain 'the economically necessary sequence of household development' (Hooper 1970: 68). Child-shifting can thus be viewed as constituting an economic benefit to two households, both the child-giver and child-receiver.

ECONOMIC SUPPORT SYSTEM AND CHILD-SHIFTING

The general characterization of child-shifting as a transaction between younger, less economically secure and older, more economically stable households is clarified by an examination of the diversity of income sources in the respective households. In each type of household, the percentage of resident adults between 18 and 65 who are employed is very similar: 85.2% of the adults in receiving households vs. 80% of those with outgoing children. Thus any difference in economic well-being does not appear to be related to the employability of resident adults. The ratio of resident employed adults to dependents in the two sets of households is also not very different, though they expectably vary slightly from the mean for all households in the sample in favour of receiving households.

Resource Multiplicity The economic difference between households with incoming and outgoing children seems to be the diversity of resources accummulated by receiving households. Indeed, if one measures the resource multiplicity of all households in the sample as the number of sources of income (i.e., income diversity, including cash and non-cash resources, generated by household residents and provided by non-residents) relative to household size, one finds a progression of increasing resource multiplicity with average of household as follows:

Table 6 *Average age of households relative to resource multiplicity*

Average age of household	Ratio of number of sources of income relative to number of people in household
6.5-14.9 (n=6)	.46
15.0-24.9 (n=19)	.66
25.0-34.9 (n=6)	.68
35.0-44.9 (n=7)	1.0
45.0-54.9 (n=3)	.83
55.0-64.9 (n=2)	1.8
65.0+ (n=6)	4.0

In this measure, a ratio over one means that there are more sources of income than people in the households, a number near one means that the number of sources is about equal to the number of people, while a number smaller than one indicates a household in which there are more people than sources of income. Clearly there is almost an exact progression, with households under 35 (31 households) having the lowest ratio of resource multiplicity and potentially experiencing the greatest economic stress, those between 35 and 55 (10 households) at a fairly stable level, and those over 55 (8 households) having the greatest diversity of income sources. Resource multiplicity might thus be conceived as a feature of the household development cycle (see, e.g., Chayanov 1866; Fortes 1966; Goody 1966; Smith 1956, 1978; White 1980). Although this measure of resource multiplicity does not 'weight' or compare the relative *value* of individual resources, such would be a welcome expansion of the concept. Unfortunately, even ascribing a monetary value to non-monetized resources (e.g., subsistence goods, exchange labor, provision of housing) does not fully capture the significance of the exchange network of which an individual 'transaction' is a part (cf. Olwig 1981).

Interestingly, households receiving children are above the mean for households of that age range, while households with outgoing children are about at the corresponding mean. In short, receiving households have greater diversity of sources of income relative to dependents than do child-giving households or other households of comparable age, hence would seem to exhibit greater economic security. Resource multiplicity as a life-long economic strategy provides a household with an 'economic security net,' i.e., there are other resources on which to rely should any one fail. In a context in which an individual has relatively little control over economic vagaries, such a strategy appears to be quite rational or adaptive indeed (cf. Smith 1963; Richards 1983; Rubenstein 1984).

More specifically, the 'advantage' illustrated by receiving households in part attributable to non-resident sources of income, largely from overseas kin, that are being utilized. Indeed, five of the receiving households are getting some support from a parent of the child for whom they are caring. Of those, *all* of the senders are overseas. In fact, child-receiving households are getting support from all overseas kin at a higher rate than for the total sample.

Table 7   *Households Receiving Help from Overseas Kin*

Incoming	75%
Outgoing	42.9%
Total sample	51.02%

The apparent economic advantage held by receiving households is illustrated by yet another indicator of economic well-being, the level or number of physical amenities within a household. Attention to this variable as a legitimate indicator is supported, for example, by Hackenberg *et al.* who notes that consumer goods essentially have investment value in that they 'store value,' hence serving as semi-liquid 'savings accounts' for periods of high inflation (209- 10). There are also examples of such goods being sold to obtain cash for larger expenditures, e.g., the travel costs for migrating kin (Philpott 1973), an 'expenditure' which can itself in turn be constructed as an 'investment'. Furthermore, Hart (1980) notes that non-production assets, e.g., household possessions, are highly correlated with both primary (e.g., land) and secondary (e.g., home gardens and livestock) production assets.

Based on inventories of 111 possible household 'possessions' and access to modern infrastructure (e.g., electricity, water source, type of fuel), a 10-point scale was devised for the sample households. The household rating 10 (1 household in the sample) had a maximum number of such physical amenities, while those ranking 0 (11 households) had almost no such amenities. The distribution of households from the total sample along that scale was as follows: the mean for the total sample was thus 4.3 PA. Households engaged in child-shifting, however, again deviated from the mean in expectable ways, even allowing for differences in average ages. Clearly, by various 'measures', child-shifting seems to be occurring between households of differential economic well-being.

Table 8   *Distribution of households at various levels of physical amenities (PA) in total sample population*

High PA, 7-10 (n=16)	10:	1
	9:	3
	8:	7
	7:	5
Medium PA, 3-6 (n=16)	6:	4
	5:	6
	4:	4
	3:	2
Low PA, 0-2 (n=18)	2:	4
	1:	3
	0:	11

Table 9   *Level of physical amenities (Pa) for households engaged in child-shifting relative to that of the total sample population*

	Incoming	Outgoing
Mean PA	6.0	3.4
Average ages of these households	30.85	16.32
Mean PA for households of that age range, total sample	5.83	4.47
	(i.e., 25-34.9)	(i.e., 15-24.9)
	(n=6)	(n=19)

These informal measures of 'economic well-being' are necessary because conventional SES measures, usually based on income (often *cash* income only), occupation, and education are not only unavailable for the West Indies, as for most Third World areas, but also are largely inappropriate as traditionally designed. For example, income measured only as cash income, largely or solely from wage employment, often underestimates sporadic income (e.g., that from irregular or occasional employment, gifts as from the father of a child in the household, or remittances from overseas kin). Furthermore, such a measure ignores often critical non-cash forms of income, e.g., vegetables, fish, part of the meat from a slaughtered goat — perhaps to be reciprocated in some future occasion, the provision of housing and /or land — thereby eliminating the recurrent expense of rent, or exchange labor (cf. Olwig 1981).

In fact, one cannot assume that cash income is a consistent, albeit incomplete, measure of economic resources on the basis; that such a measure ignores non-cash resources for all populations alike. Indeed cash and non–cash resources cannot always be assumed to covary (Stack 1974). Traditional SES measures often ignore not only the diversity of forms and sources of income but also the *variability* of income (cf. Wilks & Netting 1984). While many factors contribute to macro-level economic *variability* in LDC's, the point here is that, at the micro-level, households *also* experience, and with varying degrees of success adapt to, such variation. Also education below the tertiary level does not always correlate with observable economic well-being, in particular because people — especially women — who are able to muster multiple sources of income can be fairly 'well off,' or certainly have a measure of economic security, despite relatively modest educational levels either for themselves or their offspring. Finally, an internally-validated ranking of the 'status' of various forms of employment that is adapted to each of the independent countries in the Caribbean *and* incorporates indigenously defined notions of relative status is not available. For example, variations in the 'color-class hierarchy' (Smith 1978) from one island to another must be considered in occupational status rankings, and casual observation suggests that such inter-island variation does indeed exist.

Indeed, perhaps a fruitful area of future research would be the development of an internally-validated, culture-specific measure of economic well-being (cf. Rodman 1971: 98). Such a measure would not only be useful to researchers but also would, for example, allow national and international development agencies to more astutely identify households which might be 'good risks' for loans despite their failure to conform to conventional requirements in terms of collateral or income. In fact, it is quite likely that there is a substantial number of households who are *very* effectively managing their available resources and thus 'ought' to be eligible for development assistance and could well benefit from such. Households engaged in child-shifting might well illustrate the effective management of kin as a resource to more than one household's economic advantage. Indeed, it is quite improbable that the large percentage of a Third World population usually classed as 'poor' is a totally undifferentiated mass. At the very least there is documentation of some variation in household morphology and function (e.g., by developmental or life cycle; cf. Hammel 1984: 30-31), Instead, this population is more likely an amalgam of different 'subsets,' including some percentage of 'marginal poor' (cf. Hackenberg *et al.* 1984). It would, therefore, be highly useful to more analytically identify this subset of 'more successful resource managers' in a culturally-appropriate manner.

MANIPULATION OF HOUSEHOLD FORMATION AND DEPENDENCY AS AN ECONOMIC STRATEGY

Clearly child-shifting is an elastic strategy, part of the 'fluidity' of household composition (Rodman 1971) which is well integrated into and highly compatible with the available economic strategies. If domestic organization was highly rigid with strict prescriptions for coresidence and responsibility for children, then other economic alternatives — or other 'economic niches' — would have to remain unexploited.

This analysis of child-shifting as a responsive strategy is compatible with that of Hackenberg *et al.* (1984), i.e., child-shifting is an alternative household-level economic strategy, related or parallel to 'pooling' of resources. While Olwig (1981) and others have been instructive by directing attention to the economic significance of child-shifting, this argument is that the institution parallels Hackenberg *et al.'s* structure for manipulation of dependency within the household. In examing the economic strategies of Third World households in the Phillippines and Mexico, these authors distinguish among three economic levels: (1) essentially middle class households, (2) marginals, an 'upper strata' of poor or near-poor, and (3) 'the poor.' Since their designation was based largely on cash income, it is not clear what the comparable categories would be in the West Indian context which incorporates substantial non-cash income; it is quite likely, however, that one could defensibly identify comparable clusters. They argue that while households in all economic categories benefit from *more sources* of income, in the Phillippines, households expand their resource multiplicity by importing incom — earning adults, and in Mexico, by reproduction. Likewise in Antigua, households are manipulating household composition in order to manage dependency relative to resources, or 'equalize' this relationship among households within the community.

The West Indian analog, then, is elasticity in household morphology as an economic strategy to accommodate the vagaries of a largely externally-controlled economy (cf. Richards 1983). Indeed an essential and recurrent feature of low-income or marginal populations is variability in their resource base. For example, obviously an agricultural economy will typically exhibit seasonal and annual variability. Perhaps more subtle is the significance of variability embedded in an externally-controlled economy, as many Third World systems are (cf. Richards 1983). For example, many LDC's see tourism as an attractive sector for potential development in that it can require less indigenous capital investment. Yet this embraces not only seasonal variation but also vulnerability from its dependence on the economic swings within the industrialized countries and the oft-shifting 'fashionableness' of a particular tourist site. Finally, the world markets in primary commodities are notably variable (e.g, recall dramatic falls in both sugar and cotton markets which were particularly damaging to many tropical areas) and vastly beyond the control of the producing/exporting countries. Households thus incorporate substantial elasticity in their formation in order to more effectively respond to such variability.

Furthermore, this analysis suggests the value of further testing Wilks and Netting's (1984) hypothesis. They argue that when a woman's productive tasks outside the household are incompatible with a reproductive strategy requiring high fertility, then the household is more likely to be expanded to include nursemaids or surrogate mothers (p. 14). In the Antiguan context, women can and do exploit the 'economic niche' of migration, a productive activity which clearly necessitates surrogate child caretakers. At the same time, relatively high fertility is advantageous in building the elements of a life-span strategy based on resource multiplicity. Similarly, V. D. Gonzalez (1982) takes a broad view of 'sources of livelihood' and refers to a high cultural value placed on children. While Gonzalez notes that the rationale for the value of the role of mother is shifting from one of divine providence toward individual control over life changes by objective means (p. 14), that high value is nonetheless retained. Wilks and Netting argue, and this research tentatively confirms, that in such an economic context with fairly persistent high fertility, surrogate caretakers will be utilized. In the Antiguan setting not only does child-shifting occur fairly frequently as a strategy for providing surrogate caretakers, but also perhaps necessary for a household's flexibility in responding to macro-level economic vagaries and variations, including 'economic niche expansion' strategies such as migration. While more rigorous testing of this hypothesis in different culture areas is clearly called for, this research certainly seems to confirm the proposition by underscoring the economic value and significance of child-shifting.

Both development planners (e.g., UNDP n.d.: 4, 5; USAID Policy Summary: 144-145 in WCARRD 1979) and researchers (e.g., Tinker 1977: 3, 8-9; Wood 1980:9) acknowledges the need for better data on Third World households. Without more specific understandings of household morphology and functions, particularly as they might vary over a development cycle, it is impossible to understand or explain the differential success of development programs. Furthermore, there are those who argue that 'the population problem' seeming to plague much of the Third World is basically an imbalance between population and resources in line with Hackenberg *et al.*'s contention that at least at the household level dependency ratio is the most fundamental issue. Indeed, whether one is concerned with economic development, modernization, political stability or meeting some minimal standards of a 'quality of life,' the relationship between productive and dependent members of a household is the normative patterns of household formation allow for substantial elasticy in household composition. Such elasticity is not only compatible with but also a critical variable. Inasmuch as child-shifting is a mechanism for managing household morphology, it is thus of interest as a household-level economic strategy for manipulating dependency relative to resource multiplicity.

J. Gussler

ADAPTIVE STRATEGIES AND SOCIAL NETWORKS OF WOMEN IN ST KITTS

This chapter looks at the role of women in a generally poor plantation society in the non-Hispanic Caribbean, on the island of St Kitts. Factors of poverty, migration, low incidence of marriage, and a high birth rate combine to make the lives of lower-class women difficult. Within this socio-cultural system, children represent for men an affirmation of their masculinity and for women, potential support at later stages in life. Survival for a woman and her young children requires much ingenuity and diversification of effort. Women's strategies to 'get by' include the development and utilization of a network of human resources. The author discusses the implications of these networks for lower-class women's social and geographic mobility, and she contrasts their form with those of middle-class women in the society of St Kitts. The careful exploration and optimization of avenues of support, including the management of social networks, shows Kittitian lower-class women to be resourceful and often successful social actors.

A young friend wrote recently from St Kitts:

Right [sic] now I am very broke I aint even have a cent to buy decoration for the house. Cant even get a job. If you do get a job they dont want to pay you sufficient money and some times they delay you. Its a lady living side me she cant walk so good it is she who do give me little change sometime to buy milk for them [the babies] and when she dont give me they would drink the plain boiling water ....

I met this young woman in 1972 when I began field research on food distribution and social networks on the small West Indian island of St Kitts.[1] When we met she was a child of 14; in 1977 she was a 19-year–old unmarried mother of four children, living in poverty and ill health. While her plight is more serious than that of most other young women, they all share some of the problems of trying to raise families in a society where employment opportunities are scarce and incomes are low. The common difficulties faced by the women of St Kitts produced in me both personal concern and anthropological curiosity. I sought to find why, in this generally poor nation, these young women are often relatively more deprived than some other categories of people and what actions they (the women) take to ameliorate their situation.

In this chapter, I will describe the major socio-cultural and historical parameters of resource distribution, and discuss how they impinge specifically on the lives of Kittitian women. To do so, I must also describe the nature of Kittitian society in general, demonstrating how, in an individuated social system with few inclusive group structures, success often depends upon how effectively one establishes and utilizes links in the social network. Relationships of women to men, other women, even to their own children, are very often consciously viewed as social resources to be tapped now, or as investments that will pay off in the future. Before this discussion, however, I will provide a brief culture history of the social system itself.

ST KITTS: HISTORY AND GEOGRAPHY

The small island of St Kitts is a land mass of approximately 68 square miles situated in the Leeward chain of islands in the eastern Caribbean. Being of volcanic origin, it is a fertile land, even after more than 300 years of continuous cultivation. The eastern portion of the island tapers off into an arid peninsula which reaches within two miles of the smaller sister island of Nevis. The mountains of the interior of St Kitts intercept the clouds blown continuously by the trade winds, with the result that the western end of the island is well watered and lush with tropical vegetation. Here the fertile nature of the land is apparent, today yielding great amounts of sugar cane for sale in the world market.

St Kitts was apparently discovered first by the Arawak Indians, according to prehistoric records, and next by the Carib Indians, who called it Liamuiga, the Fertile Island. The Caribs were there when Christopher Columbus 'discovered' the land during his second trip to the New World in 1493,[2] and when European settlement began in the early part of the seventeenth century. The British settlers occupied the central portion of the island, and the French the east and west ends, which they named Basseterre and Capesterre, respectively. The capital of St Kitts dates to this period of French occupation. In an early spirit of cooperation, the French and British worked out a plan of coexistence that included the extermination of the Caribs. Despite the fact that the Indians had lived more or less peacefully with the settlers and provided them with food from time to time, they were killed or driven to other islands during the early years of colonization (Merrill 1958: 51; Parry and Sherlock 1957: 48).

During the later years of the seventeenth century, the British brought out French claims on St Kitts, but the French and Spanish both challenged the British hold on the island repeatedly throughout the next 100 years of their occupation. By the nineteenth century, however, St Kitts was a colony in the British Empire, and remained so until 1967 when it became an Associated State with a measure of independence.

Early colonists grew tobacco, indigo, ginger, and cotton for markets at home. However, these crops rapidly depleted the soils, and the farmers were unable to compete with the North American colonies. Thus, when sugar cane was introduced (*ca.* 1640) it quickly became the major product of the island. The establishment of sugar cane production as the economic base of the island resulted in far-reaching social change. Sugar cane requires large areas of cultivatable land, a large cheap labour force (before mechanization), and relatively expensive equipment and sophisticated technology to be profitable. The 'sugar revolution' on St Kitts and other West Indian islands had a threefold effect: first, there was a demise of independent small-scale farming and an exodus of many poor white Europeans; second, many African slaves were imported to fill labour needs; and, third, the plantation type of socioeconomic organization developed, comprised of white managers and overseers, and a large black population of dependent workers.

In St Kitts, these effects were more extensive and enduring than on most other islands. Sugar has maintained its hold on the Kittitian economy even through years of failing prosperity. And the sugar estates have maintained their hold on the Kittitian people. On some of the larger islands of the Caribbean, slaves were encouraged to grow their own foods in order to reduce the need for expensive imported foods. On St Kitts, however, it was deemed a better strategy for the estate owners to put all agricultural lands into cane production, and import foods for the slaves. Slaves were allowed to establish provision gardens on marginal lands, such as on the sides of ghauts, but these gardens were too small and unproductive to serve as the basis for a peasant farming economy after emancipation. In fact, emancipation of slaves in 1833 changed the lifestyle of most Kittitians very little. They moved out of the estate yards into independent villages, but the individuals in these villages were still dependent on the estates for their livelihood. Many are today.

During these years, many of the British colonists returned home, establishing a pattern of absentee landlordism. This later exodus of successful colonists, following upon the earlier one of poor whites, resulted in an island population that is predominantly black (98 percent 'African' or 'mixed') and poor. The poverty is partially a function of too many people competing for too few jobs in a single industry which has too many competitors in the world market. In an effort to enhance their position in the world sugar market, estate controllers have attempted both mechanization and consolidation, but the accompanying efficiency of production is a mixed blessing on an island with a large poor population. One historian has pointed out that at some time, presumably during the nineteenth century, the problem of a chronic labour shortage on St Kitts became a problem of chronic under- and unemployment (Merrill 1958:98). The lack of jobs becomes even more serious as machines take over the work of men and women, but the problem in St Kitts has been compounded by an increasingly militant and powerful labour union. When disgruntled workers stayed away from their jobs during the 1960s, the men who controlled the sugar industry were encouraged to get new machines to do the work for them. Modernization of the sugar industry has also failed to solve another perpetual labour problem, which stems from the seasonal nature of sugar work. Labour utilization — male labour — is intense from February or March until August, but for the balance of the year only occasional estate work is available.

The labour union of St Kitts became an organized political force during the 1960s, and after the island was granted independence, the Labour Party assumed control of the government. Since that time, it has also gradually assumed control over the sugar industry, and, thus, the island's economic system. In this new position of political power, the Labour government is also attempting to stimulate tourism, which has had very little impact on the island economy up to now. Labour has not solved the ultimate problems of Kittitian economic development, but it has improved incomes for sugar workers to some degree and has helped erase the stigma of slavery from such work.

Continuing stresses from over-population and under-employment have been alleviated somewhat over the years through population migration. Throughout this century, Kittitians have moved off the island in response to economic opportunities — working on shipping fleets and navies, on the Panama Canal, and in the tourist hotels in the Virgin Islands. This movement of people has been important, not just because it has eased population pressures and job competition on the island, but because those Kittitians working overseas have traditionally sent a part of their incomes to their families back home. These remittances have long been an important source of income for the people who have by choice or necessity remained home. In fact, one official of the sugar industry admitted that Kittitians receive as much income from remittances as from sugar estate wages.

THE PEOPLE OF ST KITTS

The people of St Kitts, then, can be described as black, poor, and highly mobile. The Kittitians who remain home live in either the capital Basseterre (population, approximately 13,000) or in one of the smaller towns and villages that lie alongside the island's single major road. Out of the total population of nearly 40,000 people, more than three-quarters could be classified as 'lower stratum' on the basis of occupation, level of education attained, and features of their lifestyles. Among these features are a low incidence of marriage, a high birth rate, and a high rate of illegitimate births. The rate of illegitimate first births, for example, exceeds 90 percent, and the overall figure for all births approaches 80 percent. (These percentages include births to mid- and upper-stratum mothers, as well; thus, the figures for the lower stratum are somewhat higher). Many of the households, then, are headed by women, and some of these span three or even four generations. They also may include women, men, and children who are more distantly related or, occasionally, who are not kin at all. Economic necessity rather than kinship is the primary parameter of household composition. Men who are neither married nor living in a 'consensual union' with a woman, may live alone or share quarters with other kinfolk; again, the major constraints are availability of space and economic necessity, rather than traditional and recognized social bonds. The nuclear family household is more common in the mid and upper strata, but in some of the villages, there are few middle-class families and the elite may not be represented at all.

Adaptive opportunism is also reflected in the economic pursuits of lower stratum folk in St Kitts. Very few of the poorer people can afford to tap only one resource. A man, for example, may work in the cane fields several months of the year, raise a few vegetables and sell the surplus to a 'turnhand' (a market woman, equivalent to the Jamaican 'higgler'), break rock and sell the gravel, help another man construct a house, and receive a small money gift from an overseas relative. None of these activities will bring a man much money, perhaps the equivalent of $500 to $1,000 U.S. dollars for the year. For a woman, the situation can be more serious, since there are relatively few jobs for women on the sugar estates. Lower-class women can and do garden. However, it is a long and hot walk to the gardens in the mountains, made more difficult by pregnancy (a common state) and the necessity of caring for small children. Even with the occasional help of a good friend or close relative, working the hilly land with nothing more than a heavy bladed hoe will usually yield only enough yams and sweet potatoes for family consumption. A woman with several children may have no surplus to sell to turnhands.

While these Kittitian women have to shoulder the burdens of family finances and nurturance, they also have the relative independence and self-determination that goes with being a head of household. Women in the Caribbean, and their West African ancestral counterparts, have always had significant supradomestic roles. In the plantation societies, slave women were too important economically to be merely bearers of new slaves, and their work included weeding cane fields, growing ground provisions, and marketing locally grown produce. The question of whether their gardening and marketing activities have a West African provenance or are products of a slavery system in which men's labour was strictly controlled by and for the sugar estate is immaterial. Probably the roles are an outcome of the interaction between Old World cultural remnants, ethnohistorical trends, and continuing poverty. It is necessary only to point out that these are and have long been designated women's activities, important both for the women who participate in them and for the island economy. These roles were not restricted to the house and yard, but involved the women in the daily activities of the island world outside the household. Kittitian females move freely and independently about the towns and villages, relatively unfettered by cultural constraints which relegate women in some societies to a strictly domestic role.

The 'turnhand' for example, remains the major distributor, wholesaler, and retailer, of locally grown provisions. Since the island lacks adequate transportation and storage facilities to move these fresh foods in bulk, women provide the service a few pieces at a time. Buying up extra sweet potatoes, yams, dasheens, tannias, carrots, tomatoes, cabbages, pumpkins, mangoes, and so on, they carry the items to the marketplace in Basseterre. Some turnhands are strictly 'middle people' and sell their goods to those women who are retailers; others will rent a stall and sell. These women usually establish a network of regular customers who will buy only from them. They, in turn, will save choice or scarce items for their regulars. I was fortunate to establish a relationship such as this with a turnhand, since a friend and informant was one of the woman's customers. I discovered, in fact, that these mutual obligations extend beyond the marketplace. My friend and I bought 'sweeties' for our children from a vendor woman at a cricket match in Basseterre, only to spy 'our' turnhand, who was similarly selling snacks to the fans. My friend was so concerned at this slight that she purchased more candy and peanuts with her remaining money, and the turnhand reciprocated by throwing in some free sweeties for the little ones.

Gardening and marketing are among the oldest supradomestic activities of Kittitian women, but they are certainly not the only ones. In fact, women's economic roles are surprisingly varied on this small island. Most of the villagers I observed breaking rock into gravel, for example, were female. Women work in cane fields, although they do not cut or load sugar cane. They prepare food specialities, such as sugar cakes, black pudding, and souse, and sell them in the village, in Basseterre, and sometimes in the schoolyards. None of these traditional activities provide women with much of an income, but through a combination of them they can feed their families.

Women have moved relatively easily into the modernizing and middle-class Kittitian society. St Kitts has female police officers, clerks, bank tellers, bookkeepers, factory workers, and intermediate level government officials. This involvement of women in the economic realm may, in part, be an artifact of the high rate of male migration; however, since women are now migrating too in great numbers, this is not a sufficient explanation. More important, in my observation, is that in this society the competency and significance of women are generally not challenged.

For many of the lower-stratum women, improved economic fortunes depend upon the availability of three resources over which they can, in a sense, exert no direct control: men, overseas relatives, and migration opportunities. A fortunate woman will find a man, usually the father of one or more of her children, who is willing to share some of his income with her, even if they do not share a common residence. In Kittitian society there are both social and legal pressures on men to help provide for their illegitimate children, but in fact they often do not. Although many women complain about the short-comings of men, they very rarely use the law to enforce social expectations. Instead, they assume a fatalistic world view that it is in the nature of a woman's lot to work hard and have a difficult life. Nevertheless, Kittitian females do consciously establish relationships with a series of men or, occasionally, several men concurrently in order to maximize their chances of receiving financial support. (These strategies are discussed in some detail below).

While Kittitians tend to see their island as a land of 'limited good', the world outside is perceived in terms of economic abundance and opportunity. People who expect little or nothing from local kinfolk do not hesitate to request food, clothing, even money, from those overseas. Better yet, Kittitian men and women seek the opportunity to leave the island themselves, following their kinfolk to the Virgin Islands, to New York City, to London, and Toronto in search of work. For lower-stratum women, such a move may be of considerable importance, for domestic work — one of the few types of work for which most of them are qualified — is hard to find on small islands with few tourists. In 1972 (the last year for which there are published government figures), 18,793 men and 14,066 Kittitian women left the island for at least a short time (St Kitts-Nevis-Anguilla 1972: Table 24). The availability of these opportunities, however, is unpredictable and fluctuates greatly in accordance with a variety of economic and political factors external to St Kitts and beyond the control of the Kittitian people. An important feature of lower-class economic pursuits, then, is mobility and the ability to compete for scacre, fluctuating, and sometimes remote resources.

These facts of island life, following upon a history of slavery and a plantation social system, have had a profound effect upon the quality of interpersonal relationships in St Kitts. Fragments of diverse social groups and parts of unrelated families were brought to the island as slaves, where they were seen primarily as individual units of production. The slavery system perpetuated the breakdown of kin and other social groups, as did the estate system after emancipation, as *individuals* sold their labour, and cheaply, to the sugar industry. On this small island there was no place where freed men and women might live and maintain control over resources and means of production outside the sphere of sugar industry influences. Thus, no socioeconomic groups grew in St Kitts comparable to those in peasant societies. Competition instead of cooperation characterizes relationships, even to some degree between kinsmen. Eric Wolf (1966: 82) pointed out that such an individuated and competitive social situation is common in developing states such as St Kitts, where things come to be evaluated primarily according to economic values. In my 1972-73 study of food distribution and food habits, I found that food is considered in this light in St Kitts. Most surplus foods are sold to turnhands or directly to customers, that is converted into cash, rather than used in establishing and maintaining local multistranded social ties. In other words, institutionalization of social relationships and groups through reciprocal exchanges (of food, service, and so on) is rare, presumably because such relationships would entail obligations difficult to meet in times of scarcity. In fact, my observations suggest that group obligations are an economic burden more often than an asset in this meeting.

This lack of group structures was apparent in the village in which I conducted my anthropological field research. The community lies about four miles to the east of the capital, Basseterre, and, thus, is an easy bus ride or a long hot walk from the most 'urbanized' section of the island. The village was settled by freed slaves during the mid-nineteenth century, and approximately 600 of their descendants still live there. The small frame and masonry construction houses are situated close together about the single road, but distance in social relationships is maintained through several social, physical, psychological, and even supernatural barriers which local folk have erected to ensure privacy and minimal interpersonal involvement. Most villagers, for example, have fenced in the property upon which their house is built. Fences range from fast-growing bushes to high corrugated metal structures behind which a villager may live for years with very little contact with neighbours. Reinforcing the physical separation of villagers is their shared set of attitudes concerning hospitality, visiting, and sharing. People commonly do most of their socializing on 'neutral' ground of some sort, such as on the street, at church, in a bar or rum shop, or in Basseterre, where no one has an obligation to entertain and provide refreshment. Furthermore, there is little value placed on generosity in this social setting. An individual who is the recipient of a gift or loan is vulnerable to attack by village gossip, and fear of 'being talked about' is a real deterrent to sharing. I have recorded nearly a dozen independent examples of people who have expressed a great deal of concern about being the object of such talk, have myself heard and been the victim of it on several occasions, and have seen many people take elaborate precautions to hide gifts to me and from me from the eyes of their neighbours. One time, for example, I was told by two women in the village not to drive a third younger woman to visit a 15-year–old friend of ours who had just given birth to her first child. The explanation given to me was that the young woman wanted to carry a few necessary items to the new mother, then return to the village and 'talk about her'. In another conversation, a woman with whom I have worked on a number of field research projects informed me that in the village, pregnant women could not borrow maternity clothes the way my 'friends in the States' do, because 'people would say "H. is wearing P.'s dress" and talk about me'. Finally, an individual who gets a reputation for generosity, may be considered weak and a mark for anyone willing to risk gossip for a free ride to town or a handout.

My research suggested that supernatural barriers may also reinforce and maintain social distance between Kittitians, especially older people. Among the few obvious cultural continuities with Africa still perpetuated in the culture of St Kitts is a belief in magic call 'obeah'. An obeah man is knowledgeable about how to use such things as powders to produce magic for the control of people or events, and his skills are often in demand by those who harbour a grudge against kin, neighbour, friend, or foe. One destitute old man accused his cousin of attempting to harm him with obeah powders placed in food she brought to him to ease his hunger; another old man was thought to have been disabled by a spell put upon him by a jealous brother. In both cases the men had isolated themselves, avoiding certain kinds of social contact, from the fear of obeah, and gifts made to them were suspect because they might carry harmful powders. In a sense, the avoidance of sharing and cooperative social ventures because of fear of gossip is an extension of the more specific, more tangible obeah avoidance, and both reflect a general distrust of social involvement.

I felt the impact of this sociocultural situation throughout my research in St Kitts. I found, for example, that the non-sharing ideology by the village extended to include people such as myself. In societies that are composed of a number of inclusive groups, such as kin groups, a field worker can usually count on being integrated into the organization by forming relationships with members of a major informant's primary groups. In an individuated social structure, however, the field worker faces what Morris Freilich called a lack of 'spreadibility of rapport' (1970: 218,226), requiring a relatively large number of informants, each of whom is the focus of a network of ties. Not only will a relationship with one individual informant *not* lead naturally and inevitably to ties with a circle of relatives and friends, it may actually interfere with the extension of ties, since many folk would actively discourage such attempts by making disparaging remarks about their friends and foes alike. Once I had learned the important ethnographic lesson that people, including myself, are resources in that environment, I could better understand why a friend would viciously attack her neighbours for bothering me with requests for rides to town and in the next breath suggest that we take a 'little ride around the island'.

Skill in the management of social resources, then, is an important aspect of a successful socioeconomic strategy in St Kitts, as in much of the Third World. Whitten (1970: 33) pointed out that by selectively opening, reinforcing, and terminating dyadic ties with kin and non-kin, an individual can maximize his or her opportunities for social and spatial mobility. And in the 'marginal, fluctuating money economics' (1970:33) of the Caribbean, successful strategies are often the most flexible ones, those with the greatest number of options for social and geographic movement.

In an article by Nancie Gonzalez about the Black Caribs (1970), there is evidence that the low incidence of marriage and matrifocal households, which are both common features in West Indian society, are adaptive responses to these same economic pressures. She points out that the 'consanguineal household offers financial and psychological security to the female and to the male and, thus, to the maintenance of a fairly stable home environment even when jobs are hard to find and remuneration low' (1970: 242). Gonzalez indicated that there are pressures on males who have conjugal unions with women to be 'good providers'; to fail may bring rejection from a spouse but not from consanguineal kin. The author added:

> Conversely, a woman can ill afford to cleave only unto one man, cutting herself off from other conjugal unions or from male kinsmen, for in such systems the chances that any one man may fail are high. Should her husband disappear or fail to provide regularly, a woman needs the support of other males. By dispersing her loyalties and by clinging especially to the unbreakable sibling ties with her brothers, a woman increases her chances of maintaining her children and household even when any one attached male is incapable of helping her (1970: 242).

In other words, Gonzalez has suggested that establishing a network of ties with men, none of which are exclusive or ultimately binding (except, perhaps, those with brothers) may be a successful strategy of women in these societies. These anthropological perspectives are particularly useful in explaining the lives of the women I have met on the island of St Kitts.

THE VILLAGE SETTING

The village in which I lived with my three children, gathering cultural data and attempting to understand the problems of women, has no town hall or other seat of government, because there is no local political organization. There is no institution actually, that integrates these people into an identifiable group. There are no economic, political, ritual, or kin activities that involve or even potentially involve all villagers. Church affiliation serves to integrate communities in some of the Catholic islands of the Caribbean, but in St Kitts, even religion is divisive. The largest church congregation in the village itself is Methodist, while the Anglicans, who are nearly as numerous, must walk to a nearby community to worship. There are several other smaller congregations in the village proper, Pentecostal and Gospel Hall being the most important, but members of these 'sideways churches', as they are called, often are derided by their neighbours. The Methodists and Pentecostals, especially, sustain a mutual enmity. I have heard villagers laugh at those who have 'become Christians' (Pentecostals), because joining this church requires one to adhere to a strict code of conduct and dress, as well as regular church attendance. Furthermore, the Methodists are either disdainful of or amused by the 'dancing' of the Pentecostal participants as the true believers move in response to their preaching and music to achieve possession by the Holy Ghost. The woman who heads the Pentecostal Church, on the other hand, delivers powerful sermons, often directed at the curious non-believers who watch through the church doors. The only integrative feature of the churches that I have observed, is the community centre that was built and is still maintained by the Methodist congregation. In it, pediatric clinics are held regularly by the Kittitian Health Department, and films are shown sporadically, most concerning religious themes or birth control. The local band uses the building for their practice, and young people play table tennis there.

More common than churches in the village, are the small shops of local entrepreneurs. These provide a variety of vital functions to villagers, who depend on them especially during bad times to sell on credit. Freshly baked bread, both lunch and breakfast for most villagers, is carried to the shops to be sold to regular customers. While most people shop in Basseterre each Saturday for fresh provisions and staples such as rice, flour, cooking oil, and tinned milk, they often find themselves lacking sufficient cash to purchase in quantity. When they run out of these staples in mid-week, they can purchase small amounts from the large tins and barrels in the shops. Most of the villagers with whom I worked and lived bought a great deal of their food from the shops on a meal-to-meal basis. In the long run, food costs are slightly higher, since quantities are small and unit prices somewhat higher in the villages, but this pattern does provide flexibility; people buy only what is immediately needed of stocks that are available with whatever money is at hand. Finally, the local shops are meeting places, where neighbours can visit, and men can play dominoes and discuss the latest cricket match over a beer.

This is the social and cultural context, briefly described, within which the women of St Kitts live and strive. They perceive it as a hard world, and indeed it is; however, their personal strength and patterns of dealing with a harsh and unpredictable socioeconomic order have survival value. Mobility and a flexible network of kin and friends are adaptive social features in a changing society. In the next section, these features are described through lives of the women themselves.

A WOMAN'S STRATEGY: DEVELOPMENT OF A NETWORK

A woman usually faces the birth of a baby with mixed or ambiguous feelings. Most women want babies to affirm their female social identitfy, to care for them in their old age (more about this below), or to please a man who wishes to demonstrate his virility. Or they say they simply want a little one to love. Village women, on the other hand, are very realistic about the problems involved in raising children without money and without a husband. Pregnancy is not discussed a great deal, nor is labour and the process of giving birth. There is some embarrassment in bearing an illegitimate child, despite the frequency with which this happens, but there are also remnants of traditional beliefs which proscribe discussions of birth and babies. Jumbies, for example, which are perceived as spirits of the dead, can bother a new infant, causing it to sicken and die. Thus, little fuss is made over the new one, and its name is not to be mentioned until it is christened; older children may have asafoetida tied in their hair to keep the troublesome spirits away. (The latter practice is rare today, in part due to the counsel of government physicians).

Men sometimes state a preference for male children, but mothers show little prejudice to either sex in the treatment of their babies. They are generally given adequate food and attention without being indulged, unless, of course, the babies come too quickly and too often. In this case, the mother may not be able to provide sufficient nourishment and care for each, and they may sicken and, too often, die. I have also known some mothers who have had to find other homes for one or more of their children, despite the anxiety this causes to mother and child alike. If a woman's own mother can assume part of the burden, the anxiety is less, because women feel that the grandmother will provide the love and care young ones are thought to require. No one else, the women told me, can really be trusted to adequately look after your children. Yet it often becomes necessary to send them to other kin, to friends, or to (sometimes) virtual strangers, who have the room and resources to provide for them.

Babies are generally fed according to a mixed feeding pattern, breast in the morning and evening, and the bottle in between. All the women with whom I spoke felt that women now do not have enough breast milk to feed their infants without supplementary bottles. In one sense, this shared concern itself causes problems since tinned milk is expensive, less nourishing for the babies, and must be mixed and stored under improper conditions. Some mothers spend up to one-third of their low incomes on milk alone. Yet the mixed feeding pattern does give the mothers something that may be more important ultimately — flexibility and mobility, should opportunity arise somewhere.

Most infants are off the breast completely by the sixth to ninth months, and as soon as the children begin to toddle about, less and less attention is paid to them by mothers or surrogates. This is a critical time for the children, both socially and physically, for their mobility brings increased vulnerability. The youngster is extricating itself, in a sense, from the mother and her enveloping network of resources, neither a dependent extension of the mother nor yet an independent and self-sufficient member of the household. He or she may not yet have a place at the table or a set of eating utensils. (Two women expressed surprise that a place was set for my one-and-a-half-year-old son). The child is not considered 'ready' or in need of adult food and may subsist primarily on gruels and porridges made with milk and meal or flour on into the second year. Since nutritional needs are changing throughout these months, it is not surprising that the diet of these youngsters is very often sub-standard, and is especially low in protein. Gastro-intestinal disorders plague the lower stratum toddlers of St Kitts, as they do in many developing tropical nations, and are the most common cause of hospitalization in children of this age category.

Between the ages of three and five, boys and girls usually begin to spend greater amounts of time with peers, relatives and friends, with whom they play. Actually, much of their play involves gathering and stealing food of many different kinds. By the sea, for example, they may collect whelks, moray eel, and sea grapes; in the pastures they chase down tululu (small land crabs); and in the mountain they find mangoes, guavas, coconuts, almonds, tamarinds, gineps, and so on. Since my middle child was integrated into one of these peer groups, I had the opportunity to follow closely some of the scavengers, whose ages ranged from four to twelve. Most of the children in this particular group were siblings and cousins from a large family who had been left with an old woman who was grandmother and great-grandmother to them. Since she was ill and feeble, they actually had to watch out for one another most of the time. In fact, I observed and was told by several informants that many of these children that 'run the streets' are those whose mothers have left to work overseas. While many of these youngsters fall short of the high standards for conduct held by villagers (obediency, respect for authority, helpfulness), the importance of the foodstuffs they gather in this context of marginal food resources is considerable.

During these childhood years, both boys and girls attend classes in the overcrowded one-room school house in a neighbouring village. Virtually all of them stay in primary school for a few years, thus achieving at least minimal literacy, and many even complete the sixth level. However, only about 5 percent according to 1970 census figures, go on to secondary schools or other higher education (University of the West Indies 1975: 156, 157).

During these years of childhood, there are few major differences in the socialization of boys and girls. Both engage in active, physical, sometimes rowdy play, often involving the administration of 'licks'. When girls play card games, for example, they usually play 'for licks', which gives the winner the right to strike the loser as hard as desired, one hit per point lost. I myself received a number of licks from the girls who came to know me well, and although they were delivered in the spirit of play and fun, I can attest to the strength and enthusiasm of the delivery!

Girls are not molded into dependent, subordinant, passive, and strictly domestic roles; such training would be obviously incompatible with the 'real world' of lower-class adults in St Kitts. Instead, girls acquire a sense of independence, a competitiveness, a resourcefulness, sometimes an aggressiveness that makes them seem harsh at times to outsiders, but that can assure them survival under the existing socioeconomic conditions. Most lower-class Kittitian women spend many years as mothers without also being wives, and many never have a man 'to take are of them'. In such an environment, socialization to independence is adaptive.

Despite the lack of sexual segregation of childhood activities and roles, the lifestyles of boys and girls begin to diverge as they approach adolescence. Girls are more likely than their male peers to be given child care responsibilities, helping their mothers who have several more younger offspring, or caring for younger siblings left in their charge by mothers who must work. Child care is not entirely a sex-typed activity, but girls are more likely than boys to assume it. One girl of 12 was our constant companion during the summer months of 1972, when I first began my field research in St Kitts. Because she was such a quiet, unassuming girl, I could not understand the constant criticisms I heard of her from friends and neighbours. 'Don't harbor her', I was told on several occasions. I found that her mother, who was 29–years–old, had seven other children which the girl was expected to look after. Her mother kept her home from school most of the time, and the other girls teased her because she could not read. Yet all the sympathy of fellow villagers went to her mother, who had such a disobedient child. A niece of my major informant was 13–years–old that same summer. She was responsible for the care and feeding of five siblings, since her mother was working in St Croix. I tried to arrange for her to go with us on outings to the beach, but her aunt always pointed out that the girl had to stay home with the little ones and cook for them. My obvious sympathy for her was not shared by my Kittitian friends, who saw the girl's plight as one of the facts of life: a woman must become accustomed to hard work and a hard life.

Another fact of Kittitian life is sexuality. Children learn of sexual behaviour and reproduction early in those small houses in which the family all sleep together. Furthermore, the body and its various functions are considered 'natural', and people do not attempt excessively to hide them. Children experiment sexually at an early age, and full heterosexual relationships are not at all unusual by the age of 12. It is not surprising, then, that many girls are pregnant by the time they are 14 or 15. Health workers report that venereal disease is common among children 13 and younger; I personally know two girls who had their first babies during their thirteenth year. And of the approximately 25 village women of all ages from whom I got this type of information, all but two had become pregnant by the age of 17, most during their sixteenth year.

In this way, the adulthood of Kittitian women begins. For many of the lower-class females, this is also a difficult time — babies to care for, a household to establish if their mother will not allow them to stay, no job, and a boyfriend who bolts or has no money. I know of only one young mother who has found employment in Basseterre. A few have left the island, especially in upwardly mobile families, with the encouragement of other family members, who are embarrassed about the illegitimate birth. Most of these teenagers, however, must be constantly searching for sources of money, food, and clothing for themselves and their babies. The young mothers are now considered independent adults, no longer to be cared for by nurturing relatives, and as such they must assume adult roles and responsibilities. This independence is sometimes reinforced by the departure of the teenager from her natal home, either by her own choosing or by the choice of her relatives. One friend and informant of mine told me of her own difficult existence when she was told to leave her mother's home after she bore her second illegitimate child at the age of 17. Yet because a teenage mother is now adult, she must give up most of the foraging activities that provide supplementary foods for children. She is burdened with her baby, of course, but beyond that, foraging is not considered appropriate adult behavior in most cases. At this age, the search for a livelihood must take the form of an extension of one's rudimentary social network through the establishment of additional and hopefully fruitful social relationships.

Among the most significant of these relationships are those with men. During the early years of adulthood, a young woman may have a series of boyfriends — and, perhaps, a series of babies — and find not one with whom to establish a tie involving mutual economic responsibility. While these contacts with men virtually always involve sex, the women are not promiscuous, for there are recognized standards of conduct. For the duration of the relationship, for example, the couple is expected to remain faithful, although according to the local double standard this fidelity applies primarily to the female. Unless the relationship is very casual, the young man often takes a proprietary view of 'his woman,' and jealously guards her from attentions of other males. If a woman violates the unspoken vows of fidelity, or if her boyfriend imagines that she has, he may erupt in jealous anger and beat her. Several young women I know have either been beaten, one badly, or threatened with violence, and while they have been given some degree of sympathy from their friends and relatives, they rarely use legal means to punish the men.

One young attorney in St Kitts is particularly concerned with what he perceives as maltreatment of women. He told me that the men like to 'chat up the girls,' and, indeed, to get them pregnant as a demonstration of their masculine prowess. A man who does not produce offspring is sometimes said to have 'sand in his seed'. The young women, left with babies and no money coming from the fathers of them, complain of their lot, but will rarely use the existing laws to force child support payments. Instead, the attorney said, they tell him that a woman's life is supposed to be hard. Furthermore, he had been constantly frustrated in his attempts to get women to use the law to protect themselves from boyfriends and husbands who mistreat them physically or mentally, or who use them simply as sources of income without reciprocation of duties. He said he felt that they hesitate to bring legal action because they see courts as a place for criminals; because of their resistance to swearing oaths (especially members of fundamental religions); and because of their fatalistic world view.

The existence of such a double standard in a society where women are independent and relatively free from the social constraints that inhibit women in many places, results in stormy male-female relationships. One young man told me, in fact, that 'in St Kitts, men and women don't like each other very much'. While this is no doubt an exaggeration, I did observe a great deal of visible tension and outright battles between the sexes during my stay. In one case, a young married man had gone to a neighboring village to visit his girlfriend on an evening that a fete was being held at our house. We had invited the couple, so the young woman came alone. When her husband returned and found her there, he became jealous and very angry. During the argument that ensued, she screamed that she was going to kill him and went after a knife. Eventually friends restored order, but the couple's relationship was strained for some time thereafter.

Despite the potential tensions, even unmarried women generally are faithful to their boyfriends, and virtually always know who the fathers of their babies are. Informally, in fact, many illegitimate children use their fathers' surnames, even though legally they should not. Even this public expression of paternity, however, does not force support. During my last field trip to St Kitts I, interviewed seven young mothers, ages 16 and 17, who had between them 13 children, most of them fathered by different men; not one of these young women was receiving financial help from any of the men.

There are, of course, a number of reasons why women still consort with men — social, recreational, and sexual reasons. Yet as I interviewed the women of St Kitts, I could see that their reasons were often highly practical, for they would suggest in subtle ways that eventually a woman should find a man who will help her. If the man is not married and the relationship is reasonably stable and children born of it, they may even establish coresidence. Some women, however, told me the best situation is to have a man provide them with money, goods, and services of various kinds without moving in, since he is less likely to try to dominate and control under these circumstances. Coresidence often means the man moves into the woman's established household, and under these conditions he nearly always asserts what he perceives as his proper dominance. One informant told me she actually had some regrets about her boyfriend moving in, despite the fact that his income provided her with some economic stability. Another younger woman angrily explained that men move into your house and then run around with other women anyway. She wanted a man to help support her, not live with her. However, the search for a stable relationship may be difficult and long. One young friend of mine (whose letter appears at the beginning of this Chapter) had had a series of boyfriends since her first baby was born when she was 15. After she found out she was pregnant for the fourth time, she told me that each child had a different father — an admission which caused her much embarrassment — and that although she 'went' with men who might eventually help her out, all she got from them was a baby. I heard a number of tales such as this during my last field research on the island. While I was investigating the socioeconomic context of infant feeding, the word was spread that I was interested in talking with young mothers about the problems they have in taking care of their families; several of them came to me, volunteering to talk for no other motive than to have an opportunity to express their most important concerns.

Occasionally a young woman will marry her boyfriend after the first child is born, particularly if she comes from a middle-class or upwardly mobile family. Most young adults, however, establish and terminate a succession of relationships with sexual partners that are relatively casual, entailing neither coresidence nor a wide range of mutual responsibilities. For the young mothers, lacking a husband or steady beau, friends with regular incomes, adult children earning a living, or steady employment, these years may, indeed, be hard. In the language of network analysis, these are the years when the range of social networks is narrow; that is, the women have relatively few direct contacts and few types of contacts in their personal networks. The links that do exist in these 'webs' of relationships are often not productive resources anyway, since they are usually peers who are in the same stage of life and facing essentially the same problems. To state the problem in a different fashion, at this stage of the life-cycle, most Kittitians have relatively few social resources to tap.

Another sure investment in the future expansion of social networks is expressed in the bearing of children. I am not suggesting that women make conscious decisions to have eight or ten children in order to add a number of links in their networks of social resources: most of them do not make decisions about having babies, a matter that seems to them to lie outside their control. Nevertheless, the young mothers who are struggling to feed their families now know that those youngsters will grow up to help them when they are older and, perhaps, unable to care for themselves. To that extent, children are an investment, a short-run expense that usually pays off in the long run. This view of children is a realistic one. One young woman, now a mother of six children, was discussing with me the plight of an old man in the village who was ill and going blind. After 40 years of working in the sugar cane fields he had retired from the estate with a pension that provided him with the equivalent of about one U.S. dollar a week. He was the same man who rejected help from a cousin in the village who brought him food, because he feared she was trying to poison him with obeah. 'If he had children,' my friend told me, 'he would not be hungry.' 'Your children will feed you when you are old.' Time and again I was told that the only people you can trust to help you are your mother, your grandmother, and your children. They are your social security.

My ethnographic observations confirm the value of offspring to older people. One of the women with whom I worked in the gathering of cultural data on several occasions is a 75-year-old great-grandmother. She and her husband expanded their house a few years ago, making it one of the largest dwellings in the village and comfortable for themselves and the four great-granddaughters who live with them. When we discussed her financial security, I found that her husband still works and she still gardens in the mountain; I also heard about all the friends and relatives that send her remittances. She has a large network of people-children, grandchildren, nieces, nephews, and their kin — who provide her with all kinds of goods and services, and she speaks of her success in terms of these social resources. Of course, not all the childless older villagers are living in the poverty of the old cane worker above, nor are all grandparents as successful as my informant; however, for many, having children who recognize the traditional obligations of lineal kinship is the only way to assure even a minimally comfortable old age.

The implications of this social situation and perception of the value of children for family planning programs are important. Dissemination of birth control information and paraphernalia has had little impact on the high Kittitian birth rate. Although a variety of cultural features (such as demonstrations of masculinity) interferes with the success of such programs, this need for a personal network of resources as a hedge against poverty in old age is a major contributing factor. However, a letter from a friend I received just a short while ago suggests that the problem of birth control goes beyond these simple explanations:

Yes V. has her baby and if she dont be careful she will end up getting a next one. The baby is getting on fine for the present. A lot of these young girls presently now is pregnant I hope Im finish with that I have enough on my hand they are taking a lot out of me. Even those who was on the pill for a long period still find themselves pregnant. With the cost of living so high I just cant see hoe we will survive in this land at all. The Government here is seeking for independence and this place is so full of unemployed people? What is going to happen later.

Instead of seeing both the men and children in a woman's life as economically and, perhaps, psychologically draining, we must view them as a part of a larger strategy in which being involved in a variety of relationships with a large number of people in different geographic settings under a variety of economic conditions maximizes a woman's life chances. Either these people will send remittances to her in St Kitts, or she may join them where they live and work herself. Having such a social network broadens and extends the economic base of an individual female.

Other people, such as friends, employers, and so on, are incorporated into networks in the same way. I gained a great deal of information about the formation and function of social networks through personal involvement in several. During my first field trip, I met a young woman who worked for the landlord of the house I rented, who also was hired to help me with the care of my children. Our relationship was relatively impersonal for the first three months, separated as we were by social distance imposed by our racial, cultural, and class differences. Eventually, the distance diminished, and on subsequent trips to St Kitts I hired her in the capacity of 'research assistant,' and we have worked together on several subsequent projects. Nevertheless, I was somewhat disturbed by the regular requests for clothing, magazines, and other items 'from the States'. When two other close relationships began to involve similar requests, I came to realize more clearly how important overseas ties are to Kittitians, and in what ways being kin or friend to someone on the island means being a social resource. Two of these relationships were clarified and structured recently by the extension of fictive kin ties to me. One woman, my friend and assistant, told me that I had 'come as a mother' to her, and at Christmastime I received a beautiful Christmas card from her designed 'for mother'. I knew that she meant that I do things for her that one's mother usually does, providing economic help, support, and advice. The economic bond between us was also reinforced by affection and mutual respect. In the second case, my young friend whose plight is suggested in the opening paragraph, named me the godmother of her new baby.

Gradually, then, a young woman builds her network. If she is successful in her strategy, she may have a number of links that provide her with money and other items, either regularly or sporadically, and be fairly secure in this socioeconomic niche. Because my friend above is a hardworking female, and thus a generally respected member of the village, she has been largely successful in this fashion. She has an employed boyfriend with whom she lives, another ex-boyfriend (father of her first three children) who provides money and clothes from time to time, a mother in St Croix who occasionally sends money, a neighbour who provides food when she can, a friend in whose garden she sometimes works in exchange for produce, and myself.

Figure 9.1   *Two overlapping socioeconomic networks*

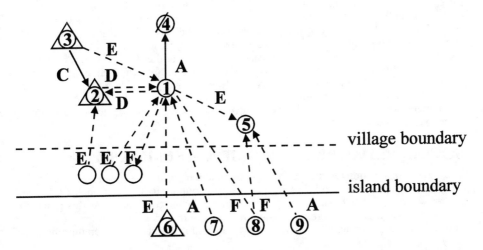

The contrast between the rudimentary networks of teenage mothers, who are transitional between childhood and adulthood, and those fully developed networks of older women is generally impressive. In order to demonstrate the difference, the following figures of two overlapping networks are included. Figure 9.1, for example, presents most of the primary figures in the networks of two young women whom I know well; one was 17 when the data were collected, and the other was 29–years–old. Individual number 1 is the older of the two. She, H., is the person discussed above, who is living in consensual union with her boyfriend, number 2. Both of them work whenever and wherever they can, and each contributes to the maintenance of the household, which also contains six children. Number 3 is a neighbor who is relatively well off and provides work for H. and her boyfriend, at a variety of tasks. His wife also gives them foodstuffs when she has extra items. H. gave food and money to her grandmother, in turn, until the old woman died recently. Both she and her boyfriend know people in other villages from whom they receive bits of food from time to time, in exchange for little favors, such as picking up packages for them in town, helping them dig sweet potatoes, and so on. (These individuals have not been numbered.) Number 6 is H.'s ex-boyfriend, and number 7 is her mother; number 8 is the village anthropologist, myself.

Figure 9.2   *Network of teenaged female*

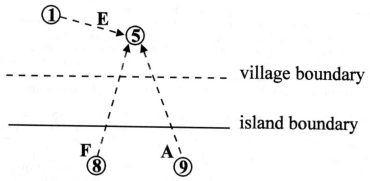

H. also helps out number 5, V., when she can because V. is 'something to' her boyfriend; that is, H.'s beau is a cousin of V., and H. feels some obligation to help the unfortunate girl. As figures 9.1 and 9.2 illustrate, V. has very few social resources in the form of helping relationships. Only H., her mother, and I come to her aid, and none of us is a regular patron. She and her four small children live with a cousin who is 13 and her baby in a two-room, two-bed, shack. V.'s children are all ill and grossly undernourished, their apathy and listlessness, their bloated bodies and fine, discolored hair suggesting too little protein. She herself is not well, and each pregnancy causes her increasing difficulties. The severity of her plight is exceptional, even though the general problems are common among the very young mothers. She is, in part, a victim of acts that are considered deviant by Kittitian standards: when her mother left the island to look for work, she did not adequately provide for the care of the three children she left behind, requiring V. to be essentially on her own before she was an adolescent. Furthermore, her mother rarely sends her remittances even now, as she should according to custom. The general features of her condition, however, are not unusual for a lower-class female of her age category.

SOCIAL NETWORKS OF WOMEN: A SUMMARY

The broad lines of this research on socioeconomic networks of Kittitian women indicate three major stages of network involvement during adulthood. The first begins at adolescence, when sexual behaviour — and often maternity — commence. At this point, the roles of boys and girls diverge, as girls often must assume adult roles and responsibilities and their male peers 'lime,' which is to say, do nothing, but with a certain amount of style. Women, who perceive themselves as hardworking people, often condemn these boys as 'worthless'. In truth, for many of them no legitimate work is available, and they mark time until they get an opportunity to go overseas. For them there is no clear-cut rite of passage into adulthood that motherhood provides their girlfriends. Having relatively few relationships with employed males, employed friends, and potential employers, the teenage mothers have few social resources to exploit. Yet they can begin to build more ties, which can be activated in time ot need, and gradually extend the range of their social networks. As adults, many of these women may be receiving help from a number of different men with whom they have had sexual relationships, friends with jobs or land to work, well-to-do neighbors, and kin in strategic places. Certainly adult women in the lower socioeconomic stratum of Kittitian society do not themselves become well off; most of them do not even become comfortable by U.S. standards. Few ever have indoor plumbing, many do not have electricity. Most continue to live in homes that are much too small for the whole family, even by their own standards. But the large majority of these adult women have enough food to feed their families adequately; many can provide sufficient clothing for themselves and their children.

As these women mature and reach the later years of adulthood — and the last stage of network involvement — network links begin to die or move on. While some older people continue to maintain small gardens by their homes or in the mountain, actual wage employment is unavailable, and income drops. Some old women try to live on the welfare payments, which are grossly inadequate. Living conditions are not so grim, however, for old women with a large number of lineal kinfolk working. Some of these women actually do quite well with all their remittances coming in regularly, especially if they have only a few relatives (such as grandchildren in the home) to support. For them there is adequate money and sufficient food. For old women without such kin network links, primarily those that remained childless, or for many old men, aid from social sources is minimal.

MODERNIZATION, THE MIDDLE CLASS, AND THE ROLE OF WOMEN

Much of the contemporary literature concerning women of the world deals with the effects of industrialization, urbanization, and other trends of modern society on the traditional roles that they have played in the past. A great deal of this material dwells on the destruction and major changes in the life-style of women that accompany technological and economic modification, focussing on the alterations in the basic institutions of societies, such as the family. Since women in many parts of the world were restricted to the 'private' or family domain, and their major roles were those associated with being a wife and mother, changing family life virtually required changing female roles.

Some of this impact has been felt in St Kitts. Here, however, the major changes have been political, rather than technological and economic. Over the years that St Kitts was a British colony, and especially since 1967, when the island state of St Kitts-Nevis-Anguilla was granted independence, there has been a trend toward self-government and democratization. Control over internal affairs now rests with the government in Basseterre, and the political bureaucracy grows each year. As career opportunities open up for black Kittitians, both men and women, the island's middle class also grows. The village in which this research was conducted contained such a growing mid-stratum, in part because of its advantageous position vis-a-vis the government and business offices of Basseterre. Only two of the women in the circle of friends and informants involved in research could be classified as middle class by virtue of their educational level, occupation, and life-style; however, ethnographic observations of village women suggested some of the ways that upward social mobility specifically affects them. First, relationships with men are different, since marriage is essential in the middle-class life-style. These women rarely have children by several different men, and they do not live in consensual union with boyfriends. They are likely to marry earlier in life than lower stratum women and to remain married to the same person, since divorce is rare. Having ties with many males, which is adaptive for poor women, is neither necessary nor proper for those in the Kittitian mid-stratum, since their men are very likely to have stable, nonseasonal, jobs or professions and adequate incomes. Furthermore, women of this class usually continue to work, as well, providing the family with two incomes. Middle-class accoutrements, such as electricity, indoor plumbing, refrigeration, television sets, are thus made possible by the efforts of two employed individuals.

Middle-class Kittitian women also lead more private lives than those in the lower stratum. Some of them interact very little with the neighbors in the village, and are rarely seen at social functions in the countryside, outside of church services. The married women of the middle class, of course, are likely to have more roles to play in the private domain, being both wives and mothers, than their lower stratum counterparts; furthermore, there is a certain amount of social distance between the classes, even in the small villages of St. Kitts. I have heard middle-class women complain that all their neighbors do is sit around and gossip, while those neighbors accuse them of snobbery. One of the middle-class women was critically called 'The Queen of C. village' by some of the older children. The females in this higher social stratum tend to have more 'urban' relationships, actually, than local relationships in their networks. Their employers and many of their friends live in the capital.

In a sense, there are more restrictions and constraints on the women in the higher socioeconomic levels than on those in the lower, less flexibility and less mobility. The former are tied, to an extent, to their homes by their private roles. One reflection of their different life-style lies in the narrowing of their networks, the relatively few people (men,children,employers,neighbors) with whom they have regular, sporadic, or potential relationships involving mutual help. The middle-class women depend less on a broad range of social relationships, any one of which may fail at some point, than upon a narrow network composed of generally stable links.

CONCLUSION

This ethnographic evidence indicates that the traditional patterns of life of most lower-class women on St Kitts are changing relatively little under the impact of modernization. The history of slavery and continuing domination of sugar estates restricted the development of local groups, such as kin groups, which operated as subsistence and economic units, and in which the women might have played a specific and formal part. Instead, the individuated social structure and the patterns of social and geographic mobility developed as people, both men and women, sought ways of exploiting fluctuating and unpredictable resources beyond their direct control. The success of women, the domestic unit, and the social system itself depended upon the ability of the female to be mobile, flexible, and resourceful, rather than tied to a specific structure or role. Women were never totally relegated to strictly domestic roles; indeed the traditional system in the lower stratum mitigated against such constraints. Because of its very nature, generalized and adaptive, rather than specifically adapted, the socioeconomic system and women's roles within it are changing relatively little. Activities and life-style of the women in the lower stratum of society in St Kitts need change little, as long as the new technologies and economics can be reached and exploited by a link in a social network.

NOTES

1. This research was funded by NIMH grant 1 FO1 MH51587-01. I conducted further work on infant feeding in 1976 with a grant from The Human Lactation Center. My thanks, too, to Ms Sue Wolkow for the network figures, and to M. Cathey Maze for perspectives on the adaptive features of networks.

2. Christopher Columbus named the island St Christopher, but it quickly was nicknamed St Kitts. The official name is still St Christopher, but the shorter 'St Kitts' is used far more commonly.

REFERENCES

Freilich, Morris 1970 'Mohawk Heroes and Trinidadian Peasants.' In *Marginal Natives*, M. Freilich, ed. New York: Harper and Row.

Gonzalez, Nancie 1970 'Toward a Definition of Matrifocality' In *Afro-American Anthropology*, Norman Whitten and John Szwed, eds. New York: The Free Press.

Merrill, Gordon C. 1958 *The Historical Georgraphy of St. Kitts and Nevis, The West Indies*. Instituto Pan Americano de Geografia e Historia. Mexico, No. 232.

Parry, John H. and P. M. Sherlock 1956 *A Short History of the West Indies*. London: Macmillan.

St Kitts-Nevis-Anguilla 1972 *Digest of Statistics* No. 8. St Kitts: The Statistical Department.

University of the West Indies 1975 *1970 Population Census of the Commonwealth Caribbean*, Vol. 6, Part 3. Kingston, Jamaica: Census Research Programme.

Whitten, Norman 1970 'Strategies of Adaptive Mobility in the Columbian-Ecuadorian Littoral,' in *Afro-American Anthropology*, Norman Whitten and John Szwed, eds. New York: The Free Press.

Wolf, Eric R. 1966 *Peasants*. Englewood Cliffs, New Jersey: Prentice Hall, Inc.

K. F. Olwig

THE MIGRATION EXPERIENCE: NEVISIAN WOMEN AT HOME AND ABROAD

Anthropologists have long been interested in the special role of women in the West Indian family. Family studies from the 1950s and 1960s noted an absence of men in many of the domestic units and emphasized the central role of women as *de facto* household heads, rearing and providing for the children. Due to this importance of women, the family was designated matrifocal. This family system was, furthermore, often described as a variant, caused by the heritage of slavery and poverty, of a European nuclear family ideal inculcated in the Afro-Caribbean population by the colonial churches and schools (Smith 1956, 1973; Gonzalez 1970; Smith 1966). During the 1970s increasing attention was paid to the fact that although women tend to manage domestic affairs, they do this with networks of relatives and neighbours, who help with child rearing, grant economic support and provide the necessary labour. These networks have been seen to derive in part from the Afro-Caribbean heritage of the West Indians and in part from their adaptation and resistance to the constraints of oppression (Brown 1977; Gussler 1980; Olwig 1985; Sutton and Makiesky-Barrow 1977).

The focus on kin networks has drawn attention to the fact that, while women may play a central role in domestic units, men do in fact contribute to the household through support networks, though their economic assistance is often less regular than that of women. Furthermore, male support may be given to several different households, including the maternal one, the domestic units of current and prior spouses, as well as to those of their offspring. The importance of men in the extra-domestic sphere has also been emphasized in studies of men's social life (liming) in the public arena (Wilson 1971; Tobias 1975; Lieber 1976; Brana-Shute 1976; Abrahams 1983).

While women are tied to one particular domestic unit for which they assume responsibility, men have considerable freedom with respect to membership in a domestic unit and may, in fact, display allegiance to several domestic units at one time. Furthermore, women and men are delegated to different spheres; women to the private, domestic arena with its social reproductive functions, supported by a network of kin, including men; men to the public sphere outside the home, where they engage in the money economy and associate with friends.

These two spheres reflect an ideal conceptualization of family structure, which emphasizes the importance of keeping women in the home, supported by men who act as bread winners and represent the family in the society at large. This ideal reflects British cultural values and has been introduced largely by colonial officials through the church and schools (Wilson 1969; Abrahams 1983; Olwig 1987, 1989). It does not, however, match the social and economic reality of West Indian society and West Indian women cannot be characterized as primarily dependent housewives confined to the home. Despite the fact that, since the formative stage of West Indian society, women have been jural minors and linked *ideologically* to 'domestic' activities' (Smith 1987: 167), they have played crucial roles in extra-domestic affairs, including economic ones.

West Indian women, therefore, have had to deal with the fact that they are actively involved in the greater society, even though the family ideal restricts them to the private domestic sphere. As one might imagine, this situation is less problematic within the local community, for women situate their activities within networks of domestic relations, which cushion the effect of the women's involvement in extra-domestic affairs. The women's position is more difficult (and the strategies they devise to deal with it more apparent) in the migration situation, in which they leave their home community in search of wage employment. While male migration would seem to be a natural extension of the men's position in the wider, public community, and their attempt to play the role of provider for their families, such migration on the part of women clearly constitutes a break from their domestic world of relatives and neighbours. The main problem for the women who emigrate, therefore, appears to be that of reconstituting their network in the migration destination. This process, ironically, is made difficult by the fact that, even though migrant women have left the protective sphere of the network of their natal community, they remain important in it as social and economic resources. Thus they continue to have strong obligations in their home island, which make it difficult for them to generate their own network abroad.

IMPORTANCE OF MIGRATION

Nevis has been heavily affected by migration since the abolition of slavery in 1834. It had little to offer the freed slaves other than poorly paid menial jobs as labourers on plantations that had dominated the island for centuries.[1] Emigration in search of economic opportunities abroad was an attractive alternative and, as early as 1835, 157 Nevisians left for British Guiana. By 1846, 2,441 had migrated to Trinidad (Richardson 1983: 88). Emigration from the island continued throughout the nineteenth and twentieth centuries to the gold mines in Venezuela, to the large sugar plantations in Cuba and the Dominican Republic, to help construct the Panama Canal, to the domestic and industrial sectors on the east coast of the US, to the oil refineries on the Dutch West Indian islands (see Chapter 2), to the industries and public services in Great Britain, and to tourism in the Virgin Islands and the Dutch island of St Martin (see Richardson 1983). While much of the early emigration was temporary and tied to short-term economic opportunities, the more recent emigration to England and nearby West Indian islands, which has involved thousands of Nevisians, has been more permanent (Richardson 1983: 147).

In many ways Nevis presents a classic case of the effects of out-migration. During the 1960s Richard Frucht (1972: 279-81) carried out a community study on the island in which he documented the migration of thousands of Nevisians to England and the Virgin Islands. More than half the households he studied had migrant members; almost 45 per cent consisted of grandparents and grandchildren; and over 70 per cent of the households heads were above 50 years of age. A study of the island's folklore by Roger Abrahams (1983: 10-18) at about the same time showed that, as the local community disintegrated through heavy out-migration, many of the social events and cultural traditions, such as Christmas celebrations and the tea party, were on the verge of dying out.

Geographer Bonham Richardson (1983), who did research on the island during the 1970s, documents the huge impact of emigration on the island's agriculture, the mainstay of its economy. The cultivation of subsistence and cash crops on small farms, which had taken the place of plantation production by the middle of the century, declined markedly with the loss of so many economically active members of the community; in its place emerged a pattern of extensive cattle grazing which needed little labour. Furthermore, these herds of animals were 'walking banks' for the emigrants who had largely financed the increasing cattle population by investing in livestock on the island. The 1980 census (Population Census of the Commonwealth Caribbean 1980-81: 4) recorded a population of 9428, the lowest since the abolition of slavery.[2] Today it is estimated that the majority of the Nevisian-born population has settled in destinations as far away as England, the US and Canada, as well as on the nearby British, US and Dutch islands.

Though emigration has taken a heavy toll on the island society, it is incorrect to speak of a breakdown of the Nevisian community as such. Rather, the Nevisian community has redirected itself outwards to include and centre on Nevisians living and working abroad. Richardson (1983: 48) suggests that 'outside remittances account for more disposable income on the two islands than any other source, including the St Kitts' sugar industry'. The dispersed families are united primarily at burials and cultural events such as carnival celebrations, which are supported by returning migrants (Richardson 1983: 51-4, 174, 181; Sutton 1986). Nevisian geographer Carolyn Liburd (1984: 57) made a detailed study of the nature of the remittances sent to Nevis from abroad, in which she documents the increase in calls by ships transporting goods from nearby West Indian migration destinations from 61 calls in 1969 to a peak of 163 calls in 1979. A closer examination of the content of one boat arriving in November 1983 revealed not just luxury items such as antennas, mixers and liquor, but also household necessities such as beds, tables, chairs, plastic buckets, mops, brooms and foodstuffs (Liburd 1984: 59-60). Nevisians have clearly come to depend on the migrants even for the everyday essentials of life.

PARTICIPATION IN MIGRATION

Throughout the history of emigration from Nevis, men have left the island in greater numbers than women. This is reflected in population censuses of Nevis, which reveal a consistent, female bias.

Table 9.1 *Sexual composition of Nevis population, 1844-1970*

Year	Men		Women	
1844	4418	46%	5153	54%
1861	4734	48%	5088	52%
1871	5433	47%	6247	53%
1881	5436	47%	6248	53%
1891	5945	45%	7142	55%
1901	5605	44%	7424	56%
1911	5521	43%	7424	57%
1921	4678	40%	6891	60%
1946	5062	44%	6326	56%
1960	5653	44%	7117	56%
1970	5186	46%	6064	54%
1980	4426	47%	5002	53%

Sources: Richardson 1983: 93, 132, 146; Population Census of the Commonwealth Caribbean 1980-81:4

Though men have been more prominent in migration, women have also been active. Statistics on post-emancipation emigration from Nevis to Trinidad show that 44 per cent of the migrants were women (Richardson 1983: 88). Female participation seems to fluctuate as employment opportunities for women vary. Thus, during the first two decades of this century, when canal work in Panama provided the major attraction for migrants, male emigration predominated and, by 1921, the proportion of males in the Nevis population had dropped to 40 per cent. During recent decades, when tourism and industry have provided ample opportunity for female as well as male employment abroad, women have emigrated in large numbers. The 1980 census of Nevis found that women constituted 55 per cent of the net migration from Nevis between 1970 and 1980 (Population Census of the Commonwealth Caribbean 1980-81: 4) and that the proportion of males in the Nevis population had correspondingly increased. Women have been involved in migration both in staying behind in the domestic unit to care and provide for a residential family and in leaving to exploit economic opportunities outside the island. Family networks have provided an important basis for women's lives both within the rural community of Nevis and in the complex societies of the migration destinations.

FAMILY NETWORKS

The basic building block in kin networks, which provides continuity and stability in the Nevisian community, is the tie between mother and child. In General, the parent-child tie involves, on one hand, the obligation to clothe, feed and care for the child and, on the other, the right to expect help and support from the child as soon as it is able to contribute in any way. In the West Indies the parent-child tie tends to be concentrated on the mother-child relationship, partly because it is common for young Nevisians to engage in a number of child-bearing sexual unions before settling down to one mate. This typically results in the fathers having children in several households, whereas the mothers usually have all, or at least most, of their children living with them.[3] The relative unimportance of the father-child tie in the domestic unit is reflected in a survey of Nevisian school children carried out in the mid-1980s, which showed that single mothers cared for the greatest proportion of children (38 per cent), followed by grandparents (29 per cent) and both parents (26 per cent) (Edwards n.d: 44).

The female bias in the parent-child relationship is strengthened by the fact that children are reared in the female sphere of the household or yard, a fenced-in area inhabited by a family living in one or more houses (see Chapter 3). Though very young children can impose a heavy burden on women, they constitute an important source of labour power at quite an early age. In the rural communities, which dominate on Nevis, most households are involved, not just in domestic activities such as child care and housework, but also in some farming, including cultivating a vegetable plot and rearing livestock. Women manage these household affairs with the help of older children, who do most of the work outside the domestic unit, including fetching water at the public stand-pipe, collecting firewood or tending animals in the bush. In this way the women are able to concentrate on activities in the yard or fields, which the family either owns or leases. With the help of children women can therefore maintain an appearance of remaining within the domestic sphere, even though they are, in fact, actively involved in economic activities that extend beyond the household.

Few, if any, Nevisian households depend entirely on the limited income that can be generated from farming. Unless they have the educational qualifications to obtain a civil service job, work opportunities for women on Nevis are limited and confined to wage employment in tourism and light industry. While wage employment is regarded as attractive and suitable for women, for it takes place indoors in respectable surroundings patronized or owned by people from Western countries, it is poorly paid and often rather irregular. Remuneration is further decreased if the women must pay for child care and transport to and from work. Wage employment therefore does not grant them any sort of economic security. On the contrary, they remain dependent on the domestic units of the rural communities for basic subsistence produce and child care. For the vast majority of women, a respectable and secure life therefore depends on their ability to build networks of mutual aid and support, both on Nevis and in the various migration destinations outside Nevis.

A sexual relationship constitutes an important basis for developing networks among young women. In the short run it brings some support from the man and in the long run it produces children, who are vital future links in the mother's networks. As long as the sexual tie endures, the man usually provides some support for the woman and her eventual children; but as soon as it is cut off and the couple begin to turn toward other relationships, it is not uncommon for the man to stop providing any kind of support.

This is largely because, since the father has children with other women living in different domestic units, father-child ties are subject to conflicting demands. The mother-child tie, however is usually permanent and free of such conflicts of interest; women are therefore often the main providers for children and the main beneficiaries of support from adult children. Many young women with small children, who have only limited networks of their own, therefore prefer to remain in their mother's yard, where they can benefit from the remittances she receives.

For women without a family network, rearing children to adulthood can present great problems. For example, I. N. was 26–years–old and expecting her sixth child. Her five children aged one to 12 years, all boys, were fathered by two different men and the sixth was with a third. The two fathers provided no support for the children and she would not take them to court, but her present boyfriend helped out. Without his support she would have found it difficult to manage on her part-time job as a maid. She lived by herself and her only external support came from an aunt on St Kitts, who had taken care of her when her mother died during her infancy. She placed great hope in her children and was supportive of her oldest son's desire to become a doctor. She wanted the rest to follow him in this, 'to become something big'. Her hopes were rather unrealistic, for it would be difficult for her to provide proper education for so many children on her limited resources.

This woman's expectations for her children were not unusual. The inculcation of high ambitions in children by their parents, particularly their mothers was quite apparent in a questionnaire survey I carried out among schoolchildren on the island in 1981. It showed that most children were very career oriented, hoping to obtain white collar jobs as teachers, civil servants or professionals, even though their educational qualifications were often inadequate and their actual chances of obtaining the required training limited (Olwig 1987: 162-4). The mothers' desire to see their children do well does not merely reflect their wish for a better life for their children than they have had themselves. It also reveals that, after many years of struggles and personal sacrifice, mothers hope to see the fruits of their labour in terms of financial support from their offspring. This was emphasized by another woman, who put it more bluntly than most. 'People get children to get help, help in the home and yard, and when they become grown up they can give back what you have spent on them.'

The mother-child tie thus links women into the kin network. With help from their young children they can maintain an appearance of respectability in the domestic unit, even though their economic activities extend beyond it. As the children grow older they form links in wider networks, which provide an important economic and social context for women's lives. On an island as heavily influenced by migration as Nevis, the networks cannot be confined to Nevis, but must extend to the migration destinations within which Nevisians are involved.

HOME COMMUNITY

The impermanence of sexual relationships, the difficulties in obtaining support from children's fathers and the dependence on economic assistance from one's offspring are all accentuated in the migration situation. Many of the women interviewed on Nevis had lost touch with their children's fathers through emigration, or found it difficult to put pressure on men living abroad to send them money.

One difficulty women experience in bringing up their children is that, with the influx of food, clothing and other material goods sent by migrants abroad, Nevisians have grown accustomed to a Western life style, which costs far more than the women living on Nevis can earn. The young women most satisfied with their situation were either living with mothers receiving support from abroad, or were closely connected with emigrant relatives. Some of the greatest difficulties were experienced by married women dependent on husbands living at home. One woman whose husband was a mason complained: 'If the father is not working, because he can't find any work, it is hard to find something to give the children. When there is no food in the house, the children can't understand nothing is there, and when there is no money you cannot buy the clothes that the children want. All I have is an auntie in England, who sends things sometimes, but she has children herself to look after.' This woman was looking forward to the possibility of her husband obtaining a visa to go to St Croix, so that he could work there and send money back for her and the children. She hoped that some of her children would leave the island 'to get something outside'.

It is instilled into children from an early age that if they have any 'mind' and ambition they will emigrate so that they can help the family left behind.[4] From children's answers to a questionnaire about why they wanted to emigrate, it became apparent that maternal pressure was an important factor. One young student simply replied 'because my mother told me so' (Olwig 1987: 164). Most children, who see all wealth coming from abroad, quickly perceive the importance of emigration. One woman proudly explained that her six–year–old boy was already talking about whom he was going to support when he was earning good money abroad. When asked about the ideal number of children they would like to have, the women usually took it into account that some of them would be leaving the island and one warned against having too few, saying: 'If you have only one or two children, they might go away, leave you alone. But with more children, one will stay behind.'

The benefits of having reared a number of children properly and taught them to appreciate everything that their mother had done for them accrued to the older generation of women on Nevis, the parental generation of mothers. These women had seen their children leave the island during the large-scale migratory movements after the Second World War and it was quite apparent that some of them were flourishing, resting on the laurels of their good work, while others had not been quite so fortunate.

One woman who had done well was Mrs L. She had a son and daughter in England, three daughters (of whom one was a teacher) and one son in the Virgin Islands, and one daughter (a nurse) in the US. The sons seemed to be 'afraid of pen and paper' and rarely wrote, but the daughters sent letters regularly, including some money for their mother. Before writing home, the daughter in England often called her brother and he would send a message and some money; the sisters in the Virgin Islands sometimes did the same thing with their brother. The children had paid for the building of an addition to Mrs L's house and the installation of electricity and running water. Mrs L was well satisfied with her lot and refused to move to the Virgin Islands to join her children there, as they would like her to do, preferring to stay in her own house in her home village. She explained her children's help as a mother's just reward: 'Look, I reared them, and now they keep me up, because they send me food, they send me clothes, they send me money. I reaped my reward, you understand. You sow good seed, you reap good fruit.' Her situation was in marked contrast to that of another elderly woman living down the road who received no support because she had no children. She lived in a tiny shack with no electricity or water and had to go begging for food.

For these women, migration was thus less about people leaving the island to live and work elsewhere than about extending the domestic unit to include people working abroad, in some cases thousand of miles away. The idea of the household not necessarily being a residential unit, but rather a tight network of exchanges of support, seems to be commonly accepted among the Nevisians. Many of the schoolchildren who answered the questionnaire I gave them in 1981 were unsure about whom to include in their household and a number of them listed relatives working abroad (Olwig 1987: 156-8). Ties between the domestic unit on Nevis and those who have emigrated from it are apparently so close that the emigrants are regarded as part of the household. This view is also reflected in Liburd's (1984) research on migration from Nevis since 1950, which showed 96 per cent of the households studied to have members living abroad.

In the Nevisian migration community the household is therefore less of a residential unit than a group of people engaged in the 'pooling of goods and services, placing at the disposition of its members what is indispensable to them' (Sahlins 1972: 94). Perhaps it is not so strange that West Indian households conform to those of the primitive societies analysed by Sahlins, for in many ways West Indians have become 'hunters and gatherer's in the modern world economy, on the look out for new economic opportunities.

LEAVING THE ISLAND

Great Britain and the United States have been important migration destinations for West Indians looking for unskilled work, and several thousand Nevisians have settled in these two countries over the past few decades. Today the small US Virgin Island of St John (which is dominated by tourism) and the industrial city of Leeds in northern England contain sizable Nevisian populations. While these destinations have provided widely different social and economic conditions for these migrants, Nevisian motives for emigration to them were similar: they wished to 'better' themselves. Men and women express this wish for betterment, however, in rather contrasting ways.

In a study of out-migration from Grenada, Tobias (1975: 135, 214) suggests that 'manliness and liming are central to Grenadian migration' and that 'freedom implies the ability to leave Grenada with the least fuss, leaving the fewest obligations behind'. For the men, who may not be tied to a particular domestic unit, with its social and economic obligations, and who are allowed to, even expected to, spend much of their time outside the home, migration in search of personal freedom and exciting adventure can be seen as a natural extension of their wide array of extra-domestic activities.

For women, however, migration presents problems. With their close association with the domestic sphere, most of them are vital members of a household (usually their mother's) when they migrate and have a moral obligation to support it, especially since many of them leave one or more of their children behind in the care of their mother. In the case of St John, over a third of the women I interviewed had left children on Nevis (usually with their maternal grandmother) and felt strongly indebted to their mothers for enabling them to emigrate. Many of the men had been able to pay much, or all of the cost involved in emigrating, having had wage employment on Nevis and being subject to fewer domestic demands than the women. The women, on the other hand, left from their parental household and, directly or indirectly, their mothers provided the money for their passage, for the young women were in no position to earn enough on Nevis to pay for it themselves. In many cases the mother also used her extensive network of friends and relatives to make arrangements with a Nevisian abroad to receive her daughter and help her find work and a place to stay, while in the case of men, it was often male friends who helped one another in the migration situation.

By the time the young women left Nevis, they therefore knew that their mothers had already expended considerable effort and money to help them. (See also Philpott 1968: 469.) There was little doubt in the young women's minds that they were expected to remain important sources of future help and economic support to the family left behind on Nevis. This was further impressed on the children as they saw the older ones leave home and realized that their chances of migrating depended on their older siblings paying back the passage money that had been expended on them. In one case, doubts about a daughter's willingness or ability to provide support for her family on Nevis actually led a mother to refuse to give her daughter the passage money when it became her turn to emigrate:

> Three of my sisters went to England before I left for the Virgin Islands. My mother did not want me to go to England, and when one of my sisters sent passage money for me, she refused to spend it on me, but decided to repair the house instead.
>
> I had one child for a young man who had gone to England some years previously. He left with a lot of promises, but after a few months he never sent any support for my child. My mother refused to send me to England fearing that I would get together with my old boyfriend have more children with him and forget all about my mother and the one child I left behind. My mother told me that she had no shots to waste on hawks, and she later sent out one of my sisters who left behind five children.
>
> As it turned, out this sister married soon after going to England and had four more children. She never sent anything and I had to help support her five children, who stayed in my mother's household, after I finally managed to emigrate to the Virgin Islands on my own and with the help of my brother on St Martin.

For women, the ability to send a money order back home after having received their first wages became an important proof of their continued loyalty. For many, however, the price of that first money order was much greater than the cash paid at the counter, for it became apparent that conditions at the new location were far more difficult than expected.

SETTLEMENT ABROAD

(a) St John

In the 1950s, West Indians began to migrate to the US Virgin Islands in order to find wage employment in the rapidly developing tourist industry. Most of them entered the islands during the 1960s under a special labour certification programme that made it possible to hire aliens on a temporary basis, provided they were guaranteed 40 hours of work and the US minimum wage. This programme began to be phased out in 1972, but most Nevisians still lived and worked on the islands under the tenuous conditions of the certification programme.[5] For many years Nevisians therefore remained in limbo, not knowing whether their visas would be terminated and they would be forced to return to Nevis. Perhaps because of this long period of uncertainty, the Nevisians I interviewed during the late 1970s had maintained even stronger ties with their family on Nevis than they might have done had they been more secure in their migration destination.

Nevisian women found in St John a rural island that in some respect reminded them of Nevis. Until the 1950s the St Johnian population lived in scattered communities and subsisted on small-scale farming, supplemented by wage employment and remittances from migrant labourers. In the mid-1950s tourism began to develop rapidly in the Virgin Islands and St John attracted an increasing number of visitors. The island was transformed from a peaceful, rural community to a major tourist resort, attracting US investors as well as workers from nearby West Indian islands among them Nevisians. This led to fierce competition among those attempting to take advantage of the tourism and hostility on the part of Virgin Islanders seeking to preserve their island community in the face of drastic change (Olwig 1985). While Nevisian women could enter the Virgin Islands legitimately in search of employment, they found they were resented by the local population and exploited by their employers — a situation made worse by the US immigration system.

According to the law, to qualify for a work permit the migrants had to be offered full-time employment at minimum wages. Most of the available female employment was in domestic work in private homes or hotels (guest houses), where few employers were able to offer full-time jobs or were willing to pay standard wages. Many women made informal arrangements with employers, who agreed to certify them under the conditions stipulated by US immigration law so long as they were not expected to live up to the requirements of the contracts — that is they might pay less than the minimum wage or offer only part-time or seasonal employment. If the women reported this to the authorities they would lose their certification and be forced to leave the Virgin Islands.

Most women were willing to put up with deplorable working conditions to get the desired labour certificate. Those who failed to obtain one before their temporary tourist visa expired had to return to British territory and re-enter the US islands on a new visitor's visa. One of the women interviewed had endured one and a half years in the Virgin Islands before she finally received certified employment:

> I came to my sister in St Thomas in 1967. She had planned for all of us to come, but I was the only one who made it, so I regard myself as the lucky one. I came on a visitor's visa and I had to go to the British Virgin Islands every time the visa expired. Sometimes I got two weeks' extension, sometimes as little as two days. While I was on a visitor's visa I lived with my sister and made a little money doing odd jobs, cleaning, ironing and baby-sitting for anybody who needed a little help. Of course, I was paid less than the minimum wage. Finally, after one and a half years, I found a certified job on St John and settled there. I did not go back to Nevis, because I had come here to help my home, and I felt that I had to stick it out. I knew there was no work on Nevis.

As soon as they started to work the women began to send regular remittances to their families on Nevis, irrespective of whether or not they could really afford it. By Nevisian standards they earned good salaries on St John (easily two to three times as much as they would have made on Nevis); however, much of this income was spent on rent and food. It was therefore quite difficult to set aside money to send to their Nevisian families, but they usually chose to eat less well or to delay paying a bill rather than disappoint their relatives. Many women also contended with poor housing, for they were unable to afford the rents demanded for better accommodation in the highly inflated tourist economy. They would resign themselves to their lot with statements such as, 'I know that I can't do better than stay where I do, because this is not my home.' This statement was typical, in fact most of them said that they did not feel at all at home on St John, but merely regarded it as a place to work and make money, not to have fun and relax. Furthermore, many stated that they did not like to 'keep company' and emphasized that they spent most of their free time at home with their children.

The only extra domestic sphere in which they all felt free to participate was the religious one. Although the women had by and large belonged to Anglican or Methodist churches on Nevis, on St John most of them chose to join more fundamentalist denominations such as the Baptists or Seventh Day Adventists. These churches offered them a warm, often emotional environment and provided various forms of social and moral support, as well as minor economic assistance to members experiencing problems. This support was generated from the other members, however, and most of the churches actually presented a rather heavy drain on their members' economic resources, expecting them to tithe and in some cases even offer additional donations. The churches therefore constituted a parallel to the women's support networks on Nevis, also they did not encourage the women to engage in local social and economic affairs, but rather preached resignation and obedience to the word of the Bible.

In general the women found that they felt much freer on Nevis, where they had relatives and could move about as they pleased; some would try to visit Nevis every year. Several of those who were married to Nevisians had built houses on Nevis after emigrating to St John; and they regarded these houses as their real homes even though they occupied them for no more than a few weeks a year. But many of the women visited Nevis far less often than would be expected given their close attachment to their family there. One reason was that, despite the short distance of only about 180 miles, the plane ticket was quite expensive. But a more important reason was that returning migrants cannot apparently come empty-handed but must live up to their Nevisian family's expectations of their great affluence abroad. As one woman explained: 'When you go back to Nevis on vacation, it is almost necessary to bring a big bag of money and six suitcases of clothes. All my relatives and godchildren come and ask me right to my face to give them something. It is really quite a rat race to go home.' Some women said they were not much better off than their family on Nevis, which was supported by all the relatives who had left the island. They did not, however, want to cause disappointment and, rather than admit that they had nothing to bring, some chose to visit less often.

One solution to the double bind of living and working on St John while maintaining expensive ties with relatives on Nevis, was to bring the relatives to the Virgin Islands. And a few early migrants did succeed in relocating their families on St John, thereby both fulfilling their family obligations on St John and drawing on their families in their everyday lives. A minority of the Nevisian women managed to resettle to the extent of forming their own families on St John and reorienting their future networks to the migration destination. These tended to be women who had their children in the Virgin Islands, either through having them sent from Nevis or having them and marrying on St John. This reorientation was most marked among those who had married St Johnians or men from other West Indian islands.

Furthermore, as they received permanent visas and entered the stage of having lived most of their lives on St John, even those who expressed the strongest attachment to Nevis and sent the most regular support, experienced a gradual distancing from their Nevisian family, especially when their parents died and they lost their main link with the home island. With the death of parents the obligation to send support to Nevis disappeared, especially if any remaining siblings on the island received remittances from their own children abroad. As all the immigrants have become more settled on the island they have begun to merge with the local population to generate a new West Indian community.

(b) Leeds

The pattern of relocation abroad was much more pronounced in Leeds. This was partly because Nevisians had not experienced the same visa problems in England as they had in the Virgin Islands. Almost all of them had settled in England by 1962, when further immigration from the West Indies was severely restricted. In England, Nevisians found themselves in a completely alien society, which forced them to establish their own, separate, West Indian community.[6]

The Nevisians who emigrated had great expectations of England as the imperial mother country. Going to England meant going to the centre of the old empire. When they found, instead, a racist society on the verge of serious economic depression, offering only menial labour at subsistence wages, they were deeply disappointed and many wished to return to Nevis. But their economic situation and obligations to their families back home prevented them from doing so.

For many of the women, the encounter with the old mother country was a long string of humiliating experiences, as one woman related:

I went to England with my oldest sister, who was 21 and came here to get married. My mother decided that I was to go with her, I was sixteen and a half .... I was leaving my parents, yet I was glad to go to England. I had gone to an Anglican school, and the minister was a white man, and he used to tell stories about England .... He used to go to England on holidays, and we would ask him to bring back pictures for us. He then took pictures in parks and other nice areas and showed the slides on a screen. We were very impressed and thought that England was paved with gold, and I day–dreamed under a tree about going to England and seeing the places the had told me about ....

I didn't like what I saw — I kept seeing chimneys and thought that all the houses were factories .... I cried non stop to go home. I didn't want to stay, and it took me ages before I got used to it.

My first job was in a bread factory .... Only three blacks worked there .... I was naive, I noticed that I did the dirty work, but didn't realize that we were put to do it .... Later I did domestic work, but I said to myself: 'Why leave home to do domestic work for others? I will do it for my parents, but not for others.' Then I got a job in a restaurant at £4 a week as a waitress, but I had to leave again as the £4 couldn't even keep me.

We stayed in rooms, where we had to share the kitchen and work in it at the same time. I didn't like that so I waited until late at night .... My parents had their own house with no one talking, spitting into you pot. I used to cry over it.

I married young and became a mother. I just did the necessary things a wife is supposed to do, stayed at home, looked after the kids, watched telly. I never knew what a pub looked like inside. Never left the kids except in the evening for work.

Despite Nevisian women having associated British culture with respectability, the norms related to female respectability were precisely those that were most offended in England. Women, who were supposed to remain in the domestic sphere or perform light work outside, could only find employment that was physically hard and dirty. Women accustomed to being autonomous in the domestic sphere found themselves confined to rooms in a flat. Not only had their traditional sphere of operation diminished to the point of being 'boxed up in packages', as another woman put it, but even the heart of female family-oriented activities, the kitchen, was intruded by total strangers, men as well as women. To make matters worse, the economic reward for this type of life was extremely poor, making it difficult for the women to fulfil their obligations to their families on Nevis. But despite the initial despair, most of the women not only succeeded in sending support (however small it may have been) to their Nevisian families, but they also managed to regain their respectability. In Leeds this was done largely through marrying and establishing an independent home.

Because of the problems West Indians encountered in England, they tended to settle in their own communities, where they are shielded against such examples of racism as signs indicating that rooms will not be rented to coloured people. However, the difficulties of finding adequate accommodation encouraged some West Indians to speculate in housing in the West Indian areas. In Leeds, West Indians live in Chapeltown, a formerly affluent section of the city with many spacious houses amenable to subdivision and rental at high prices to newcomers with little choice about where to live. Through overcrowding and exploitation the houses deteriorated to the point that many had to be abandoned. While Chapeltown still contains some boarded-up houses, many streets have been subject to urban renewal and today contain modern flats and terraced houses that can be rented or purchased at reasonable rates.

If they were able to afford it, Nevisians chose to purchase a house as soon as possible (no matter how run-down it might be) and renovate it on their own, for they realized that only through having their own home could they lead the kind of life they wanted. This required great sacrifices; the husbands often worked overtime while their wives cared for the children during the day and then worked an evening shift. But the reward was, for the men, getting a place, albeit within their home, where they could associate with other West Indians in the way they wanted to — playing calypso, having domino games and drinking. The women were able to reconstruct the domestic space they were used to having as their own. In this way they created their own version of the West Indies in England, as one young woman who was born in England experienced it:

> My home has always been West Indian. I live in Britain, but when we are within the four walls of the home we are in the West Indies: the music, the language, the cooking, the atmosphere are West Indian .... My mom and dad always talk about back home. Outside the home we are black British, at home we are West Indians.

The presence of a distinct West Indian community in Leeds, which, apart from a strong Nevisian presence also has a large number of Kitticians and increasing numbers of Jamaicans, has allowed Nevisian women to form their own ties outside their home island. These provide an important context for their social lives. The West Indian Ladies Association, formed in the late 1970s, is led mainly by Nevisian women, with six of the eight chairpersons in 1987 being Nevisian. The association organizes meetings, outings and dances for its members, thus offering a respectable place for women, otherwise confined to the home, to socialize with one another. Dues are collected every month so that flowers can be sent to members who are in hospital. The association also attempts to collect money to send to the hospital on Nevis. In 1986 the Caribbean Women's Dramatic Society was formed to present plays about the West Indian community. Its first performance was in the summer of 1987 — a play by a Kittician woman about the migration experience from a woman's point of view.

For many of the women the churches provided an important place for social activities, as well as worship. Some attended Methodist and Anglican churches, while others, as on St John, drifted toward the more fundamentalist Baptist and Pentecostal congregations. Church attendance was less regular than it had been on Nevis or St John and seemed to be a less essential aspect of the woman's lives.

While the Nevisian women were actively developing a new, respectable West Indian community in Leeds, they were also (over the 30 odd years of them having lived in Leeds) gradually developing their own family networks. These local networks have made them less dependent on the male-headed nuclear family, which many of them had established in England. The husband's social independence is offset by the woman's relative economic independence based on wage employment. Some of the women have asserted their newfound independence by refusing to tolerate their husbands' life style, seeing that divorce is a respectable solution to an unhappy marriage in Great Britain:

I made my own life and independence here. I have a right to decide what happens to me. My husband was a Nevisian, and he said to me that if we had lived in Nevis I would not have divorced him. But I replied that we were here, and I would do what the British do. In Nevis a woman wants to be a respectable wife, but then the husband will have other wives as well. My husband had other women, and I didn't want to change him, though I wanted him, if he wanted to change and saw the need to change. Black women get me mad. The husbands run around, and they accept it. I don't see why they should be so unhappy, if they can get peace for themselves.

The Nevisian women have, for such reasons, redefined their cultural value in the new situation of social and economic opportunities in which they have found themselves. In this way they have created a new life in England, which is not easily brought back to Nevis. This emerging sence of alienation from Nevis is reinforced by the fact that many of those from the older generation, who emigrated from Nevis, now have children and even grandchildren in Leeds, who generally speaking do not regard Nevis as their home island and have no desire to move there. At the same time many of the migrants no longer have close relatives on Nevis. While these women still identify themselves as West Indian and feel a close attachment to Nevis, most of them no longer wish to return to the island. Ironically, they have reached this conclusion at the very time that they are actually able to retire, sell their house and move back to Nevis.

I have been to Nevis three times, and the last time was in 1983, when I went back to stay there. When I came there many had left [the island] for work, so many of the people I had known were not there any longer. And those who were there didn't understand what I was talking about, because they had not been in England, and they didn't understand what had happened there.

I returned to England in 1984. The heat almost killed me, and I was homesick for my four daughters and one son in England. I have my own family life in England, they care for me. I have family and grandchildren in Nevis, but didn't know them so well. And the grandchildren didn't like me telling them anything.

CONCLUSION

In this study of Nevisian women I have examined what happens when women leave their home community to look for wage employment abroad. While emigration constitutes a break from the domestic sphere, this is not caused by women being confined to the domestic unit on Nevis. Rather the break occurs because, when they emigrate, the women leave the protective sphere of the family network on Nevis, which helped them integrate the ideal of confinement to the domestic sphere with their actual integration into the greater society. The network had provided a flexible context within which they could provide and care for their children without losing respectability. It also provided an important avenue of support which made it possible for women to discharge their duties without the help of a husband. Furthermore, the network enabled women to explore economic opportunities entirely outside the domestic economy both in wage employment on Nevis and work abroad.

With emigration, the Nevisian network lost its importance as a context of everyday life. Nevertheless, being under a strong obligation to provide support for their mothers who had reared them and, in most cases, helped them emigrate, the women remained vital members of the network. In this way, the network, which acted as centripetal force encouraging women to leave the island to become wage earners in an industrial economy, also locked the women into the Nevisian domestic economy, giving them a form of responsibility that was difficult to reconcile with their new life. Furthermore, while the female networks on Nevis operated within the flexible domestic sphere of the small rural communities of the West Indian island, in the migration destinations they extended to individual women, isolated in the limited private space associated with the domestic sphere of more compartmentalized and complex societies.

The success of the migrant woman therefore depends on the extent to which she can meet the conflicting demands of her obligations to her mother (as a vital person in the maternal network) and the need to develop her own networks at the migration destination. A woman who devoted all her attention to her own family abroad as soon as she emigrated would be berated for having failed in her duty to her mother. But if she remained too closely tied to her family on Nevis she soon found that her new existence abroad was reduced to work alone and that only during her short visits to Nevis did she truly live. Those who managed to lessen their obligations to the Nevis family and to develop new family networks abroad gradually found a new life outside Nevis. The women in Leeds seem to have come furthest in this process, with their obligations to Nevis now partly taken care of by the West Indian Ladies Association. Furthermore, to them migration has become a thing of the past, perhaps to be written about in plays.

The migration situation reveals how the twin poles of the Afro-Caribbean female-centred family ideal work together to create a contradictory situation in which a woman is forced to leave home in order to maintain its ideals. Immigration has enabled some of them to realize the ideal of the nuclear family (and even the status of divorcee which is predicated upon it), but the network nevertheless maintains its importance. The Afro-Caribbean family form can thus be seen to persist, even where its outward manifestation has changed. It remains, therefore, both as an ideal and as a highly concrete socio-economic reality, a vital link to the Caribbean and its cultural heritage.

NOTES

1. Further documentation and analysis of the Caribbean diaspora can be found, for example, in Thomas-Hope (1978, 1986), Marshall (1983) and Chaney (1985).

2. Barry Higman's study of slave populations in the British Caribbean shows that toward the end of slavery, the island's population was below present levels. In 1822 a total population of 9,274 was registered on Nevis (Higman 1984: 413).

3. Some women place their children in other households if they have difficulty maintaining them on their own. These households are commonly those of the children's grandparents, childless relatives, or, more rarely, strangers (see, for example, Sanford 1975; Goossen 1972; Olwig 1985). The importance of child fostering in migration is analysed by Soto (1987).

4. Philpott (1968: 468-9) makes a similar point in his discussion about migration from Montserrat.

5. For a discussion of the migration regulations in effect in the US Virgin Islands, see Committee on the Judiciary (1976). A briefer and more up-to-date summary of the migration situation in the Virgin Islands is found in Miller and Boyer (1982).

6. Various aspects of the West Indian migration experience in Great Britain are discussed in Philpott (1973), Lamur and Speckman (1975), Foner (1979), Brock (1986), Carter (1986) and Gilroy (1987).

REFERENCES

Abrahams, Roger D. (1983) *The Man-of-Words in the West Indies*. Baltimore: The Johns Hopkins University Press.

Brana-Shute, Gary (1976) 'Drinking Shops and Social Structure: Some Ideas on Lower-Class West Indian Male Behaviour'. *Urban Anthropology* 5 (1) 53-68

Brock, Colin (ed.) (1986) *The Caribbean in Europe: Aspects of the West Indian Experience in Britain, France and The Netherlands*. London: Frank Cass.

Brown, Susan E. (1977) 'Love Unites Them and Hunger Separates Them: Poor Women in the Dominican Republic'. In R. R. Reiter (ed.) *Towards an Anthropology of Women*, New York: Monthly Review Press, 322-32.

Carter, Trevor (1986) *Shattering Illusions: West Indians in British Politics.* London: Lawrence & Wishart.

Chaney, Elsa M. (1985) *Migration from the Caribbean Region: Determinants and Effects of Current Movements.* Washington DC: Centre for Immigration Policy and Refugee Assistance, Georgetown University, Hemispheric Migration Project, Occasional Paper Series.

Committee on the Judiciary (1975) *Non-immigrant Alien Labour Programme on the Virgin Islands of the United States.* House of Representatives, 94th Congress, Washington DC: US Government Printing Office.

Edwards, Elkanah D. (n.d.) *Socioeconomic Factors Contributing to Learning Difficulties among Primary School Children in Nevis.* Report, Charlestown, Nevis: Public Library.

Foner, Nancy (1979) *Jamaica Farewell: Jamaican Migrants in London.* London: Routledge & Kegan Paul.

Frucht, Richard (1972) 'Migration and the Receipt of Remittances'. In *Resource Development in the Caribbean,* Montreal: Centre for Developing-Area Studies, 275-81.

Gilroy, Paul (1987) *'There Ain't no Black in the Union Jack': The Cultural Policies of Race and Nation.* London : Hutchinson.

Gonzalez, Nancie L. Solien (1970) 'Towards a Definition of Matrifocality'. In N. E. Whitten and J. F. Szwed (eds) *Afro-American Anthropology,* New York: The Free Press, 321-44.

Goossen, Jean (1972) 'Child Sharing and Foster Parenthood in the French West Indies'. Paper presented at the American Anthropological Association, New York City.

Gussler, Judith D. (1980) 'Adaptive Strategies and Social Networks of Women in St Kitts'. In E. Bourguignon (ed.) *A World of Women,* New York: Praeger, 185-209.

Higman, B. W. (1984) *Slave Populations of the British Caribbean 1807-1834.* Baltimore: The Johns Hopkins University Press.

Lamur, Humphrey and John D. Speckman (eds) (1975) *Adaptation of Migrants from the Caribbean in the European and American Metropolis.* Amsterdam: Department of Anthropology & Non-Western Sociology, University of Amsterdam/Leiden: Department of Caribbean Studies, Royal Institute of Linguistics & Anthropology.

Liburd, Carolyn G. (1984) 'Migration from Nevis since 1950'. BA thesis, University of the West Indies, Jamaica

Lieber, Michael (1976) '"Liming" and Other Concerns: The Style of Street Embedments in Port of Spain, Trinidad'. *Urban Anthropology,* 5(4) 319-34.

Marshall, Dawn (1983) 'Toward an Understanding of Caribbean Migration'. In *US Immigration and Refugee Policy: Global and Domestic Issues,* Lexington, Mass: Lexington Books, 113-21.

Miller, Mark J. and William W. Boyer (1982) 'Foreign Workers in the USVI: History of a Dilemma'. *Caribbean Review,* 11(1) 48-51.

—Olwig, Karen Fog (1985) *Cultural Adaptation and Resistance on St John: Three Centuries of Afro-Caribbean Life.* Gainesville: University of Florida Press.

—(1987)'Children's Attitudes to the Island Community: The Aftermath of Out-migration on Nevis'. In J. Besson and J. Momsen (eds) *Land and Development in the Caribbean,* London: Macmillan Caribbean for Warwick University Caribbean Studies, 153-70.

(1989) 'The Struggle for Respectability: Methodist Missionary Activity on Nevis'. Paper presented at the 14th Annual Conference of the Society for Caribbean Studies High Leigh Confrence Centre, Hoddesdon, Hertfordshire, England, 4-6 July.

Philpott, Stuart B. (1968) 'Remittance Obligations, Social Networks and Choice among Montserratian Migrants in Britain'. *Man,* 3 (3) 465-76

—(1973) *West Indian Migration: The Montserrat Case.* London School of Economics, Monographs on Social Anthropology No.47, London: The Athlone Press.

Population Census of the Commonwealth Caribbean (1980-81) St Christopher/Nevis, 3 vols.

Richardson, Bonham C. (1983) *Caribbean Migrants.* Knoxville: The University of Tennessee Press.

Sahlins, Marshall (1972) *Stone Age Economics.* Chicago: Aldine.

Sanford, Margaret (1975) 'To Be Treated as a Child of the Home: Black Carib Child Landing in a British West Indian Society'. In T. R. Williams (ed.) *Socialization and Communication in Primary Groups*, The Hague: Mouton Publishers, 159-81.

Smith, M. G. (1966) 'Introduction'. In Edith Clarke, *My Mother Who Fathered Me*, London: George Allen & Unwin

Smith, R. T. (1956) *The Negro Family in British Guiana: Family Structure and Social Status in the Villages*. London: Routledge & Kegan Paul..

—(1973) 'The Matrifocal Family'. In J. Goody (ed.) *The Character of Kinship*, Cambridge: Cambridge University Press, 121-44.

—(1987) 'Hierarchy and the Dual Marriage System in West Indian Society'. In J. F. Collier and S. J. Yanagisako, (eds) *Gender and Kinship: Essays toward a Unified Analysis*, Stanford: Stanford University Press, 165-96.

Soto, Isa Maria (1987) 'West Indian Child Fostering: Its Role in Migrant Exchanges'. In C. R. Sutton and E. M. Chaney (eds) *Caribbean Life in New York City: Sociocultural Dimensions*, New York: Centre for Migration Studies of New York 131-49.

Sutton, Constance and Susan Makiesky-Barrow (1977) 'Social Inequality and Sexual Status in Barbados'. In A. Schlegel (ed.) *Sexual Stratification: A Cross-Cultural View*, New York: Columbia University Press, 292-325.

Sutton, Joyah Junella (1986) 'Culturama: An Analysis of a Nevisian Festival'. BA thesis, University of the West Indies, Cave Hill, Barbados.

Thomas-Hope, Elizabeth M. (1978) 'The Establishment of a Migration Tradition: British West Indian Movements to the Hispanic Caribbean in the Century after Emancipation'. In C. G. Clarke (ed.) *Caribbean Social Relations*, Liverpool; Centre for Latin American Studies, 66-81.

(1986) 'Caribbean Diaspora, the Inheritance of Slavery: Migration from the Commonwealth Caribbean'. In C. Brock (ed.) *The Caribbean in Europe*, London: Frank Cass, 15-35.

Wilson, Peter J. (1969) 'Reputation and Respectability: A Suggestion for Caribbean Ethnology'. *Man* 4(1) 70-84.

(1971) 'Caribbean Crews: Peer Groups and Male Society'. *Caribbean Studies*, 10(4) 18-41.

N. L. Gonzalez

RETHINKING THE CONSANGUINEAL HOUSEHOLD AND MATRIFOCALITY

In 1956, in describing the social organization of the Black Caribs as I saw it at that time in Livingston, Guatemala, I used the term 'consanguineal household' to refer to a domestic group whose members are related through a series of consanguineal ties, and in which no two members are bound together in an affinal relationship (Gonzalez 1959, 1969: 4), thus emphasizing coresidence as the defining characteristic of households. I further suggested that kinship, rather than either residence or function, might be viewed as the most central and binding element of the family, even though the members might be residentially dispersed (Gonzalez 1960). Others at that time and later saw the 'grand-mother' or 'matrifocal' family as the primary Caribbean domestic pattern (Henriques 1953; Smith 1956). Although I dealt with matrifocality as a variable independent of the structure of the household, I agreed with others that it was especially strong and wide-spread in the Caribbean area (Gonzalez 1970).

Over the years I have continued to pursue field work among these people, and have tried to incorporate into my original explanatory framework new data which do not always fit. In what follows I present a new interpretation to which I have been converted as a result of my own longitudinal studies in Livingston, archival research in England and Guatemala during 1982-83, and reading the impressive findings of historians and anthropologists who have been digging into the past of our own and many other societies (See Kent 1977; Laslett and Wall 1972; Stone 1977; among many others).

It is particularly striking, I believe, that the peculiar residential alignment of consanguineal kin I found (and still find) among the Black Carib, (or Garifuna, as they prefer to be called) never appears in any of the historical records for Europe, China, colonial America, nor was it even prominent among New World slave societies (Gutman 1976). Aside from other areas in the Caribbean, the closest we come to a comparable form is the 'female-headed household' of the contemporary United States, Latin American, and African urban ghettos, though this often consists only of a mother and her unmarried children, without the assortment of other kinfolk so common among the Garifuna. Increasingly, of course, the female-headed household is also found among the middle classes, especially in the United States. This suggests that poverty is not a sufficient explanation for its existence everywhere, as some have thought.

Though I formerly called the consanguineal household a 'type' (Gonzalez 1969: 4), I would now reject that except in the most general sense, for it is clearly not merely one of several alternative forms associated with different ethnic groups or religious or other culturally defined population segments. Nor does it seem to be one which young people consciously select as a lifestyle. Neither can it properly be called a phase in the developmental a cycle of the domestic group, since although most people live in such a group at some time(s) in their lives, there seem to be no predictable patterns for such behaviour. Rather, most individuals can expect to find themselves part of such groupings time and again, at different points in their own life cycles, though perhaps, especially if they are male, settling down in a stable marital and familial setting in their old age.

In 1975 I repeated a census first taken in 1956 in Livingston, this time covering a 25 per cent sample of the population. Although my 123 informants were volunteers, and thus may constitute a biased sample, their homes turned out to be distributed quite evenly among the various barrios in the town, and I was unable to define any systematic source of bias. Collectively, they reported on some 525 persons coresiding with them, as well as on 129 others who regularly contributed to the household income.[2] Preliminary analysis of the data, presented in Tables 1-5, shows that living arrangements are remarkably evenly divided between what I formerly called 'consanguineal' and 'affinal' (read conjugal) types. In fact, the percentages of each did not differ significantly from what I found in 1956.

My first reaction to this was that if the consanguineal household was, as I had suggested earlier, a response to poverty and to male out migration, one would expect it to persist to the extent that it provided a means to maximize the number of male wage earners for a given household. The argument was more complex than this, but it is not necessary here to go into it in detail. Suffice it to say that the teleology of such an explanation did not bother me (or many others) so much then as it does now. Although I still believe, and my recent data appear to confirm, that there is a demonstrable advantage for many of the women who form the core of these households, this is not sufficient to explain why, at any given time, we find both consanguineal and conjugal units almost in equal numbers. Nor, as it turns out, is the migration of men any longer a crucial variable.

We must start from scratch in explaining Garifuna household structure, as Yanagisako (1979) and others have urged we do generally. But it is hard to know where to start. Years ago, in reference to Jamaica, Edith Clarke (1957) said we might as well start with the house, since it is there, and one can walk up to it and ask who lives there. But Yanagisako (1979) suggests we start by asking what activities are central to domestic relationships involving productive, ritual, political, and exchange transactions in the society being studied. We can then go on to ask what kinds of kinship or locality-based units engage in these activities, thus deriving a more complete and less biased view of the social structure.[3] She (Yanagisako 1979: 195) also emphasizes the importance of marriage form in the creation of different types of domestic groups.

While mulling over these ideas, I began to reanalyze my data from both the 1950s and the 1970s and came up with some fundamentally different, and at first blush, startling interpretations of what was happening in the Garifuna domestic world.

THE DATA

First, the Garifuna have only a domestic, or private world of their own. At least in Guatemala, they are completely without power in the society at large. Not only do they form a tiny minority of the total Guatemalan population, but even in Livingston, where they constitute a large majority, they have almost no public or political life. They have never elected one of their own as mayor *(alcalde)*, for example. This has been so from the time they were first brought to the Central American mainland from St Vincent back in 1797. In the few instances in which they became (usually unwittingly) involved in the political affairs of one or another town or country, it was always to their individual or collective detriment.

Although at one time the Garifuna produced most of their own food, this is no longer the case, at least in Livingston. A few people still plant cassava and some have small kitchen gardens close to their houses, but most purchase foods either from the local shops run by Chinese and Ladinos or in the market and stores of the small city of Puerto Barrios, an hour and half distance by public launch. In only a few cases can the local domestic unit today be said to be the productive unit. Nearly all Garifuna are dependent on cash income from outside the town, often from outside the country.

The various residential units in Livingston have overlapping, fluctuating memberships. Often the same person will be listed by two or more units as 'belonging' to them. When one examines individual behaviour, it is not uncommon to find a person eating, sleeping, storing belongings, or 'hanging out' in more than one house at a time. This is particularly true for men, but women also may divide their time between two or more households. Children are switched around frequently, sleeping for several weeks or months with a grandparent, then going off to stay with an adult sibling, then back again with their mothers, and so on. Children may also be sent to another town for schooling, or to live in a fosterage situation with another family (Sanford 1971).

Men come and go from the town, often giving little or no notice of their intentions, and over the past generation women too have more often left to seek work elsewhere when left alone with no means of support. Sometimes they simply board up their houses, placing their children with relatives; others take them along to Guatemala or New York. They may return a few months later with little fuss, or they may remain away for years. Young single women may similarly go off to see what fate New York has in store for them, and if they are successful in obtaining work, may send money back home to one or both parents.

Now, given all this, what does the observed distribution of people in domestic units in Livingston mean? How important is it that some houses contain a conjugal pair and others do not? Are there differences between what the Cambridge Group[4] calls 'simple' and 'extended' families? What is the nature of domesticity in Livingston, and how does it relate to the residential units?

As can be seen in the tables, there are several surprises. Table I divides the households according to the classification proposed by Laslett and Wall (1972) and others. Note that my consanguineal/affinal household classification crosscuts this, for there are both simple and extended forms to be found in each. Table 2 matches the division with the classification I have previously presented for the Garifuna, starting in 1959. Tables 3 and 4 present figures showing how the sexes of various age groups are represented in the different types of units, as well as how they show up in the sample generally. Finally, Table 5 shows the numbers of persons who contribute economically to each household, as well as the location in which the work is performed.

DATA ANALYSIS

The following are the points I consider most salient for present purposes:

1. Females outnumber males in all age categories, but especially between the ages of 18-54, considered the most able-bodied period for both sexes (Table 4).

2. All men older than 55 live in affinal households (except for two solitaries). This is in sharp contrast to older women, who are more likely to be found in consanguineal households (Table 5). Not only do women live longer on the average than men, but there is customarily at least a five to ten year gap in age between partners, the men tending to choose even younger women as they themselves age. If their earning power has gone up in middle age, men will have no difficulty attracting new partners (Table 3).

3. Both men and women migrate (79 males: 50 females) and send money back to affinal, as well as consanguineal households. But the latter are more than twice as likely to have outside contributors (87 compared with 42). Consanguineal households averaged 1.3 outside earners, compared with 0.8 for affinals. (Table 5).

TABLE 1   *Sample of livingston households in 1975 according to typology of the Cambridge group.*

Household Type	Number	Per cent
Solitaries	7	5.7
No Family	10	8.1
Simple		
Married Couples Alone 12		
Married Couples & Children 21		
*Widows or Widowers & Children 24	57	46.3
Extended (Upward, Downward or Laterally	49	39.9
Multiple (Stem, Joint, etc.)	0	
	123	100.0

SOURCE: Laslett and Wall 1972: 31.

Note that 'widowhood' among the Black Carib bears no relationship to either marriage or to death. Since there is no other category provided in the Cambridge model, I have here grouped together all single women (or men) with children.

4. The average size of the two 'types' of households is significantly different. Consanguineal units averaged 4.2 members, while affinals averaged 5.7. However, when outside contributors are added to the total population in each unit, the differences are slightly less marked, resulting in averages of 5.5 for consanguineal and 6.8 for affinals. These figures are even more meaningful when divided as follows:

   a.   Consanguineal households averaged 2.5 children under eighteen, while affinal households contained an average of only 2.1.

   b.   Consanguineal households averaged 1.8 adults, while affinal households averaged 2.8. When outside contributors — all adults — are added, the affinal households have an average of 4.6 adults, compared with only 3.1 for consanguineals. (Table 3)

DISCUSSION

The notion that consanguineal households are superior to affinals because they maximize the number of males who may be called upon to contribute to the household economy does not hold up in the face of the present evidence. This may be related to the fact that women, as well as men, now migrate to seek work. Fifty, or 39 per cent of the outside contributors are women (Table 5). Certainly, the sex ratio (0.6) suggests that many more men than women are lost to the system, though at least for some of them this may be only a temporary phenomenon.[5]

The increased migration of women reflects the decline of horticulture, which has been their primary productive activity for many generations. Kekchi speaking Indians have infiltrated the tropical forest lands once cultivated by the Garifuna, and many now reside on the very outskirts of Livingston itself.[6] Ethnographic research, even in 1956, but especially in 1975, indicated that most younger Garifuna women were not fond of 'going to the bush' anyway, so the Indian presence seems not to have produced much, if any, felt competition or pressure upon them. Few men had ever undertaken farming which was looked down upon by them as women's or Indian's work. Their only contribution in earlier times was in clearing and burning.

TABLE 2   *Numbers, types and percentages of households in 1975 livingston sample, grouped by categories defined in Gonzalez (1969:68).*

Type	No. Hshlds.	No. Members	Ave. Size	% All Hshlds	% Tot. Pop.
Consanguineal	66	277	4.2	53.7	52.8
Single Person	7	7	1.0	5.7	1.3
Affinal*	38	217	5.7	30.8	41.3
Couple Only	12	24	2.0	9.8	4.6
TOTALS	**123**	**525**	**4.3**	**100.0**	**100.0**

'Affinal' roughly corresponds to 'conjugal'. However, the intent was to contrast allegiances owed to marriage or mating, to those derived through 'blood' ties. Affinal households are those containing at least one marital pair. (In fact, I found none containing more than one).

Similarly, fishing, once a primary source of food, has declined drastically as more men find it necessary to migrate to seek wage-paying jobs to support themselves and fulfill the expectations held by their mothers, sisters, wives, and children. It was also said in 1975 that commercial fishing, often by foreigners, had significantly diminished the supply of fish in nearby waters.

As a result, the Livingston Garifuna household, like the community itself, is primarily a unit of consumption rather than of production. Kinfolk cluster together in various ways to share what for many are only temporary living quarters and housekeeping chores. Childrearing and care of the aged remain among the most important functions of the domestic group. Although people in both of these age categories may contribute to income generation within the community in various ways, they are primarily assigned to housework, leaving those able-bodied adults who live in the household free to seek odd jobs about the town or in the nearby city of Puerto Barrios.

TABLE 3   *Distribution of population by age group in consanguineal and affinal households in Livingston sample, 1976.*

Ages	Consanguineal			Affinal		
	M	F	Total	M	F	Total
55+	0	43	43	36	27	63
18-54	15	60	75	28	42	70
6-17	58	78	136	35	49	84
-6	15	15	30	10	14	24
TOTAL	**88**	**196**	**284**	**109**	**132**	**241**

TABLE 4   *Totals and percentages of total population in various age groups in Livingston sample, 1976.*

Age Group	Males	% of Pop.	Females	% of Pop.	Total	%
55+	36	33.9	70	66.1	106	20.2
18-54	43	29.6	102	70.4	145	27.6
6-17	93	42.3	127	57.7	220	41.9
-6	25	46.3	29	53.7	54	10.2
TOTAL	**197**	**37.5**	**328**	**62.5**	**525**	**99.9**

In great part because there are so many more of them, and because they tend to migrate less often and for shorter periods than do men, mature women are especially important in everyday household decision-making. As I have suggested (Gonzalez 1983a), they are the ones who manage the labour pool potentially available to the household in such a way as to maximize its size and the income its members can generate. They are the magnets who draw their adult sons and daughters back home and influence them to help support those who remain in Livingston. Kerns (1983) has shown how their managerial role also extends to the ceremonial sphere, largely directed toward honouring the dead ancestors, bilaterally reckoned. But women do these things regardless of the kind of household in which they live.

TABLE 5 *Selected comparisons between consanguineal and affinal garifuna households in Livingston sample, Guatemala, 1975.*

	Consanguineal		Affinal	
	No.	% of T.	No.	% of T.
Households	66	54	51	46
Resident Males Over 17 yrs.	15	20	61	80
Absent Male Contributors	53	67	26	33
Total Able-bodied Males	68	44	87	56
Resident Females Over 17	102	60	68	40
Absent Female Contributors	34	68	16	32
Children 6-17	136	62	84	38
Children under 6	30	56	24	44
Total Absent Contributors	**87**	**67**	**42**	**33**

For many years scholars have struggled to understand the origin and nature of the consanguineal household and to describe how it differs from those containing a marital pair (McCommon 1982; Smith 1956; Stack 1974). Earlier, I postulated there might be differences in the way children viewed women (Gonzalez 1970). But subsequently I found that Garifuna children of both sexes and from any type of household tended to draw females first in the Goodenough Draw-a-Person test (Gonzalez 1979). This suggests that women are probably recognized as authority figures in general — a support for calling the society matrifocal.

Brown (1975) was able to demonstrate significant differences between the households and lifestyles of monogamous women and what she called 'multiple maters' in the Dominican Republic. However, unlike the ethnographic setting in which Brown worked, I found that there was a continual flow of people in and out of Garifuna households and that most people lived in a variety of situations over their lifetimes. This has made it impossible to find samples of each 'type' which would remain stable long enough to test for hypothesized functional differences.

Looked at another way, Garifuna households may be seen as ephemeral, transitory agglomerations of kin who cluster together when their personal needs compel them to seek succor and subsistence, or when they can be drawn in (even coerced) to help support others. In such a setting, marriage might be expected to be an important means of establishing rights and obligations. However, marriage, in the sense of forming contractual obligations, is rare. Becker (1981) has suggested for the United States that when there is little economic gain from marriage, it will decline in importance. Among the Garifuna, when two people assume a marital relationship there is no transfer of property, no public ceremony or announcement, no transfer of rights in children. Many couples enter their union lightly, and with the general expectation that it will not last. The couple may or may not reside in the same house, and if they do, that too may be only a temporary arrangement, just as are most household alignments. The colloquial United States' 'sleeping together' and 'living together', which emphasize the sexual and coresidential bases of some unions, may be as good as any other terms.

Another common occurrence is for distant relatives to appear, expecting to stay a few weeks or months. They are welcome, so long as they contribute to the household chores and do not freeload too long. They are expected to buy food if they are able. There is a generalized notion of reciprocity, as well as a special sense of obligation to one's relatives. I heard one of my elderly informants lecture her 42–year–old son on how he must be 'true' to his latest partner, for she was a distant kinswoman, and therefore deserved more from him than the others. Marriage consecrated by the church and formalized through the legal system is recognized and idealized, but seldom undertaken until a couple is very old. It is not at all uncommon to find marriages recorded only days, and sometimes hours before the death of one of the partners.

Interestingly, I was never able to elicit terms for either 'household' or 'family' nor does Taylor (1952) report them. There are terms for 'house' (muona); the collective family decide (gubida); parents or elders (agoburigu); and kinsman or kinswoman (iduhe, pl. = iduhara). However, when I pushed for translations of the English or Spanish *familia*, I got only 'kinsmen', or sometimes 'kinsmen who live in the same house'.

CONCLUSIONS

If we cannot distinguish between these two 'types' of household on linguistic or economic grounds, nor in terms of reproductive success or the assignment of authority, in what sense may they be said to exist at all? I am no longer so sure they do in either an etic or an emic sense. Contrary to what I once argued, I now believe it might be more useful to think in terms of transformational theory, or as Geertz and Geertz (1951: 3) suggested for Bali, the diversity of kin groups observed may be seen as variations on a set of common ideational themes.

The first of these, I believe, is individualism. In spite of their loyalties to the ethnic group, to their community of birth, and to their relatives, Garifuna tend to live out their lives from earliest childhood as individuals who become attached to, then detached from, various other persons and/or households for varying periods of time. Unlike the early English individualism, as described by Macfarlane (1980), the individual, rather than the nuclear family, becomes the basic unit, or building block.

The second ideational theme is matrifocality. Women have become central, perhaps by default. They seem not to have been so on their arrival in Central America, though that may only reflect the male biases of the eighteenth century European chroniclers. On the other hand, if one were deliberately to set out to 'feminize' an entire sociocultural system, there could be no better way than to remove the institutionalized male functions'. In the seventeenth and eighteenth centuries, men alone hunted and fished, served as religious leaders, as warriors and as headmen. In the earliest days of migratory wage labour (eighteenth century) this was also a masculine endeavour, and one which led to both economic success and personal glory. But bit by bit these roles have been either removed from the Garifuna culture completely, or, as in the case of migration and religious leadership, women now participate as well. As one male informant put it in 1975 — there is nothing a man can do that a woman can't do as well or better.

A basic feminist argument today is that the overall status of women in a society is related to the nature of the roles they are allowed to fill. The Garifuna case is almost a mirror image of what has more often happened to women since the onset of the industrial revolution. That is, the roles assigned to men have been deleted or diluted to the point that men as a class seem somehow less important than women. The general situation which remains has struck many observers, themselves members of a different kind of social order, as being 'matrifocal'.

The third theme, already alluded to, is migration. Livingston, like so many similar towns and villages in the Third World, is today completely dependent upon the outside world; yet it has nothing to sell but its most able-bodied as labourers. Most adults now must leave the town for a good portion of their lives merely to subsist. It is likely that without migratory wage labour the town would long ago have ceased to exist. At the same time, the historical record shows clearly that Garifuna men started working off-island (St Vincent) by the third quarter of the eighteenth century, and when they arrived in Central America, they were immediately recruited by the Spanish as soldiers and by the British as woodcutters. It might be argued that without wage labour they might not have survived at all, nor gone on to establish Livingston or other towns. Indeed, many of their earliest settlements were founded in spots where wage labour might be easily obtained.

My sense today is that I was not too far off back in the late 1950s when I emphasized that Garifuna culture, including their 'series of household forms' as I called it then for lack of a more precise understanding, was largely a new or 'neoteric' thing — created out of a hodge-podge of elements from several sources and molded by poverty, stress, and outside forces beyond their control. A more detailed story of their removal from the island of St. Vincent in 1797 can now be told, and it includes a devastating epidemic which cost them 55 per cent of their total population in the space of four months, leaving a total of only 2,026 who actually arrived on Roatan (Gonzalez 1983b). Somewhat fewer than that were left two months later when they crossed over to the mainland of Central America, and contemporary censuses I have discovered list them as individuals, even though Indians, slaves and European settlers were always listed by families or household groups. It is impossible to know why this was done, but it may have been because family groups were not discernible as such by the European authorities at that time. Certainly there must have been the need to regroup and revitalize in order to survive those first difficult years. We must assume that St Vincent families had been broken up by two years of warfare, the epidemic, and the hardships of the journey to Central America. One account speaks of the dying and recently dead having been abandoned in their hammocks (War Office 1797). It may have been then that the individualistic spirit first arose — much like that described by Turnbull (1972) for the Ik under similarly difficult circumstances.

But clearly, individualism alone need not lead to the kind of domestic organization that characterizes their society today. Nothing in Macfarlane's (1980) description of English individualism and the rise of the nuclear family matches the Garifuna case, especially in relation to matrifocality. I suggest that the answer lies in the nature of the larger society in which the domestic groups lie embedded. In England, and indeed in Europe generally as well as in most of the rest of the world, the supradomestic domain, even during modernizing periods, continued to provide a set of institutions and spheres of activity in which both migrant and stay-at-home males were expected and encouraged to predominate. This was not the case in the West Indies, and this may be the key to understanding not only the Garifuna, but West Indian domestic organization in general. The Caribbean situation is indeed different from that found in areas with deeper historical traditions, and if not pathological, as even mainline social science once characterized it, there is a sense in which these matrifocal family and consanguineal household institutions might be thought not to be healthy for those living in them — particularly for males. Yet adjustments have occurred such that some of the suggested detrimental effects of father-absence have apparently been avoided (Mertz 1978). At least one writer has suggested that the West Indian male seems to cope well with life Wilson (1973), and Whitehead (1978) has showed how both men and women successfully juggle residence and marital arrangements, with survival as the common denominator.

But so long as Garifuna towns like Livingston remain encapsulated within their national societies, existing primarily to furnish labour to an exterior market, they cannot be complete societies, and their domestic institutions will reflect that. Neither can they be truly integral parts of their nation or region. For those few individuals who manage to attach themselves relatively securely to the larger society and to its institutions, monogamy and the nuclear family may be achieved. The vast majority, however, do not expect to live this way; indeed, only eleven out of my 123 households were centred on marital partners who had never borne children with anyone other than their current spouse.

From the perspective of those who may espouse the ideal of lifelong monogamy, the more typical Garifuna life appears as a lonely journey from mate to mate and from household to household — always striving for stability, but never quite finding it. But most Garifuna seem not only to survive, but to flourish under the system I have described. Not only have they shown remarkable reproductive success since their arrival in Central America in 1797, but they have also kept alive and even enhanced their sense of ethnicity, their language, and their culture (even though much of the latter has been borrowed from others). Perhaps it is more sensible and closer to reality to conclude that for them marital and residential instability is not only the norm, but an adaptive strategy that has served them well.

Helms (1981), in taking issue with my view that the Garifuna culture patterns had relatively shallow roots, suggests that the Island Carib from the seventeenth century on, also had consanguineal households. What she describes is the typical tropical forest village organization in which women, their unmarried daughters and small sons inhabit independent huts, while the men congregate in a communal men's house for most residential purposes, visiting their wife (or wives) only occasionally, presumably primarily for sexual purposes. Although superficially this does resemble what we see today, it is institutionally very distinct. The entire set of interrelationships between men and women seem very different from what I read in the same early accounts to which Helms refers. Again, I believe the difference lies in the ways in which the various roles are structured for men and for women and in the ways in which the differenct roles were valued in the past in comparison with the present day. Congregating in a man's house keeps the men out of the woman's abode, but it seems more homologous than analogous for purposes of analysis.

Where I find Helms (1981) more convincing is in her observation that the consanguineal household (as defined by me and as found today) has fit admirably into several different economic circumstances. Not only has it facilitated women's co-operative agricultural activities and migrant wage labour of the men, perhaps for as long as two centuries, but as women move increasingly into the job market, the consanguineal household continues to provide a stable and secure home for their children, their siblings, and their mothers who remain behind. The latter is what I tried to document in 1975, and as I have shown here, it may well be so, but affinal households seem to serve as well.

Thus, I suggest that household structure is a function of household composition, and that for the Garifuna, and perhaps for other societies with similar characteristics, composition is unpredictable except in broad terms, and is dependent upon immediate circumstances. Thus, it does not help to try to correlate this or that characteristic with the different 'types' since, in effect, the latter really exist only in the minds of the ethnographers. Once we abandon this misconception, we will make more progress in understanding the way in which Caribbean social organization really works.

NOTES

1. This paper was read at the meetings of the Society for Economic Anthropology in Iowa City, April 22, 1983. Fieldwork in Central America and in New York City over the years has been supported by the Doherty Foundation, the Ford Foundation, the National Science Foundation, and Boston University Graduate School. I am grateful to all of them for having given me the opportunity to return to the Garifuna time and again, thus permitting the accumulation of a longitudinal data set through which we can study process.

2. In 1956, with the assistance of three Garifuna, I recorded data for every household of that ethnic group. In 1975, because time was more limited, and because I had multiple research goals, I asked that people come in to see me who might be interested in having their blood tested. The response was overwhelming, and it was in connection with this that I obtained the present data set.

3. David Aberle taught a course entitled Primitive Society at Michigan in the 1950s in which he used an almost identical scheme, building upon models suggested by Marion Levy.

4. This is the term used to refer to the group of British demographic historians who met at Cambridge (England) in 1969 under the chairmanship of Peter Laslett to consider the results of data concerning household composition in former times in Europe. Their conclusions about the size and composition of families, especially in England, were based upon computerized analyses of various censuses carried out between 1574 and 1821, and were startling, to say the least (Laslett and Wall 1972).

5. The sex ratio at birth and during early childhood is also lower than expected, which contributes to the situation, of course.

6. For descriptions of the Kekchi migrations as they affected the Izabel/Toledo (Belize) area generally, see Carter (1969) and Wilk (1981).

7. I am indebted to my colleague, William T. Stuart, for having suggested this line of thinking.

BIBLIOGRAPHY

Becker, G. 1981. *A Treatise on the Family*. Cambridge.

Brown, S. E. 1975. "Low Economic Sector Female Mating Patterns in the Dominican Republic." *Women Cross Culturally: Change and Challenge*, ed. R. Rohrlich-Leavitt, pp. 221-239. The Hague.

Carter, W. E. 1969. *New Lands and Old Traditions*. Gainesville.

Clarke, E. 1957. *My Mother Who Fathered Me*. London.

Geertz, H., and C. Geertz, 1975. *Kinship in Bali*. Chicago.

Gonzalez, N. L. 1959. The Consanguineal Household in Central America. Ph.D. Dissertation, Univ. of Michigan.

—1960. "Household and Family in the Caribbean", *Social and Economic Studies* 9:101-106.

—1969. "Black Carib Household Structure", Seattle.

—1970. "Toward a Definition of Matrifocality" *Afro-American Anthropology*, eds N. E. Whitten, Jr. and J. Szwed, pp. 231-243. New York.

—1979. "Sex Preference In Human Figure Drawing by Garifuna (Black Carib) Children" *Ethnology* 18:355-364.

—1983a. "Domestic Groups, Family Wealth and the Mobilization of Labour in Modern Peasant Societies" (Ms.).

—1983b. New Evidence on the Origin of the Black Carib. *New West Indian Guide* (in press).

Gutman, H. G. 1976. *The Black Family in Slavery and Freedom, 1750-1925*. New York.

Helms, M. W. 1981. "Black Carib Domestic Organization in Historical Perspective: Traditional Origins of Contemporary Patterns", *Ethnology* 20:77-86.

Henriques, F. 1953. *Family and Colour in Jamaica*. London.

Kent, F. W. 1977. *Household and Lineage in Renaissance Florence: The Family Life of the Capponi, Ginori, and Rucillai*. Princeton.

Kern, V. 1983. *Women and the Ancestors*. Urbana.

Laslett, P., and R. Wall 1972. *Household and Family in Past Time*. London.

Macfarlane, A. 1980. *The Origins of English Individualism*. London.

McCommon, C. 1982. "Mating as a Reproductive Strategy: A Black Carib Example". Ph.D. Dissertation, Pennsylvania State University.

Mertz, R. 1976. "The Effect of Father Absence on the Development of Psychological Differentiation Among Male Black Carib Students in Belize." Ph.D. Dissertation, Univ. of Arizona.

Sanford, M. 1971. "Disruption of the Mother-Child Relationship in Conjunction with Matrifocality: A Study of Child-Keeping among the Carib and Creole of British Honduras." Ph.D. Dissertation, Catholic University of America.

Smith, R. T. 1956. *The Negro Family in British Guiana*. London.

Stack, C. B. 1974. *All Our Kin*. New York.

Stone, L. 1977. *The Family, Sex and Marriage in England 1500-1800*. London.

Taylor, D. M. 1952. 'The Black Carib of British Honduras', Viking Fund Publications in *Anthropology* No. 9. New York.

Turnbull, C. 1972. *The Mountain People*. New York.

Whitehead, T. 1978. "Residence, Kinship and Mating as Survival Strategies", *Journal of Marriage and the Family* 40:817.

Wilson, P. C. 1973. *Carib Antics*. New Haven.

Wilk, R. R. 1981. "Households in Process: Domestic Organization, Land Pressure and Cash Crops Among the Kekchi Maya of Belize." (Ms).

War Office 1797. I/82, f. 683. Public Record Office, Kew, England.

Yanagisako, S. J. 1979. "Family and Household: The Analysis of Domestic Groups" *Annual Review of Anthropology* 8:161-206. Palo Alto.

4
Ideology and Culture

The most recent contribution to the understanding of family in the Caribbean high-lights ideology and culture, historically generated and interpreted by Caribbean people themselves. The approach directs attention to the meaning and symbols embedded in social action and interaction. By asking simple, open questions like: 'What is Caribbean kinship?' and 'What do Jamaicans, St Lucians and other West Indians think about their family patterns?' and listening closely to the ideas and concepts through which informants give meaning to their family lives, researchers take us back to basics, providing a fresh start by clearing away the misconceptions of imposed theoretical concepts and principles. The return to culture and history reminds us of the work of Herskovits which we reviewed in Chapter II, but the probe into family ideologies and practice over time provides us with a more sophisticated analysis than his notion of cultural persistence and the straightforward collection and classification of African survivals. Additionally, the question of structure, which so dominated the paradigms of structural functionalism and its variants, now takes a back seat to the study of meaning in social action. The pioneers of this new approach are Raymond Smith, who with these insights provided a thorough revision of his earlier work, and his group of research assistants which included Jack Alexander (1973, 1976, 1977, 1978, 1984) and Diane Austin (1984). They were joined by other anthropologists such as Henrietta De Veer (1979), Mindie Lazarus-Black (1991), and Lisa Douglass (1992) and by historian Barry Higman (1984) who recognised the limitations of his demographic studies of slave household composition, to which we refer in Chapter VI, and proceeded to investigate the meanings embodied in kinship terminology used by the slaves.

The search for meaning in kinship practice also avoids the somewhat myopic character of earlier investigations that focussed on the contemporary black lower class; firstly, by restoring a historical perspective and secondly, by introducing comparisons across class and race.

With reference to the first, structural functionalism initially dismissed history as unimportant to the central concern with contemporary family structure. When the model was later adjusted to incorporate notions of 'equilibrium', 'evolution' and 'modernization', some understanding of social change was achieved, but the emphasis on continuity and stability remained dominant. Leaving behind these unsatisfactory conceptualisations, Smith (1984: 4) has placed history at the centre of Caribbean family studies:

> More attention should be paid to the particularity of the historically generated cultural forms characteristic of this area, and to the social practices through which those forms operate in the specific conditions of contemporary society.

Similarly, Joseph Manyoni (1977, 1980) in his studies of illegitimacy and of extra-marital mating patterns, which, he argues, 'are a consequence of the historical forces deriving from the pervasive socio-economic plantation system of the 17th and 19th centuries', demonstrates the value of archival research.

Secondly, as we noted in earlier chapters, the concept of pluralism applied to Caribbean societies brought with it the perception that each socio-cultural segment has its own status in the social hierarchy, economic base and distinctive cultural patterns. Studies of family and kinship therefore assumed that lower-class, black villagers have unique and 'abnormal' patterns of family, marriage, descent and the like which, while they may reflect those found in communities of similar race, class and economic marginality, are markedly different from those of higher-status persons, which were assumed to be 'normal', that is European-nuclear (Henriques 1953: 160, Davenport 1961: 420). Communities, therefore, qualified as units of investigation often in isolation from the rest of society. Smith (1984: 18) has challenged this view:

> Although it is difficult to keep the general characteristics and the historical experience of a whole continent within one's field of view, some means must be found to avoid undue preoccupation with discrete segments and their supposed survivals, continuities, and ecological adaptations.

And in response, Smith, Alexander, Austin and Douglass, though they remain a minority, have extended family studies to include the elite and the middle class of Jamaica.

Caribbean creole societies are hierarchically arranged by race, by indicators of class such as achievements in education, occupation and wealth and by status refinements and etiquette. These patterns of stratification are acknowledged and reinforced by pervasive, central ideologies. However, according to this approach, cultural diversity, established with the arrival of immigrant groups in the Caribbean, has not led to the establishment of semi-autonomous, socio-cultural groupings. Diversity, division and conflict are contained within a Creole cultural continuum of shared symbols and experiences, passed down and transformed through the generations and subscribed to, at one level or another, by *all* members of the society. Contained within this continuum are meanings and practices relating to family, affinity, illegitimacy, motherhood and so forth.

By adopting this perspective, investigations of family and kinship also avoid the narrow, essentially empirical perspectives and the perception of change as individualistic and utilitarian, which, to a greater or lesser degree, characterised the studies reported in the previous chapter. Individual community members are no longer seen as having virtual free range to make personal choices for their own material benefit, but are social beings fully embedded in a culture, their family patterns influenced by principles and meanings passed down through the generations. The search for the fundamental ideological continuity of family and kinship, while acknowledging that families are not immune from economic forces, also avoids the pitfall of conceptualising the family as the dependent variable, squeezed into new shapes and purposes by the economic forces of slavery, plantation systems, modernisation and poverty. As Douglass (1992: 15-16) has stated:

> In Jamaica, there are two points that dispute the assumption that kinship practices directly reflect economic position. One is that despite general improvements in the living standard of the majority of West Indians over the past century, the practices and patterns of kinship remain today, much as they were just after emancipation over 150 years ago. The second is that Jamaicans of all economic levels participate in many of the same patterns of kinship practice. Jamaicans are not isolated into classes or groups that live apart from one another, but rather they all form part of a creole society. What I seek to demonstrate is that the kinship patterns, practices, and sentiments of the family elite are at once unique to this group, yet they fully conform to the cultural principles that characterize Jamaican kinship and society generally.

The demise of what we have referred to as the 'adaptive response' approach came with the realisation that neither structural functional analysis nor its offshoots could provide the framework within which to fully understand social change. This also provided the stimulus for studies of kinship to progress by recognising the importance of meaning and symbolism.

With these theoretical innovations, Caribbean families can be studied in their own right, with their own structures and historical patterns of change, not as evolutionary stages en route to the nuclear ideal or as African survivals. The approach requires the investigator to shed those theoretical preconceptions that have resulted in repeated misrepresentations as social scientists have distorted field data by imposing knowledge and ideology.

> This is a particular problem in the study of kinship where it has generally been assumed that kinship is nothing but the recognition of the 'real' facts of consanguinity and affinity. The distortions produced by the imposition of this European concept upon the observations of other societies can be avoided by a careful study of native concepts defining the meaningful units within the domain of kinship and family (Smith 1984: 19).

Methodology

The methods adopted for these studies are varied. All the researchers, however, used in-depth techniques that allowed them to interpret meanings through the words and ideas of their informants. Smith (1988) and Alexander (1984, see Article 1 at end of chapter) collected detailed genealogies from selected informants, the idea being to arrive at an understanding of kinship by attending to what they say and do about their own families, those of others and about family life in general. The methodology is meticulous and time-consuming. The objective is not to aim for statistical representation, though Alexander's sample was carefully selected according to occupation, place of birth, age, colour and marital status to represent different social categories within the middle class. Similarly, Smith's sample of 51 men and women from Guyana and Jamaica, within which Alexander's informants and those of seven other research assistants were included, covered variations in class and race, residential area, occupation, age, birthplace and marital status (Smith 1988: 19). For Smith's study, the collection of information on each individual's genealogy took anywhere from 20 to 150 hours with each session being tape recorded and transcribed, often verbatim (Smith 1988: 10). Alexander spent nearly two years with his eleven Jamaican informants, supplementing lengthy sessions with shorter interviews with another twenty-three informants and with participant observation (Alexander 1977: 370).

These techniques constitute a decisive departure from the traditional collection of quantitative data by relying on household questionnaire surveys incorporating mainly pre-coded questions based on predetermined kinship categories.

> In following a procedure which is open to so many criticisms for its lack of methodological rigour, I can only argue that the exercise is worthwhile because of the novelty of its point of departure, and for what it may suggest concerning the sterility of the ever-more refined and methodologically elegant studies of statistical data on mating and household composition.

> Undue concentration on household studies, and the false functionalist assumption that stable co-residential conjugal unions are necessary for the proper upbringing of children — and for the firm establishment of kinship ties — has served to bias both observation and analysis. An extension of genealogical case studies of the type reported on in this paper will throw new light upon the whole question of family formation and the dynamics of family development. To do this is especially important in view of the rapidly expanding historical scholarship focussed upon family relations which draws most of its material and ideas from concentration upon the household. Even with a limited number of cases such as I examine here, we are able to see much more clearly the interaction between individual households and the more extensive networks of mutual aid and interaction which permeate their boundaries. Surveys and censuses dealing only with household composition tend to obscure these relationships because they require boundary definitions to be made with some degree of rigidity in order to facilitate the data collection process. Such definitions are necessarily a priori and they either ignore or attempt to pre-guess the definition and demarcation of meaningful categories used by the population being studied. As I have stated above, in many cases the observer's definitions grow out of his own assumptions about the 'natural' or social-functional characteristics of familial and domestic relations. The method used here seeks to avoid such premature closure of the analytical scheme and includes the actors' definition of the situation as a part of the data of observation (Smith 1978: 336).

The 'genealogical universe' of each informant is very broadly defined and the process is described as a 'total kinship exploration', a technique which 'employs a minimal definition of what constitutes a 'genealogy' and which keeps open the question of where lies the boundary of the domain of kinship' (Smith 1978: 337). Accordingly, informants were asked to 'give a picture of your family life' (Alexander 1978: 5) or to respond to a preliminary statement such as 'Please tell me all your relatives' (Alexander 1984: 148) or 'Could you list for me all the people you consider to be related to you?' (Smith 1988: 32). Queries from informants were turned back to them for their own interpretation and, on the occasions when interviewers asked additional questions, these followed through from statements made by informants rather than from the interviewers' preconceptions.

> The aim of the interviews was to get informants talking freely, with a minimum of interviewer stimulus, about family life, kinship relations, and associated aspects of social life. The genealogy, containing the informant's knowledge of all individuals related in any way through consanguinity, conjugal unions or kinship links created in other ways ... was used as a framework on which the informant was expected to hang a great deal of

general comment. This comment would, it was hoped, reveal basic assumptions about the nature of kinship and status (Smith 1988: 10-11).

Also discussed in this chapter are the studies conducted and methods used by George Roberts and Sonja Sinclair on the conjugal and reproductive patterns of women in Jamaica, by Mindie Lazarus-Black on male-female relations and child support in Antigua, by Janet Brown, Patricia Anderson and Barry Chevannes for the Caribbean Child Development Centre (CCDC) in Jamaica on the male contribution to the family in Jamaica and by Joseph Manyoni on legitimacy and illegitimacy in Barbados. Their methods incorporated larger samples, relying on the more traditional techniques of structured surveys and semi-structured interviews. Nevertheless, the collection of information on culturally defined attitudes and meanings remained central.

Roberts and Sinclair followed their own plea for attitudinal and qualitative information by adopting an extensive, nineteen-page questionnaire with several open-ended questions. They supplemented this with tape recordings of the interviews in their entirety.

> From every standpoint the use of tape recording of interviews has proved rewarding. Not only has it made possible the checking of material recorded on the questionnaire by the interviewer, but the recording conveys the attitudes, feelings and values of the respondent in a way which no other approach could capture (Roberts and Sinclair 1978: 252).

Lazarus-Black's investigation combined case histories of women who take the fathers of their children to court with interviews of litigants and lawyers and observations of court proceedings (Lazarus-Black 1991: 126, see Article 5 at end of chapter).

The CCDC study used a two-tier methodology combining a questionnaire survey and participatory group discussions. The survey was directed at men and contained 110 pre-set questions, nearly half of which were attitudinal and open-ended. The group sessions, which were taped in full, included women as well as men and prompted lively and often heated views about fatherhood. This project methodology enabled researchers to return data to the people involved in the research in written manual and video format so as to generate local understanding and problem solving (Brown et al. 1993: 24-32, 49). Historical material was also important to the studies. Manyoni (1977, see Article 4 at end of chapter), for example, sought archival material in relation to illegitimacy. By adopting these detailed, innovative research techniques, researchers sought to arrive at an understanding of the cultural image of kinship shared by informants, what Alexander referred to as sets of 'collective representations' of kinship embedded in the psyche, which represent social reality and which 'combine on a conglomerate level to create domains — such as family — that are guides for action' (Alexander 1984: 148).

For the remainder of this chapter, we examine the new insights provided by these studies as they examine conjugal relationships, matrifocality, male marginality and illegitimacy from the perspectives of Caribbean kinship ideology and practice. We then examine how history has been reintegrated into this theoretical perspective.

Conjugal relationships

Caribbean family studies have been dominated by the assumption that marriage is the union of the middle class while members of the lower class enter into visiting and common-law unions, marrying, if at all, only in the last years of life. And yet, in their study of family life in Jamaica and Guyana, every one of the genealogies collected by Smith and his colleagues, irrespective of class or race, contained legal marriages as well as common-law and visiting unions.

> We have collected no genealogy in Jamaica or Guyana that does not show legal marriages, common law marriages, visiting unions and illegitimate births resulting from casual affairs. One cannot conclude that it would be impossible to find extensive genealogies on which 'irregular' unions did not occur, but this evidence shows no sharp dividing line between classes or segments with different institutionalized forms of mating. Status differences affect relations between kin. In the lower class, legal unions are distinguished from non-legal, but all West Indians recognise the entire range of forms that conjugal unions may take. The types form a coherent series in which each one is defined by contrast with the others. All West Indians understand these contrasting categories in much the same way, and share the valuation of their status ranking. All forms of mating are practised by West Indians of all classes (Smith 1988: 112).

Indeed, in the genealogies of the lower-class informants, the rate of marriage was surprisingly high, constituting between 78 and 80 per cent of all unions (Smith 1988: 113). The proportions of each union were, however, found to differ with the status of informants, with common-law and visiting unions increasing as one moved down the social scale from middle to lower class (Smith 1988: 112). The proportion of these two unions is also higher in the genealogies of those aspiring to enter the middle class than among those already well-established there (Smith 1988: 123). Additionally, there is a greater incidence of multiple unions in the lower class. The important point, however, is that 'this is a difference of rate of occurrence and not a difference in systems of mating' (Smith 1978: 377).

The type of conjugal relationship does not therefore change as we move up the social hierarchy to anything like the extent we have been led to believe. Classes do not exist in isolation from one another and do not exhibit and protect their own unique forms of conjugal union. We proceed by examining the recent literature as it provides answers by referring to kinship ideologies, to questions about the cultural meaning of marriage and other conjugal unions.

Alexander's work on middle-class Jamaicans also focussed on what he called 'the domain of marriage'. For his informants, conjugal love is the main prerequisite to marriage and an essential ingredient. Marriage occurs as friendship is transformed into love — intense, exclusive, absolute, involuntary and constant. After marriage the meaning of love changes from 'being in love', an inwardly directed feeling of emotion and passion, to practical actions in the public and social arena. One of Alexander's informants, for example, stressed that her husband, although sexually unfaithful, had always taken care of her and the children, thus shifting the main criterion according to which she measured his love, thereby maintaining the belief that it was still going strong (Alexander 1978: 11). As we move to the lower class, however, love is less central to marriage and other criteria, such as social status and colour, not altogether absent from the middle class, begin to carry more weight. Here marriage is a symbol, perhaps the most important, of upward social mobility and is therefore associated with middle-class status and civilised behaviour. Indeed, marriage to someone of lighter complexion who is also educated, socially refined and preferably a member of an established religious denomination, virtually ensures escape from one's roots.

Although informants claimed that colour should no longer be important in assessing someone as a suitable marriage partner, in practice it still counts. Mrs Sears, one of Smith's well-established, middle-class informants, presented a somewhat hesitant and contradictory argument. While stressing various indices of civilisation as major criteria in the selection of a spouse, she eventually came round to the question of race as she recounted the experiences of her sister.

> We naturally would like our children to marry people like ourselves, similar background and education, but what if she turns up with a boy who isn't? The only thing I think that I would — what would hurt me most, is that if the boy, I don't care what nationality or what colour he is, I only ask that he be, have a similar background and home and, um, education ... the thing that would hurt me most is say if she went and married somebody, well say the gardener boy, with whom there would be so little in common .... But I have to think through the other differences and put them in their proper perspective. They really don't matter ....

> One of my sisters married a very black man. And when I was growing up at a very impressionable age, this happened. And it was one of the reasons my father objected to the marriage .... One of the reasons ... but as you grow up you have to think these things through for yourself ... it's not important really if a fellow is from a good home, well educated, and in every way could make her an admirable husband (Smith 1988: 121).

For all this rationalisation and despite the fact that the husband's occupational and financial status ranked him as equal to other men of the family, the sister became an outcast. For men, the choice of a partner and marriage is associated with settling down, with the renunciation of running around wild with many women and the virtually unlimited freedom of their younger years. For women it means domestic economic security, a respectable, religiously blessed family life and the improved welfare of the children (Smith 1988: 115-117). The reality of married life may, of course, be very different.

Similar views are reported by Roberts and Sinclair (1978: 63-67, see Article/ extract 3 at end of chapter) as they compare the attitudes of Jamaican women to marriage, common-law unions and visiting relationships. Although the women view marriage as the most respectable union for themselves and their children, as well as the most stable and secure, with legal protection and religious approval, it by no means receives unqualified support. Women in common-law unions suffer all the disadvantages of marriage with none of the benefits. The drawbacks of both unions are a function of co-residence which limits a woman's freedom, ties her down to performing domestic chores for her partner and may also expose her to conjugal violence. These problems are, however, seen to be less likely within marriage, for husbands have legally and religiously pledged their commitment to the relationship. It is the value placed by the women on visiting relationships that is perhaps the most surprising, given the conclusions of earlier studies. Quite positive attitudes are expressed as women in these unions are seen to be free, independent and safe from the dangers of domestic violence. Less intensive contact between the partners is conducive to greater harmony and, since the relationship is viewed as a prelude to marriage, it does not attract the moral and religious condemnation of common-law living in sin.

Another frequently commented on characteristic of Caribbean conjugal unions is late entry into marriage. In the sample of women interviewed by Roberts and Sinclair, the average age at marriage was 27 years and only 22 per cent married before bearing children. The researchers explored the implications in their study, noting that young women who seemed to consider themselves ready for motherhood, claimed that marriage would be inappropriate because they were too young.

However, the most interesting aspect of late entry into marriage is the opinion of several women that they are too young for marriage. This rationale is also applied to common-law unions and is generally used when explaining their initial unions, namely visiting, giving rise to their first pregnancies. For example one woman aged 19 at the birth of her first child and whose partner was 28 years old stated that 'she saw him and loved him', and he visited her as that was the type of union most convenient for their age group. She broke off the relationship on discovering her pregnancy and said that 'even if she had been older at the time she does not think she would have lived with him or married him.' She in fact married when she was aged 30 ....

Another woman states that 'I could not go in another union type as I was too young' (aged 19). According to her, in the visiting union there is much freedom, whereas in marriage and common-law there is much violence and unfaithfulness. This woman did in fact get married when she was aged 23 ....

The reasoning behind a female of 19 or 20 ... claiming that she is too young to live with a man, while obviously having no hesitation in mothering a child or children, is not clear from these data. Cognizance must be taken of the fact that many of these women do have older relatives, often their mothers, to assist them with their child rearing. In view of these attitudes we are led to question the rationale which allows a woman to assume the responsibility for rearing an infant, with its many psychological, physical and social demands, when she possibly feels that because of her young age, she lacks some of the attributes necessary for a meaningful relationship with her partner (Roberts and Sinclair 1978: 177).

The rationale for these attitudes obviously requires more investigation, but in practice may indeed be linked to the presence of female kin to assist with child rearing while the young mother remains at home and in a visiting relationship, whereas marriage and relocation would mean having to cope with the responsibilities more single-handedly. Managing a co-residential conjugal relationship may be seen as more difficult than dealing with a young child. It is significant that economics was not mentioned in this discussion. One might conclude, therefore, that these young women remained in visiting unions because marriage is culturally inappropriate, rather than because their partners, as young men living in unemployment and poverty, were unable to save enough for the wedding ceremony and for a home. The statements of these Jamaican women on the meaning of marriage clearly imply that women of 19 or 20 years of age are too young and immature to become wives, though motherhood is culturally approved.

In another contribution to this debate, Smith (1988: 134-148, see Article/extract 2 at end of chapter) provided a model for the study of conjugal union variation by examining gender roles and relationships. It has been well-recognised for some time that the roles of men and women in any society are not biologically determined, but culturally prescribed, and therefore subject to change and almost infinite in variety. Smith noted that as societies structure the meaning of sex, 'attributional' and 'relational' aspects are distinguished. The attributional aspect stresses a gender dichotomy as a result of fundamental differences between men and women, physically and in terms of temperament, talents and abilities. Male roles are thus distinguished from those of females, husbands and fathers being markedly different to and separate from wives and mothers. The relational aspects emphasise the complementarity and unification of the sexes (Smith 1988: 135). Societies vary in the relative emphasis placed on each and notions of gender roles and relationships differ. Where attributional aspects are dominant, gender roles are expected to be distinct, to be performed in separate domains and relationships to be segregated. Conversely, where relational aspects dominate, the emphasis is on the unity and complementarity of the sexes and joint co-operative activity between conjugal partners is expected in the several spheres of social life - domestic, employment, leisure and so on.

With this analytical perspective in mind and following the earlier work of Elizabeth Bott (1957) on urban family patterns in England, Smith pursued the distinction between 'dissociated', 'segregated' and 'joint' conjugal role patterns. The dissociated pattern stresses independent organisation with exchanges between two distinct and different entities, male and female. This is a characteristic of most visiting unions, especially those that are short-lived, though it may also be present in co-residential unions, both common-law and marital. Generally, this pattern suggests the absence of intense emotional involvement and full commitment to the relationship. The partners tend to maintain close supportive ties with their own kinship networks and may be simultaneously involved in other sexual relationships.

The segregated pattern places emphasis on complementary activities, on the combination of the distinctive qualities and contributions of husband and wife to the running of the family. The pattern is common in the Caribbean, especially in co-residential unions (marriage and common-law) in both the middle and lower classes. The male partner should be responsible for family protection and economic support while the female's contribution is in the area of domestic work and child care, much, it would appear, like the ideal nuclear family pattern. In practice, over the generations many women have worked to provide economic support for the family. This is not perceived as a threat to her partner's role and identity. The foundations of masculinity, especially for the lower class, are to be found more in sexual prowess and in maintaining a reputation among other men than in employment and occupational status. Correspondingly, domestic chores diminish masculinity (Smith 1988: 146-148).

The marital relationship of Mrs Cook of Jamaica illustrates this segregated role pattern (Smith 1988: 168-171). She stopped work as a secretary when her first child was born to devote her time to child care and domestic work. Mr Cook worked hard, prospered and provided well for the family, though she never knew how much he earned. He also remained close to his children. Throughout the marriage she kept in close contact with her mother and sisters, while he also remained attached to his kin. When he became involved in an affair with his secretary, she tolerated it, made no fuss and waited for him to return. Though the affair separated the couple, he continued to provide for them and eventually returned. She describes the segregation between herself and her husband:

Well you see I don't know what I expected — I suppose it was more or less companionship you look forward to, and well you see my case is sort of different, because I was never a demanding person and I know the things I put up with, I don't think the young people of today would put up with it ... I mean they may not be big things but still. For instance as I say I never asked my husband where he was going, why he was going, or when he was going. He just say, 'I'm going out this evening' and he's gone; and now that's not going to suit most people and they want to know where he's going and why he's going. Now I never ... I figured if he wants to tell me he'd tell me, and maybe some later date I'd hear it you know. But because he was the type ... I don't know, I always feel that he had a ... I don't know how to explain it. There was a sort of a reservation to him, I'd hear him telling his sister things for instance that he'd never told me, and I'd overhear them talking about it with his sister. And maybe it's just something in business but I know when he came home he always said he didn't want to be bothered with business and so I never bothered him with business you know. And I always felt that when a man came home in the afternoon they didn't want to be bothered with household things and .... But he didn't know what was going on in the house you know. He just expected his house to be run properly and he never got any of the details. He didn't know how to open the fridge or to take out a tray of ice — and I mean for instance he would go any place he felt like going but he always had the feeling that I should be here when he came home (Smith 1988: 170).

The joint conjugal role pattern involves the partners doing things together with little concern about what constitutes a 'male' activity or a 'female' activity (Smith 1988: 146). Thus both partners in the relationship engage in all activities necessary to the family — income-generating work, domestic chores and child care — as well as leisure activities. This pattern is rare in the Caribbean though there is evidence that the younger generation of the middle class is moving in this direction as the above quote from Mrs Cook implies. To return to the point made earlier, it is within this joint pattern that male and female are defined in relational terms and not as different and separate. In other words, women are no longer seen in contrast to men, as dependent and submissive, caring and nurturing and home-based, with their menfolk strong, sexually active and dominant and operating in the public domain, each efficiently performing the tasks to which they are best suited. Indeed, the joint pattern is often held up as the ideal against which the other models are unfavourably compared.

An interesting addition to this perspective on gender relationships is provided by Lazarus-Black (1991, see Article 5 at end of chapter) in her investigation of what it means when women in Antigua take men to court for child support. Her analysis supports the interpretation of Caribbean conjugal roles and relations as distinct and segregated. Mothering involves nurturing, feeding, teaching, disciplining and generally caring for the child, and although a father also provides care, his main task is to ensure economic maintenance. Men take pride in fatherhood and rarely deny paternity. The relationship between the child's mother and father should embody 'respect' (politeness and discretion), even after the couple has separated (Lazarus-Black 1991: 127-8). Among Antiguan lower-class males, 'big men' are distinguished from the rest as those with respectable jobs, regular income, leadership and other masculine qualities. Big men are also expected to conform to standards of family life which require that they support their wives and 'outside' women as well as all their children, legitimate or not. It is when they fail that women use the law. They are taken to court for violating fundamental moral principles. There they are ritually shamed and their status as 'big men' is challenged.

With this argument, Lazarus-Black took issue with models which interpret lower-class family relationships as economically motivated. If this were the case, she asked, why was there no sustained increase in requests for affiliation and maintenance in Antigua when, in 1982, the maximum awarded as child support was doubled (Lazarus-Black 1991: 126)? Additionally, not all legally defaulting fathers are taken to court. An irregular supporter is exempted, especially if his mother helps out. But he exposes himself to the risk of legal procedures if he disrespects her, for example, by insulting her in public. A woman takes her case to court for 'justice', to correct a breach in the moral codes governing gender relations and family life.

Matrifocality revisited

The phenomenon of matrifocality, the focus of much misunderstanding, as we have noted, has also been reinterpreted. Smith (1973) linked matrifocality to other cultural principles of family relationships and to the system of social stratification. According to him, the Caribbean kinship system is bilateral with a marked sexual division of labour operating within a system which separates the domestic domain from the wider political and economic arena. Women's roles in child-rearing and household chores are concentrated in the domestic sphere and, while men are segregated from that domain, they are nevertheless tied in as 'consumers of services, providers of support, and as linking elements between the domestic group and the external systems of social, economic, political and ritual activity' (Smith 1973: 139). Caribbean matrifocality is not simply centred on women, but is specifically mother-focussed for the reason 'that "mothering", or child-rearing, is the central activity of the domestic domain and is productive of the intense affective relations which pervade it' (Smith 1973: 140). Matrifocality is also linked to another principle of the Caribbean kinship complex, that is, the association of close and enduring family ties with the mother-child bond, not the conjugal relationship which is characterised as loose and unstable and is not generally expected to be otherwise.

The race and class distinctions of the wider system of social stratification and the circumstances of lower status and poverty are admittedly conducive to the development of matrifocality. But matrifocality is not the inevitable result. Neither is matrifocality necessarily confined to people living in these poor economic conditions, for there is no inherent reason why higher-status women should not also provide the central focus for domestic activity and kinship relations (Smith 1973: 142).

> I believe that there is value in retaining the term 'matrifocal family', and I also believe that its genesis and reproduction in the West Indies is closely related to the hierarchical structure of these societies. But it is not peculiar to the lower class, nor is it simply the consequence of certain functional problems within an ideally conceived nuclear family. It is part of a complex of meaning and action that constitutes the West Indian creole kinship system, a complex that necessarily involves all classes and status groups (Smith 1988: 8).

Matrifocality is reinterpreted and explained within the context of a historically established kinship complex of gender roles and relationships defined and symbolised within a Caribbean social hierarchy.

> Matrifocality arises from the way in which kinship and family life is practised, and that practice is rooted in the cultural meaning of social life developed over several hundred years. It can and will change, not as a response to increases in the level of living, but only if, and when, there is a change in the structure of social hierarchy and a change in the definition and meaning of sex roles. Matrifocality in domestic relations arises at the conjuncture of social hierarchy and marked sex role differentiation (Smith 1988: 180).

Male marginality revisited

The identification of the lower-class, black male as 'marginal' to the family in the Caribbean has become all too familiar. As we have noted, studies have consistently analysed male marginality, along with matrifocality, by constructing a chain of causes from underdevelopment and poverty through male unemployment to the inability of men to undertake the responsibilities expected of them in familial roles. Recent investigators who have listened to what men and women say about the principles and practices of male involvement in the family have challenged these interpretations of male marginality. We refer to three studies which tackle the issue from very different perspectives. The first analysed the meaning and performance of fatherhood among lower-class men in Jamaica and came to the conclusion that they are not 'marginal'; the second, an on-going and as yet un-reported study in Barbados, tested the 'male marginality' thesis within the extended rather than the nuclear family; the third, set in Jamaica, sought to explain why the middle class perceives its men as 'marginal'.

The study conducted by Brown, Anderson and Chevannes (1993) for the Caribbean Child Development Centre dealt in detail with the contribution of men to the family in six lower-class communities in Jamaica. The project concentrated essentially on the father role, and concluded that the performance of Jamaican men should not be rated as 'marginal' in this regard. Fathering was defined and judged by what the men and women in the study said about these roles so that the Caribbean cultural meaning of fatherhood constituted an integral part of the study.

In terms of gender roles and relationships, the researchers found that the expectations of fatherhood were minimal, defined to include economic maintenance and the discipline of children, especially sons. The satisfactory fulfillment of these duties ensures the male's status as head of the household (Brown et al. 1993: 76). Not only are responsibilities narrowly defined, but allowances are made for non-performance and community sanctions are weak. Additionally, fathering does not require the male's presence in the home on a regular basis. Women, especially those in visiting and common-law unions, expect that they will share the responsibility of generating income to support the family, at least during some phases of their life cycles, and paternal disciplinary measures are more in the form of threats, as actual punishment is administered by mothers. The high level of female-headed households in the Caribbean is an accepted fact of life.

Most significant from our perspective in this chapter are the project findings on what it means to be a father. The male respondents in this study expressed positive views. Fatherhood is perceived as central to male self-definition, 'a declaration both of their own manhood and their movement into maturity' (Brown et al. 1993: 132). The majority indicated that they would not marry an infertile woman and would feel fundamentally unfulfilled without children.

The powerful and even primordial feelings which men held about fatherhood came tumbling out in response to the question on how they thought they would feel if they had no children. This intensity was evident from the language in which they phrased their replies:

- I would feel like a bird without a wing

- I would feel like a tree in a forest without leaves

- I would feel no good as a man

- Like a eunuch

- I would feel haunted

- Like I am wasting my time

- Jealous of others who have

- I would run away from my wife

Other adjectives included: useless, empty, lonely, embarrassed, irresponsible, unbalanced, strange (Brown et al. 1993: 139).

Interestingly, the study also reported that respondents linked the fathering of children to cementing the relationship between themselves and the mother of their children. Even so, the parental roles of mother and father are segregated. The rearing of children is 'woman's work' and the domestic domain is hers. The performance of men as fathers requires little but, even then, many respondents expressed dissatisfaction with their own performance and might well have rated themselves as 'marginal'. But the meaning of the biological fact of fatherhood is anything but marginal. Men boast about having children, not about their contributions to rearing them (Brown et al. 1993: 198). Being a father is a most important part of being a man.

The second study (Barrow forthcoming/b) recognised the ethnocentric biases inherent in conclusions of 'male marginality' which were based solely on the nuclear family of procreation. In this respect, two assumptions inherited from structural functional theory persist in Caribbean family studies. The first is that adult male familial roles are assumed to be confined to those of the nuclear family and the second that males as adults complete the transfer, physically and emotionally, from the family of orientation into which they were born to the family of procreation within which they produce children. Accordingly, they are perceived and judged to be 'marginal' solely as 'husbands' and fathers. Their roles as sons in particular and also as brothers, uncles and others in the extended family, while recognised and reported as ethnographic data, are not incorporated into discussions of male marginality.

Within the Caribbean family, a man's most intensive and enduring relationship is the one he has with his mother. It is a relationship of close emotional and material interdependency, first he on her, then she on him. The relationship survives and he may live at 'home' with her until her death, often a devastating period in the life of the son. The mother-son relationship constitutes the pivot of Caribbean family structure around which the other family relationships revolve.

Much of this was recognised in earlier ethnography. Clarke (1970(1957): 163-164), for example, described the mother-son bond as 'exclusive and often obsessive' and cited the cases in which sons continue to depend on their mothers well beyond adolescence, often postponing co-residence with a conjugal partner and continuing to live at home.

Boys also are tied to their mothers and sometimes postpone leaving home for many years. They do not as a rule set up house with their girlfriends until they are well on in the twenties. Although they may themselves be fathers they live in their mother's yard. One man of about 33 whose eldest child is ten neither brings his woman and children home, nor goes and lives with them. He is very kind to them and proud of the children so this does not seem to be motivated by dislike. He is just very tied to his mother. Once when she was ill he sat on the bed holding her in his arms for hours. When she wanted to vomit it was he who held the pot and helped her, not the women of the household (Kerr 1952: 70)

Mothers do not give up claims on their sons. Sons are expected to support their mothers financially and emotionally and seem to honour these obligations without hesitation. Smith (1956: 120) summed up the situation in Guyanese village life:

> Unmarried sons stay on as nominal members of their family of orientation even when they begin to go to work away from their village, but although they usually send money home to their mothers or otherwise assist in the maintenance of the household, there is no well-defined place for them in the family group except as sons who are obliged to show deference to their mothers. It is mothers who often show jealous when their sons contemplate breaking away and getting married, and cases occur of women resorting to some form of Obeah practice to try to prevent their sons leaving their home. On the other hand, sons will rarely have an open breach with their mothers and even after they set up their own households they continue to send money and gifts to them if they can afford it. The tie between mothers and adult daughters is effected more through their common interest in their children and their solidarity as mothers, whereas the mother-son bond finds maximum expression in economic co-operation of some kind. We saw earlier that sons help to build houses for their mothers, and they may also take on the responsibility for the payment of rates on their mother's land if she is left alone without a spouse (Smith 1956: 120).

The end result is that women generally manage to secure company and support for their old age through their roles as mothers and grandmothers, whereas many elderly men fear loneliness and neglect, especially with the death of or separation from their conjugal partners through whom they might otherwise have maintained a close, affective link to the wider kinship network.

Though research has not, as yet, pursued an in-depth analysis into what we might call the 'cultural domain of motherhood', along the lines proposed by Alexander, there is evidence that the mother-daughter tie differs from that of mother and son. Mothers and daughters are linked through the fact of common lifestyle, their joint involvement in bearing and raising children and the elder woman's assumption of the role of grandmother. Indeed, studies have suggested potential conflict between the two if the daughter becomes a mother and remains in the same household (Smith 1956: 144-145). But the intensely affective relationship between mother and son persists. According to informants in the CCDC study, to which we have just referred, women 'bring up their sons to remain sons' and neither prepare nor encourage them to enter conjugal relationships (Brown et al. 1993: 55,81). Conflict between a son's conjugal partner and his mother is virtually inevitable as the mother does all she can to prevent the son from leaving home and as the two women jealously make competing demands on his financial resources and emotional commitment. In addition, male familial roles as siblings are also important. As elder brothers, their responsibilities included providing guidance and support, often financial, for their younger brothers and particularly their sisters. They are particularly involved in protecting and defending the honour of their sisters through adolescence and early sexual experience and, by extension, often develop close supportive relationships as uncles, especially with their sister's children (Barrow forthcoming).

Third is Jack Alexander's analysis of male marginality (Alexander 1977) which was based on in-depth and detailed interviews with middle-class Jamaicans. His discovery that the Jamaican middle class perceives its males as 'marginal' to the family refutes previous notions of economic causality and also the assumptions that middle-class males are perceived to perform their roles as husbands and fathers adequately.

According to Alexander, lower-class male marginality may have preoccupied Caribbean researchers, but it is not of major concern to the people they have studied. Middle-class Jamaicans, however, are very concerned about male marginality. The reason has to do with how essential the husband/father is to the family. Among the middle class, his responsibilities as authority figure and steady income provider for important long-term investments is crucial. If he fails to fulfil these duties, the family is threatened and he is perceived as marginal. In contrast, among the lower class he is not indispensable to the family and the group is not threatened if he is not around.

> It is easier to demonstrate that anthropologists have focussed on the marginality of lower-class black fathers than it is to demonstrate that lower-class blacks themselves do not focus on the marginality of fathers. Since most anthropologists have focussed on matrifocality they have asked about it and have received the answers they were looking for. However in my experience with and observation of lower-class persons ... there is little emphasis on this problem. The probability that a male will play a dominant or equal part in the family with the mother is neither more nor less important than most realities lower-class persons need to calculate. Lower-class women seek a man to 'response' for them, but it is not a central preoccupation of theirs (Alexander 1977: 372).

Middle-class perceptions of male marginality are also tied in with fundamental cultural principles of family and society in Jamaica, in particular male dominance, the sharp differentiation of sex roles, the segregation of conjugal partners and the ideology of civilised male behaviour. Alexander also reported that female gender roles are identified primarily with the domestic domain. It is here that she has responsibility and authority, while the sphere of male activity and authority is the world of work and public affairs. Though women engage in income-generating employment outside the home, they should not assume dominance in the relationship. Common to both men and women is the perception that women are committed to the family; men are not and are 'irresponsible'. It is also said that women actually encourage male marginalisation in the family. As mothers, they spoil their boy-children and as wives, resourcefully manage household and business matters, leaving nothing for the men to do. The major indicator of middle-class male weakness and 'irresponsibility' is sexual infidelity, the same behavioural pattern that has been associated with the lower class. Alexander's informants assert,

> that men in the middle class 'run around' just as much as in the lower class, but are simply careful to maintain proper appearances with a public home, wife and offspring and private outside relations. It is important to note for the purpose of our analysis that the marginality of the middle-class male is formulated in the same moral terms as the marginality of lower class males: sexual indulgence vs. the 'responsibilities' of a 'serious covenant' (Alexander 1977: 377).

And yet, middle-class men are seen as marginal by others of their class, while lower-class men are not. Indeed, the behaviour of the 'marginal men' among Alexander's informants is not unequivocally 'irresponsible'. There are those men who are not continually unfaithful, who spend time at home, who are often very much involved with their children and who work hard to support and care for their families. In addition, in other societies in which family life is similarly structured, males are not characterised as marginal. Adding to the confusion is the fact that sexual unfaithfulness is also admired as a mark of higher status so that a man can at one and the same time be 'irresponsible' and acquire prestige. Why then, is it only the Jamaican middle-class men who are perceived as marginal and why is this the case when much of their actual familial behaviour is not irresponsible and some of the irresponsible behaviour may actually be admired?

The answer to the paradox, according to Alexander, lies in viewing the definition of Jamaican middle-class male marginality as part of an ideology and to focus on the way in which the evaluation of male behaviour in the public arena influences perceptions of men as husbands and fathers. A man's public behaviour is defined by how 'civilized' he is, 'civilization' being a quality of culture that is imparted in the educational system and reflected in domestic life. As Alexander (1977: 386) explained:

It is my contention that the subordinate position of non-white men in the public domain is conceived of in terms of their not possessing enough 'civilization', which is prerequisite of gaining responsibility, and this lack of civilization is symbolized by the definition of the male in the family. For the essence of the definition of the male in the family is that he is irresponsible and follows his natural uncivilized inclinations, most noticeably his sexual inclinations. Thus the ideology that evaluates the male in the family negatively is a way of talking about his position in the public domain.

He concluded:

The middle class must constantly strive toward an ideal it can never achieve in order to avoid falling into the lower class. The middle-class public decrial of lower-class male irresponsibility and its private acknowledgement of middle-class male irresponsibility perfectly expresses its attempt to separate itself from the lower class while fearing it has failed (Alexander 1977: 387).

Illegitimacy

Just as non-legal and 'outside' unions are a part of family life in all classes so, it follows, are illegitimate and 'outside' births. Alexander, for example, found that illegitimacy featured in the genealogies of all his middle-class informants. This fact of kinship practice in the Caribbean has also been ignored, again largely due to data collection methods. Illegitimacy has been viewed from the perspective of the mother and while it is true that the father is generally also lower class and, in the case of co-residential common-law unions, easily identified, illegitimacy is also the result of relationships across class. The structure of illegitimacy in these cases is such that it is the father of the child that is usually of higher status. In virtually all cases the child lives with the mother or one of her kin with the result that, in surveys which focus on household composition, the father remains invisible and illegitimacy is assumed to be confined to the lower class. As Manyoni (1977: 418, see Article 4 at end of chapter) explained, illegitimacy is largely considered from the perspective of maternity rather than both maternity and paternity. Since lower status women tend to be the sexual victims of higher status males, and the physical evidence of childbirth is unequivocally linked with the woman, illegitimacy is thus often associated with her and the status group to which she is ascribed. Sociological results inevitably tend to draw correlations between the incidence of 'illegitimate' births and lower status women and to associate the phenomenon with the value system of their status group.

Adopting alternative methodologies has made it quite clear that illegitimacy is a structural feature of family life in all classes of Caribbean society. According to Alexander, among the middle class in Jamaican society, illegitimacy is expected and there are no structurally generated sanctions against it (Alexander 1984: 160). Indeed official attitudes have become less condemnatory in recent years as evidenced particularly in the passage of legislation to formally remove the legal distinction between illegitimate and legitimate children, for example in Barbados (The Status of the Children Act, 1979) and in Jamaica (The Status of the Children Act, 1976). Nevertheless, as reported for Jamaica, the birth of 'outside', illegitimate children among the middle and upper classes is 'stigmatised' and 'the social and emotional significance remains' (Douglass 1992: 188). This suggests that there are class and gender differences in attitudes towards illegitimacy.

For Alexander's middle-class Jamaican informants, illegitimacy is 'improper' and 'provokes shame and silence'. In one of his case-studies, which details word for word a conversation between himself and an informant, illegitimacy is 'frowned on' as something to 'keep very quiet' and 'away from the family' and illegitimate offspring are 'avoided', 'shunned' and potentially embarrassing (Alexander 1984: 159-160, see Article 1 at end of chapter). On the other hand, Alexander (1984: 158-159) also quoted an informant whose testimony suggests that the well-established, middle-class male appears to suffer no shame and his wife may even take his 'outside' children into their home. The case of Mrs Brown's family demonstrates much the same middle-class response to illegitimacy.

> Mrs. Ester Brown's grandfathers were pillars of respectability; both had outside unions and outside children. The maternal grandfather acquired a lady friend only after his children were grown up and he had sold the large family house, replacing it with a series of smaller ones — for his wife, each of his married children, and his mistress. He was seventy-three years old when his outside son was born. The other grandfather had five children with his outside lady, their birth paralleling that of his legitimate children. He often fathered two in one year; one outside and one inside. The children of both grandfathers received an adequate middle-class education and are now fully accepted as part of Mrs. Brown's family circle (Smith 1988: 118).

For established middle-class men, having so-called 'bastard children' seems to be no disgrace and might have quite the opposite effect as such 'irresponsibility' enhances their masculinity. It appears therefore, that they may have more in common with their counterparts in the lower class than they do with young men of their own class for whom illegitimate children are a definite drawback as they aspire to consolidate their status.

For women, the meaning of illegitimate births is not articulated in quite the same way (see also Douglass 1992: 187-196). In general, giving birth to illegitimate offspring is unacceptable for middle-class women and for some it is nothing short of disaster. Though cases seem to be relatively few, they do occur, mainly among young girls where they are generally perceived as the mistakes of youth and inexperience and are dealt with by other family members.

> On Mrs. Brown's genealogy there were many cases of young, middle-class women having babies that were looked after by other family members; cases of covering up premarital pregnancy by sending the girl abroad; and cases where the child is just accepted into the girl's family of orientation until she marries. All informants suggested that premarital pregnancy affects the chances of making a good marriage, but in practice it seems to make very little difference. Middle-class women who had illegitimate children married men with good occupations. These pregnancies were youthful errors; the result of affairs where the father was of the same class background. Sometimes a marriage would result, but if the child were born illegitimate it would be brought up in a middle-class milieu, acquiring all the benefits of its class, including the all-important 'good' education (Smith 1988: 122).

Manyoni's Barbadian informants included female patients attending a rural public clinic, a sample of women selected with the assistance of the Family Planning Field Unit and female occupants of a sample of rural households (Manyoni 1977: 423, 425). He makes no reference to the social status of his informants, but it is likely that they were predominantly lower class. In Barbados, the women who attend public clinics and who utilise family planning services are mainly from the lower class as are the occupants of most of the households in the outer rural parishes included in the investigation. According to Manyoni, none of these women expressed resentment or shame at revealing very personal details of sexual and familial experiences. While they went to great length to hide the extra-marital relationships in which they were involved, the resulting pregnancies were perceived fatalistically. No attempt was made to conceal illegitimate births and no social disgrace was attached to them.

This evidence suggests that the implications of illegitimate births are different according to class and gender. For lower-class women they are natural and inevitable, while for their middle-class counterparts they bring a measure of shame and disgrace. For men, fathering illegitimate children is evidence of masculinity and an assertion of status. For all, however, illegitimacy is a fact of life, a fundamental principle of Caribbean family structure.

The importance of history

If the understanding of Caribbean kinship is to be sought within cultural ideology and practice, rather than in contemporary functions, adaptations or individual transactions, then a study of how that culture has developed is essential. While scholars have not yet provided us with anything like a comprehensive history of kinship in the Caribbean, all the researchers quoted in this chapter have turned their attention to the analysis of kinship and sexual attitudes and practices in historical perspective. The meaning of modern family and conjugal relations within and across the boundaries of race and class has a long Caribbean history dating back to the slave period.

The basic principle concerning marriage and legitimate children established during slavery and perceived from the perspectives of white dominant culture, defined these as appropriate between status equals. Concubinage and 'outside' children were associated with those who were socially unequal. The consolidation of property and the pursuit of business and political interests through marriage and legitimate sons created Caribbean family dynasties of great power and influence. These marriages, however, were not necessarily associated with the formation of nuclear family households. Mortality rates were high, especially for men, and widowhood and remarriage a familiar pattern for women so that compound families were common.

Planter households contained a variety of relatives and other inhabitants, attended by a retinue of domestic slaves and servants, all of whom appeared on occasion to be members of one large extended family in all but blood. Also present were the domestic units consisting of concubines and their 'bastard' children. The majority of white men in plantation society did not live with wives and children in family groups. Most were unmarried and highly mobile. They sought temporary sexual unions with black and coloured women as indeed, did the married planters themselves.

> The turnover of white employees on sugar estates was remarkably high; on the average sugar estate in Jamaica there was a constant procession of young, single white men passing through the estate, moving on to better jobs or falling ill and dying. The life of the white staff was organized around the overseer's house and catered to by cooks, washers and cleaning servants provided by the estate, but it was customary for white men to form semi-permanent attachments to women — slave or free — who provided services beyond those laid down in the estate code (Smith 1988: 156).

The women involved may have been 'sexual victims' in some cases, but in others they actively pursued concubinage relations with higher-status men, coloured as well as white, for the material advantages which ensued and also, in Jamaica for example, with the view to lightening the colour of their children, a process which over the generations would result in the legal redefinition of these children as white.

Although planter society condoned sexual liaisons across the colour line, marriages would have been viewed with horror. It would seem, therefore, that coloured women may have faced reality in terms of the possibilities of their relationships with white men, chosen to form temporary sexual unions and managed their own matrifocal households containing the children from these various partners. A case in point is that of Mulatto Kitty whose history Smith (1988: 96) adapts from the account written by Michael Craton (1978).

> Mulatto Kitty, daughter of Robert Ellis, white bookkeeper and overseer, and Amy, black creole field slave, was born in 1795. Because of her colour she was put to work as a house slave in the overseer's quarters. The rapid turnover of white employees on Jamaican estates during the slavery period is well documented and explains the child-bearing history of this woman. She had six quadroon children by three different white men — bookkeepers and overseers — and two sambo children by two black men whose names are unknown. As Craton suggests, it is likely that Kitty became housekeeper of the overseer's house, a position of some authority and she was probably the most permanent and stable member of that household in which she brought up her eight children. What happened to her, or her children, after emancipation is not known but her life seems to have been the very archetype of what is now regarded as the unstable domestic life of the lower class, and the very archetype of the 'matrifocal' household.

It was reported from Barbados that for coloured women it was just as virtuous and respectable to be the mistress of a white man as it was to be married to one of their own colour (Manyoni (quoting from Sewell) 1977: 420). Some of them actually lived in the households of their masters and had their offspring accepted into these households by their masters' wives, a practice which was reported to have survived at least until the last generation in Jamaica (Alexander 1984: 159). Coloured men were often left with little choice but to marry or engage in concubinage relationships with women of lower status and darker colour, with the result that their children were generally darker than themselves.

Racial and gender beliefs also formed an integral part of these ideologies of sex and family. Black slaves were stereotyped by the white population as promiscuous, licentious and incapable of forming enduring marital relationships based on civilised love and commitment. Only in their later years were they thought to be able to settle down, control their animal-like sexual urges and form faithful and stable unions. Even then, they were considered to be outside the domain of Christian civilisation.

Adding to the overall picture are contrasting images of women, black and white. As members of their race, black women represented unrestrained sexuality, quite the reverse of the fragile, white woman whose role in life was to be married, cloistered, protected and to produce sons. Perhaps coloured women were perceived as combining the positive characteristics of the two, a more physically attractive and refined version of black sexuality. The point is that these images and ideologies reinforced illegitimacy, concubinage and the virtual absence of marriage across the colour line and within the slave population. Among the slaves, marriage was prohibited until the latter days of the slave regime, so that notions of legitimacy and illegitimacy had no meaning except for those with wealthy, white, married fathers. The structural principles of family life in the Caribbean as determined by dominant patriarchal planter culture were established many years ago. Conjugal union types, the nature of family relationships and the structure of households correlated with race and class and intersected in the lives of well-to-do men.

The kinship system incorporating these principles is important to those involved in it not only from the perspective of survival, but also because it provides meaning. This point can best be illustrated with reference to what Alexander calls the 'origin myth' of the Jamaican middle class (Alexander 1984: 173-175). It is necessary to understand this myth in order to understand their interpretation of their position in Jamaican society and the negative image which they have of their family life. All of Alexander's informants traced their genealogies back to a founding ancestral couple whom they believed to have existed, but could not specifically identify. All were convinced that they originated as the coloured offspring of a white master and a female slave and assumed a status midway between them. This origin myth contains within it the fundamental structural principles of Jamaican society, the juxtaposition of English, white and civilised and African, black and uncivilised, and the conjunction of these in the middle-class, coloured male. Kinship and affinity are central to the myth, for just as the two races mixed but did not amalgamate, so legal and non-legal conjugal unions and legitimate and illegitimate children are distinguished but also linked through male irresponsibility. Contemporary Jamaican, middle-class men are not sufficiently civilised and responsible in the public domain, a characteristic which is symbolised in family life where they combine proper behaviour with irresponsible, natural instincts.

Conclusion

The principles of Caribbean kinship have become thoroughly institutionalised at all levels of society. Taken together, they form a kinship system at the level of ideology and practice, irrespective of class and colour. Differential incidences of marriage and other patterns occur as we move from one class to another so that the proportion of visiting, common-law and multiple unions is higher in the lower class as is the degree of matrifocality. For the middle class, marriage with status equals contrasts with concubinage relationships with those of lower status and often darker colour, while among the lower class, marriage occurs, if at all, at a later stage of life. But these are variations of incidence, not plural systems of kinship. From among the common principles mentioned in this chapter we might highlight the centrality of the mother-child bond, matrifocality, sex role differentiation, conjugal union segregation, male sexual infidelity, close enduring bonds with one's own kin and the prevalence of non-marital unions and illegitimate children, none of which is the special preserve of any one class or racial group. To those with even a cursory knowledge of contemporary family life among the different classes in the Caribbean, these patterns must appear familiar.

Caribbean kinship patterns have acquired stability and tenacity over many generations. Lower-class family patterns were not a function of slave status or of economic conditions of the slave and post-emancipation periods. When the abolition of slavery removed legal distinctions on the basis of race and colour, there was no rush to marry among the ex-slaves despite pressure from missionaries and priests. Neither, it would appear, was there any reduction in 'outside' unions and 'outside' children. From a contemporary perspective, even though the standard of living and consumption patterns of the lower class in Caribbean societies have improved enormously since the 1940s and 1950s, marriage rates have hardly changed and illegitimacy remains high. Referring to Jamaica, Roberts and Sinclair (1978: 8-9) support the point.

> There have been therefore marked social and economic changes in the island during the post-slavery era. But it is contended here that there is no evidence of any change in mating forms over this period ....

> Statistically, two sets of complementary data available since 1878 can be relied on to support this. The first of these is the series of marriage rates. These have remained almost unchanged since the introduction of vital registration, at between 3 and 4 per 1,000. The only important departure from this level occurred in 1907, and this can be attributed to an act of God, the destruction of Kingston by earthquake and fire in that year. During the year 1906-7, the number of marriages celebrated amounted to 5,500, and 1,228 of these took place within one month of the disaster. In the following year the number rose to 6,200, giving a marriage rate of 7.7, the highest ever recorded in the island. In keeping with our hypothesis, we may consider this dramatic rush to marriage as a collective effort on the part of the society to seek closer conformity with formal religion at a time of natural disaster. But apart from this short-lived upturn in the marriage rate and a slight decline during the period of world-wide economic depression of the early 1930s, marriage rates have not moved very much.

> The second series, the rates of illegitimacy, also have shown no real change over the period covered by vital registration. As in the case of the marriage rates the only departures were in the years 1906-7 and 1907-8 during which a concomitant decline was observed in illegitimacy rates. These rates have been, by European standards, extremely high, that is in the high 60s and low 70s. This was the phenomenon which attracted most attention and comment in the early reports of the first Registrar General of Jamaica, S. P. Smeeton. He protested strongly against what he called 'this Hydra-headed evil' and even for a time had the names of fathers entered in the registers —although this contravened the law — in the hope of reducing this high level of illegitimacy. But

there has been no change in this level, which remains the strongest evidence in support of our argument that no fundamental change in family forms has taken place since emancipation.

Finally, we hasten to add two points. Firstly, the perspective adopted for studies of Caribbean kinship ideology and practice may well tend to overestimate the degree to which creolisation has generated shared symbols and common experiences. The danger here is to assume a clear family culture to which everyone agrees. As Smith (1982: 121) himself cautions, the principals of Caribbean family must not be overformalised in such a way that 'eliminates the ambiguity, uncertainty and contradictions which are an integrated part of the system.' Elites and the poor, as well as male and female, young and old, view marriage, infidelity, male marginality, illegitimacy and outside children differently. Even persons of the same status may not structure their family lives in the same way. There are those, for example, for whom common-law unions are a socially acceptable alternative, while for others they are avoided and condemned as 'living in sin'.

Secondly, these theoretical insights must not be taken to imply that Caribbean family patterns are fixed for all time. An important example of change is the rise to middle-class status of coloured and black women in the post-emancipation period and their change of attitude and behaviour as they subjected themselves to the civilising forces of Christianity and education and renounced concubinage. For them marriage and legitimacy became an obsession as they sought respectability for their families. They vociferously denounced what they saw as the promiscuity and immorality of the lower classes and promoted proper family life increasingly based on western patterns of faithful marriage, legitimate children and nuclear family households. But they were faced with their own husbands, fathers and sons, firmly embedded in Caribbean culture, for whom peer group popularity, non-domestic activity, marital segregation, concubinage and outside children had become a way of life. It remains to be seen whether the demands for marital fidelity, domestic togetherness and joint social activity on the part of young, contemporary, middle-class women will result in a change to these long-established structural principles of Caribbean kinship. But for now, we can agree with Smith (1988: 166) that 'there has been little or no change in the pattern of domestic and kinship relations consequent upon 'economic development' or, we might add, as a result of social, legal and religious pressure.

READINGS

J. Alexander

LOVE, RACE, SLAVERY AND SEXUALITY IN JAMAICAN IMAGES OF THE FAMILY

INTRODUCTION

Lady Maria Nugent, daughter of an American colonist and wife of the British governor of Jamaica, kept a diary during her stay in Jamaica from 1801 to 1805. In her diary she recounts a visit to one of the 'better' sugar plantations in the island:

> As you enter the gates, there is a long range of negro houses, like thatched cottages, and a row of cocoa-nut trees and clumps of cotton trees. The sugar-house, and all the buildings, are thought to be more than usually good, and well taken care of. The overseer, a civil, vulgar, Scotch officer, on half-pay, did the honours to us; but, when we got to the door of the distillery, the smell of the rum was so intolerable, that ... I left the gentlemen, and went to the overseer's house, about a hundred yards off. I talked to the black women, who told me all their histories. The overseer's *chere amie,* and no man here is without one, is a tall black woman, well made, with a very flat nose, thick lips, and a skin of ebony, highly polished and shining. She shewed me her three yellow children, and said, with some ostentation she should soon have another. The marked attention of the other women, plainly proved her to be the favourite Sultana of this vulgar, ugly, Scotch Sultan, who is about fifty, clumsy, ill made, and dirty. He had a dingy, sallow-brown complexion, and only two yellow discoloured tusks, by way of teeth. However, they say he is a good overseer. (Wright 1966, p. 29)

In this essay we will find the image of the overseer, his *chere amie* of polished ebony, and their yellow children hidden in and structuring the everyday perceptions of family life experienced by middle-class Jamaicans.

Our informants will eventually lead us to their understanding of their place in Jamaican society, for that understanding permeates their family lives. We will find that the power of their image of the family lies in its ability to resolve the paradox of legitimacy in a colonial society. What characterizes the 'colonial situation' is a racial, social, and cultural split between the dominators and the dominated, whereas on the other hand legitimacy — 'the means by which ideology is blended with power' (Fried 1967, p. 26) — is a cultural phenomenon consisting of beliefs that justify the exercise of power. How can there be legitimacy, which requires a common culture, when the essence of the colonial situation is a total split between the dominators and the dominated? It is the image of the family that formulates legitimacy in the Jamaican colonial situation. Thus this essay heeds the contention of Smith 'that more attention should be paid to the particularity of the historically generated cultural forms characteristic of the area and to the social practices through which those forms operate in the specific conditions of contemporary Latin American societies'.

The collection and analysis of the data in this essay have been based on the method and theory of David M. Schneider and Raymond T. Smith, (Schneider 1972, (1968) 1980; Schneider and Smith, (1973) 1978). The data consist of a set of interviews with eleven middle-class Jamaican informants collected between 1967 and 1969. Interviews were approximately weekly and lasted between one and two hours. The shortest set was seven interviews over two months; the longest set was thirty-one interviews over fourteen months. All interviews were taped and transcribed, a process that provided a set of texts to analyze.

The analysis assumes that culture consists of a pure level of domains, such as kinship and age, which consist of a set of collective representations that cohere, and that pure domains combine on a conglomerate level to create domainssuch as the family — that are for action (Schneider 1972, pp. 40-41). Therefore the analysis begins with a description of domains, proceeds to describe how these combine into the domain of the family, and finally shows how the cultural domain of the family is related to action in the society.

KINSHIP

The first interview with each informant began with the request 'Please tell me all your relatives.' Requests for clarification of the question were turned back on the informant, who was encouraged to clarify the question for him or herself. The aim of the technique is to set a framework in which informants choose how to present their relatives so that their presentations represent their own conception of relatives and can be analyzed as such.

Informants asked for two types of clarification. With one kind of question the anthropologist was asked, on the basis of his presumed superior knowledge, to define for the informant exactly what a relative is, the informants believing themselves to have an imperfect concept of this term. Thus, these informants' collective representation of kinship may be said to reside in an ideal or objective realm. The informant fills this collective representation with personal meaning, listing not 'Father' but 'my father' and listing relatives by personal name. The intimate tie and analytic distinction between the informant's collective representation and the personal meaning given to it is illustrated by the fact that, if we construct this collective representation, we can see how the informant manipulates it and thus reveals personal meanings. For instance, kin listed and the order of kin are highly consistent among informants, yet one informant did not mention her father at all in the first interview. Our suspicion that this absence tells us something about her is amply confirmed at the beginning of the second interview. 'I left out a most important person .... In the days when my mother was a girl, to have an illegitimate child in a small district was a great disgrace .... I was illegitimate, an unfortunate thing. So after I came to the age of discretion, I personally felt a great remorse. And I still do.'

Examples of the second kind of question are 'Do you want the dead ones?' 'Do you want more than the close ones?' Having defined *relatives* for themselves, the informants still need further clarification in order to determine which persons are relatives. The collective representation *relatives* is ambiguous when put to use.

These two kinds of original questions express from the outset two related themes that run through the interviews — a collective representation of kinship conceived by the informant to exist in an ideal, objective realm and an ambiguity in the use of this collective representation.

When also asked to define *relatives*, informants have difficulty producing a definition they find adequate, and if they come up with a definition they find adequate, it is easy to push them into a position where they become uncertain. Informants offer two reasons for this difficulty. One is that kinship concerns feelings that are illogical and difficult to conceptualize. The second is that having referred to their feelings as an essential part of the meaning of *relative*, they find that their feelings do not consistently distinguish between relatives and non-relatives, because one component of the meaning of *relative* is independent of their feelings: 'I was interpreting family in one conversation as consanguinity, as blood relationship, and another time I was interpreting it as a sort of emotional, inclusive group, and I think people vary between the two posts, as least I do, according to circumstances.'

If we examine more closely informants' feeling of kinship and their idea of blood relationship, we can discover why the conceptual vagueness and inconsistency do not normally disturb them.

The most common feeling informants associate with kinship is the feeling of belonging.

A: So the relationship isn't distinguished by the fact that you help those people more than others?

I: No.

A: Or that you feel closer to them.

I: No. There is a — how can I find the right word? there is a feeling of belonging. That's all there is.

A: A feeling of belonging.

I: A feeling of belonging. That's the best way I think I can describe it. But it does not obligate you all.

The objective fact of blood relation is the possession of a common physical substance. Though informants regard blood relationship as an objective fact of nature, it has a further meaning to them: 'I would very much like to know, which I will never know, where the various families I'm comprised of come from .... My parents accentuated the white side. Well, we all know it's a healthy mixture. The fact that we know we're so mixed up .... there's nothing we can do about it. We must just accept ourselves as we are.'

Thus, I am, in some way and to some extent the physical substance I consist of and insofar as I share some of the substance with others, we are the same. For informants a blood relation means that they share the same substance and to the extent share a common identity. It is this sense of common identity that the biological fact of blood relationship conveys to them.

The feeling of belonging and the meaning of a common substance fit together and reinforce each other. The impact of the collective representation, consisting of these two apparently disparate elements, is revealed in the following observation by a male informant:

I: Now, I feel a person outside could not have the same love for a child that a mother would have.

A: How about a father?

I: A father too. I don't know, Jack, but I never thought about it. I tell you something. When I got married, my wife went to the hospital; I said, 'Now, there's one thing, I ain't touching that child. Do you hear me? No, sir, I ain't looking after no pickney, you know.' And it just never, well, I just, and I wondered what I would do. I never had any feeling. I don't know how to explain. And yet, the evening when I came home from work and stopped off at the hospital and the nurse showed me, well, that is your, when I go and looked on it, a feeling passed through me that changed my entire, something inward took place, a transformation, instantly I felt it, and I knew that I was no longer a single person, and I had a responsibility, and I had something, my child, and it has never left me since. I don't know if it has happened to you?

Here we see the power of symbols. The stimulus of a newborn child is endowed with a meaning that produces a powerful feeling that manifests itself in the world of ideas as a sense of common identity ('I knew I was no longer a single person') and a sense of belonging.

We can state the collective representation of *blood relatives* as follows: blood relatives share a common substance that is a part of nature, and thereby and to that extent, they share a common identity, which gives them a feeling of belonging. Thus, the symbol of blood relations, of substantial unity, creates meaning in certain physical objects in the world, persons defined as relatives, and this meaning arouses feelings in the actor.

What has from the beginning of the section appeared to be an inconsistency and even contradiction between two elements of the collective representation of relatives turns out to be highly consistent and mutually reinforcing.

Having revealed the collective representation of relatives that lies behind and gives shape to the accounts of individual informants, let me show that the meaning this representation gives to experience can best be understood as the resolution of a problem of meaning arising from action.

The collective representation of relatives asserts the fact of a permanent fundamental mutuality of interest between persons defined as relatives in the sense that the welfare of one is the welfare of the other; it asserts what Schneider terms 'enduring diffuse solidarity' ([1968] 1980, p. 50) or what Fortes terms the 'axiom of amity' (1969,p. 219). This cultural assertion of a permanent mutuality of interests between persons focuses on part of the inherent characteristics of social experience and proclaims this part to be the whole. Insofar as persons are social beings they are interdependent. Therefore, they are means to one anothers' ends, and this interdependence creates a mutuality of interests. This same interdependence also creates the possibility of a conflict of interest, because by withholding him or herself a person can thwart the achievement of the ends of someone else with whom he or she has a social relation. Therefore, the collective representation of relatives, which asserts a total and permanent identity of interests, operates as an ideology that marks off a category of relations for which it asserts the reality of one aspect of social experience, mutuality, at the expense of another aspect, conflict.

The ideology of relatives asserts the permanent mutuality of interests in a particular symbolic form. A physical identity is asserted, the meaning of which is a feeling that is formulated as a feeling of belonging. This physical identity is asserted to be a natural, given, permanent condition.

Thus, perceptual experience — for instance, a newborn child — is given thinkable form by the symbol of shared physical substance, the meaning of which is a feeling that takes thinkable form as a feeling of 'belonging'. Now the thinkable form, the symbol of shared substance and belonging, can make most sense, for an anthropologist, if we assume that people think in order to act. Anthropologists will most fully explain the collective representation *relative* if we suppose that humans give meaning to experience in order to formulate choices and in order to live with the consequences of choices, for they must choose; the choice can be formulated only by humanly attributed meanings. Can we say anything about why (1) the symbol for 'enduring, diffuse solidarity' is shared physical substance and a feeling of belonging, and why (2) the symbol splits into what is formulated by the culture as an objective and a subjective aspect?

The answer to the first question is that in order to assert the existence of a category of social relations in which mutuality is inherent and conflict is not, the mutuality is expressed as a natural phenomenon, that is, one over which humans have no control. Mutuality is formulated not as a possibility, opportunity, or obligation, all of which imply human choice, but as a fact outside the realm of human choice. How is this formulation a solution to a problem of meaning arising from action? If we impute to humans the experience of choice, then the definition of an unchangeable mutuality of interest will make sense only if it is defined as outside the realm of human choice.

Let us turn now to the second question — the split of the collective representation *relative* into objective and subjective aspects. The formulation of *relative* as a given natural fact in a sense lifts *relative* out of the realm of human choice. However, it is a characteristic of Jamaican culture that phenomena defined as outside the realm of human choice are conceived of as outside the realm of human responsibility. An American example is the effort currently being expended to choose the fate of one's ascribed sex role. A Jamaican example is the fact that in Jamaica race is an ambivalent phenomenon; on the one hand, it is conceived as a very deep, given component of the person, and on the other hand, precisely because it is a characteristic over which a person has no control, informants treat it as an extraneous fact for which they take no responsibility. Within kinship itself its ascribed character can be and often is taken as grounds for denying its relevance for action: 'you can choose your friends, but not your relatives'.

In short, on the level of meaning, what is defined as an objective fact of nature cannot be in itself a meaningful ground for a motive of action. Because action involves choice, any reason that denies the realm of choice is senseless as a reason for choice; it does not, so to speak, give a reason for effort. It is only what is formulated as a subjective state for example, calculating the benefits to be gained from alternative actions or a feeling of belonging — that can make sense as a basis for action.

In fact, the area marked off as *relatives* is experienced as an area of action; whether informants' behaviour is in accord with the norm of enduring, diffuse solidarity or not, it is experienced as an action, not a reflex. It is this experience of action that demands, so to speak, a subjective aspect in the collective representation of relative. It is the permanent, given aspect that demands an objective aspect in this collective representation.

In everyday life the collective representation *relative* works smoothly, for after all, that is what it is designed to do. It is only in marginal situations that its nature as a solution to an intractable problem of meaning in action appears.

In addition to a spontaneous kin list, a genealogy was collected from each informant. In the genealogy each link was explored for further links, so that the genealogies were much larger than the spontaneous kin lists. One feature of these genealogies is especially relevant for our present purposes. In eight cases the genealogies trace back to an ancestral couple; in three cases they do not. The eight informants who donot have ancestral couples are all of middle-class origin; the three informants who do not have an ancestral couple are all of lower-class origin. The significance of the ancestral couple can be understood by examining one case more closely. The following are an informant's descriptions first of her ancestral couple and then of another ascendant couple.

I: From what I was always told, my great-grandmother who married McManus, she was supposed to be the daughter of a slave.

A: And a planter, did you tell me?

I: Well it's always these people that came out on the plantations, some of them may have been overseers, I don't know which, but he would have been a, probably would be English.

A: My mother's mother's mother had eleven or twelve children, but my mother's mother was the only one that lived to hâve children .... And she didn't live very long either, because she married first at eighteen, and then she married at twenty-one, and then she died when my mother was seven, so she must have been about twenty-eight or thirty when she died .... The first husband was an old man named Dixon. She wanted to marry somebody rich, and he died and didn't leave her a farthing. He left it to her if she didn't marry again .... When she was twenty-one, she married Mr d'Estaing. She died seven years after.

For the ancestral couple, the color and legal status of the woman are crucial; for the mother's mother legal status and color are not mentioned, whereas the facts that she was the only of many siblings to survive long enough to have children, that she died very young, and that she married twice in that short time are crucial. The fact that she died young is mentioned twice and is connected with the fact that it is the mother's mother's mother who raised the informant's mother. For the male member of the ancestral couple, place of origin, color, and occupation are crucial; on the other hand, what is crucial for the mother's father is a series of facts (not given in the quotation) such as his place of origin and the fact that he died shortly after his wife. Family experiences do not enter into descriptions of ancestral couples as they do in the descriptions of other ascendants. Ancestral couples are presented exclusively in terms of impersonal characteristics that define social position in the society-color, nationality, and occupation. Relatives who are ascendants are defined by characteristics that are of significance only to the informant and those close to him or her; these characteristics are meaningless to outsiders. Ancestral couples are defined by characteristics that are of common significance, such as class, status, power, and race. Later we will see how informants link these contexts.

AFFINITY

The collective representation of marriage formulates the experience of diffuse, enduring solidarity as created, in contrast to the give solidarity of consanguinity. The collective representation of marriage is approached here through an analysis of an account of courtship. In this account the contrast between love and friendship reveals the nature of the collective representation of affinity:

1   She was in one dorm and I was in another and she used to pass through my dorm and I saw her and I thought she was nice-looking and all that, but just remained there, you know. (A friend introduced her, and our informant invited her to a Christian Conference.)

5   So I went, and when we were there we chatted at times. I realized that I was getting too interested in her, because I understood that she had another boy-friend .... So I didn't go back. For a while. But we both were involved in this Christian group and through this we saw each other .... We developed a deeper interest in each

10   other and we went on .... I suppose for her there was this conflict. There wasn't such a conflict for me, because although I liked her, I saw her when I wanted, and I when out with her went I wanted, and we had good times, and it didn't really affect me that there was somebody else; at any rate I didn't sort of consider her being my

15   girl-friend. Well, she always felt that she liked this fellow .... We were just friends. I mean we went out together and had a good time. (Then one weekend the group took a mountain-climbing trip.) We travelled together. The whole trip sort of made us realize that we were in love with each other. So it wasn't just a matter of friend-

20   ship. We really found that we loved each other. But there is this other fellow.
(Summer came; they separated to follow their independent plans.) We both wrote each other. And I suppose in writing a lot of things are sort of set down .... and when we came back we realized that

25   we can't sort of fool ourselves. Because we used to deny it. We used to tell our friends we were friends, but it was nothing .... As this new year went on we developed in our friendship, and I don't think any real significant things happened except that we got closer, got more friendly. (She was now in her final year at the university, and

30   he was one year behind her.)
But I realized the big question was there. Was I to sort of make up my mind now as to whether I wanted her or not? I made up my mind that we would do something. So we got engaged. That summer she went home. This was sort of a test to see .... whether we

35   would wake up in absence, and for her to think away from me and the whole artificial situation on campus.... We wrote a lot, and during this time we really realized that we wanted each other. One night after she returned I just said 'Let's get married,' and she said 'yes.' .... I had remembered that she always dreamed of wak

40   ing up on Christmas a new bride .... So I said 'Let's get married Christmas Eve.' And we did.

There are seven elements that structure the contrast between love and friendship. Some of these contrasts may appear obvious, but it is important to make the analysis systematic.

1.   Love and friendship are distinguished by intensity, love being a more intense form of personal relationship. 'The whole trip sort of made us realize that we were in love with each other. So it wasn't just a matter of friendship' (lines 18-20).

2.   The difference in degree of intensity amounts to a qualitative difference, because one can have several friends, but only one lover. 'We really found that we loved each other. But there

is this other fellow' (lines 20-21). These two facts are incompatible and demand some resolution. Thus love is an exclusive relation.

3.   It is striking that, though love follows on friendship, after the couple are described as in love our informant reverts to describing the relationship as a friendship (lines 25-27). Why this apparent contradiction? Because the word *friendship* can apply to the development of a relationship, but the word *love* cannot. Therefore, when our informant wishes to describe the development of the relationship, even if it has already advanced to the state of love, he must revert to the word *friendship*. For our informant two persons 'realize' they are in love (lines 18, 24, 37) or 'find out' that they are in love (line 20), but love does not develop. In contrast, the two 'develop' their friendship (line 27) or get 'more friendly' (lines 28-29); they do not 'realize' or 'find out' that they are friends. Thus love either does or does not exist, whereas friendship can become greater. Where friendship admits of degrees, love is absolute.

4.   From this same contrast between 'realizing' the existence of love and 'developing' a friendship we can also conclude that love is involuntary and friendship is voluntary. A person does not decide to be in love; the person finds out whether he or she is in fact in love. In contrast, friendship develops by choice: 'we developed in our friendship' (line 27).

5.   Love is constant; friendship need not be so. As friends 'I saw her when I wanted, and I went out with her when I wanted, and we had good times' (lines 11-13). In contrast, the best proof of love is constancy through separation: 'That summer she went home. This was sort of a test' (lines 33-34).

6.   Love arouses a sense that there are two aspects to the personality. For our informant to say that 'we realized we loved each other,' and 'we found we loved each other,' he must assume that love was part of each of them and they were unaware of it. It follows that the existence of love is not dependent on one's awareness of it. Nor is it simply a question of being aware or unaware of love; it is possible to have a false awareness .... It is possible to think one is in love when one really is not. Thus their separation was an occasion to see if they were dreaming or 'really' in love. In contrast, because the informant does not 'discover' that he has been a friend, there is no assumption in friendship of two aspects of the person in imperfect communication.

7.   What difference does it make whether the person is aware of love? Awareness provokes the necessity of a decision. Given the awareness of love it becomes necessary to decide whether to make a commitment. 'Was I to sort of make up my mind now as to whether I wanted her?' (lines 31-32). Why the necessity to make up one's mind? For it might be thought that if two persons love each other, they will, of love's accord, stay together, and if they do not love each other, what could be the point of making up one's mind on the matter? What assumptions could underlie our informant's perspective? A possible explanation is that love remains incomplete without conscious assent. The informant's account assumes not only that two aspects of the person – unconscious and conscious – exist but also that these two aspects embody contrasting principles. One aspect is associated with the awareness of choices and with decisions; choices and decisions do not exist when the person is unaware. It is as though the impelling force of love has a source outside awareness and that integration of the person requires assent of the conscious aspect of the person, which is given by the faculty of decision, which is a faculty of consciousness.

Thus there are seven elements that structure the contrast between love and friendship. (1) Love is an intenser, friendship a milder, relation. (2) Love is an exclusive, friendship a nonexclusive, relation. (3) Love is an absolute, friendship a graded, feeling. (4) Love is involuntary; friendship, voluntary. (5) Love is a constant, friendship a fluctuating, feeling. (6) Love provokes an awareness of conscious and unconscious aspect of the person; friendship does not. (7) Love provokes an integration of the conscious and unconscious aspects; friendship does not. The components of the contrast between love and friendship provide a structure of collective representations in terms of which the informant can relate his unique experience of courtship.

There are two conclusions to draw from this analysis. In contrast to friendship, love is linked to a collective representation of the personality that consists of two elements: and unconscious, involuntary element and a conscious, voluntary element. Furthermore, love orients persons to the problem of integrating these two elements of the personality.

Conjugal love and marriage involve two elements, an unconscious, involuntary element of the personality as well as the voluntary element discussed above. Although marriage is a voluntary decision the decision is made with reference to what is experienced as an integration of the voluntary and involuntary aspects of the personality.

The cultural structures of cognatic and conjugal love have similarities. In both cases there is a voluntary and an involuntary element. Still, it is true that in cognatic love there is an element of substance — blood — and is in conjugal love this element is absent. This difference between the structures of cognatic and conjugal love arises from the fact that diffuse, enduring solidarity is conceived as coeval with existence for blood relatives and as created for spouses. Appropriately, cognatic love is symbolized by bodily substance, which is coeval with a person's existence, and conjugal love is symbolized by a sudden emanation of love.

Once again we see that diffuse, enduring solidarity asserts a permanent mutuality of interests between persons, when in fact social relations inherently contain the possibility of conflict as well as mutuality. The fact of alternatives is covered by the assertion that diffuse, enduring solidarity arises from a realm where there are no choices — the unconscious, involuntary realm. Because in fact there are alternatives (conflict or mutuality), there must be an experience of choice in action, and this choice is represented in the voluntary, conscious aspect of the person. The power of the collective representations lies in their capacity to express and, most important, to integrate these two aspects of experience. It is the power of the collective representations of kinship and affinity in integrating two aspects of the experience of action that makes them effective means of talking about other aspects of social life.

ILLEGITIMACY

Such other aspects of social life have already entered into our informants' speculations. Early in the section entitled 'Kinship,' our informant referred to her illegitimate birth, a notion that has nothing to do with the solidarity of kinship and affinity. Illegitimacy is a feature of every informant's discussion of family life, and its relation to kinship and affinity is well illustrated by these two quotations:

I: I know a rather respectable middle-class man who has had a string of outside children, and his viewpoint is it doesn't say a man must not have bastard children, but he must take care of them. He has given them all his name, he has educated them very well, and he still occupies his position of respect in the community, but if his sister or his daughter did produce a bastard, I think she would have to pay her penalty in terms of loss of regard in the community.

A: In a case like this people would know?

I: Yes.

A: Nobody would go around and fuss about it?

I: No.

A: Does it make a difference how he treats these outside children?

I: No.

A: Is there any concern with how the women are treated?

I: No.

A: How do the wives take all this?

I: It would differ with the personality of the wife. Some would be very angry and repudiate any knowledge or association; some would take them into the homes.

A: You mentioned to me the first time we were talking that one of your brothers has an illegitimate son.

I: Yes.

A: Was he in the home at all?

I: No. Illegitimacy is sort of frowned on by the family and by any people, so the mother not being the type that we had expected, he grew away from us. Occasionally he calls on one of the family. Whenever he meets one member of the family he introduces himself.

A: Is this something that your brother and the rest of the members of the family keep very quiet?

I: Yes, he was born when my brother was teaching, and many teachers have lost posts because of that.

A: Was this something that caused upset in the family?

I: The mother might have been somebody like that one you see coming up here (informant points out the window to a poor, black woman walking up the street); that type of person. He had to keep it away from the family.

A: Is it something that would ever be discussed in the family?

I: My sister would mention it to me that 'Imagine this chap came and tried introduce himself.'

A: Has he ever got in touch with you?

I: Yes, he came introducing himself as my nephew. I found I wasn't going to take any responsibility for him .... I avoided him. He has the tendency to embarrass the father. The mother was that type; the grandmother. You see illegitimacy can turn out to be something that some people can make capital out of, or try to. Which is normal to a certain extent, and abnormal in one way. In that the normal affections that a child would expect from whoever is supposed to be his father are not met in the home. Therefore they have to be abnormal in their approaches. Well, I personally can't accept any responsibility for him .... Interesting enough my nephew said this chap came and introduced himself. He had never known of him. And he said he was at some friend's place and this chap was there and introduced himself as my cousin. He felt rather funny about it .... When he introduced himself as a cousin my nephew wasn't sure which side of the family, from his mother's side or from his father's side. So he had to ask him all these things to get the story. When it did get around, he shunned him.

These quotations show us first that illegitimacy is an improper yet expected feature of middle-class Jamaican life. It provokes shame and silence, yet there are no structurally generated sanctions against it; indeed, it is a structural feature of middle-class family life. The pervasive presence of illegitimacy means that there is a contrast between legitimacy and illegitimacy and that this contrast overlays the cultural structure of kinship and affinity. The contrast between legitimacy and illegitimacy is a contrast between responsibility and irresponsibility. Legitimacy brings with it the 'normal' expectation of affection and responsibility. Illegitimacy brings with it irresponsibility in the sense that the terms of kinship relationship are subject to personal preference. Whether a man supports his 'outside' children and whether his wife takes them in are matters of personal preference. The contrast between responsibility and irresponsibility shows itself in many ways in our interviews. For instance, the responsibility of legitimacy can be experienced as an onerous obligation in contrast to the spontaneous genuineness of illegitimacy, or it can be experienced as a fuller expression of kinship than the passing, lustful relation of illegitimacy. Yet no matter how the contrast plays itself out, it always has the effect of driving a wedge between the unconscious and the conscious elements of kinship and affinity. Insofar as legitimacy enters into the definition of kinship relation — and it always does to some degree — it shifts the content of conscious choice in kinship and affinity from an element that flows from the unconscious given to an element that flows from imposed responsibilities.

The contrast between legitimacy and illegitimacy invariably brings with it, in our informants' accounts, other domains of culture. Illegitimate relations, our accounts show, are acceptable for middle-class men, but not middle-class women, so that illegitimacy automatically brings with it notions of the sexes and of class. Illegitimacy also always entails notions of race. Therefore we follow our informants to their notions of sex roles, race, and class.

THE MALE IN THE FAMILY

This section focuses on the collective representation of men in the family. The marginality of males in the Caribbean lower-class family is a standard focus of Caribbean scholarship. Our middle-class informants are as interested in the marginality of lower-class males as are scholars, though with a more explicitly moral evaluation: 'The Jamaican man has a great responsibility to see to it that motherhood and childhood do not deteriorate into becoming casualty listings from some wild game he sets out to play in the field of sexual indulgence, but rather that these be developments growing out of a serious covenant into which he enters with loving care and sober commitment. If he is slow in acknowledging this responsibility, the state must have ways of reminding him.'

Here the marginality of men is formulated in the moral contrast between 'sexual indulgence' and a 'serious covenant' undertaken with 'responsibility'. Interestingly, here the reference is to Jamaican men in general, not just lower-class men. The image of the male as marginal to family life appears as a major focus in the middle class as well as the lower class.

In the middle class there is much argument between men and women over their proper roles in the family. Much of this argument can be understood as a symptom of changing sex roles in the society; but the issue is formulated by the participants in moral terms — the greater commitment of the woman than the man to the family. The woman does more of the work in the family, say informants, because the man is not sufficiently committed to it:

I: I have met so many men who have had to be a burden of the family responsibility.

A: I'm, not talking of the lower class.

I: No, no. Middle class. In fact, I believe sometimes they are worse off than the lower class. Because people tend to believe that they belong to the middle class and they are reasonable. I know too many women, especially teachers with families, and they have to just shoulder the responsibilities. A large number. The men either gamble it out or have other women, that sort of thing.

The belief in male lack of commitment — irresponsibility — might be a weapon wielded by women against men, but men hold the same conviction. The depth of this belief in male irresponsibility is revealed in the image of the father held by middle-class male informants. 'My father was an unusual man. In my young days I thought of him as a very happy-go-lucky person who valued a good time, valued "the boys." I thought him in those days somewhat irresponsible, and it was my mother who kept the family together.'

The image of the marginality and irresponsibility of the male in the family must be understood against the background of the counter-expectation of the man as the dominant authority figure in the family. One informant, who was a teacher, worked briefly as a domestic in the United States: 'Family life in the United States is really shocking. Here men are kings; there women are queens. Here, if there is a limited amount of food the man gets a proper share, and then the rest is divided up. I realize my husband works hard and has many responsibilities; though I work hard at school, not as hard as he, and I don't expect him to do housework .... In America, a woman would shout her husband down; here you just couldn't do it.' The assumption that male dominance is the suitable state of affairs is clear. Therefore, insofar as the male is perceived as lacking, it is in comparison to the dominant authority figure he is expected to be.

The indicator par excellence for middle-class Jamaicans of the male's irresponsibility and weakness is his sexual unfaithfulness. An example comes from one of my earliest and most frequently repeated field experiences. When middle-class persons asked me what I was doing in Jamaica, and I told them I was studying family life, they usually laughed and told me that there is no family life in Jamaica. Often they then launched into a discussion of illegitimacy and promiscuous mating in the lower class in order to demonstrate their point. However, permitted to run on in this way, they invariably came to the point of saying that the middle class was not really so different. The evidence they presented for this assertion was always the same: that men in the middle class 'run around' just as much as in the lower class, but are careful to maintain proper appearances with a public home, middle-class wife, and legal offspring and private 'outside' relations with a lower-class mistress and illegal offspring. It is important to note that the purpose of our analysis that the marginality of the middle-class male is formulated in the same sexual and moral terms as the marginality of lower-class males: sexual indulgence versus the responsibilities of a 'serious covenant'.

So the irresponsibility that, informants assert, distinguishes the lower class from the middle class turns out to be, informants also assert, a characteristic of the middle-class male as well. What does distinguish the middle-class from the lower-class male is that the middle-class male operates on two tracks at the same time. In her study of sex roles in a Jamaican town, de Veer (1979) shows that in the lower class, men are considered to be irresponsible in comparison to women. For a male to become a responsible family member he must undergo a religious transformation that will control his general, irresponsible inclinations (p. 96). In contrast, the middle-class male has both a 'responsible' legal family and an 'irresponsible,' illegitimate, 'outside' relationship. (This fact has been discussed in the literature; see Braithwaite 1953; Jayawardena 1962.)

There is one final feature in the image of the male, because his irresponsibility is also defined as an assertion of status: 'The moment they are rich, men now earning a good salary, or what we call, going back to our middle-income group, going up in more salary, he must have one or two girlfriends, outside you know. He has to share his time between his home and things like that.'

Summarizing this description of the collective representation of the male in the family, we find that he is stereotyped as marginal to family life, and this marginality is evaluated morally as irresponsible and is so by contrast to a counter-expectation in which the male is dominant and the authority in the family. The flaws in the male are most powerfully expressed in his sexual indulgence, which is contrasted to a 'serious covenant'. Finally, the very sexual indulgence that is the mark of inadequacy is also judged to be a mark of status. In my analysis I will show that the representation of the male is a bridge between the domestic and the public domains and that the image of the male in the family is a reflection of and an expression of this image in the public domain.

RACE

I begin the analysis of the collective representation of race by considering very briefly the use of racial terms by informants. The vast majority of racial descriptions are of physical appearance. However, these elements of physical appearance are significant because they are taken to be outward signs of race. Race is conceived to be a component of the inner bodily substance, which is passed down from generation to generation. At the same time, physical appearance is considered a somewhat unreliable indicator of race. For instance, it is freely acknowledged that siblings who have the same racial composition can have very different physical appearances.

The relation of appearance to race is further indicated by the fact that informants have a restricted and general meaning for racial color terms. The restricted meaning refers specifically to skin color; the general meaning refers to a number of features — skin color, hair, eye color; and facial features. One must have both meanings in mind to make sense of this remark: 'His wife is quite dark, but beautiful black hair. Dark in complexion, but beautiful black hair .... down to her shoulder.' To say that a woman was dark but had long hair would be unnecessary unless *dark* in itself implied some other kind of hair. At the same time, if *dark* had only the general meaning then the fact that the person has long black hair would require the informant to change her term rather than restrict its meaning. The general meaning encompasses a number of physical features in addition to skin color, because in theory color and these features are related. Thus white skin goes with straight hair, blue eyes, and fine features — all Caucasian racial features. Similarly, a black man, by virtue of his African descent, is assumed in the absence of contrary evidence to have curly black hair, brown eyes, and heavy features. Yet, just as informants recognize that appearance is an unreliable indicator of blood, so do they realize that color and other physical features may in fact not vary together.

What sense can we make of the fact that informants use terms that apply to appearance when they are interested in appearance as sign of race yet know that appearance is an unreliable indicator? Originally, color terms were accompanied by a set of terms that referred directly to racial composition: *sambo, mulatto,* and so on. These terms, however, have almost entirely dropped out of use in favor of color terms. Even the term *mulatto* to indicate any degree of Negro 'blood' has been largely replaced. One informant answered the question as follows: 'I suppose I describe more from the point of color, because most of us are sort of mixed up.' Thus the use of color terms for racial description makes possible the continued identification of persons in terms of their racial mixture, when the exact mixture is unknown. For color to act as a sign of racial mixture, informants assume a continuum from pure Caucasian, or pure white, to pure African, or pure black. This continuum expresses the principle that despite the generations and centuries of racial mixture, racial identity consists not of a homogeneous type but of varying mixtures of two distinct racial types — 'white' and 'black'.

When we analyze informants' talk about race (as distinct from their use of racial terms) several themes appear: (1) the significance of race as both a deep and a superficial phenomenon, (2) the relation of race to identity, (3) the relation of race to a hierarchy of social honor, (4) the justification of this hierarchy, and (5) the relation of race to solidarity.

1. Informants are intensely ambivalent about the importance of race: 'As far as my sister Mary, you wouldn't imagine that she had colored blood at all .... I don't think it means anything much to Jamaicans. Do you think so? I mean, in talking to different Jamaicans? What matters to them is when a person is in a different class. People are terribly conscious of hair. I'll try to label these persons (racially), but this is something that we probably haven't thought of, or it just rolls off the tongue without your having given it much thought.'

Ambivalence over the significance of race has two sources. One source is the impropriety of caring about race; because it makes invidious distinctions between persons, race is something that ought not to be important. The other source is the ambivalence over the relative importance of achieved and ascribed characteristics. On the one hand, informants believe that people are what they make themselves; because they have no control over their race it is irrelevant. On the other hand informants believe that within rational people who choose their destinies, there are also forces that are part of them, but over which they have no control. During the research a large riot erupted in Kingston, and many people feared that civil order was threatened. One informant, who had previously described the decline of racial consciousness in Jamaica, told me that the Kingston Gun Club had enlisted as special marshalls and were patrolling with loaded rifles. 'And,' he concluded, 'you know what color they are' (Gun Club members tended to be at the white end of the color continuum). The informant assumed that race is the ultimate basis of solidarity.

Thus the subject of race immediately raises a conflict for informants over its relative importance as an ascribed characteristic.The conflict is not resolved. The assertion that race is or is not important rarely remains uncontradicted for long, and consequently it is expressed above all in ambivalence.

2. Insofar as it is conceived to be important, race is thought of as having a specific ascribed significance, which is illustrated in the following notes of an interview:

> Color played a very great part in his life. When he asked about his ancestry and his father told him it went back to a slave woman that was very important to him. Made him realize where he really belonged. Which had troubled him. He could say he was a Jamaican, but that was not really satisfactory. Would ask himself where do I really fit in. Is there such a thing as a Negro quality? The writing of Aimé Césaire and others helped him. Made him realize there was such a quality .... It was not an artificial development, but a question of discovering what was there. Black was identified with poverty and one tended to identify with whites and colored. Now he has a feeling of kinship, having discovered himself as a Negro.

In constructing their own identities persons find it sensible to refer to their race, and in considering race they find it sensible to consider their identities. In what way is race an attribute of identity for informants? A comparison can be helpful. Erikson suggests that the definition of American identity is that of the person who has a wide range of options and chooses among them on his or her own (1963, pp. 285-87). The identity established for our informants more commonly focuses on group membership: 'I'm considered Chinese .... I am really in a sense three-quarter Chinese. Am I? Yes, three-quarter, I am ... of course, our physical features stamp us Chinese.' In contrast to American identity, Jamaican identity focuses less on a typical mode of action and more on a community of action. Erikson has pointed out that identity includes an image of a person's place in the community (1968, pp. 45-53). This aspect of identity is what the cultural definition of race formulates. However, the effect of the cultural definition of race is to fragment and make problematical this identity, because it defines, as we have just seen, the community as composed of two distinct elements (white and black) and their mixture, a mixture that does not amalgamate. For some, this racial identity leads very far into the experience of mixture and fragmentation. One informant presented the fact that his family does not suffer from sickle-cell anemia, albinism, or rope scars at healing (all believed to be inherited black characteristics) to demonstrate that 'from my immediate bloodstream I don't know of any that are really colored'.

3. Informants frequently deny that race is hierarchically evaluated; therefore it is important to note that, consistently, when they feel that they have received less than the respect due an equal, they suspect that race is the cause. One informant recalled an incident when he was twelve years old: 'He was standing around at a gas station eating mangoes. A car came in for gas, and the station attendant gave him the gas cap to hold while he filled the tank. The driver grabbed the cap away and cursed him fiercely. He felt he was being treated as a menial. It might have happened even if he had been white, after all his hands were dirty with mango juice; still it was the way the man spoke to him.'

4. Less evident than the hierarchical evaluation of race is the ambivalence with which this hierarchy is conceived. This ambivalence is expressed in the touchiness with which the subject is discussed. Informants all framed the matter the same way: race is a subject people do not discuss freely and openly; it remains understood.

The reasons for this ambivalence are revealed by informants' discussion of color prejudice. Informants can easily expand on the wickedness of color prejudice; to claim superiority on the grounds of race is wrong. Yet they cannot discuss racial differences without implying superiority and inferiority; hence the ambivalence.

Ambivalence over racial status exists because there is no cultural justification for distinctions based on race. In India, for example, status is justified by the ideology of purity, but there is little evidence for such an ideology among our informants. Indeed, if racism is to be strictly defined — 'the doctrine that a man's behavior is determined by stable inherited characters deriving from separate racial stocks having distinctive attributes and usually considered to stand to one another in relations of superiority and inferiority': (Banton 1967, p. 8)-then it might be argued that there is little evidence of racism as part of the culture of our informants. Though informants do see race as associated with superiority and inferiority, the association is not biological. For informants racial hierarchy is the result of a historical association of race with both social dominance and style of life. They define being white as superior to being black because whiteness has brought with it advantages in the society. Secondly, white is superior to black because it is associated with a superior style of life; white is civilized, black is uncivilized.

What is crucial to see is that the association between race on the one hand and superior life-style and dominance on the other hand is, from the point of view of informants, a matter of historical fact, not biological necessity. (This type of ideology is more common than might be supposed. See Arendt's 1951 discussion of race thinking before racism.) For informants, whites did dominate, speak English, practise certain conjugal customs, eat certain foods, and so on.

Thus the culturally defined superiority of white over black follows from the culturally asserted historical association of white with superior social position and superior style of life. The earlier analysis of the use of racial terms revealed that appearances are interpreted as signs of an inner physical condition; the analysis of the significance of race to informants reveals that it is significant for its association with a superior style of life and dominance. Whereas the link between appearance and race is conceived to be biological, the link between race and superior style of life and social position is conceived to be the result of historical events, the association of superior and inferior power and style of life is conceived to be the result of historical events, the association of races with distinctive power and styles of life is conceived to be the consequence of an intrinsic property of race.

5. Racial differences imply hierarchical and invidious distinctions between persons; conversely, racial similarity implies equality and solidarity. The idea that people of the same color are equal and belong together is most clearly expressed in the discussion of marriage. Much has been made by scholars of a white bias, especially as expressed in the desire to marry up in color. What is as true, but much less noted, is the bias toward marrying someone of the same color: 'If a man is a doctor or lawyer ... if he earns money he could marry a girl from that class, he could. Because they have the feeling that it will upgrade their children. But the funny thing about it is that by and large the colored people resent this kind of action in a colored person. Because they feel that he would be turning against his group. And women in particular felt there were girls out here of educational standing good enough that he could have found a wife. This desire on his part to marry out of his color they didn't accept.'

Furthermore, the notion of union between persons of different races has an air of illegitimacy around it: 'You hear people talking, just describing other people and say "She's a mulatto; her father was a Scotsman." It's a good word, but it is also used as a curse word. 'She was the product of a promiscuous relationship.'

Finally, informants formulate the illegitimacy of unions between races in their beliefs about the origin of Jamaican society. For informants the origin of contemporary society is in the illegal union of a white male master and a black female slave and their illegal mulatto offspring.

In the cultural definition, the solidarity that arises out of racial sameness is an intrinsic property of that racial sameness. People stick together because they have the same blood, and there is no more explanation necessary. At the same time the definition of race as a continuum consisting of an unamalgamated mixture ensures that racial solidarity will be a fragile condition easily dissolvable by the racial differences that the culture always formulates. Let us now return to the problem of the cultural definition of race and hierarchy.

Although solidarity is defined as an intrinsic property of racial sameness, the hierarchy of racial difference is defined as an accidental property resulting from historical events. As we have already noted, there is little evidence of a belief in intrinsic racial superiority (that is, little evidence of racism); the superiority of white arises from its association with superior social position and life-style, and not vice versa. We can make most sense of this complex of beliefs by inferring that for informants common lifestyle and common social position are results of racial solidarity; because persons of the same blood stick together they develop the same life-style and function as a group to maintain or improve their position in society. Consequently, although the superior social position and style of life of whites are not biological consequences of race, they are still essentially and not accidentally white. That is why a colored person who lives according to the superior life-style or who marries a white person is pursuing a life-style that is not 'really' his own and is marrying outside his group; just as a colored person, no matter how white he may look, is never 'really' white. Thus, although life-style and social dominance are in one sense achieved characteristics-persons can acquire proper speech and wealth- in another sense they are defined as intrinsically white and therefore as ascribed characteristics.

The relationship between race and hierarchy as defined by informants leads to the relation between the collective representations of race and those of class and status.

CLASS AND STATUS

Scholars have often asserted that race is a language for talking about class interest or the subjective form that objective class interest takes. My own observation is that informants have no difficulty talking about class interests when that is what they want to talk about, and in general they are keenly aware of class interests. Furthermore, informants can talk about race without referring to class. Nevertheless, there is a relation and a tension between race and class, because from one perspective they are conceived to be distinct and from another perspective they are conceived to be related.

From one perspective there is, for informants, a fundamental distinction between race on the one hand and class and status on the other: 'Mark you, this woman is of good station; I mean socially. Physically-wise she is considered black, but her attributes are definitely of his social status.' From the other perspective class and race are related, because they are conceived to be aspects of a single hierarchy. A person who is middle class is expected to be also midway in the racial hierarchy. In order to understand the tension between race and class let us proceed to an analysis of the culture of class, particularly the impact of the pure domain of class on the conglomerate level of family life.

Though informants find it difficult to define classes, the same criteria appear consistently in their discussions: income, education, standard of living, occupation, group membership, and attitude. 'Those cousins are able to earn as much money as those of us who were able to pass our exams. It's only that because of their limited education and their whole social outlook their life is at a very low ebb. The question of having a nice home, nicely furnished, with books, possibly getting married, and having a settled home, that is not the sort of thing you would find them doing. They would prefer to have drinking parties, to play the horses, and just live and let live.' Here one can observe how rapidly education, standard of living, attitude, and group membership can be interchanged, and how they are contrasted to income. Education, standard of living, attitude, and group membership should be considered different aspects of the same basic feature, in contrast to income.

One can understand the contrast between income and the other features by first grasping the meaning of education for informants. Education can refer to skills acquired through formal schooling, and informants are keenly aware that education provides skills that influence occupational possibilities and thereby income. But it is in another sense that education is contrasted to income. Historically, in Jamaica education has been defined as a Christianizing, civilizing force. Thus a prominent minister wrote in 1853:

> Unallured by the enjoyment of civilized society and by whatever is sublime and beautiful in natural scenery; — the dwarfs of the rational world, their intellect rising only to a confused notion and imperfect idea of the general objects of human knowledge; their whole thoughts, indeed, confined within the range of their daily employments and the wants of savage life. By some writers they have been described as an inferior species of the human family ....

> Acquiring a taste for knowledge and a love of virtue, they will receive into their midst the term of all vitality and the secret of all strength .... When gently led forward by the humane of every nation they shall, under the *egis* of an overshadowing Providence, run a career of honourable progression in all that adorns and elevates the species, with the boasting inhabitants of more privileged climes.

> To realize these anticipations nothing is required but the introduction of a liberal and enlarged scheme of sound education among the more respectable classes of the coloured and black population. (Phillippo 1843, pp. 191, 211-12)

Thus, in Jamaica education came to mean a training in civilization, particularly manners. Our informants continue to accept this historical meaning of education. For them, to be educated means to know how to behave properly, in a civilized manner. 'The middle class is defined by education, not money. The education they have had, which gives them the responsibility of setting standards, the tone, the pattern of behavior.'

Standard of living has two meanings also for informants: it can refer to material possessions or to decency and propriety. In the second meaning the significance of material possessions arises out of their role in maintaining a decent and proper way of life. Having such possessions as a house and a car is part of decent living, as are speaking English and being well mannered. It is the second meaning that is contrasted to income as a defining characteristic of the middle class:

You will find some of the loveliest homes. Yet, as far as I know you would never think of classifying those people as middle class. Because the standard of living is altogether on a lower plane .... So I think we would have a more proper gauge if we were to take it on an educational basis .... The general feeling there is I haven't got an education and I can find the money I want to spend just the same.. So standard doesn't matter to him at all. You have that basic middle class where money is not the sole object, but they believe in living a decent life, having a good family life, educating their children as best as possible, and living a clean, decent life.

To understand the complex of features that are contrasted to income, it is necessary to consider the meaning of income for informants. In the face of the consistent assertion that it is education, style of life, and so on that define the middle class, one wonders why income is introduced at all. Income stands for the ability to appropriate valued goods and resources: 'In the past teachers told children there was no point trying to achieve a bank job on account of their color. If your people had money you were going to do medicine or something like that, well that's different .... But I mean if you were just a mediocre middle-class family.'

Informants feel the need to justify their income. They all introduce the theme of working hard and struggling to establish and maintain a position in society. Yet the middle-class sense of dignity rests more on the ends for which income is utilized than on the means by which it is gained. Informants deserve their income by virtue of the morally superior uses to which they put it. These uses are the educated standard of living on which so much emphasis is placed in the discussion of class.

We can clarify the meaning of the middle-class self-definition by contrasting it to the middle-class definition of lower and upper classes. Although informants realize the competition from below, there is little attention to classes as conflicting groups or quasi-groups. Rather, informants conceive of a moral hierarchy and focus on the moral superiority of the middle class:

I: For example, if you go to St Elizabeth you'll find the squatters on the estate. They never own an inch of land for themselves. They work on the sugar cane estate and they are just like coolies .... They generally live on the outskirts and they build up a big community like that. But those are not holdings. They just pitch a house here, pitch a house there and they live in that sort of fashion. And the standards of living are very low. It's just a question of living on the little that they earn on the estate from week to week .... We've had families that are poor people, but they are on their own farm and you couldn't classify them as lower class; you 'd have to classify them as middle class. Their outlook is different altogether. There is a greater ambition standard there, that type does everything for his child's education. .... Whereas the other is just a hit-or-miss livelihood.

A: What makes people upper class?

I: Well, because of money. And inheritance .... A man couldn't just get himself up there unless he was born of wealthy parents .... There isn't the urge, that deep necessity for striving as the middle-class man would have. So you find that the upper-class boy might eventually just come with a little basic training back home and continues on his daddy's property.

Thus informants characterize the upper and lower classes in the same way. The lower class is basically 'careless,' though there is a segment that does care but is simply too poor to be middle class. The upper class has money without having to work for it and tends not to concern itself with leading a moral life. The assertion that the middle class works for its money and, most important, uses it in a moral and civilized fashion expresses the sense of dignity of the class.

Now we can understand the relations among our informants' conceptions of race, class, and status. Race and class are conceived of as distinct in that race is a 'physical thing' and class is the money one has; race and status are similar in that both connote a hierarchy, and that hierarchy is expressed in a civilized style of life. It is the civilized style of life that links race and status to a single hierarchy and creates the presumption of consistency among race, class, and status and the strain that arises when they are inconsistent. Precisely how the links among race, class, and status are forged will be described in the following section. A crucial part of the civilized style of life, the sense of dignity, is family life, to which we now turn.

For the middle class marriage is a prerequisite to living together and having children, whereas for the lower class it is not. Therefore the contrast between marriage and nonlegal union has class meaning. Illegitimacy and nonlegal unions, as we have shown earlier, are framed in the light of a contrast between seeking immediate pleasure without consideration of its consequences and responsibility or acting with consideration for the consequences of one's actions — 'sexual indulgence' in contrast to 'loving care, sober commitment, and more than token responsibility'. Because illegitimacy and nonlegal unions are signs of putting immediate pleasure above responsibility, it follows that legal marriage is a sign of placing responsibility equal with or above immediate pleasure, accepting obligations regardless of their impact on the immediate satisfaction of needs. It also follows that the middle-class commitment to legal marriage is a commitment to responsibility over immediate pleasure. Yet this commitment is flawed, for in the middle class's own view of itself men participate in non-legal unions with lower-class women as well as in legal unions with middle-class women. Middle-class men are distinguished from lower-class men not by their capacity to rise above immediate pleasure, but by their split orientation toward pleasure and responsibility. (It is important to keep in mind that we are describing middle-class beliefs, not practices.) Finally, the very behavior that is a sign of flawed honor — male nonlegal unions — is also an assertion of middle-class male power, as was noted in the section entitled 'The Male in the Family.'

Why is there this cultural focus on the two faces of men's family behavior? Studies of family life in many societies show that outside relations are common for men without being the subject of cultural focus. The answer to the question requires us to integrate our analyses of the domains of kinship, marriage, sex roles, race, class, and status.

THE MYTH OF ORIGIN

The situation we are analyzing appears to be a curious one. Weber observed that 'even pariah people … are usually apt to continue cultivating … the belief in their own specific honor' (1968, p. 934). In the Jamaican middle class we appear to have a group that harbors a belief in its own dishonor. Why the flawed self-image of family life presented by our informants?

In order to understand the self-image of the family we must understand the origin myth that is the charter of the middle class, and perhaps of the society.

Informants believe that the middle class originated in the nonlegal union of a white male master and a black female slave, which produced an illegitimate brown offspring of status midway between slave and master. This belief is clearly expressed in the genealogies of those informants who see themselves as of middle-class origin; as mentioned earlier they all trace their genealogies back to a white male master, black female slave, and illegitimate mulatto or brown offspring. It is at this point of origin alone that class, status and race correlate directly. It is here that the link connecting race, class, and status is forged, that class terms have direct implications for race terms and vice versa. There are two class terms that have an automatic race significance, slave and master. Slave automatically implies black; master automatically implies white.

How is the story of the origin of the middle class to be taken as a myth? It operates to anchor current practices in their origins and does so by a distinctive sense of time. This mythical time has been analyzed clearly by Levi-Strauss: 'On the one hand, a myth always refers to events alleged to have taken place long ago. But what gives the myth an operational value is that the specific pattern described is timeless; it explains the present and the past as well as the future' (1963, p. 209).

The myth of middle-class origin operates in just this way. It relates events that have taken place in the past and that are yet still in the present, not simply as past causes of present conditions, but actually present. The origin myth formulates in the minds of informants the underlying, fundamental principles of the society against which all variations are measured.

The distinctive mythical time is expressed by race: white blood and black blood have been passed down from the beginning of society, from generation to generation, endlessly mixed and still distinct, into the present. Race thus establishes the historical rootedness of the society and its members' place in it, and does so in a way that locates the historical rootedness directly in the experience of persons' bodies, thus to a certain extent fusing the continuity of the person with the continuity of the society. The tension between race and class expresses change; it is an experience of the present as a contrast to the past. Every time people experience inconsistency among race, physical appearance, status, and class, they are referring the present to a past which in the beginning there were two groups — one English, white, civilized, master, and solidary; the other African, black, uncivilized, slave, and solidary — who mixed without amalgamating. Every time people perceive themselves or others in terms of race they commit themselves to a view that sees the present as the result of a long process of mixture in which the two elements are always kept track of — because they have never really joined.

In the myth of origin the family plays a central part, and thereby the myth links the domains of kinship and affinity with the domains of race, class, and status. The myth distinguishes the part of society and integrates them in terms of male irresponsibility and the distinction between legal and nonlegal union. These are of course precisely the features of family life that draw the attention of scholars and natives alike. It is puzzling that middle-class males are perceived as marginal by our middle-class informants, for they are in reality more commonly a part of the family than are lower-class males. For instance, a male is far more likely to be the head of a middle-class than of a lower-class household. Furthermore, the features of male behavior that are pointed to as evidence of male marginality are commonly found in many societies with sharp sex-role differentiation.

The answer to this puzzle lies in the relation of man's place outside the family to his place inside the family. Here I wish to study the interaction between the evaluation of the male outside the family and the evaluation of him inside the family. I wish to show that the evaluation of the male in the family can be influenced by the evaluation of the male in the public domain, and that this influence can operate independently of what the male actually does in the family. The phenomenon to which I refer has been described well for another group:

> The Eastern European Jewish ... type of family is in many respects mother-centered and mother-dominated .... Mother exercises control over the daily run of affairs and over her children's behavior, as well as over most of the practical aspects of her husband's life. The father's authority tends to be so remote that it does not impinge much upon the details of the children's daily lives. Father may be, according to modern psychiatric concepts, a 'dependent personality,' ...; but — and this is the decisive point-there is not stigma attached to his so-called dependency. He has well defined privileges and rights, many of which are denied to the mother. His prestige is largely based on the religious value system ....

> The mother acts mainly as the manager of the household and the father acts as a representative of the family in the community and of the community in the family .... The community may be a religious collectivity sustained by a common value system. In such a social setting, whether or not father dominates family life, the respect he commands among its members is sustained by the values of the community. (Coser 1974, pp. 365, 367)

Thus in the Eastern European Jewish community the values of the society bestow prestige on the male in the public domain, and this prestige penetrates the domestic domain irrespective of what the male does there. In colonial Jamaica the values of the society demean rather than support the nonwhite male, as is reflected and expressed in a double definition of the middle-class male within family life.

In the dominant ideology, non-English men are in a subordinate position in the public domain because they do not possess enough 'civilization', which is a prerequisite to gaining responsibility; and this lack of public responsibility and civilization is symbolized by the definition of the male in the family. The essence of this definition is that the male is both responsible and irresponsible and that he follows his natural uncivilized inclinations, as well as channe ling his inclinations in a civilized way. Thus the ideology that links race, class, and status to the family through the male is a way of talking about his middle-class position in the public domain. It is to the position of the middle class in Jamaican society that we now turn.

THE MIDDLE CLASS FIELD OF SOCIAL ACTION

The origin of the middle class lies in the freedmen of Jamaican slave society. The freedmen were an utterly distinctive product of Jamaican slave society and in time became a dynamic force in their own right in that society. Freed slaves and the descendants of freed slaves, they were frequently the offspring of white free masters and black female slaves. They occupied a position midway between slaves and free men, no longer slaves but lacking the full civil rights of free men. Though whites and blacks had their origins in Europe and Africa, Jamaican plantation slave society required substantial adaptions that gave the Jamaican slave society its own distinctive character. Whites, surrounded by a sea of black slaves, developed a cohesiveness and spirit of equality, despite their economic differentiation, that was unparalleled in Europe. Africans, though they came from diverse tribes and though they were internally differentiated economically, were united by their common lot as slaves and plantation laborers.

Several social principles characterized this society. The plantation combined European capital with a large supply of unskilled African labor and tropical land to produce crops (primarily sugar in the Jamaican case) for export to the European market. This economic activity was the central but not the only principle that determined social relationships. Certainly the threat and use of force were essential to the maintenance of social relationships, as is evidenced in the frequent incidence of individual and group slave rebellion and the violence with which it was repressed. Certainly the ideology of racism flowered from its seed in England into a central principle of the society. The assertion of the superiority of 'civilized' whites over 'uncivilized' blacks was common among whites. There is no way of knowing how widely or deeply racism was accepted by blacks, but it established for blacks an inescapable frame of reference. Finally, in complex relation to the use of force, which divided white and black, and to racism, which defined the division, was a private world of personal relations and common customs that crosscut the social groups. The Scottish overseer, his ebony woman, and their yellow offspring illustrate the web of personal relations and common custom created in Jamaican society:

> Every unmarried white man, and of every class, has his black or brown mistress, with whom he lives openly: and of so little consequence is this thought that his white female friends and relations think it no breach of decorum to visit his house, partake of his hospitality, fondle his children and converse with his housekeeper .... The man who keeps his black or brown mistress in the very face of his wife and family and of the community has generally as much outward respect shown him, and is as much countenanced, visited, and received into company especially if he be a man of some weight and influence in the community, as if he had been guilty of no breach of decency (Stewart, quoted in Dunker 1960, p. 60)

Though demographic dates are sketchy, it is estimated that 9 percent of the population were freedmen by 1820 (calculated from Brathwaite 1971, p. 169). Freedmen filled interstitial occupations in the economy, primarily as artisans, tradesmen, and clerks; by 1823 they provided half the militia (Dunker 1960, pp. 76-83, 199).

By the end of the eighteenth century freedmen were exerting pressure for increased rights; though on the whole in a conservative way. They argued their rights by virtue of their white fathers, their loyalty to whites, their possession of English education and manners, the property interests they held in common with whites, and finally their status as the only true natives of Jamaica (Dunker 1960, pp. 153-74). On the other hand, their claim to full rights, however conservatively stated, challenged a social order legitimized by a racial ideology, and furthermore, they were willing to use the support of the Abolitionists in the British Parliament.

In 1832 freedmen were granted full rights, and in 1838 slavery was abolished. White, 'civilized' owners and black, 'uncivilized' slaves were no longer owners and slaves, and so the racial and status ('civilized') components defining these two groups came to the fore. The colonial government substantially expanded church and school, both of which were to inculcate white, English, civilized values that would turn black Africans into good citizens without eliminating the ultimate superiority of whites (Smith 1966, 1982, first developed this notion of post-emancipation society, which he labelled 'creole society').

By the end of the nineteenth century the middle class that was developing and expanding was diverse in character and changing in personnel, yet showed itself to be a development of the freedmen of slave society. By means of education this group came to fill positions in the expanding civil service, teaching, religious, legal, and clerical occupations. A prosperous group of farmers and produce traders also developed, who, though they did not owe their position to education, tended to provide the rural support for the 'civilizing' educational and religious systems.

The middle class articulated its interests in a way that clearly built on that of its predecessors, the freedmen. It came to assert its achieved English civility as a justification for its position and as a status line separating it from the lower class. Because English civility was ultimately a white characteristic, the same argument that justified the middle-class superiority over the lower class also justified its subordination to the white upper class. The continuity between the middle class and the freedmen of slave society is also revealed in the fact that this class, like the freedmen before it, was disproportionately colored, rather than white or black.

In the twentieth century some members of the middle class began to achieve economic power and demand more political power. Middle-class leaders articulated a democratic nationalist ideology in justification of their claims. The roots of nationalism lay in the eighteenth-century freedmen's claim for the rights of natives. What was new in the ideology was its democratic and anti-racist character. But there it was deeply ambiguous. It could be said that the new elite was trained in schools with English models and that its nationalistic demands were in large part claims that it had mastered the English lesson and could function as effectively as the English. Its anti-racist character was a claim that persons should be judged by their ability to act like civilized Englishmen, regardless of their race. The racism that had supported authority remained as a strong tendency of the elite to separate itself from, while it led, the lower class: 'Leaders are what the labourers want. Good leaders, Temperate Speeches, work within the bounds of British Principles and Policies, with grim determination you must win' (quoted in Post 1969, p. 382).

The ideology of democratic nationalism embedded in racism, fashioned by the middle class in the pursuit of its interests, clearly developed from the original freedman interests and ideology. It is this ideology that we finally reached in the analysis of our informants' beliefs about their family lives. Thus the middle class of Jamaica symbolizes, acts out, and makes real for itself its conception of its legitimate place in a colonial society through the definition of the male role in the family.

ACKNOWLEDGEMENTS

The ethnographic present is 1967-69, when most of the fieldwork on which this essay is based was done. That fieldwork was supported by the National Science Foundation through a grant (NSF-GS-1709) to a project directed by Professor Raymond T. Smith, and by NIH Training Grant No. 1-FI-MH-34477-01A2 (CUAN). The fieldwork and its analysis benefitted greatly from the advice of Raymond T. Smith. Sections of this essay have previously appeared in Alexander 1976, 1977a, 1977b, and 1978. I am grateful to the editors of the *American Ethnologist* and the *Journal of Comparative Family Studies* for permission to reproduce them here.

REFERENCES

Alexander, Jack 1976. 'A Study of the Cultural Domain of Relatives.' *American Ethnologist* 3:17-38.

—1977a. 'The Culture of Race in Middle-Class Kingston, Jamaica.' *American Ethnologist* 4:413-35

—1977b. 'The Role of the Male in the Urban Middle-Class Jamaican Family: A Comparative Study.' *Journal of Comparative Family Studies* 8 (no. 3): 369-89.

—1978. 'The Cultural Domain of Marriage.' *American Ethnologist* 5:5-14.

Arendt, Hannah 1951. *The Origins of Totalitarianism*. New York: Harcourt, Brace.

Banton, Michael 1967. *Race Relations*. New York: Basic Books.

Brathwaite, Lloyd 1953. 'Social Stratification in Trinidad.' *Social and Economic Studies* 2:5-175.

Brathwaite, Edward 1971. *The Development of Creole Society in Jamaica: 1770-1820*. Oxford: Oxford University Press, Clarendon Press.

Coser, Rose Laub 1974. 'Authority and Structural Ambivalence in the Middle Class Family.' In *The Family: Its Structures and Functions*, edited by Rose Laub Coser, pp.362-73. New York: St. Martin's Press.

de Veer, Henrietta 1979. 'Sex Roles and Social Stratification in Rapid Growing Urban Area — May Pen, Jamaica.' Ph.D diss. University of Chicago.

Dunker, Sheila 1960. 'The Free Coloured and Their Fight for Civil Rights in Jamaica: 1800-1830.' M.A. thesis, University of London.

Erikson, Erik 1963. *Childhood and Society*. 2d ed. New York: W. W. Norton and Co.

—1968. *Identity: Youth and Crisis*. New York: W.W. Norton Co.

Fortes, Meyer 1969. *Kinship and the Social Order: The Legacy of Lewis Henry Morgan*. Chicago: Aldine Publishing Co.

Fried, Morton 1967. *The Evolution of Political Society: An Essay in Political Anthropology*. New York: Random House.

Jayawardena, Chandra 1962. 'Family Organization in Plantations in British Guiana.' *International Journal of Comparative Sociology* 3:43-64.

Levi-Strauss, Claude 1963. *Structural Anthropology*. Translated by Claire Jacobson and Brooke Grundfest Schoepf. New York: Basic Books.

Phillippo, James M. 1843. *Jamaica: Its Past and Present State*. Philadelphia.

Post, Ken 1969. 'The Politics of Protest in Jamaica, 1938: Some Problems of Analysis and Conceptualisation.' *Social and Economic Studies* 18:374-90.

Schneider, David M. 1972. 'What Is Kinship All About?' In *Kinship Studies in the Morgan Centennial Year*, edited by Priscilla Reining, pp.32-63. Washington, D.C.: Washington Anthropological Society.

—1980. *American Kinship: A Cultural Account*. Chicago: University of Chicago Press. Original publication Englewood Cliffs, N. J.: Prentice-Hall, 1968.

Schneider, David M., and Smith, Raymond T. 1978. *Class Differences in American Kinship*. Ann Arbor: University of Michigan Press. Original publication, *Class Differences and Sex Roles in America Kinship and Family Structure*, Englewood Cliffs, N. J.: Prentice-Hall, 1973.

Smith, Raymond T. 1966. 'People and Change.' In *New World: Guyana Independence Issue*, edited by George Lamming, pp.49-54. Georgetown, Guyana: New World.

—1982. 'Race and Class in the Post-Emancipation Caribbean.' In *Racism and Colonialism: Essays on Ideology and Social Structure*, edited by Robert Ross, pp. 93-119. The Hague: Martinus Nijhoff.

Weber, Max. 1968. *Economy and Society: An Outline of Interpretive Sociology*. 3 vols. Edited by Guenther Roth and Claus Wittich. New York: Bedminster Press.

Wright, Philip, ed. 1966. *Lady Nugent's Diary of Her Residence in Jamaica form 1801 to 1805*. Rev. ed. Kingston: Institute of Jamaica.

R. T. Smith

SEX ROLE DIFFERENTIATION

The sexual division of labour is nothing else than a device to institute a reciprocal state of dependency between the sexes.

Lévi-Strauss 1956

Sex role differentiation is a cultural recognition that males and females differ, but also unite to create what neither can produce alone. They are separate but cannot properly exist without each other; different but complementary; integral parts of a larger totality. In all societies these differences extend to social activity. This division of labour by sex is so pervasive, and seemingly 'natural', that it is often taken for granted and assumed to be an inevitable consequence of physical difference. Only when dramatic inversions of normal sex roles occur is normality itself reconsidered. But 'normal' behaviour also varies between societies, and even between groups within the same society. It is now widely recognized that sexual differences impose few limits on behaviour. Sex roles are culturally constituted.

West Indians have specific ideas about the behaviour appropriate to males and females at various stages of the life cycle, at various positions within the social hierarchy, and within the occupational system. The distinctive features of sexuality are clear and unequivocal because they are physical rather than social; they do not vary from class to class, race to race, or at various stages of an individual's life cycle. Males and females are readily distinguished by the presence of male or female sexual organs, and it is by reference to these distinctive features that the sex of each individual is established at birth. Sex role is not the same thing as physical sex, any more than kinship is the same thing as reproduction. Certain aspects of sex roles are uniform within West Indian society irrespective of class or race. Men are thought to be stronger and more dominating and are expected to be more active. They should be 'providers' while women need someone to be 'responsible' for them. The nature of man is such that he needs sexual intercourse; the nature of woman is such that she needs children. Needless to say, these stereotyped ideas are very different from reality.

In this chapter I discuss some general ideas about gender, or sex roles, in order to bring the West Indian material into a wider comparative framework.

1. THE CULTURAL DIMENSION OF SEX ROLE DIFFERENTIATION

Schneider and Smith (1978) distinguish two aspects of the meaning of sex in American culture. There is a relational aspect, in that the symbol of sex stands for the unification of opposites through the joining together of naturally differing elements. An attributional aspect may also be distinguished, when sex stands for the absolute separation that is believed to arise from the biological and temperamental differences of male and female (Schneider and Smith 1978, pp. 70-7).

The distinction between relational and attributional aspects of sex at the level of cultural meaning is a special application of the distinction between quality and performance, or ascription and achievement, a distinction made by Talcott Parsons (1951, pp. 58-67, 180-200). Part of the 'pattern variables' scheme for the analysis and classification of value systems, the ascription-achievement distinction is highly abstract. Here the attribute-relation distinction is more limited, and does not have the same general theoretical implications.

In the West Indies, as in the United States, both relational and attributional aspects are always present in the structuring of the meaning of sex; what varies is the relative emphasis placed upon each.

i. Attributional dominance

Where the attributional aspect of sexuality is dominant, primacy is given to the differences between the sexes over a wide spectrum of social and psychological perception. It is believed that males and females are fundamentally different, not only in physical characteristics, but also in temperament, aptitude, and ability to perform certain roles. Where these beliefs are embodied in social action they produce a sharp separation of the spheres of activity of males and females. For example, one might find that women monopolize — or are believed to monopolize — the 'female' tasks of child care, cooking, washing, sewing, cleaning, and the various extensions of these tasks such as obtaining food, firewood, shopping for clothes, and so forth. Their major social intercourse is with other women and takes place in a predominantly domestic setting. For women, child bearing and child rearing may be considered the major attributes of their sexuality: tasks for which they are uniquely fitted. These cultural emphases do not always coincide with actual behaviour. For example, it has been assumed that lower-class West Indian women dominate the 'domestic domain' while men are active in the 'outside' world of occupations, politics and status determining activities generally. This assumption is shared by informants themselves, but does not correspond with observed activities. Women have always been involved in such 'masculine' pursuits as heavy agricultural labour, road work, and animal husbandry. On slave plantations the strongest women took their place beside men in the 'Great Gang', which did all the heaviest work (see Roughley 1823, p. 99; Craton and Walvin 1970, pp. 128, 138). Sex was not used as a major criterion in allocating labour in the most labour intensive agricultural tasks; black women were assumed to be more suited for heavy labour than lighter coloured individuals of either sex. Only at the higher skilled, levels of the occupational scale did gender affect who would become a sugar boiler, carpenter, mason, cooper, washer or seamstress. Theories that assume a total separation of male and female activities are ill-founded, even where attributional dominance is present (see R. T. Smith 1987). Where attributes dominate ideas about sex it is found that relations between men and women are stylized and circumscribed, at least until the sex role element ceases to be the most active element in the relationship. Old age diminishes sex role differences, and eases relations between men and women. Relations between husband and wife can grow in mutuality and intimacy over time, but 'the war of the sexes' is more usual, especially where a relational element is coming to be seen as necessary or desirable, but attributional concepts still dominate. Courtship embodies a particular kind of attributional stress. In the West Indies three patterns of courtship may be distinguished, with differing frequencies of occurrence in different classes. They may be called the companionship pattern, the chaperone pattern and the uncontrolled pattern. The first is appropriate to relational dominance and will be discussed later.

The chaperone pattern is the ideal of the West Indian lower class; it assumes that if young people of opposite sex are left alone they will be carried away, intercourse will be inevitable, and pregnancy will follow. A third party must be present until they are placed in the right social situation for their sexual natures to combine. That situation is marriage. To say that this is the 'ideal' of the West Indian lower class is only approximately accurate; it is the lower-class conception of how relations between young men and women should be ordered to embody the status enhancing act of early marriage. In practice it is rare for young people to court and marry in this way, except among Indo-Guyanese where marriage is arranged at an early age. The exaggerated emphasis placed upon proof of virginity at marriage in one Guyanese village has been reported previously (R. T. Smith 1956, p. 172), and other case material has been collected on courtship carried out under very close supervision (R. T. Smith 1978a, p. 355). A man should always write to a girl's guardian if he intends to be her friend, whether the object be marriage or some other form of union. These ideals of chaperonage and close control are not accompanied by concepts of family honour comparable to those found in Mediterranean society, and this makes them difficult to understand.

In practice, the most common form of early sexual experience is an uncontrolled encounter that is generally furtive and brief. Women often claim that their first experience of sexual intercourse was shrouded in ignorance (Blake 1961, pp. 52-7). Doubtless it was; not ignorance of what sex is all about, as Blake supposes — most unlikely in a predominantly rural society where sexual reference is frequent and explicit — but ignorance of the actual experience of sexual contact and intercourse. Stress upon sexual attributes as part of the nature of males and females requires a process of learning how to manage the attributes as they develop, much as one has to learn to walk or speak. Sexual intercourse is considered to be a normal and expected activity for both men and women (the lack of which can lead to illness and even insanity); therefore the definition of maturity includes sexual intercourse. In the absence of any general concept of a relationship of friendship between young people of the opposite sex, the first sexual intercourse is likely to be thought of in retrospect as an isolated and even traumatic act, as when a woman refers to 'the man who fall me'.

Further development of sexual maturation leads to parenthood; symbolic of maturity for women, and virility for men. Parenthood is an attribute of each parent separately, and not an expression of the relationship between them. It does not have to be embodied in a conjugal tie and certainly not in a coresidential union. For men, a further dimension of sex role attributes is the development of 'responsibility' but this is not expected until the man is much older, and is always modified by the supposition that economic factors may make it difficult, or even impossible. Where attributes are stressed, solidarity arises through likeness; in Durkheim's terms it is 'mechanical' and not 'organic' (Durkheim 1947, pp. 71-110). If sex roles are considered in isolation, men have nothing in common with women and everything in common with other men. Men and women are to each other only necessary objects for the achievement of their respective ends. Men need women for sexual satisfaction, to prepare food and wash clothes and do other tasks defined as being inappropriate for men; women need men for economic support, and less urgently for sexual satisfaction. No joint activities are involved necessarily, except for sexual intercourse itself. Women's joint activities are with other women in the immediate domestic and neighbourhood environment, and the women most likely to be there are mother, sisters and daughters. The specifically female tasks of child care and domestic activity constitute the core of the interaction of such groups even when the women work out for wages.

For men the focus of solidarity and joint activities is the peer group; not the unit of father and sons, or even of brothers. This asymmetry is interesting. There is no field of activity for closely related men comparable to the domestic life of women. Young men begin to work out for wages as soon as possible since this is the means by which they assert their independence. Rarely are farms large enough to require the labour of a large body of men, even in the rice farming areas. Among Indo-Guyanese, where the ideal of filial dependence is still strong, sons expect to be set up on land of their own as soon as they mature and get married. Jobs most readily available to young men are in large concerns — sugar plantations, bauxite mines, government projects — where fathers and sons may work side by side, but equally subordinated to higher status supervisors. The difference between solidary groups of female kin and solidary groups of male peers is not a product of functional necessity; it is produced by the way in which sex roles are defined.

Where the attributional aspects of sex roles are stressed, conjugal relations are affected. Intimate relations develop between husband and wife but they rest upon a kinship, rather than a sex role, basis. There is an interesting contrast between Indo-Guyanese and Afro-Guyanese communities. In the former it is customary to marry a woman from a different village who is then incorporated into the family of her husband. The position of the young bride is notoriously bad; she is not yet a part of the female group within the household, and her husband often ignores her. When she becomes a mother she gradually becomes a part of her husband's family, and may grow to be the dominant element in the household. Among Afro-Guyanese, and other West Indians, the stress tends to be the other way. Women who go to live with a man in a common law or a legal union are mistress in their own house from the beginning. If possible they stay close to their mother, and their sisters. Where close relationships develop between husband and wife it is because one has become absorbed into the family of the other. It is more likely that the relationship continues to be 'segregated' with the man marginal to the solidary relationships of the household, and to his wife's matrilateral group.

ii. Relational dominance

Where the relational aspect of sex role is dominant the emphasis is all the other way. Rather than stressing the separation of the sexes, rooted in their respective attributes, the focus is upon the 'unity — physical, spiritual, emotional ... the coming together into a single whole, ... the bringing of opposites together ... the inseparability and interdependence of the differentiated parts ... enduring or "eternal" solidarity, and so on' (Schneider and Smith 1978, p. 73). Where this aspect of sex roles is most fully developed, attributional differences are minimized in favour of equal cooperation in whatever activity contributes to the unity of the relational whole. The unity and complementarity of the sexes is stressed, rather than their differences, and so one expects joint activities as the working out of the relationship. These joint activities can extend over a wide area of social life. They can be manifest in domestic life where each does what is necessary without reference to whether it is a 'male' or a 'female' task; they can be manifest in leisure activities where each contributes to the pleasure of the other and the compatibility of the couple is the focus of attention; they can be manifest in joint efforts to enhance the social status of the couple, and they can be manifest in sexual intercourse itself where the emphasis is upon the creation of unity and mutual transcendence by whatever means seems appropriate without reference to the orthodoxy of 'male' and 'female' actions. Companionship is stressed as the essential part of courtship during the period after the couple 'fall in love' and are getting to know each other. Neither chaperonage nor an uncontrolled relationship are deemed appropriate; the first because it interferes with the interpersonal bond and the second because it contravenes the notion of mutual regard and equality.

A stress on the relational dimension of sex role differentiation links to the symbolism of kinship in a particular way, once it is brought into conjunction with the idea of production of offspring. Schneider has dealt with this issue at length in his treatment of the components of middle-class American kinship, where he shows that the master symbol of coitus 'stands for' the creation of unity out of difference, and the holding together of parents and the children who are created and sustained by conjugal love and unity. Thus, argues Schneider, the nuclear family becomes the embodiment of both conjugal love and consanguineal love, the archetype of all kinship relations, since they are rooted either in common substance or in the relationship of diffuse, enduring solidarity. The nuclear family based on the relations between spouses is the conjunction of all these factors and represents the interpenetration of the kinship and sex role domains (Schneider 1980 [1968]).

Schneider's analysis seems to be logical, an economical interpretation of the generative elements in the symbol system, but it does not satisfy many middle-class Americans. In a review of Schneider's book remarkable for its tone of disparagement, but still forced to conclude that the essay brings many fundamental issues into focus, Wallace denies that marriage in American kinship is a relationship in law, as opposed to the relationship in nature that characterizes consanguineal kin (Wallace 1969). Wallace distorts the argument by omission of certain of Schneider's qualifying statements; for example, 'sexual intercourse is an act which is undertaken and does not just happen. Yet as an act, it is natural. Its outcome is conception, which is followed by birth, and these are natural, too' (Schneider 1980 [1968]), p. 38). However, Wallace is correct in pointing to informants' uneasiness over the deriving of all kinship concepts from the master symbol of coitus, a symbol that, according to Schneider, joins the relationship in law of the conjugal partners to the relationship in nature of the parents and offspring.

Without attempting to argue from the West Indies to the American middle class (or the other way), it is interesting that West Indians are similarly uneasy. Mrs Brown, a middle-class Guyanese of mixed racial origin, was explaining the difference between 'family' and 'relatives'. Family, she said, are related by some direct connection, while relatives are connected by marriage. As soon as we began to discuss non-legal (irregular) unions, the distinction began to break down. I asked whether her sister's husband was part of her family. 'He's a relation — he's not family — he's not a "begat"'. When asked the same question about her own husband the response was different and more complex. 'He is my family but their relative.' 'Why is he your family?' 'Because I married him; he is the father of my children.' At this point she was confronted with the clear distinction she had made between family and relatives. 'I know, but you can't call your husband a relative — it is ridiculous .... All those who are from the same grandparents will be family; the in-laws would be relatives, but the husband would be a third category. The two of us would be the beginning of another family'.

Schneider's analysis makes more sense of these West Indian data than does Wallace, who lays primary stress on the natural quality of 'love' as a state into which one gets, or 'falls'. Alexander has made a similar point (1978, p. 7). Mrs Brown, in the interview cited above, is not discussing 'love' in that sense at all; rather she is pointing to the fact that marriage creates a tie of natural generation which is comparable to a blood tie and in fact results in the creation of blood ties. 'Love' as a state of being is beside the point. This variability in the symbolization of kinship arises because of the differential stress upon attributes and relationship in the domain of sex role differentiation.

In Schneider's middle-class cases the relational element in sex role differentiation is dominant in the conjugal bond — or so it seems. Between 'husband' and 'wife' a relationship is actively created, leading to unity through love, expressed in mutual activity, sexual intercourse being the most complete and intimate activity. However, sexual intercourse is also a fact in nature giving rise to the generation of offspring. The American middle-class informants (and Schneider) separate these two aspects, so that Schneider interprets the master symbol of coitus as embodying and combining two separate elements — kinship as law (spouses), and kinship as nature (parents and children). In the West Indies the configuration is different because of the differing emphases in sex role definition and differentiation.

Where attributional elements dominate the domain of sex, two kinship outcomes are possible. The conjugal bond may be separated from consanguineal kinship. A woman's 'husband' becomes 'the baby father' or 'Jean's daddy'; that is, her tie to him is defined in consanguineal terms — through the child. The relatives 'in-law', such as the baby's father's mother, are classed in the same way. They are the baby's blood relatives and as such it is the duty of the mother to see that the ties of blood between them and the child are given recognition and expression.

The other possible outcome is to model marriage or common law marriage on consanguinity. One informant described how her children's father goes with her when she visits her relatives.

> Yes man. For my relatives are now his like too you know. We live together long now; it is not like say the children don't have a common father. They are all for him, and he come in like one of us now. But his family different like. They don't move so close, so he come more to mine, except the mother like how I told you.

What she said about his mother was:

> Agatha Wilson — she is my husband's mother and she lives at Hermitage. I visit her regularly, but I don't know any other from his family. But his mother is different; she come in like sort of family.

Thus, sex role definitions play an important part in the constitution of kinship, even at the cultural or ideological level. As an element in the constitution of social relationships and normative structure, they are even more important.

2. SEX ROLE DIFFERENTIATION IN THE SOCIAL STRUCTURE

The logical implications of stress on attributional or relational aspects of 'sex' are built into culture and norms. How do sex roles vary according to their differential positioning in social structure? More specifically, what are the class variations in sex roles, and what effects do they have on kinship and family structure? At least three patterns of conjugal relationship can be distinguished in West Indian kinship. These patterns are not 'types' into which all unions must be sorted; they are models constructed to show how a sex role component enters into the constitution of conjugal unions. Elizabeth Bott, in *Family and Social Network*, found, after a process of elimination, that the organization of family activities could be classified as 'complementary', 'independent' and 'joint'.

> In complementary organization the activities of husband and wife are different and separate but fitted together to form a whole. In independent organization activities are carried out separately by husband and wife without reference to each other, in so far as this is possible. In joint organization activities are carried out by husband and wife together, or the same activity is carried out by either partner at different times (Bott 1957, p. 53).

All three types of activity are found to some extent in each of her families, but in some families complementary and independent types of organization predominated and in those cases she described the relationship of husband and wife as a segregated conjugal role relationship. Where joint activities predominated, the relationship was termed a joint conjugal role relationship. The revised version of her book has a chapter of 'Reconsiderations' in which she discusses the close correspondence between conjugal roles and general sex role differentiation.

Bott's terminology is widely known and will be adopted here, with the added distinction that segregated conjugal role relationships should be divided into two types, and the word 'relationship' replaced by 'pattern'. These patterns are dissociated conjugal role pattern and segregated conjugal role pattern. The introduction of a distinction between 'dissociated' and 'segregated' is not entirely satisfactory, linguistically or anthropologically, but we need to distinguish independent organization from complementarity in family activities, rather than treating them both as being segregated role patterns.

i. Dissociated conjugal role patterns

The dissociated pattern of conjugal roles has a minimal relational element; it is found in many, but not all, visiting unions, and in many coresidential unions — legal and non-legal. Where this pattern occurs it is difficult to think of activities constituting a unitary whole; the stress is on exchange between two distinct entities, male and female, which differ in certain ways. Even sexual relations are conceived as 'giving' one to the other rather than as the joint activity of a couple. Intense affect is not necessary. This does not mean that unions approximating this pattern are without love or affection; it means that intense emotional involvement is not essential. Each partner probably continues to be closely involved in a network of consanguineal relationships that provide emotional support and reciprocity.

The social arrangement embodying this pattern most completely is the short term visiting union. Each partner may be involved in more than one union simultaneously, or one partner may invest very little in the union, while the other is more committed. Most usually this is described as male 'exploitation', but there is no necessary bias in that direction.

Alice Smith lives with her six children in a small house built on the edge of a plot of 'family land' in Kingston, land in which she acquired residence rights through her father. In Jamaica, no member of the kindred can be denied accommodation on such land. Her parents separated when she was an infant and she spent most of her childhood with paternal relatives on this family land, supported by small contributions from her father. She first became pregnant when she was sixteen, and she now says that she 'didn't know what was happening'. Alice Smith always refers to the father of her first child as 'the chap' and says that being a boy he was more experienced than she was. When she realized she was pregnant he took her to the doctor and contributed to the expenses of the delivery. They remained friends and he fathered a second child. During this period she shared a room with her father's sister's daughter, her husband and four children. After the birth of the second child she moved out, into a small one room structure built originally by her father, but occupied recently by a cousin. She has lived there since, alone with her children. She is not really 'alone'; the family land is well populated with 'relatives'. Although she claims not to get along with them, they provide child care services (for which she pays), and this enables her to work — she began as a domestic servant and now works in a dry cleaning factory. The father of her first two children developed other ties, and he now lives with the mother of his other children. Alice Smith's next friendship resulted in the birth of two more children, a girl and a boy, but she drifted away from that man because, she says, he is not 'collective' (mentally stable). He lives with his aunt, and contributes no money to the support of his children. Alice's fifth child, a girl, is nearly three years old: the father lives with another woman. He gives Alice some money occasionally and she appears to be on good terms with him. Her youngest child was born just before the beginning of the field interviews. The father was a regular visitor to the home until about a month before the baby was born, and then he stayed away for about four months, claiming that one of Alice's children had been rude to him by not saying 'goodnight' when he arrived. This exquisite sensibility was only part of the story; it turned out that another woman had just given birth to his child — this in addition to his three children in the country and a daughter attending school in Kingston. Alice was upset about his staying away because 'it looked bad' that he had not even been to see the baby. Eventually he resumed his occasional visits, giving a small contribution now and again for the support of the child. Alice was not sure whether he was actually living with the other woman or merely visiting each of them.

Miss Smith's relationships with her gentlemen friends (the local term) are typical of many such cases. She refers to them, and addresses them as 'Mr so-and-so'; the absence of deep personal involvement implied in such terms is characteristic. In principle Alice Smith would like to settle into a stable monogamous relationship with one man, but she has avoided moving in with a man who might turn out to be unreliable, preferring to maintain her own job and her own house. She has great hopes for her sons. One is already working as a TV and radio repair technician, bringing in money for household expenses, while the second son is almost ready to start work. She says that she would never have had so many children had she known what she knows now, and her conversations are punctuated with yearnings for a better life. She hopes to move into a better neighbourhood before the girls get older, and is always talking about her 'ambition', especially her desire to migrate to the United States as a domestic servant. The men with whom she has had relationships remain insubstantial. She knows them of course, and maintains contact with them and their families, but they are not now, nor do they appear ever to have been, figures of deep personal significance. How else could she have been unaware of their other, simultaneous, sexual relationships?[1] In terms of the classificatory system suggested above, it appears that the attributional aspect of sexuality is dominant in these dissociated conjugal relationships. In the following case, there seems to be less detachment, but in spite of a considerable emotional component, attributes dominate the explanation of the breakup of each of the unions.

Lester Chase, thirty-two years old, has a steady job in a biscuit factory just outside Georgetown, Guyana; he has just broken up with a 'girlfriend' with whom he has been living for the past three years. He has two children by other women; the first was born as a result of an affair with a young girl he met through the church. She was seventeen when the baby was born and he had some idea of marrying her, but nothing came of it. His second child was born while he was in a coresidential, non-legal union with Vernel Payne, a domestic servant who already had several children. He says he got along extremely well with Vernel.

Yes man, fine. She was what you would call a housewife. The nice type. The only difficulty I find with her was that she had these many children. I found it difficult with them. I asked her to give them to the rightful parents and so on. I would even consider marrying her. But she won't agree. She said she would give some of the children to their fathers and one girl she was going to keep because she didn't have any girl children. But I couldn't agree to that so eventually we split down the middle. It wasn't an easy task.

How big were the children? from fourteen right down. The little girl was about nine. But I know that if I had kept the girl the father would have come there to see the child. In so doing conversation might have reached a stage where she might have accepted something from him. Eventually they would be in bed and I would be the comic in the middle. Once there is that spark there's always some kind of feelings so I think it was wise.

I don't have that trust in people on the whole, because on many occasions I've tried and people let me down. Women are like rain — there's no telling when it might fall. But this girl was really great. When I say great I mean great. There wasn't a thing I wanted she won't share. Suppose I get sick — I would get great care from her. Moreover she had nice ways. But we just couldn't agree about the children. One time I struck her and the little boy she had was about ten. He said, 'Don't strike my mother. You're not her father, nor mine.' And that boy used to eat out of me. I said to myself, in years to come he would break me up, even if I talk a little harsh to her. It would be a very one-sided affair. To prevent these things from happening I thought it best for me to leave.

His most recent union was even more turbulent. Peggy is three years older than he is, has a good job as a clerk in a small business and is separated from her husband. She has three children ranging in age from nineteen to fifteen who live with her husband's family. Lester met her by chance one evening and then ran into her again a couple of weeks later.

We went into the restaurant down the road there and had a few beers. A friend of mine came in the same time and tell me about a sport [dance] up in La Penitence. I asked her if she would go. She told me she wasn't dressed and had to get home early. Anyhow I tell her to come along — we would only stay two hours or so. When we get there — I am a drinking man — I moved over with the boys — then me and a fellow put together and buy a large [a quart bottle of rum]. If you see this woman drinking down this rum! I take her out on the bicycle and we went to my room. Six o'clock next morning is when she leaving — although she had to get home!

Anyhow, I gone to Bookers and buy that bed; not even sheets. And she move in. She live there for three years until last week.

Why did you break up?

From the beginning when I see what a trickster she was I tell her straight — 'look Peggy I don't want to like you so you leave me where I am and go your way'. But she got more brains than U Thant. [He then launched into a long account of her unfaithfulness and deceit]. Any woman can come in my house but she isn't hanging up anything.

It's a bad way I know — a man needs a foundation and stability in life but you can't trust no woman.

This Peggy, I had to let her go because she was too hot. It was the same thing with her husband. She only want to know the size of every man's cock. Women are a barbarous set of people.

In this case, as in the last, the unions involve sex and the mutual provision of other services, but failure to adjust the practical details of that mutuality quickly leads to the break up of the union, especially if one partner has independent resources. Lester Chase's union with Vernel Jones was less dissociated but his marginal position in relation to her and her children, made it unstable.

ii. Segregated and joint conjugal role patterns

The pattern contrasting most strongly with the dissociated pattern may be termed, following Bott, the joint conjugal role relationship pattern. Here the emphasis is upon the partners doing things together with a minimum of concern about the separate attributes of each sex, and no assumption that each should have reserved activities. Either partner will do what is necessary for the common good, whether it be preparing a meal, painting a room, cleaning the house, or taking care of the children. Husband and wife share leisure activities; a visit to friends, a trip to the beach or a night at the cinema. Emphasis is placed on 'the family' meaning the family of husband, wife and their children — the unit to which primary loyalty is owed. If both partners work, their income is pooled for the common good.

This pattern has been most fully described for Europe and North America. It does occur in the West Indies, but the segregated conjugal role pattern is more frequent, and is often compared unfavourably with the joint pattern. In the segregated pattern the stress is on complementary activities; upon the meshing together of the distinctive attributes of husband and wife as male and female, with each person having a clearly defined area of competence into which the other does not venture. This pattern of conjugal role structure is found in both the lower and middle classes, but with differing consequences and content.

The cultural definition of complementary activities in segregated conjugal role patterns says that men should provide support and general protection while women engage in child rearing and domestic work. Some supplementary provisions may be added, as when rural women may be expected to market the produce of jointly operated farms.

When the male contribution to the conjugal union is defined as the provision of economic support, the occupational system must influence male familial activities. However, occupational roles do not determine family roles. The independence of conjugal role patterns was shown by Bott in her study of London families (1957, p. 111). Male familial roles are not confined to the conjugal relationship. Men play an important part in the family as sons and brothers, and occupation does not determine what that part shall be, even if it sets limits to what it can be. The occupational system in the West Indies has made it difficult for men to be reliable providers, and has made it possible for women sometimes to earn as much as men — more in some cases. Historically women worked at the hardest tasks alongside men, and if today women do the lighter tasks such as weeding, some may still perform the heavy labour of loading bananas, breaking rock for road building, planting and harvesting rice, carrying firewood and cultivating small farms. Domestic service has always been a source of employment for women, the numbers so engaged rising and falling as the tides of economic prosperity erode or augment male earnings. Women dominate petty trade, and even 'middle-class' women sometimes make cakes, do dressmaking, or engage in other part-time, income-producing activities.

The easy availability of low-paid domestic servants, and nursemaids to take care of children, has enabled middle-class West Indian women to have full time occupations and careers. But women of different classes work for different reasons and this throws light on the relationship between employment and conjugal roles. Middle-class married women say that they work for personal satisfaction or to help out with domestic expenses and clothes for themselves and the children. Major recurrent items, such as rent or mortgage payments, utility bills, and food, are the man's responsibility, but the exact division of payment for other things is rarely a settled matter. The idea is that both partners are contributing to the needs of the family, of which 'advancement' is a major part. In practice things may not work so smoothly; where there is segregation of conjugal roles men rarely share their income openly, usually giving the woman a fixed sum for housekeeping that she supplements through her own activities. This pattern also prevails among lower-class couples, but the husband's income is more critical in the domestic economy of the middle class. It is larger in absolute terms and essential for the maintenance of the domestic budget and the status of the family. The income of the lower-class male is smaller and more erratic; since the family does not operate on a fixed budget, its income and expenditures vary from day to day.

Male roles are not defined solely in terms of economic support. When the attributional aspect of sex roles is dominant men are perceived to be strong, virile, active and domineering as well as 'responsible'. They are thought to be so by nature, not by education or effort. If a man cannot get work it does not mean that he is 'emasculated'; it is thought to be bad luck, because he 'can't do better' or because of the perversity and evil of the society as a whole. Masculinity does not depend on work performance; it is demonstrated by 'manly' activities with other men, by sexual conquest of many 'girl friends', and by 'having children all about'. Masculine role identity is established by displaying the sexual attributes themselves. Similarly women are mothers, housekeepers, sexual partners at the appropriate stages of their social development. Conjugal relations are not entered into by calculating the cost of maintaining a household. Being 'friendly' with someone of the opposite sex, or being married, is natural for adults. This is different from the idea that marriage is active cooperation for the production of a 'family', and for its progressive advancement in the social scale.

These varying patterns of conjugal roles are associated with class but the link is not absolute. In middle-class West Indian families conjugal roles are generally segregated, though young people are moving toward joint activities. There is a pervasive feeling that middle-class marital relations should be more joint than they are. Constant criticism of men's refusal to lift a finger in the house or help with the children, even when women go out to work, is not diminished even when domestic servants take care of the dirty work. In his discussion of the asymmetry in the division of labour within the conjugal relationship, Alexander points to two interesting aspects. Men believe that domestic chores diminish masculinity, but there is no corresponding feeling that women's employment is a threat to either partner's sexual identity. It is also commonly said that men's behaviour is an aspect of their identity as Jamaican, or West Indian, men, who are then compared unfavourably (by women) with foreigners. Yet these complaints about male indifference to family life are less strident when families are more prosperous and the burden on working wives less onerous. The middle-class preoccupation with male familial roles is projected onto the lower class in public discussion about the 'problem' of West Indian family life, as it has been for at least 100 years.

NOTES

1. See Roberts 1975, p. 150, note 5, for evidence from Barbados of women's lack of knowledge of visiting partners.

G. Roberts and S. Sinclair

INSTITUTIONAL AND OTHER ELEMENTS INFLUENCING MATING PATTERNS

While in the opening chapter of this study the view has been expressed that the three union types identified here have been in existence throughout the post-emancipation period, and we have refrained from being drawn into discussions of their origins, it is still necessary to bring together some observations on factors contributing to the persistence, if not indeed to the origins, of prevailing mating patterns. In the first place there were probably several institutional elements militating against the widespread resort to marriage as a means of initiating family unions. At least one line of evidence pointing to this may be cited. Up to recent years, postmistresses in Jamaica, who also performed the duties of district registrars and many other significant official functions, were not permitted to marry; it was a condition under which they occupied official houses that they should not marry. The reason behind this cruel imposition is not clear, but it is all the more relevant in the present context because these officials were responsible for the registration of births in the island. There were other female-centred occupations — notably nursing, and to a lesser degree teaching — but restrictions against marriage were evidently not in force among them. The reluctance on the part of the colonial civil service to employ married women was well known throughout the Caribbean. The opening of civil service careers to married women has materialized only in recent years.

Perhaps several other institutional factors might have played a part in establishing the existing mating forms, but it is not the aim of this study to pursue these. More relevant in the present context are the views women express about prevailing family types. It is therefore essential to consider briefly their assessments of the three union types. We begin by an examination of what they think of the common-law union. It is curious that there seems to be very little support for this form of relationship. Of the women who gave views on the subject there is only one who comes out firmly in support of it. She is a 64-year-old widow and she states her position as follows, 'You are steady and quiet even if things do not work out well, and it is better than running around and having children for different men.'

To some women the disadvantages of common-law unions mainly derive from the impact on their children. One claims that if children are involved the partner might not want 'to accept responsibilities since it is not legal'. Again, another holds that this type of union 'don't look proper for children'. On financial grounds also the impression is that several disabilities inhere in this type of union. One respondent says that the partner will give an amount of money and 'you have to stretch it and cannot ask for any more'. Also, in the words of another, the money brought by the partner has to be 'shared', whereas in a visiting union 'the money they bring is for the woman alone'. There is a general feeling among respondents that the common-law union 'demands' too much of them and accords them 'less freedom' than in the visiting union, while the woman has no certain claim on her partner. As one respondent puts it, 'If you live with a man, he will have a girl outside and everywhere you go that girl will laugh at you'; because of this, she prefers just 'to talk to them'. In the opinion of another, men in these unions usually 'stay out late at night'. Men in common-law unions also at times ill-treat their partners. In the words of one, 'When they come and stay they have too much clue to you. They want to beat you up and tell you not to go outside of the street.' And another holds, 'When people live together they usually fight and quarrel.' Thus there does seem to be much enthusiasm for the common-law union, which denies the woman much of her freedom, exposes her to ill treatment from a resident partner, does not afford much financial advantage and promises few benefits for her children.

The formal married status is much more acceptable to respondents. Indeed for the most part it appears to be an ideal type to which most women aspire. But it is important to note that many see in it disadvantages which they are anxious to spell out. Thus one argues, 'It can be very difficult if one has chosen wrong', and there is 'too much responsibility connected'. Another is skeptical of marriages because many of them 'are not working'. And one respondent concludes that the man 'leaves you at home and you suffer more'.

One of the principal benefits of marriage acknowledged concerns the 'respectability' it confers on the family. According to one respondent, it is a 'more respectable' form of association and 'better for the children'. And another expresses her support thus, 'People respect you and you are near the person you really like.' A married woman, says another 'is more honourable and she is more respected', the union is 'binding'. In the words of still another, marriage 'is more stable and other men do not try to get in so readily'. Also, 'Marriage is the best thing as you settle down one place.' Marriage, several women argue, has definite advantages for children. As one states it, 'Marriage is only good for the children's sake, so if their father dies and leaves a little house or land they can get it.' Religion has also played a part in inducing some to accept marriage. In the words of one, after 'accepting Christ' she 'just lay low with everything' and thought marriage was the best way. Also another argues that you cannot be a member of a church unless you are married. 'Marriage is the union that God requires', claims a married woman aged 26, who gives her religion as Open Bible. In fact the religious arguments form the basis for extensive support for the married state.

Comments on the visiting type are numerous and far ranging, above all demonstrating the extent to which the women in the society accept such relationships as part of their way of life. In outlining what are advanced as the benefits of this union type it is convenient to consider in the first place the views of respondents who evidently do not contemplate marriage. Their tendency is to stress that the visiting union assures 'freedom' and a measure of 'independence'. This is not to say that they hold that such a position confers licence to any form of conduct on the part of the respondent or her partner.

Underlying many of the views of respondents on the types of union is a lurking fear that living with a man, whether in common-law status or marriage, carries a strong risk of a woman being the victim of her partner's violent behaviour. This theme of violence appears to be another important aspect of the seeming preference for visiting-type unions expressed by many respondents, especially in the early stages of the family. Some even fear that their partners will take their lives, as in the case of one woman aged 51 years, who one night saw her partner with a razor and thought that he was about to kill her. This led to their immediate separation. Another, after remonstrating with her husband because he stayed out late at nights, faced his threat 'to break my bones'. One respondent in a visiting union and still living in her mother's home was re-luctant to set up her own house with a partner, for when 'you do this you usually get some lick that you don't suppose to get'. Still another in a visiting union comments that she did not want to live with any man; 'The men cannot beat you when visiting, but liv-ing together they will beat you.' It is not surprising therefore to learn that several women see in the visiting union a protection against such violent behaviour. One respondent points out that if conditions do become difficult in the union, the woman 'can leave when she wants'. This is fully spelled out in another statement, 'You can get to know the person and you can break off if it does not suit you.' Many women prefer to have short periods of isolation from their partners, and the visiting union assures them this: 'It is not every time that you want to see him', declares one respondent. 'You can get to know the person without getting tired of him, which might happen if you were living to-gether.' This means that the couple remains 'sweeter' and the woman has 'less work to do; she is free'. A poetic assessment is, 'It's better being in a visiting union, because 'ab-sence makes the heart grow fonder.'

Others supporting the visiting type do so from the standpoint of assuming that it is a prelude to marriage. These views dwell less on the aspects of freedom and inde-pendence of these relationships. In short, 'a visiting union should lead up to something, marriage'. 'One gets to know a person before marriage', is how another sums up the situation. One, mindful of both marriage and a career, argues that a visiting union 'gives one time to get a career before marriage'. Another holds that it affords the woman needed experience. She gained so much experience that she 'was able to marry a man quite a few years older than herself', which evidently pleased her. Such a marriage could not have taken place if she did not have the necessary experience 'about love and so on'.

Some disadvantages and drawbacks of involvement in a visiting union are stressed by respondents, but it is by no means the subject of general condemnation. A few express reserve about it on moral grounds. To one, this type of union 'does not look decent', while to another it is 'not nice'. But in none of the views expressing disapproval with this type of union is this position based on or in any way associated with religious prin-ciples; the closest to a religious assessment is the view of one respondent that it is 'less sinful' than presumably the common-law. Some respondents acknowledge that the free-dom of movement which this union type allows to their partners as well as to them-selves is not always to their advantage, because 'sometimes you think he is gone some-where and he is somewhere else'. Indeed, this 'coming and going' in visiting unions does not find universal approval.

The implications of this type of union for children are not stressed much by respon-dents. One claims that she obtained 'no good' from her union as she got a child which she had to support herself. More important, very few consider that the existence of this type of union in any way seriously impairs their financial position. One frequent theme is that money received from a partner does not have to be used to support him; it is en-tirely for her own use. Another goes so far as to characterize the position of the visiting union in these terms: 'It provides ready financial assistance without responsibility of a household.'

It seems fair to sum up the general assessment of the prevailing types of union in this way. To many women marriage appears as an ideal with clear advantages of many kinds, but it does not by any means command universal support. Much of the argument in favour of this union rests on religious grounds. There is strong support for visiting unions, the main contention being that it affords the women freedom and independence, as well as protects her from many abuses by her partner. Very important here is that virtually no views against visiting-type unions rest on religious grounds. There is little doubt that the common-law is lowest in the scale of values of the respondents, being disapproved of mostly on religious and moral considerations.

J. Manyoni

LEGITIMACY AND ILLEGITIMACY: MISPLACED POLARITIES IN CARIBBEAN FAMILY STUDIES

In studies of Caribbean family structure, the prevalence of customary-law unions, concubinage, and 'illegitimate' parenthood has traditionally been explained in terms of African customs, slavery conditions, and socio-economic status. Research on Caribbean mating patterns has tended to view 'illegitimacy' only from the point of view of the mother to the exclusion of the genitor. Data from recent research suggest that for a sociologically adequate understanding of Caribbean family structure, extramarital sexuality and premarital parenthood, both maternity and paternity, as well as attitudes to these behaviours, need to be taken into consideration to account for the continuation of these phenomena among contemporary Caribbean societies. Evidence is adduced to show that the prevailing forms of sexual behaviour are implicitly sanctioned, not only among the social stratum in which they are predominant, but at the social level. Hence the attribution of the concepts 'legitimacy' and 'illegitimacy' to societies in which extramarital relations and parenthood have always exceeded their counterparts is analytically inappropriate.

Theories relating to the peculiar features of West Indian family structure and marital patterns are well documented in the literature on these former plantation slave societies. These theories have sought for explanations of Caribbean family forms from diverse factors such as African origins (Herskovits, 1947); slavery conditions (Smith, 1956; Clarke, 1957; Greenfield, 1966; Patterson, 1967); colour attitudes (Henriques, 1953; Braithwaite, 1953; Hall, 1962); demography and emigration (Roberts, 1955, 1962).

It is not the intention of this paper to review these well-known theories on Caribbean family structure. Rather it will focus on the question of: whether the analytical dichotomy drawn between 'legitimacy' and 'illegitimacy' reflects the people's own conception of, and attitude to, the bearing of children out of formal marriage. I will attempt to show that sex relations and marital patterns in Caribbean societies are unlikely to be adequately explained in terms of the polarity between legitimacy and illegitimacy of parenthood without taking into consideration societal attitudes and practices in historical perspective. I further suggest that socio-economic status is a less powerful explanatory variable for attitudinal differences towards sexual behaviour among the different status categories and social groups.

The Herskovitses (1947: 16) in their study of a Trinidadian village have raised a significant question about the appropriateness of adopting the polar concepts of legitimacy and illegitimacy in dealing with Caribbean family patterns. They point to the 'false perspective on the thinking of the people ... given by the application of legal terms such as 'legitimate' and 'illegitimate' to the offspring of common-law unions. However their attempt to explain Caribbean mating patterns in terms of 'retentions and reinterpretations' of African customs (1947: 287-317) is less than satisfactory. The reason for this narrow perspective is to be found in the traditional anthropological bias of focussing upon social units in a society rather than the society as a whole.

Socio-anthropological studies of mating patterns which focus on 'Negro communities' or 'lower-class Negro groups' to the exclusion of not only other component groups but also the prevailing societal ethos provide an inadequate understanding of 'Caribbean mating patterns' or 'Caribbean family structure'. The crux of the problem would seem to be how to relate the practices among a particular segment to the overall ethical system of the society. As Smith (1971: 471) rightly points out, previous work on 'the study of Caribbean kinship and family structure raises a host of general theoretical problems' which have not been squarely faced by researchers. One of these problems stems from the traditional sociological perspective from which extramarital sexuality and childbirth are treated in Caribbean literature. Undue emphasis is often placed more on normative expectations rather than on the practical behaviour and manifest attitude of all segments in these societies.

Similarly, illegitimacy is largely considered from the perspective of maternity rather than both maternity and paternity. Since lower status women tend to be the sexual victims of higher status males, and the physical evidence of childbirth is unequivocally linked with the woman, illegitimacy is thus often associated with her and the status group to which she is ascribed. Sociological results inevitably tend to draw correlations between the incidence of 'illegitimate' births and lower status women, and to associate the phenomenon with their status group. I propose an alternative system of their status group. I propose an alternative view that takes into account the value system of *the society as a whole* in respect to attitudes to parenthood, marriage, and sex relations among all social levels. Data from my Barbados study suggests that 'illegitimacy' is a status that is institutionally accepted by the society as a whole, and not confined only to the lower segments. These data suggest there is in process a simultaneous maintenance of two contradictory moral and behavioural codes of conduct giving rise to evident discrepancies between ideal norm and sexual practice.

A consideration of the historical background to contemporary social attitudes to sexuality and marital relations is indispensable for a sociological interpretation of Barbadian data on family patterns. Present-day sexual behaviour, family structure, and value system in Barbados, as in the rest of the West Indies, derive from the pervasive system of the plantation slave economy of the seventeenth to the nineteenth centuries, as well as the quasi slavery conditions prevailing well into the twentieth century. Marital and social relations were significantly influenced by the conditions created by this peculiar institution.

HISTORICAL BACKGROUND

The history of the development of marital relations is one of the most sociologically revealing episodes in the social history of Barbados. In the earliest days formal marriage was a prerogative of the upper- and middle-class whites, but the institution of marriage existed concomitantly with the system of concubinage, which was widely practised by all sectors of the society. The lowest ranks of the population, the blacks, were considered outside the institution of legal matrimony. Both state and church shared a strong disapproval of slave marriages.

Before 1825 only one marriage between black slaves was officially performed at the Anglican Church's plantation in Barbados 'by a minister who was later subjected to persecution by his own parishioners' (Bennett, 1958: 116). The issue of slave marriage was inextricably tied to that of their Christianization against both of which the planters had very strong feelings. They strongly opposed the conversion of slaves to Christianity for fear this would 'destroy their property [and] endanger the island, inasmuch as converted negroes grow more perverse and intractable than others, and hence of less value for labour or sale' (Calendar of State Papers Colonial Series: West Indies and America, 1677-80: 611). In 1681 the same determination was reaffirmed on the ground that the conversion of slaves was impossible because 'their savage brutishness renders them wholly incapable' of Christianity (Calendar of State Papers: West Indies and America, 1681-5: 25).

One contemporary observer of plantation slavery suggested that the planter opposition to the Christianization of the blacks was a device for maintaining rigid social distinctions among the various status groups in the society (Ligon, 1673: 50). Another astute observer of the Barbados scene during the early 1700s. Père Labat, recorded that 'the clergymen do not instruct the slaves or baptize them' (1970: 126). When non-conformist sects such as the Quakers and Moravians attempted to extend religious teaching to the blacks, the Barbadian Grand Jury of 1665 at once branded these sects as heretics 'who under the pretence of piety, seduce many innocent persons from due obedience to authority and true worship of God', and were thus forbidden to have 'Negroes at their meetings' (Burns, 1954: 285). A Barbados law of 1676, besides preventing Quakers from having at their meetings 'negroes as hearers of their doctrine and taught in their principles, whereby the safety of the island may be hazarded', also prohibited them from undertaking educational activities (Southey, 1827, II: 112). Thus the unchristianized and uneducated blacks were not only effectively kept out of whatever morality there was, their womenfolk were also subject to sexual abuse with impunity.

In any consideration of sexual and marital relations under the plantation system, two factors should be borne in mind. The breeding of children was a separate consideration from that of contracting a formal legal marriage. Sugar production under the plantation system was an enterprise which depended upon both large numbers of slaves and maximum use of their physical capacity. Thus slave mortality was exceedingly high throughout the sugar plantations of Barbados, and this was exacerbated by an almost total absence of normal family life from which deficiencies in the labour force could be replenished. Marital life was a luxury incompatible with the regiment efficiency of the plantation system. The raising of slave children was considered too expensive and uncertain. The planters had to weigh the possible advantages of natural increase against the certain loss of time and labour during pregnancy and nursing. Even such an apparently humanitarian planter corporation as the London-based Society for the Propagation of the Gospel in Foreign Parts failed to maintain any significant natural increase in the slave population at its Codrington plantations. Wastage through overwork, underfeeding, and harsh treatment was so bad that in over 120 years of slave management the society could only show a net increase by natural accretion of thirty-four slaves (Bennett, 1958: 112). By 1660 the Barbados planters had devised a comprehensive system for the complete 'chatelization' of the slave. They had built a code of laws and regulations for the control of every aspect of the slave's life.

The outcome of the prohibition of family life among the blacks was the development of common-law unions and other informal patterns of mating. Informal mating was not confined to the blacks and lower ranks. The system of concubinage pervaded the whole society resulting in a socially approved habit of breeding children out of wedlock. Concubinage among all ranks of society was sufficiently rampant to have attracted the attention of virtually every observer of Barbadian sexual behaviour and attitudes to breeding children outside formal matrimony. Historian John Poyer reports that Governor Ricketts kept a coloured mistress who 'enjoyed all the privileges of a wife', and comments on the generality of this practice throughout seventeenth century Barbados (1808:639-40). Similar observations were also made by Dickson (1789:92-3), Southey (1827:198), Thome and Kimball (1838:76), Schomburgk (1848:88-90), Sewell (1862:68-70), and Caldecott (1898::37-38).

By the middle of the eighteenth century the social significance of what William Dickson (1789:54) termed the 'sacred majesty of a white skin' further encouraged the general practice of 'illicit unions' between black females and white males. Sewell (1862:70) reports that illicit sexual intercourse between white men and coloured women was widely condoned, but white Barbadians regarded with horror 'the mere mention of a matrimonial alliance with a Creole of African descent'.

TABLE 1 *Ethnic Related Population Growth 1748-1805*

Year	Whites	Coloureds	Negroes
1748	15,252	107 'free negroes'	47,025
1757	16,772	—	63,645
1773	18,532	—	68,548
1786	16,167	833	62,115
1787	16,127	2,229	64,405
1805	15,000	2,130	60,000

SOURCES: Southey, 1827 II, III; Schomburgk, 1848; Sewell, 1862; Davy, 1854.

Yet as early a the 1780s Dickson had observed during his thirteen years of residence in Barbados that 'many are not ashamed to live in such habits of intimacy with the female domestic slave .... ' (1789:92-3). Concubinage became institutionalized to the extent that members of all ranks openly participated in the practice. Barbadian sexual behaviour and social attitudes presented an apparently irreconcilable paradox: social intercourse between white and non-white was strictly taboo, sexual intercourse and concubinage between white males and non-white females were exempt from these strictures. The progeny from concubinage and other forms of unregulated sexual matings had become sufficiently numerous by the last quarter of the eighteenth century to be enumerated separately in the censuses of Barbados. The coloured Creoles were first computed as a social category in 1786 (see Table 1).

Towards the close of the eighteenth century the number of coloured Creoles had increased considerably, thus indicating that inter-colour sexual liaisons were widely practiced and condoned by the society. In less than thirty years the 'mixed-blood' population increased from 2,130 in 1805 to 5,146 by 1829, a growth rate of 5 per cent per annum. Barely twenty years later, in 1851, there were already 30,059 coloured Creoles, an incredible increase of 30 per cent per annum. It can be safely concluded from such phenomenal increase in the small coloured population that widespread miscegenation among white, black, and coloured was taking place concurrently with the existence of a social norm discouraging marriage between white and non-white. The logical outcome of the prevalence of extramarital sexuality and liaisons across the colour line was the rapid rise in the numbers of children born outside marriage up to the present day.

TABLE II *Ratio of legitimate to illegitimate births in Barbados 1892-1901*

Year	Legitimate	Illegitimate	Population	Percentage illegitimate
1892	3,167	3,910	183,000	2.13
1893	3,505	4,266	184,000	2.31
1894	3,213	4,095	185,000	2,21
1895	3,526	4,021	187,000	2.15
1896	3,125	3,861	188,500	2.04
1897	3,300	3,897	190,000	2.05
1898	3,226	3,933	191,500	2.05
1899	3,240	3,798	193,000	1.45
1900	3,389	3,948	194,500	2.03
1901	3,252	3,969	196,000	2.02

SOURCE: Colonial Reports, Barbados, No. 368, 1901-2, p.43.

Contemporary observers of Barbadian social life and sexual behaviour in the period following emancipation were often struck by the simultaneous operation of two contradictory moral principles shared by the whole society. Thome and Kimball (1838: 76) noted that 'coloured ladies have been taught to believe that it was more honourable, and quite as virtuous to be the kept mistress of *white gentlemen*, than the lawfully wedded wives of *coloured men*'. Similarly, Sewell (1862: 68) reports finding intercolour sexual unions being 'very general, and illicit intercourse ... sanctioned, or at least winked at, by a society which utterly condemns and abhors a marriage between two people of different colour'.

In a strict sense, marriage, even in the post-emancipation era, was still a privilege enjoyed almost exclusively by persons in favourable circumstances. However, marriage did not debar males of the upper level strata from indulging in concubinage with non-white women of the lower stratum. Caldecott (1898: 39) says family life in Barbados was retained only among the upper rank, 'and even with them it was too frequently marred ... by the presence within the house itself of coloured 'mistresses' and their offsprings and further notes that 'open concubinage and secret licentiousness were rampant'. The consequence of the mode of sexual behaviour which had prevailed from the mid-seventeenth century and continued to the twentieth century was the inevitably large number of extramarital children. Such children have always predominated over offspring from legal matrimony. Table III gives a clear indication of the consistency of this reproductive pattern in Barbadian society. Schomburgk's conclusion that 'in Barbados the illegitimate children exceed those born in wedlock' finds ample confirmation in these statistics (1848: 90).

TABLE III   *Ratio of legitimate to illegitimate births in the three parishes of St Michael, St John, and St Joseph, Barbados, 1835-45*

Year	Legitimatel	llegitimate
1835	418	1,109
1836	397	1,296
1837	379	1,266
1838	521	1,518
1839	509	1,497
1840	518	694*
1841	522	944
1842	704	991
1843	699	1,051
1844	707	1,078
1845	799	1,045

SOURCE: Compiled and summarized from Sir Richard Schomburgk's History of Barbados (1848:90).

NOTE: The table is not a true reflection of total births even in these parishes but only reflects children presented for baptism and registered.

*Figures for St John not available.

The societal attitude to the status of children from such unions is reflected in the manner in which official records were kept up to 1891. Population registers were first instituted for Barbados in 1661, but only recorded 'christenings, marriages, and burials'; births being completely ignored (Schomburgk, 1848: 93). Governor Hay complained to the colonial secretary in 1894 that 'the system of recording of vital statistics in the Colony is not at all satisfactory; there is no proper record of births or deaths, but only baptisms and burials ...'.

The sexual behaviour which had been the object of comment by observers appear to have taken a change for the better following emancipation. Sturge and Harvey who were observers in Barbados during the transition from slavery to freedom noted a change towards a new morality among the blacks and coloured Creoles: 'concubinage is now considered discreditable, and marriages are now fast increasing among the coloured and black population' (1838: 142). This new morality, rather than being welcomed by the white sector as a development towards social respectability, was roundly deplored. The whites complained of 'the change which had taken place in the sentiments of the coloured people, and of the presumption of the coloured females in aspiring to marriage' (Sturge and Harvey, 1838: 148). Similarly, Caldecott (1898: 37) claims that the majority of white men 'consorted with the Negro women without restraint, either from their own corrupted consciences or from public opinion'. And he estimates that 'nine-tenths of the coloured women were "housekeepers" to white men', but when such women were converted to Christianity, 'their consequent renunciation of base connections gave the greatest offence to the white community'. The evident improvement in marital condition among the black population of Barbados after emancipation impressed Schomburgk who reported that the blacks now held 'the decencies of civilized life ... in general respect ... than they were fifteen or twenty years ago; ... marriages have been more numerous' (1848: 88-9).

CONTEMPORARY MARITAL PATTERNS

The pattern of marital relations established during the plantation slavery period were further perpetuated by the peculiar ecological and demographic features of Barbados. When emancipation took place in the 1830s, no free land was available for the freedmen for residence and peasant farming. They remained trapped as tenant/workers in the same plantation system. The scarcity of land was further exacerbated by a high population density which led to a high rate of male emigration from the early 1860s to the present day (Roberts, 1955:275; Cumper, 1962:324).

TABLE IV   *Density of population in 11 parishes, 1969*

Parishes	Zone	Population	Density
1 St Lucy	Northern	9,776	698
2 St Peter	Northern	11,782	906
3 St Andrew	Northern	8,523	608
4 St James	Northern	14,790	1,232
5 St Thomas	Northern	10,779	829
6 St Joseph	Northern	9,275	927
7 St Michael	City	88,742	
	Bridgetown	12,283	5,916
8 St John	Southern	11,782	906
9 St George	Southern	18,306	1,076
10 Christ Church	Southern	36,098	1,640
11 St Philip	Southern	18,550	806
Total:		**250,686**	**Density**
			ratio:1,500

SOURCE: Barbados Family Planning Association, 1969

Large-scale emigration among the labouring sector produced a two-fold effect on the population of Barbados. Emigration for a while controlled the rapid rate of population growth and stabilized the density ratio of persons to land space. The density ratio actually decreased from 1,040 in 1911 to 940 by 1921 (Roberts, 1955: 277). However, despite continued high emigration, after the Second World War, the density ratio had increased to 1,500 persons per square mile due to a corresponding high birth rate. Prior to 1960, Barbados had a birth rate of over 33 per 1000, though still below the regional levels of between 40 and 50 in some territories (Roberts, 1962: 339). Enlightened family planning programs have reduced the birth rate to about 20:1000.

Ironically, increased emigration had another but negative demographic effect on population stability in Barbados. It created an exceedingly high sex imbalance in favour of women since emigrants were mostly males. The scarcity value of men gives them greater advantage for making sexual demands from a surplus female population resulting in a high frequency of serial matings, extramarital births, and multiple fatherhood of children from individual women. The prevalence of premarital and extramarital unions and the corresponding preponderance of premarital and extramarital births appear to be closely linked to excessive male emigration. Two-thirds of all live births in the last 150 years fall into the extramarital category. In an analysis of the 1844 Barbados census, Schomburgk (1848: 88) found a predominance of 10,190 females over males in a population of 122,198 giving a sex ratio of 100: 118.19. The present sex ratio is 100: 182. Roberts (1955: 275) estimates that 70 to 80 per cent of the 103,500 Barbadian emigrants between 1861 and 1921 were males. The 1960 census shows a preponderance of 23,000 females, 10,900 being in the 15 to 45 age group. The Barbados Family Planning Association estimates that in 1969 females exceeded males by 23,878, with 60,000 females were in the 16 to 45 age group.

Data from my field survey as well as those compiled from official registers indicate that the highest rate of extramarital births occur within the 15 to 35 age group. Census data also show that a considerable number of persons over 15 years of age have never married. Women predominate in this category (see Table VI). The number of legal marriages show a decline from 1104 in 1960 to 960 in 1968 while the ratio of extramarital to marital births continues to widen (see Table V).

THE FIELD STUDY

The data on which the ensuing analysis is based were collected in the course of field-work in Barbados extending over a thirteen-month period from 1969 to 1970. Field observations were supplemented by a study of archival material pertaining to social relations in Barbados over the last three centuries. A novel feature of the study is the inclusion of paternity as a variable in the analysis of the prevalence and frequency of extramarital births, and a consideration of demographic, ecological, and attitudinal factors as explanatory variables for understanding of the persistence of historical mating forms under contemporary conditions.

Enquiries and observations relating to motherhood patterns were initially conducted in two northern rural parishes of St Peter and St Lucy. Preliminary interviews were conducted at the Northern District Headquarters clinic in Speightstown. The researcher was introduced as a temporary member of the clinic staff, and provided with a desk strategically placed at the final exit point where the female patients were interviewed after completing their clinical rounds. The women attending the clinic came from the parishes of St Peter, Upper St James, St Thomas, St Andrews, and St Lucy. The age range was from 15 to 45, the largest category being in the 16 to 25 age group.

TABLE V *Number of live births, age group of mother, distributing and percentage of legitimate to illegitimate births*

	1965	and		1968
Live births	6,358			5,474
Percentage legitimate	33			32
Percentage illegitimate	67			68
Age-group	Legitimate	Illegitimate	Legitimate	Illegitimate
0–15	—	25	1	22
15–17	20	585	16	486
18–19	55	680	43	661
20–21	130	600	122	654
22–24	295	660	265	641
25–29	600	703	494	572
30–34	530	450	376	363
35–39	420	300	290	219
40–44	185	90	125	96
45–49	20	10	15	6
Not stated	—	—	4	3
Total	**2,255**	**4,103**	**1,751**	**3,723**

NOTE: *1965 figures compiled from information provided by the Barbados Family Planning Association. 1968 data extracted from Register of Births, Barbados Registry.*

TABLE VI   *Number of males and females of all ages, and number of males and females over 15 years by marital status*

A. *Population by sex and age category*

Females: all ages	126,808	Over 15 years	82,213
Males: all ages	105,519	Over 15 years	61,232
Excess females: all ages	21,289	Over 15 years	20,981

B. *Marital status*

	Male	Female
Over 15 years, never married	32,819	44,998
Over 15 years, widowed	1,694	7,443
Over 15 years, divorced	127	194
Over 15 years, separated	400	593

NOTE: Part A compiled from Part D Table 4, and Part B from Part D Table 13, Barbados Census, 1960.

Data recorded on the first day involved a total of twenty-eight cases among which only three were legal marriages. Information sought from respondents included: number of children and live births, number of genitors responsible for such births, age at first pregnancy. Similar information was elicited for female members of each respondent's natal family. Of the twenty-eight cases, eight girls under twenty years of age had given birth to sixteen children among them for a total of nine genitors. A further nine women under twenty-four years had mothered twenty children from thirteen genitors. In the 25 to 29 age group, five women had twenty-three children from eleven genitors, and in the age group 30 to 41, six women had forty-nine children from eight genitors. None of the women interviewed showed any signs of shame or resentment at being questioned about intimate details of their sex life and marital condition.

Girls experience first pregnancy in their teens, as early as fifteen years of age. By the age of twenty years they may have produced up to four children from various genitors. Multiple fatherhood is not uncommon particularly in the early stages of a girl's sex life. From the mid-twenties they tend to settle down with one man either in a common-law union or on a visiting relationship of a stable kind. The pattern of courtship in Barbados is partly responsible for the type of sex life young girls lead, and the resultant high rate of premarital parenthood. Courtship is not normally regarded as a prelude to marriage. It is a relationship carried on in secrecy protected from public scrutiny and prying eyes of neighbours and parents. Elaborate evasive tactics are adopted by both sexes to avoid identification or association. A man with a car has considerable advantage of evading public scrutiny of his courting habits; he avoids exposure not only by escaping the neighbourhood but also using the car as shelter.

One of the reasons for this secretive pattern of courtship is the serious lack of privacy in the frequently small houses of most Barbadian families. There is an almost neurotic public interest in other people's affairs and activities are keenly followed by pairs of interested eyes from behind louvered shutters. Men do not like being closely identified with a particular woman in public unless they have made a definite decision for a stable partnership. Women respondents were fairly open about their reasons for secret courtship. By keeping the affair private, the woman protects herself against ridicule by others when the man abandons her (as men often do). In this way the woman avoids the possibility of being asked embarrassing questions when the man no longer calls for her. Barbados is a parochial society in which everyone's business is everybody's concern and news of local events travels exceedingly fast and wide. The scarcity value of eligible men in the population tends to put the woman at a disadvantage. She either has to acquiesce to the man's whims or lose his attention. Sex activity is, of course, the centre of this submissiveness, and soon the young woman becomes pregnant and the affair is frequently ended. After childbirth she drifts to another man and the process is repeated, resulting in a number of premarital children and multiple fatherhood. Table VII gives an indication of the extent of this problem.

The prevalence of premarital and extramarital sex relations in the general population is an open secret among Barbadians of all status levels. A kind of simulated disapproval of sex mating among the young coexists with an almost fatalistic attitude to the inevitability of early pregnancy. Sex education is still a very delicate subject in Barbados. It is treated as a 'dirty' subject to talk about, and this sanctimonious attitude feeds and perpetuates ignorance about sex matters among old and young alike. There is a generally held belief among women, particularly in the lower status ranks, that it is a natural development for a woman to produce babies and as many as nature has assigned to her. Concerned school teachers have reported being embarrassed by the reaction of mothers of schoolgirls who had fallen pregnant. Some parents reacted with, 'ain't she woman? She got get baby sometime. What's wrong with she?'

TABLE VII   *Births to single women in 50 sample households by age groups, number of children and number of genitors*

Age-Group	No. of mothers	No. of children	No. of genitors
15–19	20	32	20
20–22	38	84	44
23–25	26	74	40
26–28	8	30	20
29–39	14	68	28
Totals	**106**	**288**	**152**

(P = 250, N = 50 by households).

This accommodating attitude to premarital births is further exacerbated by a profound indifference about the use of contraceptive devices. The subject of contraception, like sex itself, is shrouded in mythical beliefs about resultant 'ill health' due to 'suppressing the birth of babies nature has given' to a particular woman. Such folklore further finds support from occasional reports about medical opinion concerning possible risks of using certain contraceptive products. Information obtained from both surveys and interviews of men and women suggest these beliefs are held equally by both sexes. Men object to their women using contraception because it interferes with their sex enjoyment and may also cause 'ill-health'. Symptoms are of a generalized urological sort such as a 'weak bladder' or impotence. The reluctance of parents to face up to the recognition of the problem of premarital and unwanted pregnancies largely accounts for the perpetuation and resigned acceptance of the excessively high birth rate, especially among the young.

A sample survey involving sixty women taken with the assistance of the Family Planning Field Unit revealed that fifty-one of the sixty women had experienced their first pregnancy between the ages of thirteen and twenty, and that only fifteen of the sixty women were legally married. They ranged in age from sixteen to forty-seven. In another sample survey consisting of fifty households in the parishes of St Peter and St Lucy, none of the seventy-eight female occupants with children born out of wedlock stated that a promise of marriage was the reason for their staying faithful to the men who had made them pregnant. The general response to interviews about their marital plans was, 'well if he wants to marry me it's alright, but he never says anything about marriage'. Women thus take risks of becoming pregnant by men who show no indication of marrying them. Hence common-law unions are placidly accepted by girls as young as twenty years of age.

Apart from the historical factors pertaining to marital relations in Barbados, it is reasonable to hypothesize that the contemporary prevalence of common-law unions and the women's passive acceptance of pregnancy risks without marital prospects are closely related to the demographic imbalance between the sexes in favour of females. The scarcity value of men generates a tolerant attitude on the part of women. Since formal marriage in many instances generally takes place after the couples had experimented with a number of informal unions, it could thus be taken as an index of social status rather than the creation of a new personal bond. Hence the wedding ceremony is elevated to the highest pinnacle in the pyramid of social activities in Barbados. It is a *rite de passage* celebrated with the greatest pomp and ceremony as a public declaration of status achievement. Analysis of registered marriages taken from the Barbados Registry shows that 33 per cent of total annual marriages were among couples between the age group of 30 to 45 years. Early sexual experience and late marriage lead to the common situation whereby couples may already have grown-up children by the time *de facto* union is made *de jure*.

Public announcements of impending marriages make no effort to conceal the fact that the individuals concerned are of 'illegitimate' birth or are living in common-law union. Death and funeral notices broadcast over the radio openly state the relationship of the deceased and the bereaved. The euphemism for a common-law partner is 'the friend of Miss or Mr so and so'. In the case of engagements and marriages the caption accompanying the photograph would typically read: 'the bride is the daughter of Miss A. B. of St Michael, and the groom is the son of Miss (or Mrs) C. D. and Mr E. F. of St Peter'. From interview responses, and public announcements of personal events, there is a strong indication that no social disgrace is attached to premarital and extramarital parentage, or to extramarital cohabitation.

Implicit in the concept of 'illegitimacy' is the notion of unwanted child, a sort of accidental birth attended with moral opprobrium. There is no evidence that premarital and extramarital parenthood and parentage are viewed in this manner in Barbadian society. Historical and contemporary evidence show that at no time in the development of marital relations have 'legitimate' births and legal marriages exceeded their counterparts. To all intents and purposes, many common-law relationships are an end in themselves, and hence children born out of these relationships are socially viewed as normal progeny. A common-law union is viewed as a reciprocal domestic relationship aptly implied in the common Barbadian expression 'who lookin' after you?' Looking after someone is in the nature of man-woman relations devoid of legal fetters. Some cohabiting couples justify their informal union by saying 'we both know where we stand, getting married might spoil our relationship'. This rationale contains more than a grain of truth. Divorce statistics in Barbados show that the highest number of divorces occur between the female age-group 15 to 24 years and male age-group 20 to 29 years. The age-group 15 to 29 years accounted for approximately 63 per cent of total divorces for 1968 (see Table VIII). As remarriage is uncommon, these divorced couples inevitably settle for some form of informal extramarital relationship.

TABLE VIII   *Divorces by age of husband and age of wife, 1968*

Husband's age	Total	Wife's age								
		15–19	20–4	25–9	30–4	35–9	40–4	45–9	50+	NS
15–19	2	2	–	–	–	–	–	–	–	–
20–24	37	13	20	3	–	1	–	–	–	–
25–29	26	5	17	4	–	–	–	–	–	–
30–34	7	–	4	1	–	–	1	–	–	–
35–39	5	–	1	3	1	–	–	–	–	–
40–44	3	–	–	2	–	1	–	–	–	–
45–49	4	–	–	3	–	–	–	–	–	–
50–54	1	–	–	–	1	–	–	1	–	–
55–59	–	–	–	–	–	–	–	–	–	–
60–64	–	–	–	–	–	–	–	–	–	–
65–69	1	–	–	1	–	–	–	–	–	–
70+	–	–	–	–	–	–	–	–	–	–
NS	3	–	–	–	–	–	–	–	–	3
Totals	89	20	42	17	3	2	1	1	–	3

SOURCE: *Barbados Registrar-General's Office.*

CONCLUSION

This paper has attempted to draw attention to the inadequacy of viewing premarital and extramarital relations, parenthood and parentage, in terms of a polarity between legitimacy and illegitimacy. Once societal attitudes, as expressed in the public and personal behaviour of individuals, are taken into account, the polarity ceases to be sociologically meaningful. At best the polarity view reflects externally imposed value judgements, at worst it distorts the perception of social realities as manifested in the attitudinal and expressive behaviour of the actors themselves.

Historical evidence adduced in this paper strongly supports the view that contemporary practices in sexual and marital relations take place within a framework of socially sanctioned behaviour that takes little account of the moral assumptions implicit in the legitimate-illegitimate polarity. Field data indicate that plural sexual relations for men, and multiple extramarital parenthood for women, are socially tolerated as expected behaviour. These social expectations are further underpinned by a positive attitude that regards masculinity and female fecundity as normal sexual behaviour.

REFERENCES

Bennett, J. H. 1958 *Bondsmen and Bishops: Slavery and Apprenticeship on the Codrington Plantations of Barbados* 1710-1838. Berkeley: University of California Press, 1958.

Braithwaite, Lloyd 1953 'Social stratification in Trinidad', *Social and Economic Studies 2* (2, 3):5-175.

Burns, Alan Sir 1954 *History of the British West Indies*. London: George Allen and Unwin.

Caldecott, Alfred 1898 *The Church in the West Indies*, London: Frank Cass.

Clarke, Edith 1957 *My Mother Who Fathered Me: A Study of the Family in Three Selected Communities in Jamaica. London: George Allen and Unwin*.

Cumper, George E. 1962 (*'The differentiation of economic groups in the West Indies'*), *Social and Economic Studies II* (4):319-32.

Davy, John 1854 *The West Indies before and since Slave Emancipation*. London: Frank Cass.

Dickson, William 1789 *Letters on Slavery*. London.

Greenfield, Sydney M. 1966 *English Rustics in Black Skins*. New Haven: College and University Press.

Hall, Douglas 1962 'Slaves and slavery in the British West Indies', *Social and Economic Studies II* (4):305-18.

Hay, J. S. 1894 Report to Marquis of Ripon. Colonial Reports, *Barbados Blue Book*, No. 140, 1894:10.

Henriques, Fernando 1953 *Family and Colour in Jamaica*. London: Eyre and Spottiswoode

Herskovits: Melville and Frances 1947 *Trinidad Village*. New York: Octogon Books

Labat, Jean-Baptiste 1970 *Memoirs of Père Labat, 1693-1703*. London: Frank Cass (translated by J. Eaden).

Ligon, Richard 1673 *A True and Exact History of the Island of Barbadoes*. London: Frank Cass, 2nd Edition.

Patterson, H. Orlando 1967 *The Sociology of Slavery*. London: MacGibbon and Kee.

Poyer, John 1808 *History of Barbadoes from the first discovery of the Island in the year 1605 till the accession of Lord Seaforth 1801*. London: Frank Cass.

Roberts, George W. 1955 'Emigration from Barbados', *Social and Economic Studies* 4(3):245-88.

1962 'Prospects for population growth in the West Indies', *Social and Economic Studies* II(4):333-50.

Sewell, William G. 1862 *The Ordeal of Free Labour in the British West Indies*. London: Frank Cass.

Schomburgk, Robert Sir 1848 *The History of Barbados*. London: Frank Cass.

Smith, Raymond T. 1956 *The Negro Family in British Guiana*. London: Routledge and Kegan Paul.

—1971'Cultural and social structure in the Caribbean: some recent work on family and kinship'. pp. 448-75 in Michael M. Horowitz, ed., *Peoples and Cultures of the Caribbean*. New York: The Natural History Press.

Southey, Thomas 1827 *Chronological History of the West Indies, 3 Vols.*, London: Frank Cass.

Sturge. Joseph, and Thomas Harvey 1838 *The West Indies in 1837*. London: Frank Cass.

Thome, J. A., and J. H. Kimball 1838 *Emancipation in the West Indies*. New York.

State Papers

—1680 Barbados delegation to the Council of Trade and Plantations. *Calendar of State Papers, Colonial Series: West Indies and America 1677-80*. 8 October 1680, London: Public Records Office, p. 611.

—1681 Barbados delegation to the Council of Trade and Plantations. *Calendar of State Papers, Colonial Series: West Indies and America 1681-5*. 30 March 1681, London: Public Records Office, p. 25.

M. Lazarus-Black

WHY WOMEN TAKE MEN TO MAGISTRATE'S COURT: CARIBBEAN KINSHIP IDEOLOGY AND LAW

Every Thursday afternoon a list of 'Order in Bastardy, Maintenance, and Arrears' is posted on the wall of the St John's magistrate's court in Antigua, West Indies.[1] In a typical week, six to eight new cases are scheduled for hearing, while twenty or 30 others are brought by the collecting officer of the state against men who have neglected to pay child support. There were 1,492 cases of maintenance and arrears in 1984; 1,287 cases in 1985. Given a population of approximately 80,000 in Antigua and Barbuda, such case loads indicate that the court is frequently utilized.

Academic, legal, and popular wisdom holds that these West Indian women are going to magistrate's court for money because the babies' fathers fail to support them or to pay regularly enough (e.g., Massiah 1982; Jackson 1982; Durant Gonzalez 1982; Barrow 1986: 162; Brodber 1986: 46). They go to court because they are unemployed or underemployed with too many illegitimate children to raise and too few dollars with which to do so. But when I asked one such woman if she went to court for money, her answer surprised me. She looked at me indignantly and said, 'I carry my case up there for justice. I complain him for justice.'

This article explores ideas about justice which are integral to kinship relations in Antigua and Barbuda and which also explain why women take their children's fathers to court.[2] In contrast to the voluminous body of earlier research on West Indian families,[3] I argue that studies of kinship must encompass simultaneously the legal forms and forces of the state and the common sense understanding of kin which evolves in local communities. 'Carrying a case' to the magistrate's court exemplifies the interaction between state forms and community norms and demonstrates that certain rules and judicial processes of the Antiguan state are now constituent of local family ideology and practice. That is, Antiguan women regularly take cases to court to demand justice in their kinship relations, to assert their autonomy and rights, and to resist the pervasive hierarchical structures of gender and class.

This research also contributes to our understanding of how the legal codes and judicial institutions of a colonizing state shape, and in turn are shaped by, indigenous beliefs and practices (e.g., Cohn 1989; Comaroff 1989; Comaroff and Roberts 1981; Cooper and

Stoler 1989; Goveia 1970; Lewin 1981, 1987; Martinez-Alier 1974; Moore 1978, 1986, 1989; Nader 1989; Smith 1982, 1984, 1987; Starr and Collier 1989; Stolcke 1984; Stoler 1989; Vincent 1989; Westermark 1986). As Stoler (1989: 637) points out, 'Who bedded and wedded with whom in the colonies of France, England, Holland and Iberia was never left to change.'[4] Yet few scholars tackle the development of law and the present functioning of judicial institutions in the Caribbean. Historians concentrate on the slave codes in their discussions of 'law' (e.g., Goveia 1965, 1970; Knight 1970; Dunn 1972), legal scholars compile indexes and summations of contemporary legislation, and a few discuss women's legal status (e.g., Patchett and Jenkins 1973; Shahabuddeen 1973; Cumper and Daly 1979; Moses 1976; Forde 1981; Durant Gonzalez 1982; Jackson 1982; Boxill 1985). But as Massiah (1986: 9) points out, studies of Caribbean families continue to focus attention on women as mothers, domestics, or workers, and 'there is little attempt to see how the institutions of law, education, politics, religion, interact with each other to affect and be affected by the institution of the family'. A few exceptions to this generalization include some analyses of land tenure and inheritance practices (Smith 1955; Smith 1965; Clarke 1966), studies of marriage and family organization among Guyanese plantation workers (Jayawardena 1960, 1963; Smith and Jayawardena 1959), research by Durant Gonzalez (1982) and Jackson (1982) on Jamaica's family court, and Martinez-Alier's (1974) account of marriage, race, and class in nineteenth-century Cuba. In the main, however, Caribbean scholars neglect the legal codes and processes that influenced the development of kinship systems in this region and miss the ways in which West Indian people acknowledge and use law and legal processes today to define family and to achieve the rights and duties that belong to kin.

It is easy to appreciate why law has been overlooked in studies of West Indian kinship. The extraordinary illegitimacy rate of approximately 70 per cent (Powell 1986: 83) suggests that at least in the form of legalized unions, law is of little importance in family life. Yet law has dynamic presence in Antiguan communities. Antiguan women find in law means both to assert extra-legal familial norms and to resist the structures of domination which characterize their everyday lives. They use lawmakers' law, reinventing its meaning and purpose.

My analysis is in five parts. I first trace Antigua's social and legal history to statutes governing marriage, bastardy, and support for illegitimate children. Next, I describe the research setting because people's ideas about social class influence who takes whom to court. An account of the local courts, contemporary kinship law, and the sociological characteristics of the litigants follows. I then explain why Antiguan women take the fathers of their children to magistrate's court, and in conclusion, I suggest the implications of these findings for understanding the origin and development of family ideology and structure in the Caribbean and for studies of kinship generally.

THE LEGACY OF COLONIALISM

Scholars continue to miss the fact that British and European colonists brought to the West Indies cultural traditions in which families were legally constituted and then duly went about relegislating kinship. In the case of Antigua, as early as 1672 and at regular intervals over the next three centuries, legal codes were absolutely critical to creating and maintaining different social ranks in the colony and to regulating families, gender, and race (Lazarus-Black 1990). Local legislators wrestled with questions about who might marry whom, which persons constituted 'family', and what rights and duties such connections bestowed. The kinship order these lawmakers instituted for Antiguans departed dramatically from the rules that guided kinship in Great Britain. The legacy of colonialism included both detailed kinship laws and an elaborate hierarchy of courts.

Antigua was first colonized in 1632, mainly by English and Irish adventurers, soldiers, farmers, and labourers. Relying upon British common law which instructs 'colonists carry with them only so much of English law as is applicable to their own situation' (Blackstone in Morrison 1979: 46), the settlers established an Assembly and a judicial system. England supplied a governor and intermittent instructions, advice, and assistance. Although the Secretary of State for the Colonies could withhold royal assent of a colonial law, he had no power to make new local statutes (Hall 1971: 148).

Antigua's early lawmakers and judges consisted of a very small group of men of property, most of them planters. The switch from tobacco and cotton to sugar began in the 1650s. At that time, the colony was comprised of small farmers and a good number of European indentured servants. A century later, 93.5 per cent of the population were slaves and most worked on large sugar plantations (Gaspar 1985: 83).

The kinship laws Antiguan planters wrote were directed at controlling marriage and human reproduction, and also at reproducing the hierarchical social and economic structures of capitalism. Codes made it illegal for slaves to marry free persons, prevented indentured servants from marrying without their masters' permission, granted the right to perform marriage ceremonies only to Anglican ministers, and made white men responsible for their white bastard children (Lazarus-Black 1990: 67-86). The *Leeward Islands Amelioration Act*, passed in Antigua in 1798, also set up a separate system of marriage for slaves. According to this act, a slave marriage was monogamous but not contractual, since the nuptials bestowed none of the rights and duties implied in marriages of free persons. Nor did a slave marriage convey upon children the status or title of the husband/father. The law did include provision for a public declaration of a couple's intention to live together and monetary awards from their masters. We know that at least some slaves married under this law (Flannagan 1967: II, 97).

The colonists also established a hierarchy of courts. By the end of the eighteenth century, there was a Court of Chancery, a Court of Error and Appeal, a Court of King's Bench and Grand Sessions, a Court of Common Pleas, a Court Ordinary, a Court Merchant, and a Court of Admiralty. In addition, complaints between indentured servants and masters, and masters and slaves, were heard by itinerant justices of the peace. After 1784, a Court of King's Bench and Grand Sessions governed the trial of criminal slaves (Goveia 1965: 60-64).

Slavery was abolished in Antigua in 1834. In reality, abolition brought few dramatic changes to the lives of the ex-slaves. Limited availability of free land and the infamous Contract Act, which set new terms between workers and planters, combined to make it difficult to leave the estates. The Contract Act not only made it arduous to find a new employer, it also directed who might legally reside with whom in the estate huts, and commanded labour from each member of a man's family. Other social welfare legislation of this period made the destitute, the infirm, and the elderly the economic responsibility of their kin, and not of government (Lazarus-Black 1990: 128-155).

Lawmakers passed in 1875 *An Act for the Better Support of Natural Children, and to afford Facilities for obliging the Putative Father to assist in the Maintenance of such Children.* The statute set procedures for obtaining affiliation orders, bestowed power upon magistrates to establish relationships between illegitimate children and their fathers, and designated stipends for men to provide for their offspring. Any woman who delivered a bastard child could apply for a support order. The request had to be made within a year after the baby's birth unless she could prove that previously the man had cared for the child. At the hearing, parties could bring witnesses and had the right to counsel. Weekly support payments were limited to five shillings for the first six weeks and to two shillings and six pence thereafter until the child attained the age of twelve or until the mother married. Stipends were payable directly to the mother and she had to apply for arrears within thirteen weeks or they were forfeited. The magistrate also had discretionary power to order the father to pay the costs of the case, a payment to the midwife, and funeral expenses if necessary. He could appoint a guardian for a child if the mother died, was of unsound mind, or went to prison. A putative father could appeal his case to the High Court, but the magistrate had power to send him to jail and to sell his property for failure to comply with the bastardy order.

With only slight modifications, the bastardy law still functions today. The act exemplifies both the continuous intervention of the state in matters of kinship and the hegemonic character of legalities in local communities. The bastardy law is regularly invoked by contemporary Antiguan women, although not always for reasons envisioned by nineteenth-century and later lawmakers.

THE ETHNOGRAPHIC SETTING

Antigua's present population is almost entirely African-Caribbean. A few people have British and other European forefathers, others are descendants of Syrian and Lebanese traders who arrived early in the twentieth century, and there are some expatriate Americans and Canadians. English is the standard language, although there is a creole dialect. Most islanders are literate and most consider themselves Christian.

Historic dependence upon sugar exports prevented Antigua from achieving economic self-sufficiency. Agriculture remains in general decline today, despite a variety of efforts to revive it. Manufacturing and industry is developing slowly, but in the last two decades tourism has emerged as the most important economic sector (Henry 1985). Its direct value now accounts for approximately 21 per cent of the gross domestic product and at least 12 per cent of the labour force works in tourism (The World Bank 1985:24). Government employs about 30 per cent of all working persons (The World Bank 1985:4). Unemployment remained at around 20 per cent through the first half of the 1980s (*Statistical Yearbook* 1985).

Antiguan planters controlled local politics until labour unrest heralded a movement for social and economic reform early in this century. Unions were legalized in 1940 and adult suffrage was granted in 1951. Shortly thereafter, election rules were changed to allow greater representation of the working people. In 1969, the islands became an Associated State, gaining control over local affairs but still under British authority with respect to external relations and defense. Independence came in 1981. Antigua and Barbuda is now a parliamentary democracy with a Prime Minister, Senate, and House of Representatives. The government proclaimed a nonaligned foreign policy at independence, but maintains strongest political and economic ties with Britain, Canada, and the U.S.

Antigua's two social classes, middle and lower, can be differentiated into smaller strata based upon members' socioeconomic status and ability to wield formal political power. At the top of the present hierarchy is a small local elite which holds elected political authority. In contrast to the days when sugar dominated, this elite is Antiguan-born, black, and increasingly educated in the Caribbean. Within this same stratum are foreign businessmen and expatriates who play important roles in the economy but who are noticeably absent from the official political process. The lifestyle and domestic organization of the elite, however, are virtually indistinguishable from Antigua's middle class. Such similarities help explain why middle class persons almost always say that Antigua has only two classes. Middle class women rarely use the magistrate's court to order their kinship relations. Moreover, the ideology of class protects middle class men from being named publicly as the fathers of illegitimate children.

Quite the opposite is true of the lower class, which uses the courts regularly. In some respects, the lower class is also more heterogeneous than the middle class. Its upper stratum consists of a *petite* bourgeoisie, 'who own small amounts of productive resources and have control over their working conditions in ways that proletarians do not' (Rapp 1982: 180). *Petite* bourgeoisie men are often jacks-of-all-trades. They may own some land, raise a few cattle or goats, and work a job or two for weekly cash. Petite bourgeoisie women run their own small shops or work from their homes as seamstresses or hairdressers. In contrast, members of the working class have little or no property and only their own labour to sell. They include agricultural workers, fishermen, sales persons, domestics, hotel workers, and labourers. They are low income, hard working people for whom multiple jobs and job-sharing is common.

In contrast to Antigua, class is not relevant in Barbuda. Antigua's sister island was leased to the Codrington family in 1685 and 1705 (Hall 1971: 59). The Codringtons used Barbuda as a supply depot and manufacturing centre for their estates in Antigua. Until 1898 when the Antiguan legislature assumed financial responsibility for its government, Barbuda was virtually without political representation, welfare or educational services, or legal institutions (Hall 1971: 91-95). The island has remained sparsely populated. Codrington, the only village, is home to approximately 1,200 people — almost all descendants of Codrington's slaves. Today many Barbudan men fish for their living. Others raise cattle. Both men and women work subsistence gardens and continue to insist upon communal ownership of land outside the village despite opposition from the government in Antigua (Berleant-Schiller 1977). Barbuda has a few shops, a couple of hotels where people find seasonal work, an elementary school, a health clinic, several churches, and a few government buildings. During my field work, a room in the police station served as a temporary courtroom upon the arrival of the magistrate.

THE COURTS, THE CODES, AND THE LITIGANTS

The organization of the courts and the codes themselves partially determine who comes to the magistrate's court, the types of complaints that are filed, and how any particular case will fare.

A four-tiered court system presently serves the islands. The first tier consists of the magistrate's courts. Affiliation and maintenance cases, arrears, disputes between persons over small property claims, personal grievances, traffic matters, and minor assaults are brought to these courts. The magistrate's court serving St John's, the capital, occupies the second and third floors of a new concrete building. There are two courtrooms on the second floor, one of which was regularly used by the magistrates in 1985-1987 for kinship cases. The courts are clean, well-lighted rooms cooled by overhead ceiling fans. They are starkly furnished with a few wooden pews, tables and chairs for attorneys, two witness stands — where the litigants do, in fact, stand to tell their stories — and the magistrate's desk. On any given day, prosecution of scheduled cases may continue for several hours or for only twenty minutes.

In addition to the St John's magistrate's court, there are three 'country courts' in Antigua which meet weekly in the villages of Bolans, All Saints, and Parham. By law, the magistrate holds court in Barbuda four times a year for two or three days, depending upon the case load. The Barbuda court draws quite a crowd. Interested bystanders make humorous comments about the litigants and their cases, sometimes to the chagrin of the magistrate.

A case heard in a magistrate's court may be appealed to the second tier in the system, the High Court. The High Court also settles major property and criminal cases, and family matters such as divorce, adoption, and contested wills. The third tier, the Appellate Division of the Supreme Court of the Eastern Caribbean, meets intermittently in the different Leeward Islands. Finally, since Antigua and Barbuda is a member of the Commonwealth, cases decided by the Supreme Court may be appealed, as a last resort, to the Privy Council in England.

Kinship statutes instruct who shall use which of these courts to resolve family disputes. When I conducted field work, statutes distinguished persons on the basis of their marital status (single or married) and their birth status (legitimate or illegitimate). Married persons have the option of applying either to the High Court or the magistrate's court for legal remedy with respect to certain kinship disputes. For example, a married woman may apply to the magistrate for relief if a spouse has committed adultery, aggravated assault upon the applicant, desertion, is guilty of persistent cruelty, or is a habitual drunkard. The magistrate has authority to order that the complainant no longer be bound to cohabit with the defendant, award legal custody of children to the applicant, and direct the defendant to pay weekly support for the plaintiff and any 'children of the family' for whom the man is legally responsible. Only a woman in a legal union can ask for support for herself (*The Revised Laws of Antigua* 1962: 417-421). All conflicts between unmarried couples over child care and maintenance, however, must be adjudicated in the magistrate's court.

The persistence of these two alternative legal channels preserves the hierarchical social structure. The system, in place since the nineteenth century, funnels women with illegitimate children through one set of processes and married women through another. The law also differentiates in practice between persons of different social classes since the two courts are widely acknowledged to have quite different consequences for individuals' family ties and the economy of their households. When I asked whether the magistrate's court might be characterized as a 'poor peoples' court', eighteen of 21 attorneys concurred.[5]

There are structural, economic, and ideological reasons beyond the factor of legal jurisdiction as to why that characterization holds. First, the magistrate's court is more readily accessible to the lower class. It is cheap to take a case there: the cost of a three dollar stamp. One need not hire an attorney and, indeed, the majority of litigants with maintenance cases are not represented. Second, in 1987 a magistrate could award a maximum of fifteen Eastern Caribbean dollars per week for child support ($5.67 U.S. currency) and up to 25 E.C. dollars per week ($9.36 U.S. currency) for support for a married woman. Such small sums are unlikely to draw middle class women to the court. Moreover, since they are usually married, middle class women prefer to divide their property and arrange for the welfare of their children at the High Court where judges have much greater discretion in awarding support. In contrast to magistrates, High Court judges investigate the income and property of both parties and the ages and educational needs of the children. Finally, there are ideological reasons why the middle class avoids the magistrate's court. Members of this class, and some lower class persons as well, con-sider kinship cases analogous to 'hanging one's dirty laundry in public'. The court's long association with persons of low status — with rogues and criminals — also dissuades Antiguans concerned about reputation from bringing a case there.

For all of these reasons, the magistrates primarily hear kinship disputes of working class persons. The large number of family cases is partly due to the frequency with which men who have been adjudged as legal fathers, and ordered to pay weekly sup-port, fail to make those payments. When a man does not pay for five or six consecutive weeks, the collecting officer requests the magistrate to order the man to give reason why he has neglected to pay. At present, if he chooses not to pay he does not pay until the police track him down. Meanwhile, the number of cases against him continues to multi-ply on the books. After cases of unpaid arrears, the most frequently heard family dis-putes are those in which a woman requests that a man be judged the putative father of her child and an order be made for the child's support. These petitions constituted about 70 per cent of all new kinship cases brought before the magistrates each year between 1980 and 1986.

Excluding cases of arrears, almost all of the kinship cases heard by the court are brought by women. Women rely on the courts to establish affiliation and maintenance, to increase support orders, to deny husbands the right to cohabitation, to request main-tenance for themselves and their children, to protect the financial interests of a child if a father is about to leave the country, and to remove a youth from the home of a negli-gent parent. Men, on the other hand, file most of the requests for a discharge of a ma-gistrate's order. They have that option as soon as a minor reaches the age of sixteen, if the child comes to reside with them, or if the mother takes the child out of the state.

The plaintiff in the magistrate's court with a kinship case, almost always a lower class woman, finding herself at odds with the man, and the children neglected, files a com-plaint. The woman may or may not have other children at home to support. In a great many instances, she juggles child care and some form of part-time employment to pay for shelter and food. Usually the union between the man and woman has not been a casual one; most frequently the couple have been seeing each other for over a year and up to several years. Five of six attorneys questioned about the number of children named by plaintiffs responded 'one child usually, but two or three is not uncommon'. Of 22 such trials I observed in St John's, seven involved one child, nine involved two children, four involved three children, and two involved four children. The parties tend to be young, commonly eighteen to 35 years of age, but the vast majority were not preg-nant teens. Most plaintiffs had never been to court before and most were uncertain about what was expected of them.

The litigants usually did know, however, that a magistrate could award only up to 15 E.C. dollars per week for child support. Indeed, the amount is so low that it can make a difference only to the most indigent. Moreover, if financial considerations were the pri-mary cause why women went to court, we would expect to see a steady rise in the number of cases filed after 1982 when the stipend was raised from $7 to $15 E.C. That was not the case. My examination of the magistrates' records showed there was an im-mediate but temporary rise in the number of requests for affiliation and maintenance in St John's right after the stipend increased. As one might suppose, the publicity surround-ing the change in the law encouraged some women with easy access to this court to ap-ply for aid for the first time and others to request an increase in the support they already received. Within two years of the passage of the bill, however, the number of new requests had dropped to earlier levels. The court records also show that over the relevant five-year period there were no significant changes in the number of new cases filed in any of the country courts or in Barbuda. Apparently neither urban nor village women were motivated to go to court for purely financial reasons. Doubtless other considerations guide a woman's decision to take a man to court.

WHY WOMEN USE THE MAGISTRATE'S COURT

The case histories, interviews with litigants and lawyers, and observations of trials at the magistrate's courts show that Antiguan women take men to court when those men violate local norms about respect, support, and appropriate relations between the sexes. Women invoke the state in the name of justice, using law and forensic processes to ritually enact the meaning, rights, and responsibilities of kin. Two case histories illustrate this phenomenon.

In 1985 Cicely was 38, unmarried with four children, each of whom had a different father. Cicely supported herself and the children by cleaning offices two days a week, working in a private home one afternoon, and sometimes selling candy, cigarettes, drinks, and other small items on a street-corner from a tray perched upon a styrofoam cooler. Her regular salary was only $95 E.C. per week (about $35 U.S.) and she frequently needed help from her mother, who worked as a kitchen aid, or from her younger sister, a primary school teacher.

Her situation had improved somewhat a year later. She had a full-time cleaning job for which she earned $108 E.C. per week. She had also obtained some funds from an American organization which assisted poor children. The composition of her household had changed as well. Her oldest daughter had returned to live with her, but a little girl she had been 'minding' in 1985 had gone to live with her father's sister. One thing was unchanged; Cicely had virtually no support for her children from their fathers. Yet Cicely took only two of those men to court. The first man was a bartender, the second was a police officer. The other fathers were labourers.

Josephine's story reveals some interesting parallels to Cicely's case. Her father, Tyronne, was a carpenter and electrician. Tyronne had no formal training, but he was a master at fixing and inventing things, and could connect a house to the government electricity without its knowledge. Tyronne ran a small shop and drove a big car. When he died in 1981, Josephine met siblings at his funeral that she had never known.

Josephine's mother, Evelyn, worked as a domestic servant. Evelyn and Tyronne had not stayed together long. When Evelyn married for the second time at the age of 44, she had eight children by six different men. Only her first husband had consistently supported his two children. The other men, labourers and fishermen, went their separate ways. Only Tyronne, however, was taken to court. By coincidence, two other women also summoned Tyronne to court for maintenance on the same day and all three were awarded the maximum that the law allowed.

The timing of Tyronne's cases may have been coincidental; the fact that he, and two of the fathers of Cicely's children were brought to court, was not. The case studies show that women use the courts selectively. The profiles of these men are keys to identifying ideas about family, gender, and status which explain why Antiguan women go to court and why these particular men received summons. Moreover, these notions are intrinsic to family ideology and the even flow of family life in the community.

In the Antiguan lower class, men and women are held to have distinctly different natures. Although West Indians highly value individual autonomy and economic independence for both men and women. I found that Antiguans repeatedly stressed the biological and social differences between men and women and used those differences to support the premise that there is a proper domain for each sex. The Antiguan case is similar to that which prevails in May Pen and Kingston, Jamaica (De Veer 1979; Alexander 1973, 1984; and Austin 1979, 1984). My findings also accord with survey research conducted in Barbados, Antigua, and St Vincent (Anderson 1986; Powell 1986; White 1986). Both men and women distinguish between the 'inside' world of women and the 'outside' world of men and neither views those two domains as equal in any respect.

The creed of gender hierarchy within the family contributes to the subordinate position of women in this society. Nevertheless, as we shall see, a highly developed sense of justice ensures there are limits beyond which a man may not assert the special privileges accorded to his sex.

Antiguan men and women love and need each other — children are one consequence of that fact — but becuase their natures are so different, men and women parent in different ways. Women nurture children, cook for them, wash them, teach them, and discipline them. Men provide some of this care, but their primary responsibility is to 'feed a child', which means that the man maintains a particular kind of relationship with the child and the mother. An alliance exists in the first place because the man and the child share the same blood. Antiguan men are proud of their children and boast about their number. As another indication of their willingness to accept fatherhood, men rarely deny paternity at court, even if there are raging disagreements about how much they can afford in weekly payments. A child generally uses his or her father's surname in the community and is entitled to that man's attention and 'support'. Support may take the form of cash, gifts, food, clothing, school supplies, or services provided by either the man or members of his family. For example, a woman generally does not take a man or members of his family. For example, a woman generally does not take a man to court if his mother babysits or provides clothing for her grandchild.[6] In contrast to the law, community norms are flexible with respect to the amount and type of support due to an illegitimate child. Support may vary in amount or kind from month to month, but it must be given somewhat regularly to maintain the alliance. Finally, in addition to support, a man owes the mother of his child 'respect'. Like the notion of feeding a child, respect embodies a host of expectations. It means that even after their separation the man speaks politely about his child's mother and the people she is close to, that he acknowledges them publicly if the occasion arises, that he acts with discretion, and that he never flaunts a new relationship in her presence.

Breaking these norms which govern the alliances between men, women, and children sometimes results in a man being hauled to court. One woman I interviewed, for example, took the father of her child to court only after he had insulted her publicly in the market. Often, however, a norm involving respect is broken in conjunction with another which speaks directly about principles of hierarchy within the lower class. Consider the men whom Cicely and Evelyn brought to court; the bartender, the policeman, and Tyronne, the electrician. These men share a social stature that distinguishes them from the other fathers of Cicely's and Evelyn's illegitimate children. Locally, they are called 'big men'.[7] A 'big man' in Antigua has a respectable job with a steady income. Beyond this, he has won admiration by virtue of his leadership qualities, command of language, intelligence, wit, education, and generosity. He can maintain multiple unions, even when married, keep his women 'in order', and father and 'feed' many children. They uphold certain standards in their family relationships. They provide gifts to their wives and 'outside' women and support all of their children in a manner which accords with their standing in the community.

Violating this code of behaviour makes a big man an Antiguan woman's choice for a trip to the magistrate's court for a ritual shaming. The courtroom becomes for these men what Garfinkel (1956:89) calls a 'degradation ceremony'. When a man's name is called in court, his position as a big man is challenged. The trial indicates that he is not generous, not responsible, not a suitable father, and incapable of controlling his women.

By all accounts and my own observations, the shaming of men at the magistrate's court undeniably achieves this aim. Often a woman need only file legal papers and the man changes his ways. Those who come to court are chastised and warned that they may face prison if they fail to pay for their children. Some men refuse to attend, but in that case the suit is heard in their absence and the effect upon their reputation in the community is the same. The shaming ceremony, then, renews and validates legally constituted kinship responsibilities while mitigating the prestige of a big man.

The court ritual that challenges a man's personal competence and his status among his peers also inverts the usual hierarchical status between men and women. When she brings a man to the magistrate's court, a woman forces a conjuncture of the domestic and the public spheres; the dirty laundry is made public. During the case, she uses law, courts, forensic processes, and legal personnel to manage male behaviour and to lay claim to the rights due her and her children. If only for the duration of the ritual, she is a status equal and the public spokesman and representative for her children. Such behaviour has its costs. A woman may be chided for going to court; she may be accused of spite. Nonetheless, the achievement of equality, the validation of individual rights, and the recognition of moral duty — central elements of Antiguan family ideology — are proclaimed during the trial. These constitute a vital part of the 'justice' for which Antiguan women go to court.

Ironically, the expressed intent of the lawmakers — the regular provision of support for illegitimate children — is not nearly as effective as the threat or the actual performance of the shaming ceremony. Almost every woman I spoke with during my follow-up study complained about not receiving weekly payments. Their complaints were borne out by the collecting officer's records. Most women waited weeks between payments; some waited months. Women who take policemen to court face an added difficulty because officers are reluctant to hand warrants for failure to pay child support to fellow officers.

One last issue with respect to kinship cases at the magistrate's courts needs to be raised. There is a point at which a big man is too big a man to impugn in court, which accounts for the infrequency of inter-class family disputes in the lower courts. For at least three reasons, upper middle class status shields a man against the justice that lower class women seek from the courts. First, charges of corruption against public officials occur frequently enough so that the lower class remains cynical about the justice that poor people can expect at court when their opponents are wealthy and power people. In their view, pragmatism teaches that there is not much use in suing a middle class man whose fancy lawyer will break your case or who is himself a friend of the judge. Second, rich and powerful men are likely to be married to rich and powerful women, who are formidable adversaries in their own right because they wield considerable influence over employment and educational opportunities in the community. Finally, some lower class women do not take the wealthy fathers of their illegitimate children to court because they cherish the hope that some day these men will 'rediscover' their children, come to love them, and provide them with their rightful due. That hope is part of the ideology of Antiguan family life and is crucial to understanding why a woman has a child 'for' a man.

In short, although a maintenance case may appear to be a request for cash, it is in fact a way to substantiate familial alliances and to shame men who purport to be big men but who break a big man's code of conduct. A woman brings a case to magistrate's court to claim normative rights which regulate family, gender, and hierarchy within the lower class. They rely on and use a literal translation of Antiguan kinship law to manage male behaviour, to voice objections to their own inequality, and to reaffirm the rights of their children. They 'carry' their cases for 'justice'.

CONCLUSION

Studies of West Indian family life have neglected the historical development of indigenous kinship law and ignored the importance of legal rules and processes in everyday life. These oversights, I have argued, cause us to miss the ways in which kinship embodies state power and how law, as an agent of the state, mediates family, gender, and class relations.

Antiguan kinship was influenced from the beginning by the codes and judicial institutions of the state. British colonists constructed a hierarchical social order that was singularly devoted to the success of a sugar crop worked by slaves. Lawmakers used various kinship statutes to promote class endogamy and to prevent love and sex from interfering with the rigid division of labour required by slavery and sugar production. The legacy of colonial rule included the presumption that kinship was partly a legal phenomenon, that families could be legislated and regulated, and that courts were an appropriate arena for resolving familial disputes.

History and ethnography reveal the hegemonic force of law in peoples' lives. Antiguans continue the long-established practice of using law and formal legal institutions to proclaim, manage, or dissolve kinship ties. Yet very few Caribbeanists have asked questions of those who bring their family disputes to the courts about the meaning of those cases or about the effects of court actions over time. Scholars have assumed, along with lawmakers, that women use the magistrate's courts to obtain purely financial relief. I found instead that Antiguan women most often take men to court to right a breach of the norms which govern family, gender, and hierarchy in the community. They are concerned with misconduct involving partnering, parenting, responsibility, respect, and social status. Theirs is a distinctly creole act, an act exemplifying the dialectical interaction between state forms and community norms.

A comprehensive investigation not only of Antiguan kinship, but of kinship generally, must therefore contend both with everyday beliefs and practices and the legal forms and forces of the state. Some evidence from Jamaica (Patchett 1973; Roberts 1979, 1985; Salmon n.d.; Smith 1987), Montserrat (Fergus 1978) and Guyana (Shahabuddeen 1973) indicates that the Antiguan case is not unusual; as part of the colonization process, law has played a significant role in the formation of kinship systems elsewhere in the West Indies. Moreover, Stoler's (1989) recent account finds that race, class, gender, and kinship were also subjects for the pens of lawmakers in the Netherlands Indies and French Indochina.

Europeans made relations of consanguinity and affinity subject to legally binding duties and responsibilities wherever and whenever they colonized. The politics of writing and enforcing those codes, and the ways in which such rules and institutions altered, ignored, or mediated local ideology and practice transformed the cultures of the lawmakers and their subjects in the matters of kinship, gender, race, and class.

NOTES

1. I conducted historical and legal research at the University of the West Indies, Barbados, followed by field work in Antigua and Barbuda from January 1985 to March 1986, and again for three months in 1987. The women whose cases are reported here have my heartfelt thanks for all they taught me.

   An earlier version of this paper was presented at the American Anthropological Association Meetings in Chicago in 1987. I am grateful to Raymond T. Smith, John L. Comaroff, Lisa Douglas, Wendy Espeland, members of the American Bar Foundation, and, especially, Bill Black.

2. Following local custom, I use 'Antigua' rather than the more cumbersome 'Antigua and Barbuda'.

3. Kinship has dominated Caribbean research since the late 1930s when West Indian families were first perceived as a social problem, in part because of their high rates of illegitimacy (Smith 1982). Initial efforts to explain the diverse social and kinship organization of the region centred either upon the disruptive effects of slavery (e.g., Curtin 1955; Goveia 1965; Smith 1966, Patterson 1967) or the retention of African customs and patterns (e.g., Herskovits 1958, 1966; Mintz and Price 1976). The development of community studies inspired by British structural-functionalism next produced a variety of social, psychological, economic, and demographic variables to account for local patterns (e.g., Goode 1960; Clarke 1966; Kunstadter 1968; Gonzalez 1970; Rodman 1971). Many earlier characterizations of West Indian families are now challenged by historical analyses and recent ethnographic work; e.g., Higman (1973, 1976, 1977, 1984a, 1984b), Morrissey (1989), Bush (1990), Smith (1982, 1984, 1987, 1988), Austin (1979, 1984), Alexander (1978, 1984) and Massiah (1986). None of these accounts, however, explores in depth, the role of law and courts in the development of West Indian kinship.

4. Stoler (1989) also finds regulating marriage and miscegenation by legal statute provided Europeans the means to govern sexual morality in the colonies. As I demonstrate here, the moral duties with which Antiguan women are concerned when they use kinship law has nothing to do with sexual morality.

5. The characterization of the magistrate's court as a 'poor person's court' was first drawn by Cumper and Daly (1979: 10). A few attorneys and some of the court staff I interviewed felt it was problematic to portray the court in this fashion but conceded that the vast majority of

persons with family disputes at the magistrate's court would have to be described as lower class persons.

6. The importance of relationships among women which are traced through men is well documented in the literature on West Indian families. See, for example, Smith (1956, 1987, 1988); Smith (1962); Clarke (1966); Rodman (1971); Craton (1978); Gussler (1980); Brodber (1986); Powell (1986). Research on American Black families points to the same phenomenon (e.g., Liebow 1967; Genovese 1972; Stack 1974; Aschenbrenner 1975; Gutman 1976).

7. Carmody (1978: 326-327) discusses Antiguan 'big men' in overtly political roles distinguishing Antiguan 'big men' from the political type described for Polynesia by Sahlins.

BIBLIOGRAPHY

Alexander, J. 1973. *'The Culture of Middle-Class Family Life in Kingston, Jamaica.'* Ph.D. dissertation, University of Chicago.

—1978. 'The Cultural Domain of Marriage.' *American Ethnologist* 5:5-14.

—1984. 'Love, Race, Slavery, and Sexuality in Jamaican Images of the Family.' *Kinship Ideology and Practice in Latin America*, ed. R. T. Smith, pp. 147-180. Chapel Hill.

Anderson, P. 1986. 'Conclusion: Women in the Caribbean.' *Social and Economic Studies* 35:291-324.

Antigua and Barbuda, 1962. The Revised Laws of Antigua. Prepared under the authority of the Revised Edition of the Laws Ordinance, 1951. 8 vols. London.

—1985. Statistical Yearbook. Antigua and Barbuda: Statistics Division, Ministry of Finance.

Aschenbrenner, J. 1975. *Lifelines: Black Families in Chicago.* Prospect Heights.

Austin, D. J. 1979. 'History and Symbols in Ideology: A Jamaican Example.' *Man* 14(3):497-514.

—1984. *Urban Life in Kingston, Jamaica.* New York.

Barrow, C. 1986. 'Finding the Support: A Study of Strategies for Survival.' *Social and Economic Studies* 35:131-176.

Berleant-Schiller, R. 1977. 'Production and Division of Labour in a West Indian Peasant Community.' *American Ethnologist* 4:253-272.

Boxill, E. 1985. 'Developments in Family Law Since Emancipation.' *West Indian Law Journal* (October):9-20.

Brodber, E. 1986. 'Afro-Jamaican women at the Turn of the Century.' *Social and Economic Studies* 35:23-50.

Bush, B. 1990. *Slave Women in Caribbean Society 1650-1838.* Bloomington.

Carmody, C. 1978. 'First Among Equals: Antiguan Patterns of Local Level Leadership.' Ph.D. dissertation, New York University.

Clarke, E. 1966. *My Mother Who Fathered Me.* London.

Cohn, B. S. 1989. *Law and the Colonial State in India. History and Power in the Study of Law,* ed. J. Starr and J. F. Collier, pp. 131-152. Ithaca.

Comaroff, J. L. 1989. 'Images of Empire, Contests of Conscience: Models of Colonial Domination in South Africa.' *American Ethnologist* 16:661-685.

Comaroff, J. L., and S. Roberts 1981. *Rules and Processes.* Chicago.

Cooper, F., and A. L. Stoler, 1989. 'Tensions of Empire: Colonial Control and Visions of Rule.' *American Ethnologist* 16:609-621.

Craton, M. 1978. *Searching for the Invisible Man.* Cambridge.

Cumper, G., and S. Daly 1979. *Family Law in the Commonwealth Caribbean.* Jamaica.

Curtin, P. D. 1955. *Two Jamaicas: The Role of Ideas in a Tropical Colony 1830-1865.* Cambridge.

De Veer, H. 1979. 'Sex Roles and Social Stratification in a Rapidly Growing Urban Area — May Pen, Jamaica.' Ph.D. dissertation, University of Chicago.

Dunn, R. S. 1972. *Sugar and Slaves: The Rise of the Planter Class in the English West Indies 1624-1713.* New York.

Durant Gonzalez, V. 1982. The Realm of Female Familial Responsibility. *Women and the Family,* ed. J. Massiah, Women in the Caribbean Project, pp. 1-27. Barbados.

Fergus. H. A. 1978. 'The Early Laws of Montserrat (1668-1680): The Legal Schema of a Slave Society.' *Caribbean Quarterly* 24:34-43.

Flannagan, Mrs 1967 (1844) *Antigua and the Antiguans: A Full Account of the Caribs to the Present Free Labour Systems; The Statistics of the Island, and Biographical Notices of Principal Families.* 2 vols. London.

Forde, N. M. 1981. *Women and the Law.* Barbados.

Garfinkel, H. 1956. 'Conditions of Successful Degradation Ceremonies.' *The American Journal of Sociology* 61:420-424.

Gaspar, D. B. 1985. *Bondmen and Rebels: A Study of Master-Slave Relations in Antigua.* Baltimore.

Genovese, E. D. 1972. Roll, Jordan, *Roll: The World the Slaves Made.* New York.

Gonzalez, N. L. S. 1970. Toward a Definition of Matrifocality. *African-American Anthropology,* eds. N. E. Whitten, Jr., and J. F. Szwed, pp. 231-244. New York.

Goode, W. J. 1960. 'Illegitimacy in the Caribbean Social Structure.' *American Sociological Review* 25:21-30.

Goveia, E. V. 1965. *Slave Society in the British Leeward Islands at the End of the Eighteenth Century.* New Haven.

—1970. The West Indian Slave Laws of the 18th Century. *Chapters in Caribbean* History 2, eds. D. Hall, E. Goveia, and R. Augier, pp. 9-53. Barbados.

Gussler, J. D. 1980. Adaptive Strategies and Social Networks of Women in St. Kits. *A World of Women: Anthropological Studies of Women in the Societies of the World,* ed. E. Bourguignon, pp. 185-209. New York.

Gutman, H. G. 1976. *The Black Family in Slavery and Freedom, 1750-1925.* New York.

Hall, D. 1971. *Five of the Leewards 1834-1870.* Barbados.

Henry, P. 1986. *Peripheral Capitalism and Underdevelopment in Antigua.* New Brunswick.

Herskovits, M. J. 1958 (1941). *The Myth of the Negro Past.* Boston.

—1966. *The New World Negro,* ed. F. S. Herskovits. Bloomington.

Higman, B. W. 1973. 'Household Structure and Fertility on Jamaican Slave Plantations: A Nineteenth-Century Example.' *Population Studies* 27:527-550.

—1976. *Slave Population and Economy in Jamaica, 1807-1834.* Cambridge.

—1984. Terms for Kin in the British West Indian Slave Community: Differing Perceptions of Masters and Slaves. *Kinship Ideology and Practice in Latin America,* ed. R. T. Smith, pp. 59-81. Chapel Hill.

—1984. *Slave Populations of the British Caribbean 1807-1834.* Baltimore.

Jackson, J. 1982. Stresses Affecting Women and their Families. *Women and the Family,* ed. J. Massiah, Women in the Caribbean Project, pp. 28-61. Barbados.

Jayawardena, C. 1960. 'Marital Stability in Two Guianese Sugar Estate Communities.' *Social and Economic Studies* 9:76-100.

—1963. *Conflict and Solidarity in a Guianese Plantation.* London.

Knight, F. W. 1970. *Slave Society in Cuba During the Nineteenth Century.* Madison.

Kunstatder, P. 1968. Divisions of Labour and the Matrifocal Family. *A Modern Introduction to the Family,* eds. N. W. Bell and E. F. Vogel, pp. 368-376. New York.

Lazarus-Black, M. 1990. 'Legitimate Acts and Illegal Encounters: The Development of Family Ideology and Structure in Antigua and Barbuda, West Indies.' Ph.D. dissertation, University of Chicago.

Leeward Islands 1930. The Federal Acts of the Leeward Islands containing the Acts of the General Legislative Council in force on the 31st Day of December, 1927. (Revised Edition).

Lewin, L. 1981. 'Property as Patrimony: Changing Notions of Family, Kinship and Wealth in Brazilian Inheritance Law from Empire to Republic.' Paper presented on Theoretical Problems in Latin American Kinship Studies, Mexico.

—1987. *Politics and Parentela in Paraiba.* Princeton.

Liebow, E. 1967. *Tally's Corner: A Study of Negro Streetcorner Men.* Boston.

Martinez-Alier, V. 1974. *Marriage, Class and Colour in Nineteenth Century Cuba.* Cambridge.

Massiah, J. 1982. Family Structure and the Status of Women in the Caribbean with Particular Reference to Women Who Head Households. *Women and the Family,* ed. J. Massiah, Women in the Caribbean Project, pp. 66-130. Barbados.

—1986. 'Women in the Caribbean Project: An Overview.' *Social and Economic Studies* 35:1-29.

Mintz, S. W., and R. Price 1976. *An Anthropological Approach to the Afro-American Past: A Caribbean Perspective.* Philadelphia.

Moore, S. F. 1978. *Law as Process: An Anthropological Approach.* London.

—1986. *Social Facts and Fabrications.* Cambridge.

—1989. History and the Redefinition of Custom on Kilimanjaro. *History and Power in the Study of Law,* eds. J. Starr and J. F. Collier, pp. 277-301. Ithaca.

Morrison, D. 1979. 'The Reception of English Law in Jamaica.' *West Indian Law Journal* (October):43-61.

Morrissey, M. 1989. *Slave Women in the New World: Gender Stratification in the Caribbean.* Lawrence.

Moses, Y. 1976. 'Female Status and Male Dominance in Montserrat.' Ph.D. dissertation, University of California, Riverside.

Nader, L. 1989. The Crown, the Colonists, and the Course of Zapotec Village Law. *History and Power in the Study of Law,* ed. J. Starr, and J. F. Collier, pp. 320-344. Ithaca.

Patchett, K. W. 1973. 'Reception of Law in the West Indies.' *Jamaican Law Journal* (April):17-35; (October:55-67).

Patchett, K., and V. Jenkins 1973. *A Bibliographical Guide to Law in the Commonwealth Caribbean.* Barbados.

Patterson, O. 1967. *The Sociology of Slavery.* Rutherford.

Powell, D. 1986. 'Caribbean Women and their Response to Familial Experiences.' *Social and Economic Studies* 35:83-130.

Rapp, R. 1982. Family and Class in Contemporary America: Notes Toward an Understanding of Ideology. *Rethinking the Family: Some Feminist Questions,* ed. B. Thorne, pp. 168-187. New York.

Roberts, G. W. 1979 (1957). *The Population of Jamaica.* Millwood.

—1985. 'Some Observations on the Social Background: The Family Law in the Caribbean.' *West Indian Law Journal* (October):21-28.

Rodman, H. 1971. *Lower-Class Families: The Culture of Poverty in Negro Trinidad.* New York.

Salmon, V. n.d. Nullius Filius: 'A Historical Study of His Quest for Legal Recognition and Protection in Jamaica. Thesis (LL.B.), Faculty of Law, University of the West Indies, Barbados.

Smith, M. G. 1962. *West Indian Family Structure.* Seattle.

—1965. The Transformation of Land Rights by Transmission in Carriacou. *The Plural Society in the British West Indies.* Berkeley.

—1966. Introduction. *My Mother Who Fathered Me.* E. Clarke, pp. i-xiiv. London.

Smith, R. T. 1955. 'Land Tenure in Three Negro Villages in British Guiana.' *Social and Economic Studies* 4:64-82.

—1956. *The Negro Family in British Guiana.* London.

—1982. Family, Social Change, and Social Policy in the West Indies. *Nieuwe West Indische Gids* 56:111-142.

—1984. Introduction. *Kinship Ideology and Practice in Latin America*, ed. R. Smith, pp. 3-31. Chapel Hill.

—1987. Hierarchy and the Dual Marriage System in West Indian Society. *Gender and Kinship: Essays Toward a Unified Analysis,* eds. J. Fishburne, C. Junko, and S. Junko Yanagisako, pp. 163-196. Stanford.

—1988. *Kinship and Class in the West Indies: A Genealogical Study of Jamaica and Guyana.* Cambridge.

Smith, R. T., and C. Jayawardena 1959. 'Marriage and the Family Amongst East Indians in British Guiana.' *Social and Economic Studies* 8:321-376.

Stack, C. 1974. *All My Kin: Strategies for Survival in a Black Community.* New York.

Starr, J., and J. F. Collier (eds.) 1989. Introduction: Dialogues in legal Anthropology. *History and Power in the Study of Law,* pp. 1-28. Ithaca.

Stolcke, V. 1984. The Exploitation of Family Morality: Labour System and Family Structure on Sao Paulo Coffee Plantations, 1850-1979. *Kinship Ideology and Practice in Latin America,* ed. R. T. Smith, pp. 264-296. Chapel Hill.

Stoler, A. L. 1989. 'Making Empire Respectable: The Politics of Race and Sexual Morality in 20th-Century Colonial Cultures.' *American Ethnologist* 16:634-660.

Vincent, J. 1989. Contours of Change: Agrarian Law in Colonial Uganda. *History and Power in the Study of Law,* eds. J. Starr, and J. F. Collier, pp. 153-167. Ithaca.

Westermark, G. D. 1986. 'Court is an Arrow: Legal Pluralism in Papua New Guinea.' *Ethnology* 25:131-148.

White, A. 1986. 'Profiles: Women in the Caribbean Project.' *Social and Economic Studies* 35:59-81.

The World Bank 1985. Antigua and Barbuda Economic Report. Washington, D.C.

PART II

5

Slave Families

Within the severe constraints of the system of slavery, which defined slaves as chattel and as units of labour, was there any room for them to develop as human beings with a family and community life? Were conjugal relations reduced to sexual anarchy and promiscuity or did the slaves develop enduring monogamous relationships? Were household and family structures truncated to mother and child units with fathers, grandparents and other kin marginalised and non-functioning or were nuclear and extended, three-generational forms established? In this chapter we examine the answers these questions that have been provided by the historical literature. Studies of slave families divide into two main phases. The early phase of travelogues, diaries and the interpretations of historians and sociologists who relied largely on them, concluded that family life among the slaves was unrecognisable, completely destroyed by the rigours of the system. More recent investigations, particularly those of demographic historians, while not denying the profound impact of the slave system, have been preoccupied with counteracting these negative images. They have reconstructed slave family life and claim that stable conjugal unions and nuclear family households were the norm among the slaves. We begin this chapter by exploring and comparing these interpretations in the literature, past and present, and then proceed to identify the hypotheses offered by the more recent scholarship to explain family form among the slaves.

Slave family: chaos or reconstruction?

In Chapter II we examined the thesis presented by Franklin Frazier (1939) claiming that slavery completely wiped out the African heritage including forms of marriage and family, that slave family life was virtually impossible within the conditions of the system and that what existed as rudimentary family forms were nothing but unsuccessful attempts to imitate white culture. We also noted the subsequent loss of interest in slave family systems as sociology and anthropology became dominated by structural functionalism. The few researchers who continued to seek at least partial explanations in history, specifically in the slave past, echoed Frazier's conclusions, that slavery prevented the development of stable conjugal unions and family forms.

In a pioneering work, published in 1967 and entitled *The Sociology of Slavery: An Analysis of the Origins, Development and Structure of Negro Slave Society in Jamaica,* Orlando Patterson provided the first detailed analysis of Caribbean slave life from a sociological perspective. Reinforcing the prevailing stereotype, Patterson (1967: 178, see Article/Extract 1 at end of chapter) stated:

> The real life situation was one in which there was a complete breakdown of all major institutions — the family, marriage, religion, organised morality.

According to Patterson, family and conjugal union breakdown was a feature of the whole of Jamaican society, not only the slave sector. The total collapse of planter morality and social sanctions governing conjugal relations resulted in a 'degree of sexual abandonment' and the 'ruthless exploitation' of female slaves more pronounced in Jamaica than elsewhere in the Caribbean (Patterson 1967: 159). The consequences for the slaves were the rape of young girls and the incidence of preteenage motherhood. Promiscuity and prostitution prevailed on the plantations and also in urban areas. When slave conjugal unions were established, they were generally short-lived. Young females avoided stable, monogamous relationships because they entailed a heavier work-load and because they 'felt silly' to be committed to one man (Patterson 1967: 164), and where these did occur, the couple was usually ridiculed by other slaves who viewed the union as inappropriate. Only among the older slaves were enduring relationships socially acceptable and more common. For the more prosperous, higher-status male slaves, such a union was often one among several as they engaged in polygamy. They conducted simultaneous relations with other women in addition to the stable union with a 'wife' (Patterson 1967: 163-164). This interpretation is reflected in other studies. For example, in Goveia's seminal work on slave society in the Leeward Islands, she 'rejects on logical grounds' the possibility of stable conjugal unions forming among the slaves and, although she acknowledges that 'the majority of slaves ... retained a very strong African element in their culture' (Goveia 1965: 248), this was not traced in terms of family and marital patterns.

With conjugal unions in disarray, slaves stood little chance of establishing family structures. Any hope of stable family organisation was continually thwarted by the sale and removal of slaves and the sexual demands of white men (Patterson 1967: 167). The family was reduced to the mother and child unit with men living apart. Unable to perform the social roles of father and husband, they assumed 'irresponsible parental and sexual attitudes' (Patterson 1967: 168). Even the close and enduring bond of mother and child did not escape the pressures of the slave system. Mothers who exhibited devotion and great affection for children, their own and adopted, also treated them with extreme cruelty as they expressed their frustration with the system (Patterson 1967: 168). In addition, the time they were able to spend with their children was severely limited so that influences other than their own played a more prominent part in their children's upbringing (Patterson 1967: 170).

Patterson (1967: 165-166) also presented a model of the slave life cycle that acknowledged the possibility of monogamous conjugal unions and stable families, but only as a later stage in the lives of men and women. But even at this stage, Patterson claimed that the family was not nuclear in structure since the resident man was not normally the father of the children and because it was the woman, rather than the man, who wielded most authority.

In a later work which adopts the same general perspective, Patterson (1982: 5-8, 38) identified the concept 'natal alienation' to describe the symbolic estrangement of slaves from their natal ties by the conditions of slavery. Natal alienation was a fundamental element of slavery which reduced slaves to 'genealogical isolates', with no rights and obligations to blood relatives, ancestors or living family members. With no family, no community and no 'social existence outside of his master', the slave was defined as socially dead.

> I prefer the term 'natal alienation', because it goes directly to the heart of what is critical in the slave's forced alienation, the loss of ties of birth in both ascending and descending generations. It also has the important nuance of a loss of native status, of deracination. It was this alienation of the slave from all formal, legally enforceable ties of 'blood', and from any attachment to groups or localities other than those chosen for him by the master, that gave the relation of slavery its peculiar value to the master. The slave was the ultimate human tool, as imprintable and as disposable as the master wished. And this is true, at least in theory, of all slaves, no matter how elevated (Patterson 1982: 7-8).

The basic premise that informed Patterson's work was his view of the planter class as wielding 'absolute power' and of slavery as a system of 'total domination', which left no place for any autonomous development of slave institutional systems, especially family and community, and very little space for the self-determination of character and personality.

> It was characteristic of slavery, as of all systems of total domination, that almost all the criteria for social and economic divisions within the enslaved group were defined by the enslaving group ... social status among the slaves has to be considered in terms of their economic function and not as part of their internal patterns of behaviour (Patterson 1967: 57).

> Of course, some of the initiative and qualities necessary for his own success must have come from the slave himself; but such qualities were largely ascribed — directly or indirectly — in terms of his value and proximity to the master (Patterson 1967: 65).

Although Patterson (1967: 16-29) identified three phases of slavery in Jamaica, the distinctions were defined in economic and political terms and not systematically linked to changes in slave family life. If anything, we are left with the impression that family destruction persisted throughout the period. In addition, while Patterson (1967: 93) admitted that 'there was a wide area in which the slaves' activities were economically and socially irrelevant to their masters' and implied that, outside of the formal plantation work situation, slaves were left pretty much to their own devices, he unfortunately omitted to explore the point. It was left to later researchers to follow through.

The contrasting position taken by the more recent history of the conditions of slavery in the Caribbean is that the system left some space, albeit severely limited, for slaves to fashion ways of life for themselves. Mintz and Price (1976, see Article/extract 2 at end of chapter), while recognising that the monopoly power of the planter class and the constant and arduous demands of the slave regime established tight constraints on the lives of the slaves, contended that there was, nevertheless, some room for them to manoeuvre and to remodel cultural patterns and community cohesion. Slave domestic life, while not immune from the power of the system and the planters who ran it, allowed a degree of autonomous recreation of cultural beliefs and practices, a slave morality relating to sexuality, childbirth, socialisation and so forth. As Mintz and Price (1976: 40) expressed the point, 'the code of the masters set the limits more than it determined the contents of that morality'. They took the point further as they contended that the planters themselves, like it or not, had to accept and even adapt to the institutions developed by the slaves.

> We would contend, then, that the institutions created by the slaves to deal with what are at once the most ordinary and the most important aspects of life took on their characteristic shape **within** the parameters of the masters' monopoly of power, but **separate from** the masters' institutions. We have in mind, for example, how slaves mended their clothes, furnished their houses, cooked their meals, fell in love, courted, married, bore and socialized their children, worshipped their deities, organized their 'plays' and other recreation, and buried their dead. If our assertions in this regard are interpreted too literally, of course, we can easily be proved wrong; in theory, the masters could determine how all of these activities were organized, given their power and its exercise. Yet we have many demonstrations of the way the masters came to accept the patternings of slave institutions as part of the daily reality and to which they, too, had to adjust (Mintz and Price 1976: 20) (Emphasis in original).

Once it was recognised that slavery was not a system of absolute power and complete domination with slaves totally reduced to chattel and automatons, mindlessly responding to continuous demands for labour and sex, it became necessary for researchers to turn their attention to the nature of the slave response to slavery. Interpretations of the process of rebuilding family and kinship among the slaves from the time of their arrival in the Caribbean have concluded generally that, although they might have drawn on fundamental cultural principles of African kinship, the particular conditions of slave society to which they were forced to adapt would have been more influential (Mintz and Price 1976: 34-35). Craton (1991(1979): 247, see Article 3 at end of chapter) summarises the conceptual approach, stressing the way in which slavery allowed the slaves to shape their family lives rather than how the system controlled them. We proceed by examining the historiography of slave efforts to recreate a culture of kinship, first in terms of conjugal unions and then family forms.

Conjugal unions: Monogamy, polygamy or promiscuity?

Recent reports of a predominance of marital-type relationships among the slaves challenge the earlier images of widespread polygamy and promiscuity. For example, Higman 1991(1973): 271, see Article 4 at end of chapter) has reported from two sugar estates (Old and New Montpelier) and a livestock pen (Shettlewood) in Jamaica that, although an initial period of casual mating often occurred, this was followed by 'relatively stable monogamy'. He cautioned that his conclusions were based on information concerning household composition and on the assumption that an adult male and female, co-resident and of similar age are conjugal partners, but nevertheless, estimated that probably 100 of the total 252 households in his sample contained a co-residential conjugal couple (Higman 1991(1973): 259-260). Craton's information from the Bahamas supported this interpretation and added that conjugal co-residence was normally established by age 20, around the time of birth of a second child (Craton 1991 (1979): 234). Beckles (1989: 128-131, see Article/extract 5 at end of chapter) arrived at a similar conclusion for Barbados, reporting that on Seawell and Newton Plantations the norm was monogamous unions established in the early years of adulthood, often after the birth of a child.

Promiscuity and concubinage relationships between female slaves and white masters were previously thought to be widespread in slave society. Contemporary historians are more careful. They have suggested, for example, that distinctions should be made between prostitution and more stable relationships, though admitting some overlap, for instance when unsatisfactory mistresses were demoted to prostitution (Beckles 1989: 148). Additionally, distinctions have also been drawn between urban and plantation contexts. The situation in urban areas with their inns, taverns and brothels and transient populations of sailors and the like in search of quick sexual satisfaction, not enduring relationships, is contrasted with that on the plantations. Nevertheless, both urban and rural slave owners were involved in hiring out their slaves and, in this regard, the hiring of female slaves for sex was merely an extension of offering their services as cooks, nannies and seamstresses.

> Slave owners and other males with capital, would commonly 'keep' black or 'coloured' mistresses primarily for sexual purposes. The evidence suggests that this was more popular in Bridgetown than on the plantations, though estate owners or managers probably had greater sexual access to a larger number of black women. In the towns, organized prostitution and resident mistresses were the general pattern, while on the estates the sexual use of black women took a less structured form. To a large extent, urban culture was influenced by the maritime activity on which it developed, and sex was as important a commodity to its economy as any other. The large, transient, maritime personnel expected to purchase it, and the more liberal values of urban society allowed for its sale with minimal restriction (Beckles 1989: 141-142).

> White males would often lease out their black mistresses and other slave women as prostitutes as a convenient way of obtaining cash. Dickson found this common practice during the 1770s, especially among men who were heavily in debt. Women were leased out to visiting 'gentlemen', ships' captains and other clients for a specified period. Monies obtained by these 'whoremasters and mistresses' frequently exceeded the market value of the women. As such, slave owners considered the prostitution of women more lucrative than 'breeding'. During the 'hard season' the number of slave women placed on the urban market as prostitutes by sugar planters would rapidly increase, as did the number of male artisans put out to sell their skill on a hired contractual basis. In both instances, rural slave owners expected a substantial proportion of the money earned, while the slaves were considered fortunate to have some degree of control over the disposal of their time and labour (Beckles 1989: 142).

> The testimony of Captain Cook, a British military officer, before the 1791 Parliamentary Committee on the Slave System, illustrates the extent to which white men in Barbados used black women as prostitutes. He visited the colony in 1780 and in 1782, and knew at first hand the social culture of Bridgetown. First, he noted that the use of black women, both free and slave, as prostitutes in all the colony's towns, 'was a very common practice'. Second, masters and mistresses in the towns would frequently send out female slaves as prostitutes for ships' crews. These slaves, he added, would 'go on board ships of war for the purpose' of selling sex for money (Beckles 1989: 143).

On the plantations, sexual relations between white men and black or coloured slave women are estimated to have been much less common than previously assumed. For example, on the Worthy Park Estate, the practice was confined to a 'small and select segment of the plantation's females' (Craton 1978: 166). Historical reinterpretations have also shed light on the nature of these relationships. For one thing, they are viewed from a less moralistic stance, with fewer accusing fingers pointed at the parties involved. The assumptions of white male control within these relationships and of the benefits accruing to the women involved have also been questioned.

While not denying the occurrence of rape and other coercive methods, recent scholarship claims that there were instances where slave women voluntarily entered into these relations, indeed were actively and aggressively engaged in seeking out white male partners (Morrissey 1989: 147-8). Total conjugal power by white males has also been refuted by the claim that, in some cases, 'slave women were clearly the dominant partners, and dictated the nature of relationship politics' and a degree of intimacy, albeit covert, was often established between the partners (Beckles 1989: 149). And yet, the perception that these relationships invariably functioned to enhance the material advantage and social mobility of the female slave and her children has also been challenged. Reinterpretations suggest that these relationships constituted a mixed blessing for those involved.

> For a black slave woman to trade her body with a white man in return for transient rewards was perhaps as voluntary as it was casual. But once conception occurred the process was inexorable. The coloured offspring of such liaisons lived in the twilight zone of the half-caste, stranded between two cultures. All were bound to attempt maximum assimilation, which for the coloured females meant becoming the bedmates of whichever white men laid claim to them.

> The rewards of domestic concubinage might include relative comforts, equivocal prestige, even some backstairs power for the concubine herself. For the offspring, it might lead to a choice of the best slave jobs and the chance of manumission. Yet even in the most fortunate cases these were scarcely compensations for a life of sexual anarchy and the loss of the most recognizable features of a stable family life. In less fortunate cases — where, for example, the children died, or the coloured slave lost favour through sterility, ill-health or advancing age — the results of miscegenation could be demoralizing to the point of alienation (Craton 1978: 242).

For Barbados, Beckles (1989: 135) has debunked the myth that manumission was common for these mulatto children and their mothers. The granting of freedom for these slave women was by no means a certainty as it depended on their own children, not all of whom were willing or able to make provisions for the purchase of their mothers. At any rate, since the children's own manumission was delayed until adulthood, many of the mothers involved had reached old age and existed as the 'hidden dependents' of their higher-status children (Beckles 1989: 136). Coloured women in urban areas were more successful in consolidating material privilege, comfortable lifestyles and higher status through their links with prominent white men (Beckles 1989: 147, Morrissey 1989: 148). But they were never fully accepted into white society. Their white partners, for example, did not marry them and, even if they managed to purchase their freedom from their own earnings, there was little else they could do to survive other than continue to function as prostitutes and mistresses. Only one or two, such as the notorious Rachel Pringle of Barbados, managed to acquire the capital to establish themselves as proprietors of shops or inns (Handler 1974: 133-137). In general therefore, for the majority of female slaves, especially those on the plantations, these relationships were either unavailable or probably perceived as undesirable in the long term.

Evidence of polygamy reported by earlier writers is supported by current histori-ography. Beckles (1989: 118, 119), for example, referred to a Barbadian slave 'social culture where polygamy was customary' throughout the period as slave men 'gener-ally kept one resident wife, with others located throughout the colony'. There is more than a suggestion, however, that the incidence of polygamy might have been exaggerated previously. Bennett (1958: 35), for example, claimed that records of Codrington Plantation in Barbados often misinterpreted transient sexual unions as polygamy. Recent demographic historians have reiterated the point. They con-firmed that polygamy occurred among slave men who were of higher status, particu-larly plantation headmen or head drivers (Craton 1978: 211-212), but suggested that the incidence among other slaves has been exaggerated. Craton's information from the Bahamas, for instance, identified 'only rare and equivocal evidence' of po-lygamy (Craton 1991(1979): 234).

Polygamous unions had definite advantages for those involved, symbolic for the elite males as multiple wives were an indication of relative wealth and prestige, and material for the economically vulnerable and exploitable female field labourers (Beckles 1989: 121). Following the argument through, we note that it was the slave women rather than the men who, during the latter days of slavery, were resisting po-lygamy and demanding monogamous Christian unions, presumably because by that time they were less economically vulnerable. The reasons for polygamy are not purely economic, but have also been linked to the 'double standard' of sexual mo-rality in the Caribbean, that is, the contrast between the conjugal faithfulness of women and the infidelity of men. Early historians observed that it was only the women whose behaviour exhibited fidelity and decency as they maintained exclu-sive unions with one man, albeit often short-lived and serial, while the men were si-multaneously engaged in relationships with more than one woman (Dickson 1814: 155, Ligon 1657: 47).

But, can we refer to these co-residential, relatively stable relationships, now ac-knowledged to have existed among the slaves as marriages? Early observations of slave family patterns have provided evidence that slave conjugal unions were socially recognised within their communities. Even though there is little or no indication of any ritual or ceremony organised by the slaves to give social recognition to the for-mation and dissolution of these unions, slaves did refer to each other as 'husband' and 'wife' and male slaves exhibited jealousy if other men paid any attention to their 'wives' (Ligon 1657: 47). At the level of the total society, however, slave conju-gal unions were not legally sanctioned or socially acknowledged. This was delayed until the amelioration period and the passage of various acts encouraging and rec-ognising marriage among the slaves, for example, the Act popularly known as the 'Sunday and Marriage Act', passed in Barbados in 1826. Even then, officially sanc-tioned marriages were rare. Based on incomplete parish returns in Barbados, Han-dler (1974: 165) estimated that only seventeen slave marriages took place in the An-glican Church between 1825 and 1830 and only four in the preceding years, 1808-1820. What we can say, however, is that it is highly unlikely that these Acts created conjugal relationships. It is much more likely that these marriages would merely have given the formal blessing of the total society to marital-type relationships al-ready in existence and already recognised within the slave group.

The slave family: Nuclear and extended or mother-child units?

Using detailed statistical evidence concerning household composition available as plantation documents and records of slave registrations, historians have also refuted earlier notions that slavery disrupted family ties and reduced functioning kinship units to those of mother and child. They have sought evidence to confirm that slaves established nuclear and extended family structures. Higman's pathbreaking work in Jamaica (Higman 1976) and Trinidad (Higman 1978, 1979) is of prime importance here. Although the unavailability of information for the earlier period of slavery left him no alternative but to focus on the 1807-1834 period, that is during amelioration when slave registration information was collected, Higman has argued that perceptions of chaotic kinship have been much exaggerated. Family life, he concluded, was not only possible, but was the norm among the slaves. Households containing nuclear families prevailed, while those containing only mothers and children constituted a minority in all but the urban areas. Among the slaves resident at Old and New Montpelier and Shettlewood, nearly 50 per cent lived in households which approximated nuclear families (Higman 1991(1973): 256), (see Article 4 at end of chapter) Similar conclusions are reflected in Craton's study of three groups of Bahamian slave households in 1822 including the Rolle slaves, the William slaves and the slaves resident on 26 Bahamian holdings. He contended that the majority (52.2 per cent) of the 3,697 slaves in the total sample lived in simple elementary family units comprising a man, a woman and children. If households containing a man and a woman and those with three-generation groupings are added to create a composite type which Craton labels as 'nuclear family', the proportion rises to 72.2 per cent. This leaves less that 30 per cent of the households in the categories 'denuded family' (man and children or woman and children) and 'no family' (single men, single women or separate children) (Craton 1991(1979): 233, 239), (see Article 3 at end of chapter).

Households containing female-headed family units, though far less common than previously thought to be the case, still constituted a significant proportion of the total. In Craton's three samples referred to above, households containing mothers and children accounted for 13.1 per cent of the total, while in Higman's samples from Jamaica, a total of 32.2 per cent of households contained mothers and their children, often together with extended family members such as grandchildren, nieces, nephews and others. Female-headed households in which male partners were absent were associated with urban residence and trans-racial conjugal relationships (Higman 1991(1973): 259). However these households, as indicated previously, are now considered to be the exception rather than the norm.

Slave families might not have been actually reduced to mother-child units, but there is no denying the enduring closeness of that relationship. Craton (1978: 166) described it as 'extremely strong' and made reference to the likelihood of 'melancholy decline' and suicidal mothers if children were taken away and sold. In contrast, relationships between fathers and their children were generally weak, if they existed at all. Beckles (1989: 119) refers to 'paternal alienation' among Barbadian slaves and, from the perspective of residence, Higman (1991(1979): 264) contrasts the rarity of identifiable cases of children living with their fathers or paternal relations with the emphasis on the mother-child bond. While their mothers lived, few slaves moved far away from them. The formation of three-generational households was common as a daughter had her first child in her parents' home, though these were probably temporary for the most part (Craton 1991(1979): 234). The percentage of households which spanned three generations amounted to between 11.9 and

12.3 per cent in the Bahamian samples investigated by Craton and only 4 per cent in Higman's Jamaican samples (Craton 1991(1979): 233, Higman (1991(1973): 257).

Additionally, 'yards' or what Higman (1976: 169) refers to as 'multiple house units' which consisted of clusters of households of maternal kin were also established. Beckles (1989: 123) drew attention to the emergence of grandmothers and great-grandmothers, powerful and well-respected within the slave community. These matriarchs cemented family solidarity and used their considerable influence to raise the occupational and social status of their children. Interesting illustrations are provided by the case-study of the female-dominated family of Old Doll on the Newton Plantation in Barbados (Beckles 1989: 127-129). On the Worthy Park Estate in Jamaica, Sarah Price, a 'veritable slave matriarch', and several other women survived to old age and established themselves as powerful figures in the slave community through their skills as midwives and nurses and as heads of extended families (Craton 1978: 209, 216-222). But circumstances in the Bahamas appear to have been somewhat different. Craton (1991(1979): 234) stated that evidence of extended family linkages was 'disappointingly meagre' and 'yards' non-existent.

In examining this evidence, we recognise several methodological problems, two of which we discuss here. The first is the fallacy, noted in Chapter III, of confusing family and household and drawing conclusions concerning family structure and relationships from data based on household composition. Higman (1976: 171) acknowledged the point in relation to linkages between adjacent households:

> The fundamental problem here is one of defining the physical limits of the premises occupied by co-resident groups of slaves. If the fence around a group of houses was more important in the slaves' concept of household than the walls of the houses, it follows that units defined above as nuclear, mother-child or solitary households should really be classified as extended, polygynous or multiple family households.

However, on the dubious assumption that the family was defined more according to the method of household resource allocation than domestic functions, he confirmed his original assumption that family and household, or 'housefuls' as he described them, are co-terminous. To quote him,

> the role of the yard in domestic functions is less certain. The most important of these functions were the provision and preparation of food, and the care of children. Since the 1825 report linked separate families to discrete houses, livestock and rights to gardens and provision grounds, it would seem that the slaves regarded these things as separate rights and possessions rather than common property. Within the slave system the care of children was often controlled by the masters, rather than being a potential function of the yard. Thus it appears that domestic functions do not provide a safe basis for deciding the relative significance of co-residence within houses as yards. But it is clear that relatively few slaves could have lived in simple family households which were grouped into extended or polygynous yards (Higman 1976: 171).

The possibility remains that among the slaves in the Caribbean, there may have been cases in which, on the one hand, more than one family occupied the same household and, on the other, family members were scattered across household boundaries. Evidence for the former is lacking, but what information we have suggests that this might have been rare. Average household size was (less than) four persons and the types of household structures identified imply that compound domestic units were rare. As to the latter possibility, several references have been made to close family ties transcending not just household boundaries but also those of the plantation. Higman (1976: 164-165), for example, gave evidence of significant proportions of residentially separated conjugal partners, a characteristic which he attributed to the sexual imbalance on individual plantations. And Beckles (1989: 119-121) referred to a 'commuting family culture' of husbands, wives and occasionally children and extensive mobility to maintain contact. He claimed that it was common for slaves living on different estates to form extra-residential conjugal unions and for runaway spouses to flee to each other.

The second methodological problem to which we direct attention and which we have also met before, concerns the question of drawing conclusions from synchronic data. It is impossible to determine the duration of conjugal unions and the stability of family structures from historical data such as plantation records of slave households, based as they are on information relating to household composition at a particular point in time. On this point, Higman (1976: 173) recognised that the 'problem of stability is an intractable one'. He, nevertheless, maintained that the previous image of family instability 'deserves serious reconsideration'. In other words, the more recent historical data is certainly sufficient to challenge and refute the earlier conclusions of families with ever-changing relationships amounting to chaos and destruction. The concluding picture of slave conjugal and family patterns with which we are left contrasts markedly with that previously presented by Patterson and others.

> In sum, it seems almost certain that while on slave plantations such as Worthy Park the 'modern' type of stable nuclear family was not always, or ever, the rule, family life of some kind was the common experience, and the resulting network of kinship a dominant characteristic. It was a reconstituted system of kinship, almost accidental in origin and almost unrecognized by the master class. It developed because heterogeneous Africans were brought and bound together, and remained in a closed social unit for generations. In time, kinship became one of the most cohesive bonds within each plantation, and the masters were the unwitting and undeserving beneficiaries of this development. So ignorant were the planters of the ties of family and kinship within their plantations that they predicted that thousands whom they had formerly succoured — such as the old, the sick, the very young — would be destitute when the slaves were freed, forming a pathetic floating army of the needy in each colony. In fact, no such burden fell upon the parish and colony authorities. Families looked after their own, as well as staying for the most part locationally rooted.

> Looking back, it seems that many a slave plantation population, after four of five generations must have been virtually one huge extended family (Craton 1978: 166-167).

Indeed several historians such as Higman (1991(1973): 265), have referred to the variety of types of conjugal union and of household and family structures which existed among the slaves and drawn parallels with family patterns among the black populations of the contemporary Caribbean.

Understanding slave families

In their efforts to provide some explanation for conjugal union types and family structures among the slaves, historians have sought reasons in the slave plantation system and planter dominance, in the African heritage, in demographic structures and in the economic circumstances and options open to the slaves. We proceed by examining these models in turn.

The slave plantation system and planter dominance

The conclusions presented by Patterson and others claimed that the slave plantation system and the master class transformed slaves into units of labour, bereft of normal family structures and social relationships. Challenging this perception is the evidence of more recent historians which, while not denying the destructive power of slavery and the slave owners, concluded that slaves did manage to carve out some space for themselves within which to develop culture and community. Indeed, historians have observed that there were times, especially during the amelioration period, when the slave system also played a constructive role by encouraging marriage and the formation of nuclear families although, for the most part, these efforts were prompted by economic, not humanitarian concerns. In other words, planter policies to encourage stable family life among the slaves did exist although they were not an end in themselves, but were motivated by considerations such as stabilising the labour force or maintaining its size through reproduction. Nevertheless, by creating the conditions within which slave families could thrive, these measures did, as it were, influence family development.

Several historians have noted the comments of early observers of slavery to the effect that planters tried to encourage co-resident, monogamous unions by maintaining a balanced sex ratio among their slaves. The rationale behind this, according to Ligon (1657: 47), was to curtail absenteeism by providing male slaves with 'wives' on the plantation, thereby putting a stop to their nightly wanderings as they went in search of female company elsewhere, only to return exhausted and unfit for labour the next day. The idea was to encourage the development of a plantation-based slave population, resident and under control. Seen in this light, the encouragement of polygamous relationships, once they were confined within plantation boundaries, is quite rational. For Barbados, Ligon (1657: 47) noted: 'For the planters there deny not a slave, that is a brave fellow, and one that has extraordinary qualities, two or three wives.' But it was during the latter half of the eighteenth century that deliberate social engineering policies by slave owners became more evident. Replenishing the slave labour force locally by natural increase had become a major concern as the abolition of the slave trade came closer to becoming a reality. While some policies were targeted at women and intended to stimulate increased fertility directly, others operated through measures designed to create what was perceived as the requisite family form. Planters believed that if slaves could be encouraged to live in nuclear family units, fertility levels would increase. We proceed by examining these policies in more detail.

Planters were convinced that female slaves were fundamentally resistant to bearing and raising children and to that end, were extending lactation for up to three years in order to postpone pregnancy and even inducing abortion or practising infanticide. Hence policies were designed to overcome and 'normalize' these attitudes. A package of incentives was offered to slave women to improve conditions of pregnancy, child-birth, child-rearing and family life, to lighten their workloads and, ultimately, to make them view procreation positively (Morrissey 1989: 126-127). Some of these measures were adopted as rules and guidelines on specific plantations; others were enshrined in the laws of Caribbean countries.

First and foremost were the policies directly intended to encourage pregnancy, as often as possible. Common throughout the Caribbean was a law manumitting slave women once they gave birth to six children and Craton (1978: 218-219), for example, cites several case-studies of women at the Worthy Park Estate who achieved their freedom in this way through the Jamaican Act of 1787. Slave owners often resorted to offering financial inducements to female slaves. In Barbados, for example, these were the norm by the late 1700s (Beckles 1989: 101, Handler 1978: 302-16). Attention was paid to improving medical facilities and ensuring that nutritional requirements, especially for pregnant and lactating women and young children, were met. On the Codrington Estates, by the early 1800s 'fresh fish for pregnant women' was supplied (Bennett 1958: 102). Nurseries were set up on many plantations and the burden of work for women was eased. In Jamaica, for example, pregnant women were exempted from field work and were relocated to lighter tasks in the second gang for up to two years as they nursed their babies (Higman 1976: 206-207). And on William Wylly's plantations in the Bahamas, Article XIX of the estate regulations stipulated that young children were to be well taken care of in the plantation nursery during their mothers' working day and that those women who were breast-feeding should remain close by (Craton 1991(1979): 235).

Early nineteenth-century laws prohibiting family separation, especially between mothers and children, were common in the Caribbean and also intended to increase fertility. In Jamaica, for example, a law passed in 1791 prescribed that when slaves were sold, family members should remain together (Craton 1978: 163, Higman 1991(1973): 251) and for the Bahamas, Craton (1991(1979): 237) reported the passage of a law in 1824 forbidding the break up of family units. He also provided evidence to show that this was followed through in practice. When, between 1821 and 1823, Burton Williams transferred 324 of his slaves from the Bahamas to Trinidad, most of them were kept in family units (Craton 1991(1979): 237-280), (see also Higman 1991(1973): 261-262).

Most important for our discussion were the policies implemented to encourage Christian marriages and co-resident nuclear families, the slave owners being convinced that this family form correlated with higher fertility rates (Roberts 1957: 159). On Wylly's plantations in the Bahamas, regulations were passed in 1815 with the clear intention of promoting sexual fidelity within marriage and punishing deviance. Article VII made provision for a home and livestock for a newly-married man and Article XI stipulated the punishment for adultery. Offenders had to forfeit their livestock and moveable property. They should be whipped, have their heads shaven, be made to wear sackcloth and be confined within plantation boundaries for six months (Craton 1991(1979): 235).

In Barbados, however, slave owners and their counterparts among the clergy were ambiguous about slave marriages and their policies were hesitant and often contradictory. At the same time as they were encouraging marriage and nuclear family formation, they liberalised restrictions on the physical movement of slaves, a measure which seems likely to facilitate polygamy and extra-residential unions, rather than encourage the consolidation of conjugal and family relations on one plantation. Perhaps it was argued that these relationships could not be prevented within a 'polygamous' slave culture and that this concession would cement family ties already built up across plantation boundaries. At a more fundamental level, a pronounced white resistance to slave marriages prevailed. It was claimed that allowing slaves to marry in church would imply social and racial equality and that, anyway, the measure was bound to fail, since 'polygamy' was so embedded in the mentality and way of life of the slaves, especially the men. Marriage rates, as we have noted, generally remained very low, though church baptisms and burials became quite common (Beckles 1989: 122, 130).

To illustrate these points, in particular the complex of attitudes and practices among the various parties involved, we present a case-study of the events which occurred prior to the acceptance of slave marriages during the latter days of the slave regime on the Codrington Plantations in Barbados. The account has drawn heavily on the book written by J. Harry Bennett entitled *Bondsmen and Bishops: Slavery and Apprenticeship on the Codrington Plantations of Barbados, 1710-1838.*

Slave marriages on the Codrington Estates, Barbados

In 1710, the Society for the Propagation of the Gospel in Foreign Parts (hereafter referred to as the Society) inherited two sugar estates in Barbados along with three hundred slaves. The experience of these plantations as regards the conversion of the slaves to Christianity, specifically the acceptance of slave marriages, is an interesting one. Headquartered in England, the Society professed itself to be a Christian missionary organisation, and yet on the Codrington Estates it functioned as a slave owner and planter. It was this basic incompatibility that forced the Society to tread an uneasy path between conflicting principles and was to prove very awkward during the later phase of the slave regime.

In the years immediately after taking over the plantations, christianising the slaves had not become an issue either for Barbadian or British society and the Society appeared to manage its double life by merely turning a blind eye and ignoring the problem. Later, by the middle of the century, although some slaves had been converted to Christianity, marriage was still not on the agenda. The manager of the Codrington Estates, Abel Alleyne,

> noted the fidelity of some Christian couples. As yet, however, the Christian marriage of chattels was scarcely to be thought of in the British West Indies. The idea did occur to Alleyne, but the Society maintained a discreet and prudent silence (Bennett 1958: 35).

Later, however, as pressures from the abolitionist movement for the full conversion of slaves to Christianity became more insistent, the Society found itself in a very uncomfortable position. At the heart of the matter was the abolitionist contention that Christianity and slavery were fundamentally incompatible and that for a Christian organisation to own slaves was totally unjustifiable. In response, the Society insisted that slaves, as slaves, could be converted to Christianity and that on the Codrington Plantations policies to that effect, along with a set of other progressive, ameliorative measures to improve the lives of the slaves, were being implemented. At a third level, were the practitioners on the spot at Codrington Estates whose attitudes and fears echoed those of the other Barbadian planters, attorneys and clergymen. They were prepared to bend only so far to accommodate abolitionist demands.

> With a few of the recommendations, such as that for the religious instruction of the Negroes, the majority of the planters were ready to comply, if only to deflect the fire of the abolitionists. Beyond these limits, however, the slaveholders would not go. There was widespread resistance to the British resolves that marriage between slaves be encouraged, that manumissions be facilitated, that women not be flogged, that the whip not be carried into the field, and that all punishments be witnessed and recorded. The planters felt instinctively that these proposals threatened to subvert the dependence and subordination of the slaves (Bennett 1958: 114).

By the early 1800s, the Society was forced to face the issue of Christian marriages among the slaves on its plantations. If they were to insist that slavery and Christianity could co-exist, then they had no choice but to implement a Christian marriage policy.

The Society attempted to support one of the British government's demands. In the age of Wilberforce and Buxton, the Society could scarcely uphold slavery as a Christian institution, unless it could show that its Negroes lived in Christian marriage. No question was more explosive in the West Indies, where Negro marriages were almost unknown. Only one marriage of slaves was performed in Barbados before 1825, and that by a minister who was later subjected to persecution by his own parishioners. After long avoiding this dangerous subject, the Society had adopted a regulation in 1819 for the encouragement of marriages at Codrington 'in conformity with the rites of the Church of England: as one of the most effectual means of refining and strengthening natural attachments and thereby paving the way to virtuous habits' (Bennett 1958: 116-117).

But the Codrington chaplain, John Pinder, continued to drag his heels. Implying that slaves were not ready to fully embrace the Christian faith, he urged that conversion had to be a slow and gradual, evolutionary process.

Later in 1819, Pinder admitted that he was reluctant to encourage marriages, despite the rule calling for him to do so. 'The Introduction of marriage into a code of Regulations for the religious improvement of a people appeared necessary,' he wrote, 'yet daily experience convinces me, how cautiously I should administer that rite. I have had no application and shall wait for one.' Four years later, ... Pinder was still passively awaiting the day when the Society's slaves would come to him and demand their right to the banns.

Pinder's cautious view of his duty was based not only on his regard for the prejudices of the white community, but also on a well considered theory that the Negroes, like other peoples in the past, must have time to adapt to the full discipline of a Christian culture. They were, he believed, slowly but surely moving toward monogamous unions (Bennett 1958: 117).

This caution and procrastination on the Codrington Plantations became a matter of concern for the Society and, ultimately, a source of acute embarrassment.

The Society sympathised with Pinder's position, but it became increasingly uneasy after 1823 in the face of government policy and British opinion. Pinder, after all, was a Barbadian living among Barbadians, whereas the Society was based in humanitarian Britain. In 1824 the Society's secretary asked the Codrington agents to suggest every means of promoting the marriage rite. Forster Clarke, the agricultural attorney, promised his full cooperation, noting that the slaves who formed permanent attachments produce 'almost without exception numerous families, of the most valuable description of Negroes'. Pinder, on the other hand, discouraged the idea of a marriage campaign, with 'strong temporal inducements to submit to the ceremony'. He would preach on marriage in the pulpit, but he and others must realize that they had to await the slow evolution of a whole people. Notwithstanding the chaplain's advice, the Society recommended in 1825 that its agents encourage slave couples to apply for marriage by holding forth 'such further inducements as superior habitation, and additional comforts of clothing, and security of the customary inheritance to their legitimate children if belonging to the Estate, and any other privileges ... as may appear ... expedient.'

Although Forster Clarke went no further than to promise 'that every mother having six children born in lawful wedlock' should be exempted from further work for the plantations, it was largely owing to Pinder that no marriages had been performed before his resignation at the end of 1826, and that the Society could not take credit for having realized at least the religious aspects of the government's ameliorative program.

It was no wonder, then, that in 1827, when the abolitionists were insistently proclaiming the unwillingness of the planters to lead their slaves toward freedom, hostile eyes were turned on the Codrington plantations. For more than a century these estates had been publicized as the outpost of Anglican humanitarianism in the West Indies, but it was clear to the antislavery leaders that they had given comfort to the enemy at every stage of the attack on the slavery interest (Bennett 1958: 117-118).

It was not until the 1830s, as pressure from the Society became more and more insistent and financial and material inducements were adopted as part of plantation policy, that Christian marriages became a regular feature of slave family life.

No part of the abolitionist criticism had stung the Society more than that on the score of Christian marriage at Codrington. It was a sore point, not only because the Society was a religious corporation, but because it had some claim to having anticipated the government's policy of encouraging marriages. There was little use in asserting that claim, however, as long as the Codrington Negroes rejected the lukewarm blandishments of the scrupulous Pinder. Some relief was afforded the embarrassed Society in May, 1827, when Pinder's successor, the Reverend John Packer, celebrated the marriage of two Codrington Negroes, who were promptly given one of the cottages in the fine new village. The Society was visibly impatient for much more evidence of spiritual progress at Codrington, and in 1828 it again asked Forster Clarke to offer 'some superior advantages' to married slaves 'as a matter of distinction, and proof of their sense of Christian obligation.' In 1829 the Society formally recorded its regret that the chaplain had so little success in promoting marriages, and asked Coleridge and Clarke to suggest 'the most efficient means of encouraging marriages among the Negroes.' The Society promised to cooperate fully, 'even if it should be necessary, at considerable pecuniary sacrifice'. The Barbadian deputies replied by giving every married woman 'of good character' the right to free Saturdays throughout the year, while the rest of the Negroes now had that liberty only on alternate Saturdays.

The Society's demands for results from the marriage campaign became so insistent that Bishop Coleridge, whose own views on the subject were much like Pinder's, was forced to plead, '**you must give us time**.' A few months later, however, he was able to report that he had attended the weddings of three respectable couples who 'had lived faithfully together for many years,' and that the banns had been read for two more couples. In June, 1830, he dutifully visited the plantations and preached on Christian marriage. It had been decided, Coleridge informed the Society, to give the wives freedom before ten o'clock each morning, in place of their extra day of liberty each fortnight. Every year the married slaves increased in privileges and number. There were twenty-two wedded couples in 1932, thirty-three in 1833, and about seventy in 1836 (Bennett 1958: 122-123) (Emphasis in original).

In the final analysis, the measures adopted to restructure slave families met with mixed success. Planter interest in increased fertility and a stable labour force got caught up in abolitionist demands for freedom and conversion to Christianity. And marriage and family morality seems to have had little effect on fertility. For his

Jamaican samples, Higman (1991(1973): 270-271) concluded that conjugal co-residential stability was a more important factor than marriage *per se* and immoral polygamous unions did not reduce fertility. The general conclusion supports the point that amelioration measures lacked success and that, ultimately, it was the slaves themselves, not the planters or the clergy, who made decisions determining their own conjugal relations and family structures (Craton 1991(1979): 234-235). An influential factor seems to have been the slave perception of the benefits of Christian marriage and nuclear family form as indicators of respectability and avenues to the advantages of inheritance and freedom (Craton 1991(1979): 243). But even then, there was no rush to marry when the opportunity to do so became available, a point we shall return to in Chapter IX.

The African heritage

In Chapter II we discussed the debate between Franklin Frazier and Melville Herskovits over the importance of the African heritage in explaining family form among the slaves in the West Indies. At the beginning of this chapter we also discussed the work of Orlando Patterson as he reinforced the interpretations of Frazier by concluding that slavery destroyed family forms, including any patterns that might have been brought over from Africa. We also noted that Mintz and Price reopened the issue by claiming that the slave regime did, in fact, leave room for slaves to redevelop culture and that, in the process of remodelling family forms, they drew on African patterns, albeit at the level of principles and ideas, rather than, as Herskovits believed, specific and concrete structures. Contemporary historians, although quick to point out the difficulties of identifying Africanisms and hesitant about aligning themselves with the speculations involved in adopting such a methodology, have nonetheless called on the African past to explain slave family patterns (Craton (1991(1979): 246).

Polygamy, in particular, has been identified as originating in Africa (Beckles 1989: 118). Craton (1978: 163), however, questioned this by pointing to distinctions in male roles and status, with fathers in the African situation described as the 'focus of power', whereas the circumstances of slavery 'devalued' this role by, among other things, legislating that slave children take the status of their mothers. However, he referred to privileged slaves in Jamaica as practising polygamy 'in African style' (Craton 1978: 211). A second problem with assuming an African source for slave polygamy is the contradictory ethnographic evidence. One would expect, for example, that African-born slaves would be more likely to practise polygamy than the Creoles. But Higman's data for Jamaica indicated that 'Creole polygynists were as numerous as Africans' (Higman 1976: 167) and that Africans tended either to live alone or to form nuclear family households, while the Creole slaves were more often to be found in female-headed households along with their children. He tentatively concluded that this might reflect the African efforts to maintain nuclear families, whereas Creole family life was more disrupted by slavery (Higman 1991(1973): 258). Similar results are reflected in statistical information from the Bahamas which has also indicated that African slaves were more family oriented. Creoles, in comparison, were less likely to live in nuclear families or with conjugal partners and more likely to live alone (Craton 1991(1979): 237). It is possible that for the African slaves the formation of nuclear families was intended as a first stage toward polygamy, but that the structural conditions of slavery curtailed the process.

There is even greater reluctance to conclude that the matrifocal family units identified in Caribbean slavery had their roots in African matrilineal kinship. This is hardly surprising, given the clear differences between the two. Nevertheless, Mac-Donald and MacDonald (1973: 192) have described matrifocality as 'a truncated derivative of matrilineages' and 'a fitting compromise between African principles of lineage and the new environment', giving rise to expectations of a link between the two systems. But ethnographic evidence again lends no support to the assumption of African origin. Indeed, households of mothers and children were most prevalent among both African and Creole slaves in urban areas, most particularly the Creole lighter-skinned domestics and, when nuclear families were established in towns, this was more likely to occur among the Africans. In Trinidad, for example, 17.8 per cent of urban Africans were to be found in nuclear-type families compared with only 5.6 per cent of Creole slaves (Higman 1978: 170-171). Craton (1991(1979): 242) confirmed the point for the Bahamas where Africans and Creoles were equally likely to form nuclear families.

Contemporary scholarship has acknowledged the importance of the African heritage to any explanation of slave family forms, though the methodological difficulties involved in the exercise of tracing Africanisms are now fully recognised. As Higman (1978: 163) put it: 'The necessary data are simply not available.' Conclusions are therefore hesitant and tentative, based on parallels in general beliefs and ideas, rather than specific customs and practices, and acknowledging impact of the structural conditions of slavery, particularly demographic and economic.

> Obviously, the full-scale recreation of any particular African family system was an impossibility. What might be expected, however, is a more subtle differential adaptation of individuals with contrasting African family experiences' (Higman 1978: 167).

Demographic structure

The marital and family patterns developed by slaves have also been attributed to the unnatural demographic structure of the slave population, especially the unbalanced sex ratio, skewed age distribution, low fertility and high infant mortality. We examine these in turn.

Unbalanced ratios between male and female slaves made it difficult to establish conjugal and familial norms, African or otherwise. Higman, for example, contended that in the final analysis, the existence of favourable demographic conditions, primarily balanced sex ratios, determined the extent to which slaves could recreate African family patterns.

> The large extended family occupying a compound was not unique to the Igbo as a familial norm. So the relative success of the Igbo in re-creating their African family system in Trinidad, under conditions of slavery, must be attributed to their absolute numbers (2,200) and their low sex ratio. Similarly, the relative failure of the Malinke (Mandingo) who held similar familial ideals and comprised a considerable contingent in Trinidad (1,098), must be explained by their high sex ratio. It must be concluded therefore, that the demographic selectivity of the slave trade determined very largely the extent to which particular groups of Africans could fulfill their familial ideals or norms. It is, however, equally important to notice that when the demographic conditions were relatively favourable, as in the case of the Igbo, slaves did establish a variety of family forms, reflecting in some measure their particular African cultural heritage. Such favourable conditions were simply a rarity (Higman 1978: 174) (Emphasis in original).

Demographic conditions are also said to have influenced nuclear family development. To put it simply, in situations where slaves could not pair off one-to-one, promiscuity and conjugal abnormality were assumed to be inevitable and, conversely, in situations where sex ratios were balanced, nuclear families could and did develop. It has also been suggested that slave conjugal and family patterns were affected by unbalanced sex ratios in the white population. White women seem to have been very reluctant to migrate to what were perceived as the physically uncomfortable and culturally barren circumstances of life in the Caribbean. The preponderance of white men and scarcity of white women encouraged trans-racial sexual relationships with black and coloured women. These, in turn, led to the development of matrifocal residential units from which male partners and fathers were absent.

The age distribution of slave populations has also been perceived as influential in family structure and stability. For one thing, since only a minority of slaves lived long enough, it is obvious that extended three-generational families were uncommon, especially in the early phase of the slave period. According to Higman (1976: 162), ageing slaves, especially those over forty years of age, commonly lived alone. Early and frequent deaths were also bound to have negatively affected family stability. Citing the influence of age as well as uneven sex ratios, Craton compared the Rolle Plantation in the Bahamas with Worthy Park in Jamaica and concluded that of prime importance in explaining the higher levels of nuclear family formation, as well as higher fertility, among the slaves in the former were the more even sex balance and favourable age distribution.

In the final analysis, slave family life of all kinds, whether matrifocal, nuclear or extended, was severely constrained by low levels of fertility and by excessively high rates of infant mortality. Even if we acknowledge variations of circumstance according to time and place, this general picture remains unchanged. For the British Caribbean on the whole, even in the later days of slavery when conditions were ameliorated, only approximately two-thirds of potential mothers actually gave birth and very few women gave birth to more than three children. On the Worthy Park Estate 'pitifully few slaves did, or could, have children' and 'as many as a third of the Worthy Park slave women may have had no children at all' (Craton 1978: 191). Even in the exceptional circumstances of Rolle's plantation in the Bahamas, which exhibited a more balanced 'unslavelike' demographic structure, only 65.8 per cent of women in the age range 15-49 years were recorded as mothers and the number of children per mother averaged only three (Craton 1991 (1979): 231-232).

Even when slave infants did manage to see the light of day their chances of survival were very slim. Accurate estimates of infant mortality rates are impossible to acquire as, more often than not, slave owners did not bother to record infant deaths, still less miscarriages, abortions and stillbirths. Nevertheless, what information we do have suggests extremely high rates, especially from tetanus (Morrissey 1989: 107-108). In general, infant mortality rates have been estimated at between 40 and 50 per cent of all live births (Craton 1978: 86-88, Goveia 1965: 124, Kiple 1984: 117). It would appear that, for virtually the whole of the slave period, neither the slave owners nor the slaves themselves showed much interest in slave fertility and child-bearing. It was not until the amelioration years that slave owners made conscious and sustained efforts to enhance the natural increase of slave populations, not only by encouraging nuclear family formation but also by direct demographic engineering. Deliberate policies were implemented to balance sex ratios, prolong life, increase fertility and improve the chances of infant survival. Statistical information on slave fertility and mortality rates is scattered and unreliable. Nevertheless, 'it appears doubtful whether these efforts influenced in any way population movements during the last years of slavery' (Roberts 1975: 4), except perhaps in Barbados where the black population experienced sustained growth from the beginning of the nineteenth century, mainly as a result of declining infant mortality rates (Kiple 1984: 114,118-119, Beckles 1989: 110-113).

Economic circumstances and options

A final perspective which has been adopted to explain Caribbean slave family forms concerns the specific economic circumstances in which the slaves were located and the choices which they made within these circumstances. Two variables, namely the importance of provision ground production and the opportunities for female economic autonomy have provided the main focus for these arguments. We examine each in turn.

From a feminist materialist perspective, Morrissey (1989: 117) put us in the picture by contrasting the situation in the Caribbean with that of the Southern United States.

> Slaves in the United States had more reasons to have children, given the economic conditions of southern plantations. With a stricter gender division of labour, males controlled much of the income-generating potential of household economies. Women had both a measure of economic security and material incentives to bear children to provide assistance in enhancing household incomes. The construction and maintenance of kin connections were also supported by child rearing, although slave-holders broke up families and kinship systems with frequency, frustrating slaves' efforts to keep family ties strong. United States slave owners encouraged childbirth to reproduce the slave population, adopting measures to ease birth and preserve infant life ....

> In contrast, eighteenth-century Caribbean slave owners did not welcome slave children and did little to conserve their health and welfare. Conditions of pregnancy, birth, and early infant life contributed to maternal and child mortality. Under these circumstances women had little reason to value children.

The situation changed towards the end of slavery. In those Caribbean territories such as Jamaica, where the allotment system became well-established and institutionalised, a gender division of labour for the growing and marketing of provisions by the slaves could best be organised by the formation of nuclear families. As Morrissey explained,

> women's best opportunity for acquiring income in the agricultural setting often lay with a nuclear family. Although her control of land and resources was less in this household arrangement than when heading a family, her access to male labour was greater, and, given males' opportunities in skilled and artisanal labour and other forms of income accumulation, male incorporation into the household was generally desirable .... West Indian slave women probably sought many means to institutionalize male help, and, with the sale of males and high mortality, creation of co-resident ties was undoubtedly the most flexible and therefore significant strategy (Morrissey 1989: 93).

Even then, land was scarce and the economic circumstances therefore not conducive to the re-establishment of polygamy.

Population density discouraged African polygamy, as it most certainly did in the West Indian islands where land for petty cultivation was scarce. The poor economic position of slave men made it difficult for them to amass bridewealth. Only men with resources had the means to acquire wives; only men with land in settings with the possibility of land expansion needed multiple wives. Therefore the structural conditions for polygamy were rarely present in Caribbean slave societies. Moreover, women had little incentive to join polygamous families unless the man's resources were great enough to raise his wives' standard of living well above what the estate provided. There was little exclusively female farming in the West Indies, a condition highly associated with polygamy in West Africa and suggestive again that polygamy was only occasional among Caribbean slaves (Morrissey 1989: 90).

In contrast, in territories like Barbados and the Leeward Islands, which imported or relied on estate-grown food, there was little incentive to form nuclear families. Morrissey (1989: 94) summarised the position from the perspective of the female slave:

> Women's economic interests may explain mother-child families in areas of food importation and estate cultivation and nuclear families among provision-growing slaves. With scant opportunities to earn cash or resources in kind, relatively more was available to a woman and her children if no adult man took a share. The labour that male field slaves could contribute was unnecessary where provision grounds, kitchen gardens, and marketing chances were scarce. And what men absorbed, at least in food, was generally greater than what was consumed by women and children. On the other hand, male slaves of high status must have been particularly desirable companions in those areas with few opportunities for women to enhance their economic and social positions. Although there is no evidence to buttress this point, it is likely that polygamous units flourished among upper-strata males in such settings. With few alternatives in land or trade, men of prestige could effectively use women as sources of greater status and authority, although women's utility for the men's income expansion was limited if the men were landless. Powerless economically, women might gladly share with another woman the advantage of liaison with a high-status male.

In urban areas and among the coloured domestics on the plantations matrifocality prevailed. Higman (1991(1973): 258-259) recognised this as he identified households dominated by women from which slave males were absent. There seems to have been a positive advantage for women in heading their own households and deliberately avoiding co-residential conjugal unions with male slaves whose presence might actually compromise their personal and economic autonomy.

> Domestic workers, especially in cities and towns, were the only female slaves able to **improve** their economic position autonomously. These female slaves had independent access to income and little need for male labour or contributions to overall resources. Their houses and household belongings were arranged for them. Moreover, the presence of a slave 'husband' may have discouraged white male advances, the most important potential source of income and freedom for slave women (Morrissey 1989: 95) (Emphasis in original).

Conclusion

In many ways, the approaches taken and the explanations proposed by social historians for the analysis of slave conjugal and family patterns parallel those of structural functional anthropology dealing with contemporary family forms, which we discussed in Chapter II. Both disciplinary perspectives were dominated by ideas of family abnormality and subsequently preoccupied with the search for nuclear families located within households and a determination to find them at some stage in the life cycle even if this meant transposing dynamic perspectives on to synchronic data. Both also perceived family patterns as constrained by forces in the immediate socio-economic environment, namely the unnatural demographic structures of slavery or of contemporary migration and the severe economic conditions of enslavement or contemporary economic poverty and marginality. Both rejected explanations from the past, especially the African heritage and were concerned with social structure, not culture. The individual disappeared, though perhaps for different reasons. As we mentioned before, early structural functional models ignore individual choice and self-determination while, for the historians, the invisibility of the slaves and their families was likely to be due to the absence of historical records on those aspects of their lives which were not directly relevant to the plantation enterprise.

Demographic reductionism in slave family studies has been criticised by Morrissey (1991(1986): 275):

> It has been argued that nuclear families were sometimes a demographic possibility: for example, where sex ratios were even or populations stable and isolated .... Thus, it is suggested that in the absence of material and ideological constraints, and given the demographic opportunity, nuclear families developed. This explanation is so broad as to be nearly tautological: nuclear families can exist, therefore they do exist. It does not offer in sufficiently specific terms the conditions that unite a variety of New World national and plantation settings that produced nuclear families.

As we saw in the previous chapter, anthropological explanations grounded in economics have also been critiqued, whether they are phrased in terms of the adverse impact of poverty and unemployment or the adaptive response of resilient families to these conditions. It must, however, be less easy to reject the explanations of slave kinship from the perspective of economic materialism. Nevertheless, even under these tight social and economic parameters, humanity, identity and culture were not entirely eliminated. Although most of the slaves' history died with them and the task of reconstructing their lives has been described as 'searching for the invisible man' (Craton 1978), historians persevere in their investigations of how slaves re-created and remodelled family ideology and practice (Higman 1984), calling on their African heritage and making choices and decisions even within the severe economic constraints of slavery.

READINGS

Orlando Patterson

MATING PATTERNS, PARENT-CHILD RELATIONS, KINSHIP, AND THE WHITE OUT-GROUP

So far we have been concerned mainly with the socialization of the slave into his work situation. We must now consider some of the more informal aspects of the slaves' development and the agents of socialization primarily responsible for their formation. Our observations will relate mainly to the Creole slaves. It should be remembered, however, that the African slaves had no other choice than to fall into the patterns of behaviour they found on the island.

(a) Sexual Behaviour and Mating Patterns

Slavery in Jamaica led to the breakdown of all forms of social sanctions relating to sexual behaviour, and with this, to the disintegration of the institution of marriage both in its African and European forms. According to one missionary 'the sanctions of marriage were almost unknown' and the institution was largely ridiculed by the slaves. 'Every estate on the island — every negro hut — was a common brothel; every female a prostitute; and every man a libertine'.[1] This breakdown of sexual mores and the institution of marriage among the Negroes occurred all over the New World.[2] But in no other area was the degree of sexual abandonment so great as in Jamaica. The reason for this is to be found largely in the similar breakdown of such mores among the dominant white group which we have examined in detail in our chapter on the whites. The scarcity of white women and the absence of moral sanctions led to a ruthless exploitation of the female slave. Sometimes this exploitation was crude and direct, being against the will of the woman, who would be 'compelled under pain of corporal punishment to yield implicit obedience to the will of the master'.[3] Another witness stated that 'if an overseer sends for a girl for such purposes she is obliged to come, or else flogged'.[4] Whitely was told by a book-keeper that he had had twelve 'Negro wives' in six months; and when he refused to participate in the custom of the country he was regarded 'with mingled contempt and suspicion'.[4] The male partner dared not complain if his 'wife' was called upon to satisfy the lust of the overseer, for if he did all he could expect was a flogging 'couched under the name of some other misdemeanour'.[5]

Quite apart from this exploitation by the whites, the sex-ratio of the slave population would inevitably have led to promiscuity. We have already discussed this problem in an earlier chapter. Purely biological reasons, therefore, prompted the female slave to promiscuity. The sex life of the creole Negroes began quite early; from one report they began to have sexual intercourse 'even at the age of nine, and with a multitude of men ....'.[6] Phillippo found that they had 'sacrificed all pretensions to virtue before they had attained their fourteenth year' and that 'hundreds were known to have become mothers before they had entered their teens'.[7] Another missionary also found that 'the men go astray as much as the women, and girls of fourteen are said to be common instruments of pleasure'.[8]

Where young girls resisted they were raped, many cases of which were reported by Mahon. Particularly gruesome was his account of the rape of an eleven–year–old girl by the attorney of Richmond Estate.[9] But rape was often unnecessary since the slave Negress soon gave in to the overwhelming pressures and made the best of its rewards, for, 'not only did these connections exempt the poor female from the toils of field labour, but it gave her many enviable exemptions in other respects, and in her own eyes especially raised her to a fancied superiority among the other slaves'.[10] Yet, within this seeming chaos, one may discern some pattern of mating and sexual behaviour. This pattern fell into five basic types of associations; prostitution; unstable unions; stable unions; multiple associations; and monogamous associations which were sometimes made legal. Each will be discussed in turn and then their relationships analyzed.

(i) Prostitution

Prostitution, in the strict sense of this term, was widespread. Long found the women, 'in general, common prostitutes' practising frequent abortions 'in order that they may continue their trade without loss of time, or hindrance of business'.[11] Cooper attributed a great part of the natural decline of the slave population to the prevalence of prostitution among the young women. On the estates there were well known pimps who procured the prostitutes for strangers, usually whites, who wished their services. According to Cooper, these pimps were usually the estate mid-wives.[12] And an overseer tells us that 'when a white man is inclined to get a mongrel or black girl for a night the usual mode is to hire a boy or old woman to procure one'.[13] But often the mother, or mistress, of a prostitute acted as her pimp. On the estates the mother of an attractive prostitute could be a powerful figure:

> Those gypsies (i.e. the prostitutes' mothers) have a wonderful ascendancy over men and have injured many, both powerful and subordinate; the poor slaves on a plantation are obliged to pay them as much adoration as the Portuguese, the Hostess or Virgin Mary, for the government of the cowskin depends in a great measure on their smiles and frowns.[14]

Prostitution was most rife, however, in the towns. Here there were many white men having no authority over slave women — clerks, sailors, soldiers, artisans and the like — who were obliged to satisfy their sexual needs in this manner. Many of these town prostitutes were free coloured women, and the majority of enslaved domestics in the towns were expected to support themselves in this manner.[15] Leslie wrote of the 1720s that some of the town Negresses 'go neat enough, but these are the Favourites of young Squires, who keep them for a certain use'.[16] It was common for the mistress of slaves in the towns to live off the immoral earnings of their slave prostitutes many of whom they trained specifically for this purpose. Moreton informs us that 'Mongrel wrenches from their youth are taught to be whores: you cannot affront one of them more than to give any hint of her being dull and unskilled in the magical art'.[17] Lewis mentions an old watchman on his estate who hired a coloured mistress from a brown man in the mountains at the rate of £30 per year. But this was a very unusual case, especially with respect to the woman being coloured. The latter were notorious for their contempt not only for black men, but men of their own colour.[18]

(ii) Unstable Unions

This type of association was perhaps the most common, especially among the young adult slaves. According to one missionary:

> They were frequently at a loss to determine which was the proper husband or wife. For instance, a female wishes to become a member of society; but was the man with whom she was then living the first she had agreed with? No; she had lived with many others; and the first man with whom she was connected had many more women since he left her; and perhaps was living with one at that time by whom he had several children ....[19]

Phillippo also mentions the 'frequent interruptions' to their alliances and gives an account of a quaint divorce ceremony in which the couple mutually divided a cotta (i.e. a head-pad made of plantain leaves) before separating.[20] But there is no evidence of this ceremony being widespread, and Edwards' remark that these unions were formed 'without ceremony and dissolved without romance' seems to have described the general pattern.

(iii) Stable Unions and (iv) Multiple Associations

These two categories will be considered together since the former usually existed within the wider framework of the latter. Among the older and more prosperous male slaves (boilers, coopers, smiths, other skilled mechanics, headmen, and the like) a stable relationship with one woman was established, in conjunction with a series of loose relationships with other 'wives' who were not only changed frequently, but were permitted to have other lovers. It was this combination of quasi-polygyny and quasi-polyandry which so shocked most of the contemporary observers. Long, who wrote before the abolition movement began, has left us the most penetrating account of these relationships:

> They are all married (in their way) to a husband, or wife, *pro tempore*, or have other family connexions, in almost every parish throughout the island; so that one of them, perhaps, has six or more husbands or wives in several different places; by this means they find support when their own lands fail them; and houses of call and refreshment whenever they are upon their travels ... perhaps becuase of the whole number of wives or husbands, one only is the object of particular, steady attachment; the rest, although called wives, are only a sort of occasional concubines, or drudges, whose assistance the husband claims in the culture of his land, sale of his produce, and so on; rendering to them reciprocal acts of friendships, when they are in want ....[21]

The economic aspects of these relationships, especially as they related to the cultivation of provision grounds, was obviously important. Coor said much the same in 1790 although he does not emphasize the reciprocal nature of these contingent economic factors:

> It was not looked upon as anyways disadvantageous to an estate for the men to have a number of wives, from one, two, three or four, according as they had property to maintain them. What I mean by property is provisions on their little spots of ground ....[22]

The pattern did not change markedly in the 19th century. In 1823 Reid observed that, 'The husband has commonly two or three wives, and the wives as many husbands which they mutually change for each other.'[23]

It is important to understand that while these quasi-polygynous relations of the males were synchronic, the countervailing quasi-polyandrous relations were generally diachronic or sequential. As Bromwell pointed out, 'Sometimes a man had several wives at the same time and the woman had many husbands *successively*, so that almost every child had a different father.'[24]

(v) Stable Monogamous and Legal Marriages

The attitude of the slave toward stable monogamous unions and (during the nineteenth century) legal marriage, tended to vary over the span of his life. Young slaves generally ridiculed the idea of stable unions of this kind. Despite his efforts, De La Beche 'could not prevail upon a single pair to marry' on his own estate.[25] Many women disliked marriage because it entailed extra work and felt it silly to be confined to one man.[26] The apparent contempt for marriage was greatest in the towns. Bickell recalls the case of a young mechanic who wished to get married but who 'had been much laughed and scoffed at by many in the town'. After the ceremony 'the rabble followed, shouting and jeering as if the newly married pair had committed some dreadful crime'.[27]

Paradoxically, one of the main reasons for the overt contempt shown to the slave who got married was the high status associated with legal marriage on the part of the slave themselves, who 'regard the marriage tie with a reverence and respect approaching to superstition'.[28]

Because marriage was so rare in the island, and because it was practised mainly by the wealthy proprietors, it inevitably became associated with the privileged, and one can well understand why the slave would jeer at one of his fellows partaking in this high caste ceremony. Marriage, was 'out of the question' even for subordinate whites, and Walker observed that 'rank and privilege, which are strongly marked in every thing, seem to turn marriage into a distinction somewhat of the nature of nobility and to reserve it in general for the proprietors and leading men of the country'.[29] It was different, however, with the old couples. Even before the possibility of legal marriage in the nineteenth century, it was common for the old Negroes to settle down in stable monogamous unions.[30]

In the nineteenth century, when the laws made it possible, such old couples sometimes got legally married, often under pressure from the missionaries; indeed 'the great amount of marriages appeared to be of this kind'.[31] In such cases, respect for the age of the couple and their proven affections, led to less skepticism and mockery from the younger slaves.

(vi) A Developmental View

So far, for the sake of clarity, we have adopted a static approach in our discussion of the five types of mating patterns found among the slaves; seeing them as distinct entities without any ordered relation to each other. In fact, these different patterns are really not distinct categories, but phases in the development of the mating habits of the creole slaves over the entire span of their lives.[32]

We may summarize this cycle of mating in the following manner. In general, there existed a system of mating which was a combination of a synchronic quasi-polygyny and a sequential quasi-polyandry. In the case of the female slaves, regular sexual activity began quite early in life with sporadic relations not far removed from prostitution.[33] Later, the plantation Negroes progressed to the phase of being either one of the temporary wives of an older and more prosperous male slave, or the lover of one or more younger males, or — more often — both. Next, she entered the phase in which she became the 'wife' of a young adult male in a series of exclusive but unstable unions. Finally, in middle or late middle age, now rapidly dwindling in attractiveness — since, naturally, women aged rapidly under the brutalizing impact of slavery — more than likely burdened with children and in need of some security, she settled down to become what Long described as 'the object of particular steady attachment' of an elderly male slave. With old age, this phase developed into an ordinary monogamous union as the male partner gave up his quasi-polygynous activities, and was sometimes legalized. Many women experienced a fifth phase which may be described as matriarchal. Often, this matriarchal phase was brought about by the death of the 'husband'. But even where the final 'husband' was present his authority dwindled beside the influence of his 'wife' in their household. This was due to the fact that none of the children in their household would have been his own since his union with his last 'wife' began after her child-bearing period, and his own children would be living with their mothers (his former wives), often on another estate. The old woman, on the other hand, would command all the respect with which (as we shall show below) children treated their mother.

The pattern was simpler for males. Regular sexual activity began at a much later date.[34] Early sexual experiences were highly irregular and took place with much younger women then going through their sporadic phase. Later, these men generally became the lovers of the temporary wives of older men. Next, they became partners in unstable unions and, after this, established a stable relationship with one particular woman while being engaged to several temporary 'wives', the number of which depended on their economic position.[35]

(b) Household, parent-child relations and kinship

So far we have considered the sexual and mating patterns of the creole slave. We must now examine how this pattern affected parental authority as well as the other authority-figures and relations who functioned in the socialization of the slave.

It is to be noted, first of all, that the nuclear family could hardly exist within the context of slavery. Such families were actively discouraged by the masters, and throughout the seventeenth and eighteenth centuries ran the risk of being brutally severed at any time by the creditors of their masters. Furthermore, even where such families did develop, the male head could not assert his authority as a husband or as a father. His 'wife' was the property of another, and as Cooper pointed out, 'the concerns of the family must be to her matters of very inferior moment, compared with the work of her owner. He insists on all the prime of her strength being devoted to his business; it is only after the toils, the indecencies, the insults and miseries of a day spent in the gang that she can think of doing anything to promote the comfort of her household'.[36] Slavery abolished any real social distribution between males and females.[37] The woman was expected to work just as hard; she was as indecently exposed and was punished just as severely. In the eyes of the master she was equal to the man as long as her strength was the same as his. In addition to this, the system gave her many opportunities to exploit her sex to her own advantage. Since her sexual services were in great demand by both blacks and whites she often found herself in intimate association with the white masters. If she became the overseer's housekeeper she could wield great power not only in the domestic affairs of the household of the great house, but also in the general running of the estate. We have already seen how even mothers of attractive prostitutes could exert considerable influence.

The net result of all this was the complete demoralization of the Negro male. Incapable of asserting his authority either as husband or father, his sexual difference in no way recognized in his work situation by the all powerful outgroup, the object of whatever affection he may possess, beaten, abused and often raped before his very eyes, and with his female partner often in closer link with the source of all power in the society, it is no wonder that the male slave eventually came to lose all pretensions to masculine pride and to develop the irresponsible parental and sexual attitudes that are to be found even today. 'Patent submission to the lash and manly feelings' as an abolitionist observed, 'are incongruous'.[38]

The woman became, then, the dominant, often the sole factor in the rearing of the creole slave during the eighteenth and nineteenth centuries, although there is some evidence that during the seventeenth century, when the policy of buying an equal number of males and females was followed, parental authority may have been shared between father and mother. Husbands certainly seem to have had more authority over their wives then, being 'very much concerned if they proved adulterous'.[39]

Long also wrote of the strong affection of Negro mothers for their children:

> In their care for their children some are remarkably exemplary .... They exercise a kind of sovereignty over their children which never ceases during life; chastising them sometimes with such severity; and seeming to hold filial obedience in much higher estimation than conjugal fidelity.[41]

He was able to detect, however, a certain degree of ambivalence in the attitude and treatment by Negro mothers of their offspring. In a later passage he tells us that 'they in general love their children, though sometimes they treat them with a rigour bordering on "cruelty". We have already seen that many women considered having children a great burden, especially since few masters bothered to make any extra provisions for them.

This combination of extreme cruelty and great love and affection for children is to be found among Negro mothers in Jamaica even today.[42] Her cruelty to her children was partly the displacement of aggression and hatred for the driver and overseer; partly her own ignorant way of inculcating respect and loyalty in her children. It should not hide the fact of her strong maternal affection and love, which struck many observers as 'astonishing'.[43] This love of children was also expressed in the willingness to adopt other slaves' children despite the burden of her own, many moving instances of which were mentioned by Lewis.[44]

Children were also seen by their parents as a form of security. In the first place, they were regarded by their mothers as their future supporters in old age. We have already referred to the wretched existence of those slaves who had no younger relations to provide for them. Secondly, the mother gained the labour of her child in working her provision ground and later, might even control the extra provision ground given to her children when they had attained adulthood. Thus slave mothers did everything to keep their children within their household and to discourage any attempt at forming permanent unions outside, one nineteenth century writer stating that to be the main reason for the lack of stable unions among the slaves, some mothers thus controlling their children 'sometimes to the age of forty years and even after'.[45] Such cases however were the exceptions rather than the rule.[46]

The respect for the mother was extended to all elders and these no doubt played some part in the upbringing of the slave. Elders were always addressed with a prefix to their names as a mark of respect. Indeed, something of the kinship terminology of West African society survived among the Jamaican slaves.

Lewis noted that:

> Among the Negroes it is almost tantamount to an affront to address by the name without affixing some term of relationship such as 'grannie' or 'uncle' or 'cousin'. My Cornwall boy, George, told me one day that '"Uncle Sully"' wanted to speak to massa"'. 'Why, is Sully your uncle George?' 'No massa; me only call him so for honour'.[47]

It was customary for persons of their parents' generation to be addressed with the prefix 'Ta' or 'Ma' (Father or Mother)[48] or in other cases, 'Uncle, Aunty, Tatta, Mama, Sister, Boda', even where no obvious blood relation existed.[49]

NOTES

1. J. M. Phillippo, *Jamaica, Its Past and Present State*, 1843, p. 218.

2. See for the U.S., F. G. Frazier's *The Negro Family in America*; also Kardiner's *The Mark of Oppression*, for Brazil, G. Freyre's The Masters and the Slaves.

3. Cooper, *Facts Illustrative of the Condition of the Negro Slaves in Jamaica*, pp. 13-14.

4. Evidence of Cook, Select Committee on Slave Trade, 1790-91.

5. H. Whiteley, *Three Months in Jamaica*, 1832.

6. Evidence of H. Coor, *op. cit.*

7. Report of Stephen Fuller (assisted by Messrs. Long and Chisholme) to the Committee of the Privy Council, 1788, in B. T. 6: 10, p. 23.

8. Phillippo, *op. cit.*, p. 42.

9. Cooper, *op. cit.*, p.42.

10. B. Mahon, *Jamaica Plantership*, pp. 69-71.

11. B. Lucock, *Jamaica: Enslaved and Free*, p. 122.

12. E. Long, *op.cit.*, Vol. 2, p. 436.

13. Cooper, *op. cit.*, p. 42.

14. Moreton, *op. cit.*, p. 132.

15. Ibid, p. 127.

16. Evidence of Mark Cook, Select Committee, on Slave Trade, 1790-91.

17. C. Leslie, *A New History of Jamaica*, p. 35.

18. Moreton, *op. cit.,* p. 129.

19. Sexual intercourse between coloured women and their male counterparts was so rare that Long stated categorically that they were incapable of having children together. Bickell wrote in 1825 that 'such is the contempt with which the men of colour are treated ... and such is the poverty of most of them that most of the brown women prefer being kept by a white man to being the wife of a man of her own colour and rank ...' (The W.I. as they are, etc., p. 112-13). This contempt for men darker than themselves was universal. Lewis wrote that, 'The difference of colour ... is a fault which no mulatto will pardon; nor can the separation of castes in India be more rigidly observed than that of complexional shades among the Creoles. My black page Cubina, is married: I told him that I hoped he had married a pretty woman: why had he not married Mary Wiggins? He seemed quite shocked at the very idea, 'Oh massa, me black, Mary Wiggins sambo; that not allowed'., p. 79.

20. Statement of Mr Bromwell; quoted in R. Watson's *A Defence of the Wesleyan Methodist Missions in the West Indies,* 1817.

21. Phillippo, *op. cit.,* p. 219.

22. E. Long, *op. cit.,* Vol. 2, p. 414.

23. Evidence of Henry Coor, *op. cit.*

24. *An Address to the Right Hon. Geo. Canning on the Present State of This Island and Other Matters, by Denis Reid, 1823.*

25. Evidence of Mr Bromwell, quoted in Watson, *op. cit.*

26. De La Beche, *op. cit.,* pp. 17-18.

27. Cooper, *op. cit.,* p. 9.

28. Bickell, *op. cit.,* p. 93.

29. G. Jackson, *A Memoir of the Rev John Jenkins, Wesleyan Missionary in Jamaica* (1832), p. 120.

30. J. Walker, *Letters on the West Indies,* pp. 165-66.

31. Bryan Edwards, *op. cit.,* Vol. 2, p. 98.

32. James Kelly, *op. cit.,* p. 45.

33. Note that the social anthropologist, R. T. Smith, in his study of the Br. Guianese Negro family (see *The Negro Family in Br. Guiana*) and in his general discussion of the West Indian family (see for ex. 'The Family in the Caribbean') analyses the 'development cycle of the household' in three papers.

34. With female slaves in the towns prostitution remained the dominant pattern for much of their lives.

35. Thus the turnover of each generation of sexually available females would be much faster than that of sexually mature males, a factor which no doubt played an important part in redressing the imbalance of the sexes.

36. While I am in no way suggesting a historical link, an analogy between the mating patterns of Jamaican slave society and the Lele of Kasai, studied by Mary Douglas, is very suggestive. While there was an equal ratio of males to females, the extreme monopolization of the young women by a small minority of old men, led to a situation bearing a remarkable resemblance to the Jamaican pattern. There was the same combination of polygyny and polyandry; extensive marital unfaithfulness on the part of wives who had lovers from among the young men; there were village wives not very different from the slaves prostitutes; and women began their sexual lives at a much earlier age than men, thus reducing the imbalance. See Mary Douglas, *The Lele of Kasai.*

37. Cooper, *op. cit.,* pp. 45-6.

38. George Jackson, *A Memoir of the Rev John Jenkins, Wesleyan Missionary in Jamaica,* pp. 113-14.

39. The Negro Slave in the Br. Colonies, by an Abolitionist.

40. Sir Hans Sloane, *op. cit.*, Introduction.

41. Long, *op. cit.*, Vol. 2, p. 414.

42. See M. Kerr, *Personality and Conflict in Jamaica*, p. 45; see also Judith Blake's *Family Structure in Jamaica*, pp. 58-62.

43. Beckford, *The Situation of the Negroes in Jamaica*, 1788, p. 24.

44. Lewis, *op. cit.*, p. 176.

45. Anon, 'Notes in the Defence of the ... Colonies', in *Jamaica Journal*, Vol. 2, No. 8, 1824.

46. The author overstates his argument to the point of contradicting himself. If it was true that young adult Negroes were dominated by their partners this would imply that families were universal and closely knit, the absence of which being exactly what he was trying to explain. His arguments make sense, however, if he was referring to female dominated household units. But it was only in a minority of such cases that mothers enclosed the provision grounds of their children since the master often intervened and re-allocated these grounds. See later chapter on provision grounds.

*This same pattern of what Edith Clarke has called the 'cycle of reciprocal dependence' still exists today, see her, *My Mother Who Fathered Me*, p. 163.

47. Lewis, *op. cit.*, p. 258.

48. Edwards, *op. cit.*, Vol. 2, p. 99.

49. Moreton, *op. cit.*, p. 159.

*Radcliffe-Brown (in his introduction to *African Systems of Kinship and Marriage*) wrote that 'There is a widespread custom of privileged familiarity between grandparents and grandchildren' in Africa based on the 'structural principle that 'one generation is replaced in course of time by the generation of their grandparent'. Now this very custom was noted by Lewis who wrote: 'Neptune came this morning to request that the name of his son, Oscar, might be changed for that of Julius, which (it seems) had been that of his own father. The child, he said, had always been weakly and he was persuaded that ill-health proceed from his deceased grandfather's being displeased because it had not been called after him' (Lewis, p. 349). Not only did the African custom of naming the grandchild after the grandparent survive, but also what Radcliffe-Brown described as 'another aspect of the same principle', namely, 'the merging of alternate generations' in which 'a man with his father's father, his son's sons and his "brother" in the classificatory sense form a social division over against his "fathers" and "sons", who constitute another division'. The terminological aspect of this principle survives even today among the Jamaican peasantry. The term 'granny' is used universally among them to designate the grandmother. Yet Cassidy has discovered that a '"granny" is not the grandparent among the folk, but a grandchild'. He also tells us that 'This is true, at least, among the Accompong Maroons.' It is well known that the Maroons exhibit the greatest degree of African cultural survivals among Jamaican peasant Communities.

S. Mintz and R. Price

KINSHIP AND SEX ROLES

We have been suggesting that a firm grounding in what is known as the past of Afro-American peoples can enhance our understanding of their present, much as the study of the present provides clues that can be carried fruitfully into archival research. Some additional emphasis on the uses of the past is called for, certainly not to the exclusion of ethnography, but as an essential corollary, particularly in the case of Afro-American cultures. Given the tension ridden initial situations in which enslaved Africans found themselves, we believe that one promising strategy — though by no means the only one — for plotting the rise of Afro-American cultures would be to focus on the beginnings, from which we can work forward, rather than simply to extrapolate backward on the basis of perceived similarities with Old World cultures.

If we force ourselves to consider in all its complexity the initial situation of Africans in any New World colony, few of the 'historical' explanations offered by scholars for current Afro-American cultural or social forms are likely to turn out to be fully adequate. In exploring the choices people actually faced during the formative years of these cultures, a broad range of variables must be taken into account from tribal composition of the slave masses or the specific and highly differentiated social conditions in a particular colony at a given time, to the geographical distribution in Africa of particular beliefs and practices. In terms of our current knowledge, it seems reasonable to expect that almost any sub-system of an Afro-American culture — whether music, speech or religion — would be highly syncretistic in terms of its diverse African origins, as well as in terms of inputs from European (and often other) sources; and we must expect it to possess a built-in internal dynamism and a marked adaptiveness to changing social conditions as well. This implies that the task of reconstructing the history of any such system or institutional complex is immensely challenging but fraught with pitfalls.

With all this in mind, we nevertheless would like to sketch in a partial outline of such an enterprise, for no other reasons than that it may help to bring some of our programmatic generalities to life and even, perhaps, to point to some promising lines for future inquiry.

For many years, the controversy about the proper theories and methods to be used in the study of Afro-American culture history centred on 'the Negro family', and much of this debate is probably familiar to the reader. It may be useful, therefore, to focus on this particular institutional complex, in order to highlight the concepts that may distinguish our general approach from more traditional conceptualization.

Melville J. Herskovits and E. Franklin Frazier were the major protagonists in the ongoing 'debate' over the Negro family, each calling upon history in the effort to explain current social forms, but with very different ideas about the nature of the Afro-American historical experience (see, for example, Frazier 1942 and Herskovits 1943). Herskovits, who tended to treat social structure as an aspect of 'culture' stressed the ultimate African origin of New World family forms. Discussing Haiti, for example, he asserted that 'the institution of plural marriage ... is obviously African' (1971[1937]: 260); in Trinidadian marriage forms, he saw 'a translation [reinterpretation], in terms of the monogamic pattern of European mating, of basic West African forms that operate within a polygynous frame' (Herskovits and Herskovits 1947: 293); and numerous similar statements could be cited.

Frazier, in contrast, viewed the Afro-American past in terms of its relevance for the understanding of contemporary institutions, as beginning only with the process of enslavement and transport. In one of his most forceful statements on the matter, he wrote that 'probably never before in history has a people been so nearly stripped of its social heritage as were the Negroes who were brought to America' (1939: 20); elsewhere, he argued that images of the African past were merely 'Forgotten Memories' (1939: Chapter 1). For Frazier, Afro-Americans were culturally deprived, frustrated Americans; and another sociologist, applying Frazier's ideas to the Jamaican slave, would conclude that his 'ideals and attitudes and morals and manners were more or less those of his masters' (Simey 1946: 49). Whether in the United States or in Jamaica, if the institutions of Afro-Americans were not identical to those of the American mainstream, it was according to this view only becuase of a long and terrible history of oppression.

Though such a thumbnail sketch of the Herskovits-Frazier positions may overstate the contrast between these views of Afro-Americans, the contrast is no less real. In one view, Afro-Americans were essentially Africans, whose commitments to their ancestral past made them culturally different from other Americans; in the other view, they were merely Americans who had not been able to acculturate fully becuase of their oppression. Clearly, this controversy is far from dead, and a great deal of argument continues as to whether Afro-Americans have a different culture or different cultures, or are simply the victims of deprivation. Yet the polemical nature of these arguments, as well as their strongly political flavor, has led many Caribbeanists to reject out of hand historical considerations in analyzing family institutions. One such authority claims that historical approaches 'only seek to explain the existence of Caribbean family systems as a general type' (Otterbein 1965. 66), and another that 'historical, cultural, structural, and psychological theories developed with such care to "explain" the peculiar Caribbean family system are primarily of value as items in the history of social thought' (M. G. Smith 1962b: 218). Though we might seek to explain what led these anthropologists to an a–historical position that is not our purpose here. Instead, we intend once again, in the discussion which follows, to argue the very real need for historical research for an understanding of the family or, for that matter, of any other Afro-American institution.

One of our major postulates has been that neither social context nor cultural traditions alone can explain an Afro-American institutional form (Mintz 1970a, 1970b) and that the development of institutions must be viewed in their full historical setting. In terms of the family, any number of simple illustrations come to mind. In one Martiniquan fishing village, for instance, current contrasts in family form (e.g., differing frequencies of female-headed households or of marital stability) are related directly to differing historical experiences. The residents at one end of the village are descended from people who abandoned plantation life only three generations ago, and the relatively 'loose' institutional complex (with its associated values) relating to 'the family' on plantations continues to influence them today. In contrast, the inhabitants on the other end of the village have a long heritage as independent fishermen on this site, dating back to pre-emancipation times, and their more stable family forms can be directly related to this fact (Price, 1970c). This argument, of course, is not restricted to Afro-Americans (Mintz 1956: 375-377). To explain family forms among East Indian estate workers in Guyana, for example one could hardly proceed without taking into account both cultural traditions and social conditions. As one student of these people has noted, their families are, in general, much less 'matri-centric' than one would expect, given their socio-economic situation (and keeping local Afro-American patterns in mind), yet much more so that one would predict on the basis of their attitudes or values (Jayawardena 1962: 63-64). And Jayawardena *(ibid.)* has shown that variations in family form among local East Indian villages can be fully understood only by examining the particular ways people turned their cultural resources to the task of adapting to new and varied social environments.

One of the problems with many traditional studies of 'the Negro-family' — and this applies to those of Herskovits as well as to those of Frazier — was a tendency to reify the concept of 'family' itself. Though anthropologists, at considerable cost, finally have learned otherwise during the past decade or so, many historians may not yet be aware of the implications of such reification. For example, in Afro-America the 'household' unit need by no means correspond to 'the family', however defined. It is, for example, common for domestic groups (those which pool economic resources, share responsibility for socializing children, etc.) to span several households; for the composition of a household to be determined by factors other than kinship; and so on. In studying family institutions, then, a number of distinctions should be drawn between those ideas and practices relating to kinship, those relating to mating or marriage, those relating to residence and household, and those relating to the allocation of domestic responsibilities (Fortes 1958, Solien 1960, Greenfield 1961, R. T. Smith 1970). Some of the processes involved in the development of kinship and sex roles among Afro-Americans will be used to illustrate the necessity for such distinctions, and also to point up the complexities involved in tracing the growth of any Afro-American institution.

Let us begin, once again, with a hypothetical aggregate of recently-enslaved African on a new plantation in the Americas. What, if anything, might have constituted a set of broadly shared ideas brought from Africa in the realm of kinship? Tentatively and provisionally, we would suggest that there may have been certain widespread fundamental ideas and assumptions about kinship in West Africa. Among these, we might single out the sheer importance of kinship in structuring interpersonal relations and in defining an individual's place in his society; the emphasis on unilineal descent, and the importance to each individual of the resulting lines of kinsmen, living and dead, stretching backward and forward through time; or, on a more abstract level, the use of land as a means of defining both time and descent, with ancestors venerated *locally*, and with history and genealogy both being particularized in specific pieces of ground. The aggregate of newly-arrived slaves, though they had been torn from their own local kinship networks, would have continued to view kinship as the normal idiom of social relations. Faced with an absence of real kinsmen, they nevertheless modelled their new social ties upon those of kinship, often borrowing kin terms acquired from their masters to label their relationships with their contemporaries and those older than themselves — 'bro', 'uncle', 'auntie', 'gran', etc. But in order for such early attempts by the slaves to invest social relationships with the symbolism of kinship to be transformed into kinship networks grounded in consanguinity, the first and essential requirement was group stability in time and place, or at least sufficient stability to permit the socialization of offspring within that same group. And it is here that the very real differences among plantations and plantation systems would be relevant.

We are assuming, remember, that in the early contact situations between the enslaved and their owners in the New World, the slaves had to develop their life-ways in the face of terrible and usually inescapable constraints. The processes of institution-building would have involved a continuing consciousness of uneven odds, of the masters' overarching power, and of the need to generate social forms that would be adaptive, even under these immensely difficult conditions. In arguing this way, we do not mean to undervalue the importance of the African backgrounds of the slaves or to imply that the slaves knew little, or remembered little, of their heritages. But we do think it reasonable to suppose that the precise ways in which those pasts could be drawn upon to generate new institutions, would depend in part upon the particular circumstances in which the slaves found themselves in the New World situation — the extent to which the slavery regime controlled, interfered with, or interdicted the recreation of institutional solutions, the stability afforded a particular slave group in its new setting, and so forth. While it would be neat and convenient to suppose that such variables can be ordered according to the aims and values of the master group in specific colonies (e.g. Spanish planters vs. English planters, or Jamaica vs. Cuba), we do not take up this mode of analysis in the present essay.

We might cite one case, however, in which there is evidence that plantation complements achieved considerable stability in early colonial times — the Para region of Suriname. As was the planters' policy here, as elsewhere in Suriname during the first hundred years of the colony's history, not to break up slave families by selling members to different masters, and special care seems to have been taken to avoid separating mothers and children (van Lier 1971: 154). Over the course of several generations in this region, important kinship groups, each with strong attachments to a particular locality, developed. These were non-unilineal descent groups, composed of *all* the descendants (traced bilaterally) of a particular person who had come from Africa. After several generations, then, any individual would have belonged to a number of such kin groups.

We would contend that these groups, based on cognatic rather than unilineal descent, developed in a social situation in which there were few if any 'tasks' for corporate groups to do (see Goodenough 1970: 52) *other than* those relating to ancestor rites. In our view, these groups, which developed during the first several generations of settlement, grew out of the social interaction and common ritual concerns among the descendants of each of the original enslaved Africans. This ritual focus, in turn, was related to widely shared ideas about the importance of kinship in structuring social relations and the central role of ancestors in the ongoing life of the community. Since maximal numbers of descendants would have been desirable for carrying out such rites, and group overlap would pose no problems, there would have been no question of applying restrictive rules for group membership. (We remind the reader that a system based on cognatic descent is able to maximize the number of people who belong to each group, in contrast to a system based on unilineal principles — whether patrilineality or matrilineality — which by definition restricts membership to only *some* of a focal ancestor's descendants — See Goodenough 1970: 53). Over the course of time these Para kin groups, originally focussed purely on rites for their collective ancestors (who were buried locally), seem gradually to have taken on a broader functional burden, playing an important role in defining lines of authority and cooperation and in regulating social relations more generally.

An interesting contrast is provided by the Saramaka maroons, many of whose ancestors escaped from the plantations of the Para region during early colonial times. Their original social groups, composed of those slaves who ran away from the same plantation (or who grouped themselves together, at the outset, in the forest) often spent years in relative isolation from one another. These small communities were organized as fighting bands, struggling to forge an independent way of life against tremendous odds (see Price 1973, 1976). Initially, these groups were mutually suspicious and often hostile, and they were fiercely proud of their own group's skills, knowledge, and accomplishments; moreover, it is probable that they began to hold land corporately almost from the beginning. By the time they had regularized social relations (including marriage) with one another, then, each group had a firm sense of community. We would contend that it was this initial sense of corporateness and the desire to perpetuate it that prompted Saramaka groups, in contrast to the slaves on Para plantations, to adopt a principle of descent (in this case 'matrilineality'[20]) which restricted an individual's membership to a single group. As in Para, however, the principle of descent was sanctioned by a whole complex of ritual and belief, the collective ancestors became anchored strongly to the soil, and time and space were merged symbolically in the cult of the ancestors.

On the relatively stable plantations of Para, there also developed a strong sense of community, though it came about more gradually than in the case of Saramaka groups. The growth of interlocking kinship ties among the slaves on each plantation certainly contributed to this sense of group solidarity (van Lier 1971: 159-160). Each local plantation developed a distinctive character, almost a 'micro-culture' of its own, as seen even in their having slightly different styles of drumming to summon their gods; and there were frequent rivalries and feuds among their respective slave complements (Wooding 1972: 259-260, van Lier 1971: 160). Upon emancipation, the former slaves of the Para region chose to remain where they had always lived and to purchase their plantations communally. We would suggest that it was becuase the non-exclusive (cognitive) kingroups of these people (1) would not function efficiently to hold land in common; and (2) by this time were so strongly institutionalized that a switch to a Saramaka-like unilineal system was out of the question, so that a different solution was reached. Here the plantation communities themselves became the land-holding corporations, with individuals gaining rights to land use through their genealogical connections to ancestors who had lived there. Kinship retained, and still retains, its central role in Para social organization, with the principles of descent and ancestry richly particularized and anchored in the land. But in terms of defining the social world of the individual, kinship is accompanied by a concept of community the roots of which are firmly in the New World and, more specifically, in a distinctive form of plantation slavery.

We have seen that the early history of the Saramaka maroons and that of the original slaves in Para was similar in that both witnessed considerable stability of personnel through time, and a consequent proliferation of genealogical ties. In each case, kinship became a major organizing force in social relations, descent and veneration of the ancestors became a central feature of the religious system, and a strong relationship developed between notions of descent and locality. The ways that these systems came to differ, in our view, can be traced to the fact that initially the people on any Para plantation were merely an 'aggregate', while those in Saramaka came to think of themselves, almost from the beginning, as members of particular groups. Although a full comparative analysis of these two kinship systems through time would obviously require a great deal of additional documentation and discussion, we believe that the kinds of variables we have singled out would figure importantly in such an enterprise.

We wish we had examples of other plantation areas where circumstances fostered a relative stability of personnel, in order to examine the nature of developing kinship institutions in those settings. One potentially revealing case is Carriacou, in the southeastern Caribbean, where the relative stability of slave personnel was reinforced by the tiny size of the island. Today, we find there the most fully articulated system of unilineal descent (other than that of the Suriname maroons) in all of Afro-America, replete with a complex ancestor cult and functioning localized patrilineages (M. G. Smith 1962a). At this point, however, our lack of detailed knowledge about the early history of this island, and our even greater ignorance of the development of its people's kinship institutions (M. G. Smith 1961a: 309-310) permit little more than a guess that the variable operating in Suriname may also have been relevant here.

The relative stability and continuity of the slave force on plantations in Suriname (and, perhaps, Carriacou) undoubtedly represents one extreme in the total spectrum of early Afro-America. We are also sure that there were those plantations on which mothers and children were separated almost routinely, where 'marriages' were brief at best, and where the slave complement was in a constant state of instability and flux. In such a case (and Saint-Domingue or Jamaica must have had many such estates at certain times in their history), the development of meaningful genealogical ties would have been severely restricted (see, for instance, Debien 1962). One imagines that the matri-central cell, composed of a mother and her children (Fortes 1962), would often have constituted the practical limits of an individual's kinship network. Relations other than those between a mother and her children, and between siblings who grew up together, would likely have been haphazard; lasting ties of paternity or collateral extension (to cousins, uncles or aunts) might as well have been the exception rather than the rule. No matter how strongly the slaves may have *wished* to use the kinship idiom in defining their social relations, in the face of the kind of instability we postulate here they would have had great difficulty in developing meaningful groups of kinsmen. With the passage of time, the very notion of kinship as an important organizing force may have lost some of its power, with other kinds of principles (i.e. dyadic, peer-type ties such as 'mati') supplementing or partly supplanting those based on kinship. We know that even in nineteenth-century Jamaica, slaves were still using kin terms as honorifics in address:

> Among the Negroes it is almost tantamount to an affront to address by name without affixing some term of relationship such as 'grannie' or 'uncle' or 'cousin'. My Cornwall boy, George, told me one day that 'Uncle Sully' wanted to speak to massa'. 'Why, is Sully your uncle George?' 'No massa; me only call him so for honour'. (Lewis 1816: 258, cited in Patterson 1967: 169-170).

Our intent is not to underplay the importance of the tiny 'family' groups which were often able to form in such systems. In spite of the difficulties these slaves faced in creating stable unions and keeping them together, we have ample evidence of small groups of kinsmen (often simply a woman, her children, and her current spouse) which were basic units of economic cooperation. As we noted earlier, provision-plot agriculture was frequently encouraged by the masters, since it served to reduce plantation costs. Over time, it became sufficiently institutionalized in some slave societies so that the masters might accept as custom the slaves' property rights in their produce and, in an admittedly different sense, their rights in the land they cultivated. An observant eighteenth-century writer on Jamaica (Edwards 1793, II:133), for instance, indicates that the slaves could even ' .... bequeath their grounds or gardens to such of their fellow-slaves as they think proper', though of course the land belonged to the plantation, and never became the slave's property in fee simple.

Though the evidence is scanty, some authors writing on eighteenth-century and early nineteenth-century Jamaica do describe *families* at work on these plots (Stewart 1823: 267; Madden 1835, I: 136-137). The marketing of surpluses by slaves, in both Jamaica and Saint-Domingue, appears early in the record (Long 1774, II: 486-487; Mintz and Hall 1960; Moreau de St. Méry 1958 [1797], I: 433-436; Girod de Chantrans 1785: 131-132), and it is clear that the profits from such enterprise belonged to the slaves themselves, in accord with accepted custom (see, for instance, Long 1774, II: 410-411; Dallas 1803, I: cviii). Hence, in spite of the lengthy and unquestionable record of the oppression of slaves in these societies, we find substantial information on their opportunities to engage in relatively independent economic activity on their own account, and at least some information suggesting that kin groups carried out such activity cooperatively. Beckford

(1970, II: 151-187), for instance, writing on Jamaica, mentions how the slaves at work on their grounds ' ... move, with all their family, into the place of cultivation; the children of different ages are loaded with baskets, which are burdened in proportion to their strength and age .... The infants are flung at the backs of the mothers, and very little incommode them in their walks or labour'. Patterson even asserts that ' ... the mother gained the labour of her child in working her *provision ground* [italics added; we could find no evidence that provision grounds were granted to women] and later, might even control the extra provision ground given to her children when they had attained adulthood' (Patterson 1967: 169). Even more striking is Patterson's claim (ibid.) that ' ... slave mothers did everything to keep their children within their household and to discourage any attempt at forming permanent unions outside, one nineteenth-century writer stating that to be the main reason for the lack of stable unions among the slaves'. Such evidence supports our contention, then, that very small kin groups, which provided a basis for economic cooperation, were able to develop within even some of the most oppressive slave systems.

Given the highly restricted nature of kinship in these slave systems and the limited possibilities for the development of ties other than those between mothers and children and between siblings, Davenport's summary of the major features of (five) modern Caribbean kinship systems takes on special meaning.

> We seem to be dealing with systems in which lineal and sibling relations are the only important ones. In contrast to these, avuncular-nepotic and more distant collateral relationships are of secondary importance. By this is meant that the relationship of ego to his grandparents, his parents, and his siblings are the only ones to which rights, duties and obligations are precisely defined, regardless of other considerations [1916b: 382].

The juxtaposition of Davenport's comments on kinship in contemporary Caribbean societies with our own, relating to the colonial period, is no more than suggestive. Yet we believe that, given sufficient data, it might well be possible to trace direct continuities between the limited growth of kinship institutions in these more heavily industrialized, mobile plantation forces of, say, the eighteenth-century Caribbean, and current forms of social organization in these same areas.

In so doing, however, one might well be surprised by the extent to which people may keep alive, even under conditions of extreme repression, the kinds of fundamental ideas about kinship which we postulated as being widespread in West Africa. After emancipation in Jamaica, for example, once individuals had gained access to land ownership, large kinship groups which may have been built in at least some ways upon African models, began to take shape in some areas of the island. Composed in theory of all the descendants of the original title holder (traced bilaterally), these late-emerging non-unilineal kinship groups, which were centred on 'family land', grew to resemble in certain ways those of the Para region of Suriname, with a ritual association between ancestors and the land on which they were buried (Clarke 1953, Davenport 1961a). Haiti witnessed a similar development following the slaves' acquisition of land in the early nineteenth-century. In some areas, groups of patrikin — co-residential units called *lakou* — grew up around parcels of land, each of which contained an ancestral shrine and was inhabited by particular deities associated with the group (Bastien 1961). Though a good deal remains obscure about the precise nature of the kin groups involved in both the Haitian and Jamaican cases, we believe that we could carry this discussion to a more detailed level. However, it is probably sufficient here simply to stress the existence of such groups, since their presence suggests that ideas — whether about kinship or other aspects of life — can be kept alive even under severely repressive conditions; further, that the nature of particular Afro-American systems of kinship — or other institutions — cannot be understood except in terms of an extremely variable and complex range of social and economic situations.

To turn our attention to a more specialized aspect of family life, that of the role expectations between spouses, we again confront the need for greater analytical subtlety and more socio-historical research. We have already noted that a major effect of enslavement was the nearly total destruction of the antecedent statuses held by individuals in the ancestral societies from which they had been torn. In spite of occasional mentions of former status distinctions being observed in the case of one slave or another by those around him — the much-romanticized idea of the enslaved prince or princess — it is not at all difficult to perceive why antecedent distinctions of rank would tend to become irrelevant or to become totally transformed in the plantation setting. However, among such distinctions, those drawn according to sex and age merit special attention in this case, since these biological dimensions against which differences can be calibrated are employed universally in the allocation of status and role. In Africa as elsewhere, distinctions were drawn between male and female, as well as between young and old, and a good deal of the channelling of life activities originated in these sociological orderings, based on socially learned perceptions of biological differences. We do not feel prepared to assess the variability of West African social systems in terms of how they dealt with such differences, but we would like to speculate on the effects exerted on the definition of sex roles by plantation slavery.

Earlier we suggested that, to a considerable extent, the slaves on a particular plantation or other colonial enterprise were able to create their own rules and to attempt to live by them — often without significant interference by the masters. But we also stressed the limiting effects of such interference, which was always a possibility and, often enough, a reality. Nowhere was the balance between autonomy and submission more movingly revealed than in the quality of slave domestic life, since it was within the confines of the slave huts and barracks that so much of the most intimate aspects of that life — sexuality, reproduction, birth, socialization, death, love and hate — were lived out. We recognize that the ultimate power of the masters over the slaves — not only over their lives, but also over their sexuality and its exercise — probably conditioned every aspect of the relationships between men and women. However, while many authors have contended with good reason that slave morality is ultimately referable to the morality of the master class, we suggest once more that the code of the masters set the limits more than it determined the contents of that morality. From the point of view of the masters, of course, individual slaves theoretically had no power over each other, since all were ultimately accountable to their owners. But we would take the position that this generality is not particularly useful in examining the everyday realities of slave life.

Orlando Patterson has asserted (1967: 167) that 'slavery abolished any real social distribution between males and females', and while he certainly is correct in emphasizing that the primary locus of power lay with the planters, we believe that the evidence about the sexual division of labour belies so sweeping a generalization. As we have indicated, in many of the colonies in which provision-plot agriculture became institutionalized, slaves were permitted to carry their own produce to market. The division of labour with regard to marketing before emancipation is not well-documented. In the case of both Jamaica and Saint-Domingue, however, there is an absence of descriptions of independent women marketers. Descriptions refer only to unattached males or to family groups. This contrasts sharply with what is known for post-emancipation Jamaica and post-revolutionary Haiti, for women emerged as the overwhelming majority of marketers in both societies. This development is all the more striking since women are today — and presumably have long been — the marketers in many (perhaps most) West African societies. Indeed, it has sometimes been argued that the predominance of women in contemporary Antillean internal market systems is to be explained by reference to the African past (Herskovits 1971 [1937]: 260; Herskovits 1947: 292).

Thus a puzzle is posed by the data: that of explaining what might appear to be a 're-version' to the African past, so far as the sexual division of labour is concerned, after lengthy periods during which women appear not to have been independent marketers in these societies. Though we do not feel ready to offer a satisfactory explanation here, we would like to make some comments which may point toward a better understanding of the problem. Upon emancipation, men seem predominantly to have taken over agricultural production in all of these areas, in spite of the fact that both men and women had worked provision grounds and done field labour during slavery. This male takeover of agriculture may represent an adaptation to the sex-role expectations of the broader European society or it may have some other explanation (*see*, for instance, M. G. Smith

1957: 42-43). The female adaptation to marketing,however, poses a more puzzling problem, since it presumably would have occurred only if the existing role expectations were compatible with the exercise of considerable female autonomy. Simple acquisition of more land by men could not be expected to have resulted in female domination of trade, if such domination were to run counter to male notions of masculine dignity or prestige. Husbands had to be willing to permit their wives to engage in economic activities away from the home and, in some cases, even to develop independent careers as marketers (Mintz 1974a).

We remind ourselves here that the idea that a man's masculinity need in no way be diminished by his wife's economic independence is not a standard part of our western cultural heritage. Many interpretations of family life, both past and present, carry implicit postulates concerning the relationship between men and women (husbands and wives) that preclude a division of authority based on a separation of economic activity. Even in a society as broadminded as our own, women who insist on banking their incomes separately are considered inappropriately unfamilistic in most circles.

In this context, it seems clear that the independence and authority exercised by a Haitian or Jamaican market woman in regard to her uses of her own capital probably have few parallels in the Western world, where individual prerogatives commonly are assumed to flow from individual male wealth, embedded in an economically indivisible nuclear family structure. The generation of separate and independent economic risk structures within a single family may be considered characteristically West African and Afro-Caribbean, as opposed to European or North American (Mintz 1971d).

We are not able yet to disaggregate the significance of the African past and the experience of slavery in fostering and nurturing these characteristic Caribbean sex-role expectations. One might wish to argue that, under slavery, with both men and women treated as property, Jamaican and Haitian males were forced to tolerate female autonomy and gradually came to expect it; and that furthermore, upon emancipation, Jamaican and Haitian females found themselves in a position to exercise more fully the autonomy, in ways remarkably consistent with those of their West African sisters. However, the case of the Saramaka maroons of Suriname suggests, at least, that this explanation may be insufficient. Though Saramaka women are in many respects strongly dependent economically on men, and have been for centuries, the *idea* that a man's masculinity or status is not tied to his wife's dependence (or lack of it) is as strong here as elsewhere in the Caribbean. Since the original New World ancestors of the Saramaka spent relatively little time as slaves, we can be skeptical that their ideas about sex roles were the product of the plantation experience. If such ideas hold, then, in Saramaka as in Jamaica and Haiti, in spite of their societies' differing divisions of labour, and in spite of the fact that Saramakas had little experience as slaves, the possibility is at least raised that certain fundamental West African concepts about appropriate male and female behaviour are involved. In fact, of course, we do not know enough about seventeenth and eighteenth century West African societies to make facile generalizations on this point. Again, we have come up against a fairly subtle level of cultural expectations, akin to 'cognitive orientations', on which we, at least, know of little definitive data. However, we might entertain, as a very tentative hypothesis, the idea that certain West African notions about the relative separateness of male-female roles were reinforced by the plantation experience, to produce what seem to be characteristic Afro-American patterns in these regards.

We think this example indicates that either-or formulations may no longer have significant place in Afro-Americanist research. We have at least suggested that surface analogies (e.g., female marketing in West Africa and the Caribbean) will not succeeded in revealing as much as less precisely defined but more critical continuities (e.g., male-female attitudes toward individual autonomy). To some extent, the question may be one of the differences among the statuses of male, female, husband and wife, and the status of the individual. To what degree is one's status as an individual compromised by increased emphasis on sex-based status? Again, to what degree is one's status as an individual compromised by the European emphasis on the statuses of husband and wife? It is obvious that we have no answers; but we believe that the questions are intimately connected to the emergence of the particular status systems that typify Afro-American societies. Our hope would be that this final example we have offered, like those advanced earlier, will prove responsive — even if our hypotheses are proven wrong — to more thorough historical research.

M. Craton

CHANGING PATTERNS OF SLAVE FAMILIES IN THE BRITISH WEST INDIES

> ... any attempt to restrain this Licentious Intercourse between the Sexes amongst the slaves in this Island in the present state of their notions of right and wrong, by introducing the Marriage Ceremony amongst them, would be utterly impracticable, and perhaps of dangerous Consequence, as these People are universally known to claim a right of disposing themselves in this respect, according to their own will and pleasure without any Control from their Masters.[1]

Writers on the West Indies have echoed the negative statements of Alexis de Tocqueville and E. Franklin Frazier on slave and modern black families in the United States.[2] In this vein, Simey, Henriques, and Goode exaggerated the matrifocality and instability of modern Caribbean families as 'deviant' results of an alleged absence of family life in slavery, while Smith and Patterson confidently backed up their analyses of modern family with assertions that 'the woman normally acted as the sole permanent element in the slave family, whether or not the male partner was polygynous', and that 'the nuclear family could hardly exist within the context of slavery'.[3]

In work published since 1973, Higman has proved these assertions to be wrong and thus has reopened the whole study of the West Indian family and its roots. Although concentrating on sugar plantation colonies and the period of slave amelioration and registration (1807-34), he has shown that family life—even in patterns recognizable to Europeans—was then the norm for British West Indian slaves. Although polygyny and other African practices persisted, the nuclear, two-headed household was extremely common among the African-born as well as Creole slaves. More remarkably, single-headed maternal households were in a minority in every area studied by Higman, save for the towns. The frequency of matrifocal families and the general disruption of slave families had become exaggerated, he suggested, because of the practices of those slaves with whom whites were most familiar: domestics and urban slaves.[4]

The purpose of this present paper is fourfold. It adds to Higman's evidence by using material chiefly from the Bahamas, a non-sugar, largely non-plantation colony. It also summarizes the evidence hitherto gathered, sketches the varieties of slave family from place to place and time to time, and finally, discusses developmental models. Despite great variations according to location, employment, and ownership (not to mention the difficulties presented by fragmentary and uneven evidence), a consistent pattern does emerge. This suggests both the place that the rediscovered West Indian slave family of the late salve period occupies in the continuum between West African roots and modern West Indian black family, and some of the ways in which the dynamics of West Indian black family have differed from those of the United States and Latin America.

As Stephen noted as early as 1824, slave conditions in the Bahama Islands were at the benign end of a scale on which the sugar colonies further south — particularly the newly acquired colonies of Trinidad and Guyana — represented the opposite extreme. An influx of Loyalist planters after 1783 had changed the tone and pace of the archipelagic colony, doubling the white population and trebling the number of slaves; but the population density remained a twentieth of that of Jamaica and a fiftieth of that of

Barbados, while the ratio of black slaves to white freemen and the average size of slave holdings remained among the lowest in the British West Indies.[5]

Most of the Loyalist emigrés settled their slaves on Bahamian 'Out Islands' until then unpopulated, attempting to replicate the plantation conditions they had left behind in the Carolinas, Georgia, and Florida. They found the climate ideal for growing sea island cotton, but the exhaustion of the thin soil and the depredations of the chenille bug left them unable to compete with American cotton once Whitney's gin became effective after 1800. Although a local planter, Joseph Eve, invented a wind-powered variant of the gin, Bahamian cotton production had almost faded away by 1820. Plantations were turned over to stock or the growing of grains and other provisions, and many of the slaves had to fend for themselves.

Figure 1 *Population pyramids, Rolle slaves and 26 Bahamian holdings, 1822.*

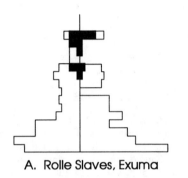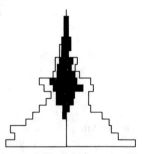

A. Rolle Slaves, Exuma   B. 26 Bahamian Holdings

Those planters who could sell up, migrated once more. Many of them attempted to transfer their slaves to the old colony of Jamaica or the new sugar plantations in Trinidad and St Vincent, where fresh slaves were at a premium after the African supply had been cut off by the abolition of the Atlantic slave trade in 1808. Although slaves were registered in the Crown Colony of Trinidad as early as 1813, this opportunistic trade was not revealed until the first returns under the Bahamian Slave Registration Act of 1812 reached London, after which it was effectively scotched by the abolitionists under Stephen Lushington in 1823. By then, perhaps, 2,000 Bahamian slaves (a fifth) had already been transferred.[6]

The meticulous triennial returns of British West Indian slaves produced by the registration laws were of great value to the emancipationists, who were able to prove the persistence of 'natural decrease' as well as to end the intercolonial trade. Modern demographers, however, can put them to much wider use, reconstituting and comparing whole colony populations by age, sex, African or Creole birth, mortality, fertility, and life expectancy. In at least two colonies, Trinidad and the Bahamas, it is also possible to discover and compare patterns of slave family. Unlike the Trinidadian instructions, the Bahamian law did not require the listing of slaves' families or households-by-name. But approximately a quarter of Bahamian slaves were voluntarily listed by their owners in such a way as to indicate family relationships, though with limits on the range of family types identifiable. Comparison between the original lists of 1821 and 1822 and those of 1825, 1828, 1831, and 1834, moreover, allows both for corroboration of relationships and the testing of their permanence.[7]

In all, it has proved possible to analyze 26 slave holdings in the first Bahamian census of 1821-22 in which owners listed slaves in family groups, rather than by alphabetical order, age, sex or any other method. This sample comprised 3,011 out of a Bahamas grand total of about 12,000, an average of 116 slaves per holding, but with a range between 20 and 840, drawn from eleven different islands. The findings not only illustrate the contrasts between the Bahamian slave population and those in sugar plantation colonies further south, but also point up the typicality of the only Bahamian slave group previously studied, that of the slaves owned by John, Lord Rolle on the island of Exuma.[8]

Figure 2 *Bahamas, 26 holdings, 1822; age differences between males and their mates*

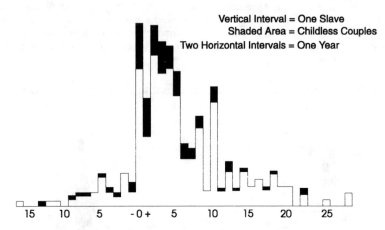

Ten times the size of the Rolle holding, this widespread fourth of the Bahamian slave population exhibited almost as balanced, 'modern', and 'unslavelike' a demographic pattern, with a broad base of youngsters and a fair number of elderly slaves. The sexes in the fertile age ranges were almost as equally balanced as Rolle's slaves, and the only features reminiscent of slave populations further south were a slight 'bulge' in the age range from 40 to 54, representing in this case survivors from the migration of Loyalists' slaves in the 1780s, and a substantial remnant of Africans, 18.8 per cent of the total. Unlike the Rolle holding, there also was evidence of considerable miscegenation, 6.9 per cent of the 3,011 slaves being listed as 'mulatto' or 'yellow'.[9]

Figure 3 *Bahamas, 26 holdings, 1822; ages of mothers at births of their children*

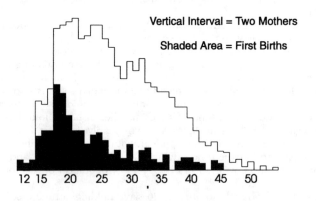

These slight differences and the less optimal work and living conditions accounted for a rather lower average net population increase than with Lord Rolle's slaves, but the incidence of family in the sample of 26 holdings was very similar. As Table 1 shows, 85.0 per cent were found in some type of family, with no less than 54.1 per cent of the 3,011 slaves indicated as living in simple nuclear families. Of the 1,356 slaves over 20 years old, 854, or 63.1 per cent, were listed in couples. The normal pattern was for

Table 1 *Household Patterns, Rolle Slaves, and 26 Bahamian Holdings, 1822*

Family Type	Rolle Slaves, Exuma				26 Bahamian Holdings			
	Total slaves	Number of units	Mean size of units	Per cent of total in type	Total slaves	Number of units	Mean size of units	Per cent of total in type
1 Man, woman, children	110	26	4.23	46.6	1,629	308	5.29	54.1
2 Man, woman	14	7	2.00	5.9	178	89	2.00	5.9
3 Woman, children	40	12	3.33	16.9	377	95	3.97	12.5
4 Man, children	11	2	5.50	4.7	16	3	5.33	0.5
5 Three-generation groups	29	5	5.80	12.3	358	46	7.78	11.9
6 Men Alone, or together	11	—	—	4.7	264	—	—	8.8
7 Women alone, or together	9	—	—	3.8	173	—	—	5.8
8 Children separately	12	—	—	5.1	16	—	—	0.5
Totals	236	—	—	100.0	3,011	—	—	100.0
A Nuclear family (1,2,5)	153	38	4.03	64.8	2,165	443	4.89	71.9
B Denuded family (3,4)	51	14	3.64	21.6	393	98	4.01	13.0
C No family (6,7,8)	32	—	—	13.6	45.3	—	—	51.1

males to be a few years older than their mates. On the average, males were some $4\frac{1}{2}$ years older, but this figure was skewed by some much older males and by the few older females. Of 397 couples who were the parents in nuclear families or were childless, in 303 cases the males were from 0-10 years older, with an average of three years and $10\frac{1}{2}$ months. Although the presence of elderly mothers whose first children had left the household or had died makes it difficult to count exactly, the average age of mothers at the birth of first children appears to have been under 20 years. As Table 2 shows, the spacing between children was regular and healthy, with the overall average almost exactly three years. Of all women in the age range from 15-49, a high proportion, 65.8 per cent, were indicated as mothers, having had on the average almost exactly three children.[10]

Besides these basic statistical findings, a study of the Bahamian returns allows for some general observations and analysis along lines followed by Gutman and other scholars of slavery in the United States. First, important implications concerning the incidence of endogamy and exogamy — or at least of in-group and out-group mating — arose from the tendency of slave families to appear most clearly in the records of the larger and more isolated holdings, which were mainly in islands distant from Nassau, the colonial capital.[11] In contrast, on New Providence (Nassau's island) and the nearer, long-established settlements of Harbour Island and Eleuthera, conjugal patterns seem to have been more disrupted. Many of the holdings were too small to include whole families and this clearly contributed to the custom of choosing mates from other holdings. But there were other factors. Among a heavily creolized population (with some slaves six generations removed from Africa), in small units, marital mobility was not only possible but probably seen as desirable to avoid too close a consanguinity. Miscegenation was also rather more common in New Providence and Eleuthera than further afield, those slaves listed as mulatto or yellow constituting 8 per cent of the few holdings analyzed and probably more than 10 per cent overall.[12]

In general, it seems that these conditions led not to familial cohesion but the reverse, with many male mates absent or even temporary. Female-headed families were most common in the listings for New Providence (where almost a quarter of all Bahamian slaves lived), not only in the several holdings that consisted solely of slave mothers and their children, but also in such groups as the 37 slaves of Elizabeth Mary Anderson, where nine men aged from 22-60 were listed together but separately from five female-headed families averaging five children each. Only in the exceptional holding of William Wylly at the isolated western end of New Providence were families distinct and clearly permanent.

Table 2   *Bahamas, 26 Slave Holdings, 1822–Average Ages of Mothers at Births and Child Spacing*

Which child	Number of mothers	Percent total mothers in each group	Average ages at births	Average spacing (years)
1st	479	100.0	22.37	
2nd	356	74.3	26.53	3.36
3rd	244	50.9	30.00	2.93
4th	170	35.5	32.60	2.93
5th	105	21.9	33.38	2.42
6th	59	12.3	35.22	2.81
7th	31	6.5	40.10	2.95
8th	8	1.7	43.46	2.67
9th	2	0.4	38.75	1.87
10th	1	0.2	38.00	1.00
Averages			34.84	3.02

In the distant, more recently established settlements, populations were on the average larger, more isolated and, perhaps of necessity, more cohesive. The choice of mates was limited, and thus relationships were likely to be not only well-known but also more permanent. In relatively large populations, consisting in most cases primarily of first and second generation Creoles, such enforced in-group mating would not yet come into conflict with any customary ban on cousin-mating that may have existed (whether derived from Africa or Europe). In all, it is possible that conditions in the Out Islands, which Nassauvians, both white and black, might consider primitive, were more conducive to stable family formation than those closer to the colonial centre. Certainly, in modern times, Otterbein has documented a greater awareness of the value of stable families in 'primitive' Andros Island than that to be inferred in the less affluent sections of modernized Nassau, which include large groups of displaced Out Islanders. Yet these conditions seem to have also obtained in slavery days, a conclusion that runs counter to Gutman's contention that the dislocating effects of urbanization postdated emancipation, at least in the United States.[13]

The listings of families headed by single females may disguise the existence of serially shifting, or even polygynous, relationships. But in the series of five censuses spread over 12 years (1822-34) there is very little positive evidence of serial monogamy, and only rarely and equivocal evidence of polygyny.[14] Naming practices were very little help in tracing family patterns. Bahamian slaves did not universally adopt surnames before emancipation, and then it is by no means certain that surnames were patronymics in the modern style.[15] The practice of taking the surname of the former owner tends to exaggerate consanguinity as well as to confuse relationships — the most extreme case being Lord Rolle's 372 slaves, all of whom took the surname Rolle in order to share common rights in their former master's land. The discernment of immediate relationships was aided, however, by the frequent practice of naming a male child after his father or grandfather, and the occasional custom of naming a female after her grandmother.[16]

Such three-generation links sometimes allowed for the identification of extended family units, but the positive evidence of wider kinship links was disappointingly meagre, and the direct evidence from the records of related families living close together in clusters of huts or 'yards' was non-existent, although such groupings are known to have been a feature of Out Island life in later times. However, the frequent listing of a young girl with her first child in the household of her parents, or mother, does permit some inferences about sexual customs. Few girls under 20 cohabited with their mates; few mothers over 20 lived with their parents, and most, as we have seen, lived with mates. Nearly all girls who bore their first children in their mothers' households began separate cohabitation at, or shortly before, the birth of their second children. It therefore seems likely that premarital sex was not uncommon, and even that virginity at marriage was not excessively prized; but that separate cohabitation in a nuclear household was the accepted norm for couples over the age of 20.[17]

The evidence proves the vigorous existence of families among Bahamian slaves during the registration period and, indeed, points to the existence of types of family classified as 'modern' by Europeans among the least modernized groups of slaves. It remains to be decided, though, whether this was a social pattern chosen by the slaves themselves — and thus likely to have existed before the recorded period — or one determined, or at least encouraged, by the Eurocentric, pro-natalist, or publicity-conscious masters.

Strong evidence for the latter conclusion is found in the case of the slaves of William Wylly, Attorney-General of the Bahamas. An ardent Methodist who arranged for a minister to preach regularly to his slaves, he came to be regarded as a crypto-emancipationist by his fellow planters because of a legal decision made in 1816, and was at the centre of a bitter wrangle between the plantocratic Assembly and three successive governors, lasting until 1820. Close examination of the evidence, however, shows that Wylly was a strict paternalist, and suggests that if he wished to turn his slaves loose it was because they were no longer profitable.[18]

By 1818, Wylly's three adjacent estates in western New Providence had ceased to grow cotton, Tusculum and Waterloo being turned over to stock raising and Clifton, the largest, being devoted to growing provisions for the slaves and the Nassau market. The Attorney-General's many enemies accused him both of allowing his slaves more time to work for themselves than laid down by Bahamian law, and of supplying them with

Table 3 Bahamas, 26 Slave Holdings, 1822 Comparison between African-Headed and Creole Families

Family type	A. African-headed families[a]				B. Creole Families			
	Total slaves	Number of units	Mean size of units	Percent of total in type	Total slaves	Number of units	Mean size of units	Percent units in type
1 Man, woman, children	830[a]	154	5.39	61.0	799	154	5.19	48.8
2 Man, woman	138[a]	69	2.00	10.2	40	20	2.00	2.4
3 Woman, children	91	21	4.33	6.7	278	72	3.86	16.8
4 Man, children	11	2	5.50	0.8	5	1	5.00	0.3
5 Three-generation groups	128[a]	19	6.73	9.4	238	29	8.21	14.4
6 Men alone or together	144	—	—	8.4	150	—	—	9.1
7 Women alone or together	48	—	—	3.5	125	—	—	7.6
8 Children separately	—	—	—	—	16	2	8.00	1.0
Totals	1,360	—	—	100.0	1,651	—	—	100.0
A Nuclear family (1,2,5)	1,096	242	4.53	80.6	1,077	203	5.31	65.2
B Denuded family (3,4)	102	23	4.43	7.5	283	73	3.88	17.1
C No family (6,7,8)	162	—	—	11.9	291	—	—	17.7

a African-headed families were taken to be those in which both parents, either parent, or the single parent were of African birth. Thus in categories 1, 2, and 5 in Section A mixed couples were included.

less than the provisions specified. In response, Wylly produced convincing proof of the degree to which his slaves were self-supporting, and stated, 'My principal object has been, to accustom them to *habits of Industry and Economy* — which I am convinced, never will be found to exist among any Slaves, in this part of the World, who are victualled by their Masters.'[19]

At the same time, Wylly forwarded a revealing set of regulations for his slaves which he had caused to be printed and published in Nassau in 1815. Apart from his concern for religious instruction and regular prayers, and details of clothing, feeding, work, and punishment regulations, these clearly illustrated his views on slave marriage, sexual continence, and motherhood. 'Every man, upon taking his first wife', read the seventh article of the regulations,' is entitled to a well built stone house, consisting of two apartments, and is to receive a sow pig, and a pair of dunghill fowls, as a donation from the proprietor.'[20]

'In cases of Adultery', read Article XI, 'the man forfeits his hogs, poultry, and other moveable effects; which are to be sold, and the proceeds paid over to the injured wife. Both offenders are moreover to be whipt; their heads to be shaved, and they are to wear *Sack cloth* (viz. gowns and caps made of Cotton bagging) for the next half year; during which time they are not to go beyond the limits of the plantation, under the penalty of being whipt.'

With far less Mosaic severity, Article XIX enjoined that, 'On working days, the children are to be carried, early every morning, by their mothers, to the Nursery, where proper care will be taken of them during the day; and their mothers are to call for them when they return from their work in the afternoon. Women who have children at the breast, are never to be sent to any distance from the homestead.'

Predictably, Wylly's slave lists in the registration returns disclose a neat pattern of families and a healthy natural increase. Since his regulations were published and his views on slave management became well known, it is possible that they became normative. The very decision to list slaves according to families and households may indicate owners who shared Wylly's concerns. Certainly, the other two Bahamian owners known to have engaged in correspondence on the management of their slaves, Lord Rolle of Exuma and Burton Williams of Watling's Island, demonstrated an awareness of the value of stable families in producing healthy, fertile, and contented slaves.[21]

It is likely, though, that such planters as Wylly, Rolle, and Williams were self-deluding if not self-serving. The widespread incidence and consistent form of slave families suggest customary choice on the part of the slaves rather than the dictates of the masters. Few plantations were owner-managed, especially in the Out Islands, and it seems strange that orderly patterns of slave family should be more common the further from Nassau (where slaves were commonly under the daily scrutiny of their owners), unless this was the slaves' own choice. Nor can the growing influence of Christianity be given unequivocal credit. The established Anglican Church, which held a monopoly on formal weddings until 1827, did not proselytize the slaves, and the few sectarian missionaries concentrated on Nassau and the nearer islands. The underground 'Native Baptists', who were active among the Loyalists' slaves in Nassau as early as in Jamaica, may have had more widespread influence. But they were known to be tolerant about informal marital ties, being regarded by whites as hardly Christians at all. Indeed, the common impression held by the whites of the mass of the slaves was that those who were not heathen practicers of *obeah* were infidel 'followers of Mahomet'.[22]

This at least suggests strong African cultural retentions, particularly in the Out Islands. Numerically the Africans were few by the registration period but, as elderly survivors, seem to have been highly respected members of the slave community. Indeed, it became clear on further analysis of the 26 holdings that the African slaves had influence out of all proportion to their numbers, and even that they were dominant in shaping family life in the Bahamas. Although most of the African-born slaves were grouped together toward the end of the rolls, in more than a third of the slave holdings analyzed an African couple was at the head of the list. This usually indicated that the owner had chosen the most prestigious married African as head driver.[23]

As in all slave communities the role of such leaders was ambivalent. They were chosen for what was termed 'confidentiality' — fidelity, reliability, and respectability. But they were known to be effective because they commanded respect and 'reputation', among Creoles as well as African blacks. For example, Wylly's African head driver and under-driver, Boatswain and Jack, practically ran his estates. Strong family men, they were expected to lead prayers at Sunday services and conduct funerals. Boatswain at least was literate, and was paid for each slave taught to read; both were rewarded with 12 guineas a year, the right to own and ride a horse, and the power to inflict punishment on their own initiative up to 12 stripes. But did their authority, ultimately, stem from their paternalistic master, or from their position as family heads and from African roots? And what did the family pattern at Clifton, Tusculum, and Waterloo owe, respectively, to memories of Africa, the examples of Boatswain and Jack, and the encouragement of Wylly?

Strong clues emerged from the discovery that, when African-headed families—those in which both parents, either parent, or the only parent were African-born—were separated from purely Creole families, it became obvious that Africans were considerably more inclined toward family formation than Creole slaves. Of the Africans, 65.3 per cent lived in couples, compared with less than 60 per cent of the Creoles over the age of twenty. Of all African-headed families, 61.0 per cent were of the simple nuclear type, with an additional 9.4 per cent indicated as extended family households. This compared with 48.4 per cent in nuclear units and 14.4 per cent in extended households among Creole families. Only 11.9 per cent of Africans lived alone, compared with 16.7 per cent of adult Creoles.

By a Bahamian law of 1824, owners were forbidden to separate slave husbands from wives by sale, gift, or bequest, or to take their children away from them before they were fourteen years old. Although the act did not expressly forbid the splitting of families by shifting slaves from island to island, or the separation of children from single parents, it would seem to have provided owners with a motive for discouraging rather than encouraging slave families. Yet the evidence strongly suggests that masters were not only forced to acknowledge slave marital arrangements and to sell or transfer slaves only in families, even before 1824, but also to consider carefully the social consequences before they shifted slaves from their customary houses, plots, and kin at all.[24]

Wylly, although an alleged emancipationist, only manumitted three of his slaves after 1822 and did not scruple to scatter them by sale and transfer between 1821 and his death in 1828. Families, however, were carefully kept together. In another case, Rolle proposed an ingenious scheme in 1826 to shift all of his slaves to Trinidad, where they were to work to earn their freedom in the Spanish style. Fortunately for the slaves, the project was vetoed by the Colonial Office. But the word must have filtered down to Exuma, for in 1828 when Rolle's agent set about transferring some slaves to Grand Bahama, all of the slaves, fearing a move to Trinidad, became so mutinous that troops had to be sent down to keep order. Two years later, when they heard that the agent planned to ship them from Exuma to Cat Island, 44 slaves (five men, eight women, and their families) actually rebelled. Under the leadership of a slave called Pompey they first fled to the bush, then seized Rolle's salt boat, and sailed to Nassau to put their case to Governor Smyth, who was widely thought to be a friend of the slaves. The fugitives were thrown into the workhouse and the leaders flogged (including the eight women). But Smyth was angry when he heard about it and none of the slaves in the end were sent to Cat Island; it can be said that Pompey and his fellows won the principle that Bahamian slaves could not with impunity be shifted against their will.[25]

The largest single transfer of slaves had been the shipment in 1823 of most of the 840 slaves of James Moss from Acklin's Island and Crooked Island to Jamaica, where their fate remains obscure. Yet the most interesting of all Bahamian transfers was that to Trinidad between 1821 and 1823 of the majority of the slaves of Burton Williams of Watling's Island and his family, since it allows for comparisons between the fortunes of those transferred and other slaves in Trinidad, and between all those and the slaves left behind in the Bahamas.

Early in 1825, after he had been in Trinidad 3½ years, Williams gave evidence to the Trinidad Council about his slaves. He claimed that in '30 odd' years of Bahamian residence he had seen the group of seven slaves inherited and 'about 100' bought augmented by 224 through natural increase. This remarkable growth (as rapid as that indicated for Rolle's slaves, and sustained over a longer period) was attributed by Williams to his own residence among the slaves, to firm management, and to the encouragement of marriage 'by giving a feast to the Gang when they come together and a sharp punishment when they part'.[26]

Figure 4   *The Burton Williams slaves, 1822, and 1825, compared with Bahamas and Trinidad slaves, 1825; population pyramids.*

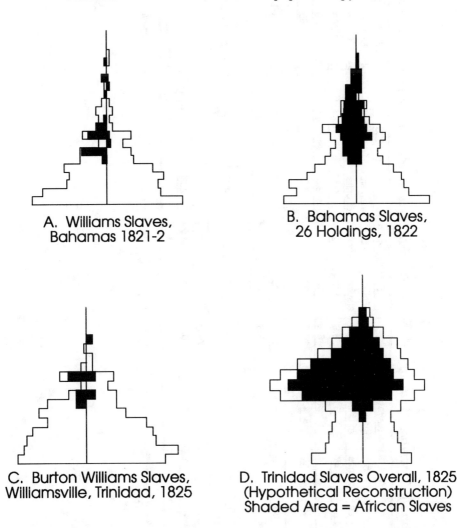

A. Williams Slaves,
Bahamas 1821-2

B. Bahamas Slaves,
26 Holdings, 1822

C. Burton Williams Slaves,
Williamsville, Trinidad, 1825

D. Trinidad Slaves Overall, 1825
(Hypothetical Reconstruction)
Shaded Area = African Slaves

Certainly, the 450 Williams slaves found in the Bahamas in 1821 exhibited an even healthier demographic balance and a higher incidence of family formation than the Bahamian average, as is shown in Figure 4 and Table 4. The proportion of young children was higher, there were only two thirds as many Africans, and yet a fair number of very elderly slaves. The proportion of slaves in nuclear families, 55.8 per cent, was some 2 per cent higher than the average for the 26 holdings analyzed earlier, and the total in some kind of family more than 5 per cent higher, at 90.2 per cent. Yet, by Williams' account, the situation in the Bahamas had become economically and demographically critical by 1821, so that he could neither clothe nor feed his slaves adequately, although

Table 4 Bahamas, Family Formation, Williams Slaves 1822 and 1825 compared with 26 Holdings, 1822.

Family type	A. Williams slaves, 1822				B. Williams slaves, Bahamas, 1825				C. 26 bAhamian holdings, 1822			
	Total slaves	Number of Units	Mean size of units	Percent of total in type	Total slaves	Number of units	Mean size of units	Percent of total in type	Total slaves	Number of units	Mean size of units	Percent of total in type
1. Man, woman, children	251	47	5.34	55.8	103	20	5.15	46.0	1,629	308	5.29	54.1
2. Man, Woman	28	14	2.00	6.2	10	5	2.00	4.5	178	89	2.00	5.9
3. Woman, children	45	10	4.50	10.0	38	14	2.71	17.0	377	95	3.97	12.5
4. Man, children	2	1	2.00	0.5	0	0	—	—	16	3	5.33	0.5
5. Three-generation	80	9	8.88	17.8	25	4	6.25	11.2	358	46	7.78	11.9
6. Single men	15	—	—	3.3	22	—	—	9.8	264	—	—	8.8
7. Single women	14	—	—	3.1	8	—	—	3.5	173	—	—	5.8
8. Separate children	15	—	—	3.3	18	5	3.60	8.0	16	—	—	0.5
Totals	450	—	—	100.0	224	—	—	100.0	3,011	—	—	100.0
A. Nuclear family (1,2,5)	359	70	5.13	79.8	138	29	4.75	61.6	2,165	443	4.89	71.9
B. Denuded family (3,4)	47	11	4.27	10.4	38	14	2.71	17.0	393	98	4.01	13.0
C. No family (6,7,8)	44	—	—	9.8	48	—	—	21.4	453	—	—	15.1

[a] African-headed families were taken to be those in which both parents, either parent, or the single parent were of African birth. Thus in categories 1,2 and 5 in Section A mixed couples were included

he owned 13,000 acres of land. Taking advantage of the inducements offered by Trinidad, he therefore transferred 324 of his slaves in five cargoes between 1821 and 1823.[27]

Although one or two couples were split and an unknown number of extended family members separated, Williams clearly attempted to transfer his slaves predominantly in family units. Comparison of the slaves settled at Williamsville, his new estate in Naparima, in the Trinidadian returns of 1825 with those left behind listed in the Bahamas returns of the same year, indicates also that the majority of the elderly and Africans were left behind, and that rather more young females were carried than young males. The transferred population therefore exhibited many characteristics sharply different from those of the generality of Trinidadian slaves. Only 5.3 per cent of the Williamsville slaves were African-born, compared with the Trinidadian average of over 40 per cent, and females outnumbered males by 7.8 per cent, more than reversing the general Trinidadian pattern. Whether using the categories used elsewhere in this paper or those employed by Higman, the contrast in family formation is even more noticeable. Because of the greater detail given in the Trinidadian registration returns, more types could be differentiated, but the total of Williamsville slaves in some type of family was as high as in the Bahamas sample, and almost twice as high as the Trinidadian average indicated by Higman. The percentage in simple nuclear households, 57.3 per cent, was slightly higher than in the Bahamas, and three times as high as the Trinidadian average. Mothers living alone with their children accounted for only 6 per cent of the Williamsville slaves, half of the Bahamas figure, and little more than a quarter of that for Trinidad as a whole.

As a consequence of the division of the Williams slaves, those left behind and increased even more slowly. However, they did increase, in contrast to Trinidadian slaves in general, who suffered an alarming depletion throughout the registration period. By the end of 1826, 33 of Williams' Trinidadian slaves had died, while 57 were born (49 having been sold and two manumitted), an annual rate of natural increase of roughly 16 per 1,000. This was half the Bahamian rate, and compared with an annual net decrease at least as high for Trinidadian slaves on the average.[28]

Although his 1825 evidence was twisted to justify the transfer, Williams had to admit that the health and morale of his slaves had suffered in the first three years — the seasoning period. 'Fevers and Agues and bowel Complaints', as well as unfamiliar 'Sores', although not great killers, were common among the transferred slaves. These ills Williams attributed to his having arrived in the middle of the wet season, settling in a wooded and marshy area, and being forced to feed his slaves on plantains and saltfish rather than their customary guinea corn (millet or sorghum). He deplored the laxity of Trinidadian morals and the effects on family life of the disparity in the sex ratio. He also pleaded that the demoralizing effects of Colonial Office regulations would encourage the idleness of slaves and limit the powers of correction of their masters. Against the evidence, he denied that the work required of slaves was harder than in the Bahamas, and claimed that slaves had more opportunity in Trinidad to dispose of the surplus food that they grew on their own allotments. However, he remarked that most of the slaves would have returned to the Bahamas if they had been given the choice.[29]

The research undertaken so far not only indicates a far wider existence of family in slave society than hitherto expected, but has also clarified the varieties of family within the range of West Indian slave communities in the late slave period. At one end of the scale were the virtual peasants of the Bahamas, Barbuda and, perhaps, the Grenadines, with locational stability, a small proportion of African slaves, natural increase, and a relatively high incidence of nuclear and stable families. At the opposite pole were the overworked slaves of new plantations such as those of Trinidad, Guyana and St Vincent, with a high rate of natural decrease, a majority of slaves living alone or in 'barrack' conditions, and a high proportion of 'denuded', female-headed families. In between came the mass of West Indian slaves, all but 10 per cent living on plantations of one sort or another, with a wide range of demographic patterns but a generally declining rate of natural increase and a rapidly dwindling African population, and varying degrees of practical exogamy, miscegenation with whites, and family formation.[30]

Unfortunately, statistical information on West Indian slave families is practically limited to the registration period, 1813-34, after the slave trade with Africa had ended, when all plantations were starting to decline, amelioration measures were being applied, and missionaries were beginning to make their influence felt. It remains to be seen whether a morphology of slave family during the entire period of slavery can be inferred, or projected, from this material alone; what additional light is shed by the white-produced literary sources from an earlier period; and, finally, what other arguments can be adduced, including the incorporation of West African material.

Table 5   *Family structure, Williams Trinidadian slaves, 1825 compared with Trinidadian total, 1813 (Higman, 1978)*

Family type	A. Williams slaves, 1825				B. Trinidadian slaves total, 1813			
	Total	Units	Mean size	Per cent in type	Total	Units	Mean size	Per cent in type
Man, woman, children	142	24	5.9	57.4	4,675	1,162	4.0	18.3
Man, woman	6	3	2.0	2.4	1,036	518	2.0	4.0
Woman, children	15	3	5.0	6.0	5,690	2,066	2.8	22.2
Man, children	0	0	—	—	357	138	2.6	1.4
Polygynists	0	0	—	—	31	7	4.4	0.1
Three–generation and extended[b]	47	8	5.9	18.9	445	97	4.6	1.7
Siblings	14	4	3.5	5.7	547	197	2.8	2.1
Siblings, children	9	2	4.5	3.6				
Man, woman, cousins	5	2	2.5	2.0	0	0	—	—
No family[c]	10	—	—	4.0	12,892	—	—	50.2
Totals	**248**	**—**	**—**	**100.0**	**25,673**	**—**	**—**	**100.0**

[a]*Data from Public Record Office, London, T. 71/513 (1825); T. 71/501-503; Higman, 'Family Patterns in Trinidad', 32.*

[b]*In the Williams Population: Man, Woman, Children, their Children (8); Man, Woman, Children, Man's Sister, her Children (7); Man, Woman, Woman's Brother, his Spouse (6); Man, Woman, Child, Man's Brother, his Spouse (5); Man, Woman, Man's Sister, her Child (4); Woman, Children, Spouses (5). In the Higman Total: Woman, her Children, her Grandchildren (227); 'Extended' (218).*

[c]*In the Williams Population, Men and Women living alone, unrelated separated Children.*

Earlier speculation led the present writer and Higman to postulate, and then to refine to the point of dismissal, two successive models. First, if one took the nuclear two-headed family as the quintessentially modern family form, it was beguilingly easy to propose its different incidence during the registration period as relating to the degree of maturation, creolization, or modernization of each slave unit, and thus to suggest a historical progression from some aboriginal African form of family. Such a progression initially seemed borne out by the closer parallels among the modern Jamaican rural communities analyzed by Edith Clarke and the Exumian slaves of Rolle, as compared with Jamaican slave plantation examples, and by the highly developed family patterns traced by Colin Clarke and Lowenthal among the completely creolized peasants of Barbuda in 1851.[51]

However, the discovery by Higman, amply corroborated by the Bahamian material examined here, that Africans were at least as likely as Creoles to form nuclear families, modified the original model. This revision, coupled with the likelihood that the registration records largely concealed the existence of extended families, and the apparent paradox that Creole men were more likely to be polygynous than Africans, led Higman to a second developmental mode, based on the seemingly progressive differences between Trinidad, Jamaica, and Barbados.[32] By this formulation, the establishment of 'elementary nuclear families' was the primary response of the displaced Africans in the first slave generation. This was the stage of fictive kin such as the 'shipmate' relationship described by Edwards. Owing to high mortality, the further shifting of slaves, and a high male ratio, families were able to practise polygyny. A second slave generation began to establish extended families based on the formation of virilocal 'yards' within single plantations; but, because mortality remained high and fresh Africans were continually arriving, the elementary family continued the dominant norm. At this stage polygyny may actually have increased, as an index of status and property. In subsequent generations, kinship networks expanded as slaves increasingly practised exogamy. This occurred earliest and most rapidly where holdings were small and contiguous, and the proportion of Creoles high. The process tended toward matrifocality rather than the nuclear family, especially where lack of slave-controlled provision grounds, money, and property deprived slaves of the chance of 'marriage strategies'.[33]

It was clearly right to de-emphasize the normative role of the slaveowners and to stress that slaves largely determined their own family arrangements. Higman's schematic formulation also properly recognized that a wide variety of family types coexisted in all periods, since different islands and sectors developed at different rates and in different ways. A closer study of the Bahamian materials, however, suggested that it was the Bahamas rather than Barbados which represented the forward extreme of slave family development. Higman's most recent analysis of the 1813 registration returns also suggested that Trinidad was a more special case than previously thought: an area directly supervised and rapidly expanding on the eve of emancipation and changing technology, rather than a frontier area exactly analogous to Barbados in 1650 or Jamaica in 1720. In particular, his scrutiny pointed up three conclusions apparent or latent in the Bahamian material considered here: the critical importance to slave family development of plantation size; the effects of urbanization; and the difficulty of tracing simple cultural transfers from Africa. Even more critically, Higman's earlier model underestimated the formative changes that occurred over the century and a half before the slave trade ended. These included great changes in the intensity of the plantation system and the gradual evolution of systems of slave management aimed at greater efficiency in general, and thus at increasing slave fertility as well. Perhaps most important of all was small and impermanent, and only for a few privileged slaves: this was the filtering down into the West Indies of evolving concepts of the 'modern' family, which gradually gained hold in the practice of creolized slaves, as well as in the minds of white masters.

It is notable that the two most important early writers on British West Indian slavery gave sympathetic accounts of the slaves' society and customs. Ligon (1657) and Sloane (1707) described the early slaves as having a great sense of decorum. Unlike Europeans, they were not ashamed of nakedness and, though with a healthy sex drive, fastidiously avoided public displays of 'wantonness'. They married when they could, and had a rigorous distaste for adultery. 'They have every one his Wife', wrote Sloane, 'and are very much concern'd if they prove adulterous, but in some measure satisfied if their Masters punish the Man who does them the supposed injury, in any of his Hogs, or other small wealth. The care of the Masters and Overseers about their Wives, is what keeps their Plantations chiefly in good order, whence they even buy Wives in proportion to their Men, lest the Men should wander to neighbouring Plantations and neglect to serve them.' The males appeared to be dominant and the practice of polygyny by no means uncommon, being enjoyed, 'by certain brave fellows ... of extraordinary qualities', from the earliest days. In contrast to later reports there was a strong bond of affection between parents and children, particularly between mothers and infants, who, in African fashion, were carried to work in the fields and not weaned for two years or even longer. Great respect and care were shown for the aged, whether or not they were actual kin.[34]

Ligon and Sloane wrote with exceptional objectivity before the plantation system was intensified, and also in a period when extended families were more important than nuclear families in Europe itself, and modern ideas of childhood and parent affection were still relatively strange. Besides, during Ligon's period in Barbados and Sloane's in Jamaica, miscegenation had not yet become institutionalized because there was still a sizeable proportion of whites of both sexes in the labouring population, and the majority of the blacks were unacculturated Africans.

Echoes of Ligon and Sloane could still be heard in later writings, but most gave a far less sympathetic account of the slaves. As Barbados, followed by the Leeward Islands and Jamaica, became dominated by sugar plantations, the planters became more callous and indifferent to slaves' social arrangements. Wedded to the plantations, the slave trade also intensified, and now men imported outnumbered women by three to two. Meanwhile, bourgeois social values increasingly added insult to injury. As far as they were concerned at all, planters disparaged as natural faults, characteristics in their slaves for which the white themselves were chiefly to blame, and often similarly guilty. Thus, although marriage and family life were practically discouraged and forcible miscegenation was rife, planters condemned the slaves' 'promiscuity', 'polygamy', and apparent indifference to their children, or even to having children at all.

Behind the planters' ignorance and exaggeration, however, lay the undoubted truth that the quality of slave life had nearly everywhere deteriorated seriously. In this phase, West Indian families were probably at a low point of integration — before extended new kinships had been built up and laws passed forbidding the separation of husbands and wives, and mothers and children. Except for the polygamous favours enjoyed by privileged slaves like drivers — the slaves' 'worst domestic tyrants' — conjugal unions were rare and impermanent, and the majority of infants lived with single mothers and grandmothers — up to 10 per cent of whom were, or had been, the casual mates of plantation whites.

In the last phase of slavery, as the profits of plantations dwindled, the price of slaves rose, and in 1808, the supply of fresh Africans was cut off and the West Indian slave-owners came under economic constraints at the same time as they were coming under pressure from metropolitan philanthropists. Writers on slave society attacked or defended plantation customs, or proposed methods of raising the dismal level of slave fertility. The encouragement of Christianity and family life was seen by some as methods of making slaves contented, peaceable, and fertile. Some measure of local reform would, moreover, vitiate the arguments of the emancipationists and undermine the sectarian missionaries, who shared none of the establishment's reluctance to proselytize the slaves and promote respectable marriage. Accordingly, in the 1820s, plantocratic Assemblies passed acts ostensibly encouraging slave marriage and actually authorizing fees to Anglican ministers for slave baptisms.

Few writers, though, acknowledged the slaves' own motives. Since all slaves yearned chiefly to be free, if adherence to the Church and its formulas were conditions of freedom, a growing number of slaves would aspire to baptism and formal marriage, with their official registrations, as potent indicators of improving social status. Most writers also ignored the degree to which slaves actually possessed property and virtual tenure of houses and plots, which they were able, in custom if not law, to bequeath to whomever they wished. Long before emancipation, a fair proportion of West Indian slaves had ample reasons, on the grounds of respectability and conformability to the laws of inheritance, to adopt the familial norms of the master class.

But nearly every commentator, from Ligon and Sloane to 'Monk' Lewis and Mrs A. C. Carmichael, did share two absolute certainties: that as to marriage, whatever the masters did, the slaves always had and always would (in the words of the Jamaican, John Quier) 'claim a Right of disposing of themselves in this Respect, according to their Own Will and Pleasure without any Control from their Masters'; and that within certain obvious constraints these voluntary arrangements were African rather than European. 'We restrain their Actions sufficiently, to our conveniences', wrote Lindsay, Rector of St Catherine's, Jamaica, 'tho' we inslave not the Inclinations of the Heart, against their Natural Habits and Native Customs, which may well be injoy'd separately from their Obedience to us.'[35]

Table 6 *West Indian family from slavery to the present: A comparison of Trinidad, Jamaica, and the Bahamas in slavery days with Barbuda immediately after slavery, and with modern rural Jamaica, 1813-1955*

		A. Trinidad, 1813		
Family[a] type	Total slaves	Number of units	Mean size of units	Per cent of total in type
1.	4,675	1,162	4.0	18.3
2.	1,036	518	2.0	4.0
3.	5,690	2,066	2.8	22.2
4.	357	138	2.6	1.4
5.	445	97	4.6	1.7
6.	} 12,892	—	—	50.2
7.				
8.				
Others	578	204	2.8	2.2
	25,673	—	—	100.0
A	6,156	1,777	3.5	24.0
B	6,625	2,408	2.8	25.8
C	12,892	—	—	50.2

		B. Montpelier, Jamaica, 1825		
Family[a] type	Total slaves	Number of units	Mean size of units	Per cent of total in type
1.	204	50	4.1	25.1
2.	76	38	2.0	9.3
3.	328	70	4.7	40.3
4.	0	0	—	—
5.	24	6	4.0	2.9
6.	} 182	—	—	22.4
7.				
8.				
Others	—	—	—	—
	814	—	—	100.0
A	304	94	3.2	37.3
B	328	70	4.7	40.3
C	182			22.6

		C. Bahamas, holdings 26, 1822		
Family[a] type	Total slaves	Number of units	Mean size of units	Per cent of total in type
1.	629	308	5.3	54.1
2.	178	89	2.0	5.9
3.	377	95	4.0	12.5
4.	16	3	5.3	0.5
5.	358	46	7.8	11.9
6.	264	—	—	8.8
7.	173	—	—	5.8
8.	16	—	—	0.5
Others	—	—	—	—
	011			100.0
A	165	443	4.9	71.9
B	393	98	4.0	13.0
C	453	—	—	15.1

Family[a] type	Total population	Number of units	Mean size of units	Per cent of total in type
D. Barbuda, 1851				
1.	425	76	5.6	67.7
2.	28	14	2.0	4.5
3.	50	12	4.2	8.0
4.	6	1	6.0	0.7
5.	90	18	5.0	14.3
6.	7	7	1.0	1.1
7.	10	10	1.0	1.6
8.	13	6	2.2	2.1
Others	—	—	—	—
	629	144	4.7	100.0
A	543	108	5.0	86.3
B	56	13	4.3	8.6
C	30	23	1.3	3.1

E. Rural Jamaica, 1955[b] 1. 'Sugartown' 2. 'Mocca'

Family[a] type	Per cent of total population in type	Per cent of total population in type
1.	} 46	42
2.		
3.	16	117
4.	3	3
5.	18	30
6.		
7.	} 17	9
8.		
Others	—	—
	100	100
A	65	71
B	19	20
C	17	9

[a] *1 = Man, Woman, Children; 2 = Man, Woman; 3 = Woman, Children; 4 = Man, Children; 5 = Three Nuclear Family (1, 2, 5); B = Denuded Family (3, 4); C = No Family (6, 7, 8). Generation Groups; 6 = Men Alone, or Together; 7= Women Alone, or Together; 8 = Children Separately Edith Clarke,* **My Mother Who Fathered Me** *(London 1957), 191-94.*

Few Africans carried their children with them into slavery, and fewer still accompanied marital partners from West Africa into West Indian plantations, let alone the members of the extended family and kinship groups which were of prime importance in West African society. The ethnic mixing which was standard plantation policy meant additionally that the legacies of Africa were transmitted in a haphazard or generalized way. Yet the impress of Africa was indelible, and African patterns were replicated where possible, and reconstituted as soon as possible where not, surviving slavery itself in modified forms.

On large plantations there were sometimes sub-cultural groups — such as 'Ibo' or 'Congo' — and some forceful cultural traditions, particularly the Akan (or 'Coromantee'), seem to have been normative. Yet the very variety of West African roots allowed for creative syncretism, or the choice of alternative customs — for example, concerning the role of women, and the acceptability of cousin-mating and premarital intercourse — as the slaves made the necessary adjustments to the new environment, the dictates of the plantation system, and the shifting demographic conditions.[36]

Some features of the plantation system, such as the expectation that women would work in the fields, that men would monopolize the skilled and privileged roles, and that slave driver and other elite slaves such as head craftsmen would be likely to practise polygyny, actually facilitated the continuation of West African customs.

Other continuities were of necessity more covert, having to exist in the narrow scope of private life left to the slaves by the master class: rites of passage, courtship and pre-marital negotiations, marriage ceremonies and celebrations, and the role of elderly slaves as 'councils of elders' to determine custom and settle domestic disputes. While the slave trade lasted, direct links with Africa were never cut, native Africans being brought in groups to expand plantations or, more commonly arriving in ones and twos to make up the shortfall in slave fertility. As Edwards testified, these Africans were welcomed into family units, especially those of their own tribe and language.[37]

From the simple pairings which were all that the planters provided for, the slaves built up extended family relationships beyond the masters' ken or concern and, in the course of generations, whole new kinship networks based on the cohesive 'village' of a single plantation holding but gradually extending beyond the plantation's bounds into nearby groups. In Barbados, a small island covered with small contiguous plantations, the process of social diffusion had gone on longest; but even there, as in Africa, the primary allegiance remained the village, the birthplace, the home and burial-place of closest family kin, and ancestors.

In 1808 the direct connection with Mother Africa was cut, but by that time the area of social autonomy had significantly expanded for most slaves. Slaves owned their own property (in some colonies even in law), bequeathed and inherited houses and land, and in some islands virtually controlled the internal market system. On declining plantations they were encouraged to be as nearly self-sufficient as possible, and on decayed plantations were left almost entirely to their own devices. Yet, contrary to the masters' pessimism, the young and the aged were better cared for than under more rigorous slave regimes, and the unfavourable ratio between deaths and births began to reverse. In the phrase of Sidney Mintz, the most fortunate British West Indian slaves were proto-peasants long before slavery ended, and made an easy transition into 'full freedom' in 1838.[38]

Four influences militated against the continued development of peasant lifestyles and family systems: the breakup of the old slave quarters and the consequent 'marginalization' of many ex-slaves; the persistence of plantations in a more impersonal form; an accelerated urbanization; and the spread of the canons of respectability. The closing down of the slave cantonments after emancipation, as plantations decayed or turned to less intensive forms of agriculture (particularly, grazing 'pens'), or ex-slaves who refused to work on the planters' terms were evicted from houses and plots, was as traumatic a change as the cutting of the African link or the ending of formal slavery itself. The more fortunate ex-slaves were able to form their own villages and develop a healthy peasant society; but many others without land of their own were forced into a marginal existence, depending on the increasingly mechanized plantations for wages, but competing with each other, and with newly imported indentured labourers, in a cruelly seasonal economy. Far fewer women worked as plantation labourers, and most of the men became transients, living in barracks or strange villages during crop-time and being unable to form permanent or stable attachments while women provided the only permanence and stability for children. A similar continuation of the worst features of the slave period occurred among the poor of the towns, which burgeoned after emancipation. The new towns had a high proportion of migrants from the countryside, a disproportionately high ratio of women, and thus a majority of impermanent, fractured, and matrifocal families.

As we have noticed, many slaves in the last phase of slavery were attracted by the apparent advantages of respectable, European-type families. After emancipation these became the norm among the small emergent middle class, many of the members of which were the coloured descendants of domestic slaves who had engaged in miscegenous relationships. Under the growing influence of the churches, a far wider spectrum of the ex-slaves continued to subscribe outwardly to the canons of respectability, especially in islands like Barbados where the Anglican Church was deeply entrenched and conditions were unfavourable for true peasant development. Yet, as Wilson has plausibly argued, the subscription to respectability is superficial among the majority of British West Indian blacks. Far more deeply engrained are the tenets of 'reputation': those elements of customs which place greater stress on community, kinship, and extended family, and place greater value on social worth, than on introspective family forms, bourgeois manners, and material wealth. In this analysis, reputation provides a continuous thread of tradition passing back through slavery to Africa itself.[39]

Therefore, in assessing the nature of slave family and its place in the continuum we emphasize not the ways that slavery destroyed or distorted family, but the ways in which the slaves' own forms of family triumphed over adversity. In this light, we evaluate slavery not by the manner in which it controlled and shaped slaves' destinies, but by the degree to which it allowed slaves to make family lives of their own.

NOTES

1. John Quier, 'Report of the Jamaican House of Assembly on the Slave Issues', in Lt. Gov. Clarke's No. 93, November 20, 1788; Public Record Office, London, C.O. 137/88, Appendix C.

2. Herbert G. Gutman, *The Black Family in Slavery and Freedom, 1750-1925* (New York, 1976), xxi.

3. Thomas S. Simey, *Welfare and Planning in the West Indies* (Oxford, 1945), 50-51, 79; Fernando Henriques, *Family and Colour in Jamaica* (London, 1953), 103; William J. Goode, 'Illegitimacy in the Caribbean Social Structure', *American Sociological Review*, XXV (1960), 21-30; M. G. Smith, *The Plural Society in the British West Indies* (Berkeley, 1965), 109; Orlando Patterson, *The Sociology of Slavery* (London, 1967), 167.

4. Barry W. Higman, 'Household Structure and Fertility on Jamaican Slave Plantations: A Nineteenth-Century Example', *Population Studies*, XXVII (1973), 527-50; idem, 'The Slave Family and Household in the British West Indies, 1800-1834', *Journal of Interdisciplinary History*, VI(1975), 261-87; *idem, Slave Population and Economy in Jamaica 1807-1834* (Cambridge, 1976) Higman's 'Family Property: The Slave Family in the British Caribbean in the Early Nineteenth Century', unpub. paper (1976), is now largely superseded by his 'African and Creole Slave Family Patterns in Trinidad', paper delivered at the Tenth Conference of Caribbean Historians (1978). See ibid., 12.

5. James Stephen, *The Slavery of the British West India Colonies Delineated* (London, 1824), I, Appendix III, 454-74. The Bahamas, with almost exactly the same total land areas as Jamaica (4,400 square miles), had approximately 10,000 slaves against 300,000 in Jamaica. Barbados, with only 166 square miles, had 65,000 slaves. In 1800, the ratio between blacks and whites in the Bahamas was about 4:1; in Barbados it was 8:1: in Jamaica 12:1.

6. David Eltis, 'The Traffic in Slaves between the British West Indian Colonies, 1807-1833', *Economic History Review*, XXV (1972), 55-64. Perhaps through a misunderstanding, there was a partial census of Bahamian slaves in 1821. Most of these were relisted in 1822, but not all. The 1822 census book gives a grand total of 10,808 slaves, but this seems to omit the slaves listed in 1821 and not relisted in 1822. The intercolonial migration was at its peak between 1821 and 1822; its volume may never be known with complete accuracy.

7. Archives of the Bahamas, Nassau; Register of Returns of Salves, Bahama Islands, 1821-1834. It was fortunate that the Bahamas Registration Act of 1821 required the listing of all slaves every three years, not just an initial census and subsequent triennial increases and decreases as in most other colonies. The Act specified what information should be given but not the order of the lists. Despite this, there seems to have been a remarkable uniformity in the method used by those owners who chose to list their slaves in family and household groups. An absolutely certain distinction between family and household was scarcely possible, but a comparison of the data on slaves transferred from the Bahamas to Trinidad (where the registration returns gave fuller details), and corroboration between the triennial Bahamian censuses, suggested that although extended families were understated, the listings concentrated on families rather than mere cohabitation, and the groups listed were almost invariably cohabiting families, rarely mere 'housefuls'.

8. Craton, 'Hobbesian or Panglossian? The Two Extremes of Salve Conditions in the British Caribbean, 1738-1834', *William and Mary Quarterly*, XXV (1978), 324-56; *idem, Searching for the Invisible Man: Slaves and Plantation Life in Jamaica* (Cambridge, Mass., 1978), 60-118.

9. The proportions of African and coloured slaves in the 26 holdings in 1822 were remarkably close to those in the overall slave population, 20.0 and 6.9%.

10. The average age of mothers at the birth of their first children given in Table 2, 22.37 years, is clearly overstated since the 479 mothers included many whose earlier children were old enough to have left the parental household, and were thus not recorded. When the 251 mothers aged 35 or more at the time of the census were excluded, the average age of the remaining 228 mothers at the birth of their first surviving child was 19.27 years. Of the females in the age range 15-49, 65.6% were indicated as mothers. In all, the 479 mothers listed had 1,456 listed children, an average of 3.02 children each.

11. Of the 26 holdings analyzed, 20 were established in the further islands, with a total of 2,634 slaves, an average of 132 per holding. Six were established in New Providence and Eleuthera, with a total of 367 slaves, an average of 61. In 1834 (the only year for which figures have been tabulated), 481 of the 730 Bahamian holdings of 5 or less slaves, and 692 of the 1,088 of 20 or less, were in New Providence and Eleuthera (including Harbour Island), but only 26 of the 107 Bahamian holdings of more than 20 slaves: Archives of the Bahamas, Nassau; Register of Returns of Slaves, Bahama Islands, 1834. The 1834 tabulation has been made by Gail Saunders.

12. The figure for 1834 was 9.6% but by that date a considerable number had been manumitted.

13. Keith F. Otterbein, *The Andros Islanders: A Study of Family Organization in the Bahamas* (Lawrence, Kansas 1966). There is as yet no scholarly study of family in New Providence, or of the huge migration that has concentrated more than half of the Bahamian population in the capital, Gutman, *op. cit.*, 444-45, 489-91.

14. In the 1822 sample of 26 holdings, 5 possible cases of polygyny occurred. One such was Jack Stewart, a mulatto slave aged 66 belonging to James Moss at Acklin's Island, who appeared to live with Phoebe, an African aged 55, Kate, a Creole aged 37, and 10 children aged between 1 and 15, all listed as mulattoes.

15. Permanent mates and their children generally shared a surname, but in female-headed families and transient unions a practice common later in the Bahamas may have been followed; children went by their mother's surname until they were 21 and then adopted their father's surname.

16. Craton, 'Hobbesian or Panglossian?', 19. Today there are thousands of Rolles in the Bahamas, including, it is said, two thirds of the population of Exuma. Male children often had a prefix or suffix added, as with Young Bacchus, Jack Junior, Little Jim, or the African-sounding Jim Jim, son of Jim. Males were often named after their fathers, females more rarely after their mothers. Out of the 67 family units of the Williams group of slaves transferred to Trinidad, there were 22 males named after their fathers and at least 1 after a grandfather; 4 females were named after their mothers, at least 3 after a grandmother, and 1 after a mother's sister.

17. In the population studied, 28 young mothers lived with their parents, their average ages being 18 years and 9 months. Only 5 were over 20 years old, and the average age at the birth of their first children was 17 years 8 months. Only 1 of the 28 had a second child.

18. Michael Craton, *A History of the Bahamas* (London, 1962), 173-74, 194-96.

19. William Wylly to President W. V. Munnings, August 31, 1818, C.O. 23/67, 147.

20. *Regulations for the Government of the Slaves at Clifton and Tusculum in New Providence, Printed at the Office of the New Gazette*, 1815, enclosed in *ibid.*

21. Of Wylly's 67 slaves in 1821, as many as 53 lived in 8 two-headed households (in 2 of which the family included a teenage single mother), with 1 female-headed family and a maximum of 9 slaves living alone, averaging 49 years old and including 6 elderly Africans. Almost certainly, 3 of the household units at Clifton were the extended family of Jack, the African under-driver, and his wife Sue. Twenty of the 67 slaves were under the age of 10 in 1821. See below, 19-23; C.O. 295/66, 53-59; 295/67, 219; 295/71, 26-35; 295/78, 233-265.

22. D. W. Rose, reporting on the slaves of Exuma, 1802; Craton, History of the Bahamas, 183.

23. Besides 10 African couples, there were 3 holdings in which an African male headed the list with his Creole mate. In these 13 holdings (half of the total) there were 187 Africans out of a total of 805 slaves or 23.2%, not significantly more than the overall average, 18.8%.

24. Act of 4 Geo. IV, c. 6; *Acts of the Assembly of the Bahama Islands* (Nassau, 1827), V, 227-28.

25. Archives of the Bahamas, Manumissions Index; Register of Returns of Salves, 1825, 1828, 1831, 1834; Public Record Office, London; Register of Returns of Slaves, St. Vincent, 1822, 1825. Craton, 'Hobbesian or Panglossian?', 19-20; C.O. 295/67, 219; 295/71, 26-35; 295/78, 233-265; Governor James Carmichael Smyth to Lord Stanley, October 27, 1830, C. O. 23/82, 368-420.

26. Evidence given on January 18, 1825, C. O. 295/66, 53-59. A population of 107 increasing at the Rolle rate for 1822;-34, 34.5 per 1,000 per year, would have reached 331 in the thirty-fourth year.

27.

		Men	Women	Boys	Girls	Infants	
July	1821	27	43	7	5	23	
February	1822	9	11	6	4	24	
July	1822	6	11	3	3	14	
March	1823	10	10	7	5	33	
June	1823	6	11	6	7	33	
		58	**86**	**29**	**24**	**127**	**324**

This compilation was made on September 27, 1823. By that time, 19 children had been added to Williams' slaves by birth, and only 7 of the total had been lost by death. This indicated a crude annual birth rate of 29 per 1,000 and a death rate around 11 per 1,000. However, of 3,239 slaves imported into Trinidad from all sources between 1813 and 1822 (1,678 being males and 1,561 females), 232 males and 156 females had died, 388 in all, against only 236 births; C.O. 295/59, 252, 255.

28. 'Return showing the number of Negroes imported into this Island by Burton Williams Esq.', enclosed in Governor Sir Ralph Woodford to William Huskisson, March 7, 1828, C.O. 295/77, 33-49.

29. C.O. 295/66, 57.

30. Craton, 'Hobbesian or Panglossian?', 19-21; Colin Clarke and David Lowenthal, 'Barbuda; the Past of a Negro Myth', in Vera Rubin and Arthur Tuden (eds), *Comparative Perspectives on Slavery in New World Plantation Societies* (New York, 1977), 510-34.

31. The argument is proposed in Craton, 'Hobbesian or Panglossian?' which was first delivered at the conference on Comparative Perspectives in New World Plantation Societies, New York, 1976. Edith Clarke, *My Mother Who Fathered Me* (London, 1957).

Barbuda Household Types, 1851

Household type	Number of units	Number of persons	Persons per unit	Per cent total persons per unit type	
1. Man, woman, children	76	425	5.59	67.57	
2. Man and woman	14	28	2.00	4.45	
3. Woman and children	12	50	4.17	7.95	
4. Man and children	1	6	6.00	0.95	
5. Three generations (i.e. two women and children)	18	90	5.00	14.31	(95.23)
6. Men alone	7	7	1.00	1.11	
7. Women alone	10	10	1.00	1.59	
8. Women together	6	13	2.17	2.07	(4.77)
	144	**629**	**4.73**	**100.00**	

Source: Colin Clarke and D. Lowenthal, private correspondence (Codrington records, Gloucester Country Record Office, England).

32.What follows is the argument proposed by Higman, 'Family Property', now superseded by his 'Slave Family Patterns in Trinidad', 1977. The change was based on the analysis of the full 1813 slave population of 25,673 (a quarter of whom lived in Port of Spain), rather than the rural sample of 1,296 previously used.

33. Bryan Edwards, *The History, Civil and Commercial, of the British Colonies in the British West Indies* (London 1801), II, 155.

34. Richard Ligon, *A True and Exact History of the Island of Barbadoes* (London, 1657), 47; Hans Sloane, *A Voyage to the Islands Madera, Barbados, Nieves, S. Christophers and Jamaica* (London, 1725), II, xlviii; Stanley L. Engerman, 'Some Economic and Demographic Comparisons of Slavery in the United States and the British West Indies', *Economic History Review*, XXIX (1976), 258-75.

35. Quier, 'Report', 492; Lindsay, 'A Few Conjectural Considerations upon the Creation of the Human Race, Occasioned by the Present Quixottical Rage of setting the Slaves from Africa at Liberty', unpub. ms. dated Spanish Town, July 23, 1788, British Museum, Add. Mss. 12439.

36. Higman, 'Slave Family Patterns in Trinidad', 14-18, 33-35. This strongly stresses the melding effect of the African slave trade to Trinidad. Only among the Ibo was there a recognizable transfer of specific African family patterns, and this was attributed to the high numbers and comparatively even sex ratio. When the African slaves were broken down by 7 general regions of origin there were no really significant variations in the proportions of family types recreated in Trinidad.

37. Edwards, British West Indies, II, 155.

38. Sidney W. Mintz, *Caribbean Transformations* (Chicago, 1974), 151-52.

39. Peter J. Wilson, *Crab Antics: The Social Anthropology of English-Speaking Negro Societies of the Caribbean* (New Haven, 1973).

B. W. Higman

HOUSEHOLD STRUCTURE AND FERTILITY ON JAMAICAN SLAVE PLANTATIONS: A NINETEENTH CENTURY EXAMPLE

It is generally agreed that the marital instability and casual mating characteristic of West Indian family structure depress fertility.[1] These conditions are traced to the mating organization of the slaves.[2] The stresses placed on the African family systems of the slaves are obvious: the continued importation of slaves, most of them young adult males; the ruthless separation of kin through sale or removal; the overwhelming authority of the master, reducing the dependence of children on their parents and the economic role of the male household head. Yet, in spite of these stresses, there is evidence of strong bonds of kinship and sense of family among the slaves.

Studies of slave family structure and its connection with fertility have so far depended on literary sources. The analysis of actual slave families might be expected to contribute to the search for other in these patterns, but the data necessary for such detailed studies are rarely available. The present study of two Jamaican sugar estates (Old and New Montpelier) and a livestock pen (Shettlewood) is based on a unique set of documents which enables the identification of households, for the year 1825, within the context of data for the period 1817-32. In spite of certain limitations in the data, it does present empirical evidence of slave household structure and its relation to fertility for the first time.

THE DATA

For the years 1824 to 1828, the Account Book of Old Montpelier estate contains five lists of the slaves on the estate, giving the name, age, sex, colour, country of birth and occupation of each slave.[4] That for January 1827 also notes the state of health of the slaves and their mothers' names (when the mother was living on the estate). That for

1828 gives both the 'old' and 'Christian' names of the slaves, and notes their 'disposition' (towards their masters). The Account Book also contains a 'Report of the State and Condition of Old Montpelier Negro Houses and Provision Grounds and the Number of Stock possessed by each family', dated 1 August 1825. The first column of this report is titled 'Names with their families and dependants, if any' and consists of groups of names, the number of individuals in each group being totalled in the margin. The second column is headed 'Conditions of houses' and links to each of the groups in the first column a description of one or more houses. These groups and their associated houses can be confidently identified as 'households'. Then follow detailed statements of the livestock, gardens and provision grounds belonging to each group, a description of the provisions planted, and remarks on the 'state of culture' of the grounds. A total of 47 households are listed in the report, but it is clear that pages have been lost from the Account Book.

In 1832 Lord Seaford, owner of the properties, presented to the House of Lords 'a report made to me, on my application, by the gentleman managing by estates', dated 1 August 1825'.[5] This was a continuation of the Old Montpelier report found in the Account Book, listing 124 households, and similar data for New Montpelier and Shettlewood. Seaford's purpose in producing this report was to impress the opponents of slavery with the comforts and wealth of his slaves, not to make any statement regarding household structure. Thus, the data are relatively neutral.

The reports contain no information about kinship. This gap can be filled, in part, by using the returns of registrations of slaves made in 1817, 1820, 1823, 1826, 1829 and 1832.[6] The returns for (28th June) 1817 list the names of the slaves, their age, colour, country and mother's name (when she lived on the same property). The subsequent returns give the same data for all slaves entering or leaving the population, whether by birth, purchase or removal, or death, manumission or sale.

These three sets of data have been collated and analyzed using methods analogous to family reconstitution.[7] The problem of the identification of individuals is partly circumvented in this study, since slaves could not enter or leave the population without record. But names did change. In July 1816 almost all of the slaves at Old Montpelier, five-sixths of those at New Montpelier and half of those at Shettlewood were baptized, thus receiving 'Christian' names and surnames before the first registration of 1817.[8] Yet the old names recurred. Three household members could not be identified at Old Montpelier, 15 at New Montpelier, and two at Shettlewood. Consequently, several single-member households and one household of six have had to be excluded from some sections of the household analysis.

The limitations of the data are fairly clearly defined. They say nothing about paternity. Even links through the maternal line are discoverable only if the mother was living (on the same property as her child) in 1817. This, together with the underrecording of births 1817-23, makes it impossible to compute completed family size or the spacing of births. The 1825 household report provides only a static picture of the residential pattern. Fertility for the period 1817-32 can only be related to household structure as it was in 1825.

THE SETTING

The limitations of the study extend beyond the data to the period and places considered. The period 1817-32 was not typical of slavery in Jamaica since it came after the abolition of the slave trade in 1807. The two estates and the pen were larger than average, and were relatively recently settled. The owner, Charles Rose Ellis (created Lord Seaford in 1826), was described as a 'humane, well-intentioned' absentee proprietor. He was the 'acknowledged head' of the West India interest.[9] In 1797 he brought in a motion which placed in the hands of the colonial legislatures, the encouragement of 'a reform in the manners and morality of the negroes' which would end polygamy, a family system he thought unfavourable to population growth.[10] But this was more a delaying tactic than evidence of genuine interest in amelioration. (The Jamaica Assembly had already, in 1791, decreed that slave families should be preserved as far as possible when sold.)[11] In 1831, Seaford invited the Moravians to instruct his slaves, but they declined since they expected the Anglicans to erect a church nearby.[12] Seaford's benevolence seems to have extended little beyond permitting the salves to run livestock on the estate pastures.[13]

Old and New Montpelier estates were located in the valley of the Great River, in the western parish of St James, about twelve miles from Montego Bay; Shettlewood pen adjoined, being on the western side of the river, in Hanover. They occupied 10,000 acres in St James and 2,000 acres in Hanover. Old Montpelier was settled about 1745 and the New Works in 1775. In the 1820s, 600 acres were in cane on the former estate and 400 acres on the latter.[14] A total of 7,632 acres were in woodland and ruinate on the two estates.[15] At Old Montpelier the works and slaves' houses covered 45 acres and the Negro grounds 350 acres. The estates produced nothing for sale, other than sugar and rum. Shettlewood pen fattened and butchered their old livestock, and bred planters' steers and mules for sale.[16]

In 1817 there were 958 slaves living on the three properties, by 1832 only 825 (Table 1). Males were in a minority throughout the period. At Shettlewood, where the male proportion declined steadily, there was a corresponding decline in the African group; but the latter process was very similar at Old Montpelier and there the sexes remained fairly evenly balanced. Whereas the rate of natural increase improved at Old Montpelier and, considerably, at Shettlewood, there was a deterioration at New Montpelier. If African mortality and fertility are excluded, it appears that there was a consistent natural increase in the creole population at Old Montpelier, that such a pattern emerged at Shettlewood after 1820, and that at New Montpelier an increase became a decrease from about 1821 (Figure 1)

TABLE 1   *Vital rates*

	1817		1820		1823		1826		1829		1832
Old Montpelier Estate											
Slave population	426		412		400		395		1829		1832
Males per 100 females	98		96		96		96		101		100
Percentage African	39		35		32		30		27		25
Births per 1,000		23		17		18		21		24	
Deaths per 1,000		33		29		22		20		30	
Natural increase		-10		-12		-4		+1		-6	
New Mountpelier Estate											
Slave population	303		353		334		319		303		288
Males per 100 females	89		93		98		96		93		91
Percentage African	46		45		42		40		38		38
Births per 1000		25		12		13		8		13	
Deaths per 1,000		27		30		28		25		29	
Natural increase		-2		-18		-15		-17		-16	
Shettlewood Pen											
Slave population	229		155		146		146		157		154
Males per 100 females	78		70		74		64		63		62
Percentage African	45		37		32		28		24		21
Births per 1,000		5		18		27		37		28	
Deaths per 1,000		41		33		25		13		21	
Natural increase		-38		-15		+2		+24		+7	

Note: Trienna ending 30 June. For 1829-32 the death of slaves killed in the rebellion of December 1831 are excluded from the death rate two at Old Montpelier and four at Shettlewood.

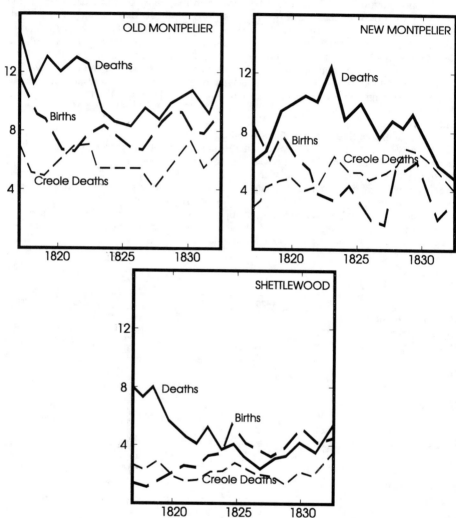

FIGURE 1 *Births, deaths (total) and creole deaths (three-year moving averages)*

The causes of all these contrasts are not apparent, but some can be explained by population movements, the maturity of the properties and the related patterns of age distribution. At least 70 slaves were moved to Shettlewood from the eastern end of the island between March 1816 and 1817,[17] and in 1819 the survivors of the 'seasoning' period went to New Montpelier. Of the 53 slaves moved, 13 of the 25 males and 18 of the 28 females were Africans, all aged between 28 and 42 years. None of the creoles in the group was more than 15 years of age. It seems that mothers were not separated from children in this move, and that siblings whose mothers died between 1817 and 1819 were kept together. The youthful age structure of the creoles at New Montpelier in 1819, which resulted from this age-specific migration and associated high fertility could not be sustained, as fertility declined throughout the period (Figure 2). By 1831 the age structure had been heavily eroded in the age-groups under 20 years. A similar erosion occurred at Old Montpelier and Shettlewood, but there growth in the under-ten-years group was renewed by 1831. At New Montpelier both the youthful age structure at the beginning of the period and the failure to grow again before 1832 can be explained by the large and augmented African section.

FIGURE 2 *Age distribution, at 1 January (the chart for Africans show all three propertities together)*

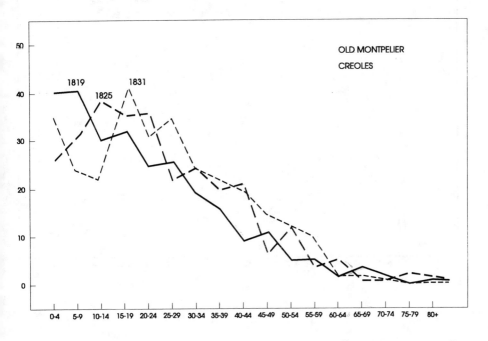

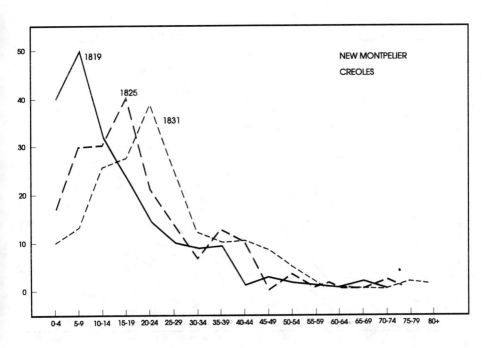

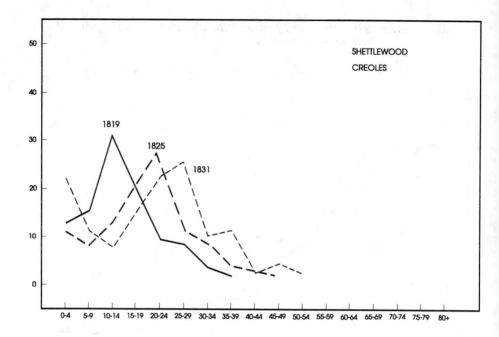

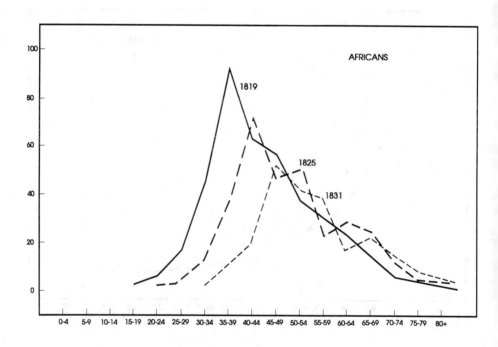

The way in which the slaves were allocated to occupations is known only for Old Montpelier. There more than half of the females worked in the fields. Men had a wider range of occupations, especially in the trades. Almost all of the males slaves of colour were put to trades, though they did not dominate the group. The female slaves of colour, however, made up almost all of those who were domestics or washerwomen. Thus, only aged or invalid black females could expect to escape labour in the fields, and it was more difficult for women to attain positions of status or relative independence. The pattern at New Montpelier must have been very similar to that at Old Montpelier. On large pens, such as Shettlewood, the slaves were organized into gangs, but there were more isolated, semi-independent tasks to be performed than on sugar estates. In 1825, about 42 of the estate slaves were listed as being occupied at 'Farm'. Farm was a part of the estate, according to Hakewill, 'which is cultivated for the supply of the estates with vegetables and ground provisions; where a range of cottages has likewise been built for the convalescent negroes or others whose health may require rest or particular attention'.[18] Farm is about 3 miles east of the Great River, elevated 500 feet above the valley floor. In 1825, many of the slaves there suffered from elephantiasis, leprosy and ulcers, but there were at least two or three healthy families whose function must have been the production of provisions.

The slave populations of the three properties were not strictly closed. At the end of 1825 seven whites lived at Old Montpelier, and there was a constant turnover of overseers. Between 1817 and 1832, white men fathered 32 slave children, ten mulattoes, 21 quadroons and one mustee.[19] Mulatto men, either slave or free, had eight sambo children by black slave women. Free coloured people lived on and around the properties, and from time to time large numbers of slaves were hired to work on the estates.

THE HOUSEHOLDS

The limitations of the 1825 household report, noted above, make it difficult to classify the households satisfactorily. An attempt to do so is shown in Table 2. In addition to the 252 households classified, there were 25 households at Farm, most consisting of single individuals. The latter have been excluded from the general analysis because of the temporary character of the establishment at Farm.

TABLE 2 *Household structure*

Household type	Number of households			
	Old Montpelier	New Montpelier	Shettlewood	Total
1. Woman and her children	10	13	6	29
2. Woman, her children and grandchildren	—	1	3	4
3. Woman, her children, her nephews and nieces (and their children)	1	—	1	2
4. Male, woman and her children	19	25	6	50
5. Male, woman, her children and grandchildren	3	1	—	4
6. Siblings, and others	2	2	4	6
7. Woman, her children, and others	19	13	3	35
8. Male	14	5	6	25
9. Female	13	3	3	19
10. Males	5	1	1	7
11. Females	2	1	1	4
12. Male and female	26	6	7	39
13. Males and females	10	13	5	28
Total	**124**	**94**	**44**	**252**

Household type	Percentage of households			
	Old Montpelier	New Montpelier	Shettlewood	Total
1. Woman and her children	8.1	15.5	13.6	11.5
2. Woman, her children and grandchildren	—	1.2	6.8	1.6
3. Woman, her children, her nephews and nieces (and their children)	0.8	—	2.4	0.8
4. Male, woman and her children	15.3	29.8	13.6	19.8
5. Male, woman, her children and grandchildren	2.4	1.2	—	1.6
6. Siblings, and others	1.6	2.4	4.5	2.4
7. Woman, her children, and others	15.3	15.5	6.8	13.9
8. Male	11.3	5.9	13.6	9.9
9. Female	10.5	3.6	6.8	7.5
10. Males	4.0	1.2	2.4	2.8
11. Females	1.6	1.2	2.4	1.6
12. Male and female	21.0	7.0	15.9	15.5
13. Males and females	8.1	15.5	11.2	11.1
Total	**100.0**	**100.0**	**100.0**	**100.0**

Household type	Number of occupants			
	Old Montpelier	New Montpelier	Shettlewood	Total
1. Woman and her children	38	36	21	95
2. Woman, her children and grandchildren	—	5	14	19
3. Woman, her children, her nephews and nieces (and their children)	7	—	8	15
4. Male, woman and her children	72	104	28	204
5. Male, woman, her children and grandchildren	18	6		24
6. Siblings, and others	7	10	5	22
7. Woman, her children, and others	111	68	20	199
8. Male	14	5	6	25
9. Female	13	3	3	19
10. Males	10	2	2	14
11. Females	5	2	2	9
12. Male and female	50	12	14	76
13. Males and females	30	43	20	93
Total	**375**	**296**	**143**	**814**

On the three properties taken together the modal household consisted of a male, a woman and her children (Type 4). This type was followed by Types 12(a male and a female), 7(a woman, her children, and others) and 1(a woman and her children). More than half the households contained consanguines (identifiable through the maternal line). The picture changes somewhat if the household types are analyzed in terms of the number of individuals they accounted for. Almost three-quarters of the slaves lived in households containing consanguines (Types 1-7). Half of them lived in households of Types 4 and 7, the latter being in many cases essentially a sub-type of Type 4. Thus, although fewer than 25 per cent of the slaves lived exclusively with identifiable kin, almost 50 per cent lived in households approximating the elementary family. This has important implications for the understanding of slave family structure. It suggests that the woman-and-children household type was far from dominant, whatever the importance of the mother-child-link.

In terms of households, Type 4 was modal only at New Montpelier, while at the other two properties Type 12 was modal. In terms of occupants, however, Type 4 was modal at Shettlewood and Type 7 at Old Montpelier. These variations highlight the origins of the importance of the elementary family type. Relatively, this type was most important at New Montpelier, the estate that was the most recently settled, suffered the greatest stresses in terms of the movement of slaves, had the highest proportion of Africans and the heaviest mortality. The implications of this pattern must be sought in the composition of the households.

TABLE 3   *The distribution between the household types of Africans and slaves of colour*

| | Africans | | | Slaves of colour | | |
Household type	Number	Percentage* A	B	Mulatto	Number Quadroon	Sambo
1	21	67.7	22.1	3	7	1
2	3	75.0	15.0	1	1	—
3	—	—	—	6	6	—
4	66	67.3	33.2	2	—	2
5	4	50.0	16.0	—	—	—
6	3	—	13.6	—	—	—
7	56	47.5	28.1	3	2	7
8	17	—	73.9	—	—	2
9	14	—	82.3	—	—	—
10	6	—	42.8	—	—	—
11	4	—	44.4	1	—	—
12	45	—	46.8	—	—	1
13	41	—	45.1	—	—	—
Totals	**280**	—	—	**16**	**16**	**14**

The A percentages exclude all 'children', while the B percentages are based on the total populations including children.

The distribution of Africans among the household types was similar to that for the total populations (Table 3). In absolute numbers, the concentrations of Africans into Type 4 at New Montpelier was greater than that for any of the household types on the other two properties. Thus, when Africans formed households, other than single-member units, they most often established those of Type 4, whereas creoles participated in the more complex Type 7. This might suggest that the Africans attempted to maintain nuclear families, while the creoles, dislocated by the experience of slavery, were unable to do so; or it may simply signify that the ramifications of creole kinship were that much greater.

The distribution of slaves of colour contrasted strongly with that of Africans (Table 3). Those with white fathers (mulattoes and quadroons) lived almost exclusively in households dominated by mothers, grandmothers and aunts. There was no place for slave mates in such households. But it is also true that some slave women had fairly long-term relationships with whites. By contrast, sambo children (whose mothers were almost always black) generally lived in households containing potential male mates (black men), but always lacking potential fathers (mulattoes).

A general consideration of the age structure of the household types is not very useful since it conceals too many other variables. Almost all of them contained the whole spectrum of ages, especially those consisting of consanguines. Slaves living alone tended to be relatively old, most being Africans over 40 years of age. As the slaves aged, the major shift was from households based on consanguines (especially the mother-and-children type) to those containing males and females who were not identifiable kin. But this pattern was confused by the connection between the African/creole ratio and age.

At Old Montpelier, at least, there was a relationship between occupation and household type. Field slaves were to be found in all of the types, except Type 3 (in which all of the slaves were coloured domestics or tradesmen). In general, field slaves comprised about half of the occupants of each type. The drivers most often lived in households containing women and children rather than non-kin. Tradesmen followed a similar pattern, but more often lived alone or in groups of males and females who were not identifiable kin. Domestics tended to live in households dominated by women. Since they were often older, slaves employed in minor field tasks frequently lived with non-kin.

Colour, country, age and occupation were not independent but related characteristics, so that some broad patterns emerge. The Africans, the ageing section of the population, formed either elementary families or lived alone. Most of those living alone were over 40 years of age and the men, who were generally employed as watchmen, could not easily find a place in the wider household system. Slaves of colour, however, with their privileged occupations allying them to the great house and the whites, formed households in which slave men had no part but were tightly organized around the maternal connection. Creole blacks, the majority of the population and of the field labour force, were widely distributed among the household types but were a dominant element in Types 7 (mothers, their children, and others) and 10-13 (groups of males and females who cannot be identified as kin). The ramifications of kinship among the creoles were important organizing factors which could not be matched by the common experience of regional origin or of being shipmates for the Africans.

MATES

Household type 4 has so far been defined as comprising a male, a woman and her children. More needs to be known about the 'male' before it can be considered an elementary family. In only three cases can the 'male' and 'woman' be identified certainly as mates. Three weeks after the household report was made, in August 1825, Charles Rose (Ellis) and Ann Ellis 1st of Old Montpelier were married by an Anglican priest.[20] They were creole blacks, Charles Rose (aged 34 years) being a mason and Ann Ellis (31 years) working in the first gang. Ann Ellis's two children lived with them, immediately before the marriage, in a 'good stone house, shingled' with a new kitchen. They possessed two cows, a steer and a bull calf, ten hogs and four chickens, and had the use of six acres of provision grounds in which were planted yams, cocos, corn and plantains. On the same day in 1825, Charles Beckford married Becky Richards of New Montpelier; they, too, were creole blacks, aged 26 and 37 years respectively. Becky Richards' daughter, aged 15 years, lived with them. Their house was of wattle and thatch and the only livestock they had were hogs and chickens; they had but one acre of provision grounds. In 1827, Richard Trail and Elizabeth Miller of Shettlewood were married.[21] Like the other couples, they were black creoles, but were younger (24 and 23 years respectively). In 1825 they had lived together, with Elizabeth Miller's two children, who were both surnamed Trail, suggesting that they were also Richard Trail's children. Their house was wattled and thatched, but in bad condition; they had a cow and three acres planted in yams, cocos and plantains. At Old and New Montpelier the mothers of the married couples had all died by 1825, but the mothers of Richard Trail and Elizabeth Miller, both Africans, lived with their other children. Thus, while marriage was confined to creole blacks who already lived together, with the woman's children, it included a wide range of ages and, probably, of statuses within the slave hierarchy.

The identification of mates in the remaining households must rest on less solid evidence. The two most obvious indicators are the age difference of the potential mates and the ordering of individuals within the household lists. All of those in household type 4 were older than 20 years and most were over 40 years of age (Table 4). At Old Montpelier, 12 of the 'males' and 'women' were separated by less than ten years, but only three by more than 20 years. At New Montpelier 13 were separated by less than ten years, 11 by more than ten, but only two by more than 20. At Shettlewood none of the six potential mates were separated by more than 11 years. Thus, the evidence from age suggests that most of the men and women living in household type 4 were mates.

TABLE 4   *Ages of male and female co-residents in household type 4*

Age of 'male'	Age of 'women' co-resident						Total 'males'
	20-29	30-39	40-49	50-59	60-69	70+	
20-29	2	3	2	—	—	—	7
30-39	—	1	4	—	—	—	5
40-49	I	3	9	2	—	—	I5
50-59	1	5	8	1	—	—	15
60-69	—	1	3	1	—	1	6
70+	—	—	1	—	—	—	1
Total 'women'	4	13	27	4	—	1	—

The evidence provided by the ordering of names within the household lists is tantalizing but inconsistent. For Old Montpelier the lists are ordered in a manner suggestive of status within the household. With one exception, all the Type 4 households in which the male and female differed in age by less than ten years are ordered thus: male, woman, her children (listed by age). At Shettlewood the form was, with two exceptions, slightly different: woman, male, the female's children. At New Montpelier the household members were divided by sex: male, the woman's male children, woman, her daughters. Thus, these data cannot be used to determine male or female headship. But only five of the Type 4 households were arranged so that the male was placed at the end of the list, and most of these involved men and women more than 20 years apart in age. Probably 90 per cent of the males and females in this type, then, were mates.

Male mates can also be sought in household types 5, 6, 7, 12 and 13. Of the four households of Type 5 (male, woman, her children and grandchildren) only two seem to be extensions of Type 4. The males in the other two households were in their twenties, whereas the women were in their fifties and seventies; they were most probably collaterals. Using the same principles, it seems that roughly half the households of Types 6 and 7 contained mates. For household type 12 (male and female) the only available evidence is that of age, and on this basis it appears that about 75 per cent of the pairs may have been mates (Table 5). In Type 13 (males and females) additional evidence can be found in the ordering of the lists, and this suggests a similar proportion to that found for Type 12; but the possible complexities, of course, are much greater.

TABLE 5   *Ages of male and female co-residents in household type 12*

Age of male	Age of female co-resident								Total males
	0-9	10-19	20-29	30-39	40-49	50-59	60-69	70+	
0-9	—	—	—	—	—	—	—	—	—
10-19	—	—	1	—	—	—	—	—	1
20-19	—	1	1	3	—	1	1	—	7
30-39	—	—	2	5	1	—	—	—	8
40-49	1	1	—	4	3	2	—	—	11
50-59	—	—	—	—	6	2	—	—	8
60-69	—	—	—	—	—	1	—	—	1
70+	—	—	—	—	—	—	1	1	2
Total females	1	2	4	12	10	6	2	1	—

In general, probably 100 of the 252 households contained mates. Almost half of these households contained only their — or rather the woman's — children. It is impossible to estimate the number of women who did not live together with their mates, but there must have been at least 30. Some of their mates had died, others lived in separate houses or even on other properties. There is concrete evidence of the latter. In 1825, James Lewis of Shettlewood cut the throat of his 'wife', Ann Thomas of Old Montpelier, and then killed himself.[22] They were aged 30 and 24 years respectively. Both were the children of African mothers who were living in 1825, and both seem to have lived all their lives on their particular properties.

POLYGYNISTS

In the 1825 report five men, but no women, were listed for two houses, all of them at Old Montpelier. In the second house for which they were listed their names appear at the end of the list, in parentheses. George Ellis, a creole carpenter aged 54 years, lived with the mother of Ann Thomas (mentioned above), her three children and the son of Ann Thomas. His second house comprised Bessy Ellis, an African nurse, her five children, and an aged invalid woman. Like George Ellis, most of the other men attributed to two houses held positions of authority on the estate. The head driver, David Richards 2nd, a black creole aged 49 years, lived in one house with an invalid creole woman aged 47, and a mulatto washerwoman and her (but not his) quadroon daughter. In his second house, the only occupant was a black creole woman aged 37, who worked in the first gang. William Squires, an African aged 50 years, who was in the first gang and acted as stillerman, lived with an African woman aged 45 years; in his second house lived an invalid African aged 41 years and her two children. Similarly, William Richards 1st was an African aged 49 years who worked in the first gang and as boiler; an African woman lived in each of his houses, one aged 45 and the other 43 years, and both working in the first gang. Finally, James Hedley, a 34-year-old creole of the first gang, lived with a creole woman aged 39 years who worked alongside him; in his second house lived another creole woman, aged 45 years, and her daughter.

Although the available evidence does not make it possible to identify these men as polygynists with certainty, it is probable that they were. Their positions within the slave hierarchy fit closely the contemporary testimony on polygamy. In every case the houses were occupied only by women and their children, excluding the possibility of co-resident mates other than the potential polygynists. It must also be noticed that, with the exception of David Richards, the two houses were always adjacent in the list which, it will be argued below, signified spatial contiguity. The creoles were as significant as the Africans but, unlike the 'monogamous' mates, the 'polygamous' households at Old Montpelier were generally either exclusively African or exclusively creole.

Polygynists living with several women in a single house are more difficult to identify. They can be looked for in household types 7 and 13. About one-third of these 63 households consisted of a man and more than one woman (and their children), but in terms of their age structure only a minority of these could have been mates.

GRANDMOTHERS

The 'grandmother family' was virtually unknown on the three properties; that is, no households were discovered consisting of a woman and her grandchildren, the mother of the children living elsewhere. In the households containing identifiable grandchildren (Types 2 and 5) the mothers lived in the same household, with the exception of three cases in which the mothers had died. But the data are limited because the link between a woman and her grandchildren is known only if the mother was alive in 1817. Thus, it is necessary to consider the possibility of grandchildren living with their grandmothers, their mothers having died before 1817. These may be sought in household types 6, 11, 12 and 13, using some basic principles; the woman and potential grandchild must be at least 30 years separated in age, the woman could not be a creole and the child African, and the mother of the child must have been dead by 1817. Applying these rules, only four of the 28 Type 13, two of the 39 Type 12, and one of the four Type 11 households could have contained grandmothers and grandchildren, all but one of them at Old Montpelier, the longest established of the estates. Thus, even in the widest sense the 'grandmother family' must have been extremely rare.

Since nothing is known about paternity, it is difficult to dissect those households which might have been headed by men in the absence of female mates. A man's potential children are not easily distinguished from potential grandchildren or collaterals. But, even with the most generous assumptions it is certain that fewer than ten households (of Types 10, 12 and 13) could have consisted of fathers and their children or grandchildren. In the absence of their mothers, children rarely lived with their paternal kin.

MOVEMENT AND SEPARATION

The 1825 household report was made six years after 53 slaves had been moved from Shettlewood to New Montpelier. What was the impact of this disruption on household structure? In 1825, some 33 of them survived at New Montpelier, being distributed among 14 households; another five lived at Farm. Five Africans and one creole (whose mother had died) moved singly into households made up of New Montpelier slaves. All of these households were of Type 13, indefinable groups of males and females, except that an African, Moses Richards, established a house with a New Montpelier African and her three children (aged 14, five and two years). But the remaining 27 Shettlewood slaves lived in eight households which contained no New Montpelier slaves. All but one of the children continued to live with their mothers. Two of the households were of Type 1, one of Type 4, and one of Type 7; the latter contained an African man and woman, her two children, and the daughter of an African who died before the move from Shettlewood. Two African men lived together, while two pairs of Africans (possible mates) established households. An African man lived with a girl, perhaps his daughter, whose mother had died in 1820. In sum, there is little evidence that the movement of the slaves disrupted the relationships of mates or mothers and children. But the Shettlewood slaves probably found it difficult to integrate themselves into the New Montpelier household system. Only Africans, who moved in with other Africans (perhaps shipmates or fellow countrymen) had any success in this respect. The women mothered very few children after going to New Montpelier, so that no child born between 1819 and 1825 was alive in the latter year. This pattern began to change only at the end of the 1820s when the girls who had come from Shettlewood reached maturity.

The impact on family structure of movement to Farm was much more disruptive, because of its selective nature. Two households there consisted of an African man and woman, and each woman's three children. Two other women lived with a single child each, but most of the slaves lived alone or in pairs. Only two of the slaves at Farm had mothers living on the estates. In part, this isolation was a result of the diseases from which the slaves suffered. The slaves living in family groups were all healthy and probably constituted the basic work force of Farm. Once again it is noticeable that the slaves who moved from Shettlewood to New Montpelier, and then to Farm, lived in a more tightly knit group than the other slaves.

SPATIAL ASPECTS

On each of the properties the slaves' houses were within 200 yards of the works or great house. At New Montpelier the houses were sited on a slope by the Great River; at Old Montpelier, one mile to the east, they were on a hill behind the works. A print produced in 1820 represents the latter, showing 14 of the slaves' houses concealed by trees.[23] These houses appear to be arranged irregularly, unlike some other estates where they were set out in lines, suggesting that the Montpelier slaves were permitted some latitude in the location of their houses. The manner in which the household reports were compiled is unknown, but since the overseer had to make a visual inspection of the houses and grounds, the listing probably follows some sort of route from house to house. Thus, it is likely that houses listed next to one another were spatially adjacent as well.

Some 'households' occupied more than one house. In many cases this was simply part of the process of decay and reconstruction; for example: 'old house, rather bad; wattled and shingled; a small new house' or 'wattled and thatched; small and bad; a new one, Spanish walled and shingled, but not quite finished'. Such cases have been ignored. At Old Montpelier two households occupied three houses, both of them consisting of women, their children and others. One of these comprised nine slaves; a male hospital attendant, a woman and her two black children (and her free brown children), an aged African invalid woman, an adolescent quadroon carpenter, a young woman whose African mother had died in 1819, a sambo woman and her black daughter. The other three-house household contained a black woman and her four sambo children (two masons and a washerwoman), a mother and her daughter, and an invalid woman. These households had the use of 12 and 13 acres of provision grounds, respectively, and held large numbers of livestock. The only other three-house unit was that listed first for New Montpelier; it consisted simply of a man, a woman and her two children, but they had far more livestock than any other household. Households occupying two houses also generally appeared early in the lists. It is evident that these households had more than one house not because of their numbers, but because of their privilege occupations and relative prosperity; many groups of similar size had to hold in a shingle house.

It is probable that these multiple-house households formed tight units or 'yards', with the houses set out around a central open area. The evidence found in the adjacence of separate households is also suggestive of yard formation. At Old Montpelier, 30 slaves did not live with their mothers, but 13 of them lived in the house listed next to their mothers' and another three were only one house further removed. At Shettlewood three slaves lived next to their mothers, six, one house removed, and seven further away. But at New Montpelier only one slave was listed next to his mother, while six lived further away. In general, 50 per cent of the slaves who did not live with their mothers were no further away than one or two houses. It is also clear that at New Montpelier fewer children moved away from their mothers; but when they did they moved much farther. Among the children not living with their mothers the differences between the sexes are of interest.

	Old Montpelier		New Montpelier		Shettlewood Pen	
	Males	Females	Males	Females	Males	Females
Living in the next house	9	4	—	1	2	1
Living in next house but one	1	2	—	—	4	2
Living further away	5	9	4	2	2	5

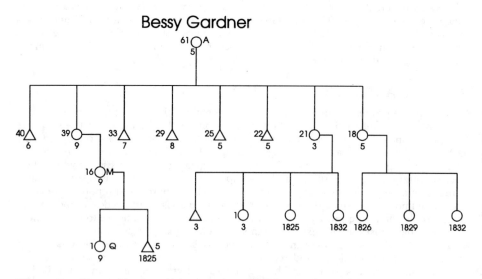

Figure 3 *Bessy Gardner's connection, Shettlewood*

Note: Numbers to the left of the male/female symbol indicate age in 1825. Numbers below the symbol indicate the household in which the slave lived in 1825. Where a date is given, 1825-32, this indicates the year of birth of children born after 1 August 1825, or, if 1817-25, the year of death of a slave dying between 28 June 1818 and 31 July 1825. All of the slaves were black and creole, unless indicated otherwise (to the right of the male/female symbol): A = African; M = Mulatto; Q = Quadroon; MU = Muster; S = Sambo

Sons most often stayed close to their mothers, with the exception of those at New Montpelier, while daughters tended to move away. In part, these contrasts were complementary, since it appears that the sons who stayed near their mothers were establishing households with other women's daughters. Daughters either moved away from their mothers to live near the mothers of their mates or, less often, lived with their children in the same house as their mother. Only one woman whose mother was living in 1825 had moved to a household lacking a possible male mate.

This pattern of movement applied not only to individual sons and daughters, but also to sets of siblings, and this resulted in groups of households, probably organized as yards, related by blood to a single woman. A clear example occurred in the households numbered 5 to 9 at Shettlewood (Figure 3). In house 5 lived Bessy Gardner, an African aged 61 years, and her two youngest sons and daughter. Her eldest son lived in house 6. House 7 was occupied by her second son and a woman who was pregnant at the time of the household report (and whose mother, an African, lived with an African man in house 23). In house 8 was her third son and an apparently unrelated man and woman (aged 20 and 22 years). Bessy Gardner's eldest daughter lived in house 9 with her mulatto daughter and quadroon granddaughter. Her other daughter, Elizabeth Miller, had moved away (though not very far, perhaps) to house 3, where she lived with her two children and the man she married in 1827.

Colour also played a role in the formation of linked household groups. At Old Montpelier all of the mulatto slaves and twelve of the 14 quadroons lived in three adjacent houses (25, 26 and 27). Further, the sambo nephew of the mulatto head of house 27 lived in house 28. Most of the slaves were domestics, hence it is probable that they were located close to the great house.

The movement of slaves also seems to have resulted in spatially linked household groups. Of the 3 Shettlewood slaves living at New Montpelier in 1825, 19 were living in houses 29 to 33. These households comprehended almost all who had retained the mother-child residential link. The one Shettlewood man to establish a household with a New Montpelier woman lived in house 31; thus, it seems that he brought her into the centre of the Shettlewood knot of houses. A simple explanation of the unity of the Shettlewood slaves at New Montpelier is that they moved into houses built for them in 1819 at a single site. In 1825 all of these houses were described as 'good; stone, shingled'. Houses 34, 36 and 37 were similarly described but by 1825 they were occupied by slaves who had lived on the estate since 1817 at least. Perhaps the spatial separation was a cause, as well as a measure of their isolation within the New Montpelier population.

In the above analysis several aspects of the spatial pattern suggest that residence may have been based on patrilocal rules, or that such rules were emerging. The pattern established by the polygynists, identified above, points in the same direction. But unfortunately the trend is not clear enough for this to be more than a suggestion.

HOUSEHOLD FORMATION

The mother-child tie was the strongest element in the creation and maintenance of households. So long as their mothers lived, very few slaves moved to separate households and about half of those who did move away went no further than one or two houses distant. All of the slaves who moved away from their mothers were creoles, of course, and almost all were black. Most of them were over 20 years of age, though at Old Montpelier a few moved away in their late teens. In 1825 the majority lived in households with their mates and children (Types 4 and 7), or simply with their mates (Type 12). Very few of them lived alone, and it has been noted already that only one woman lived with her children, apart from her mother and without a mate. Sons moved short distances to establish households near their mothers, whereas daughters moved into the ambit of their mates' mothers. Although this pattern was not universal, the point is important since it suggests that men may have played a greater role than women in the establishment of co-resident unions. And, since men living alone continued to live near their mothers, in many cases, they (or their mothers) may also have decided the stability of the relationship.

Figure 4 *The connections of Beneba 1st, Old Montpelier, and Frances Harvey, Shettlewood (for code, see note to Figure 3).*

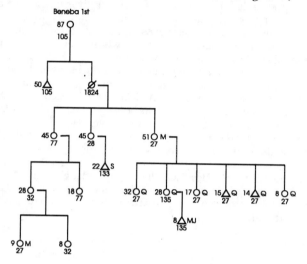

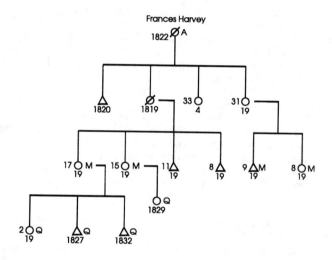

In so far as daughters whose mothers were alive formed relationships with men, they continued to live in their mothers' houses until they conceived or bore children. But very few lived with their mothers after bearing children, and most of these were coloured slaves who did not form unions within the slave population (Figure 4). The rarity of women living without a mate is suggestive of a more stable pattern of unions than Patterson recognizes,[24] unless it is argued that women parting with co-resident mates either quickly engaged new ones or returned promptly to their mothers' household. It is not improbable that slaves soon contracted new unions, but it is unlikely that these would have been based on co-residence in the first instance. The second possibility would fit neatly, if, as seems often to have been the case, the women had moved into households established by sons close to their living mothers. This point depends on the nature of rights to house and grounds, as does the whole question of stability.

If this case study is unable to solve the problem of stability, it does challenge the accepted view of household structure. Statements such as 'conditions under slavery were such that the woman and children were of necessity that family unit' (Kerr); 'normally the children resided with their mother, and the parents lived apart, singly or with different mates' (Smith); or 'the nuclear family could hardly exist within the context of slavery' (Patterson) require serious reconsideration.[25] Although the evidence is slight, this study also contradicts Patterson's argument that marriage was confined to old couples, under the influence of missionaries, being treated with contempt by the young.

Those creole slaves whose mothers were dead or had been moved to other properties were not subject to the same principles of residence. Yet it is clear that links through the maternal line remained important, so that slaves lived with their siblings, grandmothers, aunts and cousins (Figure 4). Many, however, moved into households lacking identifiable kin and containing Africans.

For the African slaves, the mother-child tie and the ramifications of kinship were missing. Thus, they were more likely to live with their mates when they formed unions and also more likely to live alone when they grew old because they lacked opportunities for alternative forms of alignment. When African men contracted creole mates they were more likely to be drawn into the ambit of their mate's mother than were creole men.

If the roots of a chaotic family system are to be traced to slavery they should be evident in the 1820s as well as in the eighteenth century. The abolition of the slave trade did not necessarily stabilize the household system and amelioration seems to have had little impact. M. G. Smith's sample of domestic units in modern rural Jamaica is not strictly comparable with the classification of households of the slave data, but the results are very similar.[26] The perception of 'chaos' in either the slave or modern periods may be a subjective matter, depending on categories of 'kinship' genealogically described which simply may not be useful indicators of the system.[27]

FAMILY AND FERTILITY

Before considering the impact of family and household structure on fertility, it is necessary to assess the quality of the data found in the returns of registrations of slaves for the measurement of fertility. Roberts, in particular, has argued that the returns take no account of children born within a triennium and dying before its end.[28] But, in fact, the Jamaica Registry Law required a record of 'the total number of births and deaths since the last return', and the practice was inconsistent.[29] On the three properties under study, 14 per cent of the births registered related to children who were born and died within a triennium, the children dying at ages ranging from ten days to two years ten months. For Old Montpelier, the Account Book throws further light on this problem since it contains 'increase' lists for 1825 and 1827. In 1827, all the children born were described as being 'nine days old at date' and all appear in the registration returns for 1829. In 1825, two children who died from tetanus on the sixth and seventh days after birth were listed in the Account Book but not registered. (The mothers of children surviving nine days received 13s. 4d. from the attorney). It would seem that, for these three properties, the underrecording of fertility was confined to mortality in the first nine days of life. Contemporary estimates placed the mortality within this period at 25-50 per cent of all live births.[30] The data can, however, be used to make comparisons between the three properties, household type and age groups, on the assumption that the extent of under registration was evenly distributed.

Table 6 *Age-specific fertility by household type and age group, 1817-25 and 1825-32.*

| | Births per 1,000 woman-years (woman-years given in parentheses) | | | | | | | |
| | 15-24 age group | | 25-34 age group | | 35-44 age group | | 15-44 age group | |
Household type	1817-25	1825-32	1817-25	1825-32	1817-25	1825-32	1817-25	1825-32
Old Montpelier								
1	— (3)	(15)	297 (37)	— (4)	135 (37)	250 (20)	208 (77)	128 (39)
2	— (0)	— (0)	— (0)	— (0)	— (0)	— (0)	— (0)	— (0)
3	— (1)	— (6)	— (7)	— (3)	500 (2)	— (4)	100 (10)	— (13)
4	40 (25)	98 (41)	333 (42)	— (22)	96 (73)	87 (46)	157 (140)	73 (109)
5	222 (9)	167 (24)	— (3)	333 (3)	154 (13)	250 (4)	160 (25)	194 (31)
6	— (12)	83 (12)	— (1)	77 (13)	— (0)	— (0)	— (13)	80 (25)
7	91 (66)	151 (93)	164 (55)	156 (51)	58 (52)	— (39)	104 (173)	120 (183)
9	— (8)	— (2)	— (13)	143 (7)	— (5)	— (14)	— (26)	44 (23)
11	— (13)	250 (4)	— (14)	— (9)	— (0)	— (5)	— (27)	56 (18)
12	— (20)	167 (18)	20 (50)	59 (17)	— (68)	— (50)	7 (138)	47 (85)
13	— (28)	59 (17)	— (35)	111 (18)	— (24)	38 (26)	— (87)	66 (61)
New Montpelier								
1	— (24)	61 (33)	56 (18)	— (19)	82 (49)	72 (14)	55 (91)	45 (66)
2	— (2)	— (14)	— (0)	— (0)	125 (8)	— (0)	100 (10)	— (14)
3	— (0)	— (0)	— (0)	— (0)	— (0)	— (0)	— (0)	— (0)
4	130 (23)	28 (72)	310 (29)	— (17)	94 (117)	18 (55)	136 (169)	21 (144)
5	— (0)	— (0)	— (5)	— (0)	— (10)	— (9)	— (15)	— (9)
6	— (2)	— (7)	— (12)	— (4)	— (2)	— (10)	— (16)	— (21)
7	— (24)	79 (66)	38 (52)	43 (23)	97 (62)	23 (44)	58 (138)	53 (133)
9	— (8)	— (1)	71 (14)	400 (5)	— (2)	71 (14)	42 (24)	150 (20)
11	— (7)	— (2)	250 (4)	— (0)	— (0)	— (0)	91 (11)	— (2)
12	— (9)	— (0)	— (11)	— (10)	— (20)	— (10)	— (40)	— (20)
13	— (25)	— (4)	— (46)	100 (20)	— (42)	26 (39)	— (113)	48 (63)
Shettlewood								
1	53 (19)	50 (20)	100 (10)	583 (12)	67 (15)	— (10)	68 (44)	190 (42)
2	133 (15)	67 (15)	— (0)	111 (9)	— (4)	— (4)	105 (19)	71 (28)
3	250 (4)	250 (12)	— (6)	— (0)	— (4)	— (0)	71 (14)	250 (12)
4	105 (19)	91 (44)	— (4)	— (7)	83 (24)	— (10)	85 (47)	65 (61)
5	— (0)	— (0)	— (0)	— (0)	— (0)	— (0)	— (0)	— (0)
6	— (3)	— (14)	— (8)	500 (2)	— (0)	— (4)	— (11)	50 (20)
7	105 (19)	53 (38)	157 (6)	200 (15)	188 (16)	— (2)	146 (41)	(91) (55)
9	— (0)	— (0)	— (0)	— (0)	— (10)	— (7)	— (10)	— (7)
11	— (0)	— (0)	— (0)	— (0)	— (3)	— (0)	— (3)	— (0)
12	— (13)	— (5)	— (4)	300 (10)	— (12)	— (8)	— (29)	130 (23)
13	—	(37)	— (42)	— (13)	100 (20)	— (10)	— (9)	— (61)	28 (71)
Total								
1	22 (46)	44 (68)	200 (65)	200 (35)	99 (101)	136 (44)	113 (212)	109 (147)
2	118 (17)	31 (29)	— (0)	111 (9)	83 (12)	— (4)	103 (29)	48 (42)
3	200 (5)	167 (18)	— (13)	— (3)	167 (6)	— (4)	83 (24)	120 (250)
4	89 (67)	66 (157)	307 (75)	— (46)	93 (214)	45 (111)	138 (356)	48 (314)
5	222 (9)	167 (24)	— (8)	333 (3)	87 (23)	77 (13)	100 (40)	150 (40)
6	— (17)	30 (33)	— (21)	105 (19)	— (2)	— (14)	— (40)	45 (66)
7	77 (109)	107 (197)	106 (113)	135 (89)	92 (130)	12 (85)	91 (352)	92 (371)
9	— (16)	— (3)	37 (27)	250 (12)	— (17)	29 (35)	17 (60)	80 (50)
11	— (20)	167 (6)	56 (18)	— (9)	— (3)	— (5)	24 (41)	50 (20)
12	— (42)	130 (23)	15 (65)	108 (37)	— (100)	— (68)	5 (207)	55 (128)
13	— (90)	16 (63)	— (94)	103 (58)	— (76)	27 (74)	— (260)	46 (195)

Table 7 African and Creole age-specific fertility, for three-year periods

Births per 1,000 woman-years (woman-years given in parentheses)

Age groups	Africans — Total						Creoles — Total					
	1817-20	1820-23	1823-26	1826-29	1829-32	1817-32	1817-20	1820-23	1823-26	1826-29	1829-32	1817-32
Old Montpelier												
15-19	—	—	—	—	—	—	98 (51)	— (54)	20 (51)	46 (66)	— (60)	32 (282)
20-24	—	—	—	—	—	—	74 (27)	30 (33)	93 (54)	250 (36)	222 (45)	138 (195)
25-29	67 (15)	83 (12)	— (0)	— (0)	— (0)	74 (27)	148 (54)	143 (42)	48 (21)	103 (27)	188 (48)	137 (204)
30-34	83 (24)	— (6)	67 (15)	— (6)	— (6)	59 (51)	102 (39)	71 (42)	125 (48)	91 (33)	167 (18)	106 (180)
35-39	22 (45)	67 (30)	134 (15)	— (12)	— (15)	51 (117)	91 (33)	139 (36)	111 (36)	67 (45)	77 (39)	95 (189)
40-44	— (30)	— (45)	22 (45)	— (24)	— (6)	7 (150)	83 (12)	56 (18)	61 (33)	77 (39)	54 (27)	— (147)
General fertility rate	44 (114)	32 (93)	53 (75)	— (42)	— (21)	35 (345)	106 (216)	71 (225)	71 (225)	95 (252)	112 (249)	91 (1197)
New Montpelier												
15-19	—	—	—	—	—	—	— (33)	— (30)	18 (57)	15 (66)	19 (54)	13 (240)
20-24	42	—	—	—	—	56 (36)	— (21)	37 (27)	111 (36)	48 (21)	157 (51)	83 (156)
25-29	111	42 (9)	— (3)	333 (6)	— (0)	— (0)	146 (21)	— (24)	— (12)	37 (27)	33 (30)	44 (114)
30-34	111	111 (36)	— (9)	47 (21)	—	104 (96)	111 (18)	74 (27)	— (15)	— (21)	— (15)	40 (96)
35-39	127	56 (36)	78 (51)	— (39)	222 (9)	100 (219)	200 (15)	— (15)	36 (27)	— (12)	— (15)	48 (84)
40-44	111	11 (81)	13 (78)	—	— (27)	17 (243)	— (0)	— (6)	67 (15)	— (21)	37 (27)	29 (69)
General fertility rate	111 (189)	56 (162)	36 (141)	45 (66)	56 (36)	67 (594)	74 (108)	23 (129)	37 (162)	12 (168)	52 (192)	49 (759)
Shettlewood												
15-19	—	—	—	—	—	—	43 (117)	16 (126)	19 (153)	51 (177)	21 (141)	32 (714)
20-24	—	—	—	—	—	— (63)	33 (60)	56 (72)	106 (132)	133 (105)	136 (147)	105 (516)
25-29	51 (39)	95 (21)	42 (24)	167 (12)	— (0)	64 (63)	118 (93)	67 (90)	133 (45)	107 (84)	136 (117)	112 (429)
30-34	111 (81)	89 (45)	— (3)	31 (33)	83 (24)	99 (162)	95 (63)	72 (69)	80 (75)	43 (69)	89 (45)	75 (321)
35-39	89 (179)	84 (84)	83 (72)	— (0)	—	82 (329)	125 (48)	88 (57)	72 (69)	63 (63)	43 (69)	75 (306)
40-44	26 (78)	6 (153)	21 (147)	— (75)	— (36)	12 (489)	83 (12)	42 (24)	33 (60)	35 (57)	61 (66)	55 (219)
General fertility rate	77 (377)	49 (303)	41 (246)	25 (120)	33 (60)	53 (1106)	79 (393)	52 (438)	67 (534)	74 (555)	85 (585)	72 (2505)

Table 6 shows broad age-specific fertility rates for each of the 11 household types containing women. A basic difficulty in this analysis is that the household type of each woman is known only for 1825. To meet this problem the rates have been divided into two periods, 1817-25 and 1825-32, but it is clear that some births will have been wrongly attributed. For example, a woman living with her children in 1825 may have borne all of them while living with a mate, the man having died before 1825. More importantly, the female children living in such a household frequently moved into the childbearing age groups after 1825, and it is probable that, if they had children, they then lived in households containing a mate. In general, it seems that the 1817-25 rates are more reliable indicators than those for the later period. In household Type 4, for instance, the 'women' bore 48 children between 1817 and 1825 and the 'children' only one, whereas in 1825-32 the 'women' bore only seven children and the 'children' nine. Thus the inclusion of 'children' in the calculation of woman-years does not greatly depress the fertility of the 'women' in 1817-25, but does so considerably for 1825-32.

Concentrating on the 1817-25 period, then, the most fertile women were those who lived with a mate and their children (household Type 4), followed by those who lived in households lacking mates (Type 1 and 2). Thus, the presence of a mate was conducive, though not essential, to relatively high fertility. Households of Type 7 (a woman, her children and others) were not as fertile since they frequently included invalids and unconnected individuals. The very low fertility of women living alone, with other women, with a man, with groups of men and women, or with siblings, may be seen as a corollary of the strong tendency for children to live with their mothers. But the women living in such households demonstrated a significant increase in fertility after 1825, suggesting that they moved into, or created by bearing children, different types. The relatively low fertility of women living apart from their mates may be explained in terms of reduced coital frequency, and this factor probably also affected some of the women living in household Type 7. In summary, the most fertile women were those who lived with a mate, followed by those living exclusively with their offspring, while the least fertile were those living with adults and who were not identifiable kin.

Excepting those household types which accounted for only a few births (Types 2, 3 and 5), the most fertile age group was always the 25-34 years group (Table 6). Within this age group the highest fertility (0.307 births per woman year) occurred among women in household Type 4, followed by those in Types 1 (0.200) and 7 (0.106). At the property level, however, households of Type 4 were the most fertile only at New Montpelier, where they were dominated by Africans (Table 3). At Old Montpelier, Type 1 households were more fertile than Type 4, since the latter had a more mature age structure, reducing the fertility of the 'women' and incorporating a larger proportion of female children over 15 years. The pattern of Shettlewood was somewhat aberrant, probably because of the small numbers involved; but if Types 4 and 7 are seen to overlap, the divergence is minor.

The results of this analysis suggest, first, that the planters' belief that fertility would be encouraged by the formation and maintenance of stable monogamous unions was not unrealistic. The missionaries' emphasis on marriage, however, seems to have had little relation to fertility. And, although the evidence is slight, polygyny seems not to have reduced the fertility of women living in such households, contrary to the view of both planter and missionary.[31] At Old Montpelier, where the evidence of polygyny is strongest, the sexes were evenly balanced so that it could hardly have exacerbated the shortage of women complained of in earlier periods. It is possible that, as some planters contended, fertility was reduced by the prolonged residence of children with their parents; certainly daughters rarely moved away before bearing children, and they were particularly infertile during adolescence, though few men remained with their parents after their twentieth birthday. These findings fit the modern consensus that marital instability and casual mating depress fertility in the West Indies.[32]

The limitations of the household data make it impossible to trace effectively changes in fertility through the period, but the general age-specific fertility rates are of interest (Table 7). Patterson has argued that the young creole slaves were indifferent to childrearing, whereas 'the habit of childbearing was too strongly rooted in the African woman for even the slave system to destroy it'.[33] But the evidence of Table 7 shows the creoles to have been more fertile than the Africans on the three properties. These data include no African women under 25 years, perhaps the most fertile years, but the creoles surpassed the Africans even in the 25-29 years age group. At Old Montpelier, the most thoroughly creolized of the properties, the creoles were most fertile throughout the period, whereas at Shettlewood a decline in African fertility was matched by a rapid increase in that of the creoles. New Montpelier, with the greatest proportion of Africans, presents a different pattern. There the fertility of the Africans exceeded that of the creoles throughout the period, possibly a result of the dominance of household Type 4 and of Africans within the type. Perhaps the high mortality of creoles at New Montpelier (Figure 1) engendered an instability which made it difficult for them to maintain households of this type.

If the evidence regarding African fertility is confused, it is certain that creoles under 20 years were most fertile (Table 7). This might be seen either as a result of quasi-prostitution (associated with abortion) or of the retentiveness of maternal household heads. Only slaves bearing children of colour demonstrated high fertility in this age group. This pattern conforms with that argued by Patterson. But following this initial infertility an early peak was reached, generally around 25 years of age, after which the decline in fertility was continuous. However generous the assumptions made regarding under-registration, the slaves were not a fertile population. If comparison is made with modern times, it is seen that the distribution of fertility among the age groups also differed, being relatively very low in the early years but approaching modern levels after 35 years.[34] Thus, to invert the argument, this pattern may be seen as suggestive of early casual mating followed by relatively stable monogamy, which corroborates the accepted view of developmental instability and gives depth to the otherwise static analysis of households.

NOTES

1. See G. W. Roberts, 'Some aspects of mating and fertility in the West Indies', *Population Studies*, VIII (1955), pp. 199-227; Judith Blake, *Family Structure in Jamaica: The Social Context of Reproduction* (New York, 1961). Cf. Anthony Marino, 'Family, fertility, and sex ratios in the British Caribbean', *Population Studies*, XXIV, 2 (July 1970), pp. 159-72.

2. M. G. Smith, *West Indian Family Structure* (Seattle, 1926), p. 250.

3. Edward Braithwaite, *The Development of Creole Society in Jamaica, 1770-1820* (Oxford, 1971), p. 204. Cf. Elsa V. Goveia, *Slave Society in the British Leeward Islands at the End of the Eighteenth Century* (New Haven, 1965), pp. 235-237, and Orlando Patterson, *The Sociology of Slavery* (London, 1967), p. 160.

4. Old Montpelier Estate, Account Book (Institute of Jamaica, Kingston).

5. *Parliamentary Papers*, 1832 (127), House of Lords, 'Report from the Select Committee on the state of the West India colonies', p. 88. The report is printed at pp. 1376-93.

6. Returns of Registration of Slaves, Liber 27, f. 37; Liber 30, ff. 42 and 49; Liber 40, ff. 83-84; Liber 48, f. 163; Liber 66, ff. 159-60; Liber 75, f. 100; Liber 85, ff. 60-61; Liber 93, f. 33; Liber 96, f. 213; Liber 100, ff. 214-15; Liber 129, f. 28 and f. 32; Liber 32, Liber 130, f. 170 (Jamaica Archives, Spanish Town). The returns at Spanish Town are copies, the originals being located in the series T. 71 at the Public Record Office, London.

7. See E. A. Wrigley (Ed.) *An Introduction to English Historical Demography* (London, 1966).

8. St James, Copy Register, Vol. 2: Baptisms, 17 July, 1816 (Island Record Office, Spanish Town).

9. Joseph Sturge and Thomas Harvey, *The West Indies in 1837* (London, 1838), p. 229; *Dictionary of National Biography Gentleman's Magazine*, XXIV (1845), Pt ii, p. 419.

10. *Parliamentary Debates*, 33, p. 257 (6 April, 1797). See also Goveia, op. cit., in footnote 3, p. 33; Alfred Owen Aldridge, 'Population and polygamy in eighteenth-century thought', *Journal of the History of Medicine*, 4, 2(Spring 1949), pp. 129-48.

11. Braithwaite, *op. cit.* in footnote 3, p. 292.

12. Minutes of the Missions Conference, 30 November 1831 (Moravian Church Archives, Malvern, Jamaica).

13. *Parliamentary Papers*, 1832 (127), *op. cit.*, p. 90; Account Book, *op. cit.*

14. James Hakewill, *A Picturesque Tour of the Island of Jamaica, from drawings made in the years 1820 and 1821* (London, 1825), Plate 19.

15. Account Book, *op. cit.*

16. Accounts Produce (Jamaica Archives, Spanish Town). See, for example, Liber 51, ff. 87, 91 and 92; Liber 62, f. 63.

17. Jamaica Almanack (1817 and 1818), Poll tax givings-in.

18. Hakewill, *op. cit.*, in footnote 14, Plate 19.

19. A mulatto being the offspring of a black and a white, a quadroon of a mulatto and a white, a mustee of a quadroon and a white, and a sambo of a mulatto and a black.

20. St James, Copy Register, Vol. 2: Marriages, 25 August, 1825 (Island Record Office, Spanish Town).

21. Baptisms and Marriages of Slaves, St James, 1827-28: Marriages, 23 December, 1827 (Jamaica Archives, Spanish Town).

22. Returns of Registrations of Slaves, Liber 93, f. 33; Liber 85, f. 60.

23. Hakewill, *op. cit.*, in footnote 14, Plate 19. Another drawing was produced by Duperly following the rebellion of 1831, but it was obviously based on Hakewill. Duperly added a further nine houses on the bare hill behind the overseer's house and stores, but these may have been mere fancy. Duperly's print is reproduced in *Jamaica Journal*, 3, 2(June 1969), p. 25. An undated, detailed map of Montpelier Estate is to be found at the Institute of Jamaica, Kingston.

24. Patterson, *op. cit.*, in footnote 3, pp. 159-70.

25. Ibid., p. 167; Madeline Kerr, *Personality and Conflict in Jamaica* (London, 1952), p. 93; M. G. Smith, 'Social structure in the British Caribbean about 1820', *Social and Economic Studies*, 1, 4(August 1953), p. 72.

26. M. G. Smith, *West Indian Family Structure*, p. 161. See also William Davenport, 'The family system of Jamaica', in Paul Bohannan and John Middleton (eds), *Marriage, Family and Residence* (New York, 1968), pp. 247-84.

27. See Rodney Needham (Ed.) *Rethinking Kinship and Marriage* (London, 1971).

28. George W. Roberts, *The Population of Jamaica* (Cambridge, 1957), pp. 3-4. Roberts seems to assume that the Jamaica and Demerara and Essequibo laws were the same, and appears to be quoting Robertson's report on the latter rather than the Jamaican law. See James Robertson's report in *Parliamentary Papers*, 1833, Vol. 26(700), 'Slave population. (Slave Registries)', p. 447.

29. Jamaica Law, 57 Geo. III Cap, XV, Section 4.

30. Robert Renny, *A History of Jamaica* (London, 1807), p. 188; John Phillippo, *Jamaica: Its Past and Present State* (London 1843), p. 144.

31. See Aldridge *loc. cit.*, in footnote 10, and Geoffrey Hawthorn, *The Sociology of Fertility* (London, 1970), p. 32.

32. Roberts, *loc. cit.*, in footnote 1 (1955). Cf. Marino, *op. cit.*, in footnote 1 (1970).

33. Patterson, *op. cit.*, in footnote 3, p. 109.

34. Joycelyn Byrne, *Levels of Fertility in Commonwealth Caribbean*, 1921-1965 University of the West Indies, 1972), pp. 58-59.

Number of households

	Old Montpelier									New Montpelier									Shettlewood								
Household type	1	2	3	4	5	6	7	8	9	1	2	3	4	5	6	7	8	9	1	2	3	4	5	6	7	8	9
1	—	2	3	2	1	2	—	—	—	—	8	2	2	—	1	—	—	—	—	1	2	2	1	—	—	—	—
2	—	—	—	—	—	—	—	—	—	—	—	—	—	—	—	—	—	—	—	1	1	1	—	—	1	—	—
3	—	1	—	—	6	—	1	—	—	—	—	—	—	—	—	—	1	—	—	—	—	—	—	—	—	1	—
4	—	—	10	3	1	1	1	—	—	—	—	11	6	4	2	1	—	—	—	—	—	2	4	—	—	—	—
5	—	—	—	1	1	—	—	—	—	—	—	—	—	—	—	—	—	—	—	—	—	—	—	—	—	—	—
6	—	—	1	—	—	—	—	—	—	—	—	—	3	2	—	—	—	—	—	1	1	—	—	—	—	—	—
7	—	—	1	6	3	4	4	1	1	—	—	1	3	3	4	2	—	—	—	—	—	1	—	—	1	—	1
8	14	—	—	—	—	—	—	—	—	5	—	—	—	—	—	—	—	—	—	—	—	—	—	—	—	—	—
9	13	—	—	—	—	—	—	—	—	3	—	—	—	—	—	—	—	—	6	—	—	—	—	—	—	—	—
10	—	—	—	—	—	—	—	—	—	—	1	—	—	—	—	—	—	—	3	—	—	—	—	—	—	—	—
11	—	5	1	—	—	—	—	—	—	—	1	—	—	—	—	—	—	—	—	1	—	—	—	—	—	—	—
12	—	25	—	—	—	—	—	—	—	—	6	—	—	—	—	—	—	—	—	7	—	—	—	—	—	—	—
13	—	—	10	—	—	—	—	—	—	—	—	10	—	2	1	—	—	—	—	—	4	—	—	—	—	1	—
Total Households	27	33	26	12	12	7	6	1	1	8	16	24	13	11	8	3	1	—	9	11	8	6	5	—	2	2	1
Total occupants	27	66	78	48	60	42	42	8	9	8	32	72	52	55	48	21	8	—	9	22	24	24	25	—	14	16	9

H. Beckles,

WIVES, MOTHERS AND FAMILY STRUCTURE

BLACK RELATIONS

In 1723, a slave from the Codrington estate named Jupiter, accompanied by Churo, another slave, in an attempt to gain his freedom, took flight from the estate and the island; both were subsequently reportedly seen somewhere in the Leeward Islands. The following year, however, Jupiter returned to Barbados and handed himself over to the estate manager, in spite of the severe punishments that awaited him. The manager, in assessing the nature of this unusual case, thought it necessary to state that Jupiter was 'much rejoiced at the opportunity of getting back to his wife and children'.[1]

Jupiter's decision to abandon his freedom for the greater pleasures of family life gives a perspective on the slaves' family relations which differs radically from that commonly presented by contemporary white commentators on slave society. There is an abundance of evidence to suggest that Jupiter's behaviour was not unusual, and this evidence can be used to illustrate the internal functioning of the slave family and aspects of male-female relations. What it also shows is the development of an intense social dynamism as family structures and sexual relations adjusted to the changing nature of plantation conditions. Yet, despite these structural metamorphoses, the slaves' firm commitment to strong and intimate family relations remained constant, not only as a survival strategy, but as the principal basis of their philosophical and aesthetic concept of social life.

F. W. Bayley, who visited Barbados during his four years' residence in the West Indies in the 1820s, presents a social image of the slaves that runs counter to this evidence. For him, the behaviour and consciousness of Jupiter was as alien to the slaves as was the planet after which he was named. Slaves, he argued, are capable of one form of strong emotional attachment, that 'to their masters and owners'.[2] In assessing the slaves' social and family lives, he stated:

> Strong attachment, either to their wives or to their children, is not common among the slaves ... perhaps partly owing to their immorality, and because they have more wives than one; and partly because any anxiety for the comfort and welfare, and lately the education and instruction, of their offspring is removed, by the conviction that all this will be attended by the owner; and it often happens that where there is little care there is also little affection. The mother who gives her infant babe to be nursed by a stranger, and only sees it occasionally, as duty requires, until it has grown out of its infancy into childhood more matured, does not feel for it the love of one who has nursed and reared it herself, who has performed for it all those sweet and tender offices which so eminently endear the child to the mother, and the mother to the child.[3]

These observations, representative of those commonly made by European visitors to the West Indies, often stand in stark contrast to the general behaviour of the slaves and comments of those white persons whose social positions placed them in close proximity to the slaves. A critical assessment of these diverse sources and opinions is an effective way to marginalize those uniformed views and bring clarity and context to those rooted in detailed observations.

Historically, scholars of slavery in plantation America have attributed a superordinate role to women in analyses of family and kinship patterns. In most instances their arguments have been related directly to women's predominant role in child-rearing and infant socialization in these undoubtedly patriarchal societies. For these and related reasons, perceptions of the West Indian slave family have been more intimately linked with women than with men. The vision of women as the human infrastructure, the bedrock of the slave family and also, by extension, the slave community, has assisted also in reinforcing an image of the male slave as marginal, irregular, tangential, and transient — an orbital figure that revolved about a female core representing certainty, continuity, and flexible but unflagging strength.

Recent scholarship on the Caribbean slave family, however, tends to present a more realistic analysis of women in the domestic context. For example, Craton has suggested the need to minimize traditional concepts in the light of new evidence which illustrates that the 'myth of matrifocality stems from the planters' emphasis on motherhood because of their need to perpetuate slavery through the female line, and their vain wish to breed rather than to buy new slaves by granting slave mothers relatively easier conditions'.[4] Opponents of Craton's thesis could easily assert that planter policy strengthened, rather than created, the matrifocal emphasis. Empirical evidence exists, however, to support both generalizations, as well as to show that African-based family structures and concepts largely give way to European systems and ideas as the slave society matured and became Creolized.[5]

A time-based typology of the factors that affected family kinship patterns (Table 6.1) illustrates the nature of the structural social changes that took place over some 211 years of black slavery in Barbados. It implies the impossibility of removing any consideration of family relations and the role of women from the colony's demographic base, though it says nothing of how women perceived their changing roles as mothers, wives and mates.

Table 6.1 *Family patterns and their social context*

1627-1720:

African-born slaves in majority; polygamous structures dominant; tendency to disintegrate family and kinship systems; planter policy indifferent to reproduction; strong tribal consciousness.

1720-1780:

Period of demographic transition; rapid Creolization of population; tribal alliances giving way to group/status differentiation; pro-reproduction planter policy; polygamy the norm.

1780-1834:

Amelioration centres on women; Creole slaves majority; Christian marriage uncommon; nuclear family common; planter policy supportive of family integration; motherhood recognized in custom/law.

The first detailed reference to the role of enslaved black women as wives comes from Ligon in his 1657 'history' of the island. He was a keen observer of black women and made several detailed statements, not only about their domestic relations, but also their physical attributes. This evidence is important, coming as it does when, for the first time, Africans were arriving in large numbers and forcing whites to adjust to the transformed social culture. For these African migrants, polygamous family structures were part of their cultural tradition, and they had no reason to believe that this norm should not continue. Ligon noted that slave owners allowed them to form unions in which partners referred to each other as wife and husband. These 'families' were neither given any legal identity, nor recognized as in any way Christian. Unfortunately, Ligon gives us no accounts of the kind of formalities and ceremonies that initiated these unions. Planters, he stated, do not deny 'a brave fellow, and one that has extraordinary qualities, two or three wives ...' 'No Woman', however, was 'allowed above one husband'.[6]

The domestic organization of these unions did not feature prominently in Ligon's account. Neither did he comment on the nature of partners' responsibility towards each other, though he did state in relation to the men: 'Jealous they are of their wives, and hold it for a great injury and scorn if another man makes the least courtship to his wife.'[7] A story that supposedly gives some idea of the manner in which women were valued by men in the family relation was related by Ligon of the slave Macow, whose wife had given birth to twins, evidence he considered of her adultery. Despite assurances from his master that such occurrences were natural and common enough he could not be prevented from resolving to hang her.[8] Eventually, he was persuaded against such an act, but only by a threat from his master that he would be punished likewise. In retreating from his purpose, Macow 'never car'd much for her afterwards, but chose another which he lik'd better'.[9]

In these formative years, Ligon noted, husband and first wife lived together in 'their little houses', none of which was 'above six feet square', but with 'several divisions' — if such space could be meaningfully divided. Both husband and wife slept on loose boards on the ground, as did the children. When a wife was about to give birth, the 'husband removes his board to another room' and leaves 'his wife to God, and her good fortune in the room … and calls a neighbour to come to her who gives little help to her delivery'. Extra rooms, made from baked mud, twigs, dried leaves, and timbers, were added as the family increased.

From Ligon's time to the end of slavery in 1838, black women in Barbados lived in a social culture where polygamy was customary. Although colonial conditions made some impact on this aspect of their African cultural heritage it took many generations of Creolization and pressure from largely European Christian sources before black males were apparently reconciled to abandoning the practice. None of the many slave laws passed between 1649 and 1824 dealt directly with the question of slave marriage, or its popular African, polygamous form. Marriage among slaves was not considered valid in law as they were not permitted to enter into legally binding, contractual relations either with each other or with whites. Families, therefore, had no constitutional or legal form, and for most of the slavery period the resident clergy made no concerted effort to alter this condition.

On most estates, white management considered polygamy among slaves as part of the general immorality which, they intimated, was common among blacks. For them, polygamy was a result of the causal and promiscuous manner in which blacks were believed to organize their domestic and social affairs. Abel Alleyne, the manager of Codrington Estate during the 1730s, believed that the slave men exacted severe social and emotional advantage of their female counterparts under the polygamous family structure. He argued: 'those that have wives, only take them as they like them, and so part with them at their pleasure'.[10] Alleyne considered that his opinion was based upon careful observations rather than upon a Eurocentric bias against unfamiliar cultural norms. In 1727, his estate's catechist, after years of effort, succeeded in inducing three men in the first gang to 'content themselves with one wife a piece'. For a while, he added, the 'christian couples' respected the importance of 'fidelity' in their relations, but the catechist was soon forced to accept that eradicating polygamy would be no easy matter.[11] For him, polygamy was also a 'perpetual bar' to administering Christianity among blacks, as the church had taken the position that the two were conceptually incompatible. Manager Alleyne believed polygamy to be 'as impossible to prevent as any one thing in the world', and therefore suggested that it should be tolerated throughout the colony.[12]

John Pinder, a Barbadian clergyman, made uncommonly detailed observations of slave marital patterns during the early 19th century. He believed slaves were willing to accept Christian marriage, but their owners refused to accept such relations as legitimate and sacred. In addition, he stated, the Bishop of London needed to issue clear instructions to colonial clergymen. In 1819, Pinder wrote:

> There is no such thing, as far as I can find, as promiscuous concubinage among them …; the slaves marry by agreement; sometimes alas! the men have two and even three wives, but these are considered in the light of wives till an actual separation takes place.[13]

Though aware that a very small percentage (7%) of the slave population was African-born in his time (1819) Pinder asserted that African cultural norms still informed the basis of slaves' marital and domestic practices. He offered no analysis of the relations between the extent of Creolization and the maintenance of African concepts of family, though he implied that no ideological differences existed between African-born and Creole slaves on matters of family and sexual practices.[14]

It was common for African and Creole slaves from different estates to enter martial unions and live separately throughout their relationship. Though planters hoped that marriages would be confined to their own estates, and encouraged slaves to marry each other, inevitably some sought partners elsewhere. Men generally kept one resident wife, with others located throughout the colony. Given the fragmented nature of these family structures, and the laws to control slave movements, planters believed that they held the key to the slaves' effective social functions. The slaves thought otherwise, and were determined to pursue distant family relations with or without their owners' permission.

Black children took the legal status of their slave mother and were the exclusive property of their mothers' owner. Paternal alienation, however, was only a physical feature of the disintegrated type of slave family. Slave owners seemed to have had little difficulty in liberalizing the application of laws designed for curbing slave movements so as to enable males to travel during their free time on conjugal missions. In general, slave owners during the 18th century believed that their slaves respected this privilege. As a result, they were probably more prone to operate an 'open' society than their counterparts in other colonies. During the 18th century there were no aborted or actual slave revolts, and planters slept comfortably at night in ignorance of their slaves' whereabouts.[15]

From his observations of the 1770s, Dickson noted that wives, regardless of rank, tended to respect marital unions. He added:

> The first wife, if still in friendship and confidence of the husband, continues to govern the household, though his appetite may be shared with one, two, three or more. The women, however, have in general a sense of decency and decorum in their fidelity under this voluntary connection; and the men have done ... Both sexes are frequently travelling all night, going to or returning from a distant connection, in order, without sleep, to be in due time to go through a hard day's labour, after their nocturnal adventures.[16]

For slaves to be free to travel was, then, a basic precondition for the effective social functioning of many families. Both husbands and wives (and sometimes children) took part in this commuting family culture. Under the 1688 Code for the governing of slaves, a ticket signed by a manager or owner was the only proof of legitimate travel. This act remained valid into the early 19th century, despite a general refusal to apply its provisions strictly.

The especially disintegrated nature of many slave families did not preclude their ability to function as socially cohesive and emotionally integrated structures. The extensive data relating to runaways, for example, can be used to illustrate this argument. Invariably, wives ran to husbands, and vice versa; children would run to either parents or to other brothers or sisters. The family served as the primary effective cover for this form of resistance, offering successful protection to its members although severe penalties were imposed on legally convicted harbourers of runaways. Slave owners were obviously convinced that strong emotional bonds within families were principally responsible for much of the successful resistance of this kind, and that kinship solidarity acted as a psychological weapon against the pro-slavery interest. During the mid-18th century, when Will ran away from his estate, his master suspected that he was being harboured by one of his two wives on two separate estates. Likewise, when Cudjoe escaped his St John estate he was suspected of being protected by his wife at Turner Hall estate in St Andrew. 'Runaway Grigg' was also thought to be under cover with one of his two wives: Binah at Mrs Ann in Bridgetown or the other at the Pool Plantation.[17]

Information in newspaper advertisements for slave runaways illustrates the complex patterns of family relations that fugitives manipulated in order to survive. It also demonstrates the extent of individuals' preparedness to reject legal obstacles in assisting their rebellious relatives. The following advertisements appeared in the Barbados Globe for 1829 and 1831 respectively.

(Reward of $5 for Amelia:)

suppose to be harboured by her father or his connections. This man has a sister or some family connections near Canewood-Moore estate, and no doubt his daughter meets with a welcome reception there ....[18]

(Reward of a Joe for Polly Grace (and three children):)

suppose to be harboured by her sister living in Mason Hall, and by her husband, James Gill, living in the vicinity of Constitution.[19]

Likewise, Mary Jane, who was married, and ran away in 1831, was suspected of being harboured by entire family, which included her mother who lived at Collymore Rock, two brothers, one who lived near Coverley in Christ Church, and the other who lived near Lowther's, and 'other relatives and connections at Newton and Seawell' Plantations.[20]

These references to slaves' family relations reflected not only the degree to which the slave population was socially integrated, but also slave owners' extensive knowledge of their slaves' genealogical pattern. It seems reasonable to assume that slave owners would have paid particular attention to these family patterns, since slaves would frequently use family obligations as reasons for their travels. Furthermore, the right to travel was one major concession granted to slaves in the amelioration policies implemented after the 1770s in an effort to encourage the domesticity of females for the purpose of enhancing their fertility.

Advertisements for runaways also illustrate the widespread nature of polygamous family structures into the late 18th century. For the majority of planters, whether slave women were incorporated into polygamous or monogamous family structures was immaterial, once fertility levels were satisfactory. Indeed, many slave owners considered the right to a polygamous family as a social concession for such privileged males as drivers and artisans. Possession of more than one wife was a status symbol in the slave community, reflecting authority and money-earning power. Certainly some field women would have improved their general material and health conditions by polygamous marriages to labour élite males, and in some instances, communal pressure would have been asserted upon these males to act responsibly by taking more than one wife. In a context of early death among field women such marriages would have enabled them to improve their overall condition. That élite males were prone to take advantage of women's individual vulnerability and exploit them as a group is evident, but it was precisely this relationship between assistance and exploitation within the polygamous family pattern that allowed for its long-term survival in the context of persistent mass poverty.

Blacks' responses to the Christian type of nuclear family structure became increasingly favourable over time, and by the end of slavery in 1838 it was a common part of the slave communities' social culture. In 1819 the Revd John Pinder stated that slave women would regularly come to him and demand the right to the banns.[21] This kind of experience convinced him that a Christian monogamous union was preferred by slave women, many of whom were now prepared to resist aggressively the polygamous family tradition. Undoubtedly, the social and material conditions of field women had improved since the late 18th century and this factor should not be excluded from a full explanation of the diminishing preference for polygamous marriages.

Slave owners, too, were becoming increasingly prepared to accept the nuclear family sanctified by the Anglican church, among their slaves, especially since the popularization of Forster Clarke's findings that slaves who formed these unions produced 'almost without exception numerous families of the most valuable description'.[22] Clarke was an agricultural attorney, whose extensive knowledge of the slaves' condition was widely recognized. His argument that female fertility was higher among monogamous households than other types encouraged slave owners to promote early Christian marriage of female slaves. In 1825, for example, the management of Codrington Plantation was encouraged to promote Christian marriage among slaves by holding forth, 'such further inducements as a superior habitation, ... clothing and security of the customary inheritance of their legitimate children if belonging to the estate, and any other privileges ... as may appear ... expedient'.[23] Forster Clarke also recommended to all slave owners that 'every mother having six children born in lawful wedlock' should be exempted from further work on the estate.[24]

In spite of there being no law to the contrary, argued Bennett, only one Christian marriage of slaves was performed in the colony before 1825. This ceremony was conducted by the Revd W. M. Harte of the St Lucy parish, who was subsequently persecuted by his parishioners. Apparently, this slave couple insisted upon being addressed as Mr and Mrs, to the great irritation of whites who considered that slaves should not enjoy this sign of social respectability. On 17 April 1827, these parishioners passed a resolution which embodied accusations against Revd Harte:

> It is with deep concern that the inhabitants of this parish have observed the frequent attempts made by the rector of the parish to destroy the distinctions which they deem so necessary to their safety ... endeavouring to alienate their slaves from a sense of their duty, by inculcating doctrines of equality inconsistent with their obedience to their masters and the policy of the island.[25]

Christian marriage, then, was perceived by whites as one way of removing the label 'heathen' from blacks, and thereby uniting the two races at a level of equality within the ideological climate of the church. There was, therefore, much resistance from the white community, and the number of blacks taking banns remained small in the final years of slavery.

Handler has provided some evidence to show that Bennett might have underestimated the number of Christian slave marriages during the 38 years of slavery in the 19th century. He suggests that during the decade before the 'Sunday and Marriage Act' of 1826, by which the church sought to promote baptism and marriage among slaves, such marriages had already taken place. Between 1808 and 1830 the number of slave marriages in the Anglican church, based on incomplete parish rectors' returns, were: 1808-14, three; 1815-20, seven.[26] Baptisms and burials, however, were far more numerous. Slave owners in general did not consider these events as threatening the ideological structure they had imposed upon the wider slave system.

But long before this legislative provision, slaves had already been accustomed to cohesion and continuity in their family life. To some extent, this was due to the unusually high level of stability in estate ownership which reduced the incidence of separation of slave families. In 1826 most estates in the colony had been owned by the same family for 100 years, so that several generations of slaves were born, raised and died in the same villages. This sense of continuity certainly allowed for the emergence of slave grandmothers and great-grandmothers as matriarchal figures on estates, empowered with immense moral and social authority in the slave communities.

Table 6.2 *Anglican baptisms and burials of slaves, 1812-1822*

YEARS	BAPTISM	BURIALS
1812	432	203
1813	317	116
1814	362	122
1815	474	144
1816	425	154
1817	544	203
1818	467	170
1819	515	203
1820	564	174
1821	NA	NA
1822	753	145

Source: Handler, 1974, p. 164

Slaves, then, from the end of the 18th century, could speak firmly about family lineage and traditions. They were also able to relate these to particular geographical locations which in turn enforced their sense of identity, as Dickson has testified.[27] He also noted that when asked to give their opinion about being moved to a neighbouring colony, slaves would invariably respond: 'here we are born, and here are the graves of our fathers. Can we say to their bones, arise and go with us into a foreign land?'[28] According to Dickson, then, Creole slaves did not allow themselves to be alienated from their families, villages, nor indeed the colony — their native land.

These forces were enhanced, not created, by the amelioration policies of the early 19th century which aimed to discourage family separation, especially of mothers and children, as part of the attempt by slave owners to encourage women to have children. Notices for the sale of women commonly made references to children, such as that which appeared in the Barbados Globe on 7 May 1829 for the sale of 'a young woman and her three children'. It is not always clear in these instances whether sellers were prepared to do business only with persons willing to buy an entire family, which in most cases was defined as a mother and her children. The Consolidated Slave Laws of 1825 did attempt to prevent the breaking up of families, and only after this date did advertisements for slaves make this a primary specification. For example, the *Barbadian* carried the following notice on Wednesday 10 April 1833:

Table 6.3   *Four matriarchs at Seawell Estate in 1796*[30]

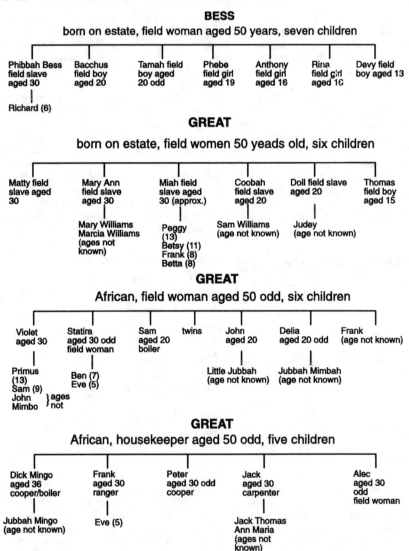

BESS
born on estate, field woman aged 50 years, seven children

Phibbah Bess field slave aged 30	Bacchus field boy aged 20	Tamah field boy aged 20 odd	Phebe field girl aged 19	Anthony field girl aged 16	Rina field girl aged 16	Devy field boy aged 13
Richard (6)						

GREAT
born on estate, field women 50 yeads old, six children

Matty field slave aged 30	Mary Ann field slave aged 30	Miah field slave aged 30 (approx.)	Coobah field slave aged 20	Doll field slave aged 20	Thomas field boy aged 15
	Mary Williams Marcia Williams (ages not known)	Peggy (13) Betsy (11) Frank (8) Betta (8)	Sam Williams (age not known)	Judey (age not known)	

GREAT
African, field woman aged 50 odd, six children

Violet aged 30	Statira aged 30 odd field woman	Sam aged 20 boiler	twins	John aged 20	Delia aged 20 odd	Frank (age not known)
Primus (13) Sam (9) John Mimbo } ages not	Ben (7) Eve (5)			Little Jubbah (age not known)	Jubbah Mimbah (age not known)	

GREAT
African, housekeeper aged 50 odd, five children

Dick Mingo aged 36 cooper/boiler	Frank aged 30 ranger	Peter aged 30 odd cooper	Jack aged 30 carpenter	Alec aged 30 odd field woman
Jubbah Mingo (age not known)	Eve (5)		Jack Thomas Ann Maria (ages not known)	

For Sale

A property of 71½ acres of land, adjoining Hallet's with eighty or ninety slaves to be sold in families, with or without the land.

It is to be assumed that the emphasis excluded buyers who had other intentions.

Plantation data for the 18th and 19th centuries illustrate the economic processes in which family developments took place, as well as the extent to which elderly women attained matriarchal status in the slave communities. Dickson claimed to have known 'a hoary headed negro woman, a great grandmother, who ... nursed, and survived, her very indulgent mistress who died about the age of 63 ...'[29] Such cases were indeed rare, as plantation records list women as 'old' and 'worn out' by the age of 50 years. Invariably, the matriarchal status of elderly women was also based upon the élite position of their children or grandchildren on the estates, whether they were housekeepers, artisans, or drivers. This situation reinforced the importance of family ties to slaves in their own career development and general opportunities. It was the norm for the sons of drivers and artisans to follow their fathers' occupation, and for housekeepers' daughters to stay close to household roles. The status of some families was considered more important than others in the slave yards. In many cases occupational continuity among kin was the guarantee of élite status.

The five leading matriarchal figures at Seawell Estate in 1796 had among them 32 children and 21 grandchildren, yet they were all listed as between 40 and 50 years old. They were also all born on the estate, which immediately suggests three-generational family structures. Grandmothers' names were generally prefixed with the word 'Great' on the estate as a symbol of the respect and moral authority which they held among kin. Fathers and grandfathers were rarely mentioned in plantation records dealing with slave families, largely becuase managers' and owners' interests were in motherhood and reproduction rather than the matriarchal nature of the slave families.

The occupational status of mothers was generally passed on to their children, unless fathers were resident on the same estate and belonged to a higher élite group. Although élite women rarely married or cohabited with field men, élite mothers' children were generally arranged at source as these women used their influence on the decision-making of managers and owners. Our four cases above illustrate this process adequately. Of this group, only Great Phebe was an élite woman, a housekeeper of long standing. Her children dominated élite occupations on the estate, Peter, Dick, and Jack being the most important artisans. On her superannuation, Great Phebe was well cared for and, with her children so well placed to assert authority in the slave community, had no fear of abandonment. On the other hand, Great Sarcy was unable to raise the status of any of her children above her own as field hand. Great Ochoo obtained prestigious occupations for two of her sons, but her daughters continued in the field.[31]

Of the 50 women on the estate, only four were listed as married, although 42 of them had children. Possibly the husbands were not estate slaves, and thus not mentioned. The eight childless women — Jubbah, Little Ochoo, Betty, Lemon, Quashebah, Bella, Jenny and Margaret — were in the age range of 30-50 years old. Two were married: Lemon to Fhit, the driver of the great gang, and Betty to Quashey, an African field hand. The 42 mothers had a total of 116 children, an average of 2.76 children each.[32]

Many of the women on Seawell's estate had children with different men, including those women listed as married. Frank, the son of Great Phebe, was married to Statira, daughter of Great Ochoo, but he is listed as having one child (Eve) while his wife is listed as having two (Eve and Ben). Tim, the head boiler, had three children, Grace, Nancy and Patience; his wife Thomasin also had three, but these were Grace, Mary Rose, and Nancy. Patience was described as 'lately born' and mothered by another woman on the estate. The majority of married couples, however, formed their unions as youngsters, and had no children outside their marriage.

The Seawell data suggest that not only were monogamous families the norm by the early 19th century, but also that family played a critical role in the life changes of individual slaves. The Newton data for the same period reinforce these findings. On this estate, the family of Old Doll, more than any other, is the best example. It is a fascinating story of an outstanding female-dominated family; one that shows how women sought to strengthen family bonds in order to maintain their élitist position at a time of rapid change on the estate.[33]

Table 6.4 Old Doll's family, 1798: Newton Estate

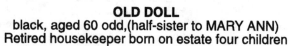

OLD DOLL
black, aged 60 odd, (half-sister to MARY ANN)
Retired housekeeper born on estate four children

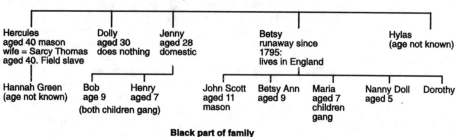

Hercules aged 40 mason wife = Sarcy Thomas aged 40. Field slave	Dolly aged 30 does nothing	Jenny aged 28 domestic	Betsy runaway since 1795: lives in England			Hylas (age not known)
Hannah Green (age not known)	Bob age 9	Henry aged 7	John Scott aged 11 mason	Betsy Ann aged 9	Maria aged 7 children gang	Nanny Doll Dorothy aged 5
	(both children gang)					

Black part of family

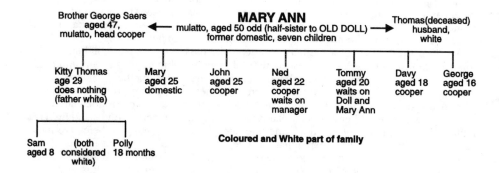

Brother George Saers aged 47, mulatto, head cooper	←	**MARY ANN** mulatto, aged 50 odd (half-sister to OLD DOLL) former domestic, seven children	→	Thomas(deceased) husband, white

Kitty Thomas age 29 does nothing (father white)	Mary aged 25 domestic	John aged 25 cooper	Ned aged 22 cooper waits on manager	Tommy aged 20 waits on Doll and Mary Ann	Davy aged 18 cooper	George aged 16 cooper
Sam (both Polly aged 8 considered 18 months white)						

Coloured and White part of family

Several features of Old Doll's family are emphasized by the plantation records dealing with the genealogical patterns of slaves: first, the low profile of men as fathers—neither Doll's father nor husband(s) are explicitly mentioned, and second, the predominant role of women in decision-making and other aspects of family life. As a former housekeeper Old Doll was retired with security, and occupied her remaining years protecting and directing the lives of her more vulnerable children and grandchildren—both males and females. As head of the extended family her authority was respected by all, including her younger mulatto half-sister, Mary Ann, who was married to a white man and had seven children, and she, in turn, was able to use her influence to ensure that her younger brother, George Saers, the estate's head cooper, made provisions for the professional training of her young sons. Uncle George took all four of his nephews under his wing as apprentice coopers, including ten-year-old George. All of Doll's and Mary Ann's sons were trained as craftsmen and their daughters protected from the scourge of field labour as adults. Certainly, the family was very successful in ensuring the perpetuation of élite status among its members at the expense of other less fortunate families. With severe competition for the few highly prized occupations on the estates, it was to be expected that élite families would close ranks and reinforce their advantage.

Even though colour was a crucial factor in status achievement and social experiences, and also enhanced ideological differences between the black and coloured communities, Old Doll's family, in spite of its clear colour division, held together closely and struggled as one. This can be attributed mainly to the intimate relations between Doll and Mary Ann, but the growing 'élite' consciousness of the colony's slave labour aristocracy was also an important factor. That this family should function in this manner suggests that perhaps within families, colour as a divisive social force was not as potent a factor as in the wider social order. Old Doll was frequently brokering on behalf of her sister's 'white' children, while her sister's slaves worked for both parts of the family. It was certainly Doll's social authority that held the family together as a surviving unit rather than Mary Ann's status as grandmother of 'white' children. Furthermore, the weak image of men that emerges from the documents enhances Old Doll's stature as head of the family, and thereby reinforces the fact that women were by no means 'second class' individuals within the slave yards.

Manager Wood's 1796 'Report' is also particularly detailed on marital patterns and family size. He stated at the outset that 'all negroes that have neither father or mother attached to their names have none alive, and all women whose husbands' names are not mentioned, having children, their husbands are men who do not belong to the estate'.[35] These data point to the significant extent to which nuclear-style families were part of the plantation's slave community.

Married couples on the Newton Estate lived in the same households with their young children, while adult offspring lived in neighbouring huts, forming a family compound. The most senior man in the slave yard was Saboy, 'former driver and overseer of the first gang', who with his wife Nancy (also retired) had five children — all boys (Moses, Bange, Sam, Adam, and Aaron). Neither Saboy nor Nancy had children outside their marriage. This was also the case with Little Peter, the head boiler, and his wife Phibbah, who had four children on the estate. Betty, however, a 40-year-old first gang field hand, had four children 'by a former husband' and one with her present husband Toby, the 30-year-old mason. Bella, a 40-year-old field woman had one child with Bob, her former husband, one with a man not known to the manager, and another with Tom Rogers, the cattle keeper and present husband. Phillida, aged 50, had a daughter, Joan, aged 30 by a 'former relation', and then five with her present husband, the distiller'.[36]

In 1796 only a minority of Newton women had husbands on the estate, although the manager seemed to have known most estate children's fathers. Of the 57 women on the estate, 14 were listed as having no children and five as pregnant. The 43 mothers had between them a total of 104 children, an average of 2.41 children per woman. Excluding Old Doll's family, the maximum number of children of any one woman was five; four women had five children; five had four; eleven had three; ten had two, and eleven only one child.[37]

Table 6.5 *Pregnant women at Newton plantations, 1796*

NAME	AGE	No. OF CHILDREN
Hagen Doll	40	3
Bookey	40 odd	5
Bennybah	40 odd	2
Fanny Ann	20	1
Willoughby	30	0

S1ource: Newton Papers, M. 523/288

Most women on the estate gave birth to their first child between the ages of 17 and 20 years, a few much earlier. For example, a field woman, Jubbah, gave birth to her first child at the age of 14 and by the time she was 30 had had five children: Alacey at 14, Phillis at 17, Chloe at 19, Robin at 20, and Lucy at 27.[38] Only a few women gave birth to more than three children, and depressed fertility levels were undoubtedly an obvious and important feature of Newton slave women into the 19th century. It was common for women to have one child before marriage with a man other than the husband, but their subsequent children were generally confined to the marital union, though the husband would father children with other women.

Anglican clergymen, and some of their planter supporters, were critical of the slaves' polygamous tradition, in which they perceived black women as the sexual victims of black men who considered the possession of wives as symbols of their virility and social status. Basically, the anti-polygamy policy was conceived as follows: in order to encourage black women to favour the monogamous family, it was necessary to Christianize them, not only in formal ways such as baptisms and church attendances, but in matters such as Christian marriage, and concepts of fidelity and chastity. Such a policy, they intimated, was doomed to failure since it would immediately encounter the impervious polygamous sexual culture which slave men were prepared to defend adamantly. According to the council's 1822 report on slaves:

> Polygamy was imported by the negroes from their native country, where it is a sort of privilege of rank; the richest and greatest man enjoys the largest number of wives; and in these colonies they no doubt consider a plurality of wives the privilege of their colour. A more effectual way of giving them a distaste of Christianity could not well be devised, than to tell them in the first instance, that it required a surrender of this their highly valued privilege.[39]

The commissioners considered that black women, unlike the black men, were morally prepared for Christian family life. Likewise, Dickson had argued in the 1770s that black women were inclined to fidelity and decency while the men could not be so described. This concurrence of opinion found expression in the report as follows:

> Chastity is not classed among the cardinal virtues by the Blacks ...., but a violation of it even in a woman not contracted to a husband, is visited by the ridicule of the gang when it is detected, and in women who are wives, want of fidelity is considered disgraceful.[40]

By the end of slavery, none the less, the Christian-style nuclear family was a common institution within black communities. The model of the white planter household, the respectability and security it offered women and the loyalty it demanded from its members, would undoubtedly have appealed to some black women whose lives were commonly characterized by economic insecurity and social uncertainty. Against the background of this model, the physically fragmented slave family stands in stark contrast. With family reunions taking place on weekends and at nights, blacks would have looked forward to a condition of permanent unity. This can be supported by evidence from the post-slavery period which illustrates that much of the so-called 'vagrancy' reported among blacks was actually due to individuals fervently seeking out and integrating their families.

WHITE MALES AND 'COLOURED' CHILDREN

Most contemporary observers considered that slave women who voluntarily engaged in sexual relations with white men were 'incorrigibly licentious'. Attempts were rarely made to unravel the context in which these relations developed, or the forces that gave rise to them. Departing from the premise that interracial relations were 'unnatural' and 'permissive', planter-politicians who occasionally commented on the social impact of such partnerships were content to discuss the matter primarily in terms of morality. Abolitionists argued that immoral white men's sexual exploitation of vulnerable black women was to a large extent responsible for their so-called sexual permissiveness and promiscuity. In making this charge, abolitionists showed a marked degree of unfamiliarity with the social values of black women. In response, some planters sought to show that the proclivities of slave women should relate solely to their specific relations with black men, and to their African-based culture in general. The urban and rural-based data, however, suggest a rather more complex set of social forces at work, most of which relate to the role and experiences of the black woman as 'mother' of the 'coloured' social groups.

The 1822 report of Council on the condition of slaves dealt in great length with black women as wives and mothers and was particularly concerned with their sexual relations with white men, especially those who worked on the estates. When the Commissioners asked Sir Reynold Alleyne:

> From your knowledge of the habits of negroes, are you prepared to say whether or not the women get husbands at an early age, and can you undertake to assert with confidence, whether or not they are restrained from contracting engagements of this kind, by their licentious intercourse with the white men on the estates?

he replied:

> Most of my young women have husbands at a very early period; whenever I have discovered any attempts on the part of the white servants to form connexions with the females of the estate, I have invariably discharged them; ... in a population of 525 slaves, I have not a single child the off-spring of a white man, since the estates have been in my possession: I took possession of my first estate in the year 1811.[41]

Likewise, when Forster Clarke was asked the same question, his full response was recorded as follows:

> Examinant saith — that although he does not think the young women do in general settle themselves very early with husbands, he is not of opinion, that they are often prevented from doing so, by their intercourse with the whites; it can seldom or never be the effect of arbitrary influence, as he attends to the complaints of every negro, and he believes that most others do the same, and such conduct would be resented and punished by the discharge of any white servant, or manager who attempted it; that an illicit intercourse does often exist there can be no doubt, but from the small number of mulatto children born in estates, it would appear that such connexions were not so often formed as might be expected.[42]

William Sharpe also admitted that white men who worked on the estates sometimes had relationships with slave women which resulted in pregnancies. There are two particularly striking elements in his testimony: first, that such sexual relationships were not considered legitimate by the estates' management, and probably by white planter society at large; and second, since some white labouring men who impregnated slave women were driven off the estates, managerial policy supported the forceful alienation of white fatherhood of such mulatto children. This is not to suggest that these white males were prepared to shoulder responsibilities for their 'coloured' progeny and black mates, but rather to illustrate the ideological hostility the plantation world directed against black women with white mates. There is also a class element implicit in Sharpe's responses; white workers were considered the culprits, the offenders of social codes, when in fact, planters and managers were largely responsible for the sexual manipulation and exploitation of black women. Whereas for the white élite these sexual relations were considered a 'right', for white labourers they were an intolerable abuse of race and privilege. Sharpe's answers to the question concerning this latter type of interracial relations were recorded as follows:

> Illicit intercourse with the whites does sometimes take place, but it is principally confined to the inferior servants on the estates, who are young men whose circumstances in life will not admit of their marrying and supporting a family: — when a connexion of this kind takes place between them and the young black women, it is done by persuasion, and because they have it more in their power to gratify the vanity of the females in their fondness for dress; punishment however awaits the offender when his improper conduct is discovered, for he seldom escapes being turned out of the estates. A manager's moral conduct is a great recommendation of him: glaring instances of immoral conduct would not be tolerated. Saith — he is of the opinion that the illicit intercourse with the whites, has but very little effect in preventing the young women on estates from having husbands at an early age. On two estates which are under his direction, and have upwards of four hundred negroes on them, only two coloured children, descendants of white men, have been born since May 1817 to the present time; and on another which he took over in 1819, with 120 negroes, there has been no coloured child born.[43]

Planters' attempts to diminish the extent to which black women mothered children for white men can, of course, be evaluated by the available demographic evidence, but such an approach would inevitably negate the full sociological and legalistic context and consequences of interracial reproduction. It is necessary, therefore, to look at slave codes, the ideology and politics of the coloured community, and of course the machinations of white males in order to comprehend the forces that were critical in shaping the social lives of these black women.

The slave codes of Barbados consistently held that all children at birth took the status of their mothers. 'Mulatto' children, therefore, born of slave mothers, were categorized as slaves irrespective of their fathers' social status. Black motherhood, by implication, was conceptually and legally tied to the perpetuation of slavery while white fatherhood was alienated from the process. This matrifocal legislative approach to slave reproduction ensured that from the point of view of white society, black women's maternity could not be separated from enslavement and degradation. Also, it meant that white men could rape, seduce, and impregnate slave women, as a normal part of their common culture, without any legal or social responsibility to spouse or progeny.

According to Dunn, from the early 17th-century beginnings of slave society:

> The English sugar planters ... slept with their slave women and sired mulatto children .... The master enjoyed commandeering his prettiest slave girl and exacting his presumed rights from her. Many planters whose wives and children lived with them in the islands openly kept black concubines.[44]

The mulatto offspring of these sexual encounters had to be accounted for legally within the scheme of things in order to remove any possibility of their claim to their father's property by inheritance. Also, slave owners wanted to ensure that landed property could not become the basis of any mulatto ascendancy over their white fathers in the socio-economic structure. To do this, legislative provisions, as well as social ideologies, had to be shaped in an effort to attach the stain of racial and genetic inferiority to the offspring of black mothers, who, according to the prevailing white hegemonic ethos, carried the seed of slavery.

Enslaved black women entered into both voluntary and involuntarily reproductive sexual unions with white men from most sections of society. Whereas white men saw such relationships as a legitimate benefit of their race and class dominance, sexual relations between black men and white women were taboo throughout the white community; this was part of the white men's general attempt to limit the sexual freedom of white women, and also to maintain their social dominance within society. For the male slave, however, sexual access to the white female became increasingly surrounded by fear of severe punishment — including death.

In the formative decades of slave society, when social ideologies were not yet fully formed, sexual relations between black men and white women were recorded as being in no way extraordinary. In the St Michael parish register for 4 December 1685, for example, a marriage is entered between 'Peter Perkins, a negro, and Jane Long, a white woman'.[45] The 1715 census shows that they had a son; three other children of such relations were recorded as:[46] Elizabeth X, a mulatto born of a white woman; Mary K, the daughter of a white woman and begotten by the extract of a negro; John L, a mulatto born of a white woman. During the 18th century, however, as the slave society matured, the role of racial ideologies became increasingly important to the white élite as tools of social control, and reports of such relations more or less vanished from official documents.

An account of the colony in 1683 mentioned the existence of 326 'mulatto' inhabitants, some of whom were free.[47] During the 18th century, planters tended to refer to all persons of mixed racial ancestry as coloured, unlike the Jamaicans, for example, who paid social and official attention to all the various possible types of interracial mixtures. In this way, black women would be conceived as representing the maternal ancestry of the majority of coloured persons in the colony, irrespective of their legal or social status. The proliferation of studies dealing with the 'coloured' racial group, especially those who were free, has hardly emphasized the special relationships that existed with black maternity. Yet an understanding of this relationship is critical for their proper social analysis.

Some whites preferred their mulatto progeny legally freed, and made arrangements for their manumission — with or without their slave mothers. These free coloured persons cherished their freedom, probably the most valuable social asset in slave society, and sought to distance themselves socially from their slave ancestry which white society defined as the undisputed mark of social inferiority. For this social group their black mothers were, therefore, generally seen as a social disability, while their white grandmothers tended to see them as a disgrace. Living within these two psychological worlds the free coloureds developed a unique perspective on society characterized by a general tendency to alienate their black maternal ancestry.

Table 6.6   *Estimated free coloured population of Barbados, 1748-1829*

Year	Number	% Total Free Non-White Population
1748	107	63.6
1773	136	54.0
1825	2,066	53.2
1826	2,169	53.1
1827	2,201	53.2
1828	2,259	53.3
1829	2,313	—

Source: Parliamentary Papers, Vol 21, 1820; Beckles, 1984a, p. 59; Handler, 1974, p. 21; Watson, 1979, p. 101.

Most white males who manumitted their coloured children did not free their black mothers. On the estates, it was not abnormal for planters or managers to free their coloured children when they reached adulthood, while their mothers continued as slaves in the fields or in the households. These children were not always the result of voluntary sexual relations; rape, duress, and other forms of coercion featured commonly in these contexts. Instances where provisions were made for black mothers were generally those in which some emotional intimacy existed, and where white fathers accepted social responsibility for their 'illegitimate' family, but these cases were few. White fathers of coloured children generally became socially anonymous, and the social and material condition of these mothers and children remained unaltered.

The majority of enslaved coloured children, then, were never freed, and the free-coloured community, which features so prominently in most sociological analyses of slave society, represents no more than the tip of the coloured 'iceberg'. In these analyses, black mothers remain hidden while the achievements and struggles of their freed sons and daughters are highlighted. It is a fact that while the free coloureds attempted to suppress the evidence of their black maternity, historians have hardly done their task of restoring to these women, their social visibility. The rise of prominent free-coloured family dynasties, such as the Belgraves, Beckles, Collymores, Bournes, and Montefiores, should not be studied without reference to this fact if historians seek to be objective and free from the ideological influence of the group under scrutiny.

Some free coloureds, however, made provisions for the betterment of their slave mothers subsequent to their white fathers' refusals to do so. For example, in 1825, Elizabeth Sarjeant, a free mulatto woman who had accumulated substantial property in Bridgetown, specified by Will that her 'reputed mother named Mary Pollard' should be 'purchased from one Samuel Game and emancipated according to the laws of the island.[48] Typically, when freed, black mothers were advanced in years and then given a low profile as 'hidden' dependents, especially when their coloured children were prominent persons. The free-coloured family of white planter Jacob Hinds, owner of the 170-acre Lodge estate in St Michael, constitutes a representative case. In his Will of 1832, by which he left extensive property to his coloured children, it is stated: 'I would call them my children but that would not be legal as I never was married'. These children were mothered by three black women from his estate. Two daughters, Jane Hinds and Elizabeth Hinds, were well known in Barbados, but little is known of their mother Mimbo Rose. Also, John's and Helen's names were to appear regularly in the records for the mid-19th century, but nothing is known of Fanny, their mother.[49]

Black motherhood, then, even when associated with white fatherhood and coloured children was never offered respectability by white and coloured élites. The 'colourism' that separated these mothers from their children was in no way less potent than the hegemonic racism which dictated that white men could not marry their black lovers. The official ideology of the ruling class held that the offspring of black women should not be distanced from the status of slavery, and legislators went to great lengths to ensure that this was incorporated into the spirit and provisions of the slave codes. William A. Green went further and argued that as Barbados was the most mature slave society at the end of the 18th century, the prejudice against the black skin was stronger than in other British colonies.[50] Certainly, Elizabeth Fenwick, who carefully observed Barbadian white racism and its subtype, 'colourism', found that the 'boundary' separating the races was 'impassable', though some of the coloureds were 'fair, light haired people' with wealth and education.

Enslaved black women, therefore, were commonly forced to endure the condition of seeing their coloured children defend slavery with the kind of intense vigour characteristic of their white fathers. For the free coloureds, the 1816 slave revolt was their most testing moment, when they were forced to take a firm position on the slavery question. Only a handful of free coloureds supported the revolt; some, according to the assembly's report, joined the black rebels probably because they had slave children whom they wanted freed and, because of their poverty, could not finance the manumission procedure.[52] One of them, Joseph Franklyn, believed by many whites to be a leading provocateur, was born a slave and freed at the age of 21 by his father, an estate owner, while his mother Leah remained a slave on the estate. He resented and rejected white arrogance, and found companionship among blacks. But élite free coloureds who fought against the slaves were commended for their 'determination to do their duty by the country', and 'devotion to the interest of the whites'.[53]

Also during the revolt, the free-coloured élites articulated their acceptance of the ideology of white racial supremacy as a social principle, with all that implied for their black heritage. This ideology was most clearly expressed by John Poyer, Creole intellectual and historian, as follows:

> In every well constituted society, a state of subordination necessarily arises from the nature of civil government. Without this no political union can long subsist. To maintain this fundamental principle, it becomes absolutely necessary to preserve the distinctions which naturally exist or are accidentally introduced into the community. With us, two grand distinctions exist resulting from the nature of our society. First, between the white inhabitants and free people of colour, and secondly between masters and slaves. Nature has strongly defined the difference [not] only in complexion, but in the mental, intellectual and corporal faculties of the different species. Our colonial code has acknowledged and adopted these distinctions .... [54]

Black and coloured slaves were defeated in their effort to remove slavery from the colony and thereby reject this racist conceptualization. The following year, the free coloureds were given a major concession by the white legislators for their loyalty: the right to give evidence in court against whites. In their acceptance memorandum they expressed agreement with Poyer's rationalization of the ideological structure of the slave society. In the letter to John Beckles, Speaker of the House, they stated:

> We are sensible that in a country like this where slavery exists, there must necessarily be distinction between the white and free coloured inhabitants and that there are privileges which the latter do not expect to enjoy .... It affords us general satisfaction to find that our conduct upon the late unfortunate occasion [rebellion] has met with the approbation of the legislator .... We assure your worships that we shall be ready at all times to give proof of our loyalty and sincere attachment to the King and Constitution and risk our lives in the defence and protection of our country and its laws.[55]

Not only were the free coloureds opposed to the armed liberation of blacks, but also to their imperial legislative emancipation. At no stage did they consider, as a group, that the black sections of their families, especially their mothers, were worthy of general emancipation. From the beginning of the 19th century when imperial legislative action was tending towards the amelioration of slaves' conditions, they had adopted a firm pro-slavery position. In an 1803 petition addressed to the Assembly, they argued:

> We have all our lives been accustomed to the assistance of slaves .... Many of our children who are now grown almost to the years of maturity have from their earliest infancy been accustomed to be attended by slaves .... Surely death would be preferable to ... a situation [of slavelessness].[56]

When in 1831, they gained full civil rights, on a par with whites, they joined the vanguard of the anti-emancipation movement in a manner comparable with their behaviour during the 1816 slave revolt. Thome and Kimball, who observed emancipation in action, wrote:

> We regret to add, that until lately, the coloured people of Barbados have been far in the background in the cause of abolition, and even now, the majority of them are either indifferent, or actually hostile to emancipation. They have no fellow feeling with the slave. In fact, they have had prejudices against the negroes no less bitter than those which the whites have experienced towards them. There are many honourable exceptions to this ... but such, we are assured, is the general fact.[57]

White slave owners, then, might have been unable to enslave all the progeny of black women, but they were able to win the active pro-slavery support of those who were freed. There were few instances where black women presided over socially cohesive families with free-coloured children, and none where legal marriage was involved. Most of those who mothered children for white men experienced no meaningful advancement in their social or material condition. Socially rejected by their spouse and children alike, many of these black women would have experienced the meaning of white racism in a unique and intense manner. Nevertheless, some women would have sacrificed their lives to have coloured children and to see them free and living among the élite.

NOTES

1. Bennett, 1958, p. 26.
2. Bayley, 1833, p. 432.
3. Ibid.
4. Craton, in *Caribbean Societies*, Vol. 2, No. 34, Collected Seminar Papers, Institute of Commonwealth Studies, University of London, 1985, p. 2.
5. See Raymond T. Smith, 1971 (first published 1957); Barry Higman, in Margaret E. Crahan and Franklin W. Knight, (eds) 1979; Michael Mulllins, 'Maroon Women', paper given at the 12th Annual Conference of Caribbean Historians, Trinidad, 1980; Herbert G. Gutman, 1976.
6. Ligon, 1657, p. 47.
7. Ibid.
8. Ibid.
9. Ibid.
10. Bennett, 1958, p. 35.
11. Ibid., p. 85.
12. Ibid., pp. 34-5.
13. John Pinder to SPG Secretary, Barbados, 29 March 1822, also 29 September 1825, MSS. Box, 3, SPG Archives, London.
14. John Pinder to SPG Secretary, 22 January, 23 September 1819, ibid.

15. See William Dickson, 1815 (reprinted 1970), (first published 1814) pp. 439-41; Minutes of the Legislative Council, 3 November 1818. C.O. 31/48, PRO; Lord Seaforth to Secretary of State for the Colonies, 22 July 1805, C.O. 28/73, f. 14. Also Beckles, in *Boletín de Estudios Latinoamericanos y d Caribe,* No. 39, December 1985, pp. 85-90.

16. Dickson, 1815, p. 360.

17. *Barbados Mercury,* 31 May 1783, 28 August 1784, 1 January and 2 February 1787; Karl Watson, *The Civilised Island,* p. 91.

18. *Barbados Globe,* 30 April 1829.

19. Ibid., 17 October 1831.

20. Ibid., 20 October 1831.

21. John Pinder to SPG Secretary, 22 January, 23 September 1819, Box 2 SPG Archives. See also Bennett, 1958, p. 117.

22. Forster Clarke to SPG Secretary, 29 June 1824, MSS. Box 3, SPG Archives. Also, Bennett, ibid.

23. Bennett, ibid.

24. Ibid.

25. Richard Schomburgk, 1848,p. 427.

26. Handler, 1974, p. 165.

27. Dickson, 1815, pp. 208-9.

28. Ibid.

29. Dickson, 1789, p. 156, footnote.

30. Report on the negroes of Seawell Plantation, their families, sexes, ages, employment, 1796, Newton Papers, M. 523/292.

31. Ibid.

32. Ibid.

33. Report on the negroes, where born, ages, employment, families, and sexes; Newton Plantation, 1796, Newton Papers, M. 523/288.

34. Correspondence of Sampson Wood to Thomas Lane, 1796-98. Newton Papers, M. 523/288 to M. 523/341. See also Karl Watson, 'Escaping Bondage: the Odyssey of a Barbadian Salve Family', paper presented at the 16th Annual Conference of Caribbean Historians, UWI, Barbados, April 8-13, 1984.

35. Wood to Thomas Lane, 1796, Newton Papers, M. 523/288.

36. Ibid.

37. Ibid.

38. Ibid.

39. A Report ... into the Actual Condition of the Slaves (1822).

40. Ibid.

41. Ibid.

42. Ibid.

43. Ibid.

44. Dunn, 1973.

45. St Michael Parish Register, Vol. 1A, RL 1/1, Barbados Archives. See also Dunn, 1973, pp. 255-6.

46. Census of Barbados, 1715, Barbados Archives.

47. See, 'An Account of Barbados and the Government Thereof', 1863, Sloane MSS. 2441, BL.

48. Will of Elizabeth Sarjeant, 21 February 1825, RB 4/63, Barbados Archives.

49. Data from Ronald Hughes, 'Jacob Hinds (?-1832). White Father of a Coloured Clan', Seminar Paper No. 2, 1982-83, Department of History, UWI, Barbados.

50. Claude Levy, 1980, p. 30.

51. A. G. Fenwick (ed.), 1927, p. 169.

52. *Report from a Select Committee of the House of Assembly Appointed to Inquire into the Origin, Causes, and Progress of the Late Insurrections* (Barbados, 1817), p. 26.

53. Minutes of the Assembly, 7 January 1817. Also Beckles, 1984a, p. 110.

54. [John Poyer] *A Letter addressed to …. Lord Seaforth by a Barbadian* (Bridgetown, 1801).

55. Minutes of the Assembly, C.O. 28/86, ff. 6 7, PRO.

56. 'The Humble Petition of the Free Coloured People, Inhabitants of the Island', Minutes of the Council of Barbados, 1 November 1803.

57. Thome and Kimball, 1838, p. 76.

6
East Indian Family Patterns

East Indians arrived in the Caribbean in large numbers in the post-emancipation period. They came from India as indentured or contract labourers to fill the labour gap on the plantations left by the exodus of ex-slaves. The survival of their Indian culture in the Caribbean, especially their caste and family patterns, constitutes a major focus of sociological attention. Most investigators have agreed that the Hindu institution of caste has all but disappeared in original form. Nevertheless, the ideology associated with caste has survived at the level of 'submerged consciousness' (Reddock 1994: 41) and dynamic elements of caste have been reconstructed, incorporating creole cultural principles. Specifically in terms of family patterns, there has been disagreement concerning survival, with some researchers like Arthur Niehoff (1959, see Article 2 at end of chapter) and Morton Klass (1961) emphasising retention, continuity and pluralism, while Joseph Nevadomsky (1980, see Article 3 at end of chapter), Michael Angrosino (1976, see Article 4 at end of chapter) and others report change and acculturation either by processes of Indian revival or the adoption of creole characteristics. This debate is tied to an issue which we noted in the last chapter in that the emphasis on continuity focusses mainly on cultural survival, while change is attributed to the process of creolisation as a result of the impact of Caribbean conditions, the most important of which are perceived to be economic. Mohammad Rauf (1974: 77) summed up the argument with special reference to the status of East Indian women in Guyana:

> It may be pointed out that the desire of the East Indians to retain their cultural identity does not necessarily imply that changes have not occurred in their traditional socio-cultural system. The arrangement of statuses has changed in response to social and economic conditions prevailing in Guyana. Economic conditions, in particular, have influenced statuses with regard to the system of division of labour in the village. Females now function in ways which once were the exclusive responsibilities of males or young adults. In the weekly village markets one finds more females than males working as salesmen. Men and young adults mostly perform the duties of helpers and assistants. The participation of women in the economic activity has resulted in **de facto** modification of their status in society. Such changes have, however, been accompanied by the

persistence of some basic cultural contents of the Indian system such as the continuity of basic status values. As such the **de jure** position of women remains the same (Emphasis in orginal).

We start this chapter by describing the traditions and ideals of Indian kinship. Then we trace briefly the conditions of arrival and settlement of the East Indians as indentured labourers in the Caribbean, paying particular attention to how these conditions affected marriage and the family. We then proceed to examine contemporary changes in family patterns in the Caribbean before returning to the argument concerning the respective influence of cultural-historical and contemporary economic factors on family form.

Indian kinship patterns

On the face of it, Indian kinship traditions appear in many respects to be the mirror opposite of family and conjugal union patterns among Afro-Caribbean people. As research conducted in Trinidad by Robert Bell (1970, see Article 1 at end of chapter) illustrates, contrasts between the East Indian patriarchal and Creole female-centred families are reflected in marriage, sexuality, parenthood, illegitimacy and child-rearing. The family as an institution and the close and enduring family bonds are at the centre of East Indian culture. The conjugal union is the focal point of the family and marriage is the norm for all East Indians. It is generally the first relationship entered into and is arranged by the parents of the bride and groom. Important to these arrangements are caste endogamy, that is marrying within one's caste, and the dowry system whereby a payment is made by the parents of the bride to those of the groom. Marriage takes place at a relatively young age and is expected to last for the rest of one's lifetime. Divorce is prohibited and visiting unions are negatively sanctioned and are relatively rare.

Kinship relations are characterised by male dominance to the extent that gender parallels age and generation in the determination of family authority and responsibility. Mothers, for example, dominate relationships with their daughters and daughters-in-law, but may play a subordinate role in relation to their sons especially in cases where the sons assume responsibilities as household heads in the absence of their own fathers (Jayawardena 1962: 48, 51). Elders, however, both male and female, are respected by the younger generation. Along with the conjugal bond, the tie between father and son constitutes the core of family relations that extend to encompass a 'joint' family, a corporate structure which includes the wives and children of the sons, all living under the same roof (Angrosino 1976: 45). Money and property are held in common and religious rituals commemorating the ancestors confirm and reinforce family solidarity. Even marriage is perceived as an alliance between two kin groups rather than a relationship between two individuals. Individualism and personal choice in family affairs, as in all other matters, are submerged and subordinated to the interests and the demands of kinship. As we shall see, however, these traditional ideals of family and marriage have undergone marked changes within the cultural, social and economic circumstances of the Caribbean.

Conditions of indenture

East Indian indentured labourers left India in an effort to escape famine and abject poverty and in response to the recruitment policies devised by West Indian planters and the British government to deal with the post-emancipation crisis in the Caribbean. Bridget Brereton (1974: 25-26) reported:

> The importation of a cheap and easily managed labour force was, to the planters, the only solution. They tried many places. The Eastern Caribbean, Africa, Madeira, the U.S. and China all supplied immigrants in the years after 1840. But each source had drawbacks; cost, or inadequate numbers, or unsuitable labourers. It was India which proved satisfactory. India had a huge population; millions of her peoples lived in destitution and so would be likely to emigrate in the hope of a better life; most of India was under British control, which meant that it would be an emigration of British subjects from one British colony to another, under the supervision throughout of the British government and with no need to deal with foreign powers. India's climate was not unlike that of the West Indies, and most of the people were accustomed to agricultural work. The cost of importation, though high, was not prohibitive as it was in the case of China. And so in the nineteenth century a vast traffic in Indian labourers was established, taking them to Assam, South-East Asia, East Africa, South Africa, Mauritius, and the West Indies.

East Indian indentured labourers began to arrive in Guyana in 1838 and in Trinidad shortly after, in 1845. Between these dates and 1917 when indentureship ended, a total of approximately 240,000 workers arrived in Guyana and about 144,000 in Trinidad. Smaller numbers were brought into other Caribbean islands, for example, Jamaica received 36,500 indentured labourers. At present, East Indians constitute 51 per cent of the population in Guyana and 39 per cent in Trinidad. In both these territories absolute numbers have contributed to the greater retention of cultural patterns, especially family patterns, while elsewhere cultural values and practices have undergone processes of creolisation and assimilation.

Brereton (1974: 28) explained the conditions of indenture:

> An 'indenture' means a contract, and the indentured Indians signed a contract before they left India which bound them to accept certain terms. For the period that their indenture lasted, they were not free. They could not leave their employer. They could not demand higher wages, live off the estate they were assigned to, or refuse the work given them to do. Once the indenture had expired, however they became free, and if they remained in Trinidad, their legal status was not different from that of the rest of the population. This is the essential difference between indenture and slavery, for slavery, of course, was perpetual.

The indentured male workers were bonded for five years, the women initially for five and then for three, after which they were granted 'industrial residence' and given a 'free paper' to prove it.

Conditions of indenture were harsh. For a working week of between 45 and 54 hours, a male labourer earned an average of one dollar, a female 48 cents. What Brereton (1974: 29) has described as the 'most obnoxious' feature of the system was the frequent and unnecessary sentencing of East Indians for petty offences, for example, even crossing a highway without their papers could result in a jail term for vagrancy. Indentured labourers suffered extremely poor health and endemic disease from the appalling conditions of barrack accommodation with poor sanitation and inadequate diets (Brereton 1974: 30-31).

On arrival in the Caribbean, East Indian indentured servants were faced with conditions that were anything but conducive to the preservation of culture and family life. Although it is generally agreed that their standards and conditions of living were not as harsh as those of the slaves, East Indians were also defined essentially as plantation labour, with culture and community patterns tolerated as long as they did not interfere with the prime purpose for which they had been brought to the Caribbean. Planters had no interest in importing family units or preserving family life, both of which they perceived to entail additional costs.

Barrack room accommodation and uneven sex ratios had a devastating effect on conjugal relations. Barracks were overcrowded with minute rooms and no privacy because partitions did not reach the roof. Sex ratios were weighted heavily in favour of men, as indentured labourers were recruited as individual units of labour, not as families (Reddock 1994: 28-31). In Trinidad during the period 1874-1917 males outnumbered females by over two to one, with numbers estimated at 63,798 (68 per cent) male and 30,148 (32 per cent) female (Vertovec 1992: 101). The sex imbalance played havoc with the traditional system of marriage and monogamy for life. Women were at a premium and the dowry system was reversed as the father of the bride demanded a 'bride price' from his prospective son-in-law's family (Brereton 1974: 31). Rhoda Reddock (1994: 42) has pointed out that bride price was the norm among lower-status Indians in North India, but nevertheless agrees that bride price became higher in Trinidad.

Reddock (1994: 30-31) has also indicated that indenture agents were unable to recruit the 'right kind of woman', that is respectable women as wives and family members. The majority of female indentured labourers were either widows escaping the misery of life with their in-laws, women who had been deserted by their husbands, unmarried pregnant women or prostitutes, all independently seeking a new life in the Caribbean. Indeed, it is quite conceivable that many used their scarcity to their advantage by pursuing improvements in socio-economic status through beneficial sexual alliances, much like their black counterparts had done previously. But white men also exploited East Indian women sexually in much the same way as they abused black slave women. Brereton (1974: 45) presented more details of the situation on the plantations in Trinidad:

> On the sugar plantations ... conditions were not conducive towards the realisation of the marital ideal. There were of course laws against seduction, but they were not always effective. Moreover, it was not infrequent that members of the non-Indian supervisory staff would be involved in such liaisons, not surprisingly, in view of the tradition of concubinage that has been associated with plantation life since the days of slavery. By the end of the nineteenth century it was being alleged by some critics that the moral effect of the indentureship system on employers was probably worse than in the days of slavery. Indeed, as early as 1854, a visitor to Trinidad told of an estate manager who had seven women returned as labourers in his account, but these were doing no work, 'being with child, all by him'.

The overall effect then, was that the intense competition for scarce women "wrecked" the traditional institution of marriage as women engaged in extra-marital unions and, on occasions, polyandry (Sharma 1986: 23-24; Jayawardena 1962: 45).

Traditional Hindu and Muslim marriages were not accorded legal sanction in Trinidad or Guyana for nearly one hundred years after the initial arrival of East Indians. Marital disputes and other domestic conflicts were settled by plantation managers according to Eurocentric family norms and values. As Chandra Jayawardena (1963: 20-21) explained:

For instance, in regulating the lives of their labourers, managers acted in terms of their own cultural norms. They housed one nuclear family in each dwelling and provided new accommodation for the children when they got married, usually in another part of the plantation. This was deliberate policy, for they wished to eliminate tensions arising from the difficult position of the resident daughter-in-law. As a rule, no married couple was allowed to reside in the parental home for longer than a few years.

The power of the father in the family was circumscribed to the extent that he was no longer the sole trustee of the economic resources of the domestic group. Adult sons and wives could evade his control in that they had access to economic resources and accommodation that were beyond his control.

Lastly, the manager was the arbitrator in all inter-personal disputes, and his solutions tended to be in terms of the norms of his own culture. He paid attention to the complaints of wives, sons, and daughters-in-law against the husband/father and, if he felt the man was behaving 'unreasonably', reprimanded him and so limited his authority. Thus the manager's intervention tended to rearrange the domestic relations of the Indians in accordance with Guianese ('European') patterns.

European family values emphasised more equality between the spouses than was the case with Indian conjugal patterns. It is perhaps not altogether surprising, therefore, that husbands often reacted violently. In the plantation conditions of Trinidad, for example:

Many an indentured woman literally lost her head — severed with a cutlass by her enraged husband or consort. At the turn of the century, when working conditions were particularly bad on the estates and the rate of imprisonment high, the frequency of wife murders caused a public outcry. **The Mirror** referred to the 'annual harvest' of murders, and claimed that the 'crude notions and customs' of the 'semi-surfs', among whom the murder of faithless wives was sanctioned, was having a demoralising effect on the 'less savage section of the population' (Singh 1974: 45-46).

Cases of wife-murder were reported for both Trinidad and Guyana during those early years, a phenomenon which might be explained as an extreme attempt to reinforce the traditional Indian pattern of patriarchal dominance and wifely submission. As Sharma (1986: 28) puts it:

Though reprehensible and condemnable, they may be seen as an extreme form of social mechanism for the establishment of the institutions of marriage and the family against all odds created by the same colonial masters who were most vociferous in condemning them.

The caste system and caste endogamy among Hindus suffered an even worse fate. With the shortage of Indian women and living conditions which violated caste rituals, such as restrictions on eating with members of other castes or with non-Hindus, the system became impossible to maintain. In addition, the tendency to choose as marriage partners men offering the opportunity of socio-economic mobility did not necessarily coincide with higher caste (Reddock 1994: 41).

Reconstruction of marriage and the family

Gradually over the generations, the destabilising impact of sexual imbalance and barrack living were mitigated and from this unstable foundation, the reconstitution of the East Indian marriage and the family began. As the labourers served their period of indenture, many chose to stay in the Caribbean and were allotted grants of land. Living in village communities more, though not completely, independent of the demands of the plantations, facilitated the restoration of Indian kinship patterns. A balance between males and females in the East Indian population was gradually achieved. Towards the end of the indenture period some effort was made to recruit family groups and the subsequent increased contribution to the population by natural increase restored sexual parity. In Trinidad, for example, this was achieved by the early 1930s. Additionally, traditional Muslim and Hindu marriages were officially recognised, for example in Trinidad by 1936 and 1946 respectively.

While these factors provided the necessary social, demographic and legal foundations, the catalyst for the revival of Indian culture was provided by a combination of circumstances, most significant of which were the pride of the East Indian population in the achievement of independence in India in 1947, the arrival of Hindu and Muslim religious preachers and artistes in the Caribbean and Indian film shows (Jha 1974: 20). Combined with the general concern that their culture was fast disappearing, this stimulated the reconstruction of a remembered system of Indian culture and identity. The family and religious ceremonies, marriage in particular, were central to this Indian renaissance. A second period of revival and 'ritual exuberance' (Vertovec 1990: 236) occurred in Trinidad with the oil boom between the mid-1970s and the early 1980s. Although much of the new-found wealth went towards consumption and business investment, 'Hindus also tended to pour money, as never before, into ritual activity .... New, or at least newly embellished rites and ceremonial events rapidly proliferated throughout the island' (Vertovec 1990: 235).

These processes, however, were not immune to the social and cultural influences of the Caribbean. Paradoxically, as East Indians reconstructed their own cultural traditions, they were simultaneously becoming creolised. While the revival of prized Indian culture was occurring, the East Indian community was not isolated from the comments of the wider society, which had already derogatorily labelled their customs as 'coolie culture'. Hindu and Moslem marriages, for example, were derided as 'bamboo weddings', a symbolic reference to the temporary tents supported by bamboo poles in which the ceremonies took place. More importantly, the spread of Christianity and of education with the concomitant increased knowledge of the English language removed the cultural isolation of even the furthest rural village.

> The role of the Presbyterian Church which initiated its proselytizing activities among East Indians in 1868 in Trinidad, almost at the same time when East Indian villages started appearing, is no less important. On the one hand, it helped in the institutionalization of marriage among the converted East Indians and, on the other, it broke the isolation of the East Indian children studying in its schools. The spread of education and knowledge of English opened windows to other traditions, especially the local creole tradition. Thus, the supposed insulation of Indian villages, which is presumed to help in maintaining the Indian culture, was undermined slowly and gradually (Sharma 1986: 27).

The younger generation led the way towards the creolisation of Indian culture, including patterns of family life.

The Indian tradition of arranged child marriages was one of the first to be compromised and changed as marital patterns were accommodated to Caribbean mainstream culture. The following passage from Rauf's study of cultural change and ethnic identity in a Guyanese village (Rauf 1974: 79-81) illustrates the transition to a freer choice of marriage partner. Most interesting are the contrasting and potentially conflicting criteria for the selection of marriage partners, the parents emphasising security, wealth and family status, while for the younger generation, love and modern, civilised ways are decisive. The youth provide the following rationalisation:

Freedom of choice in selecting life partners would make the marriage more stable; mutual selection leads to mutual compatibility; marriage by mutual selection enables the partners to know each other intimately in terms of their attitudes toward life, personal likes and dislikes, tastes and temperaments, habits and moods. Thus a deep understanding before marriage is considered by this generation a pre-requisite to a successful relationship between life partners. In the words of a female informant (17 1/2 years); 'There are many advantages in a marriage of free choice. By doing that the persons concerned will develop an understanding between each other ... and this will lead to a successful marriage because the foundation had (thus) already been laid.' For the purpose of analysis it is interesting to note that of all the reasons given in support of mutual choice marriage, the two reasons that stood out most prominently were lack of trust on the part of the younger generation in the judgements of the older generation, and the desire of the young generation to assume full responsibility for all the decisions regarding their future lives. For instance, one male (16 years) pointed out that 'the parents', who belong to the older generation, 'cannot understand the interests of the young people' and neither can they 'notice the things that we want.' He further stated that 'When I choose a girl I will not go and choose a girl once she is a girl, I will have to tackle she and I will have to meet she and get to know all about she, then I get marry to she.' Another male (16 years) expressed a doubt that if he gives his parents the right to choose his wife, they may for reasons of 'money' and 'big family', 'fix me up with a woman who is old and has about five children. I do not like this'. Yet another informant (male 15 1/2 years) remarked 'I don't know if they will choose a girl who don't know how to walk with shoe or a girl who don't know how to speak proper English language. But as far as I am concerned I will marry the girl I love, and the girl who could speak proper English.' A female informant (17 1/2 years) expressed her firm belief that 'free choice marriage is the best because you would pick up someone suitable for yourself. Your parents do not know you well so they can not select somebody for you'.

Thus, whereas the members of the older generation still see merit in the old practice of arranged marriage and support it on the grounds that arranged marriage is part of East Indian tradition and that it also provides more security, the younger generation tends to emphasize that love is the main principle on which the life partnership should rest and the family should be developed. In the absence of love the life between a husband and wife according to the younger generation is absolutely meaningless and vulnerable. Such a life leads to domestic strains, tensions, divorce, and occasionally to suicide. An observation made by a female informant (17 1/2 years) translates the attitude of the younger generation perhaps much better than any analytic description. She remarked that 'to my way of thinking arranged marriage occurred during the past when people were not so civilized. It is a long time law of far off land. Marriage without love is just like living as cats and dogs'. To this informant a departure from the old East Indian practice means a movement toward civilization.

In practice, young partners seek the consent of their parents who, in turn, seldom object unless the potential spouse is of a different race or ethnicity (Rauf 1974: 81).

Similarly, Nevadomsky (1982/3: 192) reported that in the rural village of Amity in Trinidad:

> Arranged marriages used to be the norm. Today, most marriages are based on free personal choice. In the village, 66% of the married women under 35 years of age chose their own spouses in contrast to only 17% of the married women over 35. Personal choice is to be expected where emphasis is placed on the affective bond between spouses, and young people have considerable freedom of movement in and out of the community.

He added that young girls as well as boys are given this freedom of selection of a marriage partner (Nevadomsky 1980: 46). In most cases they would subsequently seek parental approval of their choices, but in the event that this is not forthcoming, the trend is to go ahead, marry and then await a reconciliation. It is important, however, to recognise that the conflict is not always easily and amicably settled. For Trinidad, Singh (1974: 60) has reported the prevalence of,

> intrafamilial conflicts over such emotionally vital problems as romance, selection of mates and life styles. Many a young girl, traditionally under greater parental control than the boy, proved to be too vulnerable to the emotional strain that inhered in the web of cultural contradiction in which she was caught, and committed suicide.

Correlating with the decline in arranged marriages is the increased age at marriage and the disappearance of child marriages. The aforementioned law recognising Hindu marriages in fact set the minimum age at marriage at 14 for girls and 18 for boys. For the sample of East Indian women in Trinidad studied by George Roberts and Lloyd Braithwaite in 1958, 59 per cent of all initial marriages took place under age 15, the average age at marriage was 17.4 years and 90 per cent had married by the age 25 (Roberts and Braithwaite 1962: 205, 210). Nevadomsky (1980: 48) has argued that the change was not initiated by the law, rather legislation 'merely confirmed what was already a trend'. Age at marriage is now in the late teens and early twenties, with the age for girls slightly lower than that for boys (Nevadomsky 1980: 48, 1982/3: 192, Sharma 1986: 37).

In terms of conjugal union type, marriage is still the most popular union. The 1960 Census of Trinidad reported that among East Indian women in their child-bearing years and in conjugal unions, 82 per cent were married, either legally or by customary religious rites, while 15 per cent were in common-law unions and only 3 per cent were classified as visiting (Roberts 1975: 163). Since then, however, common-law unions have become more prevalent and, most significant from the perspective of creolisation is the increasing incidence of visiting unions, even though these are still comparatively rare (Abdullah 1985: 135). Younger East Indians are engaging in pre-marital sex and entering into visiting unions, a pattern that has prompted some writers to predict a trend towards matrifocal family structures (Jayawardena 1962: 63; Sharma 1986: 52). As Niehoff (1959: 182-183) has reported, this pattern is also common later in the life cycle of Hindu women who, as widows, are prohibited from remarrying and who enter visiting and common-law unions which are often quite stable and similar to those of the black population.

Traditional Indian gender relations within marriage, as already mentioned, were characterised by male dominance and female submission and sexual degradation (Angrosino 1976: 46). This extreme gender asymmetry was expressed in the Hindu doctrine of 'pati brata dharm', the wife's selfless devotion to her husband, (Jayawardena 1962: 48). Though this has not been common practice in the Caribbean, there has, as mentioned, been a concerted effort to subjugate Indian women, to suppress their personal and economic autonomy and re-establish the traditional, patriarchal family ideal, frequently by resort to violence, even murder (Reddock 1994: 44-45). A measure of success in this regard is suggested in contemporary accounts of obedient, dutiful wives. Although a wife may keep the household money, she has no control over it and must ask her husband's permission before spending it. She must also have his consent before leaving home. She serves him first and eats when he has finished (Niehoff 1959: 184). Vertovec (1992: 105) noted that older women, aged 40 years and over, 'still follow behind their husbands at some distance and avoid addressing him by his proper name', but the younger generation is experiencing a trend towards increasing equality between spouses in attitudes (Angrosino 1976: 60-61) as well as practice.

> The trend in husband-wife role relations is toward greater equality in decision-making, greater emphasis on the affectional relations between spouses, and less emphasis on the segregation of conjugal roles. **Purdah** and purdah-like practices have all but disappeared. Sex segregation at public events such as picnics and weddings is on the decline. Some men take their wives to restaurants and the cinema (Nevadomsky 1982/3: 192).

For Angrosino (1976), gender changes are of great significance for it is the role and status of the bride in Indian culture that is fundamental to the wider set of principles of intra- and inter-familial sexual politics.

Several investigators have attributed the change to Caribbean economic conditions, with much the same rationale as structural functionalists used to explain black matrifocality. Thus, increasing female authority in the household is linked to fluctuating seasonal plantation occupations, high levels of male unemployment and underemployment and the consequent inability of men to function adequately as family providers. Jayawardena (1962: 53-54) has noted that this forces the wife into the work force, the husband's dominance at home diminishing proportionately and disputes and marital separations often resulting.

The extended family and kinship networks were at the heart of Indian traditional culture, but with the impact of individualism and creolisation, these are losing their significance. The expectation that a son and his wife will live in his family home continues to be fulfilled, but the duration of their stay has been shortened. The younger generation has become more inclined towards the nuclear family form, viewing it as a sign of economic advance, independence and modernity (Nevadomsky 1980: 50). Rather than remain until the death of the father as prescribed by Indian tradition, the young couple may move out after a few months (Jayawardena 1962: 57). The move, however, depends on residential availability. In areas such as Port Mourant in Guyana, for example, where heavy pressure on scarce housing may make this impossible, couples may compromise by establishing their own kitchens or fireplaces while still residing in the parental home (Jayawardena 1962: 59-60). The Caribbean Indian ideal joint family in which all sons, their wives and their children remain in the parental home as one economic unit is not practised. Indeed, it seems that this form is deliberately avoided for it is viewed as a source of family conflict, especially between mother and daughter-in-law. Nevertheless, sons and their wives generally reside nearby, often on the same land (Niehoff 1959: 183). Increasing education and socialisation of children outside the home have reduced the formal, authoritarian nature of the parent-child relationship. As Nevadomsky (1980:

51) puts it, parents are 'respected, but no longer feared' and Jagdish Chandra Jha (1974: 4) reported as follows:

> Elders in the extended family no longer enjoy the same respect from youngsters as in the past. In some weddings the boys touch the feet of the mother-in-law but not of the father-in-law. Older women even now put **ohani** (head-gear) on their head when they are in the presence of their father-in-law or **barka** (husband's elder brother) and they eat after the male members have been fed. But in the younger generation these things are rarely found (Jha 1974: 4) (Emphasis in original).

There are also cases in which family relationships have changed to the extent that the traditional respect and care for the elderly parents no longer exists and they have been left abandoned and destitute (Sharma 1986: 47-48). Additionally, the former desire for a large number of children, especially sons, is also changing as East Indian women increasingly practise birth control (Sharma 1986: 49). The reason, according to Nevadomsky (1982/3: 196), has to do with changing economic circumstances, specifically with occupational opportunities and the hope of a better life:

> For the villager who has a good job with salary increments and the security of pension benefits, and whose rising expectations make him look forward to a better future for his children ... family planning becomes essential. A large family will tax the income of the father too heavily and spread out available resources too thinly.

From the perspective of household composition, joint household arrangements are giving way to a pattern in which nuclear arrangements are the norm and the extended household puts in an appearance only for a short period in the life cycle of the domestic group. It is important to acknowledge, however, as we did in the earlier discussion on the distinction between household and family, that residential separation does not necessarily entail a break in family relationships. As Vertovec (1992: 106) noted,

> extremely close and interdependent families continue to be the norm. Moreover, when sons do marry and move out of the paternal household, they do so quite often into houses built immediately next door to, or on the same property as, the father's house (while the last son inherits the latter for his own). This is a fact too often overlooked by writers on Indian families in Trinidad; contiguous households of kin continue to interact as 'joint' families, sharing larders, debts, childraising, recreational, social and ritual activities.

As mentioned earlier, caste was one of the first casualties of indenture. Over the years, the system has been reduced to what one author calls 'mere sentiment' (Nevadomsky 1980: 45), while another refers to Hindus 'who are unsure of their caste and others who have forgotten completely what caste they belong to' (Niehoff 1959: 178). According to a study conducted by Barton Schwartz (1964: 62-63) in a predominantly Hindu, Trinidadian village called Boodram, only 45 per cent of marriages were endogamous by caste and, if the caste groupings are expanded by classification into 'varna', endogamous marriages at 47 per cent were still outnumbered by those that are exogamous (see also Nevadomsky 1980: 47). But the virtual disappearance of caste endogamy did not lead to the open choice of marriage partners across ethnic and racial groups that one might expect with the process of creolisation. What happened was that the endogamous unit expanded to become the East

Indian ethnic group and within it a system of preferences was created. Schwartz (1964: 60) reported his findings as follows:

> The overwhelming tendency is for East Indians to marry other East Indians. This is validated by the fact that only a fraction of the East Indians in Trinidad have become significantly Creolized in spite of conscious efforts on the part of other ethnic groups to achieve admixture. I know of only one case in Boodram where this had occurred: a female East Indian married a Creole male and several offspring resulted. The children, however, did not perpetuate this situation; rather, they all married East Indians. For Boodram, ethnic group marriages are 99 per cent endogamous and only 1 per cent exogamous.

Nevadomsky's findings support the point referring to marriages between East Indians and Blacks as 'taboo', though he notes an increasing incidence of these in urban areas (Nevadomsky 1980: 47).

Within the East Indian group, the choice of spouse is made primarily on the basis of religion, with a distinct preference shown for someone of the same religious group. Among the 91 marriages investigated by Schwartz in Boodram, 69 (76 per cent) were endogamous according to religious group affiliation (see also Nevadomsky 1980: 47). Strict religious endogamy has clearly been broken, but, as Sharma (1986: 33) explained, a system which ranks alternative religious choices is in place.

> The second important violation of the norms of endogamy was a grudging acceptance of inter-religious marriages, especially between Hindus and Muslims. Inter-religious marriage between Hindus and Christian East Indians were accepted less grudgingly because Hindus considered Christian East Indians as till-yesterday-Hindus. A Christian East Indian woman told me that she would prefer a Christian or a Hindu boy for her daughter, but as far as possible not a Muslim boy. The Hindus and Muslims carried with them mutual antagonism from India which was further strengthened by separate religious organizations. Some spill-over of this antagonism still exists sub-consciously even among Christians.

There is further evidence of change when we examine the Indian tradition of village exogamy, whereby young girls were given in marriage to men of another village, while brides from outside were brought in for the young men of the village. The rationale for this practice was based on the existence of widely ramifying kinship ties within villages and the prohibition on marrying kin, together with the need to widen the range from which potential partners could be chosen on the basis of more objective criteria such as religion and wealth. Cases in which brides were brought from other Caribbean territories or from as far away as India have been noted (Sharma 1986: 34). However, village endogamy increased over the years in conjunction with the relative absence of extended family and kinship ties and also with the increasingly individual choice of a partner on the basis of desirable personal characteristics and love which was more likely to grow within a relationship with someone who lived nearby. The prediction for the future, however, is that as young people seek opportunities outside the village and become more mobile by acquiring transport, the range of personal relationships and the choice of marital partners will once again spread beyond village boundaries (Nevadomsky 1980: 47-48).

Caste groups within the traditional Indian system were arranged hierarchically according to socio-economic status, based primarily on land ownership and occupation, as well as ritual purity. Caste endogamy therefore ensured marriages between those of equal status and similar lifestyles. Class systems in Caribbean societies also exhibit intra-marital characteristics, though not as rigidly. With the decline of the caste system, therefore, one would not necessarily expect marriage to automatically begin to take place across class and status levels. The evidence we have suggests that East Indians continue to marry those of similar socio-economic status and patterns of life (Schwartz 1964: 64-65). Niehoff (1959: 178) has added that, in addition to financial position, educational levels and physical appearance have become important in choosing a spouse. Marriage with non-Indians continues to be rare. On this point, Colin Clarke has argued that, although increasing village exogamy might be expected to lead to a rising incidence of inter-racial marriage, this is unlikely despite the increased age at marriage and relaxing parental control on the choice of a spouse. A major reason is the 'socialisation of Indian youth of all religions into hostility to intermarriage (or any other action of lesser significance) with Creoles ...'. (Clarke 1993: 128).

A popular means of reviving cultural traditions among minority immigrant groups is through rituals and ceremonies. For East Indians in Trinidad, revitalised marriage ceremonies provided a primary focus for Indian identity and pride (Nevadomsky 1980: 48, Angrosino 1976: 49). Further impetus for the emphasis on the wedding ceremony probably originated in response to the denigration and lack of official legal recognition of East Indian marriages. The marriage rite is probably the most important of the religious events observed by East Indians in the Caribbean. The complex sequence of wedding rituals are outlined in detail elsewhere (see Rauf 1974: 82-93, Vertovec 1992: 202-205, Klass 1961: 123-127) and will not be repeated here. What is of interest to us is that, although weddings were at the heart of the Indian cultural revival, even they have been creolised. For example wedding ceremonies, traditionally held at night with the date determined by consulting horoscopes and confined to particular months of the year, are now held during the day on a convenient Sunday (Niehoff 1959: 181). Additionally, the traditional ban on alcohol during the ceremony has been relaxed and, although alcoholic drinks may not be served, guests will bring their own. Niehoff (1959: 182) quoted a Trinidadian Hindu pundit (priest) who lamented that a 'beautiful ceremony' had been reduced to a 'fete' and a 'mess'. Conflict often takes place between the generations, with the elders conforming to tradition while the behaviour and attitudes of the youth reflect modernity and creolisation. Rauf (1974: 92-93) described the situation in the Guyanese village in which he conducted his research:

> Marriage is an event of excitement to the members of the younger generation, not because an important religious function is being performed, but because it provides them an opportunity to drink together with their age mates. Indian film music is played and amplified on loud speakers, and young men demonstrate their skill in dancing a blend of Indian and Calypso type dances. Often they move toward the house of the bride where they attract the attention of girls participating in the ceremony. The girls do not actively participate in such dances, but give encouragement to the boys by indirect participation through smiles and gestures. This behaviour by the younger generation causes annoyance and embarrassment to the older generation. The latter wish to retain their traditional ritualistic form which symbolizes the sanctity of the occasion, but the younger generation demonstrates a ritual participation that is more in line with that of the Creole culture.

Worse still, in Trinidad young people who do not understand Hindi, the language in which the ceremony is performed, often mock and mimic what they perceive as the comic antics of the pundit (Nevadomsky 1980: 49).

Cultural history or contemporary economics?

Finally, to conclude this chapter we return to the argument raised at the end of Chapter IV. The studies examined there all emphasised the flexibility and resilience of black family structures as they adapted to the socio-economic circumstances of unemployment and poverty. From this perspective, kinship and conjugal structures become 'adaptive mechanisms' and the perspectives from culture and history are lost. We also noted that one of the paradoxes of this explanation lay in the existence of East Indian family patterns which were markedly different from those of lower-class black forms, and we have in this chapter seen just how different, despite the survival of East Indians in much the same economically marginal circumstances. In other words, if family constitutes an adaptive response to conditions of life, then how is it that East Indian patterns are so different?

The answer to this question has forced a re-examination of the issue of cultural continuity among East Indians in the Caribbean. There have been two sides to the debate. On the one hand were those who emphasised cultural retention. Niehoff, for example, in an article entitled *The Survival of Hindu Institutions in an Alien Environment,* (see Article 2 at end of chapter) concentrated on the continued existence of the joint family among Hindus in Trinidad, though he recognised that the caste system 'has become very insignificant already' and will soon be relegated to memory (Niehoff 1959: 185). The Hindu rural area in which he studied, survived the disruptive impact of indenture, 'rallied and ultimately established a clearly recognisable form of the joint family' (Niehoff 1959: 185). In comparison to caste then, the family showed 'greater persistence and inner strength', a characteristic which Niehoff attributed to small size and tightly knit relationships. Nevadomsky, on the other hand, presented a critical response in an article entitled *Changes in Hindu Institutions in an Alien Environment,* (see Article 2 at end of chapter). He claimed that, far from exhibiting conservatism and stability, the family has responded to economic and political conditions of change and dislocation in the wider society and adapted to social changes in values and lifestyles, transmitting these to its members. Traditional East Indian family patterns have been transformed by the transplant into Trinidad and the experiences of indenture and social change to create new patterns, for example, in courtship and gender roles and relations (Nevadomsky 1980: 42). Similarly, Angrosino has claimed that the contemporary 'extended' family among East Indians should not be seen as a survival or re-creation of the traditional joint structure, but as a pattern which has developed in Trinidad and which fulfills certain important functions in contemporary society.

Jayawardena has attempted to integrate the two perspectives in his study of East Indian family organisation on Guyanese plantations. Having outlined what he described as the norms of ideal family life, he proceeded to argue that the extent to which these were realised was affected by a number of considerations, especially economic. His analysis of this economic impact was essentially the same as that of other investigators. Focussing on the household, he identified low and fluctuating income and decreasing wages as the major economic factors affecting domestic relations. For example, the Indian ideal of women confined to the home as wives and mothers was broken as women had no alternative but to enter the work force and to earn income for family support. The impact on conjugal relationships as the traditional authority of the husband as household head and sole breadwinner was diminished has already been mentioned. Similarly, household composition, particularly the distinction between nuclear and joint domestic groupings, was influenced by a variety of factors, including plantation management housing policy, prevailing village economic conditions, housing availability, emigration, and individual occupational status, prosperity and social mobility (Jayawardena 1962: 57-61). For the purpose of the argument here, the important point about Jayawardena's analysis is that, even at the time he was conducting this investigation, that is in the late 1950s during the heyday of structural functional studies of Caribbean family patterns, he recognised that East Indian family changes were not unidirectional, that is, along a route determined by economic forces.

> The brake on this process is the **contrary pull of Indian cultural values** and the impossibility of rejecting them completely while remaining at the same time a member of the Indian group. Different definitions of the wife's role constitute one of the most important badges of distinction between Indians and Negroes. Adherence to certain kinship institutions is at the heart of being 'Indian' and places definite limits on the extent of deviations. Unskilled labourers abide by the traditional culture to a greater extent than clerks, although the process of creolisation is increasingly affecting all strata of the Indian population. One may add to these considerations the fact that husbands, wives and sons are socialised in the cultural norms and therefore will be inhibited from following the empirically most justifiable course of action. Hinduism, if not Islam, is closely bound up with traditional kinship institutions.

> **Economic and cultural influences flow in opposite directions**, placing the modal type of family at a point between the extremes. In the 'typical' family the power of the husband/father is less than what the norms prescribe, and more than what one expects from purely economic considerations (Jayawardena 1962: 63-64) (Emphasis added).

In conclusion the story of East Indian marriage and family patterns from indenture to the present makes an interesting case-study of cultural continuity and change. Three trends have been identified in the analysis of this process, the first two of which are familiar themes in the literature on black Caribbean family structure. The first is the survival of some kinship patterns despite the harsh conditions of indentureship. The second contradicts the first and refers to the collapse of culture through the impact of these very socio-economic conditions and the more recent dual process of creolisation and modernisation. For example, the rigidly patriarchal gender relations which constituted a fundamental structural principle of East Indian marriages and families were affected by the mediation and sanctions of plantation managers, by economic circumstances of male unemployment and by the mainstream culture of gender equality. The third trend refers to the deliberate reconstruction of family patterns, especially wedding ceremonies, as part of the conscious and active revival of ethnic identity and pride. Although individual researchers tend to emphasise one or other trend, all three have, of course, played important roles at different historical periods since the beginning of indenture. What is still missing from the literature on East Indian conjugal and family patterns in the Caribbean is a systematic study of kinship ideology and practice. Using much the same intensive, case-study methodology as we reviewed in Chapter V, investigations of family patterns among East Indians need to pursue the conceptualisations and meanings of family life as expressed by the people themselves and to understand these within the Caribbean context of cultural persistence, change and revival. To borrow Jayawardena's phrase quoted earlier, we must ask: What kinship principles and practices are at 'the heart of being "Indian"' within the Caribbean?

READINGS

R. Bell

MARRIAGE AND FAMILY DIFFERENCES AMONG LOWER CLASS NEGRO AND EAST INDIAN WOMEN IN TRINIDAD

The various power relationships that may exist between indigenous and immigrant groups have been extensively studied by anthropologists and sociologists.[1] Any two or more ethnic, religious, or racial groups in a society may fall at a stage between total conflict and total assimilation with regard to each other. Furthermore, conflict between two or more groups in a society may be dealt with in various ways. At one extreme the differences may be resolved through destruction or coercion directed by the group with the greatest power. But when the various forms of force are not used there are other social processes that may be utilized. One social process that often results from competition and conflict between groups is that of *accommodation*, which usually leads to fairly stable relationships between the groups. But the smaller and/or weaker group still maintains characteristics which it is not allowed to give up or which it is not willing to give up. Of course, this process is different from *assimilation*, where the assumption is that the smaller or less powerful group adopt the values of the dominant group and be absorbed into that group.

A third social process is that of *cultural pluralism*. This usually implies a desire for basic political and economic unity but at the same time allows for possible differences in language, religion, and other cultural variables. Gordon has pointed out that it is not possible for cultural pluralism to operate without the existence of different sub-societies. However, he writes, it *is* possible for separate sub-societies to continue their existence even while their cultural differences become progressively reduced and even in greater part eliminated.[2] This general description portrays the relationships between many Negroes and East Indians in Trinidad and Tobago at the present time. Before looking further at the nature of the relationships between the two groups, it is necessary to say something briefly of their history in Trinidad.

The island of Trinidad was originally settled by a few Spaniards along with some free coloureds and slaves. While the French never controlled the island, they did have a strong influence because a number of French settlers came to Trinidad from the French Caribbean islands. In 1797 the British captured the island. Some Negroes initially came to Trinidad as freedmen, although most originally arrived as slaves. When the abolition of slavery came in 1834 and planters throughout the West Indies had to seek a new supply of labour for work on the plantations 'Trinidad, like British Guiana, the other colony most in need of additional labour at the time, took steps to promote immigration from two main sources: (a) from the neighbouring British islands; (b) from more distant lands (especially India) through indentured immigration.'[3] In 1838, four years after emancipation, the second largest immigration movement to affect the West Indies started. During the period from 1838 to 1917 the recorded number of East Indian immigrants to Trinidad was 143,900.[4] In the years since the end of the Indian migration Trinidad has not lost population. In fact, Trinidad was not greatly affected by the large West Indian migration to Great Britain in the 1950s. Of all the West Indian countries Trinidad had the second highest rate of inter-censal (1946-60) growth and at the same time had the lowest rate of emigration to Great Britain.[5] The 1960 Census of Trinidad and Tobago showed the total population as 827,957. By racial background 43 per cent were Negro, 37 per cent East Indian, 16 per cent 'mixed' (most members in this category have an appreciable degree of Negro ancestry), 2 per cent white, 1 per cent Chinese, and 1 per cent 'other'.[6]

At the present time the relationships between the Negroes and East Indians in Trinidad are generally good, although this varies in different parts of the island and at different periods of time. In general, it appears that less racial conflict exists in Port-of-Spain than in the rural areas. Oxaal suggests there may be some differences in racial relations by religion. He writes that in general 'the more urbanized Moslem section of the East Indians — which constitutes a relatively small proportion of the total Indian population — have gotten along more amicably with the Negroes than have the Hindus'.[7] There have also been some pressures in Trinidad towards greater racial identification, although this has not usually resulted in racial conflict. For example, there continues to be a high identification among Negroes with African Congo backgrounds, although there is no African identification among other Negroes. And among a number of Indians there also tends to be strong identification with their homeland. This is partially due to the presence in Trinidad of Indian missionaries who try to contribute to an identification with India. It is doubtful that the 'old country' identifications will continue for very long.

While there are forces towards racial identification in Trinidad, there are also conditions that help reduce the potential for racial conflict. For example, one writer has pointed out that the lack of residential segregation has placed Negro, East Indian, and other minorities alongside one another in many parts of Trinidad 'and thus has produced social conditions analogous to the early multi-cultural, immigrant-filled, American metropolis. Indeed, the proximity of conflicting or disparate ways of life is even more acute in Trinidad owing to the absence of urban ghettoes'.[8]

As suggested, it is very difficult to generalize about race relations in Trinidad. Certainly most Trinidadians have learned to tolerate the differences among various groups. Oxaal argues that the common response among most Trinidad Negroes towards East Indian life patterns, 'and of East Indians toward Negro traits, is *negative indifference*, frequently accompanied by ridicule or sarcastic expressions of antipathy, mistrust and hostility'.[9] Yet, this is almost always a two-way process — Negro towards Indian and Indian towards Negro — and rarely leads to any large-scale conflict. Oxaal goes on to suggest that there is a pervasive state of mind that he calls *plural disassociation*, 'which is characterized by the attitude — a cardinal tenet in the philosophy of the Trinidadian — that each should attend to his own affairs and not go 'interfering' in the business of other groups'.[10]

Regardless of the degree of acceptance between two groups in a society, probably the last area for assimilation is that of marriage and the family. One of the best measures of the degree of community separation or assimilation is the rate of intermarriage. Gordon points out that when marital assimilation takes place the minority group loses its individual identity in the larger society. 'Prejudice and discrimination are no longer a problem, since eventually the descendants of the original minority group become indistinguishable, and since primary group relationships tend to build up an 'in-group' feeling which encloses all the members of the group'.[11] In Trinidad, intermarriage between

Negro and Indian is very limited and each group maintains patterns of marriage quite different from the other. In general, the lower-class Negro family in Trinidad has been female-centred with late marriages (when marriage occurs), low value placed on the interpersonal nature of marriage, and with minimal concern about the legitimacy of offspring. By contrast, the lower-class Indian family in Trinidad has been patriarchal, with great importance attached to early, arranged marriages and the legitimization of offspring. It is therefore suggested that distinct marriage patterns — an important measurement of cultural pluralism — are a characteristic of Negro-Indian relationships in Trinidad. The extent to which the family patterns differ between Negroes and Indians in Trinidad is the general focus of this study.

BACKGROUND OF THE STUDY

The study to be reported was carried out during the spring of 1969 in central Trinidad. The samples studied were from an area not far from San Fernando, the second largest town in Trinidad, with a population of about 40,000. However, the area where the respondents lived is primarily rural, centering around the hamlets of Bonne Aventure, Caratal, Gasparillo, and Mayo. These hamlets are in the lower regions of the Montserrat Hills. This area was first settled by Negroes who came down from the hills where they had originally worked on the cocoa plantations.[1] With the demise of the cocoa plantations they moved down to work on the sugar plantations. In about 1920 the East Indians began to move into the area although most of the Negro and Indian men in the sugar and oil refineries as well as in some farming. In the area studied many men are unemployed in the sense that they are not working for a wage. However, many of the unemployed men farm for their own use as well as for some cash crop. In fact many of the men who work in the refineries also farm in the evening. However, land for farming is becoming increasingly scarce because with large families over the years the land has been cut into smaller and smaller parcels. In many cases the land owned by a man may consist of little more than that on which his house actually stands.

A demographic view of the area of study may be drawn from the descriptions provided for the larger San Fernando area. In the area, the number of males per 100 females 15 years old and over was 89 in 1960.[12] The level of education was primary or less for 84 per cent of the males and 85 per cent of the females.[13] In the San Fernando area about two-thirds of the population are Indian and the rest Negro. Also in the area, 22 per cent are Protestant, 24 per cent Roman Catholic, 43 per cent Hindu, and 11 per cent Moslem.[14] The discrepancy in the percentages for the total Indian population, on the one hand, and those who identify themselves as Hindu or Moslem, on the other, 'apparently reflects the fact that about one in five of those regarded as racially East Indian identify themselves with various branches of Christianity'.[15]

The study area is characterized by very little racial conflict. In fact, there is a high level of mutual help and co-operation between the Indians and the Negroes. For example, there is high attendance at each others' weddings and funerals. Because the Negro has lived in the area longer and is generally more knowledgeable, he frequently sets patterns which the Indian has followed. For example, in the past as soon as an Indian boy was old enough to leave school and go to work in the fields he did so. But the Negro man has persuaded his Indian counterpart to have at least one of his sons continue his education. Increasingly the Indian is placing the same very high value on education as does the Negro. In the day-to-day interaction of the two racial groups there is generally no more conflict than one would find if the racial composition was homogeneous. Yet, given the close relationships there is very little intermarriage between the two groups and few offspring resulting from Negro-Indian parentage. In general, the daily patterns of life are the same for the two racial groups, but the values attached to marriage and the family are quite different.

Our examination of the marriage and family differences was based on interviews of two samples, drawn from the Negro and Indian populations, respectively, who were asked to respond to a 71-item questionnaire.[2] To qualify for the sample, a woman had to live within the defined area and have at least one child between one and ten years of age. In the area chosen for study, streets were picked at random and the interviewers went to each house on the street and interviewed those women who met the basic study requirement. The Negro women were interviewed by two trained Negro female interviewers and the Indians by one trained Indian female interviewer. The interviewers encountered only one refusal and found a high level of interest and co-operation. The two sub-samples to be reported on include 200 Negro women and 100 Indian women who provided acceptable interviews.

The Negro women are approximately five years older than the Indian women (37 4 and 32.7 years of age respectively). In education, the Negro women had completed an average of 5.6 standards and the Indian women 3.8 standards. Only 36 per cent of the Negro women and 18 per cent of the Indian women had completed primary education. Eighty-nine per cent of the Negro women were born in Trinidad and Tobago; the rest came from nearby islands. All the Indian women were born in Trinidad. At the time of the interview, 23 per cent of the Negro women and 6 per cent of the Indian women were working. There appeared to be no significant differences in their living conditions; for example, the mean number of persons living in the Negro households was 7.2 and in the Indian households, 7.7.

Among the Negro respondents, 31 per cent were Protestants and 69 per cent Roman Catholics. Among the Indian respondents, 56 per cent were Hindus, 33 per cent Moslems, 9 per cent Protestants, and 2 per cent Roman Catholics. The religious attendance of the Negroes was much higher than that of the Indian women, with the average attendance per month for the Negro women being 4.7 and for the Indian women 1.2. While only 13 per cent of the Negro women said they had not attended any religious ceremonies the previous month, no attendance had been the case of 67 per cent of the Indian women.

The two samples were also examined for internal variations. Among the Negro respondents no significant differences were found by marital status, except that fewer married women worked. The only significant difference in the area of religion was that older women had a higher rate of attendance. When the Indian respondents were analyzed by marital status, no differences were found. The only significant differences were found in the area of attendance at religious services: women with more children had a higher attendance rate, and Hindus showed the lowest rate of attendance. In the discussion to follow, the two samples will be examined under the general headings of marriage, parenthood, and child-rearing.

MARRIAGE

There has been a great deal of discussion about marriage patterns among lower-class Negroes in the West Indies.[16] Roberts and Braithwaite have conducted studies comparing Indians and non-Indians in Trinidad, with a special interest in fertility.[17] Those authors have shown a number of factors related to the various male-female unions of visiting relationships, common-law marriage, and legal marriage. Their studies show that the average age of marriage among East Indians is 17.4 years and among non-Indians (almost all Negroes) 27.5 years. Roberts and Braithwaite go on to point out that during the 31-year period from ages 14 to 45, East Indian women over 45 have spent 87 per cent of those years, or 27 years, in marriage. By contrast, the non-Indian women over 45 have in the same 31-year period spent only 38 per cent of that time, or 11.8 years, in marriage.[18] Because of the low average age at first marriage among the East Indian women, nearly one-half of the cohorts are married by age 15, as compared with only one per cent of the non-Indian women.

At age 20 the corresponding proportions are 73 per cent and 11 per cent respectively. Whereas the proportion of East Indian women who are married attains a maximum of 74 per cent at age 25 and then declines, amounting to 59 per cent by age 45, the corresponding proportion among non-Indians continues to increase throughout the childrearing span. By age 45 the proportion of women married for this racial group amounts to 51 per cent.[19]

When the combined time spent in marriage and common-law unions is taken for the non-Indian women, the overall average is 19.3 years, 'which is nearly 9 years lower than the corresponding value for East Indians, and equivalent to only 59 per cent of the total child-bearing span'.[20] Roberts and Braithwaite suggest that the instability of marriages among young Indians may result from the tradition of the very early parent-arranged marriages, which continues to some extent in Trinidad.[21]

> But at the same time the relative sophistication of the children means that they are not prepared to continue such arranged unions which do not completely satisfy them. Since such unions are contracted for the most part on the basis of customary rites and thus are not legally sanctioned, withdrawal from them presents no difficulties. Of importance is the fact that many of the Hindus who terminate their early marriage become single, that is they do not immediately after leaving their first marriage establish another, but remain unattached for a time.[22]

We may now compare the marriage patterns of the Negro and Indian samples in Trinidad. At the time of the study 92 per cent of the Indian women said they were married as compared with 60 per cent of the Negro women. Two per cent of the Indian, and 25 per cent of the Negro women said they were single (never married). The rest of the women in each group were widowed, separated, or divorced.

While the Indian women married somewhat younger (18.6 years) as compared with the Negroes (21.5 years), the difference was not great. The average age of marriage given by the Negro women was substantially younger than what was expected on the basis of other studies. It is possible that many gave their age at first marriage as being the age when they first entered a common-law marriage; if so this would lower the average age at marriage. However, also striking in the study was the number of Negro women who said they first entered marriage at very young ages. While 47 per cent of the Indian women had entered marriage at age 16 or young, this was also true for 25 per cent of the Negro women. It is possible that the Negro women, living close to Indian women have been influenced by them to enter marriage at younger ages. If so, this too would lower the average age at marriage.

Table 1 *Marital status of the two samples*

| | Negroes | | East Indians | |
	Number	%	Number	%
Single (never married)	49	25	2	2
Married	120	60	92	92
Widowed	5	2	—	—
Divorced or separated	26	13	6	6
Total	**200**	**100**	**100**	**100**

The two groups of women were asked several subjective questions about their marriages. The respondents were asked how, in general, they would rate their marriages: 28 per cent of the Negroes and 67 per cent of the Indians answered 'good' or 'very good'. They were also asked: 'Compared to other marriages you know how would you in general rate your own?' Fourteen per cent of the Negro women and 67 per cent of the Indian women said 'better'. Whether or not the Indian women really have better marriages than do the Negro women is not known but more of them believe their marriages are better. However, the relatively higher assessment of marriage by the Indian women does not mean they have a uniformly high value of marriage in general. For example, the women were asked: 'If you had it to do all over again would you ever get married?' 'Yes' was the answer of 27 per cent of the Negro and 35 per cent of the Indian women. Forty-five per cent and 61 per cent of the Negroes and Indians, respectively, answered 'No'; and 28 per cent and 4 per cent, respectively, answered 'Don't know'. They were also asked: 'If you had it to do all over again would you marry the same person you did?' Half of each sample answered 'No.' These findings indicate that the general assessment of marriage is low for both racial groups, although somewhat lower for the Negro women.

The women were also asked what they liked best about marriage. The most common response among the Negro women was that marriage gave them 'respectability' (41 per cent), while the most common response for the Indian women was 'home or security' (81 per cent). They were also asked what they thought was the most important thing that a woman wanted from marriage. About four out of five women in each group answered 'security'. This usually meant financial security, something most of them did not have.

One important measurement of marital adjustment centres around the definitions of sexual interaction. In patriarchal societies sexual needs have generally been seen as only important for the man, while the wife's function has been to satisfy the husband's needs, with little concern for her own sexual needs and satisfaction. The two samples of women were asked how they felt about the importance of sex in marriage for both the husband and the wife. For the husband, 76 per cent of the Negroes and 11 per cent of the Indians said it was 'very important'. The rest in each group said it was 'important' for him, and no women suggested it was 'unimportant'. As to the importance of sex for the wife, 33 per cent of the Negroes and 9 per cent of the Indians said 'very important', with 45 per cent and 86 per cent saying 'important', and 22 per cent and 5 per cent saying 'not important'. These findings suggest that in general the Negro woman sees sex as being of greater importance for both the man and the woman than does her Indian counterpart. This would suggest that Indian women reflect the patriarchal view of sex of a greater extent than do Negro women.

A further variable important to a patriarchal system is that sex will be absolutely for the husband. The study respondents were asked if they thought there was ever a time when a married man would be justified in 'running around' with another woman. Two-thirds of the Negro women and all of the Indian women answered 'No'. The women were asked if they should expect 'running around', regardless of how good the husband had been in the past, to which 97 per cent of the Negro, and 100 per cent of the Indian, women answered 'No'. The respondents were further asked if they thought there was ever a time when a married woman would be justified in 'running around' with another man. To this question 78 per cent of the Negro, and 100 per cent of the Indian, women answered 'No'. The women were also asked if the husband should expect 'running around' regardless of how good the wife had been in the past. To this question two-thirds of the Negroes and all the Indians answered 'No'. It is of interest that one-third of the Negro respondents felt a woman might run around but only 3 per cent of them felt the same might be true for the man. This would appear to be a reflection of the female focus of the marriage relationship among the Negro women. That is, because she often takes on most of the family responsibilities she also assumes for herself certain rights. It also reflects the weak stigma that is directed at many Negro women who are not sexually monogamous.

PARENTHOOD

What follows are some comparisons of the two racial groups with regard to the birth and the rearing of children. The average number of children was large for both groups: for the Negro women the mean was 6.3 and for the Indian women it was 5.7. The slightly lower rate of the Indian women is due to their being almost five years younger than the Negro women. The age at which Indian women gave birth to their first child was on the average a year and a half less than it was for the Negro mothers. The mean age at first birth for the Indian women was 18.4 years and for the Negro women 19.9 years. Twenty-six per cent of the Indian women had their first child at age 16 or younger; this was also true of 17 per cent of the Negro women. The two groups of mothers were asked: 'If you could start all over again and have only as many children as you wanted, how many would you have?' The mean number was 2.8 children for the Negro women and 3.4 children for the Indian women. But what was most striking in the responses to this question was that 26 per cent of the Negroes and 6 per cent of the Indians said they would have no children if they had it to do all over again. This is probably a reflection of the very difficult conditions under which the women had been rearing their children. Many of them may have answered that they would have no children if they could start over again because they had proven their womanhood by having children. That is, if they could start over again knowing what was ahead, but never having given birth to a child, the need to 'prove' their womanhood would probably be more important than they suggest in retrospect.

A number of the women, especially in the Negro sample, indicated minimal involvement with both the wife role and the mother role. They were therefore given the forced choice question: 'If you could only be a wife or a mother (but not both) which would you choose?' The response was 'wife' for 21 per cent of the Negroes and 5 per cent of the Indians. Seventy-three per cent of the Negroes and 93 per cent of the Indians said 'mother'. The rest answered 'Don't know'. It is possible that the somewhat higher number of Negro women answering 'wife' is a reflection of the importance of marriage status to many, especially as they grow older. In contrast, the marriage status for the Indian women is generally taken for granted. But the findings do show the greater importance of the mother role over the wife role for both the Negro and Indian women.

The importance of illegitimacy to the family system of lower-class Negro women in the West Indies has been a subject of controversy in recent years.[23] Various studies have shown a high frequency of illegitimacy with not much social stigma directed at the unwed mother and her children. There has been in Trinidad a steady decline in the number and proportion of illegitimate births. For instance, illegitimate births per 100 births annually has decreased from 72.1 during the 1921-5 period to 41.9 in 1962.[24] In the two samples studied it was possible to estimate the number of women who had had at least one illegitimate child. When combining those women who never married with those who gave birth to at least one child before marriage, it was found that 65 per cent of the Negro women and 11 per cent of the Indian women had at least one illegitimate child.

The women were also asked several questions with regard to their views on illegitimacy: for example, 'If a woman is not married and has a child, how do you think her relatives view her?' Among the Negro women only 21 per cent said 'bad' as compared to 78 per cent of the Indian women. This meant that 79 per cent of the Negroes and 22 per cent of the Indians responded that there were 'no negative feelings'. The women were also asked: 'How important do you think it is for a woman to marry for reasons of making her child legitimate?' To this 95 per cent of the Negro women and 96 per cent of the Indian women said 'very important'. These findings indicate that the Indian women have high positive marriage views with regard to the unwed mother and her child, while the Negro mothers have a high view of marriage for the sake of the illegitimate child, but not necessarily for the sake of the unwed mother.

Table 2   *Marital status at birth of first child*

	Negro Mothers		East Indian Mothers	
	Number	%	Number	%
Single (never married)	49	25	2	2
Before marriage	76	40	9	9
Year of marriage	12	6	17	17
One year or more after marriage	57	29	72	72
Total	195	100	100	100

CHILD-REARING

To further our understanding of the mother role we asked the women a number of questions about child-rearing practices. In the Indian family the punishment of children is mostly the function of the mother alone (93 per cent), while among Negro families about half of the mothers handle the punishment alone and the other half do so with the help of the father. There were differences in the types of punishments used by the two groups. 'Spanking' was used by 92 per cent of the Indian women and 53 per cent of the Negro women. Almost half of the Negro women used 'scolding' as the means of punishing their children.

Table 3 indicates involvement of the fathers with the youngest child in several activities when the child was about one year of age. Table 3 shows that there were no significant differences between the Negro and Indian groups in what they said was the involvement of the father in 'feeding' or 'playing or holding' the child. However, the findings suggest that the Negro fathers were more apt to change nappies or give a bath to the child than were the Indian fathers. In general, with the exception of playing and holding, not very many fathers in either racial group were very involved in the rearing of their young children. The mothers were asked how they felt about their husbands did with their babies during the first year. Thirty-nine per cent of the Negro, and 15 per cent of the Indian, women said 'not enough' and the rest in each group said 'about right'. Even though the Negro men had done slightly more, their wives were still more apt to think they had not done enough. This reflects a lower level of expectation on the part of the Indian women towards their husbands than was the case for the Negro women.

Table 3 *Fathers' involvement in the rearing of child when about one year of age, by race*

	Negro Fathers		East Indian Fathers	
	Number	%	Number	%
Feeding				
Never	33	17	21	22
Once in a while	109	57	44	46
Often	50	26	30	32
Total	**192**	**100**	**95**	**100**
Changing nappies				
Never	52	28	37	37
Once in a while	110	60	36	36
Often	22	12	27	27
Total	**184**	**100**	**100**	**100**
Giving a bath				
Never	41	23	45	46
Once in a while	103	57	30	30
Often	37	20	24	24
Total	**181**	**100**	**99**	**100**
Playing or holding				
Never	28	15	4	4
Once in a while	31	16	25	25
Often	132	69	71	71
Total	**191**	**100**	**100**	**100**

The mothers were also asked if they had brought up their children in about the same way in which they had been reared. While 80 per cent of the Negro women answered 'yes', only 38 per cent of the Indian women responded similarly. When asked how they reared their children differently, the mothers almost always answered that their child had more freedom than they had had. Of importance is that many of the Indian mothers appeared to reflect the breaking of traditional patterns in the rearing of their children, which seems to be part of the larger breakdown of traditional patterns among Indian families in Trinidad. By contrast, the Negro mothers' patterns represent continuity with the family patterns common to a number of earlier generations.

SUMMARY

The statistical comparisons of the two samples of Negro and East Indian women have indicated a number of important differences in their marriage and family patterns. The findings may be summarized in five related areas:

1. Marriage: Far more Indian women than Negro women were legally married, and they were married for the first time at younger ages. The Indian women tended to rate their marriages at a higher level than did the Negro women. While there is no evidence that the Indian marriages were objectively better than those of the Negroes there is the subjective belief among more Indian women to give theirs a higher rating. Yet, about half of the women in the two racial groups say they would never marry, or marry the man they did, if they had it to do all over again. In general, the findings suggest that marriage is somewhat more important to the Indian women than to the Negro women. This may be a reflection of the immediate patriarchal past of the Indian respondents. However, marriage does appear to become important to many Negro women especially as they grow older, because it is seen as the means of achieving the important status of 'respectability'.

2. Sexual dimension of marriage: The Negro women placed greater importance on sex for both their husbands and for themselves. The lower importance given to sex for themselves by the Indian women is probably a reflection of their patriarchal past which placed little importance on the sexual needs of the woman. This patriarchal influence is further reflected in the findings on the restriction of sexual experience to marriage. The Indian women reject the notion that a husband or a wife would ever have the right to 'run around' and furthermore, they do not expect that it will happen. By contrast, a significant minority of the Negro women feel it could happen especially for the woman, thus reflecting a much less monogamous view of sexual expression than the Indian women.

3. Parenthood: Both groups of women had large families and started having their children at young ages. Yet, given a choice, many of the women would now prefer to have far fewer children. (It has only been in the last few years that birth control methods have been introduced on any significant scale into Trinidad and Tobago). When the respondents were faced with a forced choice of being a wife or a mother both groups overwhelmingly chose being a mother. This reflects a commonly positive value attached to being a mother with a frequently negative or indifferent value attached to the wife role.

4. Illegitimacy: Two out of every three Negro mothers in the study had at least one illegitimate child, as compared to only about one out of every ten Indian women. The Negro women placed much less stigma on the status of illegitimacy for the mother than did the Indian women. However, both groups felt it was important to marry for the sake of making the child legitimate. For the Negro woman, this attitude does not appear to reflect a great concern for the child as he grows up; but rather the emphasis is on the ultimate or long-range legitimation of her children by her eventual marriage. In other words, the concern is not so much with getting married as soon as possible after the child is born but rather with marriage at some future date.

5. Child-rearing: The Indian women usually reared their children by themselves while the Negro women were more apt to have the help of the father (when there was one available). This difference was also reflected in the greater involvement of the Negro father with his youngest child when that child was about one year of age than was the case with the Indian father. Yet, the Negro woman, more than the Indian woman, felt that the husband could have contributed more to the care of the child. The Indian woman expected less and got less in the way of help from the father in the rearing of their children.

This study shows some sharp differences in a number of marriage and family patterns common to the Negro and Indian sample studies in Trinidad. The differences essentially reflect the patriarchal patterns of the Indians in contrast with the female-family centred patterns of the lower-class Negro women. These differences between the two groups may be greatly reduced in the next generation because there is an increasing identification among many lower-class Indians with the Trinidad culture — which in the Trinidad lower class is essentially Negro lower class. However, the present study indicates a high level of positive cultural pluralism. It is positive because there is minimal conflict in the daily interaction of the two racial groups while at the same time the marriage and family patterns are quite different, and these differences are accepted and respected by each group.

NOTES

1. I am greatly indebted to Dr. J. D. Elder, University of the West Indies, St. Augustine Branch, Trinidad, for his knowledge and insight about this area in particular and about Trinidad in general.

2. This is a part of a broader study comparing marriage and family roles among lower-class Negro women in the United States, Great Britain, and the West Indies.

REFERENCES

1. See Milton M. Gordon, *Assimilation in American Life* (New York, Oxford University Press, 1964).

2. Ibid., p. 158.

3. R. J. Harewood, 'Population Growth of Trinidad and Tobago in the Twentieth Century', *Research Papers* (Trinidad and Tobago, Central Statistical Office, December 1967), p. 71.

4. Ceri Peach, *West Indian Migration to Britain: A Social Geography* (London, Oxford University Press, for Institute of Race Relations, 1968), p. 4.

5. Ibid., p. 16.

6. Ivar Oxaal, *Black Intellectuals Come to Power* (Cambridge, Mass. Schenkman Publishing Co., 1968), p. 23.

7. Ibid., p. 22.

8. Ibid., p. 24.

9. Ibid., p. 23.

10. Ibid., p. 24.

11. Gordon, p. 80.

12. Robert T. McMillan, 'Demographic and Socio-economic Correlatives of Fertility in Trinidad and Tobago', *Research Papers* (Trinidad and Tobago, Central Statistical Office, December 1967), p. 208.

13. Ibid., p. 209.

14. *Population Census* 1960, Volume 11, A. B., Trinidad and Tobago.

15. Oxaal, p. 22.

16. See Hyman Rodman, 'Illegitimacy in the Caribbean Social Structure: A Reconsideration', *American Sociological Review* (October 1966).

17. G. W. Roberts and L. Braithwaite, 'Mating Among East Indian and Non-Indian Women in Trinidad', *Research Papers* (Trinidad and Tobago, Central Statistical Office, December 1967), pp. 148-85.

18. Ibid., p. 150.

19. Ibid., pp. 157-8.

20. Ibid., p. 174.

21. Ibid., p. 166.

22. Ibid., pp. 171-2.

23. See Rodman.

24. McMillan, p. 197.

A. Niehoff

THE SURVIVAL OF HINDU INSTITUTIONS IN AN ALIEN ENVIRONMENT

The social organization of India is highly complex and, at least in regard to one of its institutions, it is unique. Two institutions are primary in giving Indian society its distinctiveness — the caste system and the traditional or extended joint family system. The extended family is an institution found in many other parts of the world, particularly throughout Asia. However, the hierarchial positioning of individuals in hereditary, socioreligious groups, as in the Hindu caste system is not so widespread. And in the pervasiveness with which this social institution affects the behaviour of the individual, it makes Indian society differ from almost all other societies in the world. Indeed, the term caste has come to be used primarily in reference to the social groups of India and when the term is used in reference to groups in other cultures it is becuase they are similar in some ways to those of the castes of India.

Probably the only other social institution in India which affects the individual as much as caste is the family system. In the classic form of this family type a number of married couples and their children live together in the same household, all the men being related by blood (Mandelbaum 1948: 123). Money and property are held in common, usually with the senior male as the manager of the family funds. Religious rites, particularly the *sraddha* ceremony, given for the souls of the ancestral dead, are an important family function. An important duty of the family is to select spouses for its young members. Because marriage is principally a relationship between families and only secondarily a relationship between the individuals being married, the choice of a spouse and the marriage arrangements are taken care of by family elders. And although caste and family are inter-related in many ways in India, it is particularly in the institution of marriage that these two systems appear to be inseparable. Though there are a number of restrictions in the choice of a marital partner, the one, most strictly adhered to, is that the individual must not marry someone from another caste.

Many aspects of Indian culture are undergoing considerable change, and by no means the least important are the social institutions. A great part of the change that is taking place today in India is, either directly or indirectly, a result of the impact of western ideas and institutions. Culture change in the Indian village, and to a lesser extent in the urban centres, of India has attracted a considerable number of social scientists in recent years (Lewis 1958; Marriott 1955; Cohn 1955; Niehoff 1957).

The thesis of this paper is that here is another very fruitful source of data on culture change in Indian institutions beyond the continental limits of India. Such sources are to be found in the enclaves of Indians who have migrated from India, particularly during the past hundred years, to colonies of the British Union. These peoples have settled in countries, as minorities usually, where the impact of non-Indian, particularly British, institutions has been much greater than it has been in India itself. No longer did Indians have the advantage of numbers over their rulers as they have had in India. Also in these countries where Indians migrated, there has almost always been a subject people of alien culture who were numerically superior to the Indians. In South Africa, Trinidad, British Guinea these were Negroes, in Figi, native Figians, in Malaya indigenous Malayans. It would be expected that culture change would consequently be much greater among these migrant Indians, but more important than the greater general change would be the possibility of differential change. That is, some institutions might show greater persistence and inner strength than others. And from an analysis of such differential change it might be possible to learn which institutions are most vital and basic to the general structure of Indian society. Knowledge gained from such a study could then be utilized in an assessment of Indian society in India.

The following paper will be limited to a study of the changes in two institutions of Hindu social organization, the extended family and the caste system, in a community of

Indians in Trinidad. Further a comparison will be drawn between the two in an attempt to learn which is the strongest and most necessary for the continuance of a Hindu way of life in an alien environment.

The Indians of Trinidad are descendants of indentured workers who have migrated to the island between 1845 and 1916. The majority of them came from north central India, and the common language spoken is a dialectical form of Hindu. During the 113 years they have been on the island, many of them have achieved considerable economic independence in the movie industry, transportation, and shopkeeping. The majority, however, has remained in agricultural pursuits, either as workers on the sugar plantations or in growing cocoa. As an ethnic group they have acquired much agricultural land and nowadays, with the exception of the whites, they are the wealthiest landowners on the island. As a result of this interest in agriculture most Indians live in rural areas, principally in two lagoon (lowland) regions, where they can grow rice and sugar. However a considerable number has migrated to the cities and more go to urban centres each year. As would be expected, the urban Indians have become more acculturated toward western customs than the rural people. However, it should be mentioned that Trinidad is not a large island (approximately 60 by 40 miles) and the transportation system is so convenient that the differences between rural and urban Indians are not nearly as great as such differences are in India. Indians today make up about 40 per cent of the island's population and their religious affiliations are roughly 70 per cent Hindu, 15 per cent Moslem, and 15 per cent Christian. The Christians have almost all been converted from Hinduism.

The area which will be described in this report is the Oropuche Lagoon, one of the two large rural areas where Indians have concentrated. Most of the people here engage in agricultural pursuits, growing sugar, cocoa or rice, or a combination of these. Their economic position varies from that of landless workers on the sugar estate to independent cocoa growers who own several hundred acres. It should be mentioned that the village system did not persist in Trinidad. Though there are villages, these primarily serve as sources of supply to the surrounding agricultural people. Most people in this area live either in the clusters of barracks set up by the sugar companies for their workers or in houses on their own land scattered throughout the area.

During the early days of Indian settlement in Trinidad there were evidently efforts on the part of individuals to retain the prestige of their caste position, particularly if they were Brahmans. Collens, an early chronicler in Trinidad, mentions that Brahmans and Sudras did not sink to the same level. He states that 'the sceptre of the maharja Brahmin dwindles to the insignificance of a hoe handle but poor as he is he will look down on his caste inferiors', (1886: 190). Morton, a Presbyterian missionary, also states that Brahmans were not supposed to work but were to be provided for by the offerings of their disciples. He describes one Brahman who picked out his eyes so that he might not be put to work (1916: 69). It is to be doubted that such an attitude toward work was a characteristic of all Brahmans, since even in India most are in some kind of secular work. Probably what he was referring to were pundits, those Brahmans who do serve as priests. Despite the difficulties in this new environment, Brahman priests received much respect in these early days. Gamble, another early traveller in Trinidad, reports that 'There are some of the Brahman caste among them and it is revolting to see the way a woman, for instance, will drop down, touch the foot of this holy Brahmin, and then kiss the hand that has been in contact with the priest's foot ...' (1866: 46).

In the past one hundred years the practices dictated by caste membership have changed drastically, to the extent that it would be almost impossible to imagine any of the above incidents happening today. There has been almost no sympathy by non-Hindus towards the institution of caste and, moreover, there has not been any economic basis for caste differences. Where in India the agricultural land holders tend to be of the higher castes and the agricultural labourers tend to be landless labourers, or at least possession only a small amount of land, in Trinidad all men started out as plantation workers and none owned land. This is not to say though, that no caste differences have survived until today. In the Oropuche Lagoon area a hierarchy is accepted by most Hindus. Roughly the groups would be ranked as follows with those of highest prestige at the top and those of lowest at the bottom:

Brahman	
Gosain	(high castes)
Chattri	
Kurmi	
Ahir	
Koiri	(middle castes)
Lohar	
Bania	
Kayasth	
Chamar	
Dom	(low castes)
Dhobie	

This classification reflects that of North India quite well. In Uttar Pradesh, the center of the Hindi speaking area of North India, Brahmans or Chattris are generally conceded to be the castes of highest prestige and in most rural villages the wealthiest landholders are from one or the other of these two castes. The Gosains are highly regarded religious leaders from the Assam Valley (Hutton 1951: 98) and they have been accorded a place at least as high as Brahmans in Trinidad. The middle castes are those which are classified as ceremonially clean in India but well below the level of the highest castes and usually not being important landholders. The lower castes are those which in India are classified as ceremonially unclean, or 'untouchable'.

Distinctions of caste in Trinidad are mostly focussed on the high and low castes. There is some deference still shown to Brahmans, particularly those who serve as pundits. When food is served at a Hindu ritual offering (puja), Brahmans are usually taken care of first. There are still a few occasions when the Brahman's feet are touched in honourific greeting. Sometimes, also, devout Hindus bequeath land or animals to Brahman priests in their wills. A man who is a Brahman is looked up to by virtue of his birth to a certain extent, regardless, what occupation he is following. Thus, there are Brahmans in such occupations as operating service stations and practising law who are still referred to in conversations as *punditji*.

On the other hand, because many of the Brahmans as well as the Chattris have taken up all sorts of occupations, some of which are not highly respected, they have been lowered in the eyes of the Hindu community. It would be impossible for all of them to be priests for economic considerations alone. Most pundits now engage in some other occupation besides presiding over religious functions, simply becuase they cannot manage economically any other way. A majority in the Oropuche Lagoon has a certain amount of land which they tend when not serving as priests. Others get into secular occupations of one kind or another. I knew of one who worked as a taxi driver during the day and at night went off to the different religious functions as a pundit. Those who do work as pundits are found in all occupations from the highest to the lowest in prestige. There are even Brahman proprietors of rum shops in the Lagoon area. Because of the high regard Brahmans have had in the past, they are criticized more severely when they engage in such pursuits as operating rum shops than other Hindus.

On the other end of the scale are the low castes. They still carry some of the low regard which is a legacy of their caste position in India. Hindus who wish to insult each other will often use the term 'Chamar'. I was among a group of Indians on one occasion when a man was explaining how a certain spirit had appeared to him on several occasions. While he was talking, another man in the group interrupted him periodically to clarify or elaborate certain portions of the story. Finally, the speaker in exasperation addressed the intruder in the following way, 'Man, you're a jackass and from the lowest nation on earth, the Chamars, and if you don't keep quiet I'm not going to tell any more of this story.' The bystander was obviously embarrassed and though he did not leave, he interrupted the speaker no further during the recital.

There are some residence clusterings of low castes, probably to a large extent because of their habit of raising pigs and eating pork. There is a hamlet in this area known as Dom Village which is said to be inhabited by all doms. Also, one end of the town of Penal, the section where most Negroes are found, has a heavy concentration of low caste Hindus, many of whom raise pigs. Though Hindu food taboos in Trinidad have been greatly relaxed, the eating of pork by any but the low castes is still exceptional. As will be indicated further on, marriage between different castes occurs frequently and it does happen that a man of low caste will marry a woman of middle or high caste. In such instances the wives will often cook pork for their husbands but will not eat it themselves. The one other food which most Trinidad Hindus still avoid eating is beef. Cows are not treated as sacred in Trinidad to the same degree that they are in India, but it is readily noted that a considerable number of Indians keep milk cows. Bullocks are rarely used as draft animals nowadays in Trinidad as they are in India, but there are a number of water buffaloes used for such purposes in the swampy lagoon areas. In general though, motorized vehicles are rapidly displacing animal powered equipment. The cow, then, serves almost entirely as a source of food and to Hindus this consists entirely of dairy products. I know of no instances where cows were killed by Hindus.

The repugnance towards the idea of eating beef is deeply rooted in the Hindu conscience, to such an extent that many Christian Indians, whose parents were converted from Hinduism still find it almost impossible to consider eating this meat. The eating of pork, except by low caste Hindus, is almost as repugnant as beef eating.

In some cases the grown children of converted Hindus eat pork though the parents do not allow them to cook it at the same stoves they use. On rare occasions that beef is eaten either by Hindus, or Indian Christians who have been converted from Hinduism, it is likely to be canned beef from Argentina. This meat is relatively cheap and has the advantages that it can be kept without refrigeration and need not be cooked the day it is bought as must be done with fresh meat.

In India, to eat chicken or eggs is considered by orthodox Hindus as only slightly less polluting than to eat pork (Hutton 1951: 77). However, in Trinidad the attitude towards fowl has changed perhaps more than with any other meat. Almost all rural families of the Oropuche area keep a flock of scrawny chickens and there is little objection shown towards eating either the birds or their eggs. Also, it should be mentioned that fish are plentiful and cheap in Trinidad and are eaten by Hindus in large quantities.

Probably the most acceptable meat among Hindus is goat flesh, even as it is in India. Goats are relatively plentiful and there is no objection to eating them by Hindus, if they will eat any kind of meat. For food served at Hindu ritual functions meat is almost always absent. Meals are provided at weddings and at the various rituals (*puja*) that Hindus give throughout the year. The meals almost always consist of rice, *roti*, curries and various hot pickle dishes. The curries at weddings and other Hindu ceremonial functions are always made of vegetables only.

Hindus who subsist entirely on a vegetarian diet are rare. All *sadhus*, some *pundits*, and a few very devout Hindus do not eat meat, but this constitutes only a small proportion of the total Hindu population. Many Hindus do not eat much meat, restricting meat dishes to once per week, usually on the weekend. The small amount of meat eaten is primarily a matter of cost, however, since many people can't afford to buy it more than once a week.

There is little evidence of fastidiousness in the type of vessel used for eating in Trinidad. In India both the use of locally made earthenware and hardfired china is frowned upon by orthodox Hindus because it is believed these vessels cannot be properly cleaned (Hutton 1951: 77, Niehoff 1957). In Trinidad Hindus normally eat out of china dishes and the only persons I knew who used the traditional brass vessels for everyday use were sadhus and, on occasion, pundits. The *thali* is used for ritual purposes only by ordinary Indians. At Hindu weddings it is traditional for friends and relatives to give these brass trays to the bridegroom. Sometimes he gets as many as fifty or sixty of them. However, he does not keep all these trays. He either sells them or uses them later as gifts at weddings where he is the guest. These vessels, as well as all other objects of brass available in Trinidad, are imported from India.

The only evidence of touch pollution that we noticed in Trinidad was at some ceremonial functions. At these affairs there is some effort made to keep Moslems or low caste Hindus from directly touching the food being prepared. One Moslem woman I knew was much in demand for helping to cook at weddings and prayer rituals, but orthodox Hindu families would not allow her to come inside the cooking shed. She stayed outside and peeled vegetables but she could not stir the cooking pots. She was allowed to serve cooked food to the guests, however. It is also significant that my wife was allowed free access to cooking areas in Trinidad and assisted the women on many ceremonial occasions, whereas in India she could only observe cooking procedures even where a good friendship had been established with a Hindu woman.

There is particularly no connection between caste membership and occupation nowadays in Trinidad except for pundits and a scattering of individuals who follow some traditional craft. *Barhais* (carpenters) are still to be found working in house construction and, also, a few of them make traditional Indian drums. Threr are a few Kohars *(potters)* who make both traditional pottery vessels such as the *dia* for Diwali and new types which can be sold in the Trinidad markets. Also, there are some basket-makers who follow their traditional caste occupation. In general, though the economy of Trinidad is so dependent on imported goods that the craft worker has great trouble in obtaining a reasonable profit, and consequently most of them have given up the traditional occupations.

Seemingly, one of the strongest bulwarks in the caste system in India is caste endogamy. In north India marriage between castes only happens very rarely. In several recent village studies no inter-caste marriages were found (Lewis 1958: 160; Opler & Singh 1948: 471; Marriott 1950: 175). In a survey of 170 factory workers in the city of Kaapur I found *no bona* fide examples of inter-caste marriage (Niehoff 1957). And in a study of marital advertisements of north Indian newspapers, though there were found to be considerable other changes, marriage within the caste was still the norm (Niehoff 1959). Eighty-six per cent in this sample of 213 advertisements either requested spouses of their own caste or else stated their caste and asked for a suitable mate. No other specification for a spouse was listed so often. This group would consist of the least orthodox Hindus in India.

In Trinidad, marriage between castes has become quite common, with probably as many marriages, between castes as marriages within the same caste. Hindu parents prefer to get mates for their children of the same caste, but there are other considerations that they will regard just as important, or more so. Financial position and education and physical appearance are three such qualities also. In so far as people consider caste at all in choosing mates for their children, they try to avoid the extremes. High and even middle caste parents try to see to it that their children are not mated to someone from the low castes. In particular, efforts are made so that the girls will not marry someone of a lower caste. There is precedent for this in the Indian custom of hypergamy. In India, however, the bride of a lower status is from another subcaste rather than another caste as in Trinidad (Hutton 1951: 53-54). Castes have been inter-marrying between one another in Trinidad long enough by now that it is difficult for parents sometimes to decide what caste their children rightfully belong to. In general, Trinidad Hindus consider a child to belong to the caste of the parent of the highest caste status. There are even some Hindus who are unsure of their caste and others who have forgotten completely what caste they belong to.

The extended or joint family of India is similar in most ways to extended families in other parts of the world. Its interrelationship with the caste system and the seclusion of women are probably the most important. Along with the caste system, this family type was brought into an alien environment in Trinidad. The European family was not of the extended type when Indians arrived and the Negro family, by whom Indians were more strongly influenced, was characterized to a high degree by concubinage and what is called the non-legal union (Matthews 1953: 1). This union is characterized as a relationship relatively durable between two marriageable people, 'living under one roof ... without any formal religious, civil, or social ceremony'. (Matthews 1953: 2). It can be easily seen that such a marital relationship has no similarity to that brought to Trinidad by the Indians. It must be remembered also that in the early days the Indians were greatly outnumbered by Negroes and that cultural borrowing from Negroes was considerable. Right from the beginning then, the extended Indian family was challenged.

An added disability which the Indian extended family had to struggle against in the early days was the disparity of numbers between the sexes. Since the planters encouraged the indenture system solely to get field workers they were more interested in men than women. The disproportion of men to women which resulted, created social and moral problems in practically all the world areas where Indians were sent as labourers in the 19th century. Even as late as the early years of the 20th century there were still about three times as many men as women being sent to Trinidad. If the surplus Indian males had willingly accepted Negro females as spouses the kind of situation which developed might not have taken place, but there is every indication that instead of accepting Negro women, they competed among themselves for women from their own country. As a result of the demand for them, women became more independent in Trinidad than would have been possible in India. According to the early reporters when Indians came to the island, fidelity was not one of the virtues of women. 'The wives, although they have a regard for their families, and make fond mothers, are not very strict in their fidelity towards their husbands.' (Hart 1866: 101).

Morton mentions that the Indian women were quite important due to their small number (1916: 185). Jealous husbands or lovers, who often resorted to violence, are reported many times for this period and this stereotype for Indian males still exists in Trinidad. 'Coolies (Indians) do not have a good reputation with police. Negroes quarrel with their tongue, but the coolies kill. Women, being few, are often unfaithful. The coolie who learns this kills his wife without the least hesitation.' (Froude 1909: 67) 'The coolie husband is of a frantically jealous disposition .... Three-fourths of the murders in this colony may be traced to this cause'. (Collens 1886: 197)

Another disadvantage which the Indian family has suffered historically in Trinidad is that marriage as performed by Hindu or Moslem rites was not recognized as legal by the government until quite recently. Marriage as performed by a Moslem *imam* was accepted as a legal rite in 1936 and marriage by a Hindu pundit was made legal in 1946 Laws of Trinidad and Tobago (1950: 56, 69). The consequence of the legal non-recognition of Hindu and Moslem marriage rites previous to the 1930s was that such a marriage was taken seriously only by the Indian community since in the eyes of Trinidad law it wasn't marriage anyway. Children from such a marriage were considered illegitimate. And because Hindu and Moslem rites were not recognized for so long, a considerable portion of the Indian community became accustomed to non-legal 'under the bamboo' marriage; so that nowadays, when marriages can easily be registered, quite a number of Indians do not bother with civil registration.

Despite the great disadvantage the Indian family has experienced in its hundred years history in Trinidad, it still stands apart as a distinct family type as compared to the similar institutions of the other ethnic groups of the island and retains a remarkable degree of Indianness. The Indians of Trinidad view marriage perhaps as the major focal point in the affairs of the family and, undoubtedly, with more justification. It is at this time that an outsider is brought into the circle of kinship, and if this circle is to function with a considerable degree of unity the selection of the outsider has to be carefully considered. The majority of Trinidad Indian marriages are therefore arranged by the parents, or other responsible elders, even as they are in India. There is very little social intercourse between young people who are married. Indian girls do not go out on dates or to dances and a girl is usually suspect if she is seen talking to a young man on the street or road. In the Oropuche Lagoon area a Moslem or Hindu girl who went to a dance would be considered a prostitute. The only place where an Indian girl would not be censored for going to a dance would be the Himalayan Club, the one important social club for Indians in Trinidad.

After the parents have located a likely mate, the normal procedure is to bring the boy to the girl's house where she can see him and speak to him briefly. Their wishes are then weighed and if the young people agree, the parents go ahead with the rest of the marriage arrangements. It is uncommon for Indian parents to ignore the wishes of their children entirely, although they may apply considerable pressure to get them to accept a mate they have selected. When an agreement has been reached between marriage partners, the boy is often allowed to see the girl several times at her parents' home although there are still women in the Oropuche area who never saw their husbands before marriage or who saw them so briefly that they did not recognize them on the day of the marriage.

Sometimes the boy will see a certain girl on the road or market place or some other public place and will then ask his parents to arrange a marriage with her. If she seems suitable, the parents will often do this. There are even cases in which the boy, whose father is dead or who has no suitable male relatives, will make the arrangements with the girl's parents himself.

The age of marriage among Indians in Trinidad remains low, largely because parents still have primary control of the institution. The legal ages for marriage are sixteen for Moslem males and twelve for females, while Hindu males must be eighteen and females fourteen. Considering both registered and unregistered marriages, however, the majority of the Indian females are married before the age of 19 with well over a third being married before the age of 14. It should be mentioned that the *gauna* rite which in India follows the marriage ceremony by several years, and at which time cohabitation actually begins (Lewis 1958: 159), is not observed at all in Trinidad. Some older women can remember marriages of the past when this rite took place but most know nothing of the ceremony. In 85 cases of Indian women who attended the Pt Fortin birth control clinic 30 (35%) were married at 14 or under, while 45 (53%) were married between the ages of 15 and 19 (Pt Fortin 1957: 12). In 28 cases which I collected in the Penal area, 23 (82%) were married by the age of 19. Of the 42 cases in which the women were 14 or under, there were nine in which the women were less than ten years of age.

When Hindus are preparing to be married it is necessary that the pundits read their horoscope to learn whether they will be compatible and to set the time for the wedding. However, in Trinidad the planetary correspondences are largely tempered if the two individuals seem to be compatible. It was reported that many pundits, when asked to read the horoscopes of young people who were planning to be married, first tried to find out if they were satisfied with the match and then deciphered their horoscopes accordingly. A Hindu saying is current in Trinidad which illustrates this belief. 'Jo munna thiik hei, to gunna bhii thiik hai.' (When the temperaments are compatible then the horoscopes are also compatible).

It is claimed in Trinidad that according to the *jotis*, the Hindu book of horoscopes, the marriage period should be from January to April and in June. Lewis mentions that most marriages in the village he studied took place in May and June after the harvest season (Lewis 1958: 180). Nowadays there is little heed paid to these periods in Trinidad, marriages being held whenever the individuals want them. Also, the particular day of the marriage is supposed to be set by the pundit in accordance with the horoscope. Here again though, the most convenient day, Sunday, is usually arranged for instead of the day which would be auspicious according to the horoscope. It is reported that individuals nowadays don't ask the pundit which day their marriage should take place, but rather ask him which Sunday would be most propitious.

An integral part of Hindu marriage arrangements is the dowry which is settled by the parents of the couple. In Trinidad this dowry ranges in amount from a few dollars up to $500 or more and may also include material goods of prestige and wealth in the more well-to-do families. Houses, cars, and small shops are some of the things offered in such cases. In many cases when a boy is reluctant to get married, a high dowry of either money or goods is used to tempt him.

The marriage rite is one of the most important of the socio-religious events that Trinidad Hindus observe. A series of rituals begins on Friday night and lasts until Sunday evening. There is considerable expenditure for food and drinks during this time. There is much visiting, particularly at the final marriage ceremony on Sunday. Weddings are quite popular with Indian women since their opportunities for social intercourse are much more limited than those of men. Alcoholic drinks are not served at the wedding feast but individuals bring their own and, also alcoholic drinks are sometimes served in an isolated room of the wedding house to special guests. One Trinidad pundit described it this way: 'Hindu marriage is a beautiful ceremony but nowadays it's a mess. People make a fete out of it, drinking rum, smoking, and generally having a good time.'

Because of the drinking and levity that takes place at the main ceremony, it is observed during the day even though traditionally it is supposed to occur at night. This change has taken place in Trinidad during the last ten or fifteen years.

Although a man can have only one wife by registered marriage, he can have more in accordance with Hindu beliefs. In Trinidad a Hindu man can theoretically have seven wives, though a Hindu woman can marry only once. The Hindu attitude has been reinforced by the Hindu marriage law which makes no provision for divorce. It is claimed that formerly unscrupulous Hindu men would marry simply to get the dowry and then abandon the wife. The efforts to prevent this happening in registered marriages, and also the high caste Hindu objection to divorce on religious grounds, resulted in the absence of provisions for divorce in the marriage law. Today many Hindus feel there should be a divorce clause in the marriage act.

Multiple wives do occur in Trinidad, though as in all societies, they are an uncommon form of marriage for economic reasons alone. Undoubtedly, an additional pressure against plural wives in Trinidad is the fact that the social group which has been dominant politically until 1958 (Europeans), did not recognize this form of marriage. I have heard of Indian men having as many as five wives though in the cases of polygamy that I actually knew, there were only two wives for each of the men. In these plural marriages each wife usually lives in a separate house. Besides multiple wives which have been married in Hindu rites, some men live with women as 'keepers'. Hindu women, in particular, resort to the 'keeper' relationship if their husbands die because they are not allowed to go through the Hindu rites again. They are simply concubines or kept women, who live in separate houses, if the man is already married. Some such relationships prove quite stable, particularly if the man has no regular married wife by Hindu or civil rites. I knew cases of women living with men for most of all of their life and raising several children without ever being married. This kind of relationship is quite similar to that of the Negro non-legal union mentioned earlier.

After marriage the young couple stays three or four months in the husband's father's house and then moves 'one side'. This is usually a nearby house, often on the same piece of property. This kind of settlement pattern is particularly true if there is any appreciable amount of land and the sons are farmers, though even if they follow other occupations they tend to move into a house near the father's. The oldest son very often stays in the father's house, particularly if the father is too old or too weak to manage his affairs. The true extended household unit as known in India, in which all sons and their wives live in the house of the father, is a definite rarity in Trinidad. It is felt that too much quarrelling occurs if all the children are living in the same house.

Elders are respected by younger members of the family but not to the same extent as in India. The practice of greeting by touching the feet of older persons is very rarely observed. In those few cases where younger people do this, it is only to their mother or father. Most Hindus claim they touch the feet of Brahman pundits only, and by no means do all of them do this. However, this practice is usually observed when a pundit comes to a house to officiate at a *puja*. In general, the younger people are expected to do what the older people tell them to do, not to curse them, nor use obscene language in their presence and to minister their wants. The younger members of the family, particularly the wives, massage the limbs or other parts of the body that are hurting their elders at bedtime. If a son, or sons, is living with one or both parents, it is usual for the older persons to be in charge of the financial affairs. In the more traditional families the sons bring all their salary home to the father who then gives them back what he thinks they need for spending money. When the parents get very old or feeble they turn these affairs over to the son who is living with them.

The relative position of Indian men and women in Trinidad resembles that in India, though the stricter forms of seclusion and protection of women are not found in Trinidad. Women do not cover their faces when in the presence of non-related males. However, in the presence of their fathers-in-law they are expected to keep their heads covered with the *oroni*, the thin shawl or head covering that most rural Indian women wear. It has already been noted that unmarried Indian girls are expected to have very little social intercourse with non-related males. Even after marriage there are measures to restrict such mixing. At practically all Hindu religious functions men and women are kept apart. In the cases of the big Hindu pageants, the *Ram Lila* and the *Krishan Lila*, the male and female spectators are assigned to opposite sides of the play area. At Hindu prayer rituals and also at weddings men and women stay in separate areas. It must be mentioned that these practices of segregation are quite contrary to the practices found among Negroes and the other non-Indian ethnic groups on the island. At all public functions of these other groups, women mix freely with men.

In the home, the Indian woman is expected to serve and obey her husband. She serves the food and generally eats after the husband is finished. At weddings and other public functions the men are always served first. In general, the men have control of the household money. Quite often the wife keeps the money at home and gives the husband amounts as he request them. She does not spend any, however, without asking him. A dutiful wife also asks her husband when she wants to go out.

Land is normally inherited by the sons, with the oldest being favoured. This applies to Indian Christians as well as Hindus and Moslems. Male inheritance is tempered by the treatment children give their parents, however. A girl may be favoured if she had taken care of her parents in their old age while her brothers neglected them. A wife may inherit land from her husband if there are no brothers or if the brothers didn't get along well.

The position of women is brought out rather clearly by a Hindu husband's account of a famous murder that had occurred some time before our arrival in Trinidad. An Indian doctor was convicted and executed for the murder of his wife, a German woman. The interpretation of this crime by a Hindu of the Oropuche Lagoon is as follows: 'He was an important man and he wanted to marry a white woman. He married this German woman in Port-of-Spain against his father's wishes. She was a big shot and she was used to going out to functions. Now you know, an Indian wife, if she wants to go out, she asks her husband. If he says it's all right she can go out, if he said "no", then she can't. But this Indian husband couldn't tell his woman when to go out because she was white so she went out when she pleased. And then they found her body tied in a sack in the sea. And he paid the price and was hung.'

It can be readily seen that considerable changes have taken place in the two institutions of Hindu culture that have been described. This is to be expected since these people migrated to an alien environment where they were in a minority and where there was little sympathy or understanding for the culture they had brought with them. This general change will not be dealt with in this summary, however, though the comparative change will. Both Hindu caste customs and the structure of the Hindu joint family have been retained to some degree in Trinidad. However, it is my thesis that the family structure has shown much more inner strength than has the caste system. In fact, it is evident, I believe, that as a method of organizing human relationships the caste system has become very insignificant already, and that within another generation or so caste practices will remain only in the memory of the older Indian. This is not true in regard to the Hindu family. Though here too, there have been many changes, the family structure as brought from India shows a considerable vitality, and is the one important social institution that sets the Hindu community from the other Trinidadians.

To sum up the caste structure in this Trinidad community, it can first be sid that there is still a hierarchy of castes, though except for the attitudes toward the highest and lowest castes, there are very few social practices connected with these differences. Brahman pundits are still somewhat respected though those Brahmans who do not serve as priests are often highly criticized, principally because they engage in undignified or lowly regarded occupations. Anyway, the relatively high regard for Brahman pundits can be interpreted as a regard for their religious activity rather than their position in the caste structure. In this regard, it is undoubtedly relevant that the Gosains, who also act as priests in Trinidad, are regarded to be on a par with the Brahmans. The low castes such as Doms, Chamars and Dhobies still suffer some disabilities but these are very minor in comparison to the disability they suffer in most Indian villages. There is practically no problem of touch pollution in Trinidad, except on ceremonial occasions when low castes are not allowed to help cook in the communal cook-house. The problems such as castes will take food and water from which other castes are non-existent in Trinidad. The inter-relationship between caste and occupation is also practically non-existent.

Probably the most telling change that has taken place among these migrant Hindus is that caste endogamy has broken down almost completely. While parents still prefer to have their children marry someone from the same caste they make no great issue on the point. Probably at least half the marriages now are between castes. Moreover, there are even marriages between the highest and the lowest castes. One last point in the increasing ineffectiveness of caste in Trinidad is that there are Hindus now who are not even sure what caste they belong to.

The Hindu family structure has suffered as many, or more, difficulties in Trinidad as the caste system. Two of the most important disabilities were the disproportions of sexes of the migrants and also the legal non-recognition of Hindu marriage until 100 years after the first migrants arrived. Despite these difficulties, however, the Hindu community rallied and ultimately established a clearly recognizable form of the joint family. The possibility of Indian men taking Negro wives never occurred to any important extent. If this had taken place, the Hindu form of the family would undoubtedly have disapproved. Instead, Indian men competed for the few Indian women there were, and because of this competition, Indian women were quite independent at one time. However, with the passage of time and with the equalization of sexes through reproduction on the island, the relative position of men and women as found in India was re-established, though tempered. Nowadays the male is the family leader, both in public and in private. Men are served food first at home, are the holders of the family money; and inherit the family property as a rule. And although there is no seclusion of women as found in India, females are segregated from males at public functions. Also, unmarried females are expected to have no social intercourse with non-related males. Marriage is still arranged by the parents and the dowry as a means of cementing relations between the two families is quite important. Marriage age is quite low by Trinidad standards though high as compared with that of India. Elders are respected and obeyed though with less deference than in India. The predominant residence pattern is virilocal. Though there are a few homes where sons and their wives remain in the paternal household, the general practice is for the newly married couple to move into a house of their own which, however, is often adjacent to the house of the father. All things considered, the extended family in Trinidad is a going concern while the caste system has lost most of its effectiveness.

It would naturally be asked why one institution would fail under pressure and the other would survive. I believe that family structure is more basic and important to the individual than his caste membership. Both institutions had to struggle for survival in this new environment and ultimately the price of the struggle was greater than the value of retaining the institution in the case of caste. Moreover, the caste involves a much wider net of relationships than does the family, and as a consequence, it is more difficult to discipline incalcitrant members in a caste than in a family. According to this thesis, the smaller and more tightly knit the institution, the better are its chances for survival in a situation of pressure.

REFERENCES

Cohn, Bernard S. (1955). *The Changing Status of a Depressed Caste* in 'Village India', *American Anthropological Assoc.* Memoir 83,1955.

Collens, J. H. (1886). *Guide to Trinidad*.

Froude, James A. (1909). *The English in the West Indies*, Longmans, Green and Co., New York.

Camble, Rev. W.H. (1866). *Trinidad: Historical and Description*, Yates and Alexander, London.

Hart, Daniel (1865). *Historical and Statistical View of the Island of Trinidad*, Judd and Glass, London.

Hutton, J. H. (1951). *Caste in India*, Oxford University Press, London.

Laws of Trinidad and Tobago, (1950). C. T. Roworth Ltd., London.

Lewis, Oscar (1958). *Village Life in Northern India*, University of Illinois Press, Urbana.

Mandelbaum, David (1948). *Family in India* in Southwestern Journal of Anthropology, Vol. 4, No. 2, University of New Mexico, Albuquerque.

Marriott, McKim (1955). *Little Communities in an Indigenous Civilization* in Village India, American Anthropological Association Memoir No. 83, Menasha.

Matthews, Dom Basil (1953). *Crisis of the West Indian Family,* Extra Mural Department, University College of the West Indies.

Morton, Sarah E. (1916). John Morton of Trinidad, Westminster Co., Toronto.

Niehoff, Arthur (1957). *Caste, Class and Family in an Industrial Community of North India,* Ph.D. Thesis, University Microfilms, Ann Arbor, Michigan.

Opler, Morris and Singh, Rudra Datt, (1948). *The Division of Labour in an Indian Village* in 'A Reader in General Anthropology, ed. Carleton S. Coon, Henry Holt and Co., New York.

Point Forin Family Planning Clinic, (1956-57) Pt Fortin Trinidad.

Srinivas, M. N., (1955).' Castes, Can They Exist in India Tomorrow?', *Economic Weekly,* Vol 7, No. 42, Bombay.

J. Nevadomsky

CHANGES IN HINDU INSTITUTIONS IN AN ALIEN ENVIRONMENT

INTRODUCTION

In his comparative study of the family in various parts of the world, Goode (1963) observes that as societies are transformed from agricultural and non-industrialized economies to urban and industrialized ones, family patterns gradually change from the extended to the conjugal type and more emphasis is placed on the nuclear family. At the same time, however, Goode notes that as an institution the family varies greatly from one society to another and therefore one should not expect this convergence to come about in any simple, single way. Moreover, while in the long run changes in family and marriage patterns may be profound, changes between contiguous generations are likely to be relatively minor, leaving intact fundamental attitudes and behaviour. As Mandelbaum recently pointed out in his study of continuity and change in India, 'The new family ideals and the new laws have opened the possibility of systemic changes in family relations, in which the fundamental roles and processes will be redefined. Yet the motifs of behaviour ... including family relations, seem to be little affected' (1972: 655).

Like many other societies, India is in the throes of a transformation from a rural to an industrialized economy. In searching for ways to predict the impact of this transformation on the family some scholars turned to those groups of Indians that had migrated overseas. These 'Overseas Indians' would appear to provide a remarkable laboratory for the comparative sociologist or anthropologist to study the effects of emigration and dislocation on ancestral institutions and so contribute to the study of those institutions in the home country. Although many Indians migrated to East Africa and elsewhere where they became an interstitial group, it is probably among those Indians who migrated as wage laborers to sugar-producing colonies around the world under a contract system known as indenture, that social and cultural changes have been most pronounced. This evasive system of slavery subjected Indian emigrants to the vissisitudes of life in societies totally unfamiliar to them. Particularly in the West Indies, Indians entered societies that, having experienced the genocide of aboriginal populations, the importation of African slaves, and various influxes of Spanish, Dutch, French and English colonists, were still in the process of amalgamation. Indians were thus introduced to distinctive migrant groups held together by the demands of sugar production.

Some years ago in this journal, Niehoff suggested that the exposure of Indian institutions to conditions such as those found in the West Indies ought to tell us something about 'which institutions are most vital and basic to the general structure of Indian society' (1958: 172). He then reviewed changes among the East Indians in Trinidad, with main reference to what he regarded as the two central institutions of Indian society. the caste system and the traditional joint family.

Rightly concluding that the caste, system had been invalidated by indenture and was never successfully reconstituted, Niehoff went on to argue that the joint family system had fared much better, his suggestion being that the family, unlike caste, is a smaller, more tightly-knit institution, showing greater inner vitality and strength than caste, and therefore probably more impermeable and resistant to external pressures for change. And he showed how, in matters of courtship, marriage roles, household composition, and so on, the East Indian family in rural Trinidad continues to bear a remarkable resemblance to the family system typical of north India. Although Niehoff conducted his research in the late 1950s, his conclusions have, on occasion, been echoed in more recent works (e.g. Malik: 1972: 27).

Niehoff makes two important points that need to be examined here. The first concerns relating the impact on Indian institutions of emigration, indenture and adaptation to an alien environment to the possibilities of predicting family and social changes in India. This may be a doubtful procedure. Indian institutions responded and reacted to the internal dynamics of Trinidad with the result that they underwent profound transformations generated by conditions within the island society itself. As these conditions are not the same as those existing in India, the outcomes of institutional change in the societies are also likely to be different. Jayawardena prefaces his article on caste in Fiji Indian rural society with a quote by Hogbin which says that when the carriers of culture abandon one pattern for another it ceases to be. 'Other patterns have to be modified accordingly .... The totality therefore is different ...' (1971: 89). He then goes on to argue that 'the essential character of an institution lies in the manner in which its component parts are combined to form a distinctive pattern. The pattern gets mangled in the process of emigration and resettlement ... what persists is a thing of shreds and patches and not the seamless web [that existed] in the ancestral society' (1971: 114-5). For example, all that remains of the caste system among some overseas Indian groups are 'the ritual prerogatives of Brahmins and the influence of caste status on marriage' (Jayawardena 1971), elements that do not constitute the essence of caste, nor are themselves interrelated. Furthermore, if the historical conditions of settlement and the factors fostering change differ somewhat in the societies having contingents of overseas Indians, which adaptation is to be taken as the basis for predicting social change in India? For example, caste among the Indians in East Africa consists of competitive (rather than hierarchical, as in India) groups while caste in Trinidad is little more than a residual aspect of prestige limited in function to one or two social contexts.

The second point worth commenting upon, and the one I wish to emphasize here, has to do with Niehoff's relatively undeveloped assertion about the inherent conservatism and 'basic-ness' of the family, a claim that is often supported in the scholarly literature and among laymen. Goldthorpe, for example, in his review of social change and development in Third World societies, contends that, compared with changes in other social and economic institutions, the pace of change in family patterns is very slow. This is because an 'important function of the family in modern society is to provide the individual with a haven of refuge where he can rely on warmly diffuse relations' (1975: 143-4) whose stability over long periods can be counted upon. During the socialization process, family roles, being the initial set of reference points for inductees, are deeply ingrained in the younger generation making it unlikely that they would abandon the role patterns of their parents. Goldthorpe cites several studies which also suggest that people changing from old to new patterns tend to retain traditional attitudes to the family.

It is just as likely, however, that under conditions of rapid change and dislocation, the family, rather than rejecting change and preserving tradition, may actually become the agency most immediately available for adapting its members to new roles and conditions. Summarizing this point of view Levine, among others, has said that 'when an alteration in social conditions ... changes the values, beliefs and life styles of a given generation of individuals, these changes affect the ways they socialize their young. If this is true, then the next generation experiences a different pattern of child care and training than its forebears and socialization is a process promoting the cumulation of individual change over generations rather than the persistence of tradition' (1967: 216). His, and similar research, tends to counter the widely held view which takes it as axiomatic that socialization ensures the transmission of culture from generation to generation. Yet even if one wishes to accept the axiom as true, the question remains as to what culture is it that is being transmitted? The norms that family and community inculcate in their children take their essential character from causes external to them. What one generation transmits is what the society wants transmitted: the family functions as the transmission agency for the dominant institutions in the society. Reviewing general trends in family and marriage, Udry (1966: 16-17) observes that it is not the family that is the determinant of either change or stability in the patterns of society, but the economic and political forces in the larger society. If this is the case, then changes in the economic and political system are largely responsible for changes in the family and the family, 'rather that being' "basic" 'in its form, is derivative from them' (Udry 1966).

If the above argument has any merit, then it should not come as a surprise that ancestral Indian family patterns, transplanted to Trinidad, rather than constituting an impediment to the assimilation of new values, were instead transformed by the experiences of indenture and by more than half a century post-indenture social changes. Once would then expect the emergence of new courtship patterns, new relationships between the sexes, and new family roles. This is precisely what one finds. With data recently collected in a rural East Indian community, this paper describes selected family and marriage changes. The choice of the changes presented here has been dictated by those family and marriage patterns Niehoff described in his 1958 paper.

EAST INDIANS IN TRINIDAD

Trinidad is a plural society in that it is ethnically heterogeneous. Negroes (43%) and East Indians (36%) are the two major ethnic groups in a society of over one million that also includes Whites, Chinese and Levantines.

The immigration of Indians to Trinidad between 1815 and 1917 (when the system was terminated) represents a significant migration movement involving nearly 150,000 Indians (with perhaps another 300,000 going to other Caribbean societies). This important influx of Indian emigrants was a direct response to the demands of the sugar plantations whose manpower needs became critical following the exodus of ex-slave labor after emancipation. In the sending society, most of the emigrants are from the northern provinces — apparently part of a general demographic movement from rural to urban centers as a result of poverty and famine.

The 150 years of Indian experience in Trinidad can be roughly divided into three periods though it must be kept in mind that time scales tend to cordon off phenomena that span more than a single period. During the 'indenture period' (1845-1917) conditions on the plantations were not conducive to the perpetuation of Indian culture. Immigrants were indiscriminately housed together regardless of caste, plantation managers took little or no account of traditional domestic authority patterns, a severe sex imbalance freed the few available Indian women from traditional constraints of subordination and seclusion, and so on. Polyandry, intercaste marriage and common-law unions were fairly common.

It was during the 'interwar period' (1918-1940) that the East Indians may have possibly reconstituted some features of their ancient heritage. The majority of ex-indentured Indians elected to remain in Trinidad (rather than return to India) where most of them settled in rural villages as farmers and laborers. The limited duration of Indian servitude (indentures were for five years), the isolation of Indians in rural communities (35% still live in the countryside) and the 'composite memory of things past' are some of the explanations suggested for the reactivation of Indian culture. The levelling out of the sex ratio, investment in land, and successes in petty trades facilitated the reemergence of some form of patriarchal authority and extended family households. Rural settlement patterns and customary marriage procedures aided the reactivation of caste endogamy and locality exogamy. Even so, often what emerged were the bits and pieces of culture that became integrated with aspects of the local social structure into a new totality. In his study of caste among the East Indians in Guyana, Moore (1977) refers to the retention of caste 'notions', thus neatly summing up the crucial point that many retentions were mere sentiments rather than firm rules governing action. The idea of 'notions' also suggests that adherence to traditional ways was often a matter of personal inclination for no official penalties could attach to non-compliance in a society that regarded Indian culture as alien and barbaric.

If the Indians were left relatively alone during this time to tinker with the fragments of their homeland culture, this isolation came to an end in the 'post-war period' (1945-present). During the war fortunate Indians worked on American military bases and used this opportunity to get out of agriculture. Later, Indians took advantage of the post-war economic expansion to move into teaching, light manufacturing, commerce, construction and the social services. In transportation and law they gained a disproportionate share of the jobs. Although occupational representation among the island's ethnic groups remains unequally distributed generally, there is some Indian representation in virtually *all* the available occupations. With economic advancement, Indians invested in urban real estate, business, and education. Indeed, Indians perceived in education the crucial vehicle for their social mobility. With enfranchisement and decolonization, Indians reactivated their diminishing sense of cultural pride and revitalized some disused customs. But their emergence as a political force and their significant economic and educational achievements also signalled their increasing integration into Trinidad society.

THE COMMUNITY

The community from which most of the data in this paper are derived is located in the west central sugar-belt heartland. In 1972 'Amity'[1] had 953 households with a population of about 6,500: 88 per cent East Indian, the rest mainly Negro and a few Chinese. Over 90 per cent of the East Indian population are Hindu, the rest mostly Christian and a few Moslems.

The several well-kept temples and *jandi* prayer flags, and the fields of rice, sugar-cane and vegetable crops, convey the impression of a community that has successfully survived the trauma of emigration and the winds of change. Indian food, Bombay music, and the seemingly endless round of traditional wedding celebrations also suggest this. But this impression is misleading. Behind the remaining traditional ceremonial and cultural features of rural life, one sees the effects of a modernizing economy and the heavy influence of Western norms, particularly North American ones, on local social life. For example, although the village has an agricultural base, its dependence on agriculture is fast diminishing as villagers avail themselves of white-collar work and industrial employment. With Port of Spain, the capital, and other urban areas only 15 miles away, the village looks like any typical suburban community during the normal working day: only the very young, the very old and housewives remain. Except for the fact that many villagers do a little part-time 'gardening' (especially in rice), the local occupational system is rather similar to that of the wider society. The same is true of education: about 70 per cent of the males and 50 per cent of the females in the 13-35 age bracket have had some kind of training (post-primary, technical, commercial, secondary or university) beyond primary school.

If social and economic changes are measured solely in terms of physical amenities, the results are quite remarkable. More than 3/4s of the households have radios and 1/6 have television sets. Nearly 50 per cent own refrigerators, though this appliance is underutilized. The automobile, once purchased mainly by taxi drivers and a few civil servants, is now regarded by many as a necessity. Twenty years ago 70 per cent of the houses were made of mud or board; today 70 per cent are concrete block structures consisting of four or five rooms upstairs and a storage/kitchen area below. All the roads in the village are metalled and most of the homes have electricity. The majority also has pipe-borne water. Recently telephone lines have been installed.

Besides the changes in family life to be described later, the influence of urban employment, social and physical amenities, and education are responsible for changes in the local ranking system. Some years ago, aspects of retained caste and ritual status carried weight as indices of local social status. At least in this community, the local elite seems to have been composed of the higher castes and, perhaps more so than in many other rural communities, adhered fairly staunchly to traditional religious values. Land ownership and wealth were also important. Today, caste is mere sentiment and, with the declining interest in farming, there has been a separation of social status and land-ownership. Wealth is important but it is now measured in terms of income potential. There is very wide agreement that a white-collar job (of almost any kind) and at least a secondary school education, both of which tend to correlate with relatively high incomes, are the major attributes of high status. It is now the educated, white-collar elite — a category consisting of teachers, civil servants, etc. and also young people who have just completed secondary schooling — that dictates local standards of behavior and etiquette.

This change in social status can be seen by the present placement of Brahmin priests and of scavengers, two categories which traditionally represented the high and low ends of the status continuum. Today, the prestige of the local priests, and or Brahmin priests generally, is on a sharp decline. Young people are especially harsh and rank the priests very low. One reason for this is the irrelevance of many Hindu rituals to the new emerging life-styles. Also, the majority of priests are uneducated and therefore an embarrassment to educated villagers wishing to eradicate the stereotype of rural Indians as 'coolies'. Moreover, caste, the girder of priestly rank, is anachronistic. Scavengers, on the other hand, traditionally at the bottom of the status scale because of the association of their work with filth and 'pollution', have been rising. Although still the butt of jokes among a few villagers, most people realize that the job pays well and is steady government work.

MARRIAGE AND FAMILY CHANGES

Some of the obvious changes stemming from the effects of those transformations described earlier appear in courtship and marriage patterns. Except for the early indenture period, arranged marriages were the cultural ideal and the statistical norm. Niehoff (1958: 180), among others (e.g. Klass: 1961), has described this pattern including the search by parents for a suitable spouse often through go-betweens, lengthy negotiations marked by suspicion and distrust, and of course elaborate wedding ceremonies. Today, most marriages are *not* parentally arranged, at least not in the above sense. Some indication of this can be seen if the ever-married women in a random sample of village households are divided into two age cohorts: only 17 per cent of the women 35 and under, did so. The trend is clearly for a young person to find his own mate and then to seek parental approval. If approval is not forthcoming, it is not unusual for a young man to go ahead and marry the woman of his choice, then to await the reconciliation that usually follows. Young men and women, because they spend a great deal of time outside the community at work or at school, come into contact with a pool of potential spouses. This freedom of selection applies almost as much to unmarried girls as it does to young men because women have the same freedom to seek higher educational and career goals. Although parents are often fearful that the reputation of their daughter may get 'spoiled' if she is 'seen all about' (a young man's reputation is not subject to the same restrictions), at the same time they are reluctant to restrict her lest they hinder her progress. If in the past a father's essential duties to his daughters (and a source of prestige to himself) was to find them husbands and to guarantee their virginity at marriage, his principal duty nowadays is to educate them. With that achieved he knows they can take care of themselves. Village parents often remarked that an educated daughter can easily find good employment; this enhances her eligibility as a spouse, secures the respect of her husband and, in the event the marriage dissolves, ensures that she will not be an economic liability to her parents. On the whole, then, parents agree that personal choice is the 'best' method of spouse selection though, at present, there is every kind of arrangement in the community, even sometime within the *same* family.

Along with the decline of the arranged marriages other traditional restrictions have also weakened or disappeared. Caste endogamy has disappeared and *varna* endogamy is following suit. The bar to the marriage of known consanguines is sometimes relaxed once the 'second cousin' limit is reached. Restrictions on religious intermarriage apply most strictly to Hindu-Moslem marriages, but breaches occur and no sanctions follow. Marriages between East Indians and Negroes are taboo, and seldom breached in the rural areas, though they are occurring with increasing frequency in the towns.

Formerly, too, there was a definite preference for marrying outside the village, that is, local women were given in marriage to men outside the community while men received wives from other villages, a pattern also found in north Indian villages. One reason for this preference was the view that to marry a villager was tantamount to marrying a kinsman. In general marriage was forbidden with anyone to whom cognatic, affinal or fictive kinship could be traced. This does not hold today. Villagers are beginning to invoke the 'second cousin rule' as the boundary of the exogamic group beyond which marriages are possible; also fictive kinship ties have largely disappeared. The decline of locality exogamy is evident in the sample data. There is a strong bias towards exogamous marriages among women over 35 years of age (79%) and a slight bias towards endogamous marriages among women 35 years of age or younger (53%). This trend supports the argument that marriage is increasingly based on personal choice. As Smith and Jayawardena have noted for the East Indians in Guyana:

> So long as the emphasis is upon arranged marriage and a playing down of the affective quality of the marital relationship ... it is advantageous to bring in wives from outside, particularly since this widens the field of choice upon the basis of easily ascertained factors such as religion, caste, occupation, wealth and so on. As soon as one approaches a stage where primary emphasis is placed upon the nuclear family rather than an extended kinship unit, with a corresponding increase upon the husband-wife relationship and its affective quality, it seems likely that one will have to know more about the individual qualities of the intended spouse and therefore will be more likely to choose someone close at hand (1959: 362).

Their point is supported by the data here which show that 2/3 of village endogamous marriages as opposed to 1/4 of the exogamous ones were based upon personal choice. Thus personal choice seems to be highly correlated with village exogamy. It is interesting to speculate that this trend may reverse itself in the future as young people continue to seek opportunities outside the community thus coming into increased contact with marriageable non-villagers. The fact that more young people are able to buy cars these days means that they can do their courting outside the community. The difference between traditional village exogamy and a possible future trend in the same direction is that in the latter case a young villager will not depend upon his parents to find him a spouse.

These changes are also related to a shift in the age at marriage. Formerly, when parents exercised control over marriage and spouse selection, age at marriage was low and an unmarried girl of 14 or 18 was a cause for parental concern, even acute embarrassment. But by the early 1950s the age at marriage was clearly on the rise so that the enactment of the Hindu Marriage Ordinance (1946), which set the minimum legal age among Hindus at 14 years for females, 18 years for males, merely confirmed what was already a trend. Child marriages, to the extent that they ever existed, had long been abandoned and the age at marriage was usually over the minimum legal age requirement. About 70 per cent of the women who were married under age 11 had done so years before the passage of the ordinance and only 13 per cent contracted legally underage marriages after 1950. Perhaps the major effect of the ordinance was to permit the legalization of marriages celebrated according to customary rites in the home of the groom, thus conceding to Hindus what was allowed for Christians, namely, 'to have the building in which marriage ceremonies took place recognized as a place of registration'.

Some idea of the rising trend in age at marriage can be seen if again married women are divided into two age cohorts: the average age at first marriage for women over 25 is about 14 years but women 35 and under the figure is 17.5 years. A similar situation exists for men. Using an over 40/10 and underage division (because of the later age at which men normally marry) those in the former age cohort married at an average age of 19 years whereas those in the latter category married at an average age of 21 years.

Perhaps the most conspicuous feature of a 'retained Indian culture' and certainly a constant and justifiable source of ethnic identity and pride, is the traditional wedding ceremony, yet even here there have been numerous changes. Some are relatively unimportant such as the switch from night to day weddings (to avoid rowdiness and to conform to the Christian pattern), the regular use of Sundays as weddings days, and the use of white bridal gowns in the Western fashion (often in addition to a red *sari* — the former being used for formal wedding portraits, the latter for the ceremony itself).

Other features of the wedding ceremony have been retained but are becoming anachronistic. The *kanya dan*, or gift of the virgin, is not now an assurance of virginity because the rising age at marriage plus the greater freedom of movement for women makes it virtually impossible for a father to certify his daughter's chastity. The language of the ceremony is Hindi but this is not understood by most participants and English asides are necessary. Young people mock the rite by jokingly pantomiming what they regard as the incomprehensible and silly actions of the pundit.

Significantly, the manifestation in the wedding ceremony of the traditional asymmetry between bride-givers and bride-takers, the latter superior in status, is declining. Because of educational opportunities a woman may enter marriage without too great a disparity between herself and her spouse. Although traditional features of the wedding ceremony denote the superior status of the groom, the emerging equivalence of status is evident in such contemporary features as 'bridal gifts' and 'bridal showers', diamond engagement rings and the exchange of gold wedding bands. What this means is that young women no longer need come to marriage with a dowry to equalize the asymmetry in the relationship. Whereas formerly the groom was the center of attention and a wedding was an opportunity to show respect to him (and therefore to his family), the focus of attention is now shifting to the bride.

As in India, most marriages still take place in the home of the groom (though educated villagers and those living in urban areas may prefer a temple wedding). About 60 per cent of the village marriages are of this type. Formerly, these 'bamboo' marriages, as they are called (because the marriage tent is supported by bamboo poles), were not legal, though East Indians were not bothered by this. Although these customary marriages were normally advantageous to men, East Indian women may not have objected to the insecurity of marriage 'under the bamboo' because the initial scarcity of females made it easy for them to attract husbands. The marriage ordinance mentioned earlier legalized customary marriages, giving women the right to their husbands' estate and the husbands' financial support after separation/divorce. In addition, women became eligible for widows' pensions and social security benefits. Husbands, too, gained in the sense that they could claim a legal wife and children as income tax deductions.

Some villagers do not bother with the customary/legal type of wedding and simply have their marriage registered at the local courthouse. About 25 per cent of village marriages are of this type and, although one reason may be the desire to dispense with an expensive ceremony (which is not legally necessary), most often such marriages are elopements. This is suggested by the fact that 83 per cent of legal-only marriages are based on personal choice in mate selection. The remaining 15 per cent are common-law unions in which no ceremony or registration of any kind takes place.

Niehoff is correct when he says that 'the *gauna* rite which in India follows the marriage ceremony by several years, and at which time cohabitation actually begins, is not observed at all in Trinidad' (1959: 181). There is little delay between the wedding ceremony and cohabitation. The *kangan* restraining the couple from intercourse, is removed immediately after the wedding and the couple may begin sleeping together the first night. Some couples leave immediately on their honeymoon. Or, more commonly, the bride returns home for one week until the 'Second Sunday' when her husband fetches her.

Now, as in the past, nearly all couples reside with the husband's parents, though this is sometimes perfunctory and lasts not more than a month or two. Indeed, increasingly, patrilocal residence is a short term arrangement of convenience that ends when the couple has enough money to set up their own household. Among educated couples this is not too difficult, and many begin saving for it long before they marry. One difference between past and present practices seems to be the amount of time couples spend in patrilocal residence. From the sample data, 81 per cent of married men under 40 years of age settled in nuclear households within three years of marriage as compared to 21 per cent of men over 40.

Not only does the nuclear family presently constitute the longest phase of the domestic cycle, it is also the cultural norm. Although most scholars have maintained that the East Indians retained the extended or joint family as an ideal, which circumstances made impossible to put into regular practice, I found that East Indians regard the nuclear family household, consisting of a man with his wife and unmarried children living alone in a separate dwelling if possible, as the ideal. Villagers contend that this arrangement does away with 'the rattling of plates in the same cupboard' (i.e. the mother-in-law/daughter-in-law and father/married son conflicts); but a more telling reason may be that the nuclear family is looked upon as a clear sign of economic success and social independence, just as it is in the rest of society. I often heard parents criticize their unmarried sons, still living with them, for 'playing the fool' by lagging behind their more successful and independently housed peers. Indeed, it is not unusual to find parents bluntly telling their married son to 'move one side' when he shows reluctance or laziness in getting out on his own. This domestic ideal is reflected in actual living arrangements: 65 per cent of village households are nuclear and only 10 per cent qualify as fully extended. It is noteworthy that the classic joint family type (with economic control in the hands of the household 'patriarch' or his wife) is a definite rarity and occurs in less than 2 per cent of the cases. Most villagers say that such households are, as one villager put it, 'at least 25 years behind the times'.

Both marital and parental role behaviour have felt the impact of change. Such *purdah*-like practices as the use of the *orhini* by women to hide their faces in public or the restriction of married women to the rear or kitchen area of the house when male visitors call have long been discarded. When company calls, husband and wife jointly entertain their guests. Women no longer trail behind their husbands in public; indeed, some young couples walk along the road hand in hand. Some husbands take their wives to restaurants and even to nightclubs. Sundays have become the standard outing day for the entire family, to the beach or the cinema, or to visit relatives, usually those of the wife. These fairly obvious manifestations of behavioural change are indicative of new patterns of marital conduct in the direction of broadly companionate spouse relations. As yet, such changes are far from universal in the community, being stressed more by the young and educated, but virtually everyone is aware of these 'bright ways' and attempts to emulate them if possible. For example, a decent husband ought not to publicly treat his wife as an inferior: he ought not to 'ruin her with over-childbearing'; he ought to take her to visit her kinsfolk, and so on, otherwise he runs the risk of being regarded as 'coolie-ish', that is backward.

Adults complain that the young people are spoiled, undisciplined and disrespectful. If so, then their parents are partly to blame for permitting them freedom of movement and independence of thought. Socialization in 'Amity' seems to be more a process of 'acculturation' than 'enculturation' with parents actively inculcating new values. Also, the schools play a dominant part in most children's lives. A large part of a child's training is received outside the home and in an environment where the children are under the direct control of others than the parents. Formal education and the socialization of a child by 'strangers' is now an expected part of a child's development. Education has also had the effect of breaking down some of the inhibitions between parents and children. Parents are respected but no longer feared; children interact quite openly and freely with their parents, and even argue with them. In short, role relations between parents and offsprings have become more egalitarian and less gerontocratic.

It is said that in India divorce is frowned upon, widow-remarriage is not permitted and only the husband can remarry. Among the East Indians in Trinidad dissolution is easy and frequent and remarriage, usually in the form of common-law unions, and to a lesser extent legal or registered marriages, are acceptable procedures for both men and women.

East Indian marriages tend to be initially unstable: in the community about 12.5 per cent of married women have been separated permanently at least once as had 20 per cent of the men. About 70 per cent of dissolved marriages occurs within the first three years of marriage. Many reasons for separation are given including adultery, neglect and in-law interference but underlying the surface causes are deeper manifestations of change. Women nowadays refuse to play a subservient role in household affairs, to cow-tow to the mother-in-law for any length of time or to brook interference in personal matters. As noted earlier, girls marry at a later age these days, and with far better formal qualifications than before, so they have rather firm opinions about their roles as mother and housemaker. They also expect to be able to exert some influence over the husbands' behavior and income.

CONCLUSION

On the surface there are still some resemblances of the East Indian family to the family in India but beneath these similarities profound changes have taken and are taking place. Patrilocal residence after marriage still exists, but it is fast becoming perfunctory. Extended households are still found but in some the line of authority extends upwards from married son to ageing father. Paternal authority is still in evidence but is no longer authoritarian. It would seem, then, that the Indian family has been no more successful at weathering migration and the subsequent winds of change than other distinctly Indian institutions.

NOTES

1. As this is the same community studied by Klass (1961) in 1958, I have retained his pseudonym.

REFERENCES

Goldthorpe, J. E.

1975 *The Sociology of the Third World: Disparity and Involvement.* Cambridge University Press.

Goode, William

1963 *World Revolution and Family Patterns.* Free Press.

Jayawardena, Chandra

1971'The Disintegration of Caste in Fiji Indian Rural Society', in L. T. Hiatt and C. Jayawardena (eds) *Anthropology Oceania.* Angus and Robertson.

Klass, Morton

1961 *East Indians in Trinidad: A Study of Cultural Persistence.* Columbia University Press.

Levine, R., et. al.

1967 'Father-Child Relationships and Changing Life-Styles in Ibadan', in H. Miner (ed.) *The City in Modern Africa.* Praeger.

Malik, Yogendra

1972 *East Indians in Trinidad: A Study in Minority Politics.* Oxford University Press.

Mandelbaum, David

1972 *Society in India.* University of California Press.

Moore, Brian

1977 'The Relation of Caste Notions among the Indian Immigrants in British Guiana during the Nineteenth Century', *Comparative Studies in Society and History.* Vol. 19, No. 1.

Niehoff, Arthur

1958 'The Survival of Hindu Institution in an Alien Environment', *The Eastern Anthropologist*. Vol. 12, No. 3.

Smith, R. and C. Jayawardena

1959 'Marriage and the Family amongst East Indians in British Guiana,' *School and Economic Studies*. Vol. 8.

Udry, J. Richard

1966 *The Social Context of Marriage*. J. P. Lippincott Co.

M. Agrosino

SEXUAL POLITICS IN THE EAST INDIAN FAMILY IN TRINIDAD

Although the notion of 'survivals' no longer guides anthropological discussions of the Afro-American family,[1] the kinship structure of the numerically important East Indian communities of the Caribbean is all too frequently discussed in terms of the 'retentions' of ancestral forms. As Smith points out:

> Most of the work on kinship and family structure has been concentrated upon lower-class Negro groups and a number of recent publications continue this bias .... Studies of East Indian family structure in Trinidad and British Guiana have not really been brought into the same comparative framework as yet though they are crucial cases for assessing the relative effect of cultural tradition and structural constraint and for the testing of other hypotheses.[2]

This article is based primarily on data collected in Zenobia, a predominantly Indian village in Trinidad, during an anthropological field research period in 1970 and 1971, with updating in 1973. It has as its main aims the analysis of the Caribbean Indian family in its two apparently contradictory aspects:
- as a primary marker of a separate Indian ethnic identity,
- as an institution which has developed in the West Indian setting and which is thus a factor in the adaptation of the Indian group to the local setting.

THE INDIAN FAMILY

In classic ethnography, the Indian family has been described as a 'patrilocal joint family' in which a line of brothers, their wives and children live in a common household compound with the men's father as patriarch. In India, the family was a corporate unit jointly holding title to land, which was the general marker of wealth. The father was more or less the chairman of the board, but it was the brothers — ideally acting in common — who ran the affairs of the family property.[3] Such norms, to be sure, were always more common among the upper castes,[4] but they were also ideals to which upwardly mobile lower castes could aspire. As Kapadia points out, however, there was a network of interpersonal tensions beneath this surface:

> The subordination and superordination designed to regulate the lives of the different members in the hierarchy of a joint household, recognition of the family as a unit for all social relationships, the place assigned to the family as a juridical unit in family quarrels — all tend to give the family such enormous influence that the individual lost his identity in it. The social environment never provided any opportunity to the individual to feel that he had interests apart from those of the family.[5]

Thus, the Indian family is a unit whose surface appearance of collegial solidity is mitigated by the interplay of several patterns of dominance and subjugation. Of these, the most important for the following discussion are these:

- the domination of the father over his sons as a result of the greater spiritual powers of the patriarch.

- the domination of members of the consanguineal group over the affine (those who marry in).

These two hierarchies are linked by the admittedly rhetorical, but still very useful concept of 'sexual politics'. As used here, 'politics' is the art of dominance, of establishing relationships of relative power. For the Indian family this art is basically sexual, resulting as it does in the subjugation of the women who marry into the household, a practice which as will be shown, simultaneously established the domination of the consanguineal family over its affinal relatives while enabling the patriarch to express his own personal power.

In the traditional joint family, a woman was considered to be primarily a breeder of (preferably) male children in a household of strangers. As a corollary to this, she became a domestic servant to her husband's relatives, under the exacting domination of her mother-in-law; she further observed a strict avoidance relationship with her father-in-law. Despite the refinements which the Hindus have long added to the arts of sex, the sex act per se, even one sanctioned by marriage, was believed to be a deeply disgusting and polluting activity, particularly for a 'good' woman.[6] The 'good' woman, then, became a 'wife' whose sole duty was to engage in sex, and yet, who by the very performance of that duty, became a degraded and despised individual. Her every sexual act was hemmed in by taboos to keep her from polluting her husband's family.

The act of degradation and subjugation is not an expression of mindless cruelty, but is rather a mechanism for making the most out of a limited commodity, the land. The Indian social system, with caste as its most obvious feature, was a means of reifying the differences among groups of people, and thereby of justifying the harsh fact of differential access to land. As a result, temporal power, as represented by control of land, came to be seen as a symbol of purity. One possessed land, according to this system, not because one was shrewder in business, but because one was being rewarded for spiritual merit in a previous existence.

When a man's son got married, that man was by definition annexing something of value from another family — a daughter. The girl's family had to lose her labour (as well as a dowry) in return for a small, and often purely nominal payment of jewels, because it was a curse to keep an unmarried daughter on the premises. Moreover,

> If a father delays too long [in marrying off his daughter] neighbours may begin to whisper disapprovingly that the girl's parents are keeping her to care for them in their old age. Gossips may even hint that the father is sexually interested in his own daughter. The pressure, therefore, is on the father of the girl. Time is short, and the longer he waits the greater the danger of the girl escaping the vigilance of her chaperones.[7]

Furthermore,

> A woman was thought to be naturally libidinous; an unmarried girl attaining puberty would proceed to find a lover, however strictly her parents guarded her; once she had lost her virginity she would become unmarriageable and her parents would have the choice of the disgrace and expense of maintaining an unmarried daughter indefinitely, or the even greater disgrace of casting her out to become a beggar or a prostitute. From the point of view of her parents a daughter was a serious economic liability....[8]

The act of marriage, then, elevated the groom's family above that of the bride — all of whose relatives would suffer vicariously for the humiliation of one of their women being used sexually by a man of another family.[9] A good marriage for a man's son, then, would raise that man's prestige in the village, since another family had, by agreeing to that marriage, affirmed its relative pollution. The Indian family was, after all, 'a unit before the gods',[10] and the father was its chief priest. His authority, in fact, derives from his power to make the proper ritual offerings at the beginning and end of every day. Thus, the affirmation of relative purity and pollution among families was not a trivial concern, but central to the Indian notion of social structure, in that it validated a family's claim to control of land.

THE INDIAN FAMILY IN TRINIDAD: HISTORICAL DEVELOPMENT

The basic features of the Indian family were transported to the West Indies with the indentured labourers, and patrilocal residence, patrilineal descent and their several corollaries are still to be found. However, in the ensuing decades, the isolation of the Indians in Trinidad has broken down to such a degree, that to treat their family organization as something basically extrinsic to the West Indian scene is to miss Smith's point regarding the necessity of studying the Indian family in the same framework as that applied to the black family in the Caribbean.

Although pockets of Indian traditionalism survive in Trinidad, the more typical Indian village today is one with a population that is mixed to one degree or another with blacks (called 'creoles' in Trinidad by the Indians) or other groups. The village of Zenobia may stand as an illustrative example of this more acculturated type of settlement. Zenobia, which is approximately ninety per cent Indian, is located in south Trinidad, a ten-minute drive from San Fernando, the island's booming second city. The village is sufficiently far from town to remain outwardly rural in appearance, although the proximity to the town, as well as to the nearby Texaco refinery, places the Indians of Zenobia in the position of shopping with, working with — and competing with — the blacks.

The Indians of Zenobia, then, are in a position to take their place in the political and economic sphere of modern Trinidad. Although they will often express a nostalgia for 'Mother India', they know full well that their life in Trinidad, hard as it often is, is incomparably better than the round of disease, war and privation that characterizes India today. Some of the more politically aware Indians also realize that the old attitude of separation and ethnic exclusivity is counterproductive; the fate of Uganda's Indians might well be their own unless they become truly Trinidadian, as well as Indian. The dilemma of the present generation, then, is to become part of modern Trinidad without losing completely the sense of ancient heritage. Almost to a man (and woman), informants in Zenobia content that it is the family which gives the Indians strength and which will carry the group through the crisis.

Therefore, to view the Indian family in Trinidad as a collection of quaint customs lovingly preserved for over one hundred years is a sentimental distortion of the current situation. The family remains the bedrock of Indian ethnic identity, given the widespread disappearance of the Hindi language, conversions away from Hinduism and Islam, and the adoption of Indian cooking styles by the population at large. But it is the aim of this article to demonstrate that the Indian family remains a strong vehicle for the modern aspirations of the Indians primarily because it is no longer the family of classic ethnography, but something which has changed over time to meet the needs of life in Trinidad.

The following account of family life is based chiefly on the collection of ten full life histories of Zenobia people (seven men, three women) ranging in age from twenty-five to eighty-eight years. Supplemental or corroborative evidence was gathered in less systematized conversations with Indians of various ages both in Zenobia and in other parts of the island. Comparative data of the Caribbean Indian family of several years ago may be found in Davids,[11] Jayawardena,[12] Schwartz,[13] and Smith and Jayawardena.[14] Although Zenobia is not necessarily the most representative of Trinidad's rural villages, the fact of its location within an urbanizing/industrialized area coupled with its agrarian/sugar estate history makes it a good setting for viewing the current dilemma of social change among the Indians of the island.

FAMILY LIFE IN THE ESTATE DAYS

The move to Trinidad resulted in a new set of rules by which the structure of relative domination within and among families had to be arranged. In the first place, members of joint families were separated in the estate barracks to which the indentured Indians were brought. Moreover, there was a disparity between the numbers of men and of women who were imported. Men greatly outnumbered women throughout the indenture period, a fact which inevitably affected the relationships within the family.

It should be noted that Indian religious marriage ceremonies were not recognized by civil authorities until well after the indenture period had ended. Islamic marriages were declared legal in 1936, but Hindu ceremonies remained outside the law until 1946.[15] This legal double standard probably had the effect of weakening the traditional bonds of marriage, since a discontented husband could very easily abandon a woman who was not really a wife in the eyes of the law. But within the Indian world itself, religious marriages continued to have the full force of moral and social authority behind them. Indeed, the Indian character of the wedding ceremony came to be a principal marker of the group's feeling of ethnic separateness.[16]

A more critical change, as contemporary informants see it, was the loss of land as an exchange commodity. Shortly before the turn of the century, some of the Indians were given small plots of estate land by the planters as an inducement to stay in Trinidad, and others were able to save enough money to buy unused crown land following the expiration of their indenture contracts. But most of the Indians remained part of the landless labour force, a virtual rural proletariat, until the end of the indenture system during World War I.

These crises were met by changes in the nature of the Indian family. Without joint ownership of land, the corporate structure of the line of brothers disappeared, although the bond between father and son took on a new importance. Ownership of land, as noted earlier, symbolized a family's purity and spiritual merit. In the absence of ownership of land to distinguish among families, the family's only remaining power was the right to arrange marriage for its children. This duty fell to the father, who thus performed the single most important function in his son's life. Without land as the basic commodity, the bride was no longer a symbol of an exchange which had established the primacy of one family over another; she herself became the only real commodity. One elderly informant remembers the story of his father's marriage:

> They call for the girl uncle because he was a priest — or so he called hemself — and they fix the match. Now the girl family was livin' over to an estate near Williamsville, I forget the name, but it about ten mile from here. But they all did know the girl because she uncle was this holy man, and she brothers was all supposed, to be very holy, too, and they knew to read the sacred books and all. So me grandfather says, 'Eh! This will be a good match!' Me grandmother get vex and she say, 'But you is a fool, ole man! Them people poor like dirt; I hear the girl ain't got one bracelet for she own. And is this you call a match?' But me grandfather laugh at she and he tell she, 'Is you who the fool, ole woman. Them people call they self *sadhu*-this and *sadhuine*-that.[17] You see how the girl uncle wouldn't even touch the cup of water when he here in we place. Well, they well know the girl better off here — better house, better food and all — and so they give she up to we. But then you know it will be all about from here to Williamsville that this *sadhuine*-girl is we *doolahin*.[18] And they all so say, "But this man must be something all right. He get he son a *sadhuine*-girl for he marriage!"

Since the nature of estate life left little opportunity for the young man to wander around to pick out his own bride, he had to rely on the matchmaking grapevine of the elder members of his own family, occasionally supplemented by the services of the *agwa* or professional matchmaker.[19] This placed him in his parents' debt, and made him but the agent who, by having sexual congress with a girl from another family, was the instrument of elevating his father's position above that of the bride's relations. When a man's son took a woman of another family in the sexual sense, his family by definition became purer, as the Hindu value system defines the girl as being more profoundly defiled by the sex act than the boy. For this reason, it was not common for marriage arrangements to be reciprocal; a man would not want to marry his daughter to the brother or male cousin of his new daughter-in-law, since all her relatives would be considered socially lower than all members of his family. Such reciprocal exchanges were not unknown, to be sure, but they were not sought after and only occurred when it was for some reason in the interests of both families to declare an equality of status, rather than to insist on some sort of relative ranking.

Thus, to meet the challenges of the enforced breakup of the joint unit, the civil illegality of traditional marriage and the crucial loss of land, the Indians of the estate days elevated the concept of 'sexual politics' to the forefront of their social system. In India, the ownership of land indicated the possession of power both social and spiritual. But in Trinidad, spiritual power was all-important because there was no other commodity to be owned. In a milieu where trained *pandits* were rare, where the condition of barrack life made the attention to details of ritual purity difficult or impossible, and where caste per se could no longer be maintained because of the enforced togetherness, the only viable way to demonstrate one's purity was to degrade someone else; that is, marry your son to his daughter.

One overt result of this new situation was the brutalization of the young bride, the *doolahin*. In India she had no value in and of herself since she only symbolized the transfer of power. She transferred her labour from one household to another and was under obligation to produce offspring for her new family. But in Trinidad, she was property, and thus needed to be abused in order to make clear that her in-laws possessed her completely. As an informant says:

> Is like if a man have a goat and he leave the goat out in the yard all day long and don't tend with she. People go say, 'Well, this man ain't got no goat at all!' But if he go out and beat she when she eat down the bushes, then everyone go know that he care what she do. And so if a man don't beat he wife, people go think he ain't care what she do, and you know that a woman does get funny idea and she could run off, bap! unless she husband and he family and them real take she in hand.

Niehoff and Niehoff suggest that the numerical disparity between men and women actually worked to the advantage of the latter. There was fierce competition for the available Indian women since the Indian men refused to be polluted by taking black concubines. As a result, the Indian woman came to be seen as a prize.[20] Speckmann reports that the same feeling held true in Surinam.[21] But prize or not, she was still 'owned' to all intents and purposes. As such, few women have good things to say about their treatment at the hands of their in-laws, although they may view the experience as having been a necessary discipline. 'They did grind me up like *massala*',[22] says one lady, 'but it did bring them luck. I give them ten children, and now I have sons of my own.'

FAMILY LIFE IN POST ESTATE DAYS

When the indenture system ended during World War I, the private estates began to sell off some of their lands to the Indians, who eagerly began to buy. The dispersal of the families during the indenture made it difficult for the corporate line of brothers to be reestablished, and so the newly acquired land came to be thought of as the exclusive property of he who already had the recognized social power as a result of his marriage-making activities: the father, who now once again could be considered a patriarch. The land was therefore no longer a jointly held property, but was the individual property of the father, who made the ultimate decisions about its disposition. This situation had the paradoxical result of giving young men an excuse to wander or seek jobs elsewhere, since they were not personally tied to the land, and yet of binding them inextricably to their fathers wherever they happened to go, because the father retained the last word about what would happen to the property after his death. Thus, neither the joint line of brothers, nor the patrilocal household per se was retained. In their place there arose a family in which all power — social, economic and spiritual — was concentrated in the hands of the newly reconstituted patriarch.

During World War II, many young Indian men gladly joined the services or went abroad to study trades. They tasted the formerly forbidden fruits of individual autonomy and responsibility, and yet, within the context of the Indian world in Trinidad, they were under sacred obligations to the father who, in a very real sense, controlled their futures.

In the Indian value system, a man remains a child until his own father is dead, even if he has children and grandchildren of his own.

It should be noted that in discussing the Indian family, this article is not strictly concerned, as in Speckmann, with the 'household group', defined as 'a domestic unit whose members share the residence, have at their disposal a joint kitchen, and have one common purse from which all expenses are met'.[23] Despite the prevalence of such household units in Speckmann's Surinamese sample, such physical extensions of the family have been rare in Trinidad ever since the young men were 'mobilized' after the indenture ended. Particularly in the more acculturated villages like Zenobia, separate residences are inhabited by what are, to all intents and purposes, nuclear families, occasionally with what Speckmann calls 'co-resident kin' (consanguineal or affinal, usually unmarried siblings of either the man or woman, or children of a previous marriage).

The general pattern in Zenobia is now for a young man to get a job wherever he can, even if it means leaving his father's village. If the job is sufficiently far away, the young man is within his rights to decide to live away from home. People indicate that anything further than a half-hour drive if the man has a car, or a two-transfer ride by bus or public taxi would qualify as 'too far'. Of greater interest, however, are the young men who find employment within the circuit of reasonable transportation, but who are working at some sort of skilled technical or professional job. Such jobs include anything at the Texaco refinery (even 'common labour' at the refinery is considered by the people to be 'skilled' even if it entails the same sort of menial work that might be required at the sugar refinery) or anything involving the law or medicine. Curiously enough, teaching is not considered to be part of this 'skilled' occupational group. The men in the 'skilled' category, too, are within their rights to set up their own homes, either in Zenobia or in one of the several adjacent villages. In 1970-71, of the eighty men between the ages of eighteen and forty with family ties in Zenobia who fit into the 'skilled' category, seventy-four had fathers still living; sixty-eight of these, however, lived in their own houses, forty-seven in Zenobia itself. Two of the men in this group who were living with family were living not in their parents' home but with their grandparents, and in both cases, the grandparents were ill and/or senile and were completely under the care and protection of the more or less independent grandsons. By 1973, one of these sets of grandparents had died, leaving the young man fully on his own, although three of the men formerly living in their own homes had subsequently moved in with their aged grandparents who had in the interim grown incapable of maintaining their own homes.

Despite what may seem to be a trend toward the nuclear family style of family life, many of the families in Zenobia are 'spiritually' extended households insofar as they continue to celebrate family *pujas* (household prayers) in common, and insofar as all members feel compelled to support one another in terms of mutual provision of goods and services from time to time. In Zenobia, 178 out of 211 Indian residences surveyed are 'nuclear', in that they are inhabited only by a husband and wife and their children or other dependents. But when the criterion of ritual commonality is invoked, this number is reduced to only thirty-two autonomously functioning 'households'. The number is further reduced if the somewhat more tenuous links to families living in more distant villages are included.

SEXUAL POLITICS, MARRIAGE, AND THE MAINTENANCE OF THE INDIAN FAMILY SYSTEM

The figures cited above for one village certainly cannot be taken as definitive for Trinidad as a whole, but they are suggestive of a trend as people move out of the traditional world of the estates, in which the economy consisted almost exclusively of subsistence agriculture supplemented by sugar cane cultivation, the domestic unit shifts from a strictly patrilocal organization to one approaching neolocal nuclear residence at or shortly after marriage. Yet, this shift is not being accompanied by a total abrogation of the ties of family extension. A high percentage of even the nucleated domestic units remain extended households in terms of celebrating rituals; this holds true, one might add, even for Christian Indians. Since the classic Hindu joint family was seen as a 'unit before the gods', a miniature religious congregation in its own right, the fact that the ritual status survives even outward shifts in the structure should not be too surprising.

What is needed, therefore, is an analysis of what factors enable the Indian family to continue as an extended unit despite changing socio-economic factors favouring an emphasis on the nuclear family. Surely, the 'extended family' of today is no mere 'survival' of the classic joint family; it is a unit which is the product of a developmental sequence in Trinidad itself, and which fulfills certain important functions for the Indian community on the island now.

It is best to begin the analysis of the contemporary family with an examination of the role of marriage, and the attendant 'sexual politics' within the family group.

It is first of all important to clarify the Indian emphasis on marriage which has been sanctioned (either religiously or legally, preferably both). Rubin and Zavalloni, citing Braithwaite and Roberts, point out that while Negro unions in the West Indies characteristically go from 'consent' unions to legal marriages, Indians begin with marriage and then tolerate outside liaisons later in life.[24] This is because only in the ceremony of marriage, with the proper ritual exchange of gifts, are the relative positions of the two families made socially manifest. A private union between a man and a woman is not explicitly condemned, but it is in the interests of a patriarch to make sure that his son has at least one legal union to his credit, sooner rather than later, for the sake of the status of the family as a whole.

It is useful, therefore, to study not only the exterior structures of the family. but also the network of roles and interpersonal behaviours that characterize it. In the ideal situation, the key roles within the system are:

1. *The Father*. He owns the property and can demand supportive labour from all other members of the family. Such labour is provided without question by all unmarried children.

2. *Married Sons*. They need not live in the same household, although ordinarily they will live somewhere in the same, or in a nearby village. They owe a special obligation of ritual and moral support to their father, in addition to physical labour.

3. *Daughters-in-law*. They bring in dowries, but far more important, they are visible symbols of their families' willing abasement before the superior power and purity of their fathers-in-law.

These roles are animated into behaviour via the central family crisis of property inheritance. In the indenture days, only the good name of the family could be passed down, but now that land has been restored as an indication of differential status, the inheritance of the land takes on primary importance.

One artifact of the colonial condition was, as has been pointed out, the fact that Indian religious marriages were not considered legal by the British authorities until well after the Indians' reinvestment in land following the end of the indenture system. As a result, disruptive family fights could, and often did arise when one relation challenged the right of a technically 'illegitimate' child (i.e., one born of an unregistered religious marriage) to inherit automatically the property of the father. It therefore became customary for the father to make a property settlement on his heirs as he saw fit while he was still alive and able to command the action.[25] In some cases, this action, which could conceivably end his patriarchate and sharply reduce his personal power, resulted in situations in which 'ungrateful' children turned aged parents out of the house once the title to the property was transferred. On the other hand, people say that since the act of transfer was the dying patriarch's last expression of power, he could legitimately expect to continue to be treated with deference and respect for as long as he lived, as befitted the author of whatever power his heirs now controlled.

In any case, the disposal of land before his own death could very easily be an effective means to both personal and familial aggrandizement for the patriarch, particularly if he chose to vary the expected pattern by passing over his sons and settling the bulk of the property on a daughter (or, less commonly, a niece). Passing property to a daughter might reflect nothing more than the father's affection for a favourite child. But such an inheritance could be used, informants agree, as part of a complex 'power play'. That inheritance of land is inextricably bound up in the concept of hierarchical marital relationships is shown by the changes in household structure that result from the creation of a landed heiress.

In such a case, the normal pattern of patrilocal residence after marriage would be reversed, and the groom would be expected to join his bride on her own property, especially if he and his family were relatively poor. The shift to uxorilocality in this situation would achieve two major victories for the patriarch. In the first place, it would annex another son to the household, a man who would not only be a labourer for his wife's family, but who would also be obliged to rear his children under the aegis of his father-in-law, rather than of his own father. In the second place, the new residence arrangement would effectively eliminate the moral strain on the daughter, and hence upon her relatives. Ordinarily, the bride would be defiled by the sex act and her family would be viewed as lower than the family of the groom. But the groom's family, by consenting to his residence with his in-laws, affirms its own social 'impotence', and thus acknowledges the fact that the groom is in no real position to be socially polluting toward the girl.

The *doolaha* (groom) who lives in the orbit of his father-in-law is not, however, playing a role analogous to that of the traditional *doolahin*, for it would be considered an unpardonable breach of etiquette for the family to mistreat the young man either physically or verbally. But his residence requires him to give up whatever autonomy a young groom may have, and he can ordinarily play no part in general family decisions regarding money expenditures or ritual procedures. His only reason for agreeing to the arrangement is the promise that his own children will ultimately inherit his wife's property, and since the wife will usually remain something of a submissive Indian woman (although, of course, not so much as the traditional *doolahin*) he can expect to exercise some control over what she does with that property. Ultimately, the reversed residence rules are of benefit to a poor family seeking to annex its name to a prosperous group, and hoping to secure an inheritance at least for its grandchildren, and willing to pay the price of one generation of social humiliation for that privilege.

In the ideal situation, as expressed by contemporary informants, the bride is almost always the main victim of all these circumstances, since even when her husband moves in with her own family, she is more a tool in a larger power play than an independent agent. In reality, however, there are two different strategies concerning her victimization, two different ways in which the family roles can be arranged.

In one form, the main villain is the old patriarch's wife, the girl's mother-in-law, or *sas*.[26] She may treat the girl as a virtual personal slave, and Klass says that many a *sas* ceases all domestic work when her son marries; one of his informants is reported to have announced triumphantly, 'Me have a doolahin, now!'.[27] In this situation, the *sas* takes primary control over child-rearing decisions, and the bride may not even nurse her own children unless the *sas* gives her permission. It is the mother-in-law who metes out physical punishment as well as verbal abuse. The patriarch, who is addressed as 'Baba'[28] by the *doolahin*, is a figure of distant authority to whom all others defer. The husband is a passive player, as his mother's demands on the bride's time and energy take precedence over his, except when he demands her for intercourse.

This situation superficially resembles that of the classic Hindu joint family and its prevalence in many rural areas of Trinidad has led to the assumption that the contemporary Indians are merely replicating ancient forms. But the motivating dynamics of the situation are rather different in Trinidad now than they were in the India of old. In Trinidad, as we have pointed out, the primary motivation for the degradation of the *doolahin* is not because she is a coin of exchange, a debased breeding machine. Rather, it is because in the estate days, the relative ranking of families along a hierarchy of ritual pollution could only be maintained by some overt act of dominance. While it may have been cold comfort for the *doolahin* herself, she could at least take pride in the fact that she was not being abused because of any personal failing, but only because her husband's family found her the most convenient outlet for expressing their social ascendancy over her entire family.

It is because the Indian family has remained a ritual unit, despite its physical dispersal, that it continues to be necessary to adhere to the ancient social organizational principle of relative ritual ranking. As long as a joint family functioned as the corporate unit of traditional India, it could be seen as a solidary in-group in which the outsider (the *doolahin*) could be abused in an almost casual, offhanded manner precisely because she was an outsider, and hence somehow beneath contempt. In Trinidad, however, with the once collegial power of the family concentrated in the hands of the patriarch, through his almost exclusive control of family land, the family could not automatically assume its exclusive in-group solidarity. It could only become a solidary unit by demonstrating its distinction from other families, and the best way to do that was to achieve a marriage and flaunt the abused bride as the symbol of their power over another family.

According to the logic of this system, the patriarch holds the power, which he exercises through his wife. It is a paradoxical feature of the Indian marriage system that despite the position of subjugation to which the wife must continually bow, there is a very real sense of equality between a man and his wife. Such equality does not, of course, take the form of a woman being permitted to participate actively in an autonomous role, have her own career, and have her own life. Rather, she is seen as an extension of her husband, but, as such, she carries just as much prestige and power as he. In a sense, the marriage ceremony has united the two individuals into one personage, and their roles within the system of the household authority hierarchy are often interchangeable.

As Basham points out, 'the ancient Indian attitude to women was in fact ambivalent. She was at once a goddess and a slave, a saint, and a strumpet'.[29] In India, it was often said that it was the patriarch's wife who 'held the key to the chest' because she controlled the household finances.[30] In Trinidad, the potential for relatively greater freedom of the woman was doubtlessly enhanced by the fact that the majority of the migrants came from the lower castes whose women were traditionally freer from social constraint than were the women of the upper castes. Because of this somewhat greater female freedom, a situation developed in Trinidad in which a widowed matriarch would succeed fully to her late husband's position. In India, a widow would become subject to her married sons[31] but in Trinidad, the authority of the patriarch very often lasted after his own death for as long as the wife lived, particularly in landed families. For these reasons, the tyranny of the *sas* actually stood for the household power of the patriarch himself.

Meanwhile the son is powerless because he has no effective say in the control of the family property. He is, in effect, merely the agent of his father's power; his sexual congress with the *doolahin* is, after all, merely the last straw in his father's campaign to degrade her family. In any case, the son in this situation is propertyless, and hence socially impotent; one of the few ways in which he could manipulate the situation to his own advantage was to play the 'helpless' figure to the hilt by becoming an alcoholic.[32]

In the second form, however, the *sas* is reduced to the status of a supporting player, while the young groom takes over as what the Trinidadians call the 'big beater'. The old parents are expected to give frequent advice on everything from child psychology to techniques of love-making, but they are not supposed to 'interfere' with the husband's right to make demands on his wife. The husband punishes the children, and takes a more vigorous hand in their upbringing in all ways. The patriarch still gets his own way almost all the time, but instead of achieving this by fiat, he plays the role of the whining, 'cranky old man' to whom everyone caters mainly 'so we ain't got to hear he big mouth'.

Such a system of role relationships can only occur if the basis of the patriarch's power is gone; that is, if he has lost his land, or has already made an inheritance settlement. Even if the son has not become the sole heir of that property, he is definitionally an autonomous adult, because his father no longer has any recognizable power to control his activity. The young man thus becomes responsible for his own wife and children once they have been freed from their subservience to his father.

The change in styles of family relationships is evidenced in part by several published surveys on attitudes. In their survey of attitudes among Trinidadian adolescents, Rubin and Zavalloni found that:

> Changing attitudes, toward early marriage, parental choice of partners, and traditional women's roles are evident among East Indian girls. In their autobiographies, they spontaneously indicate plans to delay marriage, and eventually to combine it with a career.[33]

In fact, East Indian girls are apt to identify an outside career, rather than a traditional family role as the primary source of satisfaction.[34] Their desire to achieve such autonomy may indicate that 'they also aspire to break with the traditional pattern of male dominance in the East Indian nuclear family'.[35] One teenage Indian girl wrote in her autobiographical essay:

> My purpose for not having more [children] is because when I realize the 'trials and tribulations' my mother underwent with her large family, it just breathes hate in me to have more than three.[36]

All of this contrasts sharply with the traditional Indian women's view of women's roles. As was shown in a survey of older women,'... East Indian mothers feel their primary duty is to care for the child's happiness and well-being at the expense of other responsibilities and desires'.[37]

This shift in attitude is also illustrated by an informal survey of some fifty middle-aged ladies in Zenobia, at least forty-five of whom described themselves as having lived through the type of experience typical of the first family relationship system. Thirty-eight, however, reported that 'times has changed', since they were unable to control their own daughters-in-law in the same way. The brides, for their part, were less positive about the changes, many of them resenting the lingering authority of their mothers-in-law. But the general attitude was summed up by one recent bride who said, 'The old sow think she the boss, but I go show she. I'm gettin' a job at the dry-good store in town, and then I be out from under she hand all day long.'

The adoption of one or the other style of family relationship is not, however, a matter of personal whim. The most significant concomitant of family styles is socio-economic: families still deeply involved in land are known as the 'sugar people' (in the sense that at least half their income is derived either from selling their own cane or from working as salaried labour in the cane fields or at the sugar refinery) and they typically manifest the first role relationship style; but 'oil people' (those involved in one of the 'modern' jobs, preferably at Texaco) are moving into the second situation. In the Zenobia area, there are eighty families classifiable as 'oil people', and 124 as 'sugar people', with at least seven doubtful or marginal cases. Sixty-eight of the oil families live in the 'new' type of family relationship (as determined both by personal observation and by the assessment of a trusted key informant) while 117 of the sugar families live in the 'old' style.[38]

CONCOMITANTS OF THE CHANGE IN FAMILY STYLE

It would however, be naive to assume that changes in income were the sole causes of changes in the family structure. Getting rich is not necessarily a correlate of changing family type. There are at least three extreme wealthy sugar families in Zenobia, all of them 'traditional' in family type, although poor, barely getting-by 'modern' workers have already moved into the second style. The critical factor seems to be the social relationships characteristic of these two types of income gathering, rather than the size of the income itself.

Sugar cane, even in the modern era of nationalized estates and more or less mechanized production, is still deeply entrenched in the values of the old plantations. There, the principal social relationship was one based on clientage, a family obligation to the local authorities who owned the plantation or who ran the mill. These relationships were reciprocal, to be sure, but they were also strictly hierarchical, 'we people' ranked well below the 'big pappies' who were owed service in return for various sorts of patronage favours.

The evolving Indian family structure of the estate days fit in well with this social system. The patriarch was, in a way, encouraged to concentrate familial power (both economic and ritual) in his own hands because of the nature of sugar cultivation. Sugar cultivation requires a large labour force, ordinarily of the nature of the 'field gang', rather than of individual skilled labourers. The family, working its own little plot and selling its produce to the mill, needed to be a power-conserving unit; that is, all authority to speak for the family and to deal with outsiders had to be concentrated in one person, as the 'big pappies' could not be expected to deal individually with every one of the 'little people' on their estates.

If sugar cultivation is based on inherited, family obligations, and a group effort in production, 'oil' (a term which covers all of the 'more modern' occupations) is explicitly based on individual autonomy. One does not inherit a job at Texaco the way one inherits a position in the estate. One gets a job at the refinery on objective professional criteria, not because one has contracted to bring vegetables to the chairman of the board. Moreover, the oil field workers' union, after the fashion of most labour unions, has provided a pension that covers the worker and his family, but the union's definition of 'family' includes only the man's wife and children, not all of the other relations to whom he may owe obligations under the old system. It thus becomes necessary for 'oil people' to be involved in a style of family relationships that could fit in with the social — not the economic — aspect of their jobs. For oil people, land inheritance remains critical, not because it provides income, but because it is still a marker of differential status. The family therefore remains a vehicle for the transmission of social and spiritual rank, regardless of differences in its structural arrangements.

IMPLICATIONS IN THE CHANGE OF FAMILY STYLE

According to Mandelbaum, the Indian family even in India has traditionally been flexible enough to adapt to changing social and economic conditions.[39] As in Trinidad, one change which is becoming more clearly defined in India is the new interpretation of the 'family roles of women'.[40]

That the changing nature of family relationships, as expressed most clearly in the shifting nature of intrafamilial 'sexual politics', is responding to conditions in contemporary Trinidad beyond basic economic developments is indicated by an appraisal of some recent political developments in Zenobia.

Despite official policy statements to the contrary, Trinidad's two main political parties are 'racial' in character, i.e., a black and an Indian party. The Indian party, the Democratic Labour Party (D. L. P.) was long content to play along with the black government in order to be able to hand out patronage to rural constituents. The sterility of this policy was revealed when Black Power became a major ideological force on the island in 1970; the Indians, long proud of not being 'black', paid the price for their racism and found themselves and their property attacked (verbally more often than physically, so far) with even greater vehemence than that reserved for the whites. In the wake of the army mutiny of April 1970, the D. L. P., prompted by some of the younger members of its leadership, engineered a merger with one of the Black Power splinter parties, despite howls of outrage from conservative Indians in the countryside. The new Indian political elite realized that in Black Power the creoles had an ideology capable of effecting a sweeping renovation of the social structure of the island; at the same time, the blacks were too disorganized to put through the revolution which they so eloquently advocated. The D. L. P., on the other hand, saw itself as an extension of the Indian kin group, a factionalized, but organized set of relationships of dominance and power. The 'new breed' saw the merger as a way to channel the revolutionary potential of Black Power ideology through the organized structure of Indian social reforms. This compromise with the long-despised blacks has become even more necessary now, lest the Indians 'lose' Trinidad as their cousins have already 'lost' Uganda. The merger ultimately failed, however, because the new D. L. P. leaders continued to rely on the 'patriarchal' role of the powerful patron demanding unquestioning support from those in a more debased social position. In attempting to achieve their ends by fiat, they failed to realize that most of their adherents were already involved in the new social relationships of 'oil' and in new styles of family organization.

The political experience of the older generations of Indians was shaped by the Canefield Workers' Union, a paternalistic group which had been the power base of the now discredited older leaders of the D. L. P. The union, the *pandit's* association (which regulated the religious life of the island's Hindus) and the family were considered to be 'all one thing' by the Indians, and, indeed, the leadership roles of all three overlapped in various rural districts. The new Indian elite, however, gained its experience in the industrial trade unions which emphasize 'progress' and 'responsibility', specifically of the working man to his family — his wife and children who are supported by the union's pension, not the extended family of the old Indians. The new elite, then, uses the theme of new family responsibilities to help sell the goals of political organization and more nearly radical action. The D. L. P. leaders attempted to attain those same goals by utilizing styles of relationship that were hierarchical and 'sugar', failing to realize that the people most inclined to follow them preferred to reach their goals via the relationships of 'oil' and resented the re-imposition of the older style.

At the heart of this activity is the 'selling' of new women's roles. Typifying this attitude was a young D. L. P. worker who shocked many, but delighted others in the district by bringing his wife out as a campaign co-chairperson during the 1971 election. In this capacity, she made speeches and distributed literature while driving around the village and its environs in a loudspeaker van. As the man put it:

> I know a lot of these boys is sayin' 'Tommy ain't much of a man — he let his wife get up
> and make speech.' But them that knows me knows I'm still the boss in my house, and if
> Sarita act sassy, is 'licks for she', like they say. But you know, man, that woman is smart like
> hell, and she's a good talker, too. And we Indians is never going to get ahead in this place if
> all these intelligent women is sitting around in their dasheen-patch[41] pretending to be igno-
> rant. I ain't care what my father and them say. I running my own house, and Sarita is my
> wife, and maybe together we'll get somewhere better.

It was noted earlier that alcoholism was, in part, a significant disease of the older style of family relationships, and in Trinidad, Alcoholics Anonymous is almost exclusively an Indian club. It is therefore important to note that A. A. members enthusiastically endorse the official A. A. policy of emphasizing the role of the man's wife in his recovery, and its members in Trinidad pitch 'progress and modern living' as well as sobriety, and an important part of their message is the injunction to treat wives as helpmates, rather than as domestic slaves.

SUMMARY AND CONCLUSIONS

The Indian family in Trinidad certainly contains definite survivals or retentions of ancient forms, but the structure has undergone important changes due to social, economic and political developments in Trinidad itself.

To summarize:

1.   The Indians left India with an ideal family structure based upon the corporate, or joint organization of a line of brothers.

2.   Under the pressures of barrack life during the indenture, the line of brothers weakened and only the bond of father and son survived.

3.   After the indenture system ended, land again became the marker of social power, and the cane workers re-established an extended family organization — but one based on the concentrated authority of the patriarch, not on the corporate line of brothers.

4.   People involved in 'modern' jobs outside the sugar industry, at whatever level, tend to establish neolocal, nuclear family residences while maintaining ties to the wider family primarily on ritual occasions. The extended family remains as a meaningful social unit, despite the physical dispersal of its members.

5.   Familial power in all stages of this evolutionary process has been symbolized by the subjugation of the bride.

6.   In order for the special strengths of the ritually consecrated Indian family organization to be used by the Indians in achieving a place in the political sun of modern Trinidad, a re-assessment of the key roles of the family's women is being made.

7.   Therefore, although there is every likelihood that the spiritually extended family will survive in Trinidad, at least for another generation, it seems just as likely that the

family within the next decade will be organized around another set of principles of relationship, due to different interpretations of the role of the bride. This new style will represent the third phase of the development of the Indian family in Trinidad.

NOTES

1. Raymond T. Smith, 'Culture and Social Structure in the Caribbean: Some Recent Work in Family and Kinship Studies', in *Black Society in the New World*, ed. Richard Frucht (New York: Random House, 1971), pp. 251-72.

2. Ibid, p. 449.

3. A. L. Basham, *The Wonder that was India.* (New York: Grove Press, 1959), p. 155.

4. David G. Mandelbaum, *Society in India*, 2 vols. (Berkeley: University of California Press, 1970), p. 34.

5. K. M. Kapadia, *Marriage and Family in India* (London: Oxford University Press, 1959), p. 246.

6. Mandelbaum, *Society in India*, p. 201.

7. Morton Klass, *East Indians in Trinidad: A Study of Cultural Persistence* (New York: Columbia University Press, 1961), p. 121.

8. Basham, *The Wonder that was India*, p. 167.

9. Mandelbaum, *Society in India*, p. 99.

10. Ibid, p. 42.

11. Leo Davids, 'The East Indian Family Overseas', *Social and Economic Studies* 13, (1964): 383-96.

12. Chandra Jayawardena, 'Marital Stability in Two Guianese Sugar Estate Communities', *Social and Economic Studies* 9, (1969); 76-100; also Jayawardena, 'Family Organization in Plantations in British Guiana', *International Journal of Comparative Sociology* 3, (1961): 43-64.

13. Barton M. Schwartz, 'Patterns of East Indian Family Organization in Trinidad', *Caribbean Studies* 5, no. 1 (April 1965):23-36.

14. Raymond T. Smith and Chandra Jayawardena, 'Marriage and Family Amongst East Indians in British Guiana', *Social and Economic Studies* 8, (1959): 321-76.

15. Arthur Niehoff and Juanita Niehoff, *East Indians in the West Indies* (Milwaukee; Milwaukee Public Museum Publications in Anthropology #6, 1969), p. 101.

16. J. D. Speckmann, *Marriage and Kinship Among the Indians in Surinam*, (Assen: Van Gorcum and Comp. N.V., 1965), p. 150.

17. Sadhus (men) and Sadhuines (women) are wandering ascetics in classic Hindu tradition. In Trinidad they are more commonly learned, holy people who keep strictly orthodox rules of eating and other ritual practices.

18. The bride was called *doolahin* until she produced a male heir, although her in-laws could taunt her with her subjugated status by referring to her by this term even when she grew older. It has been pointed out to me by several readers of this article that the conditions herein described do not apply to Christian Indian women who were earlier to be educated (by the Presbyterian mission schools) and who were earlier permitted to get jobs away from the village/family network. This is clearly the case, although this article consciously omits discussion of the Christian Indians for two reasons: a) they are not numerically significant in Zenobia, the focus of this study, and, b) the process of Christian conversion is so widely ramified that this article, concerned as it is with sex roles in the typical (i.e. Hindu) family, cannot hope to do it justice.

19. Niehoff and Niehoff, *East Indians in the West Indies*, p. 102.

20. Ibid, p. 100.

21. Speckmann, *Marriage and Kinship*, p. 253.

22. Massala is an Indian cooking spice prepared by crushing various seeds together between flat stones.

23. Speckmann, *Marriage and Kinship*, p. 187.

24. Vera Rubin and Marisa Zavalloni, *We Wish to be Looked Upon: A Study of the Aspirations of Youth in a Developing Society* (New York: Teachers College Press, 1969), pp. 126f.

25. Klass, *East Indians in Trinidad*, p. 109.

26. The Hindu Word for mother-in-law, *sas*, is usually pronounced with appropriately venomous sibilance by the women.

27. Klass, *East Indians in Trinidad*, p. 127.

28. The term 'baba' means 'revered one' and is applied to pundits (priests) as well as one's father-in-law.

29. Basham, *The Wonder that was India*, p. 182.

30. Klass, *East Indians in Trinidad*, p. 133.

31. Basham, *The Wonder that was India*, p. 157.

32. The theme of 'playin' the fool' and acting like a child crops up constantly in the life stories of recovering alcoholics in Alcoholics Anonymous in Trinidad. The Indians do not necessarily see a causal relationship between their social impotence and their physical and mental dependence on the bottle (though at least two of my alcoholic informants stated this explicitly) but they recognize the link between 'never bein' responsible for nothing' and becoming a 'bad drunk'.

33. Rubin and Zavalloni, *We Wish to be Looked Upon*, p. 129.

34. Ibid., p. 136.

35. Ibid., p. 137-38.

36. Ibid., p. 141-42.

37. Helen B. Green, 'Socialization Values in the Negro and East Indian Subcultures of Trinidad', *Journal of Social Psychology* 64 (1964): 14.

38. Most oil workers are black, whereas most sugar people (considering the island as a whole) are Indian. This inter-ethnic relationship is another dimension of modernization and change for the Indians involved in oil.

39. Mandelbaum, *Society in India*, pp. 643-44.

40. Ibid., p. 646.

41. A dasheen plant is an edible, spinach-like vegetable. The term 'dasheen-patch' is here used as a synonym of the woman's household duties.

7

Child Socialisation, Relocation and Abandonment

The role of the family as the principal agent for the socialisation of children has been at the centre of the majority of investigations of Caribbean kinship. Indeed, for the structural functionalists this constituted the most important function of the family. Raymond Smith (1956: 146), for example, referred to the family or the domestic group as 'primarily a child-rearing unit'. Given the derogatory labelling and evaluation of family life in the Caribbean, we should hardly be surprised to find that, in general, families have been found inadequate in fulfilling this important task of raising the next generation to mature, responsible adulthood. However, in recent years the issue of childhood socialisation has been neglected by sociologists and anthropologists. It is only now that Caribbean social work research is beginning to step in and fill the void. In this chapter we describe briefly the experience of childhood and puberty, paying particular attention to discipline and punishment at home and in school and the familial roles and relationships involved in the socialisation process. From the perspective of socialisation, we then examine child relocation or shifting and child abandonment.

Childhood and puberty

In virtually all reports on family life in the Caribbean, sex and procreation are seen as natural, healthy activities which, if suppressed will cause men and women to be unwell. The production of children is welcome, acting as fundamental proof of manhood and womanhood. As Henriques (1953: 136) put it, 'complete social approval is given to having children'. The economic burden is recognised, but this is set against the value of children who assist in one's old age. Edith Clarke (1970(1957): 95-96) explained in her Jamaican study:

> Not only is sexual activity regarded as natural: it is unnatural not to have had a child and no woman who has not proved that she can bear one is likely to find a man to be

responsible for her since 'no man is going to propose marriage to such a woman'. Maternity is a normal and desirable state and the childless woman is an object of pity, contempt or derision. 'A child is God's gift' and 'nothing should be done to prevent the birth of a child'. A woman who does not have children is believed to suffer physically; she will also suffer from nervousness and headaches and may even go insane, if she does not have the full number that she is destined to have. A midwife told us that she was always asked after a birth how many 'knots' there were in the umbilical cord, as this is held to be an index to the number of children the mother was meant to bear. A barren woman may be referred to as a 'mule'. A man may even desert his wife because of her childlessness. There was a case in Orange Grove where the man left his wife because, although she had previously had a child, she bore none to him. In such cases the man may believe that 'he and his woman do not match'.

For a man, as we noted in Chapter V, producing children is a fundamental declaration of manhood. With the increased availability of contraception, the process of childbearing is more controlled, less inevitable, and the multiple births of former generations are avoided. Nevertheless, motherhood is still central to a woman's existence, virility a sign of manliness and a home without children empty and somehow lacking for they bring joy and constitute an essential component of family life.

As we trace the experience of childhood in the Caribbean, it is important to recognise that much has changed in the last generation of modernisation. At birth, the child still becomes the centre of attention and an object of intense affection for the whole household and family. There appears, however, to be more attempt to impose a routine during the early years of the child's life than was the case in the past when, according to investigators of the family in the 1940s and 1950s, infants were fed on demand, unrestrained and indulged. The previous shock for the child on reaching school and facing the strict authoritarianism of the early educational system might therefore be somewhat mitigated. In previous years, early childhood patterns were no preparation either for school or for the subsequent change in parental treatment.

In the past, school began at age five and continued usually until the child was 14 or 15 years of age. Although virtually all parents placed great value on their children's education, attendance was not always regular. Children often did not have suitable clothes. They had to complete chores at home or on the farm or, in the case of the eldest daughter, stay at home to look after younger siblings. School life required many adjustments on the part of the young child. The school day demanded routine behaviour, punctuality and restrictions on freedom, none of which were part of the child's early training. Separation from one's mother and submission to new formal authority figures as well as dietary regularity and changes in the food provided also took some getting used to. Additionally, discipline in school was often quite severe as male headmasters and teachers took over from mothers (Clarke 1970(1957): 165-167, see Article/Extract 1 at end of chapter).

At home, although warmth and affection prevailed, it began to be mixed with severity, a change which has been associated with the increasing economic cost of children as they grow up. As Clarke (1970(1957): 154) put it 'the child ceases to be a plaything and becomes instead a source of endless anxiety'. From age 5 to 6 years children were expected to undertake certain duties in the home and by the time they reached 8 years of age, gender distinctions were clearly defined. The responsibilities of boys were mainly outside the home as they were expected to collect water and wood and tend to the crops and livestock, while girls swept and tidied, washed the wares and began their own preparation for motherhood as they looked after their younger brothers and sisters (Greenfield 1966: 107). Many of these duties were completed before they began the long walk to school, often several miles over difficult terrain. There was little time for play and few toys to play with, although children in some rural communities might congregate on the village pasture to play after their chores were over (Greenfield 1966: 87). Games for boys included cricket 'played with a dried branch of the coconut tree as a bat', flying kites and football, while girls played ring games and skipping (Henriques 1953: 134). Today's children of the lower class are less burdened with domestic chores, but toys and books continue to be scarce. There is little recognition by parents of the intellectual and creative value of toys. Many play activities are discourages as 'dangerous' or 'messy' and few parents join in play with their children (Evans 1989: 182, Landman 1983: 43, 44).

In previous years, sexual exploration began early. From about age 14 to 15, teenagers were escaping from their parents' attention and covertly experimenting with sex. Indeed, as indicated earlier, many girls became pregnant with their first sexual experience in these casual relations while still at school. Although the incidence of teenage pregnancy in the Caribbean has declined over the years, this still constitutes an established pattern of family life and a source of concern for social welfare workers. What may well have changed is the knowledge among the girls of the female reproductive system. Several writers report that in previous years teenage girls were almost completely uninformed, their mothers, who were probably similarly ignorant of the facts, merely telling their daughters that once they reached a certain age they were to stay away from boys and men. The onset of menstruation was usually a shock and the specific cause of pregnancy unknown. Madeline Kerr (1952: 40) recorded the responses of her Jamaican informants as follows:

> In reply to my question as to what Dorrett would tell her eldest daughter if she came to her and asked her how babies come, she replied that she would 'drive her away from me'. I expressed surprise and she said she would tell her girls about babies at about sixteen after they had menstruated and not before ....

> She admitted that mothers told their girls nothing till they menstruated and that after menstruation they told them they should keep away from boys or else they would get babies. This was all they were told and Avis suggested that this was all it was necessary to tell them as boys and girls these days played together and knew everything. But the last time Estelle (aged nineteen and pregnant) came home Avis talked a lot to her, 'but it was too late then'....

> But children today were so bad. Boys and girls started having sex play with each other at a very early age. She believed that quite a number of boys and girls at about the age of fourteen really did have 'connection'. Of course, they went away and hid in the bush and did it so that parents never knew. This was not so in her day. I asked her how she explained it and she said that it was written in the Bible that what was concealed from the wise and prudent should be revealed to the babes and sucklings.

Mothers controlled their daughters in particular, to keep them away from the temptations of sexual activity and the ravages of boys and older men, by curtailing free time outside the home for dances and other entertainment.

> When she was seventeen she went to see her sister and as it was very late she stayed the night. When she went home next morning her mother would not let her in. She had to go back and fetch her sister to prove where she had been. Girls like to go to dances

at about fifteen if their parents will let them. She never learned to dance well as she was never allowed out (Kerr 1952: 44).

When the inevitable happened, the reaction of mothers was severe. Although girls tried to hide their pregnancies, their efforts were in vain and incidents of mothers who threw their daughters out of the house are legend in the Caribbean. Most researchers, however, also report that the pregnant girls would seek refuge with a relative and that, after a period of cooling off, they were able to return to their parental homes as their mothers began to delight in the role of grandmother.

From the perspective of childhood development, few boys or girls experienced an adolescent period and no attempt was made 'either at home or in school to prepare the child for the conflicts of a psychological and social nature which are attendant upon adolescence' (Henriques 1953: 134). Boys, if they did not manage to migrate, were sent directly to work alongside fully-grown men and girls became involved in housework and motherhood. As Madeline Kerr (1952: 80) commented:

> It is in fact not easy to write about adolescence in Jamaica because there is really so little to say. It is simply a period of very vague transition. It is very doubtful whether the peasants even recognise it as a phase. If a child shows adult behaviour he is sometimes called 'a force ripe man' but there does not seem to be a specific term for adolescence, at least not in the villages known to the writer. Girls and boys are children at school one month, and a few months later they may themselves be parents.

Discipline and punishment

After an easygoing first four to five years of life during which the child is petted and spoiled, discipline both at home and at school becomes severely enforced through 'shouting' and 'flogging' or 'beating'. Children are punished in this way for lying, stealing, disobedience, impoliteness and not completing their chores. 'Playing in the house', 'crying too much' and 'not eating the meal provided' also constitute misdemeanours which warrant a 'beating' (Evans 1989: 187, see Article 2 at end of chapter). But although some occurrences of child abuse have been reported in the literature (Henriques 1953: 131), these are rare. The language of punishment may be loud and brutal (Clarke 1970(1957): 156-157), but the reality does not usually involve mental or physical cruelty. For one thing, it is administered by the mother more often than not, with the more severe 'beatings' from the father usually in the form of threats (Clarke 1970(1957): 156, Smith 1956: 68, 135). Kerr's account offered a graphic description of child discipline in Jamaica in the last generation.

> If you talk with mothers about what they teach their children it appears that upbringing is strict and discipline severe. Adults, too, say how strict their mother was with them and how parents are getting very lax nowadays. Children are taught not to lie, not to steal, not to be rude. Being rude seems to vary from cursing your parents, not doing what you are told, not hearing when you are called, making slight gestures, showing you don't want to do something which you have been told to do, to forbidden sexual play or intercourse.

> Henry said he was taught not to tell lies, or steal but he still took the milk and sugar. He was flogged for doing it. His mother is not a "playing woman"; she is very serious when she is vexed and "will lash your head off" during this time when you have taken things she didn't give you. He was not allowed to join in his mother's conversations. If

there was anything he wanted to ask her when she was talking he would ask her but immediately after he "would have to find himself at the other end of the yard" or he would get a flogging after the person had left. He has been flogged many times for not running away when his mother is talking to someone. Sometimes he had to pass them; his mother would look at him and that meant that he was not to pass.

They were not to be rude to anyone, elders especially. They had to learn by experience. Their mothers did not lecture. When they did wrong they would know it was wrong only when scolded or flogged.

Nearly everyone says that he has been strictly brought up and great emphasis is laid on flogging. Yet you seldom see a child being beaten, except in the schools. What seems to happen is that a mother loses her temper and hits the child either with her hand or stick or a strap. The children do not seem to be as frightened of their parents as they would be if some of the flogging stories were not phantasy. The term flogging too, is misleading. It seems to mean generally a smacking. In some cases there is definite cruelty but not I think as often as the stories told would lead one to believe (Kerr 1952: 42).

In general, the attitude to discipline is rather a paradoxical one. As in all places, there are parents who are really physically cruel to their children, but this is not common. What is usual, however, are blood curdling threats. So again the pattern of reaction to a phantasy is promulgated. The child reacts to a cruelty pattern which does not usually exist. The pattern is so strong that if one talks to adults about their upbringing, one of the main topics is severity. Yet they are seldom able to give concrete instances. The almost ceremonial turning out of the pregnant girl is a good example of this category of behaviour. Disciplinary efforts seem to be a gesture rather than a real attempt to alter behaviour. In fact behaviour never is altered, the girl has her baby and the children go on being rude. The gesture seems to be just another attempt at lip service to this secondary pattern with its unrealisable modes of behaviour (Kerr 1952: 45).

The futility of punishment as a means of altering behavioural patterns has also been reported by other researchers. Henriques (1953: 133) has contrasted the values of home and school.

Teachers attempt to instil the virtues of truthfulness, honour, and gentleness. But it is a losing fight against the home environment. The child returns every afternoon to the meanness of perhaps one room and is unable to put what he has learned into practice. The average lower class youth is taught at home to regard anyone in a superior social position as fair game for deceit. Teachers complain that it is very difficult to make their charges realize the error of lying and the virtue of truthfulness.

Clarke (1970 (1957): 158) described parental attempts at disciplining their children as contradictory, as parents punish their children for stealing and other behaviours which they themselves exhibit and condone.

Though the punishment may be severe, the consequences have not necessarily been interpreted as all bad. In a study conducted in Trinidad in the early 1960s, Helen Green interviewed mothers and mothers-to-be in a hospital ward. Although we must bear in mind that what these women said about their child-rearing practices might not coincide with what they actually do, Green made an important point about the positive effects of the methods of punishment used by black women in instilling the qualities of self-reliance and personal independence at an early age.

> Punishments by Negro mothers are definitely of the object-deprivation or bodily punishment kind. They emphasize the child's culpability as though he alone made the decision to be bad and he alone must pay for it by harsh punishment. The child's sense of autonomy would seem to be increased through these measures (Green 1964: 12).

From a more contemporary perspective, research and information on the impact of physical discipline on children is sadly lacking. In a short paper, however, Elaine Arnold (1982) dealt in general terms with the use of corporal punishment in child socialisation in the Caribbean. She examined briefly the explanations for child 'beating' that have been put forward, including those which refer to origins in Africa (see Landman et al. 1983: 48-49) or the brutality of slavery and those which refer to displacement theory as mothers and fathers redirect and vent their frustration and anger on their children either by severe and unwarranted physical beating or by a ritualised punishment which relieves their own anxiety. Corporal punishment, she added, is reinforced by biblical admonitions to the effect that to spare the rod is to spoil the child.

The parents with whom Arnold discussed the question of discipline maintained that a badly-behaved child is seen as a public disgrace, a direct reflection of parental incompetence and negligence which ultimately led to legal liability for child neglect. It is interesting to note that Arnold's paper indicated that parents seemed unable to conceive of methods of punishment other than 'beating'. Even those parents of a higher status with potentially more opportunity to punish by withholding gratification, resorted to physical means. Socialisation by conversation and communication, talking 'with' rather than 'at' children, appeared to be virtually non-existent. As Elsa Leo-Rhynie (1993: 17) has stated:

> There is a lack of verbal interaction in many family environments: adults do not talk to children; they exclude children from their talk; they complain that the children talk too much and ask too many questions; and they do not provide experiences for children about which they can talk. Many parents are unaware of the value of developing language to be used as an instrument of thought, description and analysis and unaware also of its importance in encouraging initiative and creativity. In many homes, language is used almost exclusively to express anger and disappointment and to reprimand; children are 'shut up' because parents are tired or busy, and the silence and lack of communication among family members is masked by the noise of the television set or the radio.

Paradoxically, it is often said that Caribbean parents agree that corporal punishment is an ineffective means of discipline and, while they vividly recall their own harsh experiences of 'beatings' as children, they argue that children are expected to believe that they are beaten because they are loved. Recent research in St Christopher (St Kitts) by Ronald Rohner, Kevin Kean and David Cournoyer (1991) has challenged this conclusion. The study indicated that, although the children who were interviewed believed that beatings were an appropriate form of punishment and although beatings were less frequently administered that the widely-held belief in them would suggest, those children who were beaten perceived themselves to be rejected in direct proportion to the punishments they had received. Additionally, the researchers concluded that there was significant evidence to establish a link between physical punishment and the psychological maladjustment of the child, whether or not that child believed in the suitability of the penalty.

At the outset of this article we asked whether physical punishment is related directly to the psychological adjustment of Kittitian children, or whether punishment is associated with psychological adjustment only (or primarily) insofar as youths perceive punishment to be a form of caretaker rejection. The answer now seems to be clear: increasingly severe punishment is modestly but significantly related to youths' negative adjustment. However, Kittitian children also tend to experience themselves to be rejected in direct proportion to the frequency and severity of punishment received. And the more rejected they perceive themselves to be, the more impaired their psychological adjustment. The direct impact of physical punishment on youths' adjustment, combined with the indirect impact, mediated through perceived rejection, is substantial. Youths' beliefs about physical punishment do not appear to have a significant effect on these relationships. That is, the psychological adjustment of youths who believe parents should punish them physically tends to be impaired to the same degree as the adjustment of youths who do not share this cultural belief (Rohner, Kean and Cournoyer 1991: 690-691).

In the final analysis and from the perspective of future research, the issue of child punishment in the Caribbean continues to provide us with unanswered questions and unresolved paradoxes. Herman and Hermione McKenzie, for example, have noted the inconsistency repeatedly reported in the literature between the warm love and harsh discipline of children and made the following three theoretical suggestions for further research:

(i) Perhaps children are viewed as being quite unformed in character and naturally prone to extreme naughtiness rather than goodness, thus requiring harsh restraints if desirable characters are to be created; (ii) Perhaps adults turn to their children rather than to their spouses and other adults for warm emotional relationships, and this may lead them to judge childish misdemeanours harshly, as if they had been committed with an adult's experience and judgement; (iii) In spite of the love for children, the circumstances under which they are born and reared often create parental tensions and there maybe an underlying ambivalence which expresses itself in great rage triggered off by minor childish misbehaviour (McKenzie and McKenzie 1971: 19).

Hyacinth Evans (1989: 189-193) has explored the implication of these Caribbean socialisation patterns, for example of father absence on the development of boys' masculinity and girls' social interaction with males, of the scarcity of toys and play on children's creativity and the lack of books and verbal communication on oral expression and cognitive development, and of the frustration of parents who have high aspirations for their children but display conflicting values and actions in the home.

From the perspectives of child psychology and social welfare, Arnold proposed a solution in terms of parental counselling. Noting that much attention has been paid to the physical needs of children, she stressed that institutional support services and parents should acquire a knowledge of childhood emotional growth and development and skills in effective parenthood (Arnold 1982: 144). It is imperative that policies and programmes to improve parenting skills take place with a knowledge of the past and present of child-rearing and development in the Caribbean. A Jamaica-based association of organisations called 'Parenting Partners' has taken up the challenge by preparing a comprehensive two-volume manual (Parenting Partners n. d.) which provides training and guidelines for facilitators in the conduct of community-based courses in effective parenting. But a research gap remains. Training and counselling in disciplinary procedures, in particular, must be informed by research and information on Caribbean cultural principles and practices and guided by theoretical perspectives such as those suggested by the McKenzies.

Roles and relationships of socialisation

The researchers on Caribbean family relations mentioned in previous chapters are in unanimous agreement on the importance of the mother's role in child socialisation when compared with that of the father, which has been generally described as 'marginal'. For a Caribbean woman, public admiration is achieved through the functions of motherhood, from the rearing of well brought-up children who are a credit to her. We also noted that, although a man may take pride in his children, his reputation appears to depend less on the functions of fatherhood and more on virility; on the impregnation of women and the physical reproduction of children. According to Smith (1956: 227-228), the very marginality of the man serves to enhance the status of women as mothers. Becoming a mother constitutes a radical change to the daily routine of a woman or young girl, whereas a man's lifestyle may continue much as before. Children are said to be 'woman's business'.

The relationship between a mother and child constitutes the core of Caribbean family structure. The bond is close, combining intense love and affection with, as we have noted, some fairly harsh punishment. Mother and child are continually together in companionship and interdependence (Clarke 1970(1957): 158). The relationship is formed on the day the child is born and lasts until the death of the mother.

> The bond between mother and child is the strongest in the whole matrix of social relationships, and it endures through time as a strongly reciprocal relationship. A woman with children will always find ways to provide for them .... When a woman's children grow up she can always depend on them for help, in the form of money or presents of food, and they will make sure that she has a roof over her head as long as she lives (Smith 1956: 65).

Recently, however, research among working-class Jamaicans presents some disturbing conclusions concerning the lack of interaction and communication between mothers and their children as a result of parental migration, illiteracy, physical exhaustion from low-status employment and household chores, stress and irritability (Evans 1989: 183-184).

By extension, the child's relationship with its maternal grandmother is also close. When children live with their grandmother, they often refer to her as 'Mama' whether or not their own mother is present. She may well function in place of the mother, but the more usual relationship has been described as follows:

> There is a normal grandchild-grandparent relationship which is one of affectionate indulgence, and a kind of equality. A grandmother, in particular, will often identify herself with her grandchildren and take their part in quarrels they have with their own mother. When a young girl has been forbidden to go to a dance by her mother, she will often appeal to her grandmother for support in her pleas. It is commonly said that grandparents spoil their grandchildren, and old men certainly display far greater affection for their grandchildren than they ever do towards their own children (Smith 1956: 144).

Similarly, siblings by the same mother generally have a closer and more enduring relationship than those who share a father.

In contrast to the enduring and preoccupying role of motherhood, that of father is much less demanding. His major duty is financial, seeing that money is available for food and clothing and the necessities required for school (Greenfield 1966: 104-105). Concomitantly, the father-child relationship is formal and distant and in many cases non-existent and apparently unnecessary to the child's existence.

> If their father does not live in the same household group, then he has literally no rights over the children in the majority of cases. Children derive practically nothing that is of importance from their fathers. They do not inherit property of a kind that is crucial in affording them the means of livelihood (though they do inherit land and sometimes houses from both their parents); they do not acquire membership in any group primarily on the basis of patri-filiation and they do not suffer if they never even see their father .... Every individual must have a father of course, but it is not crucial to have a father with whom one has a concrete and definite social relationship (Smith 1957: 147).

Fathers are supposed to discipline their children but, as we noted earlier, more often then not their involvement is as a threat, more hypothetical than real. On the occasions when they do physically punish their children, the beating is severe and remembered well into adult years. Fathers are more aloof and children's behaviour in their presence is expected to be well-mannered and silent (Clarke 1970(1957): 159, 161). But the realities of what it means to be a father in the Caribbean and the father-child relationship are only now being systematically investigated, perhaps because the father has hitherto been perceived as remote and generally absent. As a result, we are left with seemingly paradoxical conclusions. Fathers are said to be 'marginal' even to be fantasy figures (Kerr 1952) and it is the mother who fathers the children (Clarke 1970 (1957): 161) and yet, the father-figure is described as 'a very real person' for the majority of children (Smith 1956: 135). Recent comments of Caribbean men on their performances as fathers and the recognition of the minimal expectations of fatherhood, warrant at least another look at the concept of 'male marginality' that has dominated the literature from the start(see Barrow forthcoming 16). The male respondents in the study conducted by the Caribbean Child Development Centre (CCDC) to which we referred in Chapter V, claimed significant levels of involvement in child-care activities. On average and on a daily basis, 67 per cent reported that they play with their children; 60 per cent 'reason' with them, that is, engage in discussions which promote maturity and an understanding of life in general; 44 per cent stay with their children; 42 per cent help with homework; and 31 per cent tidy their children (Brown et al. 1993: 164). Approximately half of the men interviewed in the study expressed satisfaction with their performance as fathers (Brown et al. 1993: 169). Even if we allow for the possibility of exaggerated reporting, these results hardly qualify as evidence of overall male marginality within the culturally defined parameters of Caribbean fatherhood (see also Evans 1989: 185, Landman et al. 1983: 42, 49). But there were exceptions. The fathering of 'outside' children was reported in the study as 'neglectful' and as 'a most disturbing finding' (Brown et al. 1993: 163-168). Given the large numbers of outside children in the Caribbean, this constitutes a cause for concern for social policy.

Relocation and abandonment

A common feature of Caribbean family life is the residential separation of mother and child as the care of young children is entrusted to other relatives. Significantly and perhaps to be expected, the search for someone to fulfil the father role does not occur, except in so far as a single woman will try to find a man to provide economic support for herself and her children. George Roberts and Sonia Sinclair have commented on the situation in Jamaica. In cases of this kind the mother relocates her children because she is unable to care for them herself. The fundamental cause is economic, relating to the mother's financial inability to support her children and her need to find someone to look after them while she engages in income-genera-ting work outside the household (Roberts and Sinclair 1978: 166). It is normally the maternal grandmother who functions in place of the mother.

> One of the commonest ways in which children are brought up in a home other than their parents' takes the form of the mother establishing a family while still a resident in her parental home and later leaving that home to set up one of her own. If this involves her migrating to some other part of the country she is often unable to take her children with her and leaves them with the grandmother, whose readiness to assume responsibility for them is a central aspect of this pattern of childrearing in the society. It may be intended that the children should spend only a limited period with the grandmother, that is until the mother is satisfactorily settled in her new community. But in most cases the result is that the children remain in the grandmother's home for a very long period. Another way in which children are brought up outside of their parents' home arises when the woman establishes her own family union away from the parental household, and then finds herself unable to support her children. In this case she may resort to the device of asking her own mother or some other relative to take care of the children. Again this may, initially, be taken as a temporary measure, but may become permanent because of the failure of the mother to improve her economic condition sufficiently to resume responsibility for the upkeep of her children (Roberts and Sinclair 1978: 161).

About 30 per cent of the women in the overall sample selected by Roberts and Sinclair had sent their children to be cared for by relatives or friends. As might be expected, the overwhelming majority of the children involved came from visiting unions and, though mothers of all ages were involved, most were in their late 20s. The majority (62 per cent) of the children who are not living with their mothers are raised by their maternal grandmothers (Roberts and Sinclair 1978: 162-163). It is interesting to note though, that in over a quarter of the cases, fathers and paternal grandmothers were involved.

In Chapter IV we examined patterns of 'child shifting' in the Caribbean and the theoretical rationale which sought to explain the practice as a 'responsive strategy' to economic circumstances. The relocation of children was perceived as an 'adaptive mechanism' whereby economic resources and responsibilities were balanced out in the context of economic marginality and flexible household composition. The general conclusion reached from this perspective was that all was well with mother and child. But the pattern also has implications for the socialisation of children, not all of which have been favourably evaluated.

On the one hand, are the conclusions of the study conducted in Trinidad by Green (1964) to which we referred earlier in this chapter. Responses by mothers to questions concerning their child-rearing practices indicated what Green calls an 'extra-family involvement' as a positive socialisation value. Children are encouraged to cope while their mothers are working or engaged in household chores and, at the same time, trained for 'social trust and belongingness' as they are taught that socialising and cooperating with other people within and outside the family circle is important. The relocation of children fits well into this cultural pattern.

Negro mothers carry most of the disciplinary responsibility in the family. In this capacity they emphasize, even for little children, the importance of cooperation and getting along pleasantly. Confidence in benefits derived from others is seen in the Negro tendency to arrange for the transfer of a child to other households better able to help him or to control him (Green 1964: 10).

Leo-Rhynie (1993: 15) also concedes that there may be some compensation for the child within the extended family circle.

Maternal deprivation, particularly in early childhood, can result in retardation of social, physical and intellectual development. The absence of the mother from the home can, however, be compensated for by the extended family unit which has, in the past, been a source of healthy, happy interrelationships within the home. In addition, the diversity of these relationships makes the environment a stimulating one where the interactions with parents, siblings, grandparents, uncles and aunts, cousins and non-kin adults and children are warm and caring. The child can gain from this diversity and grow within a stable, secure environment. These relationships also benefit the elderly members of the family who are not isolated but continue to feel a sense of human involvement. Where, however, inter-relationships are unhappy and unhealthy then insecure, unsatisfactory environments are created and the effects on the child can be very damaging.

However, in the majority of interpretations, relocation is viewed as something of a last resort with the costs outweighing the benefits (Evans 1989: 181-182). In most cases it is economic necessity or serious ill health that prevents a mother from keeping her children at home with her(Landamn et al. 1983:49). Clarke expresses concern at the impact of this pattern of familial instability on the development of the children involved, especially in cases where this entails the separation of mother and child.

So far as children in lower-class working homes are concerned therefore, the majority live, during their most formative years, in danger of the disruption at any moment of the closest kinship ties. Although it is a general pattern and not a unique individual experience, the effect of this instability in the relationships between his parents has a profound effect on the development of parent-child roles, and particularly that between father and child. The child who sees his mother turned out of the home for another woman may give expression to his hostility against the father by openly taking his mother's side .... Consciously or unconsciously he learns that it is to his mother he must look for any security or permanence in human relationships. In accordance with the general concept that children are 'woman's business', when the union breaks up the children are normally regarded as her responsibility. If she is immediately left destitute they may be sent to relatives or given away to friends or strangers. They, or some of them, may rejoin her when she is able to make a home for them but these denuded family homes seldom contained all the women's children. If and when she entered into another conjugal union it was rare for her to be able to have them with her. Thus siblings and half-siblings were separated and often distributed among a number of widely scattered households (Clarke 1970 (1957): 107-108) (Emphasis in original).

This extensive pattern of sibling separation means that brothers and sisters spend little of their childhood together and often lose touch with each other before adolescence (Clarke 1970(1957): 174). We also noted in Chapter IV that child shifting is not necessarily painless. For St Christopher (St Kitts), Gussler (1980: 196) refers to mothers,

> who have had to find other homes for one or more of their children, despite the anxiety this causes to mother and child alike. If a woman's own mother can assume part of the burden, then the anxiety is less, because women feel that the grandmother will provide the love and care young ones are thought to require. No one else, the women told me, can really be trusted to adequately look after your children. Yet it often becomes necessary to send them to other kin, to friends, or to (sometimes) virtual strangers, who have the room and resources to provide for them.

Even grandmothers, old and unable to cope, cannot always substitute adequately and most of the children who 'run the streets' as groups of 'scavengers' are those whose mothers have migrated (Gussler 1980: 197).

In a study conducted in Jamaica, Erna Brodber claims that child relocation extends into child abandonment. Noting that incidents of child abandonment have increased in recent years, she attributed this to the decline in kin group functioning, especially in urban areas, and concluded that the phenomenon is no different in kind from the pattern of child relocation which we have just examined, merely a more extreme form of a cultural pattern whereby children are 'passed on'.

> 'Passing on' as a means of dealing with problems of children seems to be an accepted solution. Leaving a child in a borrowed toilet, at a busy street corner, in someone's car, does not suggest an attempt to solve problems of child-caring by infanticide but are only more extreme forms of passing on to a father, a cousin or a woman who needs a child to help her in the market. This is essentially what happens with the child in the grandmother and extended families which Henriques and Clarke describe. Here we find grandchildren whose parents have passed on certain aspects of their caring to a member of their kin group. We find an even finer breakdown and transference of child-caring functions among 'yard dwellers' in the capital city's largest low-income areas. Responsibility for a child's sleeping or eating activity might be passed on to some other. Passing on of responsibility for the child has been developed to a fine point in this culture.

> Nor is 'passing on' a purely lower-income method of proceeding. The 'boarding out' of children with relatives or friends who can better assist in the child's social and educational advancement are acts of passing on. Abandonment differs from these only in kind. The facts and the figures dealing with social problems among children in Jamaica lead us then to the position that where child-caring units are felt to be inadequate children are passed on to someone, some generalised 'other' seen as more capable.

> This 'passing on' has now been taken to its ultimate limit — 'passing on' to the elements. Where the wide kin group no longer functions as in the city, passing on will be to 'others', non-kin, to buildings which are more numerous and more impersonal here, and 'to the elements'. Abandonment is only the most total and extreme form of 'passing on' (Brodber 1974: 49).

The characteristics of the children and parents involved and the causes of abandonment do indeed seem to be much the same as those of relocation. In Brodber's study most of the abandoned children had young mothers not involved in co-residential unions. The majority of the mothers were under 26 years of age and appeared to be single or perhaps in visiting unions with fathers unwilling to take care of the children (Brodber 1974: 24, 56).

However, there seem to be clear distinctions in circumstance and attitude between these practices. Brodber herself reports that many of the mothers who abandoned children were socially isolated and destitute and therefore presumably unable to find a relative to whom to 'pass on' their children. Additionally, mothers who send their children to another relative to be taken care of do keep in contact with them and intend to rejoin them at some time in the future, something which the abandoning mothers appear to have little intention of doing. Brodber also echoed the findings presented by Arnold (1982: 144) when she stated that the majority of the abandoned children are boys aged between 5 and 13 years who play truant and have become uncontrollable, a characteristic which prompts abandonment, not relocation. Finally and importantly, Brodber explored the attitudes of mothers towards child abandonment and its causes. Her informants were women who claimed to have known mothers who abandoned their babies and who might, themselves, be in the same position at a future date. Their opinions are therefore likely to give us an idea of the cultural context and value system of the mothers in question. As the following passage tells us, child abandonment in Jamaica, unlike relocation, may be understood, but is certainly not condoned.

Expression of sentiment was high on the general question of abandonment. Most mothers seemed to feel that it occurs because the woman cannot afford to care for her child or because she lacks help in supporting it, not simply from the father but from anyone at all; she abandons the child because she is isolated from all sources of assistance. It seems strange, however, that the majority of mothers think that such a woman should be punished for the offence. The feeling seems to be that a woman should try to support her child, however difficult the circumstances and that she should be punished for not trying.

A number of mothers attributed abandonment simply to irresponsibility and selfishness. Thirty-two of the 208 respondents thought that abandonment could be due to the fact that the mother has no place to take the child and hoped that someone else would provide it with a better home life.

Some interviewees thought that mothers might be more likely to abandon babies if they did not know who the father was. Coupled with this, possibly as a result of it, they might not have been supported during the time of their pregnancy and might be unable to foresee any means of supporting the child. Only one mother expressed the view that deformity could be a reason for abandonment (Brodber 1974: 22).

However, studies of child relocation and shifting have not pursued similar questions and it is therefore difficult to come to definite conclusions on the parallels and contrasts between these practices which separate mother and child.

Brodber expressed grave concern about child abandonment in Jamaica and followed through by asking her informants for recommendations to deal with the problem.

We thought it would be interesting to ask of these citizens who were at least in part in a favourable position to abandon their babies, 'What steps should the government take in dealing with women who abandon their babies?' As was mentioned before, a large number of mothers recommended punishment for abandoners, indicating, we think, the high value which these people place on striving to bring up the child oneself, no matter how many obstacles there may be. Some even suggested that abandoners be given back their babies and compelled by the authorities to take care of them. Only 20.1 per cent of the total expressed sympathy for the abandoners, arguing that they should be helped by the government rather than punished. Other responses in similar vein suggested that the father not the mother should be punished. Four admitted that if one were in difficulty, the hospital was a better place than any to leave a baby (Brodber 1974: 22).

To these suggestions from her informants, Brodber added her own recommendations for solving the problem. She proposed a restructuring of bureaucratic arrangements to deal with the problem and an expansion and integration of social services dealing with the family. Additionally, like Arnold (1982: 144), she stressed the need for training and counselling in the skills and knowledge of parenthood, especially in terms of preparing young mothers to adjust to a new baby and to socialise their sons as well-adjusted youths and ultimately responsible fathers (Brodber 1974: 56-58). Most importantly from our perspective here, child abandonment is perceived as a cultural problem and therefore needs to be tackled at the level of kinship ideology and practice.

Conclusion

The study of the social welfare of family life in the Caribbean has been neglected for many years now. Since Simey's inadequate and biased efforts, there has been no comprehensive and systematic investigation of the socio-psychological impact on individual members. Although the structural functionalists emphasised the important role of the family as the major agent for childhood socialisation, not all of them proceeded to give an account of exactly how the family performed in this regard. And perhaps because the investigators who followed were anxious to rid themselves of the negative evaluations of the Caribbean family characterising the writings of their predecessors, questions of childhood socialisation and the family, questions which continued to portray the 'disfunctions' of family life in the Caribbean were avoided. Indeed, many of the inadequacies of parenting and childhood socialisation have now been attributed to poverty and urbanisation rather than Caribbean family structure (Landman et al. 1983: 50). But the bulk of recent research employs survey methods yielding quantitative results and focusses on the process of child rearing, neglecting analysis of the outcome (Evans 1989: 180). All that we have been able to provide in this chapter is a minimum outline of the role of family in the Caribbean in childhood socialisation, more perhaps to indicate the gaps and inconsistencies in our knowledge than the ways in which they have been resolved.

READINGS

E. Clarke

THE DEVELOPMENT OF KINSHIP ROLES

The training of children in the home largely devolves on the mother. The teacher in the private school in Sugartown told us: 'The father is out a lot so most of the discipline is left to the mother. The mother punishes — the father only shouts. The mother has all the burdens.' There was no evidence of any widespread cruelty to children that came to our notice in any of our Centres. Yet, whenever we touched on the subject of upbringing there was hardly a case in which our informant did not expatiate upon what he called the 'floggings' he or she had received in childhood from parent and teacher and our own observations of parental discipline were of the violent manner in which even the youngest of children were often rebuked. Children are shouted at in a way which appears brutalizing to anyone outside the particular culture. The child responds to this by equally noisy and violent outcries. It was not uncommon to see a screaming infant ignored, although apparently in great distress, while the mother was occupied nearby with some trivial task or to hear fearsome yells from a nearby yard. We would, however, be assured that it was nothing to worry about — Johnny had run away and his mother had at last caught him and was beating him. The beatings we actually witnessed were rarely as severe as the outcry appeared to indicate and the child was generally more frightened than hurt. But the constant 'threatening' of children was noticeable as also was the fact that there was very little of quiet, gentle-spoken admonition.

When we consider the things for which children are rebuked and punished, as also the principles which they are explicitly taught to be right or wrong, it is clear that there is a serious conflict, in Sugartown and in similar societies elsewhere in Jamaica, between the ideal and the socially accepted pattern of behaviour. I am of the opinion that it is not that there is no intention to establish a pattern of behaviour; or that 'disciplinary efforts seem to be a gesture rather than a real attempt to alter behaviour' but rather that the behaviour pattern is one taken over from a different cultural group, and is inassimilable in the situation in which it is expected to work. For example, children are taught by their mothers (or the grandmothers or guardian in her place) that it is wrong to lie or steal but the behaviour of adults or other children around them gives little reality to the admonitions. The woman who punishes a child in the morning for 'stealing' the milk or sugar will herself take him with her later in the day when she goes to 'pick' someone else's coconuts or firewood or send him to tether the cow or goat in someone else's pasture. Within the culture 'stealing' milk or sugar from one's parents is unquestionably and recognizably wrong but the system of values holds good only in given circumstances. There was the case of the man in Sugartown, who, before a crowd of relatives and neighbours, not one of whom protested or tried to interfere, beat his wife into unconsciousness because she had, in mistaken loyalty, gone to the police station to admit complicity in a theft of coconuts for which her companion in the escapade had been caught while she had not. She had disgraced herself and him — not by 'taking' coconuts growing on estate land which was common practice — but by admitting the fact when she need never have been found out. In the same way the emphasis placed, according to so many of our informants, on truthfulness, and the tales of 'floggings' received for 'telling lies' is not to be taken to apply in any realistic way to adult behaviour. 'I can't tell you a lie' frequently prefaces a statement which completely contradicts a great deal of information previously given. The truth, in fact, is something which should only be spoken in favourable circumstances and certainly not if it is likely to create hostility, disapproval or discomfort.

We heard less of 'flogging' or of reprimand for 'stealing' in Orange Grove possibly because there was no necessity for a well-fed child of well-to-do farmers to do any such thing. If he did, he had been 'rude', but it did not, as in the Sugartown family, mean that there was no money to buy more and therefore the rest of the family had to do without. A system of ideals which, among the upper-class farmers in Orange Grove (who formed the majority and set the pattern of behaviour) was realizable within the culture, was found only theoretically operative in Sugartown where it was in conflict with the social pattern of behaviour.

In all aspects of home training the mother is the principal actor. The child's most intimate relationship in the home is with her even in those cases where the father is present and associates himself with the upbringing of the child. We have already given some idea of the extent to which mother and children co-operate in the small daily duties in the home. They are continually together. The woman depends on even very young children to fetch and carry for her. Whatever she may be doing in the yard, the children are never far away. There is constant companionship, and a constant interdependence. The girl child identifies herself with the mother while the boy has already begun to build up a type of behaviour which might be described as husband substitute.

The relationship between mother and child was not adversely affected by the harshness of the attempts at discipline or the constant demands, even on the youngest child, for exacting services, possible because these attempts were spasmodic and interspersed with demonstrations of affection and a general pattern of indulgence. The same men and women who regaled us with stories of their mother's floggings would, in the same breath, enlarge upon her devotion to them and theirs to her. One reason for this was to be found in the intimacy and stability of the relationship and the fact that it was often the only stable relationship in the child's life. But principally because the authority of the mother is never questioned any more than the child's duty of obedience to her.

The relationship to the father where he lives in the home is at best ambivalent. He is always more strict, more exacting and infinitely less well-known than the mother. While the mother's violence and threats of dire punishment are one aspect only of a behaviour pattern which includes tenderness and a sense of security, the father's discipline is often tempered by no such conditions and leaves a permanent mark. There were many references to bad fathers but criticism of the mother is rare.

There is nothing worse that can be said of a man or woman than that 'they would curse even their mother'. Fathers are far less tender and their interest in the child more usually centres on his material progress.

Where the man is earning and in a better financial position than the unskilled sugar-worker, the plans for the children are often very ambitious. There is always the desire that they should do better than their parents and raise the status of the family. In the conditions outside Orange Grove these ambitions were only too often unrealizable.

One of our most informative fathers was a barber who could make as much as sixteen shillings a day in Crop off the sugar-workers, although during the *tempo moto* he had to live 'on trust'. He had three children by his girl, the eldest five years and the youngest a baby in arms. He assured us she was not like other Sugartown girls but had been respectably brought up and it took about six months for them to get close. He wanted to get married because he loved his children and liked playing with them and he would never like to hear them referred to as illegitimate. Nor could he bear to think of them having a stepfather. He was very ambitious for his son (aged four) and had sent him to private school, as otherwise he would never have time to learn all he has to learn. In the evenings he makes the boy read to him. If he does not do his lessons he 'hits' him. His wife also teaches the children in the home. He is not having them grow up uneducated like himself. But they live in a small rented house and conditions are not satisfactory. He told us, 'You cannot bring up children properly in the crowded housing conditions. You should have a room to sit in and talk or read, then when you go to bed there should be a room for you and your wife and others for the boys and girls separately. People live badly here, which is why girls of twelve and fourteen are having babies. In Jamaica people have too many children.' His three are too many because if he does all he wants for his son what is to happen to the other two? People were talking of a law called Birth Control which he thought should be brought in. 'It should come.' Some said it was contrary to God but he did not see it like that. A man should not run about having children all over the place. He himself had made up his mind not to do that. Another devoted father whose behaviour to his children we were able to observe as they hung about him during our interview, was an East Indian living in barracks with his wife and family. In spite of the crowded conditions the rooms were spotless and tidy and the children well dressed and cared. The little girl sat on his knee and the others ran in from time to time to speak to him. They were obviously on the most intimate and friendly terms. He, also, spoke to us of his 'ambitions' for his children. They are sent to school and in the evenings after work he hears them their lessons: 'teaches them to spell cat and dog and the like'.

In another case a married couple had already decided that their small boy should be a doctor or dispenser and the little girl a nurse and should have all the educational advantages which they had not been able to get. Sugartown, we were assured, was not a good place in which to bring up children: the people were not 'up to the mark'. As soon as the husband had saved enough money they intended to move to Kingston where the children would have a better opportunity.

In the homes in Sugartown in which there was a full appreciation of parental responsibility, which might as often be where the union between the parents was still based on concubinage as when it was based on marriage, there was still the problem, within the social and economic conditions we have described, of fulfilling the parental conception of duty. Nevertheless, these children had the advantage, despite poverty, of a great deal of tender, if not always completely wise, attention and training from both father and mother and were both better fed and cared for than were children in the unstable or broken homes which we have described.

It has, however, to be said that examples of paternal devotion, and kindness were far outweighed by the cases where he was either no more than the man 'who had only fathered the idea of me [and] left me the sole liability of my mother who really fathered me' or someone remembered for neglect or harsh discipline. Where the mother was indulgent, hasty in her angers but quick to be kind again, the father was remembered for his strictness. As an Orange Grove farmer said, 'You could not fool with your father.' He recalled an incident concerning an elder sister, engaged to be married, who 'did something' on the day before the wedding which was not suitable in their father's sight. He went into the bushes and cut himself a good whip. Then he went back into the house, told her he had been planning for a long time, 'to christen her' before she left home and proceeded to give her a first-class whipping. Sons, especially, often referred to their childhood fear of their father. One boy, in recounting the 'rough beatings' he had received from him, admitted that his mother also flogged him, but that he was never fearful with her. We heard many stories of children running away to an indulgent grandmother or other member of the family because of these beatings. Sometimes they would leave home altogether. The following is an extract from one of our Sugartown records. The account has the violence of expression and is as highly coloured as were most of these stories, but social workers and probation officers in Kingston's west end will recognize the type of 'force-ripe' man.

One morning we saw a boy running and dancing in the road. When we tried to speak to him he ran like a deer. A man caught him and brought him back telling him that he was foolish to run, we might even be going to give him a short or pant, and that he should at least listen to what we had to say. He stood with great fear and told us his name. Gradually we learned that he was fourteen years of age, and was looking for work as he wanted to earn his own money. When you have money, he said, you feel big. He had never been to school and had run away from home because his father wanted to kill him with beating. From elsewhere we learned that he had recently arrived in Sugartown and was sleeping at nights on the ground underneath Miss X's house, going about the compounds during the day trying to get work and being told he was too young to cut cane. According to Miss X he was a 'force-ripe man', and she prophesied that in a few weeks he would 'be so fierce around here that you, a big woman, or a little girl would have to watch him or else he would rape you'. A neighbour added that 'it was little boys like that that make bad for their parents. The best thing would be for a man to hold him and throw kerosene oil on him and then take a match and set him afire'. (This is the method of killing mongoose when caught in a trap). Miss X said she overheard the little boy telling another boy outside her door one night about the quarrel with his father. He stole something from his father and his father tied him to a tree and flogged him and left him tied up. He had a knife on him and started to cut the rope. As he made the last cut his father appeared. He ran and his father made after him but failed to catch him. He escaped and made for the nearest town where, according to his story, he worked until three weeks ago. Then he begged a lift from a truck driver coming to Sugartown.

The failure to establish the paternal relationship and the excessive reliance upon the mother has its effect upon the young man when he grows up. A mother impresses upon her sons that it is their duty to make up to her for the hardships she endured as the sole or principal support of her children. When the boy begins to earn money he is expected to give her part at least of his earnings and while he is in the home this is the usual practice. In return she continues to cook and wash for him. When he sets up on his own he still feels that he is under an obligation to contribute to her support. Again, this is the ideal mode of behaviour; in reality it may not be possible for him to send anything appreciable or, in fact, to give her anything at all, but once they are working most young men send money back to their mother. While the amounts may be small and the payments irregular, they nonetheless represent a considerable sacrifice in view of the earning capacity of young unskilled workers in their first jobs. A young man who gave his income as between twenty and forty shillings a week said that he had to send four shillings a week to the mother of one of his children and also had to send something for his mother. He could not manage this every week but would send her ten shillings at a time, usually every three months. Another young fellow of twenty-five who earned his living by hiring a hand cart and carrying goods for people, said he used to write his mother regularly and send her between six and twelve shillings at a time. Another told us: 'If I don't send five or seven shillings a month to my mother I feel shame because she is getting old and she works hard.' A son who knew his mother to be in want, and was unable to help her, felt both guilt and failure.

This cycle of reciprocal dependence is part of the social pattern of the mother-child relationship, impressed on the child by the mother herself, and by the society into which he grows. On the other hand, the boy receives no education as to his duty as a father. He accepts from his elders the dictum that children are woman's concern and that there need be no avoidance of procreation until such a time as he is in a position to fulfil the natural obligations of husband and father. Nothing in his own experience has enabled him to learn the meaning of the paternal relationship, nor has the society helped by example or precept. This pattern is true, of course, in its fullest extent, among our Centres only in Sugartown. In Orange Grove, as we have shown, the family is so organized that there is opportunity for the paternal role to develop fully and for the parents to be complementary to one another in the care and education of their children.

One of the features of the exclusive, and often obsessive, mother-son relationship is the persistence of the son's dependence upon her into adolescence and beyond. A result of this is often a failure to develop satisfactory relationships with other people or achieve personal independence. A Sugartown man, aged twenty-five, told us that his mother had two children by his father and when he left her she bore eight more for other men. At the age of seven he was sent to live with his maternal grandparents. After a year with them he rejoined the mother. While with her he got ill and for many years she spent all she had on treatment for him. 'A man had to love his mother when she did all that for him.' After he came out of hospital he went to live with his mother's sister. He did not get on with her and wrote to his mother who came and took him home. He was then seventeen. He lived with her, worked a bit of land and handed over the sale of his produce to her. Then he got a job on a Sugar Estate but did not keep it for long. He went to live with his father's brother for a time. His uncle was very good to him and he worked lands owned by his uncle's wife. But after a while her relatives began to show him a bad face which displeased him so he left.

Where the separation from the mother is complete and permanent, less damage may be done than when the child continually passes from one relative to another, returning for short periods to the mother. One of our Orange Grove mothers felt so strongly about this that she said she refrained from visiting her child she had given away as she thought it better that he should forget her.

Another young fellow, aged twenty-three, said he had given up his job in Kingston after a year and returned home because he longed to see his mother, while yet another grown man told us he could not marry or leave the district to seek work elsewhere because he could not leave his foster-mother (his mother's sister), who had raised him and who was now dependent upon him.

Even if the child has not already been subject to the upheavals that occur in his home life when there is a change of conjugal union, or if he is 'given away' either temporarily or permanently, going to school is a major crisis and confronts the child with a new set of problems. In many cases the school may be two or three miles away from his home and even if his parents could have afforded it, there is no public transport — whatever the distance the child has to walk it. Before leaving he has had to perform the usual household tasks and the only food he has received in many homes is a little bush tea and a bit of bread. The child arrives at school, therefore, after a considerable expenditure of energy and often hungry.

Above all, however, going to school means a break in the continual companionship with the mother. Hitherto she has been 'there' — someone always present, whether hectoring or indulgent, demanding or cajoling, the person who provides every need, whose word is law, the final and undisputed authority in everything. For the first time in the child's life this authority now becomes a source of conflict. The new regime makes it difficult if not impossible for him to perform the home tasks which she requires him to do before leaving for school. If he omits them, or any of them, she will punish him. If he is late for school as a result of doing them, no heed is taken of his excuses — he is 'flogged' by his teacher. His mother, with the conventional respect for propriety, may keep him from school because his one suit is dirty or torn. He may be 'flogged', when he goes back, for having been absent. For the first time in his life his mother's authority is challenged and by someone who has undisputed control over him for the greater part of his day. He suffers not because he disobeys her but if he does what she says. In rural areas, where the parents require the help of the children in the fields on Fridays to reap the produce for the Saturday markets, children are generally kept from school. For this the teacher may scold the mother, sometimes in the child's hearing, and although she may not say much at the time, she will defend her point of view vociferously when he is gone. Of all this the child is aware. He has to choose between obeying the mother and obeying the teacher.

Most of all he has now to submit to a routine which is in violent contrast to anything he has yet experienced. Hitherto his life has been one of almost untrammelled freedom. His world has been the yard surrounding his home. He has played in it all day. He has had the companionship, not only of his mother, but of brothers and sisters and other children from neighbouring yards. Now everything is different and strange. He has to be at a certain place at a certain hour — otherwise he is punished. Once he gets to school there is the new and wholly unpleasant experience of sitting on a crowded bench for hours on end. Gone are the days when he was free to roam about the yard, dawdle over odd jobs, run to the shop or take a message to a neighbour where he could loiter to play with the children for a time. Now he is supposed, at the sound of a bell, to perform a series of actions, stand, sit, recite, copy a pattern, etc., and absorb a series of facts and follow a system of behaviour for which his previous experience has neither prepared nor fitted him.

There is another rude break with accustomed behaviour in the matter of food. In the homes the children are accustomed to eat whenever they are hungry. If there is nothing in the kitchen which they can lay their hands on, there is generally some sort of fruit-bearing tree in their own or a neighbouring yard which can be raided. Now he has to conform to the routine of waiting for the lunch hour. Secondly, there is generally a change in diet. Many schools provide free or cheap lunches which are based on an appropriate diet scale, including meat and green vegetables. There is no question of its superiority to the home diet, consisting as this generally does of a steady ration of carbohydrates seasoned with a small bit of salt fish, but the child does not like the new food. Where there is no school lunch, the children are supposed to bring money to buy from the 'food vendors' but the lure of the 'snow-ball man' or the sweet seller is often too great and the pennies go, not on bread or patties, but on these delights.

The small child has, therefore, a considerable number of adjustments to make quite apart from those involved in the beginnings of his literary education. In some cases the abruptness of the change from the haphazard discipline and freedoms of home life to the rigid routine of the school is bridged by the 'private school'. These private schools are to be found in most country villages particularly where there is no Infant school or Infant centre attached to the Government Elementary school. We came across several in our Centres and admittedly they are by no means ideal. They are run by men and women who have often no educational qualifications. At the same time the women who choose to try and earn their living in this way are usually inspired by a love of children, and a gift for handling them as well as by a sense of social responsibility. Moreover, they are invariably local persons whom the parents can meet and talk with on terms of equality especially since they have to pay for the children. The parents are on a much more familiar footing with them than they can ever be with the head teacher of the Government school who, by virtue of his office, is in every village, a person of status.

The atmosphere in these little schools is generally homely and the group small enough for each child to receive individual attention. Moreover, through her knowledge of their homes and families, the teacher starts off by knowing a good deal about each child — their background and difficulties outside the school. Taken by and large these little schools fill a need in the community and fulfil their function to bridge the gap between the carefree early home life and prepare the child for the formal work and the stricter discipline of the school.

We have already discussed the degree to which 'flogging' is part of the home discipline. Judging from the accounts by grown men and women of their childhood, corporal punishment for trivial offences was still more the pattern of school-life. Even making allowance for the dramatic over-statement which is a feature of verbal expression, our own observations lead us to conclude that there is over-reliance in the elementary schools on this method of keeping order. Also that the strap is used for trivial offences such as talking in class, and most frequently for being late, although in many instances this was the result of duties which the child has to perform before leaving home (which he will be punished by his parents for neglecting). The worst feature was that corporal punishment was also administered where the child failed to do his work properly. This was so often told us that there seems little reason to doubt its truth.

From our own observation of elementary schools we visited, all teachers made great play with the strap or switch, which most carried in their hands or displayed prominently on their desks. Theoretically only the head teacher in an elementary school may administer corporal punishment, but all were said to do so. In any case it is a constant threat and is often regarded as the only effective means of controlling the children.

On the whole it was less relied upon in the private schools. There were exceptions. In one of the neighbourhood villages the teacher was a morose-looking cripple who carried a strap and banged it down on the desk to call order and continually threatened the children with it. Nevertheless, his pupils did not appear in the least cowed and were cheerful and forthcoming. The teacher in charge of the private school in Sugartown disapproved of flogging. She said parents flogged their children very hard as a result of which after a time they took no notice of it. Some parents lost their temper and beat the children anywhere. When the children ran away they would await their return and then flog them. She believed you should never hit a child in a temper lest you hurt it. In her school she seldom had to hit a child. She tried to teach them to have good manners and not to rough the other children. She often wondered what happened to them when they went to the big school. She was often told that they behaved better than the others but that they lost their zeal.

The teacher in the private school in Orange Grove told us that three of her children who behaved quite normally at home had never spoken at school — they did not even answer their names when the roll was called. From the time they came they remained seated in one position, quite still, till school was over. The boy's father told her to beat him up to make him talk but she would not do it. Even she, however, had her strap on her desk and on one occasion threatened her little grandchild with it. We noticed that this little girl behaved very much like the spoiled grandchild, was always demanding attention and was on this occasion jumping up, asking questions or telling tales of another child. She went up to the table where the teacher was sitting. Before she could say a word her grandmother took down the strap and attempted to hit her, but the child ran back to her seat, while the teacher ignored her and went on with the lesson.

We have already given some account of the problems of adolescence and the omission of any parental instruction or guidance at puberty. The omission is not made up by any other agency. In the elementary schools there was no attempt to face up to the problem of adolescent sex-play between the children themselves or the seduction of school-girls by adult men even within the school. After school closes in the early afternoon there were no organized authorities or any other body, in any of our Centres, to divert the pre-occupation with sex which then occurs. In the case of many boys and girls their first experience of sexual intercourse took place while they were still at school. For the girl this meant, in many cases, that she became pregnant. In the case of the boy he soon ceased to be satisfied with immature experimentation with a girl of his own age and began to go with older women. We had many graphic descriptions by men of their sexual initiation by older women. While they are still at school, therefore, the physical stresses of adolescence create a new set of problems and again there are unresolved social as well as personal conflicts. The school, if it does not tacitly ignore the situation altogether, as is generally the case, is likely to prohibit a type of behaviour for which the child finds no disapprobation in his immediate home and social life. In fact, as we have shown, there is amused, and not always covert, admiration for 'the force ripe little man' no less than for the professional seducer.

This new disturbing element which has come into the child's life may abruptly terminate school-life even before the normal school-leaving age. Even if this does not occur and the child remains, he or she either becomes troublesome and difficult or sullen and resentful, and the only reaction to this appears to be corporal punishment for being 'rude' an expression popularly used to refer to sexual intercourse.

The transition to social adolescence presents no less problems, although their gravity and nature differed considerably in the three Centres. But, with the sole exception of Orange Grove, the child was invariably unprepared and inadequately equipped to deal with them. His (or her) sexual maturity is not matched by a correspondingly adult personality. Most children leave school at fourteen or fifteen. From the point of view of formal education only a proportion have attained the highest standard. Their educational equipment may go little beyond the rudiments of the three R's. Once they leave, for the large majority, any form of literary activity ceases. They may never open a book or write a line again. In none of our villages was there a library, or any clubs for boys or girls providing either recreational or educational amenities.

Once he leaves school the boy is now expected to find something to do, and, as soon as possible, earn his living or at least make some contribution to the household expenses. It was at this stage that the mother would loudly declaim that he had no father to help him. In these circumstances he is dependent upon his family or kin. If they can find the money to apprentice him to a tradesman he may become a shoemaker or a carpenter or a mechanic, according to the facilities in his particular district. Or he may in very exceptional circumstances be sent to a technical school. If they have land he may help with the cultivation as an unpaid family help. Only in Orange Grove, however, were the family in this position. In Sugartown the only after-school source of training were the Estate workshops with their apprenticeship system.

Hyacinth L. Evans

PERSPECTIVES ON THE SOCIALISATION OF THE WORKING-CLASS JAMAICAN CHILD

ABSTRACT

This article presents a review of research on the socialization of primarily one group of Jamaican children — those whose parents are of working-class origin or are unemployed. After a discussion of the family within the Jamaican context and specifically within this socio-economic group, the research is presented under three main headings—the physical/social setting, parent-child interaction and values and beliefs. The article then examines the implications of this research for the development of the child, and considers the effectiveness of this socialization in preparing the child for school and for society. The paper ends with a critical review of the research from the point of view of its coherence and its adequacy for preparing the child for school and society.

INTRODUCTION

Every individual undergoes the process of socialization into a group, society or culture. Socialization refers to the process by which one acquires the values, norms, habits, skills and knowledge necessary for effective functioning within one's group or culture. It occurs in various settings—the family, the school, peer groups, and the church, to name a few. Each socializing agent has effects that vary in their quality and permanence. The family is the most powerful socializing agent for three reasons. First, it is the primary source of influence during the child's early formative years, when he/she is most impressionable. Second, it enjoys the special impact deriving from bonds of attachment. Third, its influence is continuous over time. Socialization within the family is therefore of critical importance in the development of the child and determines the knowledge, skills, attitudes, and values which prepare or fail to prepare him/her for societal roles. Since one such role is a learner within the institutional context of the school, socialization has special significance for teachers and educators.

We cannot, however, ignore the influence of other socializing agents. The socializing influence of the wider community, group, culture or society is pervasive, exerting both a direct and indirect influence on the child. The wider social context can influence socialization in that child rearing practices are shaped and influenced by the beliefs and values widely held in the society, or by the societal consensus on how children ought to be treated.

This paper presents a review of research on the socialization of one group of Jamaican children. It examines implications of this research for the development of the child, and considers its effectiveness in preparing him/her for school and society. It also critically appraises the research data on socialization from a variety of viewpoints. The paper begins with a discussion of the family within the Jamaican context and specifically within this group, and considers the methods and approaches employed in the research reviewed. The next three sections discuss the physical/social setting, parent-child interaction, and values and beliefs. The paper concludes with some perspectives on the research and questions for further enquiry.

BACKGROUND, CONCEPTS AND METHOD

The primary concern in this paper is the socialization within the family and its immediate environment. We need therefore to consider the nature of the family within the Jamaican context. In Jamaica, there are roughly four types of family structure, each associated with socio-economic and life style variables, values, aspirations and norms for interacting with and rearing children. The typology varies (e.g. Clarke [8]; Solien [44]; Henriques [21]; Smith [41]; Foner [13]; Roberts & Sinclair [36]). Bearing in mind the distinction between family groups and household groups [Solien 44; McKenzie 29], I propose to use the following to refer to the various family or household groupings: the marriage union, the common-law union, the visiting union (where the mother still resides in her mother's house), the kinship-related household and the single-parent household. These five groups are associated with certain class and status variables [Smith 41; Roberts & Sinclair 36], and with occupational groupings [Foner 13]. The middle classes are employed in skilled, highly skilled, professional, or managerial occupations and normally choose the marriage union. The low-income groups who are mainly unskilled, semi-skilled, or unemployed, choose the common–law or visiting unions, or live in kinship-related households. There are, however, variations on the this theme. For example, because marriage is considered the ideal form of union, many low–income men and women aspire to this status, and marry later in life after childbearing is over [Smith 40, p. 133]. They may therefore progress over time from a visiting union to a common-law arrangement or a single parent household and later, perhaps, to marriage. It often happens that the mother has to leave her child with others- grandmother, aunt or friend—either to seek employment, or to set up a household with a new partner. Grant *et al.* [17] estimates that about 15 per cent of all Jamaican children, at some time, live in a kinship-related household with their parents absent.

A knowledge of these family and household forms helps us to understand the variation in the formative experiences of Jamaican children. The overwhelming majority of Jamaican children are from the low-income or lower-class groups. They form the majority in the primary, all-age and new secondary schools. Much of the existing research on socialization or child-rearing practices has been conducted on this group. For these reasons, the paper deals only with research related to the socialization of the low-income Jamaican child.

The research reported here uses a variety of methodological approaches and research designs. The majority are surveys, employing questionnaires and yielding quantitative data on aggregates and averages. There are only a few ethnographic/anthropological studies. The majority of the research focuses on processes—e.g. child-rearing techniques, or aspects of the child-rearing situation. Only four report on outcomes though these were correlated with personal rather than process variables. The research spans a period of 40 years and I indicate, where possible, changes or continuities over time.

The research is categorized under three headings — the physical/social setting, parent-child interaction, and values and beliefs.

THE PHYSICAL/SOCIAL SETTING

It is necessary to include a brief description of the physical and social setting in which the children and their parents or guardians live, because some characteristics of the environment may explain or can be linked to child-rearing practices as well as socialization outcomes. In this respect, I am influenced by Bronfenbrenner & Crouter's notion of the micro system within which the child is socialized [5]. This micro system includes not only the parent-child relationship but also the immediate physical, social and structured setting. Implicit in this formulation is the idea that 'the child's experience in a particular setting has an effect on his subsequent development' (p. 378). The description below includes aspects of the physical environment, as well as characteristics of parents/guardians/childminders.

> The children in low-income groups normally live in one of the five family or household groups previously mentioned — the visiting union (where the mother resides with her parents), common-law or marriage unions, the kinship-related household and the single-parent household. The most frequent one is the single-parent household. The percentage of female-headed households is approximately 32 per cent nationwide [Massiah 32] and may be higher in this income group. The average family size is 4.6 [Grant *et al.* 17]. In rural areas, roughly 56 per cent of low-income families live in one–or two-room houses [Grant *et al.* 17]. Many of these urban families live in yards which can be described as a residential lot with a number of small independents units (one or two rooms), each housing a separate household.

The overwhelming majority of parents in this income group have received only a few years of primary education. Many are illiterate [Grant 14; Grant *et al.* 17]. Anderson [1] found that the majority of parents are poor readers. Members of this income group account for the majority of the unemployed which nationwide in 1984 stood at 36.5 per cent for females and 15.7 per cent for males [*Social and Economic Survey of Jamaica* 43]. Among females aged 17-24 (the prime child-bearing age), the unemployment rate is 60 per cent (Powell quoted in Ennew & Young [12]). Those who work, engage in physically strenuous jobs. The majority of women in the labour force work as domestic helpers earning roughly $250 to $300 per month. In general, parents live in poverty, with scarcely enough to provide for three or more children. (In one study, 68 per cent of parents had no source of income [Grant 16]). Due to the high unemployment rate, many parents migrate overseas and locally to urban areas to seek work. In such cases, children are left with relatives or friends. In urban areas, when mothers go out to work, they leave their young children with childminders who often live in the same yard. The quality of supervision and caring provided by these childminders is usually considered inadequate [Hall 18].

Within the home with its limited physical space, reading materials for children are rarely found [Anderson 1; Grant 14; Grant *et al.* 17]. Jarrett [23] in her study of urban pre-basic school children, found that 48 per cent had picture books, though they were destroyed soon after they were received. Very few children have parents who read to them. There are also few play materials or toys and very few educational toys such as puzzles and building blocks [Grant *et al.* 17; Landmann *et al.* 27] These children also have very few personal belongings and thus minimal opportunity to develop respect for the property of others [Grant 14]. Because parents are absent or leave early for work, there is lack of systematic supervision and routine in children's lives. Anderson [1] found that under these circumstances, many children were often late for school or played truant.

As previously mentioned, the low-income Jamaican woman often moves from one type of union to another. Some of her children will, in the early years, grow up with a relative, particularly the grandmother. The majority will experience the changes in family structure and may have to relate to different step-fathers. At an early age, the older child often assumes responsibility for younger siblings.

From the preceding description of the physical and social setting, we get a picture of a home with limited space, in depressed surroundings, where there are few reading and play materials to stimulate intellectual development and creativity. Children spend little time interacting with parents, and older children devote much of their time to carrying out household chores and other tasks.

Aspects of the physical and social environment can operate in complex ways to have direct and indirect effects on socialization and its outcomes. They can influence the mother's disposition or capability to nurture and care for her children and determine the kind of child-rearing techniques which become feasible. They also have implications for play and play activities. Very limited personal space will be available to members of the household. The importance of personal space in developing an identity and some social skills has been cited by Rutter & Madge [37]. Older children who have to assume responsibility for the care of younger ones and for households chores will learn a sense of responsibility and disposition to care for others. But it is possible that some children with their natural impulse to play and interact with others may resent such demands and find few ways to reconcile these negative emotions. Such responsibility and the performance of household duties for a substantial part of the day provide the context for the child's development, substituting for one in which his/her needs, growth and spontaneous expression take precedence.

The physical/social setting may also have indirect effects on the child, and his/her socialization. From the description above, those parents who work would return home physically exhausted after doing manual and often strenuous jobs. Roughly one-half of these parents are single mothers, and they would understandably be too tired to be disposed to interact or reason with their children. But the circumstances of their lives would also prevent such interaction. For the overwhelming majority of mothers (whether in single-or two-parent households), after toiling all day, have to carry out necessary household chores such as cooking, cleaning and feeding their children, for men in the society rarely assume responsibility for such household tasks. The mothers' response to children's needs and demands would therefore be a pragmatic one — perhaps limited to giving directions. Fatigue combined with concern about finances would probably make them irritable. Bronfenbrenner & Crouter [5] cite research which suggests that working-class families — single- or two-parent — experience a higher degree of stress around the issues of co-ordinating the burdens of work, household tasks, child-rearing and child-care arrangements. Crises in families — always greater among the poor — correlates with maternal irritability and deterioration in family discussion and problem solving [Maccoby & Martin 30]. Thus, these physical/social circumstances can influence child-rearing techniques and parent-child interaction. These indirect influences support Bronfenbrenner & Crouter's claim that one must consider the social ecology or the context of child rearing and the features of the mesosystem and exosystem which can shape and influence socialization [5].

PARENT-CHILD INTERACTION

For the purpose of this section, I shall include the following under the rubric of parent: the single mother, the mother and father living together, the guardian/relative and child-minders who take care of young children while the mother works. The dimensions of the parent-child interaction include:

(a) the nature, quality and frequency of parent/guardian-child interaction;

(b) the nature, quality and frequency of interaction with other adults and peers;

(c) systematic instruction within the home;

(d) goals and aspirations held by parents;

(e) children's preparation for attaining these goals.

The evidence suggests that children in this income group have few opportunities for verbal exchange or extended conversation with the parent or guardian with whom they live. In Grant's study [14], the overwhelming majority reported that they conversed with their young children (of basic school age) only once or twice per week. This was especially marked in urban areas where 89 per cent so reported (and 10 per cent said they never had a chance to converse with their children). Because of the prevailing family structure, the irregular working hours and lack of physical space, the family does not have the tradition of sitting down together at meal times. Children often eat in the yard by themselves [Anderson 1; Grant 14; Foner 13]. Thus, they lack the conversation and dialogue which has such educational benefits for the middle-class child. Landmann *et al.* [27] in their study of a more settled suburban low-income area, found slightly more interaction between children and parents/guardians, with about one-half the mothers telling stories to their children. Nevertheless, one-half the mothers did not attach much importance to conversing with young children or answering their questions.

Though the evidence regarding the father's role in the home is conflicting, there is some evidence that they are assuming more responsibility for rearing and interacting with their children. Roughly one-half of fathers live with the family [Grant *et al.* 17; Landmann *et al.* 27]. Fathers in visiting unions spend about four hours per week with their children [Roberts & Sinclair 36; Landmann *et al.* 27]. Still one-half of all fathers never took their children on outings. We lack information on the role of fathers in rural areas.

Even though the majority of mothers/guardians work, young children, especially those in yards, spend much of their day in the presence of adults [Jarrett 23]. The yard provides much opportunity for the young child to play with peers. However, despite the constant presence of others, old and young, very little adult conversation is directed at the child [Jarrett 23; Hall *et al.* 19]. Older children's involvement in chores and work would form the social context for their development and reduce the amount of time available for play and other developmental tasks.

The lack of systematic and on-going instruction by parents has been attested to by Brodber [4], Kerr [26] and Grant [16]. Parents lack specific goals of child development and thus rarely engage in positive guidance and direction. Instead, they react to the child's misbehaviour with threats, anger and/or corporal punishment which can, at times, be quite severe. Grant *et al.* [17] found little use of praise or tangible rewards in the disciplining of children.

Goals can refer to general expectations for the life chances of the individual and specific expectations relative to a career. Foner's study suggests that rural folk perceive the class distinctions in the island and recognize that society's benefits accrue only to some groups and not to others. The rigid class structure, recognition of one's poverty and the high unemployment among adults within the community can limit the views of one's life chances. The high drop-out rate among 11 to 15-year-old boys can be attributed to this factor.

Yet as we have seen, parents have inordinately high expectations for their children and nourish a belief in the material benefits of schooling. The evidence suggests that parents do not discuss these goals or the means for their achievement with children. Indeed, their plans for schooling and their view of learning were at variance with such goals.

VALUES AND BELIEFS

The following presents research on parents' values and beliefs which influence their child-rearing practices.

Children are highly valued by all in the society. It is widely believed that motherhood validates one's womanhood [Kerr 26; Clarke 8; Grant 16]. There is evidence that the young child receives much affection up to about age 5 [Grant *et al.* 17], but that this is less so after that age, no doubt because of the arrival of other children, or the parent's engagement in work which makes her physically exhausted.

Parents do not tolerate or see as necessary children's expressive and assertive behaviour. Sixty-five per cent of the mothers in one study [Grant 14] characterized their children as very often or often stubborn. Any delay in attending to a request was interpreted as defiance and evoked the parents' anger, making them assert their authority. Nearly all parents believed that children must obey their parents, and one-half felt that children should be seen and not heard [Grant *et al.* 17]. Almost 80 per cent of parents in Landmann's study admitted that they beat their 3-year-olds with an implement such as a stick, or belt [27].

The idea that play can be beneficial is still not widely accepted by parents in this income group. Only a few parents recognize that play is beneficial to the child [Grant *et al.* 17; Landmann *et al.* 27]. Many discourage play because it is messy, and those who allow it do so because it keeps the child out of trouble. These beliefs may explain in part the absence of toys in the home.

IMPLICATIONS FOR SOCIALISATION

In this section I consider the implications of this research for the optimal development and socialization of the child. In so doing, I shall first draw on empirical research which points to relationships between some processes of child-rearing and socialization outcomes, then consider the research from two perspectives.

The ideal result of any socialization process is a person who has learned to regulate and control behaviour and to be cognizant of others' needs — in other words, one who has internalized certain rules and ways of thinking. The person also develops a healthy self-system or personality capable of feeling and forming bonds with others. Self regulation, internalization, cognitive and social functioning and personality are thus crucial elements.

Ideally, socializers of the young hope that outward forms of control necessary in the early stages of life will become internalized so that eventually the individual can monitor and regulate his/her own behaviour in appropriate ways. The child's ability to understand rules and contingencies is central to this process of internalization. This requires that the rules be explained and that efforts be made to ensure that the child adheres to them in a consistent fashion [Harter 20]. An important aspect of internalization is the adult's explaining and reasoning with the child with respect to specific situations and transgressions. The explanation is especially effective if it sensitizes the child to his/her intentions [Harter 20]. This explanation and reasoning — what Maccoby and Martin [30] call induction — have also been shown to be related to increased pro-social behaviour, among children.

The child's engagement in contingent thinking — deducing that such an action or response stems from his/her behaviour — is of enormous significance in the child's social and cognitive development. For it not only allows the child to engage in if-then inferential thought processes, it allows him/her to see connections between thoughts and actions and the external world. When a child begins to see such connections it enables him/her to develop a sense of efficacy and control over the environment.

However, such developments do not occur automatically. They require a social environment in which discussions, explanations and reasoning occur, in which the adult/parents' responses to a child's behaviour are consistent and where the child can detect cause-effect relationships. Such a structured social environment perhaps rarely exists in an ideal form. However, when we compare this picture with the research evidence discussed above, we see that the children in this group lack sufficient opportunities to engage in these processes. Not only are there few opportunities for verbal exchange with the parent, but there is also a lack of systematic instruction. Parents, for the most part, lack developmental goals for their children and in general respond to behaviour according to the exigencies of the situation.

The role of punishment and an authoritarian-autocratic pattern of child rearing have been researched from a variety of theoretical perspectives, with inconsistent findings. Though Harter [20] citing the work of Aronfreed suggests that punishment — disapproval, withdrawal of love as well as physical punishment — can lead to internalized control, there is evidence that physical punishment and an authoritarian-autocratic pattern of child rearing correlate with above-average levels of aggression, low self-esteem and an external rather than internal moral orientation. In boys they correlate with lower levels of motivation for intellectual performance. Power assertive parenting can lead to external attributions by the child, i.e. the child comes to believe that external factors — not the individual — determine outcomes of actions. This external attribution works against the internalization of values, self control and an internal locus of control. Restrictiveness and parents' insistence on obedience may be obtained at the expense of the child's spontaneity, creativity and the more positive aspects of social competence [Harter 20; Maccoby & Martin 30; Radke-Yarrow *et al.* 35].

We have seen, however, that children in the society are very much loved and desired by all parents. Parents are disposed to be indulgent and demonstrative at least up to the age of five. We do know that such affective bonds are necessary for children to be willing (i.e. without coercion) to accept parental directives [Maccoby & Martin 30], and that such affect plays an important role in developing self-regulation [Harter 20; Radke-Yarrow *et al.* 35]. However, if such demonstrativeness is limited to the younger years, the child would not have the capacity to make the necessary attributions. We do not know how much affection is displayed in later years and whether the child's awareness of these bonds operates to mediate and modify the effects of the authoritarian and punitive approaches typically employed. Kerr [26], in her study of older rural Jamaican children, found that they were aware of their parents' affection and that this made them coquettish and inclined to be amused at their parents' anger. The social context which Kerr describes, however, differs qualitatively from that evident in the research reviewed here. We need to know how children's perception of parents' affection blunts the harshness of their punitive and authoritarian responses.

We have seen that in roughly one-half the households, the father was not present. We do not know what the developmental consequences of this absence are for the low-income Jamaican child. In their review of research, Maccoby & Martin [30] suggest that both mothers and fathers are psychologically salient to the developing child and that they adopt somewhat different roles with respect to certain parenting functions. For example, fathers engage in more 'active' play than mothers. And in studies of single-parent families, it appears that fathers play an important role in young boys' development of masculinity (though not in boys over 5 years old), and in girls' social interaction with males [Huston 22]. Father absence may also lead to misconception or ignorance about male roles. Brodber [4] found that many low-income Jamaican children were unable to describe the role of the father or of the male. Societies and communities may devise ways of compensating for a pervasive problem. We need further evidence of the effects of father absence on children's development in Jamaica and the societal structures which compensate for their absence.

It is widely accepted that play in various forms relates to growth in some developmental areas. Play has been shown to be related to creativity — defined as associative fluency and ability to generate original ideas — to problem solving, to language development, certain social skills and social cognition. The mediating processes often mentioned in these studies are pretence and make-believe, perspective taking, role taking, exploration and manipulation [Christie & Johnson 6; Rubin et al. 38]. We have seen that young low-income Jamaican children, especially those in urban areas, have a limited number of ply materials and because of physical and other constraints, few opportunities for solitary or indoor play. Thus they may be denied the benefits of engaging in such processes.

However, we know from Jarrett's study [23] that younger children have ample opportunity for active outdoor play. Landmann's study [27] suggests that some younger children use found materials for constructive play - i.e. the manipulation of objects to construct and create things. Such activities may allow for some of the processes which foster the outcomes outlined above. Older children engage in many outdoor games-with-rules, which may influence social as well as physical development. We need to examine the various types of outdoor games in which Jamaican children participate and the mental and social processes which they engender in order to determine the effects of limited indoor play and play materials.

Jarrett's study [23] suggests that younger children have siblings or peers available for play and other activities. We have little research evidence on the nature of friendships and peer relations among older Jamaican children. We do know, however, that such peer relations are crucial for the child's development. For example, they allow the child to engage in what Maccoby et al. calls 'status symmetrical exchange processes' [30], and is an important task in his/her social/emotional development.

To conclude this section, I report a few research studies which point to the outcomes of the socialization and child-rearing practices here described. Jarrett [23] discovered that 4-year-olds had a limited vocabulary and were unable to give adequate descriptions in their own creole language [23]. They also lacked the ability to make coherent sentences — choosing instead a few words to express ideas, relationships, positions and so on. These findings are reiterated in an earlier study by Wein [46] in which low-income children scored significantly lower than middle-class children on test of personal, social responsiveness (body language and ability to execute tasks), associative vocabulary (general knowledge, orientation to the environment) and conceptual developments. These findings suggest limited verbal interaction and a range of experiences. One can also speculate that in contrast with children from the middle classes, children from this income group would lack the experience of organizing and presenting ideas and the confidence in expressing themselves with adults.

Watson [45], in her comparison of children from five different types of communities, found that children from rural areas with limited opportunities for play were the least independent in their 'action modalities' and the least imaginative in contrast with children from the middle-income areas who were the most independent and imaginative. She speculated that the middle-class children lived in communities in which they 'have the opportunity to give free range to their thoughts and to ... integrate thought and action ...'. (p. 194)

Mitchelmore [33] discovered that Jamaican children lag behind their American and English counterparts in their spatial ability, i.e. their ability to recognize and be sensitive to variations in shapes, sizes and mass. There were also significant differences between boys and girls in the Jamaican sample with the boys showing superiority in spatial ability.

The following section considers the evidence on socialization from the point of view of its coherence and congruity and its adequacy for preparing the child for school.

Societies and cultural groups differ in degree to which their child-rearing practices are coherent — one with another, with beliefs, values and aspirations for children, and with future role demands. When we consider the aspirations of these parents for their children's education and life chances, there is a clear contradiction. Parents express a firm belief in education as an avenue for better opportunities, as a means of upward social mobility, and as a passport to white-collar jobs. They apparently transfer their own thwarted aspirations to some or all of their children [Foner 13], and willingly make sacrifices for their children [Kerr 26; Anderson 1; Foner 13; Grant et al. 17; Landmann et al. 27]. These parents desire for their children prestigious occupations such as medicine, law or teaching, shunning more lowly occupations such as farming, carpentry or plumbing [Anderson 1]. Indeed, rural and urban parents display a negative attitude toward manual labour and farming [Foner 13; Grant 16].

Yet, despite these high aspirations, parents do not know how to help their children reach these goals. Only a few envisage secondary education and none higher education for their children [Anderson 1; Landmann et al. 27]. At the same time, the parents in Anderson's study felt that children waste too much time on their books. The parents' aspirations may not even be based on any knowledge of the child's capability or interests. In contrast with middle-income parents, low-income parents do not consult their children when planning future careers for them. Very often, they are unaware of the difficulties which children are experiencing in school, or even their present grade level [Seaga 39; Grant 14]. Nor do many low-income parents communicate with teachers regarding their child's progress.

Parents' misconceptions regarding the educational process was evident in Seaga's study conducted in the 1950s. Parents in Rural Ridge believed that children could absent themselves with impunity and catch up on their return to school. Children's academic achievement depended solely on their natural ability, and such children were quickly recognized. The others paradoxically could be kept away from school at any time, since it made no difference. But those 'With the head for learning,' the teacher was expected to flog in order to make them concentrate on their books [Seaga 39]. The belief that corporal punishment was essential to learning was also expressed in Anderson's study [1].

Evident here is a contradiction between educational aspirations and educational beliefs, and a conflict between these aspirations and beliefs and child-rearing practices. These beliefs undoubtedly result from a lack of understanding of the process of learning and education. Thus they profess a belief in education as an avenue for upward mobility, hold high expectations for their children's future and at the same time contend that their children 'waste time on books'. Such beliefs may influence the child's access to learning and education. One can also detect a conflict between these high aspirations and child-rearing practices. We have seen from the implications of the research on child-rearing practices that the child is not likely to achieve optimal development of some crucial skills and dispositions necessary for success in school.

One can judge child-rearing practices by their appropriateness in preparing children for future roles in the society. One such role is student in the institutional context of the school. The children are required not only to learn but to fit into institutional and group demands. They have to learn and adhere to rules, to remain still and wait their turn for the major part of the day, to share limited classroom resources, and to be co-operative and share with peers. They need to display a sense of responsibility and orientation to the task at hand in order to please the teacher and accomplish academic and other assigned tasks. Those children (primarily girls) who have had to assume responsibility for younger siblings and for carrying out tasks around the house may be able to display this responsibility and task orientation (though their attitudes to the task are unpredictable). And most children would have learned to interact with their peers.

However, these children have not had the benefits of regular routines and continuing supervision. Without this supervision, they may not have acquired the habit of following rules. They would have spent much of their leisure time in outdoor activities and little on reading. Consequently, they may be at a disadvantage with respect to rule following, waiting one's turn and remaining still for long periods of time. Learning to adhere to rules may be difficult since they have not had the experience of reasoning with adults and thus developing internal controls. These institutional demands of the school may not be desirable or even educational. Nevertheless, they are a feature of schools and can work to influence the child's achievement.

Academically they may be at a disadvantage. We have seen that these children have not had the continuing conversation and dialogue with adults — conversations which could help develop concepts or clarify misconceptions. They have not had extended exposure to the wider community which middle-class children would have had. And because of limited reading and play materials they may be behind in language and conceptual development, problem solving, creativity and some logical skills. Their transition to the world of the school will therefore be difficult and unless they make this transition rapidly, they will fall farther and farther behind. The evidence supports this prognosis. The claim is often made that low-income children do not do well in school. Compared with the middle classes, few gain places to the prestigious high schools. Roughly one-half leave the primary school illiterate. These outcomes can be attributed in part to what occurs or does not occur in school. But some of the variance may be attributable to the skills and dispositions with which they enter school.

SUMMARY AND CONCLUSION

This article has presented research data on the physical/social setting in which the majority of low-income Jamaican children live, on the social interaction which occurs between parents and children, and the values and beliefs which parents hold and which often affect their child-rearing practices. It examines both the theoretical literature on child development and international research on the effects of different child-rearing practices to determine the possible implications of this research for the development of the child and his/her later adjustment to school and to life. Certain conflicts and incongruities between values and beliefs on the one hand, and aspirations on the other, were revealed which may thwart the parents' and children's ambitions.

Though this examination suggests that some existing socialization practices may be deficient, it reveals several areas which need further investigation and which suggest the possible strengths which these experiences may foster in the child. The concluding comments will focus on areas needing research, some of which have already been alluded to above. For example, mention was made of the need for further research on the effects of father absence on children's development and/or the structures and relationships which often compensate for their absence. There was also reference to the lack of research on the various types of outdoor games which Jamaican children play and the mental and social processes which these games engender. Such research would help us to understand more fully the effects of limited indoor play and play materials on the child's overall development.

Most of the research can be classified on surveys, employing questionnaires as data gathering device. Only a very few employ approaches which allow the researcher to observe and get closer to the realities of individual lives and situations, to discover meanings, motivations, and the pressures which parents experience. Such studies can complement the survey research data and allow us to form a better understanding of the intervening processes through which a particular environment or context affects development. Such studies may also reveal the day-to-day experiences of this group of children and the knowledge, attitudes and skills that derive from those experiences.

If the school is to be successful in educating the child, it needs to capitalize on his/her knowledge and skills gained from prior experiences. But we know little of what the low-income child knows or how that knowledge is structured and held. He/she has developed skills, attitudes and dispositions which must also be optimized or challenged. Research is needed to discover what low-income children know and are able to do when they arrive at school.

Finally, there is a need to find out more about the socializing influence of the school and its effect on children's social and emotional development. The experiences of children in Jamaican schools need to be further examined in research studies. Such research could seek to discover the links between the school's processes and activities, and children's development or later adjustment to adult roles and requirements.

REFERENCES

ANDERSON, K. V., *An Analysis of Certain Factors Affecting the Scholastic Achievement of Lower SES as Compared with Middle SES Children in Jamaica*, Unpublished D. Ed. Thesis, Cornell University, 1967.

ANDERSON, P., "Introduction: Women, Work and Development in the Caribbean", in M. GILL and J. MASSIAH (eds.), *Women, Work and Development*, Cave Hill, UWI: ISER, 1984.

BRODBER, E., "Abandonment of Children in Jamaica", Kingston: UWI, ISER, 1974.

————, "The Child in His Social Environment", mimeo, n.d.

BRONFENBRENNER, U. & A. C. CROUTER, "The Evolution of Environmental Models in Developmental Research", in P. H. MUSSEN (ed.), *Handbook of Child Psychology*, Vol. I, New York: Wiley, 1983.

CHRISTIE, J. F. & E. P. JOHNSEN, "The Role of Play in Social-Intellectual Development', *Review of Educational Research*, Vol. 53, No. 1, 1983, pp. 93-115.

CLARK, C. G., "The Slums of Kingston", in L. COMITAS and D. LOWENTHAL (eds.), *Work and Family Life: West Indian Perspectives*, New York: Doubleday, 1973.

CLARKE, E., *My Mother Who Fathered Me*, 2nd ed., London: George Allen & Unwin, 1966.

CRAIG, S., "Sociological Theorizing in the English-Speaking Caribbean: A Review", *Social and Economic Studies*, Vol. 30, 1981, pp. 143-80.

CRAWFORD, F., "A Study of Beliefs and Practices relating to Child-Rearing in St Ann", Unpublished DCH Study, UWI, Department of Social & Preventative Medicine, 1977.

ENNEW, J., "Family Structure, Unemployment and Child Labour in Jamaica", *Development and Change*, Vol. 13, 1982, pp. 551-63.

————, & P. YOUNG, *Child Labour in Jamaica*, London: Anti-Slavery Society, 1981.

FONER, N., *Status and Power in Rural Jamaica*, New York: Teacher's College Press, 1973.

GRANT, D. R. B., *Living Conditions of Some Basic School Children: Pointers to Disadvantage*, Kingston: PECE, 1974.

————, *Life Style Study: Children of the Lesser World in the English-Speaking Caribbean. Vol. I: The Literature in Retrospect*, Kingston, UWI: PECE, 1980.

————, *Life Style Study: Children of the Lesser World in the English-Speaking Caribbean. Vol. II: Ecological Characteristics of the Target Areas*, Kingston, UWI: PECE, 1981.

————, E. LEO-RHYNIE & G. ALEXANDER, *Children of the Lesser World in the English-Speaking Caribbean. Vol. V: Household Structures and Settings*, Kingston, UWI: PECE, 1983.

HALL, R., "Backyard Nurseries Day Care - The People's Way", *Torch*, Vol. 26, No. 2, 1979.

————, J. RAWLINS & A. K. KAUMAN, "Jamaican Backyard Nurseries", *World Health Forum*, Vol. 5, 1979, pp. 136-37.

HARTER, S., "Developmental Perspectives on the Self-System", in P.H. MUSSEN (ed.), *Handbook of Child Psychology*, Vol. 4, New York: Wiley, 1983.

HENRIQUES, F., "West Indian Family Organization", in L. COMITAS & D. LOWENTHAL (eds.) , *Work and Family Life: West Indian Perspectives*, New York: Doubleday, 1973.

HUSTON, A. C., "Sex-Typing", in P. H. MUSSEN (ed), *Handbook of Child Psychology*, Vol. 4, New York: Wiley, 1983.

JARRETT, J., "A Survey of the Experiential Background of a Sample of Lower Class Pre-School Jamaican Children", Unpublished B. Ed. I. Study, Faculty of Education, UWI, 1976.

————, "An Investigation Into Classroom Procedures of Selected Early Childhood Institutions to Determine the Extent to Which They Build on the Experiential Background of the Child", Unpublished B. Ed. II Study, Faculty of Education, UWI, 1977.

KEITH, S., "Socialization in the Jamaican Primary School: A Study of Teacher Evaluation and Student Participation", in P. M. E. FIGUEROA and G. PERSAUD (eds.), *Sociology of Education: A Caribbean Reader*, Oxford: OUP, 1979.

KERR, M., *Personality and Conflict in Jamaica*, London: Collins, 1963.

LANDMANN, J., S. GRANTHAM-McGREGOR & P. DESAI, "Child-Rearing Practices in Kingston, Jamaica", *Caribbean Quarterly*, Vol. 29, Nos. 3 & 4, 1983, pp. 40-52.

McFARLANE-GREGORY, D. & A. TAYLOR, "The Socio-Economic Situation of the English-Speaking Caribbean During the 1980s With Particular Reference to the Situation of Children and Their Families", mimeo, 1981.

McKENZIE, H., "Introduction: Women and the Family in Caribbean Society", in Women In The Caribbean Project, *Women and the Family*, Cave Hill, UWI: ISER, 1982.

MACCOBY, E. E. & J. A. MARTIN, "Socialization in the Context of the Family: Parent-Child Interaction", in P. H. MUSSEN (ed), *Handbook of Child Psychology*, Vol. 4, New York: Wiley, 1983.

MARJORIBANKS, K., "Occupational Status, Family Environments and Adolescents' Aspirations: The Laosa Model", *Journal of Education Psychology*, Vol. 76, No. 4, 1984, pp. 680-700.

MASSIAH, J., "Women Who Head Households", in Women In The Caribbean Project, *Women and the Family*, Cave Hill, UWI: ISER, 1982.

MITCHELMORE, M. C., "Three-Dimensional Geometrical Drawings in Three Cultures", *Educational Studies in Mathematics*, Vol. II, 1980, pp. 205-16.

PINTRICH, P. R. & P. C. BLUMENFIELD, "Classroom Experience and Children's Self-Perceptions of Ability, Effort and Conduct", *Journal of Educational Psychology*, Vol. 77, No. 6, 1985, pp. 646-57.

RADKE-YARROW, M., C. ZAHN-WAXLER, & M. CHAPMAN, "Children's Pro-Social Dispositions and Behaviour", in P. H. MUSSEN (ed), *Handbook of Child Psychology*, Vol. 4, New York: Wiley, 1983.

ROBERTS, G. W. & S. SINCLAIR, *Women in Jamaica - Patterns of Reproduction and Family*, Millwood: TKO Press, 1978.

RUTTER, M. & N. MADGE, *Cycles of Disadvantage*, London: Heinemann, 1977.

RUBIN, K. H., G. G. FEIN & V. VANDENBERG, "Play", in P. H. MUSSEN (ed), *Handbook of Child Psychology*, Vol. 4, New York: Wiley, 1983.

SEAGA, E. P. G., "Parent-Teacher Relationship in a Jamaican Village", *Social and Economic Studies*, Vol. 4, No. 3, 1955.

SMITH, M. G., *West Indian Family Structure*, Seattle: University of Washington Press, 1962.

————, "A Survey of West Indian Family Studies", in L. COMITAS & D. LOWENTHAL (eds.), *Work and Family Life: West Indian Perspectives*, New York: Doubleday, 1973.

————, "Culture, Race and Class in the Commonwealth Caribbean", Kingston: Department of Extra-Mural Studies, 1984.

SOCIAL AND ECONOMIC SURVEY OF JAMAICA, 1984.

SOLIEN, N., "Household and Family in the Caribbean", in M. M. HOROWITZ (ed), *Peoples and Cultures of the Caribbean*, New York: Natural History Press, 1971.

WATSON, E. M., "The Non-School Environment and Children's Creativity", *Caribbean Journal of Education*, Vol. 6, No. 3, 1979, pp. 178-96

WEIN, N., *Longitudinal Study Progress Report No. 1*, UWI, Institute of Education, Bernard Van Leer Foundation, 1972.

WEINER, B., "A Theory of Motivation For Some Classroom Experiences", *Journal of Educational Psychology*, Vol. 71, No. 1, 1979, pp. 3-25.

8

Social Policy:
State, Law and Church

Systematic studies of social policy and family life in the Caribbean are sadly lacking. In very general terms, the Caribbean experience is one in which policy has operated within pluralistic conceptions of society and has been designed to restructure 'deviant', 'malfunctioning' lower-class families in accordance with the moral principles and structural forms assumed to exist among the elites and the middle classes of the Caribbean and which are invested with moral and legal confirmation as being 'right and proper'. In this overview of social policy, we examine briefly the general principles and objectives that have informed family policy before dealing in somewhat more detail with the prescriptions and policies of the law and religion.

General principles and objectives of family policy

From the days of slavery in the Caribbean, the family has been a major target of social policy. As we noted in Chapter VI, programmes of rewards and incentives designed to restructure slave families were implemented, at this stage not as an end in themselves, but because planters were convinced that the nuclear family household correlated with the higher fertility rates they required to replenish the slave labour force. In the post-emancipation years, misdirected policy efforts to establish nuclear families continued, but the rationale (Smith 1982, see Article 1 at end of chapter), was different. By then, the objective was a moral one. For colonial social ideology, it was imperative that the black ex-slave population be taught civilised ways and the way to achieve this, through education and conversion to Christianity, was by the establishment of proper family life, meaning families structured as co-resident, nuclear and based on marriage. The colonial elite and the Caribbean middle-class cadre of social workers, teachers and the like were totally convinced that policies designed to engineer a change in family structures would work. The lower classes would, without a doubt, see the error of their ways and respond positively to rational policy interventions to solve their problems of family life.

In recent times, these notions of nuclear family ideals and related policies have been supplemented by a concern with extended family breakdown and replacement by nuclear families. In Barbados, for example, it is generally assumed that the extended family provides a preferred multiple adult context for the socialisation of children which the isolated nuclear family lacks. Conceptualising the extended family as the bedrock of desirable morals and norms has been enhanced in contemporary society by increasing anti-social pressure from peer groups and the media and by rapid intergenerational social change. As Richard Carter (1992: 15) has explained, extended families in Barbados,

> typically have a (maternal) grandmother and uncles and aunts who assist in the sociali-
> sation process, especially while the mother is at work. A traditionalist strand of this the-
> sis argues that within this framework the 'sound Barbadian values' are more effectively
> transmitted since 'authoritative others' such as grandparents, uncles and aunts are
> placed in direct contact with children. In this perspective the family is presented
> as conservative (slowing the pace of social change) and monolithic (influencing
> individual beliefs in a forceful and consistent manner). Children easily internalise the
> values of the preceding generation providing for significant ideological continuity and
> resistance to extra-familial socialisation which may create pressures for social change.

On the other hand, the nuclear family,

> is less facilitative of intergenerational value transmission since both maternal siblings
> and maternal parents are physically absent. This situation is (presumably) exacerbated
> by two factors: Firstly by the increasing potency of the other socialising agencies, given
> the growing importance of the educational system, peers and the media in contempo-
> rary society. Secondly, by the rapid pace of social change which accelerates the rate of
> generational dissimilarity with respect to moral and social values (Carter 1992: 15).

Carter's article has shown that there is a lack of evidence to support the shift from extended to nuclear family norms. Most importantly, he cautioned against the dangers of basing social policy on misconceived assumptions which attribute deviance and violence among the youth of Barbados to notions of extended family breakdown which, in turn, rest on unsubstantiated conclusions.

Studies of the family in the Caribbean began with a close link between theory and policy. The early investigators, such as Thomas Simey might be better described as social administrators, with more interest in restructuring the family than in developing a sociological understanding. The role of sociology was to provide an objective understanding of the problems of family life and plans for solving them. But the investigators were not value-free and their colonialist, ethnocentric interpretations of Caribbean family patterns resulted in some crass social engineering blunders. When the structural functionalists took over, a clear division of labour between sociology and social welfare, between academic researcher and social practitioner was established. We therefore face the paradox that, although our understanding of family in the Caribbean is much improved, the contribution of sociological investigation to social policy has been reduced to a minimum. Another consequence is that Caribbean family life is perceived in isolation from the institutions of mainstream society. With reference to the law, Mindie Lazarus-Black (1991: 120) contended:

> Caribbean scholars neglect the legal codes and processes that influenced the develop-
> ment of kinship systems in this region and miss the ways in which West Indian people

acknowledge and use law and legal processes today to define family and to achieve the rights and duties that belong to kin.

The point can be extended to the State and the Church. Much of Caribbean social policy, therefore, continues firstly, to be based on assumptions of how families ought to be and what their members should be doing as mothers and wives, fathers and husbands and so forth, rather than how the roles and relationships are constructed in reality; and secondly, to refuse to recognise how family ideology and practice have all along been interacting with and adapting state, religious and legal prescription and policy.

The cultural heritage of the Caribbean continues to reflect multiple strands. Especially distinguishable are the values and practices of everyday life and those English-based patterns which have been incorporated into formal social institutions. This is evident in family studies, most clearly in the contrast between prevailing family patterns, on the one hand, and the ideologies and policies of the law and the Church, on the other. Historically, these two institutions as arms of the colonial state functioned to uphold and disseminate the high culture and morals of society. A major policy objective was to assess and upgrade social behaviour in accordance with these, especially in family life. It was important, therefore, to withhold recognition and acceptance of prevailing cultural patterns for fear that this would reinforce family deviance and instability. Gloria Cumper (1972: 10) explained the rationale with reference to the law and proceeded to argue against it.

> The point will at once be taken, and indeed must be considered, that to give legal recognition to any relationship existing outside the monogamous marriage laid down by law might be to destroy even further the already weak basis of family life. If this were to be the effect, it would be most undesirable. But the facts show that even the difficulties and hardships of family relationships which do not enjoy the protection of the law have not discouraged people from entering into such relationships. Indeed the contrary is the case, and it might well be that the imposition of legal rights and responsibilities between members of such extra-legal families might at least give the measure of stability which they now lack and provide some protection for the members.

While the law has responded with reforms that recognise the reality of Caribbean family life, albeit slowly and with great hesitation, the Church has not. The contrast between the moral principles of Christianity and family patterns in the Caribbean has been a continuous topic of debate, the most recent focus of which concentrates on the Church and the common-law union. We proceed by exploring the relationship between the family and first, the law and second, the Church.

Family and the law

Caribbean family law was derived from the laws of other countries in which family structure and patterns are very different. Much was taken from England and assumed the existence of a nuclear family norm. The result was that the majority of Caribbean people, those with 'deviant' family forms, were 'social outcasts or lesser breeds without the law' (Wooding 1972: 144). The injustice became all the more obvious and should have constituted a source of acute embarrassment to Caribbean governments and the legal profession when the situation was compared with the statements enshrined in the national constitutions of the region, many of which are closely linked to the Universal Declaration of Human Rights. Two important Articles of the Declaration read as follows:

Article 7: All are equal before the law and are entitled without any discrimination to equal protection before the law. All are entitled to equal protection against any discrimination in violation of this Declaration and against any incitement to such discrimination.

Article 25, Section 2: Motherhood and childhood are entitled to special care and assistance. All children, whether born in or out of wedlock, shall enjoy the same social protection.

More recently, however, a new approach has become evident as the countries of the region have acknowledged the continued prevalence of common-law wives and illegitimate children, despite legal disabilities, and the long overdue need to remove legal discrimination against them.

A glaring omission in the laws of the Caribbean concerned the non-recognition of illegitimate children. In English Common Law the illegitimate child, 'filius nullius', is a bastard without a father and virtually devoid of legal rights. He and his brothers and sisters in the Caribbean are in the majority by far, with, as we have seen, percentages averaging between the high sixties and mid-seventies, and reports of legal discrimination against them are legend (Fraser 1972: 124-143). Similarly, common-law wives in the Caribbean have also fallen outside the protective framework of the law and suffered the consequences. Tales are frequently recounted of women who lived faithfully and for many years with a common-law partner only to be 'disinherited' on his death.

Country people in the West Indies usually associate the making of a will with their death: and so, many fathers have died intestate and their children and common-law wives have been left penniless because estranged widows or next-of-kin have greedily seized the estate of their departed relations. Often the next-of-kin are persons with whom the deceased may not have been on good terms. In some cases they have smirked at the women who 'lived in sin' with the departed relative and have ignored her children. It is cynical to observe that in some quarters this is thought to be a highly commendable Christian attitude, said to be hallowed by divine writ, and curiously it happens to be bolstered by established legal principle when the law's concern should be the achievement of justice (Fraser 1972: 138).

Failure to marry is a long way short of a criminal offence yet the penalty is often considerable. For example when the man in the family dies his property, which the couple probably regarded as belonging to both of them may be claimed by a brother or a wife who has not been a true wife for many years, and the common-law wife may be left destitute (Cumper and Daley 1979: 224).

At the *First Workshop on Social Legislation Relating to the Family and Child in the Caribbean* held in Trinidad in 1975, among the 'fundamental resolutions' to be adopted were the following two:

The relationship between every person and his father and mother should for all purposes be determined irrespective of whether the father and mother are married to each other, and all other relationships should be determined accordingly. Legislation should lay down the rules by which paternity should be established for this purpose.

Recognition of common-law unions and the maintenance of common-law spouses should be the subject of urgent study by the respective governments in Caribbean territories (Cumper and Daley 1979: 235-236).

By 1975 Barbados had already paved the way for family law reform with the Succession Act (1975-46). The Act extended rights of inheritance to illegitimate children and common-law wives. The act redefined 'child' and 'issue' and gave illegitimate children an equal right to inherit, whether by will or intestacy, from the estates of their mothers and also their fathers providing that paternity had been legally established. Status of the Children legislation was also passed in Jamaica, St Vincent and Belize to provide for inheritance by illegitimate children (Forde 1981: 83). However, the problem of establishing paternity remains. The onus is on the mother to provide 'evidence' which is corroborated, often a difficult and embarrassing task.

In many other respects, the status of illegitimate children remained unchanged. What was important, however, was that the Succession Act of Barbados and others like it elsewhere in the Caribbean established the principle of equality of all children, whether legitimate or illegitimate, so facilitating additional reforms of the law. In 1980 when the Status of Children Reform Act (1979-32) came into effect in Barbados, the legal distinction between legitimate and illegitimate children was totally abolished. The Act states:

> All children shall after the commencement of this Act, be of equal status, and a person is the child of his or her natural parents and his or her status as their child is independent of whether the child is born within or outside of marriage.

The Barbados legislation also provided for inheritance by common-law wives, by will or intestacy. As Norma Forde (1981: 82-83) explained:

> In Barbados the Succession Act, by careful definition of 'spouse' has sought to protect succession rights of the partners in a common law union. Spouse is defined to include a single man and a single woman living together as man and wife for a continuous period of five years immediately preceding the death of either of the parties. A common law spouse who qualifies, is competent to succeed to the statutory portion of the testator's estate as a legal right.

These provisions were subsequently extended to include maintenance.

> The 1981 Barbados Family Law Act has introduced a new dimension to family maintenance by clarifying and simplifying the maintenance principles and procedure and including in the general maintenance provisions the parties to a common law union which has continued for five years or more. Now the woman in a 'stable' common law union has been given an opportunity, legally, to seek financial assistance for herself and not only for her child, should such assistance be needed (Forde 1981: 122).

The laws of several Caribbean territories have, in the last twenty years or so, moved steadily towards closing the gap between legal prescription and social reality, especially by recognising and extending protection to children born outside wedlock and women in common-law unions. However, in family matters as in others, the value of legal reforms depends on transfer from paper to practice and on the adoption of similar principles by other social institutions. In other words, disadvantage and discrimination will persist unless new laws are comprehensible and accessible to all, especially the less well-educated, and unless social institutions, such as the Church, cease to isolate the majority as second-class citizens.

Family and the Church

The conflict between religious doctrine and practice and Caribbean family values and patterns has preoccupied the clergy, missionaries and sociologists since the days of slavery, although very little has been reported in the way of systematic research and analysis. Family patterns have been perceived as 'abnormal' and 'immoral'. Dom Basil Matthews, a Trinidadian Catholic priest mentioned in Chapter II, attributed the existence of non-legal unions and illegitimacy to the slave plantation system and castigated them as:

> Those low standards and that low grade mentality which the scourge of slavery during four hundred years burnt into the souls of the subject folk. What is the bearing of this on the non-legal union? It is common knowledge that this low grade mentality constitutes the moral climate in which the non-legal union flourishes. There can be no gainsaying that fact (Matthews 1953: 35).

The solutions proposed to resolve the conflict invariably and repeatedly recommend changes in family patterns through the systematic Christian education of the ex-slave and lower-class black population to improve their domestic lives (Barrow forthcoming/a). Since the days of slavery, the Church has been perceived as the domain of those practising morally correct behavioural standards in their familial and social lives. The ideology of exclusiveness persists. From the perspective of a practising Methodist priest, Rev. John Hoad (1972: 119) stated the position:

> One of the difficulties in getting the Church to act is that Church people are often the people who have now succeeded to a certain position in life given them by their having gotten married. And when the Methodist Church last January in Jamaica called for a positive ministry to those in non-marital unions, you know we had a counter-blast against this in the newspapers, full of moral indignation, because to the person who has now succeeded, now got the marriage badge, it seems terrible that now you want to treat the others on the same level anyhow. And it's within the Church, and it's with moralism that you are going to have the greatest difficulty of a positive approach to those outside, because those inside are those who have made it and don't want to be treated on the same level as those who haven't made it.

Common-law couples have been excluded from the Church and, although their illegitimate offspring could be baptised, the ceremony had to be performed on a weekday. Sundays were reserved for babies born in wedlock. It is only now, as the Church confronts its lack of success with conversion to marriage and probably also grapples with persistent declines in the size of congregations, that the continuing problem of what to do about common-law unions has prompted a fundamental re-examination of religious principles and policies.

The traditional position of the Church is that the only morally valid sexual union is a legal Christian marriage. The legal requirements pertain to the characteristics of the couple, such as age and degrees of consanguinity and affinity, and the ceremony, including procedures such as notification and the presence of a registered marriage officer and witnesses. The marital relationship also defines certain rights and responsibilities including mutual respect and honour, exclusive sexual access, co-residence, economic maintenance and protection and the sharing and inheritance of property. Most importantly, marriage is perceived as a permanent relationship, until death do part, and the only proper context for the reproduction and socialisation of children within the Christian faith. Accordingly, for the Church, common-law unions are not marriages. Their establishment is not publicly and ceremonially acknowledged and the rights and duties of the couple are not specified and binding, especially as regards fidelity. Common-law unions are therefore viewed by the Church as impermanent and immoral, as a form of living in sin. The involvement of persons in these relationships is perceived to constitute 'a conscious and deliberate rebellion against the divine order' (Dundas 1990: 23).

A problem arises when individuals who live in common-law unions express a desire to convert to Christianity. The two are considered to be fundamentally incompatible, as Leon Dundas (1990: 4-5) has explained.

> Such persons typically face a choice between the church, which is often equated with God, and family. Unless they separate from their partner who is unwilling to enter legal marriage, they are told they cannot serve God. They also have to grapple with the fear of losing financial security and a place to live, and especially for women, the prospect of remaining single.

The following case-study highlights the extent of the dilemma for those persons involved, implying that it is women who suffer most.

> The dissatisfaction for the women stems from the conflict between their need to engage freely in the service of God and the unwillingness of the Church to accept them into its membership while they share a Common-law Union. This situation is illustrated in the true case of Liz and Ranny. They shared a Common-law Union for about thirty years, and both were in their mid-fifties. The union produced five children and a grandchild, all of whom lived in a small two apartment house. Liz was a regular visitor to the local Baptist church, but Ranny never attended church. Liz eventually decided to become a Christian, to be baptized and to assume membership in the church. When she was mentioned to the officers for baptism they decided that before she could be admitted for baptism she should become legally married. The pastor met with her and Ranny and discussed the question of marriage. Ranny insisted that he loved Liz, and was happy with her, but for several reasons he was unable to legalize their union. The efforts to persuade him were unsuccessful. On the basis of this, therefore, Liz was refused baptism by the church. She continued in the church, however, as a consistent visitor. On several occasions she wept through the worship service. She complained that she needed to get married in order that she might be baptized and be able to enjoy the privileges of church membership. Ranny, however, refused to legalize the union. Liz's experience is a typical example of the dissatisfaction and discontent which quietly plague the lives of the great majority of the women who share Common-law Unions (Panton 1992: 24-25).

Church policy in these situations is to counsel the couple, persuade them of the evil of their ways, arrange for them to be married and subsequently admit them to full Christian fellowship. The problem with this course of action is the resistance to marriage among Caribbean people, especially men, if we are to believe the literature. As we have noted in an earlier chapter, the incidence of marriage in the Caribbean has remained at much the same low level, despite the spread of education, Christian teaching and socio-economic progress. Programmes specifically designed to encourage marriage have not succeeded. If the Mass Marriage Movement of Jamaica, mentioned in Chapter II, failed despite its widespread coverage, extensive resources and systematic organisation, then how, one may ask, can individual churches make a difference? The alternative solution acceptable to the church is the termination of the common-law union before membership is granted.

The pressure to marry adopted by the Church as a solution to the problem is recognised as unsatisfactory by some members of the clergy themselves. It is seen to exclude many who would otherwise benefit from the influence of Christianity and reflects a misunderstanding of the realities of Caribbean society. Worse still, according to one priest, by avoiding the issue the Church perpetuates 'much hypocrisy and deception', prompting couples in common-law unions to falsely claim that they are married, while others deny the existence of their visiting unions (Panton 1992: 31). Adultery in marriage may be overlooked, while faithful conjugal co-residence is negatively sanctioned. The policy may even cause the break up of the very family units the church is anxious to upgrade. In 1972, a church consultation held in Barbados recorded the following concern:

> The attitude of the churches to the parents of 'illegitimate' children has been to reject their unions out of hand rather than recognize and strengthen what is good in them. We are therefore moved to challenge a great deal that has become associated with marriage in the Caribbean. Marriage has come to stand for a certain social status and the acceptance of class, rather than Christian values. We believe that Jesus' healing friendship with those considered 'outsiders' in His day should lead us to a ministry in which we begin with people where they are, not waiting until they have been processed by a church wedding before accepting them as persons and sharing with them the exploration of greater family health, responsibility, care, planning and personal growth (Haynes 1972: 16-17).

At the consultation, Dr E. A. Allen made the following recommendation:

> Christian marriage or faithful concubinage is the same thing, one is legal and one isn't, one is blessed by the Church and one isn't .... I'm suggesting that in faithful concubinage which still exists, instead of conveying the sense of 'living in sin' the Church try to find some means through the Church and through the law of the land of accepting that type (Allen 1972: 101).

The plea fell on deaf ears until the early 1990s when two Caribbean clergymen explored and analysed the mechanisms involved in the Church's recognition of the common-law union and recommended a fundamental doctrinal rethink and a departure from established policy.

In his thesis presented for an MA in Theology, Dundas proposed that theology follow sociology in making a distinction between 'purposive unions', defined as 'common-law unions which are entered into deliberately and selectively with the hope that the unions would be permanent', and 'casual concubinage', that is 'common law unions which are established fortuitously and are exploitative of unstable situations'. The former, according to Dundas, should be viewed by the Church as moral; the latter as immoral (Dundas 1990: 6). With this distinction in mind, Dundas recommended that the Church shift attention from legal prescriptions and the proper performance of the marriage ceremony to the nature of the marital relationship, a position which echoed Rev. James Springer (1972: 96) in Barbados when he asked: 'Should we in the Church preach marriage or should we preach "good" family life?' Citing evidence from Caribbean anthropology and sociology, Dundas claimed that many common-law relationships are like those of marriage in terms of the feelings, rights and duties of the spouses and the provision of a firm foundation for good family life. Although he did not completely absolve common-law partners from moral culpability, he argued that their involvement in such unions reflected their socio-economic circumstances rather than a lack of commitment to the ideals of married life (Dundas 1990: 60). He concluded:

> By implication sexual intercourse between persons who are in the process of accepting marital responsibilities and who are actually carrying through the abiding and unique implications of their sexual relationship could be confirmed by the church as married. To state the point differently, except when their relationship clearly contravenes the biblical principles of marriage, persons who live with each other as if they are man and wife could be declared to be married under God. That is, they should know that while the legal duties of spouses may not apply to them, the divinely ordained responsibilities of marriage do (Dundas 1990: 72).

Vivian Panton's work as a Baptist minister in Jamaica reflected much the same position. He reminded us that during and after slavery the emphasis of Christian missionary activity was on baptism and that, even after the passage of laws making marriage widely accessible, it was still considered by the clergy to be a privilege for the few. This meant that from the perspective of the Church, 'marriage' was very broadly defined to cover all co-residential, stable unions which promised monogamy and fidelity. It was only later that the morality of unions became tied to their legality. Panton also separated faithful concubinage from what he called 'shack up relationships' and recognised them as an integral part of Caribbean culture. In his words:

> Common-law Union should not be viewed as an immoral and irresponsible family pattern as it is generally conceived by the Church in Jamaica. It was not produced, it did not develop, and it is not being sustained in a vacuum. Instead, it might be thought of as a social institution which is rooted in, and has developed from, concrete historical realities. At present it is also being sustained by contemporary factors which are no less real than the historical ones. These factors, themselves, are the result of motives, emotions, and values that are institutionalized in the present culture. Common-law Union, therefore, as an integral component of the Jamaican culture, must be viewed as representing the Jamaican peasants' equivalent of marriage, except that it has been denied the legal protection which is provided in a Legal Union (Panton 1992: 84).

Panton backed up his views with a project organised at his church in Jamaica which included a series of sermons, discussion and reflection. The conclusion among two-thirds of the congregation was that a change of policy is required on the part of the Church to baptise and receive into the fold those in stable common-law unions (Panton 1992: 88). In his 'concluding, untraditional postscript', Panton called for the decolonisation of Caribbean theology.

> The theological understanding which the Church has of itself and its missionary nature must be adjusted to reflect the cultural and social conditions of the Jamaican people. Consequently, Common-law Union must be viewed and accepted by the Church as a social institution which is relative to the Jamaican culture and to the Caribbean region as a whole.

> The recognition of cultural relativity in regard to Common-law Union in Jamaica will carry with it its own social and moral values which need not be the same as those of

Europe. It must be stated that while the writer recognises that there are absolute dimensions to moral values, such dimensions do not relate to the pattern(s) which constitute a marriage and a family. The fact that a marriage or a family union is not modelled on the basis of the European model does not necessarily render that union immoral or irresponsible. Moral behaviour and values must be related to their social base and they cannot be extracted from the society in which they exist. If a moral system survives it is not because it is better than others, but because it is well suited to the needs of that society (Panton 1992: 85).

In the Caribbean the debate continues and the voices of those committed to changing the position, though increasing in volume, remain few and somewhat isolated. From an academic perspective, the issue prompts a reopening of research on conjugal union types in the Caribbean. Earlier investigations had generally concluded that, from a functional perspective, there was little if any difference between marriages and common-law unions. However, the sociological evidence brought to bear on the theological discussion strongly implies that, at the level of ideology, common-law unions and marriages mean something different for Caribbean people and that a clear gender distinction in meaning exists. Is it the case then, that women are anxious to become members of the church and to change their unions in order to do so, whereas men are not? And if so why? Further sociological research to inform theological argument and policy is crucial.

Conclusion

It has taken a very long time for those in control of social policy and planning to realise that their efforts to reconstruct conjugal unions and family forms have met with limited success. The modern expansion of state apparatus and bureaucratic personnel in social work, child care, family planning, probation and youth affairs and so forth, all intended to deal with the family and other 'problems' of the lower class and the poor, has made little difference. Marriage rates have remained low, illegitimacy high, men peripheral to the family and women central, often heading their households, despite years of intensive and persistent preaching, education, social welfare and legal discrimination. The point is that few people change their cultural patterns in response to ethical condemnation. Caribbean family planning programmes, for example, have been successful not as a result of moral pressure to have fewer children, but because the provision of contraception gave people options. Women, in particular, could redefine motherhood within the context of their own lives and choose whether or not they wished to spend the greater part of their adult lives bearing and rearing children.

And maybe this is the approach that policy ought to adopt. If so, then the way is open for a reversal in the rationale for family policy. The justification in Simey's day was based on the moral duty of those whose job it was to determine social policy for the establishment of proper family structures: today questions are raised about the propriety and ethics of state interference and the intervention of professionals in the private lives of citizens (Smith 1982: 13). The legal profession has redefined its strategy to recognise, accommodate and protect Caribbean families which have for generations survived in isolation from the law or suffered discrimination at the hands of the law. The clergy, on the other hand, remains divided, with some struggling to reconcile religious doctrine with the reality of family life, while others continue their closed-door policy.

READINGS

R. T. Smith

FAMILY, SOCIAL CHANGE AND SOCIAL POLICY IN THE WEST INDIES

For Europe and North America there is a large literature devoted to the evaluation of social policies; for the Caribbean it is often difficult to find out what the policies are, much less how they are actually implemented. Most social welfare agencies in the Commonwealth West Indies have the shape and direction which they acquired during the colonial period, and in spite of some recent new departures it is to that period we must refer in order to understand the present situation. The last major review of social policy in the West Indies was occasioned by the riots and disturbances of the late 1930s, which led to the appointment of a Royal Commission and the subsequent passage of the Colonial Development and Welfare Acts of 1940 and 1945. Independence from Britain has not generally resulted in a searching examination of social policy, rhetoric to the contrary. The tendency seems to be to try to bring the area into line with a universal 'modern' practice, suitable or not, for no politician wishes to appear to be unprogressive.

This paper is not intended as a review of social policy, even in the restricted area of the family. Others will have to undertake that task. Its more modest aim is to re-examine the premises on which the policies of the terminal phase of colonial rule were based, to ask how they appear in the light of more recent work on the family, and then in the final section, and with the greatest hesitation, to suggest some implications of this work for the formulation of policy bearing on the family.

The first Social Welfare Adviser to the Comptroller for Development and Welfare in the West Indies, a post created in response to the riots of 1938 and the report of the Royal Commission which investigated their causes, was T. S. Simey. An academic sociologist who eventually became Charles Booth Professor of Social Science in the University of Liverpool, he spent the years 1941 to 1945 struggling to understand the nature of West Indian society and devise policies appropriate for it, rather than just importing ready-made schemes from Europe. He believed, ardently, in the possibility of a scientific approach to social engineering.

In the modern history of social policy in this region Simey is a particularly strategic figure. Not only did he play a leading part in implementing the new colonial policies but he also absorbed the social ideas of the most progressive elements of the West Indian middle class, and particularly the Jamaican middle class. He taught the first graduates of the new Welfare Training Courses held at Mona, Jamaica in 1943 and 1944, thus helping to set the pattern for future training. Most importantly he embodied his ideas and his experience in a book which is an indispensable guide to the thought of the period. Internally contradictory in many ways, *Welfare and Planning in the West Indies* raises all the important issues, and he regarded it as 'the record of the beginning of a fascinating and supremely important experiment in the planning of society and human relationships' (Simey 1946: 30).

Simey is also relevant to our topic in that he regarded the family as a central institution, with a formative influence on personality, and thus on society as a whole. In this he followed the conventional wisdom of his day and foreshadowed many subsequent interpretations which also found 'looseness' of family relations to be a major factor making for persistent poverty (M. G. Smith 1966; Moynhan 1965).

The bedrock of Simey's thinking is a series of ideas which are still with us in the 1980s, the simplest being that the West Indies are impoverished economically, disorganized socially and deficient culturally. 'The symptoms of serious disease in the body of modern society are only too obvious in the Colonies in general, and in the West Indies in particular' (Simey 1946: vi). Although his task is to 'investigate the causes of the ills which lie behind [the symptoms] and propound a really effective cure' he has decided *a priori* that colonial society is a special kind of problem. 'Life in the Colonies is, indeed, lived in a backwater from the main stream of human affairs, at one and the same time in several centuries, the social philosophies, moral values, and customs of which are mingled together in the wildest confusion (ibid.).' How this differs from Britain with its ceremonial royalty, vestigial aristocracy, nineteenth century utilitarian economic ethic and the beginnings of a twentieth century welfare state, he does not say.

In the circumstances of the 1940s political independence appeared to be some way off, contingent upon a series of intermediate factors. Self-determination would not be possible without adequate wealth, and that was dependent upon a 'social dynamic' powerful enough to drive the economic machine. Modern sociology was to provide both the understanding of the problems and the techniques for solving them; techniques for generating the 'social dynamic' that would set the machine of progress in motion. 'The work of the academic sociologist is being steadily translated into the language of the administrator, and a new method has been developed whereby social relationships and social problems can be studied objectively' (Simey 1946: viii). These are brave words and upon their promise has grown up a veritable industry of survey research, data banks, training programmes in social and political administration, experts, advisers and consultants. Sociology as an academic discipline would have been better served if it had claimed less and had fewer impossible demands placed upon it. It is a pity that Simey had not been influenced more by Karl Marx and Max Weber who knew, each in their own way, that the naive positivism of a supposedly value-free social science does not provide a set of blueprints for utopia.

In proper scientific manner Simey begins with a discussion of the infra-structure, a discussion reminiscent of Durkheim. Distances, densities, communications, population characteristics (deploring the lack of adequate statistics), are all dealt with before he turns to the issue of economic production, housing ('the most striking fact about the West Indian peoples, as exemplified in their houses, is their poverty'), income distribution, nutrition (Simey 1946: ii). And thus we come to the family by way of a direct comparison with Britain and America, in spite of the equal value of all ways of life.

> In Great Britain and North America nutrition centres on the family, and it is impossible to arrive at a clear understanding of social conditions in the West Indies without some consideration of the problem of family organization. The wages earned in Barbados for example, are insufficient to support family life of the type common in Great Britain; in the West Indies all members of a working-class family have to work if the budget is to be balanced (Simey 1946: 14-15).

He goes on to contrast the way in which a common family meal in Britain acts as a prop to family solidarity, whereas in the West Indies because the working class do not possess the necessary furniture this integrating activity is absent. This kind of crude, and simple-minded, determinism crops up again and again, even though in other places he makes many astute observations which totally contradict the idea that poverty determines all. The crux of the matter for Simey is that (1946: 15):

> The prevailing type of West Indian family which is encountered over and over again in all the colonies is very loose in organization. It is rarely founded on the ceremony of marriage, and the relationships between its members are often very casual indeed. There is little control over the children, who may receive plenty of maternal affection ... but little in the way of careful general upbringing.

It is fateful for the subsequent argument that poverty becomes the prime factor in shaping family relations. Men cannot discharge those obligations which are accepted without question in Britain and North America. But poverty is only part of a wider condition; along with lack of resources and inadequate nutrition there is more general 'weakness in social organization'. Only the church 'stands out as a rock round which the welter of disorganized human life surges' (Simey 1946: 18). However, the church does not seem to be able to fill the cultural void left by the forcible divorce from African culture and the as yet incomplete possession of the western way of life. Without the binding power of a common culture, and internally divided by racial cleavage, the picture is very like that drawn by J. C. Furnivall for the 'plural societies' of the Far East — as we were repeatedly to be reminded by M. G. Smith during the next two decades. Unlike M. G. Smith, both Simey and Furnivall stressed the solvent power of modern capitalism, and both called for cultural renewal or a new form of secular religion, nationalism (See R. T. Smith 1966 for a discussion).

Simey's treatment of religion runs curiously parallel to his discussion of the family. In neither case are African forms suitable for life in the West Indies. Some aspects of African religion persist in the form of superstitions embodied in sects which he dismisses contemptuously as sapping the energies of the people and undermining their economic life. Similarly sexual activity filled a need for self-expression and gratification among slaves, and like superstition it continues to function in the same way in the present. From the baseline of the slave plantation one can follow the functional adaptation of behaviour right up the present. If Haitian peasants have several wives it is because they need them to work their holdings; similarly Jamaican farmers must have the right to chop and change among partners in the interest of keeping up production. Migration within a particular territory, or to find work outside, leads 'naturally' to the creation of several families and the man has to stop sending support payments to the previous partner. So, economic factors account for 'the prevalence of the maternal family', but not totally; the patriarchal nature of the 'true peasant family' (described in almost the same terms as were used subsequently by Henriques 1953: 109), tends to prejudice 'the vast majority of young women against marriage as such' (Simey 1946: 87). Indeed he recognizes that in the towns, where prosperity is greatest, one finds the least marital stability.

When we have peeled back all the layers of Simey's discussion we come to a series of ideas about personality which, while not unique to him, have a decided effect upon his policy proposals. Juvenile delinquency is widespread he says — without offering any evidence for the assertion — and he follows this surprising observation with some speculations about child care and discipline. Children grow up without 'that close association between father and child' which is taken for granted in Great Britain and North America. Children are allowed to run wild outside but are harshly disciplined at home. Adults, not being 'schooled in self-control' cause children to grow up suffering from 'excessive anxiety and feelings of insecurity' (Simey 1946: 90). Add onto this the frustration engendered by racial discrimination and what do you get? Aggression, often disguised as unreliability, laziness, sensitivity to insult and even physical hostility.[2] The middle classes are subject to even more stress than the lower class; efforts to dissociate themselves from the masses, combined with the excessive individualism and competitiveness of modern life, creates hostility, a domineering attitude to the lower class and a 'profound spiritual *malaise*' (ibid: 104). This is all the more significant for Simey since middle class patterns of behaviour have to be adopted by the whole society. 'There is no going back, no possibility of founding a new culture on working class society alone' (Simey 1946: 103).

Recognizing that the West Indies cannot divorce itself from the rest of the world, and contending that things are getting worse rather than better, he calls for a total reorientation of administrative thinking. Recruitment of a better type of colonial administrator, efficient, selected by modern methods of psychological testing, open to scientific knowledge and dependent upon the dispassionate views of sociologists and anthropologists to guide the West Indian peoples toward self-determination via community organization and group therapy. All that nasty aggression, laziness and sexual self-indulgence must be treated by methods developed for dealing with disturbed ex-prisoners of war. Through group therapy they have been restored to normalcy without any recourse to moralizing. Ultimately Simey's vision is a polity ruled by an élite, a specifically West Indian élite to be sure, guided by cadres of social researchers providing blue-prints for middle class leaders.

> A specifically West Indian plan of action must be adopted, and the preparation of the essential blue-print is the task facing the sociologist (Simey 1946: 239). From the West Indian point of view, the future lies with the middle classes. Given a collaboration between them and their friends in Great Britain, progress towards the building up of a mass political movement of which they will become the leaders should be steady and secure (ibid: 258).

And who is to say that it has not been steady and secure? It is true that he regarded Bustamante with apprehension, but he would surely have approved of Sir Alexander Bustamante. The West Indies now have an abundance of planners, blue-print makers, analysts of social ills and fabricators of new cultural orientations — frequently disguised as discovered 'roots'. And there is no doubt that things are better in many ways now than they were in 1945. There is more education, better health and nutrition, better housing, people are better clothed, and there is even better public transportation, water supplies and power. To what extent these things are the result of careful planning and not just a shrewd political response to widespread public demand, a response made possible only because of a period of worldwide economic growth, is an interesting question — which I do not intend to pursue. What is interesting though is that *there seems to have been very little change in family structure.*

Simey had one flash of insight. He failed to follow it up but it does provide me with a convenient lead into the next section, which is an examination of West Indian kinship in the light of some recent research.[3]

WEST INDIAN KINSHIP AND FAMILY STRUCTURE

> The exploitation of the women of the masses by the men of the upper classes has brought with it a general lowering of standards of behaviour which is now a part of a West Indian culture common to people of all races. The upper classes have set a bad example which it will take many generations to efface, and it is by no means certain that as middle class standards become more widespread in the population the situation will show any tendency towards improvement (Simey 1946: 100-101).

Here we are suddenly spirited away from all that poverty and lack of furniture and absence of a common meal, into a far different realm; a realm of power and exploitation — words which Simey uses quite rarely. Simey has hit upon a most important truth, though he does not pursue it very far. In order to understand West Indian kinship it must be seen in the context of class, and classes are not discrete, separate groups, each with its own culture and way of life; they are entities in relationship with each other. The fate of one is intimately bound up with the fate of the other. Simey's idea of 'a bad example' is silly, as though West Indians were children. This is a system of social relations and a structure of ideological concepts which were in place almost from the beginning of settlement in the West Indies.

THE ESTABLISHMENT OF A STRUCTURE AND ITS TRANSFORMATION

The early settlements on St Christopher, Nevis, Montserrat, Antigua and Barbados came closest in form to those established on the North American mainland. Richard Dunn (1972: 18) says that 'Until the 1640s the Barbadians formed a simple community of peasant farmers.'

By 1640 the population of Barbados was about the same as that of Virginia, but its tobacco exports were considered to be inferior to those of the mainland colonies. The tobacco period, from 1627 to about 1640, was one of rapid population increase but it was not an economically successful period, nor did it produce a family based society; the settlers were mainly young and there was a chronic shortage of females. The growth of sugar cultivation between 1640 and 1660, accompanied by the importation of African slaves, ensured that Barbados would not follow colonies such as Massachusetts in creating a family system close to that of England. Henceforward slavery impressed its mark upon all social institutions, including kinship and the family, though not quite in the way it has generally been suggested. Barbados was not unique; it was merely a forerunner of developments in all the West Indian territories.

Britons and Africans together created a creole society. The Britons no more preserved their customs than did the Africans; between them, and out of their hatreds, exploitations, copulations, mutual dependencies and sometimes even love, they created a new social order, an order that has been accorded any social value with only the most grudging reluctance.

The next two centuries saw the growth and spread of plantation agriculture using slave labour, a system which, whatever else it was, represented an advanced form of rational agriculture with careful accounting and calculation at all stages of production, transport and sale. The slave was property of course, and not all aspects of life were yet 'commodetized'. Planters made conscious calculations about the relative costs of replacement or reproduction of the labour force. The plantation mode of production had enormous influence upon every aspect of the lives of those involved in it, but it was not the sole, direct determinant of family and kinship relations. Port Royal in the seventeenth century had 'yards' with kinship units reminiscent of those of modern Kingston; Belize and the Bahamas had 'West Indian kinship' without plantations. The crucial factor seems to have been the establishment of a hierarchical social order in which racial categorization was fundamental, and in which a dual marriage system was institutionalized. Such systems are not unique to the West Indies, or even unusual, but Caribbean kinship has not yet been placed in a full comparative framework (See Smith 1982).

Recent historical scholarship on the West Indies and North America has begun to establish a series of propositions which reverse prior thinking about the influence of slavery on family structure. Gutman (1976), Genovese (1972) and Fogel & Engerman (1974), in their various ways, argue that slave families in North America were far more 'normal' than previously had been thought. They attribute the 'disorganization' of black families more to the conditions, and especially the economic conditions, which faced freedmen after emancipation, especially with the hardening of racial prejudice which locked them out of economic opportunity. For the British West Indies Craton has summarized the recent revision of the picture of slave families as follows:

> If one took the nuclear two-headed family as the quintessentially modern family form, it was beguilingly easy to propose its different incidence during the registration period as relating to the degree of maturation, creolization, or modernization of each slave unit, and thus to suggest a historical progression from some aboriginal African form of family (Craton 1979: 25).

> The discovery by Higman ... that Africans were at least as likely as Creoles to form nuclear families, modified the original model. This revision ... led Higman to a second developmental model ... the establishment of 'elementary nuclear families' was the primary response of the displaced Africans .... A second slave generation began to establish extended families based on the formation of virilocal 'yards' within single plantations ... in subsequent generations, kinship networks expanded as slaves increasingly practised exogamy .... The process tended

toward matrifocality rather than the nuclear family, especially where lack of slave-controlled provision grounds, money, and property deprived slaves of the chance of 'marriage strategies' (ibid.: 26-27).

Craton accepts Higman's more differentiated model and elaborates the context of changing plantation organization, increased miscegenation, and the deteriorating quality of slave life. In spite of his tendentious use of such terms as 'nuclear family' and his misuse of the concept of matrifocality (he seems to think it means female-headed households), and in spite of his belief in the importance of the 'filtering down into the West Indies of evolving concepts of the 'modern' family (ibid.: 28), he recognizes, more by a kind of feeling than from any real evidence, the importance of continuing African traditions especially as regards marriage (ibid.: 31).

The general direction of Craton's argument accords with that being presented here, though he appears to underemphasize the importance of creolization. It was not so much the 'filtering down' of 'concepts of the "modern family"' as it was the growing involvement of Blacks in the dual marriage system of creole society and in the system of social relations structured by class and colour values. However, he is right to stress the peculiarity of the marriage system of Africans which, to oversimplify, generally makes a sharp separation between sexual relations and the contract of marriage which establishes political rights, rights over the pro-creative powers of women (regardless of 'biology'), and rights of inheritance and succession. Even in some highly patriarchal, patrilineal societies, such as the Nuer, there may be great freedom in making and breaking sexual unions while marriage remains stable. One can speculate that there was a certain compatibility between the freedom to make and break sexual unions, and the developing structure of the dual marriage system of creole, class society. While the two are by no means the same, they could converge. However, speculation is not history, and what is needed is detailed evidence as to the nature of such convergence.

It is proposed here that the different forms of family found in the West Indies are generated by a set of principles which find differential expression in varying social and economic contexts. These principles are not to be found enunciated in oral tradition or set out in any document; they must be inferred from a wide range of manifestations, both historical and contemporary. Over-formalization of these principles eliminates the ambiguity, uncertainty and contradictions which are an integral part of the system. Unfortunately it is necessary to provide a summary which involves just such over-formalization, but it is hoped that case material will go some way toward restoring the uncertainty of real life.

THE SYSTEM OUTLINED

The West Indian system of kinship, marriage and the family consists in a differentiated series of forms generated by

1) a **mating system** which enjoins marriage with status equals and non-legal unions with women of lower status

2) a **kinship system** which places a lower priority of solidary emphasis on conjugal than on consanguineal ties

3) a **family system** which is matrifocal but not matriarchal

4) a **domestic system** which does not confine relations within an easily defined and bounded 'household'

5) a **system of sex role differentiation** which stresses the segregation of conjugal roles, permits the participation of women in the occupational system, allows men to disperse economic resources, but requires that women concentrate them.

6) **cultural assumptions** which assign specific characteristics to 'West Indian' sexual and marital patterns.

Unwieldy though this statement is, it has the advantage of bringing together a number of controversial issues which have usually been the subject of quite one-sided arguments. We may take these points one by one.[4]

A mating system which enjoins marriage with status equals and non-legal unions with women of lower status.

Simey apparently appreciated the importance of this dual marriage system when he wrote the statement quoted earlier, but he quite failed to follow the origin of this system of hypergamous marriage back to 'slavery' as will any middle class West Indian in discussing the origin of the middle class itself. Alexander (1977: 431) has documented what he terms the myth of origin of the Jamaican middle class; their ideas about the descent of the middle class from 'a white planter and a black slave'. The equation of middle class status with mixed racial origin is an interesting aspect of the way in which class is conceptualized, but the myth also encapsulates certain generic ideas about the embeddedness of the 'inside/outside' distinction in the marriage system. While there is no formal rule sanctioning 'outside' unions — indeed extra-marital sexual relations are formally condemned — it is clear that non-legal unions, whether coresidential or not, are generally accepted. In private conversation a Jamaican judge pointed out that adultery is almost never advanced as grounds for divorce in Jamaica. A petitioner will usually cite her husband's taking up with another woman as the beginning of a series of acts of cruelty, or as precipitating desertion. In the case reported in *The Star* on February 10th 1982, the petitioner said that the marriage 'went well for the first few years and then they started having very serious problems ... in June 1976 her husband told her that he was seeing a young lady. She spoke to him and told him to break off his relationship with the young lady, but he told her that he had no intention of so doing'. Eventually he started living with the other woman, while continuing to live with his wife, and she had a child at the end of 1977. However, the petition for divorce was based on numerous assaults and acts of cruelty during the period 1979 to 1981, and not on grounds of adultery.

The origin of the dual marriage system lies in the formative period of West Indian society, when customs common in Europe acquired an intensification and special quality when practised in a slave based society. Whatever the origin of the system, contemporary research shows that it is deeply embedded in the fabric of West Indian life (see Austin 1974; DeVeer 1979; Alexander 1977; R. T. Smith 1978, 1982). Alexander's discussion of the 'myth of origin' of the Jamaican middle class, especially the 'established' middle class or people born to middle class status, was referred to earlier. To find the same kind of concept in working class areas was quite surprising. Diane Austin, on the basis of field research in a working class neighbourhood in Kingston, reports as follows (1979: 500).

> I found that many working-class informants claimed descent from a European, generally a planter, whether or not they could establish the genealogical links. So common was this claim, that where at the outset I had pursued diligently any suggestion of a European relation, I came to treat such claims as fictive. They represented first and foremost a mythic statement of identity in colour-class terms.

Austin (1979: 500) provides a full discussion of the genealogy of a Mrs Mills, a 'near black' woman from the rural parish of St Mary, now married to a welder. Mrs Mills gave this account of her background.

> My father's father, he is an Englishman for the mother of my grandfather was a fair woman, and the father was an Englishman. I know my grandfather pretty well. He has blue eyes and has silky blond hair .... My father is pretty nice looking, Indian looking man.

It turned out that Mrs Mills is indeed the outside child of an outside child, and does have a whole collection of fair-skinned relatives in high status occupations — as Austin was able to observe at the funeral of Mrs Mills' great-aunt. Mrs Mills is unusual only in that she has more contact with these relatives than other working class informants who have higher status relatives. However, the point is not that all lower class West Indians have kinship ties with white, fair or high status people — which would be absurd — but that class and status differences are inserted directly into the kinship system by virtue of a dual marriage system which operates at all levels of the society. Nancy Rogers is a hairdresser living in another working class area in Kingston. Previously married, she separated from her husband who later migrated to England and died there. Born in the country, Mrs Rogers claimed that her father had been a 'planter' and not simply a 'cultivator'. She proclaimed her ambition over and over again and was much preoccupied with questions of colour. In the matter of marriage she proclaimed that

> You have to choose a man who can give you children good colour, and make them brighter than you and more upstanding. If you come from black and go married black again, they no going improve. I not saying you must marry for the sake of colour alone, for there are plenty good black men — teachers and doctors and so on. They have education, so the children born with more sense and refinement.

She herself had two of her three children before she was married. '... when I was sixteen I have Joan .... Is a man name Gordon fall me. He was quite an upstanding man you know'. Her special plea to have this man's name omitted from the genealogy, precisely because he was 'an upstanding man' is interesting. The name used here is fictitious of course. Mrs Rogers was very hard on her Aunt Ellie who, she said, was totally lacking in ambition. Aunt Ellie was actually her maternal grandmother.

> My granny did have flat mind. She live in the bush there and just like pure black nigger man. So that's why we now don't have better quality. Aunt Ellie did have flat mind man; she just go, go so, with any black man.

Mrs Rogers, like Austin's informants, has been referred to as 'working-class'. However, the question of whether one has to draw lines within the lower class is a difficult one. Is there a point in the movement down the status scale where the reference points change? Do we reach a point where there is no question of claiming even mythical descent from a European ancestor? A point where a new stability emerges, unaffected by the dynamics of class interaction though perhaps determined by class position? Is Aunt Ellie's 'flat mind' characteristic of a much greater body of people who do not care about status, or if they do are so discouraged that they rest tranquil in a different way of life? The evidence is to the contrary.

Austin (1979: 502) goes quite far in suggesting that 'through this class principle in kinship ... life itself is defined by class, and class is legitimated in the process as a universal principle of social organization — for some families and not others, it is true'. She points to the important fact that women constitute almost half the labour force, that forty-two per cent of household heads are women — most of them working women — and that female unemployment was running at 35.6% in 1976 in Jamaica (ibid.: 502fn4). However, it is not just economic need that induces women to enter into non-legal unions. Where neither property, status nor economic need are crucial considerations the structure is still operative, generating an array of visiting, common-law and legal marriages as alternatives, and sometimes as alternatives which are taken up sequentially by the same couple over a lifetime.

A kinship system which places lower priority of solidary emphasis on conjugal than on consanguineal ties.

In view of the preceding discussion it is permissible to ask what is meant by 'conjugal ties' in this statement. To which part of the dual marriage system does it refer? By 'conjugal ties' is meant the relationships which are found in the whole array of types of union. This aspect of West Indian kinship has been particularly well documented, though information on the middle class (or on the upper class if such can be said exist), is sparse. The statement on priority of solidary emphasis has been carefully formulated and should not be taken to mean more than it says. It does not say that conjugal bonds are weak (though they might well be); it does not say that marriage in the West Indies is unstable (though that can be measured); it does not say that 'love' is not an important element in conjugal relations (Alexander 1978 has documented its ideological importance among the Jamaican middle class). It means precisely what it says; there is a relatively greater emphasis upon consanguineal solidarity than on conjugal ties. More careful research will be needed to establish the range and variability in these relationships, and I would be hard pressed to provide a definition of 'solidary' that would permit of easy measurement. However, the results of this relative emphasis can be seen, even in the familial relationships of the stably married. This structural principle articulates very closely with the next two.

A family system which is matrifocal but not matriarchal.

Men dominate West Indian society. Sex role differentiation has a definite hierarchical dimension. But if men are dominant they are also, in their role as husbands and fathers, apt to be marginal to the cluster of familial relations which focus upon women in their role as mothers. There has been a great deal of misunderstanding of the meaning of 'matrifocal', deriving in large part from issue of the concept (see R. T. Smith 1956; 1973; 1978b). It has nothing to do with female-headed households, or if it has the two should be treated separately. The matrifocal nature of family relations is a structural principle which combines with the relative lack of emphasis upon the conjugal relationship to produce a distinctive pattern of feeling and action within the family system. There is a close link between this and the dual marriage system, though the link is at the level of structural principle rather than specific events.

It has been common to think of the matrifocal family as being a lower class phenomenon produced by poverty, but there is a splendid historical example which shows the importance of power rather than poverty. An almost archetypical case of a matrifocal family is described by Michael Craton in his book *Searching for the Invisible Man* (1978).

> This family was part of a complex network of kin springing from the various unions of white men and Coloured women in the area of Lluidas Vale, Jamaica, occupied by the Worthy Park Plantation. One branch of the family stemmed from the various unions of Dr John Quier, the famous physician; another from the union of Peter Douglas, owner of Point Hill Estate, and Eleanor Price — originally a mulatto slave, but freed by Peter Douglas in 1789, she bore him ten children and lived as the mistress of his house at Point Hill. Before Eleanor Price became the Kept Mistress of Peter Douglas she bore one child, Lizette. The father was probably a white bookkeeper named Nash. Lizette was a quadroon, being the child of a mulatto mother and a white father, and she caught the eye of Rose Price, great-great-grandson of the founder of Worthy Park Estate who was in Jamaica from about 1792 to 1795 putting the source of the family fortune in order.

> When Rose Price, then about 24–years–old, first took up with Lizette she was a thirteen year old slave girl. Rose Price arranged for her manumission and she bore two children for him. He returned to England, married a woman with aristocratic connections who bore him fourteen legitimate children and helped him to acquire a baronetcy. Rose Price left Jamaica before the second child, a son, was born, and Lizette went to live with her mother Eleanor Price, in the house of Peter Douglas. All this sounds quite familiar to anyone who has studied modern West Indian kinship. The subsequent development of the family is of great interest.

> Rose Price arranged with Peter Douglas that when his outside children reached a suitable age they should travel to Britain for further education. Elizabeth, the daughter, eventually married a Scots clergyman and never returned to Jamaica. John, the son, after studying engineering, returned to Jamaica in 1823 to live with his mother, grandmother, aunts, uncles (the children of Peter Douglas), and his cousins in what was clearly a matrifocal household even when Peter Douglas was alive. Both his grandmother and his mother lived to a ripe old age, and in a surviving letter which John Price Nash wrote to his sister in Scotland he speaks of them both with affection and respect.

This case embodies the structural principles of the system in a vivid way, and it also shows the process by which legitimate and illegitimate lines diverge, becoming polarized in class terms. Elizabeth and her descendants disappeared into the Scottish population until Craton uncovered the Jamaican connection; John and his descendants became part of the Jamaican middle class but as they were absorbed back into the Jamaican population they became progressively darker when declining material fortune made 'good' marriages more difficult to achieve. (See Craton 1978: 331-339 for details).

In our contemporary middle class material we find cases where a husband-father is perceived to be 'irresponsible' by virtue of his 'outside' activities of drinking and womanizing. But we also find cases where faithful, sober, devoted husbands are concerned about their children's regard for them.

Mr Benton, explained at length the tendency for Jamaican children to disparage and belittle their fathers.

> I have found that very often young people tend to have — young people who are progressing toward adulthood, they tend to regard their father as just a convenience ... and this kind of general attitude makes it difficult for the father to play his role properly ... and it also seems to me this way, that very often, ah women who are grown up in homes where they didn't have a father — I mean they didn't you know receive the care and protection of a father in a definite way — they seem to grow up without understanding the true role of the father in the home and ahm sometimes they tend, I think too, to believe that everything should revolve around them.

Although he and his wife have 'worked out a plan' he is always conscious of the tendency toward a matrifocal bias in the internal relationships of the family, a bias which he sees clearly as coming from men ultimately, and their 'outside' activities. This is not just the result of Benton's experience; it is an integral part of the culture of the Caribbean, brought to a sharp focus in the consciousness of the upwardly mobile who are striving to live a planned, careful, orderly, clean, religiously informed life as opposed to what our lower class informants (and Professor Simey), call the 'loose', 'dirty', 'careless', 'up and down' life of common experience.

A domestic system which does not confine relations within an easily defined and bounded 'household'.

This has been discussed in previous publications (R. T. Smith 1973; 1978a; 1978b). Activities such as child care, the acquisition, cooking and consumption of food, washing, sleeping, sexual relations and other activities generally regarded as 'domestic', are not neatly confined within the bounds of a single 'household'. Still less can we assume that the typical household contains a nuclear family, appearances and survey data notwithstanding. These are complex issues and space does not permit their extended discussion. Our case materials remind us over and over again that although people are quite prepared to play the game into which they have been educated by several generations of census and survey takers, and provide a neat list of household members, further investigation quickly dissolves the image of the isolated nuclear family.

> The family of Mr and Mrs Black in the village of August Town, Guyana, was listed in 1953 as living on a particular lot in a particular cluster of wooden buildings — two frame houses and a separate kitchen. Mr Black, a carpenter, already had several outside children, and he owned a house in another village in which he had installed a lady friend and their son. Two of the Black's daughters were living in August Town with spouses, one married and one in a common-law union. As recorded in 1956, these daughters spent a good deal of their time in the family home with their mother and their children (who always called their maternal grandmother 'mama'), ate there frequently, played with Mrs Black's younger children who were about their age, and often slept there. Mr Black divided his time (somewhat unpredictably) between his two homes. By 1975 things had changed a good deal. Both Mr and Mrs Black were dead. The family home, considerably worse for wear, was now occupied by the youngest daughter and her three children (by three different fathers) and a son — now a police constable. The rates on the land were paid by another daughter now living in the United States of America. For periods the policeman would give a weekly allowance to his sister who then cooked and washed his clothes, but at other times he would complain that she was wasting his money and 'board' with a married sister in the village — that is pay her a weekly sum to provide food for him. These married sisters had by now their own grown-up children with whom they maintained close interactive relations that can only be described as

'domestic' even though the people involved were apparently distributed over a number of 'nuclear family' households. This kind of pattern is not peculiar to rural Guyana. There is no need to labour the point but it is necessary to remember that lists of occupants of 'households' do not constitute an adequate guide to family and domestic relations.

A system of sex-role differentiation which stresses the segregation of conjugal roles, permits the participation of women in the occupational system, allows men to disperse economic resources, but requires that women concentrate them.

Until recently the significance of sex-role differentiation as an important component of family structure has been underestimated. Elizabeth Bott, (1957; 1968) in her pioneering work on English families, did not at first recognize that her 'segregated' and 'joint' patterns of conjugal role activity were but special instances of differences in sex roles.

Implicit in many historical discussions of the family is the idea that a 'normal' family is a nuclear family; this assumption is reflected in the very terminology when reference is made to 'denuded' families. Another pervasive assumption is that stable, normal families exist when a male in the position of husband-father is possessed of authority and control over economic resources. In many discussions of the slave family and the transition to free labour, the weakness of the family (or the supposed weakness), is attributed to the insecurity of the husband father becuase of his inability to command steady and adequate income. The concept of a 'normal' family consisting of a man who is active in the politico-jural and economic domains, a wife who has responsibility for the domestic domain, and their children to whom legitimate status is transmitted by virtue of the parents' marriage, is a concept with far-reaching consequences. It is embedded in all English thinking about welfare policy since the beginning of the seventeenth century, and inevitably it has deeply affected West Indian discussion of these issues. Unfortunately it bears little relation to the realities of West Indian working class life, nor to English working class life for that matter (see Land & Parker 1978).

KINSHIP AND THE ORGANIZATION OF WORK

Thomas Roughley's *The Jamaica Planter's Guide* (1823), a source mined to exhaustion by writers on slavery, has some interesting things to say about work organization. At this period the slave trade had been abolished for some time and planters were concerned about the reproduction of their labour force since that seemed to be the only method of replacement. Roughley had a lot to say about child care, the treatment of pregnant women, the care of the aged and so forth, and all these discussions are clearly and overtly linked to the problem of running the plantation. The 'great gang' is composed of the strongest and most skilled men *and* women, attended by a field cook who is to see that they are fed well and on time. The second gang is made up of weakly people, youths, sucking mothers and the aged, attended by nurses who look after the infants while the mother is at work in the fields. Mothers get an occasional break in order to feed their children. (Substitute free labour for slave and a factory for a plantation and all this might sound quite 'modern'). The third, or 'weeding gang' is composed of children from five to six years and upwards under the direction of a driveress. Roughley appears to be as solicitous of the welfare of these children as any modern social worker. He (1823: 104) points out these children are,

> drivers, cattlemen, mulemen, carpenters, coopers, and masons, as it were in embryo .... Even in common life, throughout civilized Europe, the welfare of the child is the grand object of the parent. The owner and the overseer of those valuable shoots should act the part of a parent, fosterer, and protector, looking on them as the future prop and support of the property.

He details the age at which children should be weaned (12 to 14 months), the desirability of 'inoculation for the cow or smallpock', the daily feeding of weaned children with soup, and the monthly dosing with worm medicine and castor oil. By the age of three they graduate to a group supervised by an old woman who keeps them clean, fed and busy, each child aided by a 'wineglass of acidulated sugar, and a taste of good rum to each, as an enlivener' (Roughley 1823: 122). Surely preferable to the laundanam with which the children of the English working classes were rendered tranquil while their mothers laboured in the textile mills of Lancashire.

The old, the sickly and the incapacitated are not neglected. The old 'should be allotted to those kinds of occupations which do not bear hard upon them'. But, 'something they should always have to do, to keep their minds employed, and their bodies in easy activity'. Similarly with the invalids, 'Though much cannot be expected of them, yet it is best to keep them at some employment,' such as planting and cleaning fences (ibid.: 113).

Roughley's experience was on the large Jamaican sugar estates. Such paternal solicitude and precise management was less likely to be found on small properties, and indeed we do not know to what extent it was actually practised anywhere. We do know that he describes a pattern of labour utilization which was widespread and continued on plantations using indentured labour after slavery had been abolished. We also know that indentured labour on Guianese plantations received better medical care, crude though it might have been, than did the free labourers who lived in villages. This is reflected in mortality statistics.

This is not the place to review the wide range of economic circumstances which existed after the abolition of slavery. It was unusual for the ex-slaves to be able to constitute themselves into a stable and prosperous 'peasantry'. Indeed, few of them tried. What they attempted to do was to alter the conditions under which they sold their labour power, and to remove themselves from the control of the plantations. British Guiana saw the most successful movement of slaves into independent villages, but, as Walter Rodney (1981) has recently reemphasized, they did not become 'peasants' (see R. T. Smith 1956, 1962).Like settlements in other parts of the West Indies they were constituted around a christian church with its attendant school, and the villages, far from withdrawing from creole, colonial society, were drawn ever more closely into it. Legal, christian marriage in the hierarchical system of creole society was a sign of status and it came to be associated with women's cessation from work outside the home. It was a class defined institution, opposed to other forms of union within a system of unions, and so it remains today. Only in this context does 'poverty' make any sense as the precipitating cause of non-legal unions.

Of course, women were out of luck in post-emancipation society. They remained actively involved in occupations outside the home, while at the same time losing whatever services were provided by the plantation; services such as day-care for their children, a cook to provide food at work, free medical services and maternity leave. Now they had to work outside and take on domestic responsibilities at home. In view of the history of the West Indies and of women's labour it is remarkable to what extent the very concept of womanhood continues to be bound up with mothering and with the performance of such domestic activities as cooking, washing and cleaning.

Erna Brodber (1975), in her study of Kingston yards, has provided some revealing insights into the way in which quite independent women allow men to dominate them. These women rent rooms in yards, into which they admit boy-friends who may or may not contribute significantly to household expenses. They go out of their way to cook attractive food, keep the men's clothes in order, and generally play the role of obedient wife. If there is a TV set it is the man who chooses the programme, even if the woman is paying the rent; if the man wants to sleep after lunch the children are chased away. Although middle class women have 'helpers' to do the dirty work, the kitchen and the house remain their domain. One middle class woman told us that her late husband had never been in the kitchen; with a wife, two daughters and a maid he never even brought himself a glass of water.

Ideologically there is a close association between the 'inside' domain and activities of women and the 'outside' life of men. Both Austin (1974) and DeVeer (1979), in their work in Kingston and May Pen respectively, have shown how deep-seated and pervasive are these ideas about sex-roles. The aspect to which attention is drawn here is the way in which men tend to use income, be it in cash or in kind, to fulfil obligations which are often dispersed over a number of domestic groups. They may give contributions to their own mothers, the mothers of their children, current girl friends and of course to their own wives or common-law wives. Such material as we have on this question shows that lower or working class men may have a remarkable number of claims on their income. In a study carried out among lower class men in Kingston, Anderson Parks (pers. comm.) describes how a delivery van driver with a steady, but not large, income tends to run up debts for such items as stereo equipment, regularly drops off money to pay the rent of a current girl friend, passes by to leave a contribution to the support of an outside child, visits his mother with a gift and eventually arrives home to his wife with a considerably reduced pay-packet, some of which will be kept back to meet his entertainment expenses.

There is no reliable measure of the extent to which this pattern is general, or the extent to which it is confined to the lower class. As usual there is a great deal of variability and one could point to cases where married middle or working class couples pool their resources for the purchase of a house or the education of children. However, our women informants are quite articulate about the propensity of men to 'wander'; field materials, some of them going back as far as 1951, confirm that it is quite common for men to disperse resources while women concentrate them. It is easy to devise functional explanations for this flow of resources; it avoids the reliance of any one domestic unit upon a sole source of income which is apt to be cut off in an unstable labour market. Like all functionalist explanations this one fails to explain why this particular solution should have emerged rather than another.

'I feel a woman can control their nature more than a man. I just have that feeling. I mean, a woman will easier be satisfying with one man when a man can't be satisfy with one woman. Right?' (DeVeer 1979: 108). This statement of a male Jamaican could be regarded as a rationalization of his own behaviour, or as special pleading. It couches the argument in universalistic, 'natural' terms, against which moral arguments carry little weight. But West Indians also claim special characteristics, as though nature had singled them out from the rest of mankind.

Cultural assumptions which assign specific characteristics to 'West Indian' ways of behaving

'Jamaicans love a whole lot of woman, you know. Lot of woman, not just one. They don't stick to one, they must have girls outside, that's just the way .... They love sport [laugh]. Married men, unmarried men, it don't matter.' (DeVeer 1979: 150). This happened to be a working class woman, but much the same sentiment can be found at every level of the society.

West Indians do not have a monopoly on polygynous tendencies, nor is it unusual for men to use positions of power to secure access to women. Many young Africans seethe with resentment at the monopolization of young women by old men; not necessarily out of sexual frustration, but because access to women is itself a sign of power, prestige and maturity. Nineteenth century European society had a well-documented under-life. The male members of the British Royal family, or some of them, were renowned for their sexual exploits. Karl Marx fathered a bastard son on his domestic servant and Friedrich Engels had a Kep' Miss from the Lancashire working class; it may have shown a democratic impulse, but of course he did not marry her.

The rising divorce rate and the increase in female-headed households in the United States sometimes appear to indicate that they are following in the wake of the West Indies. The appearance is false. There is no loss of faith in the monogamic ideal in the United States, even among that growing number of people for whom the Census Bureau had to devise a new term, POSSLQ or Person of Opposite Sex Sharing Living Quarters. The rate of re-marriage is exceedingly high. The West Indies are closer to Victorian England than to the egalitarian customs of the modern youth of North America and Europe with their apparent mastery of the techniques of birth control. Certainly the ideology is different; divorce and re-marriage is really a searching for the one, true, right person and is not based upon a notion that monogamic fidelity is impossible.

POLICY IMPLICATIONS

Social policies which bear directly upon the family are surprisingly uniform in modern bureaucratic societies, and all states, regardless of their level of economic development or the nature of their political system, tend to adopt similar policies (Kamerman & Kahn 1977). Cadres of professional 'social workers', 'family case workers', 'probation officers' and the like are to be found everywhere and are increasing in number. They are an integral, and perhaps inevitable, part of the modern state apparatus; that is, the state apparatus which increasingly regulates the lives of its citizens. Michael Foucault and his associates have shown how recent is this development (Foucault 1965, 1970, 1973, 1978a, 1978b; Donzelot 1979). The invention of modern institutions such as the prison, lunatic asylum, orphanage and workhouse went hand-in-hand with the growth of that scientific approach to planning which so captivated Simey. Poverty, marital stress, child neglect, bastardy, and unemployment came to be seen as aspects of 'social pathology' to be studied, regulated and (optimistically) cured by rational intervention on the part of paid servants of the state. The ideology of rational intervention continues to motivate social policy in the face of growing skepticism as to its efficacy. Some students regard this bureaucratic apparatus as a part of the regulatory, or police, function of the state, particularly since its clients are the poor and the unruly. Whatever the truth or otherwise of that idea, it is clear that the general trend toward more social intervention in family life is unlikely to diminish, whatever is said here. However, our previous analysis suggests that there are certain aspects of West Indian family structure which are neither pathological nor amenable to cure by concentrating on the poor.

We must agree with Simey (1946: 100-101) in his one flash of insight, that 'as middle class standards become more widespread in the population the situation will [not] show any tendency toward improvement' in the exploitation of women, though in the interest of neutrality we might re-phrase it to read, 'will [not] show any tendency to change'. Far from the system showing 'looseness', 'disorganization' or 'disintegration', it appears to be very stable. The dual marriage system is intact. Illegitimacy rates have not fallen significantly. Whether one likes the pattern of West Indian kinship or not, one cannot realistically say that it is disorganized. West Indians have extensive kinship ties, and at all levels of the society kin tend to be supportive, loving and kind — with occasional lapses of course, and allowing for the divisions created by class. It is not that West Indian kinship is weak; it is that it has distinctive patterns which need to be recognized.

These distinctive patterns are not 'caused' in any simple way by 'poverty'. That is not to say that poverty is not a grave social problem in the West Indies; poverty, along with unemployment, underemployment, lack of opportunity and absence of adequate bases for self-respect, must all be addressed by social policy. But these things are not caused by the family system any more than the family system is caused by them. They are all part of the structure in place, produced by the political economy of the West Indies, by its historical experience and by the manner in which class has been structured in West Indian society.

In the almost forty years since Simey wrote *Welfare and Planning in the West Indies*, there has been a great deal of change in this region. Most of that change has been in the direction envisaged and advocated by him. The expansion in the size of the middle class, effected by widening educational opportunity and the increase in bureaucratic, service and sales occupations, has been made possible mainly by increases in the export of bauxite and oil, and by the development of the tourist trade. It would have surprised Simey to see how little of this increased prosperity has come through agriculture, but he would have been gratified by the growth in local industry to substitute for imports and to provide housing. As is widely recognized, these changes have not altered the basic structure of dependence of the region on the industrialized countries. With the possible exception of Cuba, and the very peculiar case of Guyana, all these developments have been based squarely upon the expansion of the middle class, and upon the extension of middle class aspirations to an ever-widening circle.

It is difficult to imagine any fundamental change in these trends in the immediate future. Social policy seems to incline toward a local form of welfare capitalism. National Insurance schemes for the employed; generous pension, housing, medical and other perquisites for the upper middle class — be they in business, government service, politics or the military — and for such of the rest of the middle and working classes as can bargain for these perquisites; and very little left for the growing numbers of the poor. High rates of population growth coupled with the closing off of migration outlets and the apparent impossibility of economic growth outpacing population growth, seem to guarantee high levels of unemployment, crime and inadequate social services. Under these circumstances it would be unrealistic to expect any drastic change in family structure. For the lower class it is only the mutuality of kinship and community that keeps the very poor afloat at all, and given the continuation, and even the intensification, of class relations it does not seem likely that the dual marriage system will disappear.

It is tempting to attribute present circumstances to 'colonialism' or to 'slavery' or 'the plantation', and a case can be made for each such attribution. An even better case can be made for explaining much of the present difficulty in economic life to the continuing pattern of relations between the developed and underdeveloped parts of the world. But when it comes to family structure the case is somewhat different. When people declare, with some measure of pride, toleration, or amusement that 'Jamaica man can't satisfy with one woman' then it does not seem quite fair to blame it all on people like William Montagu, Viscount Mandeville and 5th Duke of Manchester who, as Governor of Jamaica from 1808 to 1827, left more than place names behind him. According to Edward Braithwaite he had numerous brown-skinned progeny, and at least five of his illegitimate children were at school in Kingston in the 1830s. However, his wife, Lady Susan, daughter of the Duke of Gordon, a great beauty and a woman of independent spirit, had run off with one of her footmen even before he left for the West Indies. Interesting as these historical events undoubtedly are, we must remember that the present day system is being maintained, being reproduced every day, by the actions of independent West Indians exercising their prerogatives of freedom, privilege, dominance and submission. It is nonsense to say that West Indians cannot afford to marry, that unstable unions and female headed households are an adaptation to poverty and economic insecurity (why that adaptation and not some other and why did East Indians, who were equally poor, not make that adaptation?), and it is nonsense to say that Jamaican men can't satisfy with one woman and must have outside children. All these things are a part of the system as it developed and as it is being maintained.

Repeated attempts have been made to try to swing this system into conformity with so-called 'nuclear family pattern' or 'the christian family'. More than one hundred and fifty years of intensive persuasion from the pulpits of the churches has had little discernible effect; perhaps the persuasion was directed at the wrong people. Attempts to enforce the bastardy laws have not been conspicuously successful, especially when the fathers were respectable members of the middle class. There is often a great deal of confusion about what is being aimed at when policy is discussed. The churches have been trying to alter behaviour by expounding a code of christian morals, but a great deal of social policy and legislation is aimed at something different.

One common approach is to try to solve some of the problems of poverty and excessive population by forcing men, as it is said, to 'live up to their responsibilities'. But even the early census reports, cited by Simey, noted that women in stable unions have more children than those in common-law or visiting unions which are short-term, because they are more constantly exposed to the possibility of pregnancy. Population increase will not be checked by getting all women into stable unions, unless there is also an increased use of contraceptives, freely available abortion, or as in India, a policy of paying people to undergo sterilization procedures. India has a family policy in that sense, just as countries which need population increase sometimes pay child allowances.

The problem of poverty will not be solved by getting everyone into nuclear families, unless there is also a vast increase in available income and employment. To get everyone living in nuclear families might well exacerbate the situation — always a risk with any policy. As it is now the working people share a great deal of their income with the really poor in one way or another, though we do not know just how that is accomplished.

In recent years attempts have been made to alter the existing pattern of family structure by legislating away those features deemed undesirable. The new constitution of Guyana has a clause which says that henceforth there shall be no difference between legitimate and illegitimate children. There is as yet no enabling legislation so we do not know just how this is to be accomplished, but Jamaica has laws with the same intention. However, the father has to make proper recognition of an illegitimate child, and even if he does so there is nothing to prevent discrimination against outside children in bequests. Such laws do have limited use in regularizing the position of children in inheritance cases where the father's intention is clear, but they will not change the family system unless they are accompanied by procedures for the establishment of paternity of a degree of severity which seems unlikely to gain acceptance.

Policies which may do most to bring about change in West Indian family life are those which enhance the status and rights of women, to the point where they are not constrained by traditional concepts of their role. Equal pay for equal work, equal job opportunities, adequate day care facilities, freely available abortion under safe and hygienic conditions, and all the things which make it possible for people to choose freely how they will manage their affairs. It is not for the state to dictate how people should behave in their private lives, and one may doubt the degree to which professional intervention should be used in family affairs.

If this long discussion has taught us anything it is that a family system such as that of the West Indies arises in a particular kind of class society with particular kinds of sex roles, and it is unlikely to change until the pattern of class relations changes. Even then there is no guarantee that family and sex roles will immediately be transformed. These are what Ferdinand Braudel calls structures of the *longue durée*. As yet the social sciences have very little idea as to how, and at what rate, they change.

NOTES

1. A much shorter version of this paper was presented as a lecture in memory of Professor Chandra Jayawardena, delivered at the University of the West Indies, Mona, Jamaica on March 15th 1982. Although it does not deal with the joint work we carried out, I am happy to acknowledge how much of my thinking on these matters was influenced by him. I am also grateful to those who attended the lecture for their comments, and to Mrs D. Powell and the members of the staff of the Depaertment of Sociology, and to Dr Vaughan Lewis, Director of the Institute of Social and Economic Research, for their kind hospitality.

2. These are all ideas which have surfaced in one way or another in the discussion of poverty in the United States. See for example the remarkable paper by Walter Miller (1958) which purports to locate the causes of gang activity and crime in the specifics of a lower class culture made possible by personality characteristics very similar to those described by Simey.

3. Most of the material cited in this section is drawn from the results of a series of studies carried out during the late 1960s and the 1970s under the direction of the author, and involving the collaboration of the University of the West Indies and the University of Chicago. I am grateful to the National Science Foundation and to the Lichtstern Research Fund for the financial support which made most of these studies possible. Fuller accounts of this work will be found in R. T. Smith 1973, 1978a, 1978b; Alexander 1973, 1976, 1977; Austin 1974, 1979; DeVeer 1979; Fischer 1974.

4. The material on which the following analysis is based consists not only of the by now voluminous body of census and survey materials, but also of many painstakingly collected genealogies and case studies — family histories really. My assumption is that one can only understand family life if one studies what kinship means to people, and if one is able to comprehend the whole range of individuals' experience. In this research the same individual was interviewed many times, sometimes for as much as 100 hours stretching over many months. Quick surveys have their uses but they yield data very different from those reported here. For each person interviewed we constructed a genealogy; some of them are enormous, containing as many as 800 to 1000 individuals. See R. T. Smith 1978a,1978b, and Alexander 1976 for further details.

REFERENCES

Alexander, Jack 1976. 'A study of the cultural domain of relatives'. *American Ethnologist* 3:17-38.

—1977. 'The culture of race in middle-class Kingston, Jamaica.' *American Ethnologist* 4:413-435.

—1978. 'The cultural domain of marriage.' *American Ethnologist* 5:5-14.

Austin, Diane J. 1974. Symbol and ideologies of class in urban Jamaica: a cultural analysis of classes. Chicago: University of Chicago Ph.D. dissertation.

—1979. 'History and symbols in ideology: a Jamaican example.' *Man* (N.S.) 14:497-514.

Bott, Elizabeth 1957. *Family and social network*. London: Tavistock Publications — 1968. *Family and social network*. Second edition with new material.

Brodber, Erna 1975. *A study of yards in the city of Kingston*. Mona, Jamaica: Institute of Social and Economic Research, Working Papers, No. 9.

Craton, Michael 1978. *Searching for the invisible man: slaves and plantation life in Jamaica*. Cambridge, Mass: Harvard University Press.

—1979. 'Clanging patterns of slave families in the British West Indies'. *Journal of Interdisciplinary History* 10:1-35.

DeVeer, Henrietta 1979. *Sex roles and social stratification in a rapidly growing urban area — May Pen, Jamaica*. Chicago: University of Chicago Ph.D. dissertation.

Donzelot, Jacques 1979. *The policing of families*. New York: Pantheon Books.

Dunn, Richard S. 1972. *Sugar and slaves: the rise of the planter class in the English West Indies, 1624-1713*. Chapel Hill: University of North Carolina Press.

Fischer, Michael 1974. 'Value assertion and stratification: religion and marriage in rural Jamaica'. *Caribbean Studies* 14, 1:7-;37; 3:7-35.

Fogel, Robert W. & Stanley L., Engerman 1974. *Time on the cross: the economics of American Negro slavery*. Boston: Little, Brown and Company.

Foucault, Michael 1965. *Madness and civilization*. New York: Pantheon Books.

—1979. *The order of things: an archaeology of the human sciences*. New York: Pantheon Books.

—1973. *The birth of the clinic: an archaeology of medial perception*. New York: Pantheon Books.

—1978. *The history of sexuality. Volume 1: An Introduction*. New York: Pantheon Books.

Genovese, Eugene D. 1972. Roll, Jordan, Roll: *The world the slaves made*. New York: Pantheon Books.

Gutman, Herbert G. 1976. *The black family in slavery and freedom, 1750-1925*. New York, Pantheon Books.

Henriques, Fernando 1953. *Family and colour in Jamaica*. London: Eyre & Spottiswoode.

Kamerman, Sheila B. & Alfred Kahn, (eds) 1978. *Family policy: government and families in fourteen countries*. New York: Columbia University Press.

Land, Hilary & Roy Parker, 1978. United Kingdom. In *Family policy* (Kamerman & Kahns eds). New York: Columbia University Press.

Miller, Walter B. 1958. 'Lower class culture as a generating milieu of gang delinquency'. *Journal of Social Issues* 14:5-19.

Moynhan, Daniel P. 1965. *The Negro family: the case for national action*. Washington, D.C.: Office of Policy Planning and Research, U.S. Department of Labour.

Robotham, Donald 1970. *National integration and local community structure in Jamaica*. Chicago: University of Chicago M.A. thesis.

Rodney, Walter 1981. 'Plantation society in Guyana'. *Review* 4:643-666.

Roughley, Thomas 1823. *The Jamaica Planter's Guide*. London: Longman, Hurst, Rees, Orme, and Brown.

Simey, Thomas S. 1946. *Welfare and planning in the West Indies*. Oxford: Clarendon Press.

Smith, Michael G. 1966. 'Introduction'. In Edith Clarke, *My Mother Who Fathered Me*, i-xiiv. London: George Allen and Unwin.

Smith, Raymond T. 1956. *The Negro family in British Guiana*. London: Routledge and Kegan Paul.

—1962. *British Guiana*. London: Oxford University Press. (Reprinted 1980, Greenwood Press, Westport, Connecticut).

—1963. 'Culture and social structure in the Caribbean: some recent work on family and kinship studies'. *Comparative Studies in Society and History* 6:24-45.

—1973. 'The matrifocal family'. In Jack Goody, ed, *The character of kinship*, 121-144. Cambridge: Cambridge University Press.

—1978a. 'The family and the modern world system: some observations from the Caribbean'. *Journal of Family History* 3:337-360.

—1978b. 'Class differences in West Indian kinship: a genealogical exploration'. In Arnaud F. Marks & René A. Romer, eds., *Family and kinship in Middle America and the Caribbean*. Co-publication of the University of the Netherlands Antilles, Curaçao and the Department of Caribbean Studies of the Royal Institute of Linguistics and Anthropology, Leiden.

—1982. Kinship, class and race in the Caribbean. Unpublished ms.

West India Royal Commission 1945. West Indies Royal Commission Report (The Moyne Report), Cmmd. 6607. London: HMSO.

9

Conclusion:
Themes and Perspectives

After nearly fifty years of intellectual, practical and emotional energy devoted to Caribbean kinship, what do we really know about family and conjugal union patterns in the region? The period has generated several substantial books, over one hundred articles and a seemingly endless series of conferences, seminars and workshops. Armies of social workers and other professionals have been trained and departments, centres and homes set up to deal with family problems. More than any other social institution in the Caribbean, the family has been the focus of research, debate and policy. But where has all this got us? Public cries of 'family breakdown' and 'families in crisis' are becoming louder and the evidence of problems escalates. Public wisdom condemns men for avoiding their responsibilities as fathers and husbands while mothers are overburdened, parenting skills are inadequate and divorce rates are increasing, youths are delinquent and children abandoned. Is it that family life has deteriorated or are these problems just more evident? In either case, the situation in Caribbean countries raises searching questions about the record of family research and policy. We do not pretend in this book to have provided all the answers to these grand and soul-searching questions. We hope, however, to have shed some light on the issues. In order to summarise, we revisit the six themes with which we began and which have informed the discussion throughout. By way of reminder these are: definitions of family and conjugality; plural and creole models; social structure and human action; gender roles and relationships; methodology; history and social change.

In terms of the first theme of definitions, research and policy on family in the Caribbean got off to a poor start in the post-World War II colonial period, with culturally inappropriate conceptions of what constitutes 'a family' and 'a conjugal union' and predetermined ideas on the functions and importance of the family as a social institution. By definition, according to European standards, families were stable units composed of a mother, a father and their children, owned or officially adopted, living together in one household. Conjugal unions were defined as marriages — legally and religiously sanctioned, co-resident, permanent and based on love and togetherness. Families, so constituted, performed several indispensable functions for the society, the most important of which was the socialisation of children. To fulfill these functions properly and efficiently, male and female roles were distinct, but complementary. As head of the family, the man belonged in the public domain, earning economic support for his dependent family. As father and husband, he played an important part in disciplining and training his children and protecting and representing the family within the wider society. A woman's place was in the home, comforting her husband, bearing and rearing children and doing the housework. Within the conjugal relationship, the man was the authority and decision-maker: the woman submissive and obedient. According to this way of thinking, the family was the most important social institution of society. It was the cornerstone which, by way of these functions, sustained the moral and social fabric of the society. If something was wrong with the family, the whole society would suffer and 'wrong' meant badly constructed with the wrong people inadequately performing the essential roles.

Family patterns in the Caribbean could hardly have differed more from these Eurocentred ideals. Households were incomplete and headed by women. Women had too many children and they were left alone while their mothers went out to work. Conjugal partners lived apart and, even when they were co-resident, they were unmarried, the relationship was temporary and there was little joint activity or love and affection. Children were illegitimate and 'outside'. They were shifted from one home to another. Parents migrated and aging grandmothers were left with the responsibility of training and disciplining the children. Boys, in particular, grew up without their fathers as male role models. All in all, families were deformed and malfunctioning and constituted a threat to the social order.

Accordingly, the task of colonial officials was to restructure these families and change the patterns of relationships. What existed had to be removed, not understood. Social policy, therefore, along with the Church, the educational system and the law, set about constructing proper families in the Caribbean, in accordance with European ideals. Those mandated to do the job were convinced that their policies and programmes would be appreciated and successful. Nearly fifty years later their intensive efforts have had very little effect.

In the effort, social policy received virtually no help from social research. Eurocentric ideologies of family and marriage dominated all intellectual thought on Caribbean kinship for many years. Instead of bringing a clear, unbiased and indigenous understanding of Caribbean kinship ideology and practice, the thinking of anthropologists, sociologists, demographers and historians has been blocked by these models of family ideals. According to their definitions, conjugal unions were only authentic if the partners were co-resident and families consisted only of those living together within a household. Families were 'matrifocal', men were 'marginal' and children were 'fathered' by their mothers. Years of meticulous data collection in several Caribbean countries merely served to reinforce these stereotypes and devaluations of families as 'denuded', 'disfunctional' and 'unstable' and conjugal unions as 'promiscuous' and 'loose'.

By the early 1970s an intellectual reappraisal of Caribbean families had converted all these negatives into positives. Family 'instability' was redefined to become family 'flexibility' and 'adaptability'. Matrifocality and female-centred, widespread kinship networks extending across households and across national boundaries were recognised as real family patterns. They were also interpreted as the most suitable for the conditions in which people lived. In Caribbean circumstances of poverty and economic marginality, rigid nuclear family structures with specified roles and relationships were unrealistic and unworkable. If people were constrained by nuclear family expectations, they would not be able to leave their marriages, delegate their responsibilities to others and shift their children in order to take advantage of economic opportunities at home and abroad.

With this new perspective, Caribbean kinship patterns were no longer perceived as abnormal, they were appropriate: no longer a problem, but a solution to the problem of living in economic deprivation. Definitions were expanded, to some extent localised and derogatory labels were shed, but the earlier notions of family and conjugality as dependent variables persisted. Whether as a problem or as a solution, kinship was still seen to be determined by prevailing economic conditions. Families appeared to be forever bending into different shapes to adapt to economic opportunities and constraints and individuals to be living in a cultural vacuum, making personal choices to their own material advantage.

Only in the last fifteen years or so have anthropologists finally got around to shedding all, or at least virtually all, of the preconceptions determined by their own backgrounds and intellectual training and asking Caribbean people for their own definitions and evaluations of family life. The process focusses on kinship ideologies and practices, historically developed in the Caribbean social systems stratified by race and class and by dominance, conflict and accommodation, and identifies Caribbean meanings for the various 'domains' of Caribbean kinship. The image that we receive is very different from that of earlier Caribbean ethnography.

The centrality of the mother-child bond has been highlighted and families are no longer seen as requiring and being built on a conjugal union. Conjugal co-residence, especially marriage, is culturally defined as a segregated relationship. It is a difficult relationship to manage and therefore best postponed until the partners are more mature and they have undergone a period of testing. Marriage may be more respectable, but visiting relationships are easier to handle. They allow more personal autonomy and ensure an escape from conjugal violence. Child-bearing, on the other hand, can take place in a woman's mother's home, before tackles the potential difficulties of a co-residential union. In terms of the roles of men, 'marginality' seems to mean different things to different cultures. If Caribbean culture defines fatherhood as providing economic support and, when necessary, discipline for their sons and men claim to be fulfilling this role, then we must ask, can they be described as 'marginal'?

Our second theme is that of plural versus creole culture and the question of whether we perceive lower-class black kinship as distinct from that of other racial and class groups in Caribbean society or as similar? Scholars investigating Caribbean kinship were not only influenced by foreign backgrounds and theoretical paradigms, but also by the models they created to better understand Caribbean society. The dominant perspective was one which assumed that societies were plural, divided by race and ethnicity into discrete 'socio-cultural segments', each with its own cultural patterns. Lower-class black culture contrasted with that of the middle and upper class, whether because of inherited African patterns or the experience of slavery and contemporary economic conditions. Earlier socio-historical interpretations of slave family patterns reflected these images by emphasising the destructive forces of the slave regime. Even recent accounts, concerned to portray marital-type relationships and nuclear households among the slaves, continue to refer, for example, to a polygamous African tradition. Contrasts drawn with the family and conjugal patterns of other racial and ethnic groups, notably the East Indians, also reinforce images of pluralism. On the other hand, there were those who emphasised a process of acculturation occurring in Caribbean society, the end result of which was assumed to be the creation of an integrated Creole culture. This perception made it possible for the earlier researchers to perceive deviant conjugal and family patterns as potentially capable of being properly reshaped through the process of creolisation, as well as social policy, once economic and social conditions were favourable.

Both theoretical dimensions have informed studies of change among the East Indians of Trinidad and Guyana. Some researchers stressed change within the Caribbean cultural context, especially with the decline of patriarchy, joint family structures and child marriages. Others emphasised cultural continuity and the active and conscious revival of East Indian traditions, particularly through elaborate wedding ceremonies, either in response to the perceived loss of cultural traditions or to the devaluation of their patterns as 'coolie culture'. Still others identified the contradictory pulls of all three processes — change, persistence and reassertion.

Plural theoretical assumptions, reinforcing ideas of cultural difference between black lower class and brown middle class, assumed, without any evidence to confirm or refute this, that the family patterns of the latter conformed to Eurocentric norms. It is only in recent years that family among the middle class in the Caribbean has become a focus for research. The results have challenged plural perceptions of family culture. Kinship diversity is contained within a framework of common structural principles. Genealogies from persons of all social strata contain evidence of visiting and common-law unions as well as marriage, illegitimacy as well as legitimacy. Middle-class men are also 'marginal' to the family, perhaps even more so than their lower-class counterparts for whom marginality is not a constant preoccupation. The incidence of these patterns may differ, but the experiences are shared by all classes. This conclusion must not, however, lead to assumptions of Creole family uniformity, especially in terms of the meanings of specific family practices such as common-law unions and 'outside' children

The third theme which has guided the anthropology, sociology and history of the family in the Caribbean is that of social structure versus human action. The dominant perspective has been the former, as scholars have adopted the main tenets of structural functionalism, the view that the society predominates over the individual, moulding and controlling that individual. They interpreted their task as that of providing an analysis of family structures, these structures being determined by the prevailing social and economic environment. The dominance of circumstance, namely poverty, economic marginality, community organisation and male unemployment accounted for 'matrifocality' and 'male marginality'. These perceptions were also evident in historical studies, perhaps with more reason given the character of slavery which allowed very little room for individual creativity and manoeuvre. Accordingly, slave families were interpreted as a function of the oppression, economics and demography of the regime.

With the reintroduction of human action into theoretical perspectives, interpretations of family life in the Caribbean were significantly changed. Even slaves were seen to exercise choices and, within whatever personal space the regime permitted, to restructure family and community. But some reinterpretations took things to a theoretical dead end by virtually eliminating social structures and, along with them, systems of norms and values. Individuals were given free rein to 'stretch' values out of existence and operate purely pragmatically, according to circumstance and in response to unbridled self-interest. The theoretical reassertion of values and meanings, which provide a set of guiding principles for understanding and behaviour, is most welcome.

Theoretical interpretations of gender in Caribbean family life, our fourth theme, have also undergone much transformation, more so, however, with female roles than with male. Structural functional images defined women as mothers and wives preoccupied with household and child-care duties in the domestic domain and economically dependent on and subordinate to their menfolk. Women's productive work in the wider economy and female household headship was mentioned only in passing, as a phase confined to the later stages of the life cycle. Feminist writers in the 1970s and others who began to look at family patterns from the perspectives of 'adaptive response', presented a turnabout in the evaluation of women's roles and status. In historical and contemporary perspective, families were perceived not merely as matrifocal, but matriarchal as female-headed households and extensive kinship networks with local and migrant linkages within which women established themselves as personally and economically autonomous individuals. Successful matriarchs were, however, redefined as the exception, rather than the norm when demographic information showed that, in general, women who headed households were among the 'poorest of the poor'.

Images of men in the literature have not undergone the same transformation. Notions of 'male marginality' in the Caribbean family have persisted, although some modifications have occurred as Caribbean men and women have provided their own definitions of male familial responsibility and 'irresponsibility'. Interestingly, this has provided us with the paradox that, although middle-class men are more involved in family life through their roles as fathers and husbands, they are more likely than lower-class men to be labelled 'marginal' by the women and men in their families. All in all, it is more than time for researchers to ask men and women of the Caribbean, including those of East Indian and other ethnic descent, how they define and interpret their changing family roles as mothers and fathers, 'husbands' and 'wives', grandmothers, uncles, sons, cousins and the like.

Our fifth theme concerns methodology. Apart from an initial, short period when scholars were more interested in providing solutions to family problems than in finding out about kinship patterns in the Caribbean, family research has defined its methodology as 'scientific' and 'objective' and been preoccupied with providing detailed statistical reports of family structure (usually defined as household composition) and conjugal union types within selected lower-class, black communities. Comprehensive household surveys covering all houses in these communities were used to collect the necessary information, which was then classified into elaborate typologies which added a series of ever more meaningless categories. Although meticulous, in-depth participant observation was often also conducted for many months and some reports include case-study material giving details of how individuals viewed and interpreted their family lives, the significance of these in terms of the meaning of the family was lost in the major thrust to provide a value-free picture of kinship regularities.

After many years of imposing definitions and interpretations by using inappropriate theoretical models, several scholars are turning their attention to what Caribbean people say about their own family lives. The intensive collection, tape recording and verbatim transcription of genealogical material from a select few individuals who are allowed to talk about their family experiences and values, forgoes statistical representation in favour of intensive detailed attention to meanings, attitudes and symbols of Caribbean family life.

Closely related to methodological techniques, is our sixth and final theme, that of history and social change. During the 1960s anthropologists and sociologists were most anxious to carve out a clearly defined disciplinary domain for themselves as 'scientists'; to distinguish their fields of study from others, especially history. The task of sociology was to study the social structure of a functioning system and, to this end, avoid preconceptions of earlier social patterns. The past was the concern of historians and for the anthropologist or sociologist to look back constituted dangerous speculation. Informants' memories were said to be weak and unreliable and, anyway, no significant changes were thought to have occurred in family structures, this of course being linked to persistent poverty and male unemployment over the generations. Both anthropologists and sociologists reduced history by condensing notions of social change into life cycle time frames by the dubious practice of rearranging synchronic household data into an assumed chronological order.

History, as history, is now being restored to Caribbean family studies, not as a search for African retentions and survivals, but as the recognition of long-established 'cognitive orientations' and 'structural principles'. This is not happening without difficulty and has had to await the redefinition of the subject matter of history. Until recently, history has defined as worth recording only the acts of famous men in the public arena, mainly in politics and war. Family matters were unimportant and much historical evidence died with the ancestors. Nevertheless, the imaginative interpretation of what archival material remains is providing a more holistic understanding of Caribbean kinship ideology and practice and its intersection in history with ideologies of patriarchy, race and class.

Finally, there is the theme of social change. Are Caribbean family patterns best understood by notions of continuity or transformation? Theoretical interpretations have shifted from a perspective which assumed that families would respond to social policy to restructure and, in the process, upgrade themselves and that all that was required was education and social engineering programmes such as mass marriages, to the realisation that this perception was based on the complete lack of knowledge and understanding of family structures and values. Families were then seen as appropriate to the social and economic environment and, as such, were reinterpreted as resilient and stable. The family, scholars noted, had changed very little, if at all, and they quoted data on marriage and illegitimacy rates to support the point. The dialectic of continuity and change has also informed investigations into East Indian family patterns in the Caribbean, but here, in contrast, recent studies have leant towards an emphasis on change. East Indian families are perceived as undergoing a far-reaching and often painful transformation in many respects, including choice of a marriage partner, age at marriage and the collapse of joint family structures, of gender inequality and of patriarchal authority and deference.

Although changes in family structures may not be evident in census data, there are suggestions, though not systematic scholarly evidence, that Caribbean men and women are in the process of redefining their family roles and relationships. Perhaps the most important is a change in the significance of motherhood in the lives of Caribbean women. The successful implementation of widespread birth control schemes has acted as a catalyst revolutionising women's lives by facilitating the postponement and control of the period of their life cycles spent in mothering. Whereas their own mothers and grandmothers experienced no adolescent phase, began to give birth in their teens with their first sexual experiments and were preoccupied with mothering and grandmothering for most of the rest of their lives, women of younger generations are able to make choices, to balance motherhood with education, career and other activities. Conversely, there is some suggestion, though less clear, that young men are defining fatherhood into their lives more than their own fathers and grandfathers did, not merely as the manly kudos achieved from biological reproduction, but as the involvement in rearing and nurturing their children. There is also a suggestion that young married couples have begun a process of renegotiating gender relationships from patriarchy and segregation towards greater equality and togetherness, albeit slowly and often painfully, especially within East Indians conjugal relations.

Much exciting scholarly investigation demands attention. The way has been opened by the reconceptualisation of the anthropology, sociology and history of the

Caribbean domain of kinship through the study of ideological principles and practices and the redefinition of methodology to allow us to listen to Caribbean people as they talk of their experiences, values, attitudes and aspirations in their complex of familial roles and relationships.

Bibliography

Abdullah, N. (1985) *Trinidad and Tobago, 1985: A Demographic Analysis*. Guyana, Caricom Secretariat.

Agrosino, M. (1976) 'Sexual Politics in the East Indian Family in Trinidad', *Caribbean Studies*, 16, 1, 44-66.

Alexander, J. (1976) 'A Study of the Cultural Domain of Relatives', *American Ethnologist*, 3, 17-38.

Alexander, J. (1977) 'The Role of the Male in the Middle Class Jamaican Family: A Comparative Perspective', *Journal of Comparative Family Studies*, 8, 3, 369-389.

Alexander, J. (1978) 'The Cultural Domain of Marriage', *American Ethnologist*, 5, 5-14.

Alexander, J. (1984) 'Love, Race, Slavery and Sexuality in Jamaican Images of the Family'. In R. T. Smith (ed), *Kinship Ideology and Practice in Latin America*. Chapel Hill, University of North Carolina Press, 147-180.

Allen, E. A. (1972) 'Discussion'. In L. Haynes *Fambli: Church's Responsibility to the Family in the Caribbean*. Cariplan, Bridgetown, Barbados, 101.

Arnold, E. (1982) 'The Use of Corporal Punishment in Child Rearing in the West Indies', *Child Abuse and Neglect*, 6, 141-145.

Austin, D. (1984) *Urban Life in Kingston, Jamaica: The Culture and Class Ideology of Two Neighbourhoods*. New York, Gordon and Breach.

Bagenstose, H. (1964) 'Socialization Values in the Negro and East Indian Subcultures of Trinidad', *Journal of Social Psychology*, 64, 1-20.

Barrow, C. (1977) 'Migration from a Barbados Village: Effects on Family Life', *New Community*, 5, 4, 381-391.

Barrow, C. (1986) 'Finding the Support: Strategies for Survival', *Social and Economic Studies*, 35, 2, 131-176.

Barrow, C. (1988) 'Anthropology, the Family and Women in the Caribbean'. In P. Mohammed and C. Shepherd (eds) *Gender in Caribbean Development*. University of the West Indies, Women and Development Studies Project, 156-169.

Barrow, C. (forthcoming/a) '"Living in Sin": Church and Common-Law Union in Barbados,' *The Journal of Caribbean History*.

Barrow, C. (forthcoming/b) Men an a family in the Caribbean: 'Marginality' Revisited.

Beckles, H. (1989) *Natural Rebels: A Social History of Enslaved Black Women in Barbados.* London, Zed Books Ltd.

Bell, R. (1970) 'Marriage and Family Differences among Lower-class Negro and East Indian Women in Trinidad', *Race,* XII, 1, 59-73.

Bennett, J. H. (1958) *Bondsmen and Bishops: Slavery and Apprenticeship on the Codrington Plantations of Barbados, 1710-1838.* Los Angeles, University of California Press.

Berleant-Schiller, R. (1972) 'Mating is Marriage in the Caribbean', *Montclair Journal of Social Sciences and Humanities,* 1, 1, 66-79.

Blake, J. (1961) *Family Structure in Jamaica: The Social Context of Reproduction.* New York, Free Press.

Bolles, L. (1988) *My Mother Who Fathered Me and Others: Gender and Kinship in the Caribbean.* Working Paper No. 175, Michigan State University.

Bott, E. (1957) *Family and Social Network: Roles, Norms, and External Relationships in Ordinary Urban Families.* London, Tavistock Publications Ltd.

Bourguignon, E. (1980) *A World of Women: Anthropological Studies of Women in the Societies of the Third World.* New York.

Braithwaite, L. (1953) 'Social Stratification in Trinidad', *Social and Economic Studies,* 2, 2/3, 5-175.

Braithwaite, L. (1960) 'Social Stratification and Cultural Pluralism', *Annals of the New York Academy of Sciences,* 83, 5, 816-836.

Brathwaite, E. (1971) *The Development of Creole Society in Jamaica, 1770-1820.* Oxford University Press.

Brathwaite, E. (1974) *Contradictory Omens: Cultural Diversity and Integration in the Caribbean.* Savacou Monograph, No 1, Kingston, Jamaica.

Brathwaite, E. (1977) 'Caliban, Ariel and Unprospero in the Conflict of Creolization: A Study of the Slave Revolt in Jamaica in 1831-32'. In V. Rubin and A. Tuden (eds.) *Contemporary Perspectives on Slavery in New World Plantation Societies. Annals of the New York Academy of Sciences,* Vol. 292, New York.

Brereton, B. (1974) 'The Experience of Indentureship: 1845-1917'. In J. La Guerre (ed.) *Calcutta to Caroni: The East Indians of Trinidad.* London, Longman Caribbean Ltd, 25-38.

Brodber, E. (1974) *Abandonment of Children in Jamaica.* Jamaica, Institute of Social and Economic Research, University of the West Indies.

Brodber, E. (1975) *A Study of Yards in the City of Kingston.* Jamaica, Institute of Social and Economic Research, University of the West Indies.

Brown, J., Anderson, P. and Chevannes, B. (1993) *Report on the Contribution of Caribbean Men to the Family: A Jamaican Pilot Study.* The Caribbean Child Development Centre, School of Continuing Studies, University of the West Indies.

Buvenic, M. with Von Elm, B. (1978) *Women-Headed Households: The Ignored Factor in Development Planning.* Washington, D.C., International Centre for Research on Women.

Carter, R. (1992) 'Questioning the 'Extended-to-Nuclear' Thesis of Family Breakdown in Barbados', *Bulletin of Eastern Caribbean Affairs,* 17, 4, 14-27.

Clarke, E. (1970(1957)) *My Mother Who Fathered Me.* London, George Allen and Unwin Ltd.

Craig, S. (1982) 'Sociological Theorising in the English-Speaking Caribbean: A Review'. In S. Craig *Contemporary Caribbean: A Sociological Reader* (Vol. Two). Trinidad, Susan Craig.

Craton, M. (1978) *Searching for the Invisible Man: Slaves and Plantation Life in Jamaica.* Cambridge, Mass., Harvard University Press.

Craton, M. (1979) 'Changing Patterns of Slave Families in the British West Indies', *Journal of Interdisciplinary History,* X, 1, 1-35. (Reprinted in H. Beckles and V. Shepherd, 1991, pp.228-249)

Craton, M. and Walvin, J. (1970) *A Jamaican Plantation: The History of Worthy Park, 1670-1790.* London and New York, W. H. Allen.

Cumper, G. (1972) *Survey of Social Legislation in Jamaica*. Institute of Social and Economic Research, University of the West Indies, Jamaica.

Cumper, G. and Daley, S. (1979) *Family Law in the Commonwealth Caribbean*. Department of Extra Mural Studies, University of the West Indies, Jamaica.

Dann, G. (1987) *The Barbadian Male: Sexual Attitudes and Practice*, London, Macmillan Publishers.

Davenport, W. (1961) 'The Family System in Jamaica', *Social and Economic Studies*, 10,4, 420-454.

De Veer, H. (1979) *Sex Roles and Social Stratification in a Rapidly Growing Urban Area: May Pen, Jamaica*. Chicago, University of Chicago, PhD Dissertation.

Dickson, W. (1789) *Letters on Slavery*. London.

Dirks, R. and Kerns V. (1976) 'Mating Patterns and Adaptive Change in Rum Bay, 1923-1970', *Social and Economic Studies*, 25, 34-35.

Douglass, L. (1992) *The Power of Sentiment: Love, Hierarchy and the Jamaican Family Elite*. Boulder, Westview Press.

Dundas, L. (1990) *The Morality and Marital Status of Caribbean Common-Law Unions*. MA Thesis, Kingston, Jamaica.

Ebanks, G. E., George P. M. and Nobbe C. E. (1974) 'Fertility and Number of Partnerships in Barbados', *Population Studies*, 28 (3), 449-461.

Evans, H. (1989)'Perspectives on the Socialisation of the Working-Class Jamaican Child', *Social and Economic Studies*, 38, 3, 177-203.

Foot, H.(Sir) (1970 (1957) 'Preface'. In E. Clarke *My Mother Who Fathered Me*. London, George Allen and Unwin Ltd.

Forde, N. (1980) *The Status of Women in Barbados: What has been done since 1978*. Barbados, Institute of Social and Economic Research, University of the West Indies.

Forde, N. (1981) *Women and the Law*. Institute of Social and Economic Research, University of the West Indies, Barbados.

Fraser, A. (1972) 'The Law and the Illegitimate Child'. In L. Haynes *Fambli: Church's Responsibility to the Family in the Caribbean*. Cariplan, Bridgetown, Barbados, 124-143.

Frazier, E. F. (1957) 'Introduction'. In V. Rubin (ed) *Caribbean Studies: A Symposium*. Jamaica, Institute of Social and Economic Research, University College of the West Indies, v- viii.

Frazier, E. F. (1966 (1939)) *The Negro Family in the United States*. Chicago, University of Chicago Press.

Gerber, S. (ed.) (1968) *The Family in the Caribbean: Proceedings of the First Conference held in St. Thomas, Virgin Islands*, March 21-23, 1968. Rio Piedras, Institute of Caribbean Studies, University of Puerto Rico.

Gerber, S. (1973) *The Family in the Caribbean: Proceedings of the Second Conference held in Aruba, Netherlands Antilles*, December 1-5, 1969. Rio Piedras, Institute of Caribbean Studies, University of Puerto Rico.

Gonzalez, N. L. (1960) 'Household and Family in the Caribbean', *Social and Economic Studies*, 9, 101-106.

Gonzalez, N. L. (1970) 'Toward a Definition of Matrifocality'. In N.E. Whitten and J. Szwed (eds) *Afro-American Anthropology*, New York.

Gonzalez, N. L. (1984) 'Rethinking the Consanguineal Household and Matrifocality', *Ethnology*, 23, 1-12.

Gordon, S. (1987) 'I Go To 'Tanties': The Economic Significance of Child-Shifting in Antigua, West Indies', *Journal of Comparative Family Studies*, 18, 3, 427-443.

Goveia, E. (1965) *Slave Society in the British Leeward Islands at the End of the Eighteenth Century* New Haven, Yale University Press.

Great Britain (1945) *Report*. West India Royal Commission, 1938- 1939.

Green, H. B. (1964) 'Socialization Values in the Negro and East Indian Subcultures of Trinidad', *The Journal of Social Psychology*, 64, 1-20.

Greenfield, S. (1966) *English Rustics in Black Skin: A Study of Modern Family Forms in a Pre-Industrialized Society*. New Haven, Conn., College and University Press.

Greenfield, S. (1973) 'Dominance, Focality and the Characterization of Domestic Groups: Some Reflections on 'Matrifocality' in the Caribbean'. In S. N. Gerber (ed.) *The Family in the Caribbean*. Institute of Caribbean Studies, University of Puerto Rico, Rio Piedras, 31-49.

Gussler, J. (1980) 'Adaptive Strategies and Social Networks of Women in St. Kitts'. In E. Bourguignon (ed.) *A World of Women: Anthropological Studies of Women in the Societies of the World*. New York, Praeger.

Handler, J. (1974) *The Unappropriated People: Freedmen in the Slave Society of Barbados*. Baltimore: The Johns Hopkins University Press.

Hart, K. (ed.) (1989) *Women and the Sexual Division of Labour*. Consortium Graduate School of Social Sciences, Mona, Jamaica.

Haynes, L. *Fambli: Church's Responsibility to the Family in the Caribbean*. Cariplan, Bridgetown, Barbados.

Henney, J. (1980) 'Sex and Status: Women in St. Vincent'. In E. Bourguignon *A World of Women: Anthropological Studies of Women in the Societies of the World*. New York, Praeger Publishers.

Henriques, F. (1953) *Family and Colour in Jamaica*. London, Eyre and Spottiswoode.

Henriques, F. (1973(1949)) 'West Indian Family Organisation.' In L. Comitas and D. Lowenthal *West Indian Perspectives: Work and Family Life*. New York, Anchor Press/Doubleday, 320-333.

Herskovits M. (1958 (1941)) *The Myth of the Negro Past*. Boston, Beacon Press.

Herskovits M. (1973 (1945)) 'Problem, Method and Theory in Afroamerican Studies.' In L. Comitas and D. Lowenthal *West Indian Perspectives: Work and Family Life*. New York, Anchor Press/Doubleday, 247-270.

Herskovits M. and Herskovits F. (1947) *Trinidad Village*. New York, Alfred A. Knopf.

Higman, B. (1973) 'Household Structure and Fertility on Jamaican Slave Plantations: A Nineteenth-Century Example', *Population Studies*, 27, 3, 527-550 (Reprinted in H. Beckles and V. Shepherd, 1991, 250-273).

Higman, B. (1975) 'The Slave Family and Household in the British West Indies, 1800-1834', *Journal of Interdisciplinary History*, VI, 261-287.

Higman, B. (1976) *Slave Population and Economy in Jamaica, 1807-1834*. Cambridge, Cambridge University Press.

Higman, B. (1978) 'African and Creole Slave Family Patterns in Trinidad', *Journal of Family History*, 3, 163-180.

Higman, B. (1984) 'Terms for Kin in the British West Indian Slave Community: Differing Perceptions of Masters and Slaves'. In R. T. Smith *Kinship Ideology and Practice in Latin America*. University of North Carolina Press.

Hoad, J. (1972) 'Discussion'. In L. Haynes *Fambli: Church's Responsibility to the Family in the Caribbean*. Cariplan, Bridgetown, Barbados, 103-118.

Horowitz, M. (ed) (1971) *Peoples and Cultures of the Caribbean: An Anthropological Reader*. Garden City, New York, The Natural History Press.

Jayawardena, C. (1962) 'Family Organisation in Plantations in British Guiana', *International Journal of Comparative Sociology*, 3, 43-64.

Jayawardena, C. (1963) *Conflict and Solidarity in a Guianese Plantation*. London, University of London, The Athlone Press.

Jha, J. C. 'The Indian Heritage in Trinidad'. In J. La Guerre *From Calcutta to Caroni: The East indians of Trinidad. London*, Longman Caribbean Ltd., *1-24*.

Kerr, M. (1952) *Personality and Conflict in Jamaica*. Liverpool, Liverpool University Press.

Kiple, K. (1984) *The Caribbean Slave: A Biological History.* Cambridge, Cambrige University Press.

Klass, M. (1961) *East Indians in Trinidad.* New York, Columbia University Press.

La Guerre, J. (1974) *From Calcutta to Caroni: The East Indians of Trinidad,* London, Longman Caribbean Ltd.

Landman, J., Grantham-McGregor S. and Desai. D. (1983) 'Child-Rearing Practices in Kingston, Jamaica', *Caribbean Quarterly,* 29(3 and 4), 40-52.

Lazarus-Black, M. (1991) 'Why Women Take Men to Magistrate's Court: Caribbean Kinship Ideology', *Ethnology,* 30, 2, 119-133.

Leo-Rhynie, E. (1993) *The Jamaican Family: Continuity and Change.* Grace Kennedy Foundation Lecture, Jamaica, Institute of Jamaica.

Ligon, R. (1657) *A True and Exact History of Barbados.* London.

Lightbourne, R. E. and Singh S. (1982) 'Fertility, Union Status and Partners in the WFS Guyana and Jamaica Surveys, 1975-1976', *Population Studies,* 36, 201-225.

MacDonald, J. S. and MacDonald L. D. (1973) 'Transformation of African and Indian Family Traditions in the Southern Caribbean', *Comparative Studies in Society and History,* 15, 171-198.

Mahabir, K. (1992) *East Indian Women of Trinidad and Tobago.* Trinidad, Chakra Publishing House.

Manyoni, J. (1977) 'Legitimacy and Illegitimacy: Misplaced Polarities in Caribbean Family Studies', *The Canadian Review of Sociology and Anthropology,* 14, 4, 417-427.

Manyoni, J. (1980) 'Extra-Marital Mating Patterns in Caribbean Family Studies', Anthropologica, XXII, I, 85-118

Marks, A. and Romer, R. (1978) *Family and Kinship in Middle America and the Caribbean.* Department of Caribbean Studies of the Royal Institute of Linguistics and Anthropology at Leiden, Netherlands.

Massiah, J. (1983) *Women as Heads of Households in the Caribbean: Family Structure and Feminine Status.* Paris, UNESCO.

Matthews D. B. (1953) *Crisis of the West Indian Family.* Caribbean Affairs Series, Trinidad, University College of the West Indies.

McKenzie, H. and H. (1971) *The Caribbean Family.* Paper presented to Workshop "Family Life Education", Bureau of Health, Ministry of Health, Kingston, Jamaica, July 13-31, 1971.

Mintz, S. and Price R. (1976) *An Anthropological Approach to the Afro-American Past: A Caribbean Perspective.* Philadelphia, Institute for the Study of Human Issues.

Mohammed, P. 'Structures of Experience: Gender, Race and Class in the Lives of Two Indian Women in Trinidad', Paper Presented to Second Disciplinary Seminar, 'Women, Development Policy and the Management of Change', Barbados, 3-7 April, 1989.

Monagan, A. (1985) 'Rethinking Matrifocality', *Phylon,* XLVI, 4, 353-362.

Morrissey, M. (1986) 'Women's Work, Family Formation and Reproduction among Caribbean Slaves', *Review,* IX, 3, 339-367. (Reprinted in H. Beckles and V. Shepherd, 1991. pp. 274-286)

Morrissey, M. (1989) 'Female Headed Households in Latin America and the Caribbean', *Sociological Spectrum,* 9, 197-210.

Moses, Y. (1977) 'Female Status, the Family and Male Dominance in a West Indian Community', *Journal of Women in Culture and Society,* 3, 1, 142-153.

Nevadomsky, J. (1980) 'Changes in Hindu Institutions in an Alien Environment', *The Eastern Anthropologist,* 33, 1, 39-53.

Nevadomsky, J. (1982/3) 'Changing Conceptions of Family Regulation among the Hindu East Indians in Rural Trinidad', *Anthropological Quarterly,* 55, 4, 189-198.

Niehoff, A. (1959) 'The Survival of Hindu Institutions in an Alien Environment', *The Eastern Anthropologist,* 12, 3, 171-187.

Olwig, K.F. (1993) 'The Migration Experience: Nevisian Women at Home and Abroad'. In J. Momsen (ed) *Women and Change in the Caribbean*. Kingston, Ian Randle; Bloomington and Indianapolis, Indiana University Press; London, James Currey, 150-166.

Otterbein, K. (1965) 'Caribbean Family Organization: A Comparative Analysis', *American Anthropologist*, 67, 66-79.

Panton, V. (1992) *The Church and the Comon-Law Union*. Kingston, Jamaica.

Parenting Partners (n.d.) *Pathways to Parenting: A Caribbean Approach*. Vols. I and III. UNICEF Caribbean, UNICEF Jamaica, Save the Children (UK), UNFPA (UN Population Fund).

Patterson, O. (1967) *The Sociology of Slavery: An Analysis of the Origins, Development and Structure of Negro Slave Society in Jamaica*. London, MacGibbon and Kee.

Patterson, O. (1982) *Slavery and Social Death: A Comparative Study*. Cambridge Mass., Harvard University Press.

Patterson, O. (1982a) 'Persistence, Continuity and Change in the Jamaican Working-Class Family', *Journal of Family History*, 7, 135-161.

Powell, D. (1986) 'Caribbean Women and their Response to Familial Experiences', *Social and Economic Studies*, 35, 2, 83-127.

Rauf, M. (1974) *Indian Village in Trinidad: A Study of Cultural Change and Ethnic Identity*. Leiden, Netherlands, E. J. Brill.

Rawlins, J. (1986) *Recent Research on the Family in the Caribbean: An Annotated Bibliography*. Institute of Social and Economic Research (Eastern Caribbean), University of the West Indies, Barbados.

Reddock, R. (1994) *Women, Labour and Politics in Trinidad and Tobago: A History*. London, Zed Books.

Roberts, G. (1975) *Fertility and Mating in Four West Indian Populations*. Jamaica, University of the West Indies, Institute of Social and Economic Research.

Roberts, G. and Braithwaite L. (1962) 'Mating among East Indian and Non-Indian Women in Trinidad', *Social and Economic Studies*, 11, 3, 203-240.

Roberts, G. and S. Sinclair (1978) *Women in Jamaica: Patterns of Reproduction and Family*. Millwood, New York, KTO Press.

Rodman, H. (1963) 'The Lower-class Value Stretch', *Social Forces*, 42, 205-215.

Rodman, H. (1966) 'Illegitimacy in Caribbean Social Structure: A Reconsideration', *American Sociological Review*, 31, 673-683.

Rodman, H. (1971) *Lower Class Families: The Culture of Poverty in Negro Trinidad*. London, Oxford University Press.

Rohner, R., Kean, K. and Cournoyer, D. (1991) 'Effects of Corporal Punishment, Perceived Caretaker Warmth, and Cultural Beliefs on the Psychological Adjustment of Children in St. Kitts, West Indies', *Journal of Marriage and the Family*, 53, 681-693.

Rubenstein, H. (1977) 'Diachronic Inference and the Pattern of Lower Class Afro-Caribbean Marriage', *Social and Economic Studies*, 26, 2, 202-216.

Rubenstein, H. (1980) 'Conjugal Behaviour and Parental Role Flexibility in an Afro-Caribbean Village', *Canadian Review of Sociology and Anthropology*, 17, 4, 330-337.

Rubenstein, H. (1983) 'Caribbean Family and Household Organization: Some Conceptual Clarifications', *Journal of Comparative Family Studies*, 14, 3, 283-298.

Rubin, V. (ed) (1957) *Caribbean Studies: A Symposium*. Institute of Social and Economic Research, University College of the West Indies, Kingston, Jamaica.

Schlesinger, B. (1968) 'Family Patterns in Jamaica: Review and Commentary', *Journal of Marriage and the Family*, 136-148.

Schwartz, B. (1964) 'Caste and Endogamy in Trinidad', *Southwestern Journal of Anthropology*, 20, 58-66.

Sharma, K. N. (1986) 'Changing Forms of East Indian Marriage and Family in the Caribbean', *Journal of Sociological Studies*, 20-58.